JUNIOR CERTIFICATE HIGHER LEVEL

CONNECT with MATHS 2

This book is complemented by:
- Free Student **Workbook**
- Extensive **Teacher Resource Book**
- A full suite of easy-to-use and stimulating **Digital Resources** for teachers at edcodigital.ie/connectwithmaths2

Hanna's Bookshop
270 Rathmines Rd Lr. €16·65
01 4967398
www.alanhannas.com

JOHN McKEON
MICHELLE KELLY
GILLIAN RUSSELL

The Educational Company of Ireland

First published 2014
The Educational Company of Ireland
Ballymount Road
Walkinstown
Dublin 12
www.edco.ie

A member of the Smurfit Kappa Group plc

© John McKeon, Michelle Kelly, Gillian Russell, 2014

ISBN: 978-1-84536-612-4

Editor: Lyn Imeson
Design: Mark Loughran, Liz White
Layout: Compuscript
Cover design: Design Image

Photograph, artwork and other acknowledgements:

Alamy, Martin Bates, *CensusAtSchool* (www.censusatschool.org.uk), cso.ie, Inpho, Irish Rail, istockphoto, Roger Fereday, Brendan Howard, Meunierd, recycledproducts.com, Science Photo Library, Kim Shaw, Shutterstock, Thaves

Note from the authors:

The authors would like to thank Emer Ryan, Meike Sommer, Declan Dempsey, Anna Clarke, Ruth Hallinan, Martina Harford, Julie Glennon and all at Edco whose endless patience, support and expertise was so important in bringing this work to fruition.

A special word of thanks to the students and staff of Maynooth Post-Primary School, past and present. Many happy years of teaching there have contributed hugely to this book.

Dedications:

To Emily, my wife and best friend, for her love and encouragement. To our wonderful sons Robert, Barry, Stephen and Kevin and to our inspirational granddaughters Adi May and Isla Rose. Also to the memory of Charles and Elizabeth McKeon, my primary educators – John

To my family, especially my husband Oscar, thank you all for your support and guidance through this process – Gillian

To my family and friends who have been very patient and supportive, in particular David, Jack, Katie and Conor – Michelle

While every care has been taken to trace and acknowledge copyright, the publishers tender their apologies for any accidental infringement where copyright has proved untraceable. They would be pleased to come to a suitable agreement with the rightful owner in each case.

At the time of going to press, all web references in this book were active and contained information relevant to the topics in this book. However, The Educational Company of Ireland and the authors do not accept responsibility for the views or information contained on these websites.

All rights reserved. No part of this publication may be reproduced, stored in a retrieval system, or transmitted in any form or by any means, electronic, mechanical, photocopying, recording or otherwise, without either the prior permission of the Publisher or a licence permitting restricted copying in Ireland issued by the Irish Copyright Licensing Agency, 25 Denzille Lane, Dublin 2.

Contents

Introduction vi

Chapter 1 Sets 1
1A Review 1
   Describing a Set 2
   Problem Solving with Two Sets 3
1B Venn Diagrams with Three Sets 6
   Drawing a Venn Diagram with
   Three Sets 9
1C Operations on Sets 13
1D Problems Involving Three Sets 16
   Drawing a Venn Diagram
   Involving Three Sets 17
Chapter Summary 26

Chapter 2 Number 27
2A Review of Fractions, Decimals
   and Percentages 27
2B Division Involving Zero 31
   Why Can't We Divide by Zero? 32
2C Indices 33
   Rules of Indices 34
2D Equations in Which the Unknown
   is an Index 35
2E Recurring Decimals 37
2F Irrational Numbers 38
   Locating $\sqrt{2}$ on the Number Line 39
   Real Numbers $\mathbb{R}$ 40
   Working with Surds 41
2G Scientific Notation 45
2H Exploring Even, Odd and
   Prime Numbers 48
Chapter Summary 52

Chapter 3 Algebra 1 – Expressions 54
3A Review 55
3B Multiplying Expressions 60
3C Evaluating Expressions 62
3D Factors 63
3E More Factors 65
3F Adding and Subtracting
   Algebraic Fractions 68
3G Long Division 70
Chapter Summary 73

Chapter 4 Algebra 2 – Linear Equations 74
4A Revision: Linear Equations 74
4B More Linear Equations with
   Fractions 76
4C Solving More Problems using
   Linear Equations 77
Chapter Summary 86

Chapter 5 Algebra 3 – Linear Inequalities 87
5A Review of Linear Inequalities 87
5B Solving More Inequalities 90
5C Solving Compound Linear
   Inequalities 92
5D Applications of Linear
   Inequalities 95
Chapter Summary 100

Chapter 6 Algebra 4 – Simultaneous
Equations 101
6A Review of Simultaneous
   Equations 101
6B Applications of Simultaneous
   Equations 104
Chapter Summary 113

Chapter 7 Algebra 5 – Quadratic
Equations 114
7A Solving Quadratic Equations
   using Factors 114
7B Forming a Quadratic Equation
   given the Roots 118
7C Solving a Quadratic Equation
   using a Formula 118
7D Solving Quadratic Equations with
   Algebraic Fractions 121
7E Solving Problems using Quadratic
   Equations 122
Chapter Summary 126

Chapter 8 Algebra 6 – Manipulating
Formulae 127
8A Manipulating Formulae 127
8B Working with Everyday
   Formulae 131
Chapter Summary 136

Chapter 9 Geometry 1 137
9A Review 137
9B Proofs of Theorems 4, 6 and 9 148
9C Constructions 3 and 4 154
9D Theorems 11, 12, 13 and
   Construction 7 158
Chapter Summary 168

Chapter 10 Geometry 2 169
10A Right-angled Triangles 169
   Theorem 14: The Theorem of
   Pythagoras 170
   Theorem 15: The Converse of
   The Theorem of Pythagoras 170
   Proof of Theorem of Pythagoras 173

	10B	Angles in Circles 176
		Proof of Theorem 19 176
		Four Corollaries of Theorem 19....... 177
	Chapter Summary................................. 183

Chapter 11 Applied Measure 184

- 11A Area and Perimeter of a Triangle............................... 184
- 11B Parallelograms and Circles 188
  - The Area of a Parallelogram........... 188
  - Arcs and Sectors of Circles............ 188
- 11C Prisms.. 193
  - Total Surface Area of a Prism 197
- 11D Cylinders 202
  - Net of a Cylinder 203
  - Surface Area of a Cylinder 203
- 11E Spheres and Hemispheres 207
  - Spheres 207
  - Hemispheres.................................. 208
  - Combined Shapes.......................... 208
- 11F Cones 211
- 11G Problem Solving Involving a Range of 3D Shapes..................... 216
  - Equal Volumes 216
  - Displaced Liquids 217
  - Flow Rate 217
- Chapter Summary................................. 222

Chapter 12 Co-ordinate Geometry............. 224

- 12A Distance and Mid-point Between Two Points...................... 224
  - Distance Between Two Points.......... 224
  - Mid-point between Two Points....................................... 225
- 12B Slope of a Line............................... 228
  - Parallel Lines 228
  - Perpendicular Lines........................ 229
- 12C The Equation of a Line 233
  - The Equation of a Line in the Form $ax + by + c = 0$ 233
  - How to Draw a Line Given its Equation 235
- 12D Finding the Slope of a Line from its Equation 239
- 12E Intersection of Lines....................... 242
- Chapter Summary................................. 247

Chapter 13 Probability 248

- 13A Review of Probability 248
  - Using Relative Frequency to Estimate Probabilities 250
- 13B Combining Two Events 255
  - Mutually Exclusive Events............... 256
  - Independent Events 256
  - Finding Probabilities with Tree Diagrams 257
- 13C Connecting Probability with Sets 262
- Chapter Summary................................. 269

Chapter 14 Statistics 271

- 14A Review... 272
  - Types of Data................................. 272
  - Being a Statistically Aware Consumer....................................... 273
- 14B Collecting Data: Sampling............... 275
  - Simple Random Sampling 277
  - Bias in Sampling 278
- 14C Estimating the Population Mean... 280
- 14D Numerical Analysis of Data 282
  - Measures of Central Tendency 282
  - Mean of a Grouped Frequency Distribution.................................... 283
  - Measures of Spread of the Data 287
  - Finding Quartiles and the Interquartile Range 288
  - The Five-number Summary 289
- 14E Graphical Analysis of Data 292
  - Shape of a Distribution 293
  - Back-to-back Stem and Leaf Plots....................................... 296
- Chapter Summary................................. 310

Chapter 15 Applied Arithmetic 312

- 15A Percentage Profit and Loss 312
  - Mark-up and Margin 313
- 15B Compound Interest......................... 318
  - Annual Percentage Rate (APR) and Annual Equivalent Rate (AER) 318
- 15C Income Tax 323
  - Standard Rate Cut-Off Point (SRCOP)....................................... 323
  - Statutory and Non-statutory Deductions 324
- Chapter Summary................................. 335

Chapter 16 Functions 336

- 16A Quadratic Functions....................... 336
- 16B Applications of Linear and Quadratic Functions....................... 344
- 16C Exponential Functions.................... 350
- 16D Transformations of Linear and Quadratic Functions................ 355
- Chapter Summary................................. 368

Chapter 17 Trigonometry........................... 369

- 17A Sine, Cosine and Tangent................ 370
  - Angle of Elevation and Angle of Depression 370
- 17B Degrees, Minutes and Seconds... 375
- 17C Special Angles: 30°, 45° and 60° 377
  - Working with an Angle of 45°... 377
  - Working with 30° and 60°............. 378

17D	Problem Solving	381
	Chapter Summary	389

Chapter 18 Speed, Distance, Time and Graphs 390

18A	Average Speed, Distance and Time	390
	Average Speed for Two-part Journeys	390
	Units	392
18B	Distance–Time Graphs with Constant Speed	393
	Constant Flow Rate Graphs	395
18C	Speed–Time Graphs	401
18D	Distance–Time Graphs with Varying Speed	405
	Chapter Summary	415

Appendix Problem Solving 416

Problem-solving Strategies 418
More Problem-solving Strategies;
Combining Strategies 422

Answers 431

Introduction

Connect with Maths 2 completes the syllabus for the **Junior** Cycle **Higher Level**, building on the preparatory work done in *Connect with Maths 1*. It is envisaged that Higher Level students would use this book towards the end of year 2 or from the start of year 3.

Connect with Maths 2 includes the following student-friendly features:

- A **Learning Outcomes** section at the start of each chapter
- Clearly laid-out **worked examples** with step-by-step instructions
- Plenty of **well-constructed graded activities** so that students of different ability levels are challenged
- Blue **definition boxes** to highlight key points
- **Key Points** boxes to emphasise important information
- **Revision activities** for each chapter
- **Exam-style questions** for each chapter
- **Class activity** boxes to encourage class discussion
- **Key Words** section and **chapter summary** at the end of each chapter
- **Connections boxes** where feasible linking the topic to other strands
- **Problem Solving Appendix** outlining possible strategies for tackling problems.

A **Student Workbook** comes free with *Connect with Maths 2*. This includes activities related to each chapter and can be used independently of the main book for revision, class tests or extra class work. The workbook can be used at any stage once the relevant chapter in *Connect with Maths 2* has been studied. Fully worked-out solutions are available to the teacher online.

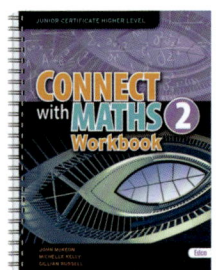

A separate **Teacher Resource Book** is packed with helpful notes on each chapter and **fully worked-out solutions** for every activity in *Connect with Maths 2*.

A **full suite of digital activities** is available online at www.edcodigital.ie/connectwithmaths2

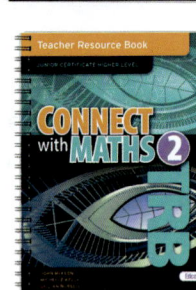

Connect with Maths 2 follows the aims and objectives of the Project Maths initiative with an emphasis on:

- Teaching and learning for understanding by investigation and discussion
- Developing problem-solving skills
- Making connections between the five strands of the syllabus so that students are able to transfer their skills from one topic to other seemingly unrelated topics. This is a central aim of *Connect with Maths 2*.
- Making mathematics relevant to everyday life
- Making the learning of mathematics enjoyable
- Challenging the students of every ability level to achieve their goals.

Many years of teaching experience and much effort and consultation has gone into the writing of this book. We hope that students and teachers will find it enjoyable and rewarding.

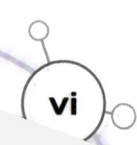

Sets

Chapter 1

Learning Outcomes

In this chapter, you will learn about:
- Working with two sets (review)
- The operations of intersection, union, set difference and complement for three sets
- The associative property of sets in relation to intersection, union and difference
- The distributive property of union over intersection and intersection over union in sets
- Using three sets to solve word problems

Section 1A Review

In this section, we revise the concepts we met previously in *Connect with Maths 1*.

Symbol	Meaning	Example
$\in$	is an element of	$a \in \{h, a, t\}$
$\notin$	is not an element of	$p \notin \{h, a, t\}$
$\emptyset$ or $\{\}$	the empty set	The set X is the set of days of the week that begin with L. $X = \{\}$
$\subset$	a subset of	$\{a, t\} \subset \{h, a, t\}$
$\not\subset$	not a subset of	$\{c\} \not\subset \{h, a, t\}$
#	cardinal number of a given set (the number of elements in a set)	If $A = \{h, a, t\}$ then $\#A = 3$
U	Universal set	The set of all elements for a given question
$A \cap B$	A intersection B (Elements common to both sets)	$A = \{h, a, t\}$ and $B = \{c, o, a, t\}$ $A \cap B = \{a, t\}$
$A \cup B$	A union B (Elements which are in both A and B)	$A = \{h, a, t\}$ and $B = \{c, o, a, t\}$ $A \cup B = \{a, c, h, o, t\}$
$A \setminus B$	A less B (Elements which are in A but not in B)	$A = \{h, a, t\}$ and $B = \{c, o, a, t\}$ $A \setminus B = \{h\}$
$B \setminus A$	B less A (Elements which are in B but not in A)	$A = \{h, a, t\}$ and $B = \{c, o, a, t\}$ $B \setminus A = \{c, o\}$
A'	A complement (Elements which are not in A)	$A = \{h, a, t\}$ and $B = \{c, o, a, t\}$ $A' = \{c, o\}$

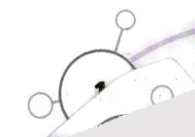

Describing a Set

We have three ways of describing a set:

1. The written method
2. The list method
3. The rule method (also known as set builder notation).

Example 1

C is the set of prime numbers between 1 and 20. Write this set using:

(i) the written method
(ii) the list method
(iii) set builder notation.
(iv) Explain what is meant by (iii).

Solution

(i) The **written method**

C is the set of prime numbers between 1 and 20.

(ii) The **list method**

$C = \{2, 3, 5, 7, 11, 13, 17, 19\}$

(iii) **set builder notation:**

$C = \{x \mid x \text{ is a prime number between 1 and 20}\}$

(iv) C is the set of all x such that x is a prime number between 1 and 20.

Example 2

$U = \{1, 2, 3, 4, 5, 6, 7, 8, 9, 10, 11, 12, 13, 14\}$

$A = \{2, 4, 6, 8, 10, 12, 14\}$

$B = \{1, 2, 3, 4, 6, 12\}$

(i) Describe each set given using set builder notation.
(ii) Represent the information above on a Venn diagram.
(iii) List the elements of:
    (a) $A \cup B$ (c) A' (e) $A \backslash B$
    (b) $A \cap B$ (d) $(A \cap B)'$ (f) $(B \backslash A)'$
(iv) Find the value of:
    (a) $\#(B \backslash A)$ (b) $\#(A \cup B)'$ (c) $\#(U \backslash (A \cap B))$

Solution

(i) The set $U = \{1, 2, 3, 4, 5, 6, 7, 8, 9, 10, 11, 12, 13, 14\}$ can also be written as:

$U = \{x \mid x \text{ is a Natural number from 1 to 14 inclusive}\}$

The set $A = \{2, 4, 6, 8, 10, 12, 14\}$ can also be written as:

$A = \{x \mid x \text{ is a multiple of 2 which is less than 15}\}$

The set $B = \{1, 2, 3, 4, 6, 12\}$ can also be written as:

$B = \{x \mid x \text{ is a divisor of 12}\}$

(ii)
- Fill in (A ∩ B)
- Fill in the elements in sets 'A only' and 'B only'.
- Fill in the elements in (A ∪ B)′.

(iii) (a) A ∪ B = {1, 2, 3, 4, 6, 8, 10, 12, 14}
(b) A ∩ B = {2, 4, 6, 12}
(c) A′ = {1, 3, 5, 7, 9, 11, 13}
(d) (A ∩ B)′ = {1, 3, 5, 7, 8, 9, 10, 11, 13, 14}
(e) A\B = {8, 10, 14}
(f) (B\A)′ = {2, 4, 5, 6, 7, 8, 9, 10, 11, 12, 13, 14}

(iv) (a) #(B\A) = 2
(b) #(A ∪ B)′ = 5
(c) #(U\(A ∩ B)) = 10

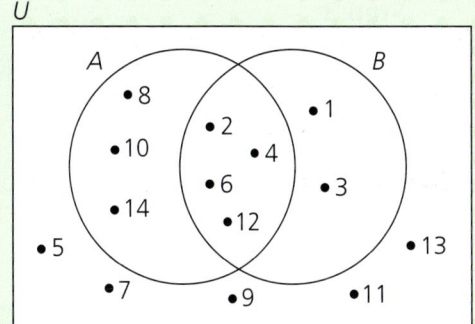

Problem Solving with Two Sets

Example 3

In a group of 50 teenagers, 26 have a laptop, 19 have a desktop PC and 9 have neither.
(i) Draw a Venn diagram to represent this information.
(ii) How many teenagers have both?

Solution

(i) **Step 1:**

Fill in the information given.

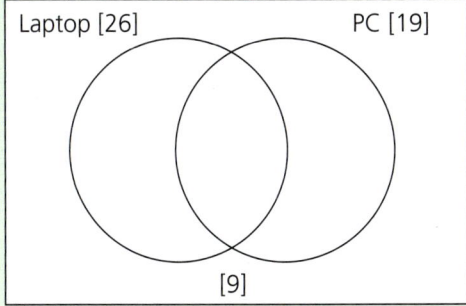

Step 2:

Find the intersection of the sets Laptop and PC.
#(Laptop ∪ PC) = 50 − 9
= 41 teenagers

#(Laptop) + #(PC) = 26 + 19
= 45 teenagers.

The difference between them is
45 − 41 = 4 teenagers.

So, 4 teenagers have been counted twice.

Therefore

#(Laptop ∩ PC) = 4 teenagers.

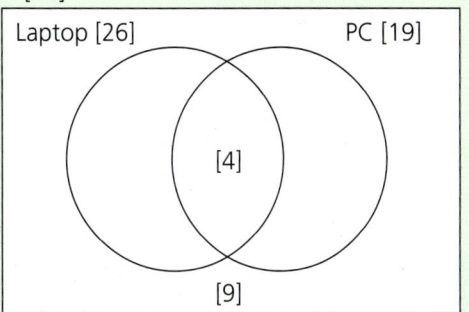

Step 3:

Fill in the remainder of the sets given.

'Laptop only' = 26 − 4
= 22 teenagers

'PC only' = 19 − 4
= 15 teenagers.

(ii) 4 teenagers have both a laptop and a desktop PC.

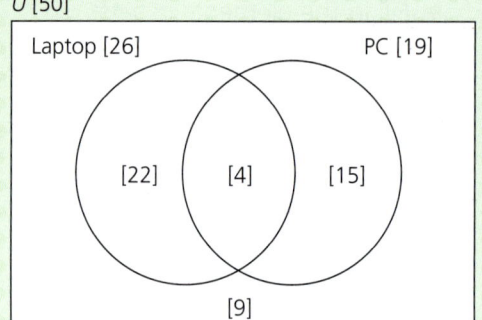

Activity 1.1

1. Two of the sets below are null sets. Identify which two and explain your answer.

    A = {the items in a mathematical set}
    B = {the set of DVDs in a given box set}
    C = {the set of months in the year with more than 32 days}
    D = {the letters in the word 'calculator'}
    E = {the set of triangles with 5 sides}

2. Write each of the following sets using:
    (i) the **list** method
    (ii) the **rule** method.

    Set A: The set of numbers from 20 to 40, inclusive, which are divisible by 5.
    Set B: The set of letters in the word 'division'.
    Set C: The set of the first five composite Natural numbers.
    Set D: The set of letters in the word 'vowels'.

3. $A = \{x \mid x \text{ is a factor of } 6\}$
    (i) List all of the elements of A.
    (ii) List all the subsets of A.

4. Set C and set D are shown.

    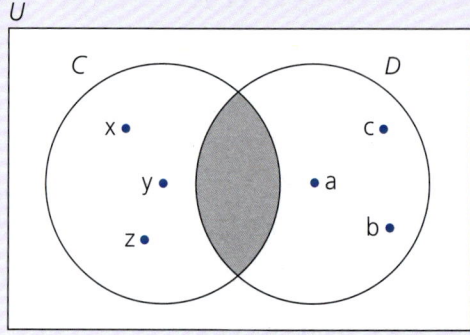

    (i) List the elements of:
    (a) C (b) D (c) C ∪ D (d) C ∩ D
    (ii) Write down the value of each of the following.
    (a) #(C\D) (b) #(D\C) (c) #(C ∩ D)′

5. Using the Venn diagram shown, state which statements are true or false.

    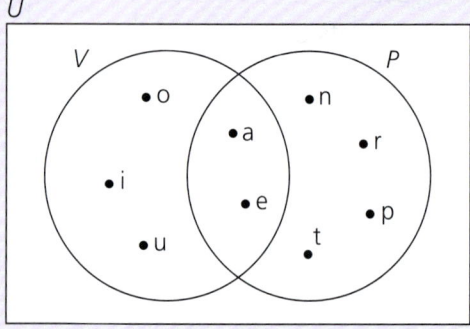

    (i) {e, r} ⊂ V
    (ii) #P = 6
    (iii) V ∪ P = {a, e, i, n, o, p, r, t, u}

(iv) V = {a, e, i, u}
   (v) {a, e} ⊂ V
   (vi) #V = #P
   (vii) { } ⊂ P
   (viii) a ∈ V ∩ P
   (ix) n ∉ V ∪ P

6 X = {the students in the class who are left handed},
   Y = {the students in the class who study Art}.

   Describe, in your own words, the members of the following.
   (i) X ∪ Y   (iv) (X ∪ Y)′
   (ii) X ∩ Y   (v) X\Y
   (iii) X′

7 U = {1, 2, 3, ..., 18}
   R = {x | x is a multiple of 3}
   S = {x | x is a factor of 15}
   (i) Draw a Venn diagram to represent sets U, R and S.
   (ii) Find the value of each of the following.
       (a) #R   (d) #(S ∪ R)′
       (b) #S   (e) #((S ∪ R)\(S ∩ R))
       (c) #(S\R)

8 U = {x | x > 19 and x < 36, x ∈ ℕ}
   Y = {x | x is a multiple of 2}
   Z = {x | x is a prime number}
   (i) Draw a Venn diagram to represent the sets U, Y and Z.
   (ii) Find the elements of the following sets.
       (a) Y   (d) Y\Z
       (b) Z′   (e) (Y ∪ Z)′
       (c) Y ∩ Z   (f) (Z\Y)′

9 A school has 175 Transition Year students. The year head asks them if they want to perform in a musical or a play at the end of the year. The results are shown in the Venn diagram.

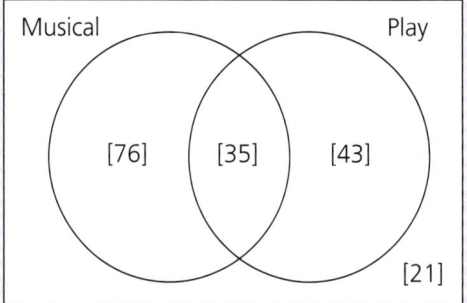

   How many students wanted to:
   (i) perform in a musical
   (ii) perform in a play only
   (iii) do neither
   (iv) do either?

10 A survey asked 50 people if they had ever visited Spain or Italy.

   23 people said they had visited Spain, 17 people said they had visited Italy and 12 said they had visited neither.
   (i) Draw a Venn diagram to represent the information given.
   (ii) How many people had visited both countries?

11 X and Y are two sets.
   #X = 28, #(X ∪ Y) = 34, #(X ∩ Y) = 9.
   (i) Represent this information on a Venn diagram.
   (ii) Hence, find the value of #(Y).

12 U is the Universal set and S and T are two subsets of U.
$\#S = 58$, $\#T = 49$, $\#(S \cup T) = 84$,
$\#(S \cup T)' = 15$.
Find the value of:
(i) $\#(S \cap T)$ (ii) $\#U$

13 U is the Universal set, M and N are two subsets of U.
$\#U = 125$, $\#M = 83$, $\#N = 69$
(i) Find the minimum value of $\#(M \cap N)$. Use a Venn diagram to illustrate your answer.
(ii) Find the maximum value of $\#(M \cap N)$. Use a Venn diagram to illustrate your answer.

14 U is the Universal set, J and K are two subsets of U.
$\#U = 82$, $\#J = 47$ and $\#K = 27$.
(i) Find the minimum value of $\#(J \cup K)'$. Use a Venn diagram to illustrate your answer.
(ii) Find the maximum value of $\#(J \cup K)'$. Use a Venn diagram to illustrate your answer.

15 U is the Universal set and R and S are two subsets of U.
$\#U = 50$
$\#(U \setminus (R \cup S)) = 5$
$\#(R \cap S) = x$
$\#(R \setminus S) = 3x$
$\#S = 3(\#R)$
(i) Draw a Venn diagram to represent the information above.
(ii) Find the value of:
  (a) $\#S$ (b) $\#R$ (c) $\#(R \cup S)$

16 U is the Universal set and C and D are two subsets of U.
$\#U = 76$
$\#C = 45$
$\#(C \setminus D) = 2x$
$\#(C \cap D) = 12 + x$
$\#(C \cup D) = 68$
(i) Draw a Venn diagram to represent the information above.
(ii) Find the value of:
  (a) $\#D$
  (b) $\#(C \cup D)'$
  (c) $\#(D \setminus C)$

Section 1B Venn Diagrams with Three Sets

We will now work with Venn diagrams involving three sets. Study the following Venn diagram carefully. It has eight regions.

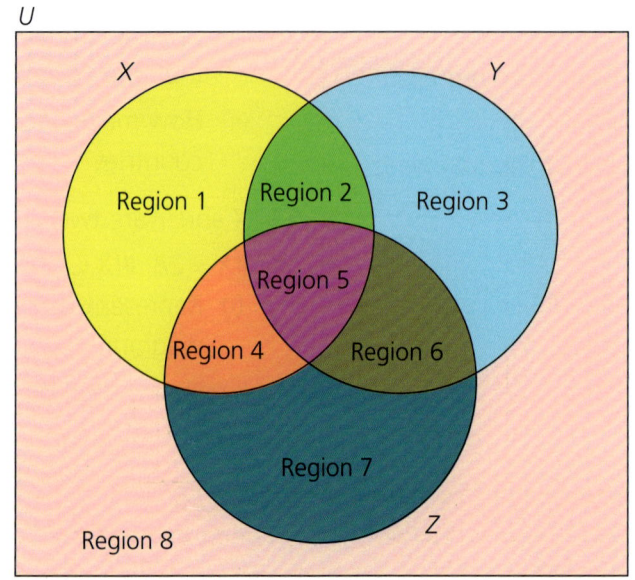

Region	Symbol	Meaning
1	$X \setminus (Y \cup Z)$	X less (Y union Z): Elements in X but not in Y or Z
2	$(X \cap Y) \setminus Z$	(X intersection Y) less Z: Elements common to X and Y less the elements in Z
3	$Y \setminus (X \cup Z)$	Y less (X union Z): Elements in Y but not in X or Z
4	$(X \cap Z) \setminus Y$	(X intersection Z) less Y: Elements common to X and Z less the elements in Y
5	$X \cap Y \cap Z$	X intersection Y intersection Z: Elements common to X, Y and Z
6	$(Y \cap Z) \setminus X$	(Y intersection Z) less X: Elements common to Y and Z less the elements in X
7	$Z \setminus (X \cup Y)$	Z less (X union Y): Elements in Z but not in X or Y
8	$(X \cup Y \cup Z)'$ or $U \setminus (X \cup Y \cup Z)$	(X union Y union Z) complement Elements in the Universal set that are **not in** (X union Y union Z) Universal set less (X union Y union Z) Elements in the Universal set less the elements in (X union Y union Z)

Example 1

Given the Venn diagram below, list the elements of each of the following.

(i) $X \cup Z$

(ii) $(X \cup Y \cup Z)'$

(iii) $Y \setminus Z$

(iv) $(X \cap Y \cap Z)'$

(v) $X \setminus (Y \cap Z)$

(vi) $(X \cap Y) \cup Z$

(vii) $(X \setminus Z)'$

(viii) $(X \cup Z)' \setminus Y$

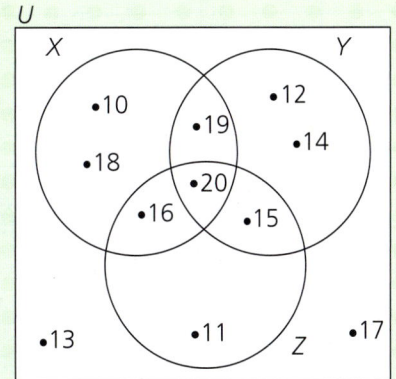

Solution

(i) $X \cup Z$

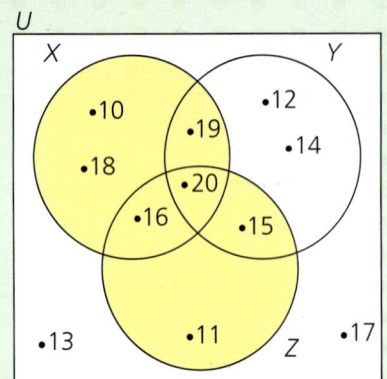

$X \cup Z = \{10, 11, 15, 16, 18, 19, 20\}$

(ii) $(X \cup Y \cup Z)'$

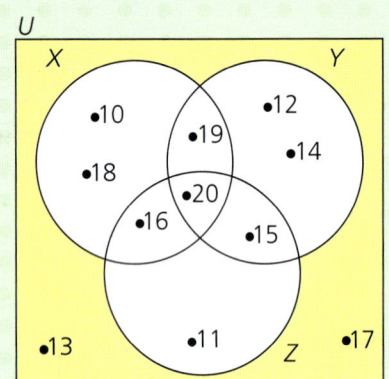

$(X \cup Y \cup Z)' = \{13, 17\}$

(iii) $Y \setminus Z$

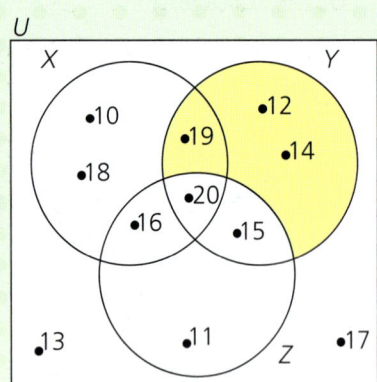

$Y \setminus Z = \{12, 14, 19\}$

(iv) $(X \cap Y \cap Z)'$

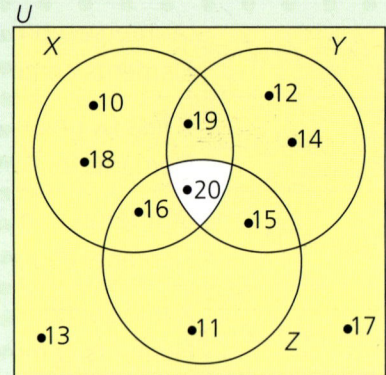

$(X \cap Y \cap Z)' = \{10, 11, 12, 13, 14, 15, 16, 17, 18, 19\}$

(v) $X \setminus (Y \cap Z)$

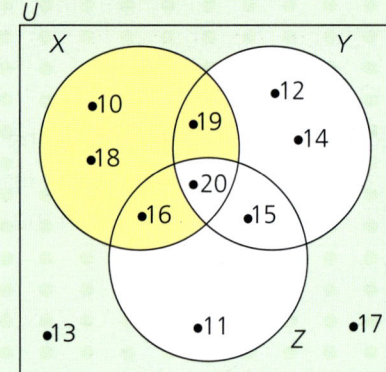

$X \setminus (Y \cap Z) = \{10, 16, 18, 19\}$

(vi) $(X \cap Y) \cup Z$

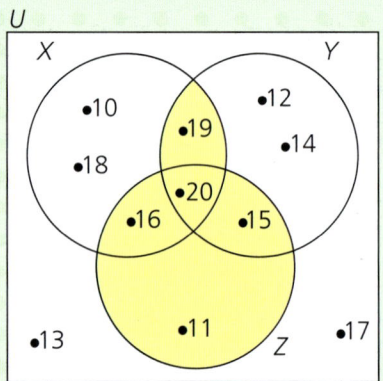

$(X \cap Y) \cup Z = \{11, 15, 16, 19, 20\}$

(vii) $(X \setminus Z)'$

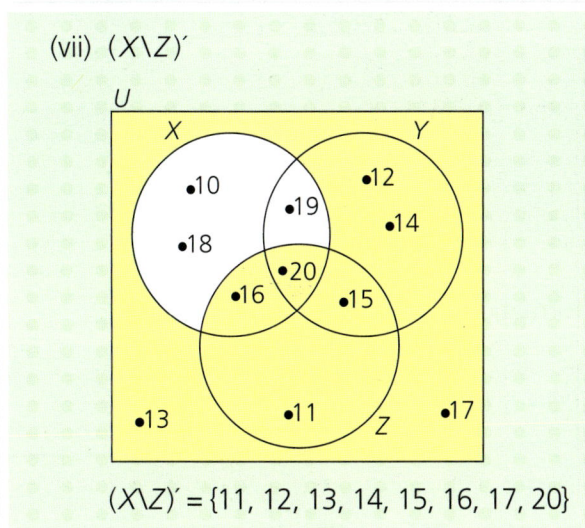

$(X \setminus Z)' = \{11, 12, 13, 14, 15, 16, 17, 20\}$

(viii) $(X \cup Z)' \setminus Y$

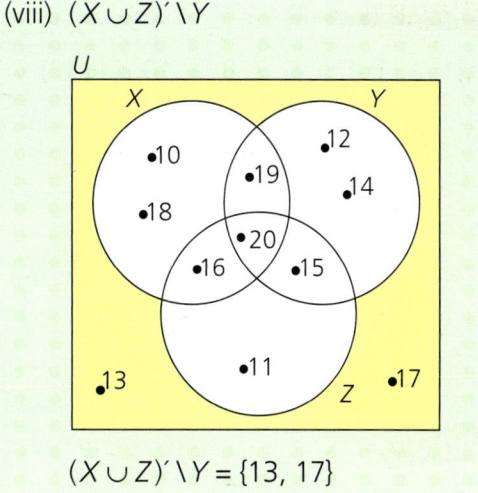

$(X \cup Z)' \setminus Y = \{13, 17\}$

Drawing a Venn Diagram with Three Sets

When asked to represent three sets on a Venn diagram, we generally follow these steps:

Step 1: Fill in the elements that are common to all three sets in the given question.

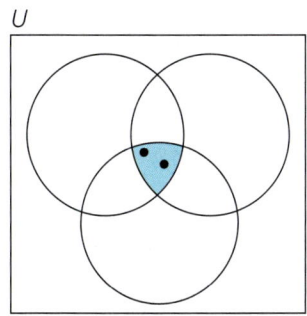

Step 2: Fill in the elements that are common to two sets.

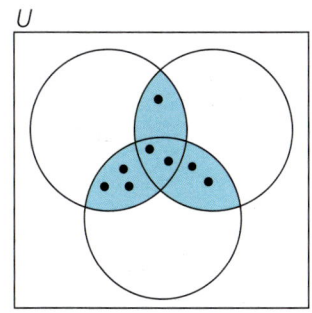

Step 3: Fill in the elements that are unique to each set.

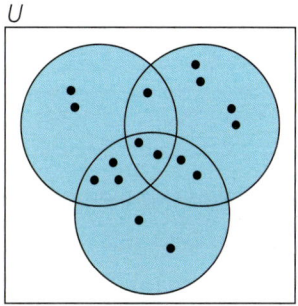

Step 4: Fill in any remaining elements listed in the Universal set.

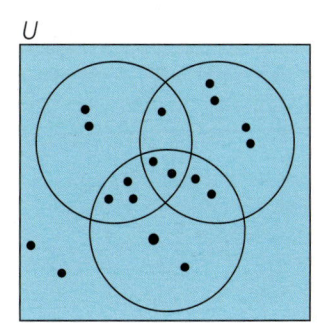

Example 2

$U = \{1, 2, 3, 4, 5, 6, 7, 8, 9, 10, 11, 12\}$

$A = \{2, 3, 4, 5, 7, 9\}$

$B = \{2, 4, 8, 10, 12\}$

$C = \{2, 3, 6, 12\}$

(i) Draw a Venn diagram to represent the information given.

(ii) List the elements of:

    (a) C' (b) $(A \cup B)'$ (c) $(A \cap B) \cup C$ (d) $(A \setminus B) \setminus C$

Solution

(i) **Step 1:** Fill in the elements that are common to all three sets.

- $A \cap B \cap C = \{2\}$

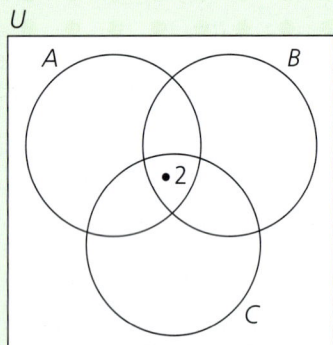

Step 2: Fill in the elements that are common to two sets.

- $(A \cap B) \setminus C = \{4\}$
- $(A \cap C) \setminus B = \{3\}$
- $(B \cap C) \setminus A = \{12\}$

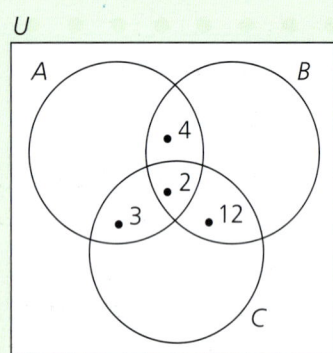

Step 3: Fill in the elements unique to each set.

- $A \setminus (B \cup C) = \{5, 7, 9\}$
- $B \setminus (A \cup C) = \{8, 10\}$
- $C \setminus (A \cup B) = \{6\}$

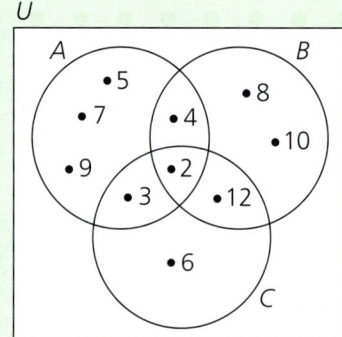

Step 4: Fill in any remaining elements listed in the Universal set.

- $(A \cup B \cup C)' = \{1, 11\}$

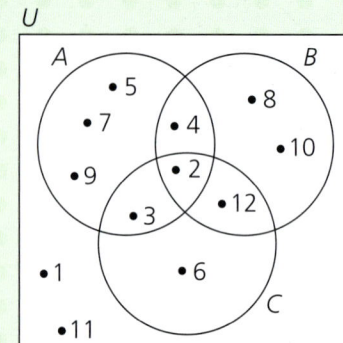

(ii) From observation, we can see that:

(a) $C' = \{1, 4, 5, 7, 8, 9, 10, 11\}$

(b) $(A \cup B)' = \{1, 6, 11\}$

(c) $(A \cap B) \cup C = \{2, 3, 4, 6, 12\}$

(d) $(A \setminus B) \setminus C = \{5, 7, 9\}$

Activity 1.2

1 Use the Venn diagram to list the elements of:

  (i) $A \cup B$
  (ii) C
  (iii) $(B \cap C) \setminus A$
  (iv) $(B \cap C) \cup A$
  (v) $A \setminus C$
  (vi) $A \cap B \cap C$
  (vii) $(A \setminus B) \setminus C$

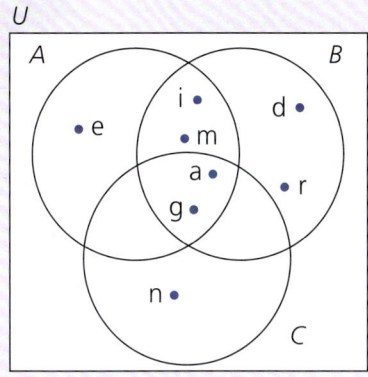

2 Use the Venn diagram to list the elements of:

  (i) J
  (ii) K
  (iii) L
  (iv) $J \cup L$
  (v) $(J \cap K) \setminus L$
  (vi) $(J \cup K)'$
  (vii) $J \setminus (K \cup L)$
  (viii) $(L \cup J) \cap K$
  (ix) $(K \cap L) \setminus J$

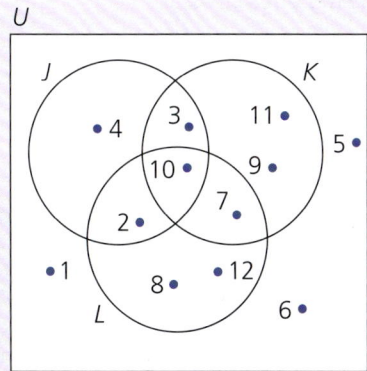

3 $U = \{1, 2, 3, 4, 5, 6\}$
$P = \{1, 2, 3, 4\}$
$Q = \{2, 3, 5\}$
$R = \{1, 3, 4, 5, 6\}$
List the elements in each of the following.

  (i) $(P \cup Q) \cap (R \setminus Q)$
  (ii) $(P \setminus Q) \cup (R \setminus P)$
  (iii) $(R') \cap (P \setminus Q)$

4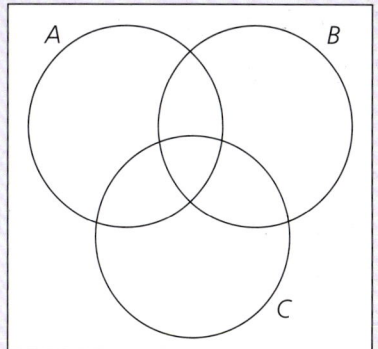

Copy the Venn diagram four times and shade in the following regions.

  (i) $(A \cap B) \cup C$
  (ii) $(A \setminus B) \setminus C$
  (iii) $(A \cup C) \setminus B$
  (iv) $(A \setminus B) \cap (C \setminus B)$

5 $U = \{x \mid x$ is a letter of the alphabet from a to n inclusive$\}$
$B = \{x \mid x$ is a letter in the word 'beamed'$\}$
$D = \{x \mid x$ is a letter in the word 'defined'$\}$
$L = \{x \mid x$ is a letter in the word 'cable'$\}$

  (i) Represent the information above on a Venn diagram.
  (ii) List the elements of:
    (a) B'
    (b) $(B \cup D)'$
    (c) $B \setminus (D \cap L)$
    (d) $(D \cap L) \cup B$
    (e) $(B \setminus D) \setminus L$
  (iii) Find the value of:
    (a) $\#(B \cap D \cap L)$
    (b) $\#((B \cup D) \cap L)$
    (c) $\#(B \cap L)'$

6 $U = \{2, 3, 4, 5, ..., 30\}$, $A = \{$multiples of $2\}$, $B = \{$multiples of $3\}$, $C = \{$multiples of $5\}$.

  (i) Find $\#(A \cup B \cup C)'$, the number of elements in the complement of the set $A \cup B \cup C$.
  (ii) How many divisors does each of the numbers in $(A \cup B \cup C)'$ have?
  (iii) What name is given to numbers that have this many divisors?

JCHL 2014 Sample Paper

7 $U = \{1, 2, 3, \ldots, 20\}$

$Q = \{x \mid x \text{ is a factor of } 20\}$

$R = \{x \mid x \text{ is a multiple of } 2\}$

$S = \{x \mid x \text{ is a prime number between 1 and } 20\}$

(i) Draw a Venn diagram to represent sets U, Q, R and S.

(ii) Find the value of each of the following.

   (a) $\#Q$

   (b) $\#R$

   (c) $\#(Q \backslash R) \backslash S$

   (d) $\#(Q \cup R)'$

   (e) $\#((Q \cup R) \backslash (S \cap R))$

   (f) $\#((Q \cap R) \cup (S \cap R) \cup (Q \cap S))$

8 $U = \{x \mid x \text{ is a letter in the word 'numerically'}\}$

$N = \{x \mid x \text{ is a letter in the word 'name'}\}$

$M = \{x \mid x \text{ is a letter in the word 'miracle'}\}$

$R = \{x \mid x \text{ is a letter in the word 'rally'}\}$

(i) Represent the sets above on a Venn diagram.

(ii) List the elements of the following.

   (a) U (e) $(N \cup R) \cap M$

   (b) M (f) $(R \cap N)'$

   (c) R (g) $(N \backslash M) \backslash R$

   (d) R' (h) $U \backslash (R \cup N)'$

9 $U = \{\text{the students in a class}\}$

$M = \{\text{the students in a class who are afraid of mice}\}$

$S = \{\text{the students in a class who are afraid of spiders}\}$

$W = \{\text{the students in a class who are afraid of wasps}\}$

Describe, in your own words, the members of the following sets.

(i) $(M \cup S)$ (iv) $(M \cap S) \backslash W$

(ii) $(M \cap W)$ (v) $(M \cup S \cup W)'$

(iii) $W \backslash S$

10 $U = \{\text{the people who live in Ireland}\}$

$A = \{\text{the people living in Ireland who own a pet}\}$

$B = \{\text{the people living in Ireland who like dogs}\}$

$C = \{\text{the people living in Ireland who have pet insurance}\}$

Describe, in your own words, the members of the following sets.

(i) $(A \cup B) \backslash C$ (iii) $C \backslash (A \cap B)$

(ii) $(A \cap B \cap C)$ (iv) $(A \cup B \cup C)'$

11 U is the Universal set and D, E and F are three subsets of U.

$\#U = 154$

$\#(D \cap E \cap F) = x$

$\#(D \backslash (E \cup F)) = 21$

$\#((D \cap E) \backslash F) = 18 - x$

$\#(F \backslash (D \cup E)) = 5x$

$\#(D \cup E \cup F)' = 3 \, \#(D \cap E \cap F)$

$\#(E \backslash (D \cup F)) = 10 + x$

$\#(E \cap F) = 23$

$\#((D \cap F) \backslash E) = 10$

(i) Draw a Venn diagram to represent the information above.

(ii) Find the value of x.

(iii) Find the value of:

   (a) $\#D$ (c) $\#F$

   (b) $\#E$ (d) $\#((D \cap F) \cup E)$

Section 1C Operations on Sets

From our previous working with two sets, we know that:

- Union of sets is **commutative**, i.e. $A \cup B = B \cup A$ where A and B are any sets.
- Intersection of sets is commutative, i.e. $A \cap B = B \cap A$ where A and B are any sets.
- Set difference is not commutative, i.e. $A \backslash B \neq B \backslash A$ where A and B are any sets.

When working with numbers, we found that:

- Addition of numbers is **associative**, i.e. $(a + b) + c = a + (b + c)$ where a, b and c are any three numbers.
- Multiplication of numbers is **associative**, i.e. $(a \times b) \times c = a \times (b \times c)$ where a, b and c are any three numbers.
- Division of numbers is not associative.
- Subtraction of numbers is not associative.

We will now investigate some operations on three sets.

Example 1

Let $A = \{a, n, t\}$, $B = \{c, a, t\}$, and $C = \{m, a, t\}$.
(i) Show that $(A \cup B) \cup C = A \cup (B \cup C)$.
(ii) Show that $(A \cap B) \cap C = A \cap (B \cap C)$.
(iii) Show that $(A \backslash B) \backslash C \neq A \backslash (B \backslash C)$.

Solution

(i) LHS $= (A \cup B) \cup C$
$(A \cup B) = \{a, n, t\} \cup \{c, a, t\} = \{a, c, n, t\}$
$(A \cup B) \cup C = \{a, c, n, t\} \cup \{m, a, t\}$
$\quad = \{a, c, m, n, t\}$

RHS $= A \cup (B \cup C)$
$(B \cup C) = \{c, a, t\} \cup \{m, a, t\} = \{a, c, m, t\}$
$A \cup (B \cup C) = \{a, n, t\} \cup \{a, c, m, t\}$
$\quad = \{a, c, m, n, t\}$
$\therefore (A \cup B) \cup C = A \cup (B \cup C)$

(ii) LHS $= (A \cap B) \cap C$
$(A \cap B) = \{a, n, t\} \cap \{c, a, t\} = \{a, t\}$
$(A \cap B) \cap C = \{a, t\} \cap \{m, a, t\} = \{a, t\}$

RHS $= A \cap (B \cap C)$
$(B \cap C) = \{c, a, t\} \cap \{m, a, t\} = \{a, t\}$
$A \cap (B \cap C) = \{a, n, t\} \cap \{a, t\} = \{a, t\}$
$\therefore (A \cap B) \cap C = A \cap (B \cap C)$.

(iii) We need to show that LHS $\neq$ RHS.
LHS $= (A \backslash B) \backslash C$
$(A \backslash B) = \{a, n, t\} \backslash \{c, a, t\} = \{n\}$
$(A \backslash B) \backslash C = \{n\} \backslash \{m, a, t\} = \{n\}$

RHS $= A \backslash (B \backslash C)$
$(B \backslash C) = \{c, a, t\} \backslash \{m, a, t\} = \{c\}$
$A \backslash (B \backslash C) = \{a, n, t\} \backslash \{c\} = \{a, n, t\}$
$\therefore (A \backslash B) \backslash C \neq A \backslash (B \backslash C)$

Key Points

The Associative Property of three sets
- **The Associative Property for Union** of sets states that the order in which the sets are grouped does not change the result.
  $(A \cup B) \cup C = A \cup (B \cup C)$
- **The Associative Property for Intersection** of sets states that the order in which the sets are grouped does not change the result.
  $(A \cap B) \cap C = A \cap (B \cap C)$
- Set difference is not associative.
  $(A \backslash B) \backslash C \neq A \backslash (B \backslash C)$

When working with numbers, we found that:

- Multiplication is **distributive over addition**, i.e. $a(b + c) = ab + ac$ where a, b and c are any three numbers.

We will now investigate whether we can operate like this on sets.

Example 2

Let $A = \{1, 2, 3, 4\}$, $B = \{2, 3, 5, 7\}$, and $C = \{2, 4, 6\}$.

(i) Show that $A \cup (B \cap C) = (A \cup B) \cap (A \cup C)$

(ii) Show that $A \cap (B \cup C) = (A \cap B) \cup (A \cap C)$

(iii) Show that $A \backslash (B \cup C) \neq (A \backslash B) \cup (A \backslash C)$

(iv) Show that $A \backslash (B \cap C) \neq (A \backslash B) \cap (A \backslash C)$

Solution

(i) LHS = $A \cup (B \cap C)$
$(B \cap C) = \{2, 3, 5, 7\} \cap \{2, 4, 6\}$
$= \{2\}$
$A \cup (B \cap C) = \{1, 2, 3, 4\} \cup \{2\}$
$= \{1, 2, 3, 4\}$
RHS = $(A \cup B) \cap (A \cup C)$
$(A \cup B) = \{1, 2, 3, 4\} \cup \{2, 3, 5, 7\}$
$= \{1, 2, 3, 4, 5, 7\}$
$(A \cup C) = \{1, 2, 3, 4\} \cup \{2, 4, 6\}$
$= \{1, 2, 3, 4, 6\}$
$(A \cup B) \cap (A \cup C) = \{1, 2, 3, 4\}$
$\therefore A \cup (B \cap C) = (A \cup B) \cap (A \cup C)$

(ii) LHS = $A \cap (B \cup C)$
$(B \cup C) = \{2, 3, 5, 7\} \cup \{2, 4, 6\}$
$= \{2, 3, 4, 5, 6, 7\}$
$A \cap (B \cup C) = \{2, 3, 4\}$
RHS = $(A \cap B) \cup (A \cap C)$
$(A \cap B) = \{1, 2, 3, 4\} \cap \{2, 3, 5, 7\}$
$= \{2, 3\}$
$(A \cap C) = \{1, 2, 3, 4\} \cap \{2, 4, 6\} = \{2, 4\}$
$(A \cap B) \cup (A \cap C) = \{2, 3, 4\}$
$\therefore A \cap (B \cup C) = (A \cap B) \cup (A \cap C)$

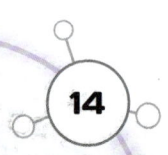

(iii) LHS = $A \setminus (B \cup C)$
$(B \cup C) = \{2, 3, 4, 5, 6, 7\}$
$A \setminus (B \cup C) = \{1, 2, 3, 4\} \setminus \{2, 3, 4, 5, 6, 7\}$
$= \{1\}$

RHS = $(A \setminus B) \cup (A \setminus C)$
$(A \setminus B) = \{1, 2, 3, 4\} \setminus \{2, 3, 5, 7\} = \{1, 4\}$
$(A \setminus C) = \{1, 2, 3, 4\} \setminus \{2, 4, 6\} = \{1, 3\}$
$(A \setminus B) \cup (A \setminus C) = \{1, 3, 4\}$
$\therefore A \setminus (B \cup C) \neq (A \setminus B) \cup (A \setminus C)$

(iv) LHS = $A \setminus (B \cap C)$
$(B \cap C) = \{2\}$
$A \setminus (B \cap C) = \{1, 2, 3, 4\} \setminus \{2\} = \{1, 3, 4\}$

RHS = $(A \setminus B) \cap (A \setminus C)$
$(A \setminus B) = \{1, 4\}$
$(A \setminus C) = \{1, 3\}$
$(A \setminus B) \cap (A \setminus C) = \{1, 4\} \cap \{1, 3\} = \{1\}$
$\therefore A \setminus (B \cap C) \neq (A \setminus B) \cap (A \setminus C)$

Key Points

- Distributive Property of **Union over Intersection**
  $A \cup (B \cap C) = (A \cup B) \cap (A \cup C)$
- Distributive Property of **Intersection over Union**
  $A \cap (B \cup C) = (A \cap B) \cup (A \cap C)$
- Set difference is not distributive over union.
  $A \setminus (B \cup C) \neq (A \setminus B) \cup (A \setminus C)$
- Set difference is not distributive over intersection.
  $A \setminus (B \cap C) \neq (A \setminus B) \cap (A \setminus C)$

Activity 1.3

1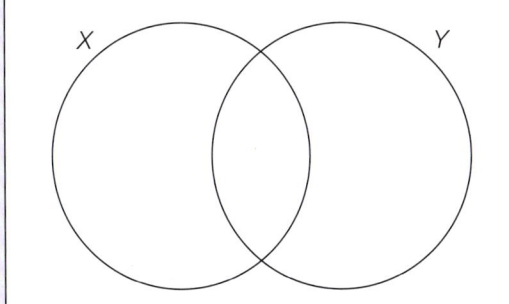

(i) Copy the Venn diagram four times and shade in:
  (a) X'
  (b) Y'
  (c) $X' \cap Y'$
  (d) $(X \cup Y)'$

(ii) Is $X' \cap Y' = (X \cup Y)'$? Explain your answer.

2 $U = \{10, 11, \ldots, 20\}$
$A = \{10, 11, 12, 13, 14\}$
$B = \{10, 12, 14, 16, 18, 20\}$
$C = \{10, 13, 17, 20\}$

(i) Draw a Venn diagram to represent the sets above.
(ii) Show that
$A \cup (B \cap C) = (A \cup B) \cap (A \cup C)$.
(iii) Show that $(A \cap B) \cap C = A \cap (B \cap C)$.
(iv) Show that $A \setminus (B \cap C) \neq (A \setminus B) \cap (A \setminus C)$.

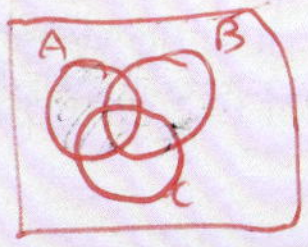

3 $U = \{x|\ x$ is a Natural number between 24 and 36$\}$
   $C = \{x|\ x$ is an odd Natural number between 24 and 36$\}$
   $D = \{x|\ x$ is a prime number between 24 and 36$\}$
   $E = \{x|\ x$ is a multiple of 3 between 24 and 36$\}$
   (i) Draw a Venn diagram to represent the sets above.
   (ii) Show that $(C \cup D) \cup E = C \cup (D \cup E)$.
   (iii) Show that $C \cup (D \cap E) = (C \cup D) \cap (C \cup E)$.
   (iv) Show that $C \setminus (D \cup E) \neq (C \setminus D) \cup (C \setminus E)$.
   (v) Investigate whether $(C \setminus D) \setminus E = C \setminus (D \setminus E)$.

4 Identify the property of sets illustrated in each of the following statements and draw Venn diagrams to show each property.
   (i) $X \cup (Y \cap Z) = (X \cup Y) \cap (X \cup Z)$
   (ii) $X \cap Y = Y \cap X$
   (iii) $(X \cap Y) \cap Z = X \cap (Y \cap Z)$
   (iv) $X \cap (Y \cup Z) = (X \cap Y) \cup (X \cap Z)$
   (v) $Y \cup Z = Z \cup Y$
   (vi) $(X \cup Y) \cup Z = X \cup (Y \cup Z)$

5 $U = \{$all people who live in Ireland$\}$
   $B = \{$all people who own their own home$\}$
   $C = \{$all people who own a car$\}$
   $D = \{$all people who are married$\}$
   Describe in words:
   (i) $B \cup (C \cap D)$
   (ii) $(B \cap C) \cup (B \cap D)$
   (iii) $(B \cup C) \cup D$

6 (i) From the Venn diagram shown, list the elements of:
   (a) $P \cup Q$
   (b) $Q \cap R$
   (c) $P \cup (Q \cap R)$

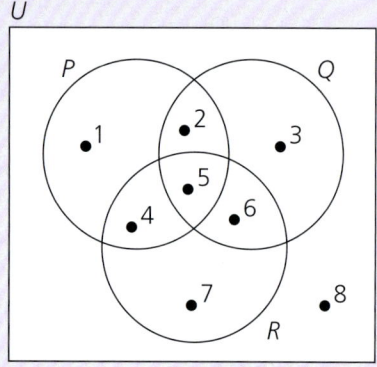

   (ii) Miriam says, 'For all sets, union is distributive over intersection.' Name a set that you would use along with $P \cup (Q \cap R)$ to show that Miriam's claim is true for the sets P, Q and R in the Venn diagram.

   JCHL 2014 Sample Paper 1

Section 1D Problems Involving Three Sets

We have already met problems involving two sets in *Connect with Maths 1*. In this section, we will solve problems involving three sets.

> **Key Point**
>
> When dealing with problems involving three sets, we use the **cardinal number** of each set in Venn diagrams. This is indicated by [ ] brackets.

Example 1

A group of Transition Year students were surveyed and asked whether they watch TV, read or sketch to relax. The results are displayed in the Venn diagram.

(i) Find the number of students who participated in the survey.

Using the Venn diagram, find the number of students who relax by:

(ii) reading
(iii) sketching
(iv) watching TV
(v) only one option
(vi) two options only.

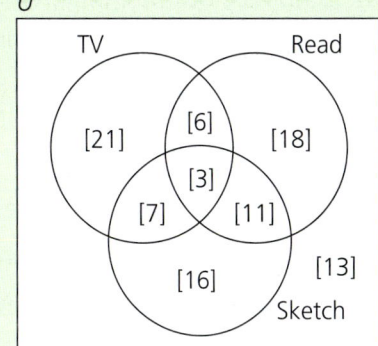

Solution

(i) The number of students who participated in the survey is:
   21 + 6 + 18 + 7 + 3 + 11 + 16 + 13 = 95 students.

(ii) The number of students who read is:
   3 + 6 + 11 + 18 = 38 students.

(iii) The number of students who sketch is:
   7 + 3 + 11 + 16 = 37 students.

(iv) The number of students who watch TV is:
   21 + 6 + 3 + 7 = 37 students.

(v) The number of students who relax using only one option:
   21 + 18 + 16 = 55 students.

(vi) The number of students who relax using only two options:
   7 + 6 + 11 = 24 students.

Drawing a Venn Diagram Involving Three Sets

To solve these types of problems, we generally use the following steps.

Step 1: Fill in the cardinal number for members that are common to all three sets in the given question. So fill in #($A \cap B \cap C$) first.

Step 2: Fill in the cardinal numbers for members that are common to two sets only.

Step 3: Fill in the cardinal numbers for members that are in one set only.

Step 4: Finally fill in the cardinal number for any remaining members listed in the Universal set.

Example 2

A school PE department have to decide on the colours for their new school tracksuit. The school colours are blue, white and red and the tracksuit must have at least one of these colours or a combination of them. The PE department survey the students and the results are as follows.

- 142 students wanted all three colours
- 231 students wanted blue and red
- 205 students wanted blue and white
- 41 students wanted white and red only
- 321 students wanted blue
- 256 students wanted white
- 52 students wanted red only.

Based on this information:

(i) Draw a Venn diagram to represent this information.
(ii) How many students want only one colour on the tracksuit?
(iii) How many students are in the school?

Solution

(i) **Step 1:** Fill in the cardinal number for members that are common to all three sets in the given question. So fill in:

$\#(\text{blue} \cap \text{white} \cap \text{red}) = 142$ students

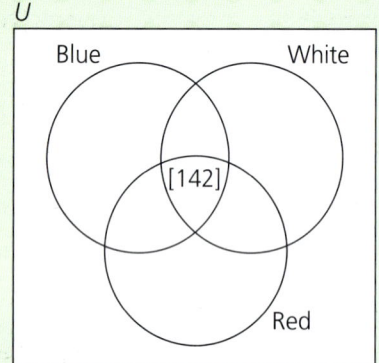

Step 2: Fill in the cardinal numbers for members that are common to two sets only.

- $\#(\text{blue} \cap \text{white}) - 142$
  $= 205 - 142$
  $= 63$ students
- $\#(\text{blue} \cap \text{red}) - 142$
  $= 231 - 142$
  $= 89$ students
- $\#(\text{white} \cap \text{red}) = 41$ students

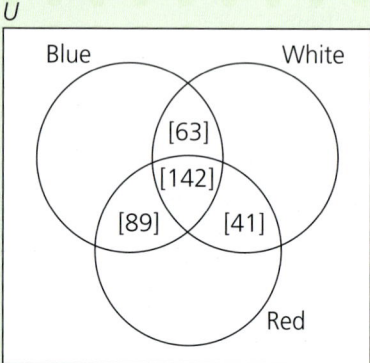

Step 3: Fill in the cardinal numbers for members that are in one set only.

- $\#(\text{blue only}) = 321 - (63 + 142 + 89)$
  $= 27$ students
- $\#(\text{white only}) = 256 - (63 + 142 + 41)$
  $= 10$ students
- $\#(\text{red only}) = 52$ students

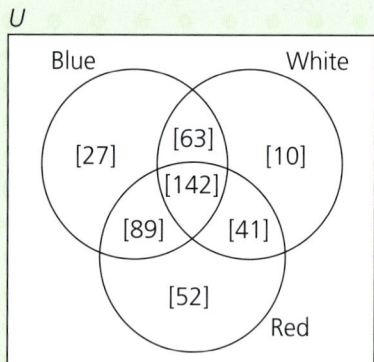

(ii) $(27 + 52 + 10) = 89$ students want only one colour on the tracksuit.

(iii) Add all values included on the Venn diagram:
$27 + 63 + 89 + 142 + 10 + 41 + 52$
$= 424$ students

Example 3

A survey carried out on 200 First Year Arts students of a university showed that:

- 76 study English
- 62 study History
- 81 study Maths
- 18 don't study English, History or Maths
- 11 study Maths and History
- 16 study History and English
- 18 study Maths and English
- x study all three subjects.

(i) Draw a Venn diagram to represent the information given.

(ii) How many students study all three subjects?

Solution

(i) **Step 1:** Let H = History, E = English and M = Maths.

Fill in the cardinal number for members that are common to all three sets.

$$\#(H \cap E \cap M) = [x]$$

U [200]

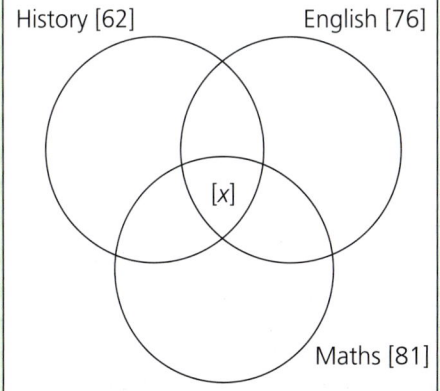

Step 2: Fill in the cardinal numbers for members that are common to two sets. Make sure to subtract $\#(H \cap E \cap M)$ each time.

- $\#(H \cap E) - \#(H \cap E \cap M) = [16 - x]$
- $\#(H \cap M) - \#(H \cap E \cap M) = [11 - x]$
- $\#(E \cap M) - \#(H \cap E \cap M) = [18 - x]$

U [200]

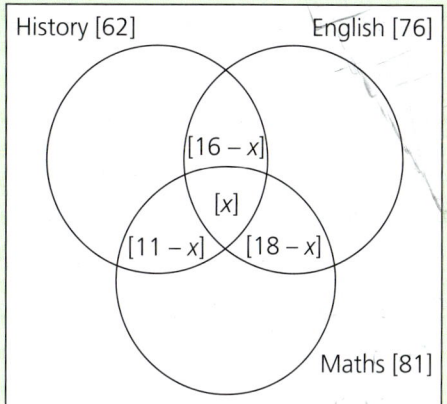

Step 3: Fill in the cardinal numbers for members that are in one set only.

- $\#H$ only $= 62 - (16 - x + x + 11 - x)$
  $= 62 - (27 - x)$
  $= 62 - 27 + x = 35 + x$

- $\#E$ only $= 76 - (16 - x + x + 18 - x)$
  $= 76 - (34 - x)$
  $= 76 - 34 + x = 42 + x$

- $\#M$ only $= 81 - (11 - x + x + 18 - x)$
  $= 81 - (29 - x)$
  $= 81 - 29 + x = 52 + x$

U [200]

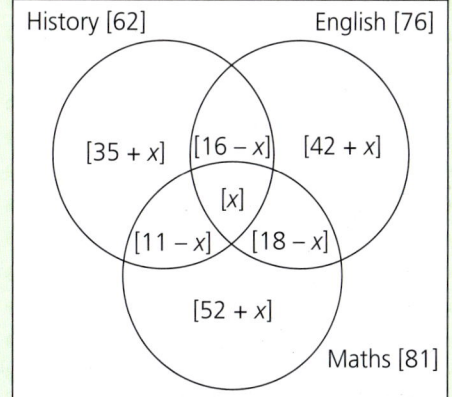

Step 4: Finally, fill in the cardinal number that represents the members of the Universal set that are not in any of the sets given.

$$\#(H \cup E \cup M)' = 18$$

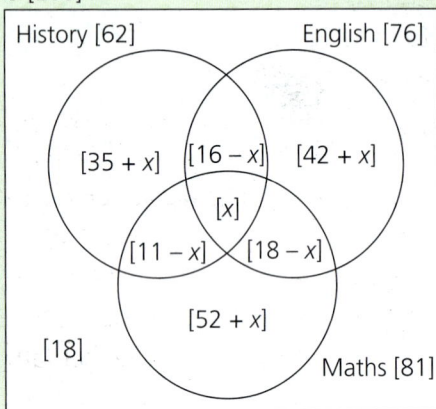

(ii) $\#U = 200$, the total number of students who did the survey.

Form an equation in x:

$(35 + x) + (16 - x) + (42 + x) + x + (11 - x) + (18 - x) + (52 + x) + 18 = 200$

$\Rightarrow \quad 192 + x = 200$ (subtract 192 from both sides)

$\Rightarrow \quad x = 200 - 192$
$\qquad\quad = 8$

Therefore, 8 students took all three subjects.

Activity 1.4

1 A group of 280 shoppers were surveyed as they entered a shopping centre. The survey asked which of the following facilities in the shopping centre could be improved upon:

A: Public toilets
B: Child care
C: Lifts

The results were as follows.
- 73 people said all of the facilities mentioned
- 106 people said the public toilets and the child care facilities
- 31 people said public toilets only
- 82 people said the public toilets and the lift facilities
- 127 people said the lifts and the child care facilities
- 212 people said the child care facilities
- 162 people said the lift facilities.

(i) Represent the above information on a Venn diagram.

(ii) How many people choose more than one facility to improve upon?

(iii) How many people said none of the facilities needed improvement?

2 A maths teacher gave a revision test to her class of 32 students.

The test had three questions:
Q1 – Algebra
Q2 – Statistics
Q3 – Probability

The results from the test were as follows:
- 17 answered question 1 correctly
- 21 answered question 2 correctly
- 18 answered question 3 correctly
- 12 answered both questions 1 and 2 correctly
- 8 answered both questions 1 and 3 correctly
- 13 answered both questions 2 and 3 correctly
- 7 answered all three questions correctly.

(i) Draw a Venn diagram using the following notation:

Set A = Students who got Q1 correct

Set B = Students who got Q2 correct

Set C = Students who got Q3 correct.

(ii) How many students didn't get any of the questions correct?

(iii) How many students got only two questions correct?

3. The Venn diagram represents the results of a survey carried out on 149 people at a train station. They were asked what mode of transport they used to get from the train station to their homes. They were given three options: walk, cycle or car.

U [149]

Walk, Cycle
[38] [x] [44 – x]
[3] [4]
[47 – 2x]
[3x] Car

(i) Find the value of x.

Based on the results, how many:

(ii) Walk and cycle
(iii) Walk
(iv) Use a car
(v) Don't use any of these
(vi) Use just two different modes of transport
(vii) Only use one mode of transport
(viii) Use all three forms of transport?

4. 70 teenagers responded to a survey based on holiday destinations. 30 had travelled to France, 26 had travelled to Spain and 28 had travelled to Italy. 12 had travelled to both France and Spain, 8 had travelled to both Spain and Italy, while x had travelled to both France and Italy only. 4 teenagers had travelled to all three countries. Twice as many teenagers had never travelled abroad as had travelled to France and Italy only.

(i) Represent the above information on a Venn diagram.
(ii) Find the value of x.
(iii) Find the number of teenagers who had travelled to France only.

5. In a survey, 250 people were asked if they like plums, kiwi or grapefruit. The results were as follows.

- 124 said that they like plums
- 101 said they like grapefruit
- 147 said they like kiwi
- 72 said they like kiwi and plums
- 38 said they like grapefruit and plums
- 21 said they like grapefruit and kiwi
- x said they like all three fruits
- $4x$ said they didn't like any of the fruits.

(i) Represent the information above on a Venn diagram.
(ii) How many people like all three fruits?

6. A group of 272 students were asked if they had an account on any of these three different social networking sites: Facebook (FB), Twitter (TW) or Myspace (MY). The results were as follows.

- 183 have a Facebook account
- 127 have a Twitter account

- 156 have a Myspace account
- 89 have both Twitter and Facebook accounts
- 5x have a Twitter and Myspace account but not a Facebook account
- 48 have a Myspace and Facebook account
- x have all three accounts
- 18 stated that they did not have any of these accounts.

(i) Draw a Venn diagram to represent the information given.

(ii) Use the Venn diagram to solve for x.

(iii) Hence, calculate the number of students who only have one of these accounts.

7 A survey of 109 students was carried out to find how many students owned an MP3 player, an iPod or a smartphone. The results were as follows.

- 18 own a MP3 player and an iPod
- 19 students own none of these
- x students own all three
- 15 own an iPod only
- 24 own an MP3 player only
- 39 own a smartphone
- 3x own an MP3 player and a smartphone but not an iPod
- 25 own an iPod and a smartphone.

(i) Construct a Venn diagram and solve for x.

(ii) Hence, calculate the number of students who own one item only.

8 A sports club want to improve the facilities at their centre. They ask all 336 members which of the following equipment they should invest in: new rowing machines, treadmills or abdominal crunch machines. The results are as follows.

- 174 said new rowing machines
- 210 said new treadmills
- 91 said new abdominal crunch machines
- 35 said they should get all three different machines
- 19 members said that no new equipment was needed
- x said they should invest in rowing machines and treadmills but not abdominal crunch machines
- 53 said they should invest in abdominal crunch machines and rowing machines
- 6x said they should get treadmills and abdominal crunch machines.

(i) Construct a Venn diagram and solve for x.

(ii) Hence, calculate the number of members who think that the club should get two different machines.

9 A GAA club surveyed 143 junior members to find out which of the following sports they have played at the club:

hurling (*H*), basketball (*B*) or Gaelic football (*G*).

- 65 members have played hurling
- 49 have played basketball
- 47 have played Gaelic football
- 20 have not played any of these sports.

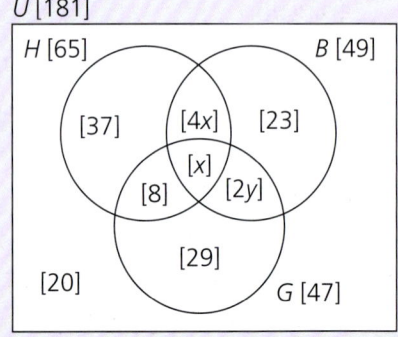

Based on the information given above and the Venn diagram, answer the following questions.

(i) Find the value of x and the value of y.

(ii) How many members have played only two of these sports?

10 An English department in a school surveyed 110 Third Year students to see if they watch the news, dramas or documentaries on TV.
- 32 watch the news
- 50 watch dramas
- 55 watch documentaries
- 11 watch both news and dramas.

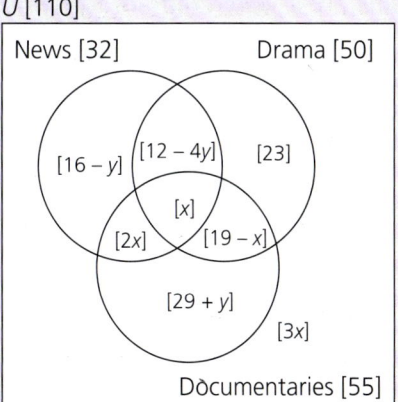

Based on the information given above and the Venn diagram, answer the following questions.

(i) Solve for x and y.

(ii) Verify your answers for x and y.

(iii) How many students watch at least one type of programme?

Revision Activity 1

1 Set A and set B are shown in the Venn diagram.

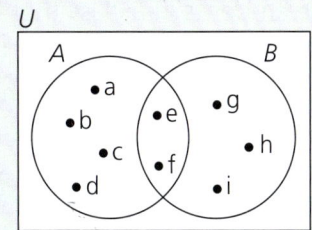

(a) List the elements of:
(i) A (iii) A ∪ B (v) (A\B)
(ii) B (iv) A ∩ B

(b) Write down the cardinal number of each set in part (a).

2 A leisure centre has 650 members. The gym (G) is used by 459 members and the swimming pool (S) is used by 532 members. 29 members do not use either of these facilities.

(a) Draw a Venn diagram to represent this information.

(b) Find the number of members who use the gym and the pool.

3 A and B are two sets and U is the universal set.

$\#U = 60$, $\#A = 34$, $\#(A \cap B) = 7$ and $\#(A \cup B) = 56$.

Find the value of:

(a) $\#B$ (b) $\#(A\backslash B)$ (c) $\#(B\backslash A)$

4 U is the universal set and P and Q are two subsets of U.

$\#U = u$ $\#(P \cap Q) = c$
$\#P = p$ $\#(U\backslash(P \cup Q)) = d$
$\#Q = q$

(a) Represent the information given on a Venn diagram.

(b) Hence, express u in terms of p, q, c and d.

(c) Show that if $p > q$, then the minimum possible value of u is $d + p$.

5 (a) Draw a Venn diagram to represent the following information.

$U = \{a, b, ..., l\}$
$V = \{a, b, c, d, e, f\}$
$W = \{a, d, g, j\}$
$X = \{e, g, i, k\}$

(b) List the elements for each of the following.
   (i) $V \setminus W$
   (ii) W'
   (iii) $V \cup W \cup X$
   (iv) $X \cup (W \cap V)$
   (v) $(V \cup X)'$
   (vi) $U \setminus (V \cup X)$

(c) Show that
$W \cap (V \cup X) = (W \cap V) \cup (W \cap X)$.

(d) Which property is being illustrated in part (c)?

6 U

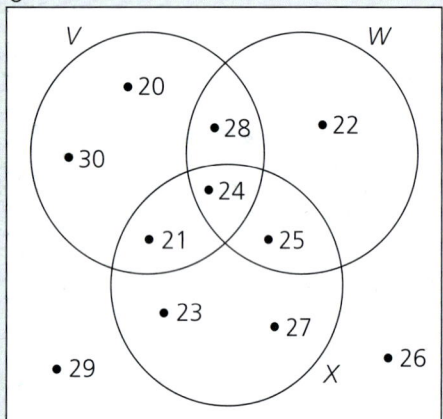

Using the Venn diagram, state which of the following is true or false.

(a) $\{21, 24, 30\} \subset V$
(b) $\#W = 7$
(c) $X \cup W = \{21, 22, 23, 24, 25, 28\}$
(d) $V' = \{22, 23, 24, 25, 26, 27, 29\}$
(e) $X \setminus V = \{23, 25, 27\}$
(f) $\#X = \#V$
(g) $\{\} \subset W$
(h) $V' = (W \cup X)'$
(i) $X \setminus (V \cup W) = \{23, 27\}$
(j) $(W \cap X) \setminus V = \{25\}$
(k) $\#U = 10$
(l) $\{29, 30\} \subset (V \cup W \cup X)$

7 U

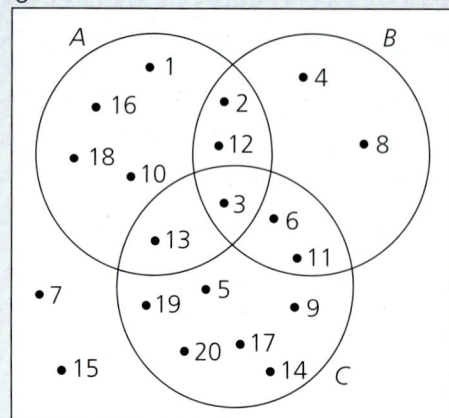

Using the Venn diagram, list the elements of each of the following.

(a) $A \cup B \cup C$
(b) $(A \cup B)'$
(c) $B \setminus C$
(d) $(A \cap C)$
(e) $(A \setminus B) \setminus C$
(f) $(C \cup B) \cap A$
(g) $A \cap B \cap C$
(h) $(A \setminus C) \cap B$
(i) $C \setminus (A \cap B)$
(j) $(A \cap B \cap C)'$

8 U = {all the students in a given class}
A = {the students in a class that have been to America}
S = {the students in a class that have been to Spain}
F = (the students in a class that have been to France}

Describe, in your own words, the members of the following.

(a) $(A \cup S)$
(b) $(A \cap S \cap F)'$
(c) $S \setminus F$
(d) $(A \setminus F) \cap S$

9 A group of 50 students were asked which of the following they liked: ice cream, chocolate or crisps. 28 said they like ice cream. 26 said they like chocolate while 26 said they like crisps. 8 said they like all three. 17 said they like chocolate and crisps. 11 said they like crisps and ice cream. 5 said they do not like any of these. Let x represent those students who liked ice cream and chocolate but not crisps.

(a) Represent the above information on a Venn diagram.
(b) Calculate the value of x.
(c) Calculate the percentage of students who like one choice only.

Exam-style Questions

1 $U = \{1, 2, 3, ..., 12\}$. P is the set of prime numbers less than 12. E is the set of even numbers less than 12. O is the set of odd numbers less than 12.

(a) Represent these sets on the Venn diagram.

(b) Name any set on this diagram (after part (a) has been completed) that is a null set.

(c) If a number is drawn at random from set P, what is the probability that it is even?

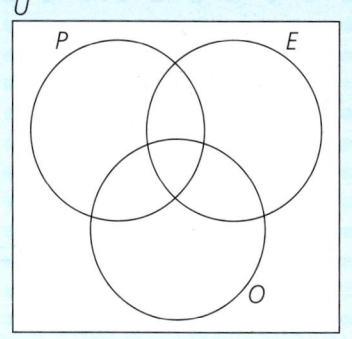

JCHL 2013 Paper 1

2 (a) For diagrams (i) and (ii) below, shade in the named region.

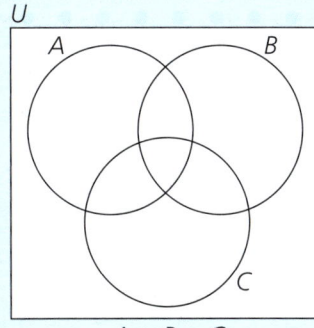

(i) $A \cap B \cap C$

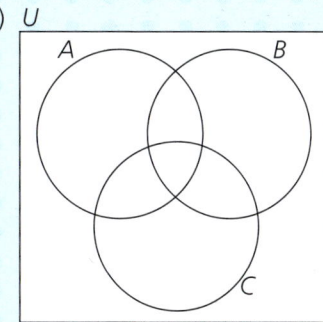

(ii) $(A \cap B) \setminus C$

(b) The box contains six statements (**note**: P' is the complement of set P). A number of the statements are incorrect. Write down one incorrect statement.

Statements

(i) $(A \cup B) = (B \cup A)$
(ii) $(A \cup B) \cup C = A \cup (B \cup C)$
(iii) $(A \setminus B) \setminus C = A \setminus (B \setminus C)$
(iv) $(A \cap B)' = U \setminus (A \cap B)$
(v) $A \setminus B = B \setminus A$
(vi) $B \setminus (A \cup C) = (B \cup C) A \setminus C$

(c) A group of 38 students were asked if they had ever been to France or Spain. The number who had been to Spain only was 3 more than the number who had been to both countries. Twice as many had been to France as Spain. 4 students had not been to either country. Find how many had been to both countries.

JCHL 2013

KEY WORDS AND PHRASES

- Associative property
- Distributive property

Chapter Summary 1

- To represent three sets on a Venn diagram:

  Step 1: Fill in the elements that are common to all three sets in the given question.

  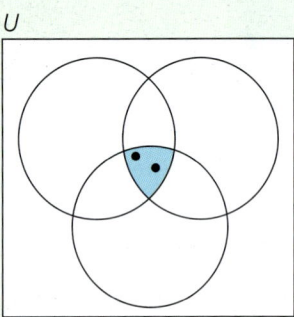

  Step 2: Fill in the elements that are common to two sets.

  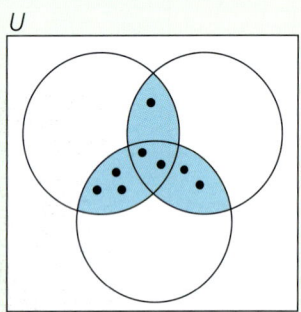

  Step 3: Fill in the elements that are unique to each set.

  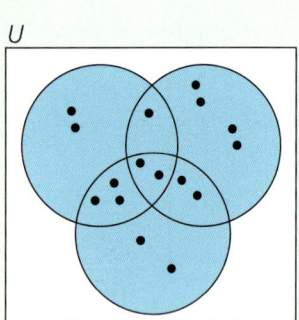

  Step 4: Fill in any remaining elements listed in the Universal set.

  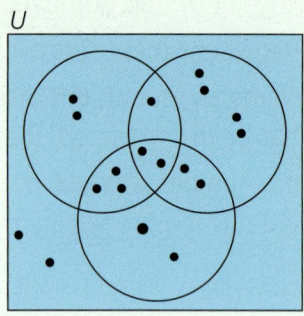

- To fill in a Venn diagram for word problems involving three sets:

  Step 1: Fill in the cardinal number for members that are common to all three sets in the given question.

  Step 2: Fill in the cardinal numbers for members that are common to two sets.

  Step 3: Fill in the cardinal numbers for members that are unique to each set.

  Step 4: Finally, fill in the cardinal number for any remaining members listed in the Universal set.

Number

Chapter 2

Learning Outcomes

In this chapter, you will learn about:

- Fractions, decimals and percentages (review)
- Division involving zero
- Indices
- Equation in which the unknown is an index
- Reciprocals
- Recurring decimals
- Irrational numbers
- Some properties of even, odd and prime numbers

Historical background

Leonhard Euler, from Switzerland, was one of the greatest mathematicians ever to have lived. We have already learned that he was the first to put forward the notion of a mathematical function. But a lot of people know him for his formula which contains the five most important numbers in mathematics:

$$e^{i\pi} + 1 = 0$$

This is considered to be one of the most beautiful formulae in all of mathematics.

Leonhard Euler 1707–1783

You are familiar with three of these numbers: 0, 1 and π. You will meet the other two numbers, e and i later in your studies.

Section 2A Review of Fractions, Decimals and Percentages

In mathematics we have different categories of numbers.

1. The set of **Natural numbers** $\mathbb{N} = \{1, 2, 3, 4, 5, \ldots\}$
   We can think of them as the numbers we use to count natural things: 1 dog, 2 mountains etc. We can show these on the number line:

   The Natural numbers allow us to **add** and **multiply** always. That is, if we add two Natural numbers, we always get a Natural number and if we multiply two Natural numbers, we always get a Natural number.

However, we cannot always subtract or divide Natural numbers and get an element of ℕ as an answer. For example, if we subtract 3 from 2, we don't get a Natural number.

So we need more numbers.

2. The set of **Integers** ℤ = {..., –4, –3, –2, –1, 0, 1, 2, 3, ...}

   The Integers have all the Natural numbers along with 0 and the negative whole numbers.

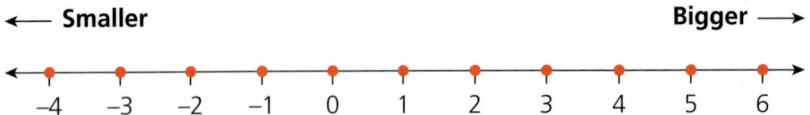

These allow us to **add**, **subtract** and **multiply** always.

However, we cannot always divide and get an element of ℤ as an answer.

This is where fractions (Rational numbers) are needed.

3. The **Rational numbers** ℚ = the set of all numbers which can be written in the form $\frac{p}{q}$ where p and $q \in$ ℤ and $q \neq 0$.

   This means that a Rational number is any number which can be written as a fraction with whole numbers as numerator and denominator.

   Of course, the sets ℕ and ℤ are included in ℚ, since any whole number can be written as a fraction with 1 as the denominator.

   We cannot show all the Rational numbers on the number line, but this diagram shows a small selection of them:

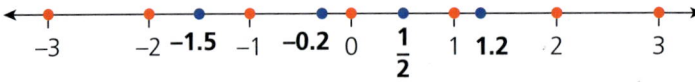

We can see that ℕ ⊂ ℤ ⊂ ℚ and we can represent these sets of numbers on a diagram like this:

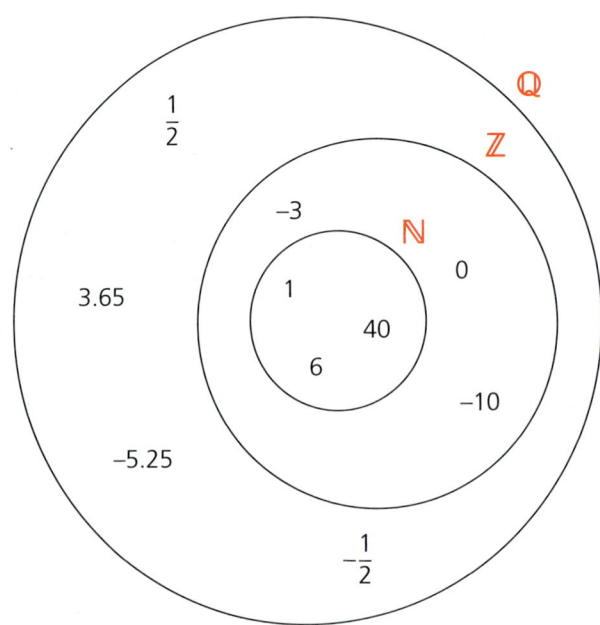

Note: The definition of a Rational number $\frac{p}{q}$ above says that q must $\neq 0$. We will discuss why this is in the next section.

Activity 2.1

1. (i) Write down a fraction between $\frac{1}{3}$ and $\frac{1}{4}$.

   (ii) Can you list two fractions between $\frac{1}{3}$ and $\frac{1}{4}$?

2.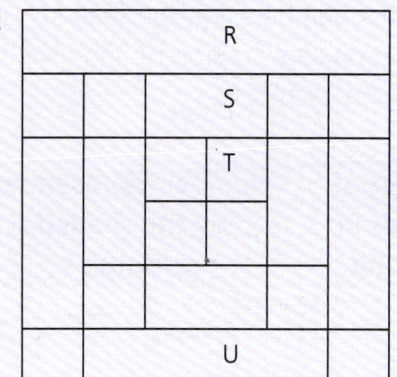

   (i) What fraction of the whole square is R?

   (ii) What fraction of the whole square is S?

   (iii) What fraction of the whole square is T?

   (iv) What fraction of the whole square is U?

3. Calculate:
   (i) 30% of €26
   (ii) 125% of €12
   (iii) 40% of 80% of €25
   (iv) $\frac{1}{3}$ of $\frac{1}{3}$ of $\frac{1}{3}$ of 81

4. Which of these rectangles has $\frac{3}{4}$ shaded in? Is there more than one?

   (i)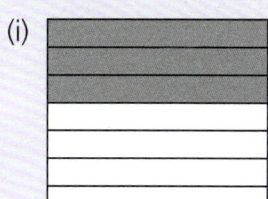

   (ii)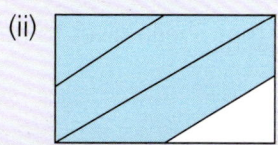

   (iii)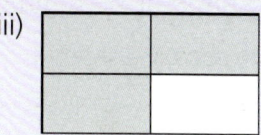

   (iv)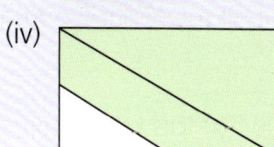

5. Kate gave $\frac{1}{5}$ of her pocket money to charity. Joe gave $\frac{1}{5}$ of his pocket money to another charity. Joe said that he gave more money to charity than Kate did. Explain how Joe could be right.

6. (i) Decrease €16 by 20%.
   (ii) Increase €8 by 70%.
   (iii) Decrease 50% of €3.60 by $\frac{1}{6}$.

7. Students were asked to explain why $\frac{5}{6}$ is greater than $\frac{4}{5}$. Which of the following explanations is the correct one?
   (i) Because 5 is greater than 4
   (ii) Because 6 is greater than 5
   (iii) Because 5 + 6 is greater than 4 + 5
   (iv) Because $\frac{5}{6}$ is closer to 1 than $\frac{4}{5}$

8. Which of these fractions is smallest? Explain your answer.
   (i) $\frac{3}{7}$ (ii) $\frac{1}{4}$ (iii) $\frac{2}{5}$ (iv) $\frac{1}{2}$

9. Tanya started her new job as a trainee. After 6 months she is to get a 50% rise in pay. After a further 6 months she will be due a second rise in pay of 50%. 'This is great', said Tanya, 'One year from now I will have double my present pay.' Is Tanya correct? Explain your reasoning.

10 Here are three number lines all of which are the same length.

This number line shows $\frac{2}{3}$ shaded.

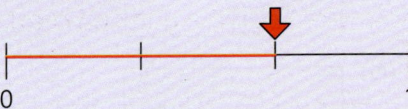

(i) What fraction of this number line is shaded?

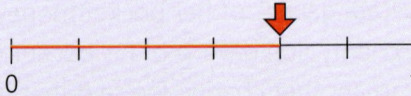

(ii) What fraction of this number line is shaded?

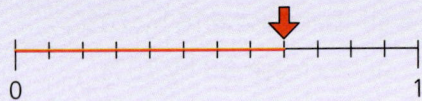

(iii) What do these three fractions have in common?

11 The diagrams show two circles of the same size.

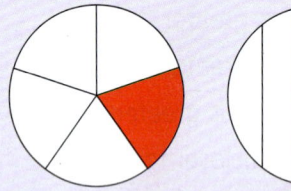

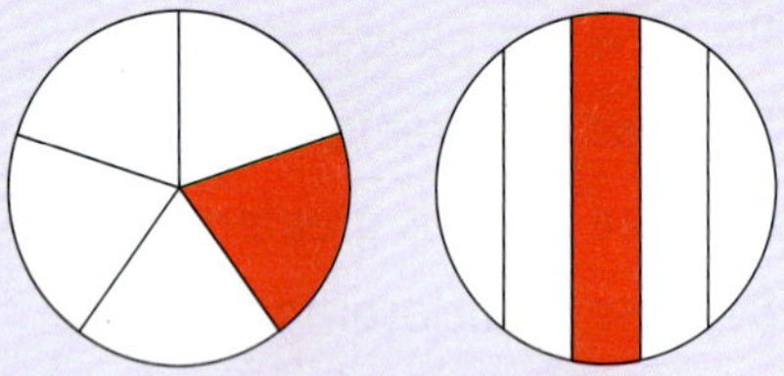

Are the shaded portions in each the same size? Explain your answer.

12 The diagram shows $\frac{2}{3}$ of a garden.

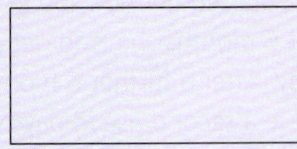

(i) Copy the diagram into your copy.
(ii) Modify the diagram to show the whole garden.

13

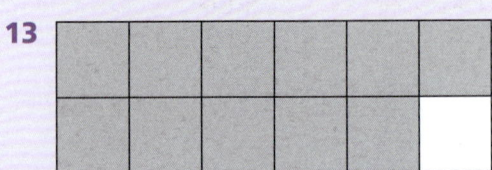

(i) If the shaded portion represents $2\frac{3}{4}$, how many small squares make a unit?

(ii) Using the same unit, what would 6 small squares represent?
(iii) If 3 shaded squares represent a unit, what number would be represented by the total number of shaded squares?
(iv) On a copy of the table, list some other numbers that the shaded portion could represent and give the unit in each case.

Number of squares in one unit	Number represented by the shaded rectangles

14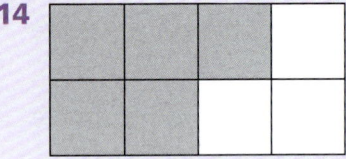

The shaded part of this diagram could represent the numbers

A: 5   B: $2\frac{1}{2}$ C: $\frac{5}{8}$ D: $1\frac{1}{4}$

Identify the unit in each case.

15 Tony tiled $\frac{4}{5}$ of a bathroom wall. Next day he grouted $\frac{7}{8}$ of the tiled section. What fraction of the bathroom wall had grouted tiles?

16 Sheila buys $\frac{5}{6}$ kg cheese. She keeps $\frac{3}{4}$ of it and gives $\frac{1}{4}$ to her sister.
What is the weight of:
(i) the cheese that Sheila keeps
(ii) the cheese that Sheila gives to her sister?

17 A shop's sales of ice cream in August was €700. In September, their sales went down to €500.
  (i) What fraction is this of August's sales?
  (ii) By what fraction must €500 be multiplied to get back to August's sales figures of €700?

18 (i) The diagram below shows three-fifths of a rectangle. Copy the grid and complete the rectangle.

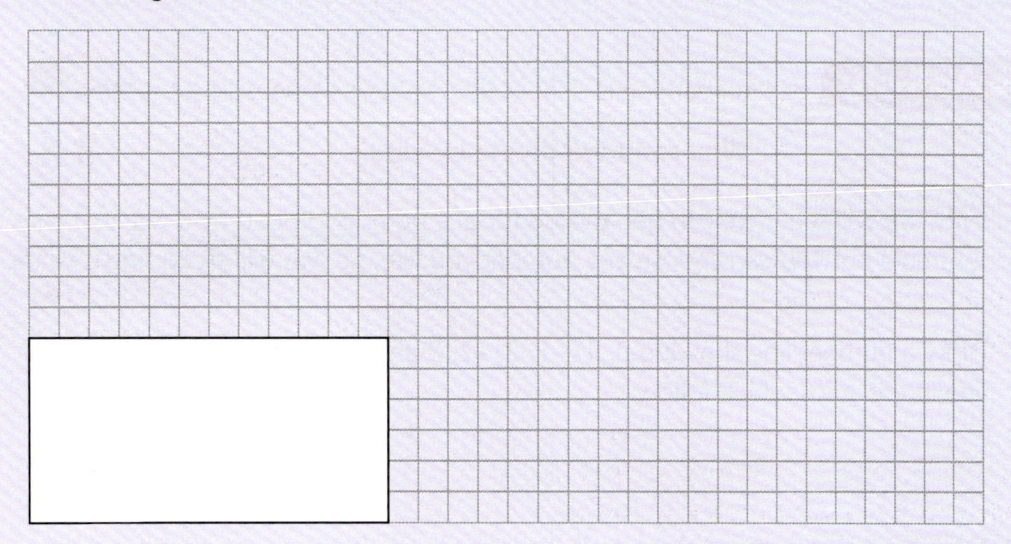

(ii) Copy the diagram below and by shading appropriate sections of the strips below, show that

$$\frac{1}{3} + \frac{2}{6} \neq \frac{3}{9}$$

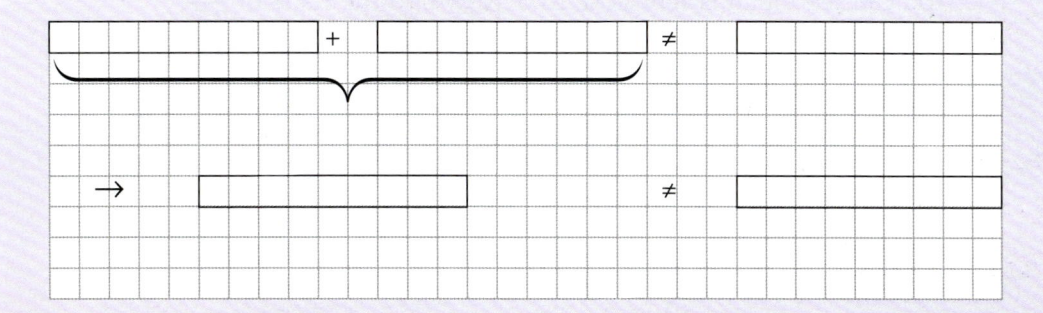

JCHL 2012 Paper 1

Section 2B Division Involving Zero

Division involving zero needs to be looked at carefully.

1. **Zero as the numerator**
    What does $\frac{0}{3}$ mean? It could mean that we are dividing €0 among 3 people.
    Each gets €0. So $\frac{0}{3} = 0$.

    > Thus, if a fraction has zero as numerator, its value = 0.
    > Rule:
    > If $\frac{a}{b} = 0$ then $a = 0$ If $a = 0$ then $\frac{a}{b} = 0$ (provided that $b \neq 0$)

CONNECT WITH MATHS 2

2. **Zero as the denominator**

What does $\frac{2}{0}$ mean? Key this into your calculator. You get 'math error'. Why is this?

Put in simple terms, **we cannot divide by zero!**

The next activity explains why.

Class Activity

Why can't we divide by zero?

In this activity, we will see if we can get a value for any number divided by 0 (we will take 5 for this example but you can choose any number you like, i.e. we will try to find a value for $\frac{5}{0}$).

Step 1 Draw a number line showing 0, 1, −1, 2, −2, 3 and −3. You will use this number line in the steps which follow.

```
—•———•———•———•———•———•———•—
−3  −2  −1   0   1   2   3
```

Step 2 Now we pick a number **close to 0**. Let's choose 1. (You can see that it is right next to 0 on the number line.) Now find the value of $\frac{5}{1}$. Your answer is 5. Since 0 is close to 1, we could say that $\frac{5}{0}$ is close to $\frac{5}{1}$ which = 5.

Step 3 Now let's pick a number **closer to 0**. Let's choose 0.5. Mark it in on your number line. You can see that it is very close to 0. Now find the value of $\frac{5}{0.5}$.
Write down its value.
Is this close to the value of $\frac{5}{0}$?

Step 4 Now take another number which is **closer still to 0**. Let's choose 0.1. Mark it in on your number line. It is really close to 0. So now we find the value of $\frac{5}{0.1}$.
Write down its value.
Is this close to the value of $\frac{5}{0}$?

Step 5 Now let's take another number which is **closer still to 0**. Let's choose 0.01. Mark it in on your number line if you can. It is really very close to 0. Now find the value of $\frac{5}{0.01}$.
Write down its value.
Are we close to the value of $\frac{5}{0}$?

Step 6 One more time, let's take another number which is **really close to 0**. Let's choose 0.001. Point to where it is on your number line if you can (you won't have space to mark it). You can imagine that it is really very close to 0. Now find the value of $\frac{5}{0.001}$.
Write down its value.
Surely the value of $\frac{5}{0.001}$ is near to the value of $\frac{5}{0}$?

Step 7 In order to clearly see the pattern, copy and complete this table using your answers from above and a calculator.

Value of a	$\frac{5}{a}$	Value of $\frac{5}{a}$
1	$\frac{5}{1}$	5
0.1	$\frac{5}{0.1}$	50
0.01		
0.001		
0.0001		
0.00001		

Step 8 We have divided 5 by numbers which are very close to 0. When do we get to 0? What then is the value of $\frac{5}{0}$?

We cannot get a value for $\frac{a}{0}$ where a is any number, so we say that $\frac{a}{0}$ is **undefined**.

Note: You might ask 'what about $\frac{0}{0}$?'

Now this is really complicated. Mathematicians call this 'an indeterminate form'. We won't deal with this here!

Section 2C Indices

We know already that 2^4 (we say '2 to the power of 4') is a short way of writing $2 \times 2 \times 2 \times 2$.

The number 4 is called the **exponent** or **index** (plural indices).

The number 2 is called the **base**.

The expression 6^2 is pronounced 'six to the power of two' or 'six squared'.

The expression 6^3 is pronounced 'six to the power of three' or 'six cubed'.

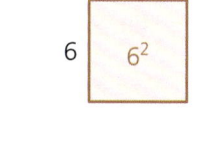

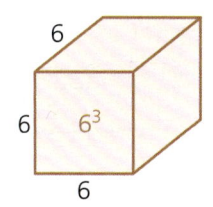

nth Roots

Since $6^2 = 36$, we also say that $\sqrt{36} = 6$.

Since $2^3 = 8$, we also say that $\sqrt[3]{8} = 2$.

Since $3^4 = 81$, we also say that $\sqrt[4]{81} = 3$.

Since $2^5 = 32$, we also say that $\sqrt[5]{32} = 2$.

Note: $\sqrt{9}$ stands for the **non-negative** square root of 9, so $\sqrt{9} = 3$.

We have learned some rules of indices which we will now extend to include negative powers and fractional powers.

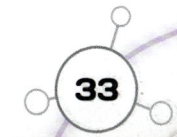

2. Rules of Indices

Rules of indices	Examples
Rule 1: $a^m \times a^n = a^{m+n}$	$5^3 \times 5^6 = 5^9$
Rule 2: $\dfrac{a^m}{a^n} = a^{m-n}$	$\dfrac{3^7}{3^5} = 3^2$
Rule 3: $a^0 = 1$	$27^0 = 1$
Rule 4: $(a^m)^n = a^{mn}$	$(3^2)^4 = 3^8$
Rule 5: $a^{-m} = \dfrac{1}{a^m}$	$5^{-3} = \dfrac{1}{5^3}$
Rule 6: $a^{\frac{1}{q}} = \sqrt[q]{a}$	$8^{\frac{1}{2}} = \sqrt{8}$
Rule 7: $a^{\frac{p}{q}} = (\sqrt[q]{a})^p$	$27^{\frac{2}{3}} = (\sqrt[3]{27})^2 = 3^2 = 9$
Rule 8: $(ab)^m = a^m b^m$	$(3\sqrt{2})^2 = 3^2 \times (\sqrt{2})^2 = 9 \times 2 = 18$
Rule 9: $\left(\dfrac{a}{b}\right)^m = \dfrac{a^m}{b^m}$	$\left(\dfrac{2}{3}\right)^3 = \dfrac{2^3}{3^3} = \dfrac{8}{27}$

These rules are on page 21 of the *Formulae and tables* booklet.

Example

Write as rational numbers: (i) 2^{-3} (ii) $27^{\frac{1}{3}}$ (iii) $(32)^{\frac{3}{5}}$ (iv) $\left(\dfrac{4}{9}\right)^{-\frac{3}{2}}$

Solution

(i) 2^{-3}

$= \dfrac{1}{2^3}$ ...Rule 5

$= \dfrac{1}{8}$

(ii) $27^{\frac{1}{3}}$

$= \sqrt[3]{27}$ ...Rule 6

$= 3$

(iii) $(32)^{\frac{3}{5}}$

$= (32^{\frac{1}{5}})^3$ ...Rule 4

$= (\sqrt[5]{32})^3$ ...Rule 6

$= (2)^3$

$= 8$

(iv) $\left(\dfrac{4}{9}\right)^{-\frac{3}{2}}$

$= \dfrac{4^{-\frac{3}{2}}}{9^{-\frac{3}{2}}}$ ...Rule 9

$= \dfrac{9^{\frac{3}{2}}}{4^{\frac{3}{2}}}$ ...Rule 5

$= \dfrac{(9^{\frac{1}{2}})^3}{(4^{\frac{1}{2}})^3}$ ...Rule 4

$= \dfrac{(3)^3}{(2)^3}$ ...Rule 6

$= \dfrac{27}{8}$

Activity 2.2

1. Simplify:
   (i) $a^4 \times a^5$
   (ii) $\dfrac{a^6}{a^2}$
   (iii) $\dfrac{a^3 \times a^7}{a^8}$
   (iv) $(a^3)^4$
   (v) $(a^3 b^2)^3$
   (vi) $(ab^4)^5$

2. Complete the following by filling in values for ?: $a^0 = \dfrac{a^0 \times a^7}{a^7} = \dfrac{?}{a^7} = ?$

3. Complete the following by filling in values for ?: $a^{-5} = \dfrac{a^{-5} \times a^5}{a^5} = \dfrac{?}{a^5} = \dfrac{?}{a^5}$

Evaluate the following.

4. $25^{\frac{1}{2}}$
5. 6^{-2}
6. 77^0
7. $16^{\frac{1}{2}}$
8. 5^{-1}
9. $9^{\frac{1}{2}}$
10. $9^{-\frac{1}{2}}$
11. $100^{\frac{1}{2}}$
12. $100^{-\frac{1}{2}}$
13. $1000^{\frac{1}{3}}$
14. $16^{\frac{1}{4}}$
15. $\left(\frac{4}{9}\right)^{\frac{1}{2}}$
16. $8^{\frac{2}{3}}$
17. $27^{\frac{1}{3}}$
18. $9^{\frac{3}{2}}$
19. $32^{\frac{3}{5}}$
20. $\left(\frac{1}{1000}\right)^{\frac{1}{3}}$
21. $\left(\frac{8}{9}\right)^0$
22. $216^{\frac{1}{3}}$
23. $81^{\frac{1}{4}}$
24. $243^{\frac{1}{5}}$
25. $243^{-\frac{1}{5}}$
26. $125^{\frac{1}{3}}$
27. $125^{\frac{2}{3}}$
28. $\left(\frac{16}{81}\right)^{\frac{1}{2}}$
29. $\left(\frac{16}{81}\right)^{\frac{3}{2}}$
30. $\left(\frac{27}{64}\right)^{\frac{1}{3}}$
31. $\left(\frac{27}{64}\right)^{\frac{4}{3}}$
32. $\left(\frac{16}{81}\right)^{\frac{1}{4}}$
33. $\left(\frac{16}{81}\right)^{\frac{3}{4}}$
34. $\left(\frac{81}{16}\right)^{-\frac{3}{4}}$
35. $\left(\frac{169}{25}\right)^{\frac{1}{2}}$
36. $\left(\frac{8}{125}\right)^{\frac{1}{3}}$
37. $\left(\frac{8}{125}\right)^{\frac{2}{3}}$
38. $\left(\frac{8}{125}\right)^{\frac{4}{3}}$
39. $\left(\frac{27}{64}\right)^{-\frac{2}{3}}$
40. $\left(1\frac{24}{25}\right)^{\frac{3}{2}}$
41. $\left(3\frac{1}{16}\right)^{-\frac{3}{2}}$

42. Write each of these in the form x^m, where $m \in \mathbb{Q}$.
    (i) $\sqrt{x}$
    (ii) $x\sqrt{x}$
    (iii) $\frac{x^2}{\sqrt{x}}$
    (iv) $\sqrt[4]{x}$
    (v) $(\sqrt{x})(\sqrt[3]{x})$

43. Answer true or false to these statements. Explain your answers.
    (i) $3^2 + 2^2 = 5^2$
    (ii) $5^8 \times 5^{-6} = 5^2$
    (iii) $(4^2)^3 = 4^5$
    (iv) $(4^2)(3^3) = 12^5$
    (v) $5^{-1} = -5$
    (vi) $4^{\frac{1}{2}} + 9^{\frac{1}{2}} = 13^{\frac{1}{2}}$
    (vii) $36^{\frac{1}{2}} - 25^{\frac{1}{2}} = 11^{\frac{1}{2}}$

44. Write $4\sqrt{2}$ in the form 2^n where $n \in \mathbb{Q}$.

45. Write $\frac{27\sqrt{3}}{3^{-2}}$ in the form 3^n where $n \in \mathbb{Q}$.

46. Write $\frac{125^{\frac{2}{3}} \times \sqrt{5}}{25^{\frac{1}{2}}}$ in the form 5^n where $n \in \mathbb{Q}$.

Section 2D Equations in Which the Unknown is an Index

In an equation such as $3^x = 81$, the unknown variable (x) is an index.

To solve such equations, we use the following rule:

If $a^x = a^y$ then $x = y$.

To solve such equations:
- Write all numbers as powers of the same number
- Use the rules of indices to write each side of the equation as a power of the same number
- Equate the indices and solve.

Example 1

Solve for x the equation $3^x = 81$.

Solution

$3^x = 81$

$\Rightarrow 3^x = 3^4$ ...write 81 as a power of 3

$\Rightarrow x = 4$ ... equate the indices.

Example 2

Find the value of x for which $4^{x-1} = 32$.

Solution

$4^{x-1} = 32$

$\Rightarrow (2^2)^{x-1} = 2^5$ ... write 4 and 32 as powers of 2

$\Rightarrow 2^{2x-2} = 2^5$ ... rule 4 of indices

$\Rightarrow 2x - 2 = 5$ ... equate the powers

$\Rightarrow 2x = 5 + 2$

$\Rightarrow 2x = 7$

$\Rightarrow x = \frac{7}{2}$

Example 3

Solve for x the equation $4^{x+2} = 8^{1-x}$.

Solution

$4^{x+2} = 8^{1-x}$

$\Rightarrow (2^2)^{x+2} = (2^3)^{1-x}$ ... write all numbers as powers of 2

$\Rightarrow 2^{2x+4} = 2^{3-3x}$ .... rule 4 of indices

$\Rightarrow 2x + 4 = 3 - 3x$ ... equate the indices

$\Rightarrow 2x + 3x = 3 - 4$

$\Rightarrow 5x = -1$

$\Rightarrow x = -\frac{1}{5}$

Example 4

If $\dfrac{5^2 \times 125^{\frac{1}{3}}}{25^{\frac{5}{2}} \times 5^3} = 5^n$, find n, where $n \in \mathbb{Z}$.

Solution

$\dfrac{5^2 \times 125^{\frac{1}{3}}}{25^{\frac{5}{2}} \times 5^3} = 5^n$

$\Rightarrow \dfrac{5^2 \times (5^3)^{\frac{1}{3}}}{(5^2)^{\frac{5}{2}} \times 5^3} = 5^n$ ... write all numbers as powers of 5

$\Rightarrow \dfrac{5^2 \times 5^{3 \times \frac{1}{3}}}{5^{2 \times \frac{5}{2}} \times 5^3} = 5^n$ ... rule 4 of indices

$\Rightarrow \dfrac{5^2 \times 5^1}{5^5 \times 5^3} = 5^n$

$\Rightarrow \dfrac{5^3}{5^8} = 5^n$ ... rule 1

$\Rightarrow 5^{3-8} = 5^n$ ...rule 2

$\Rightarrow 5^{-5} = 5^n$

$\Rightarrow -5 = n$

i.e $n = -5$

Activity 2.3

1. Solve each of the following equations:
   (i) $3^x = 27$
   (ii) $2^x = 64$
   (iii) $5^x = 125$
   (iv) $10^x = 1000$
   (v) $5^{3x} = 5^{15}$
   (vi) $7^{x+2} = 7^3$
   (vii) $3^{x-2} = 3^5$
   (viii) $2^x = 256$

2. Solve each of the following equations:
   (i) $2^x = 8^2$
   (ii) $3^{3x} = 9^6$
   (iii) $4^{2x} = 8^2$
   (iv) $10^{2x} = 100^2$
   (v) $5^{2x} = 25^8$
   (vi) $7^{x+5} = 49^3$
   (vii) $3^{x+2} = 27^5$
   (viii) $2^{4x} = 8^{x+1}$

3. Find the value of x for which $2^{x+5} = 4^x$.

4. Find the value of x for which $25^x = 5^{9-x}$.

5. Find the value of x for which $\dfrac{5^x}{2} = \dfrac{5^6}{50}$.

6. (i) Find the value of 3^6.
   (ii) Write 81 in the form 3^k, where $k \in \mathbb{N}$.
   (iii) Solve for x the equation $81 \times 3^x = \dfrac{1}{729}$.

7. (i) Evaluate $8^{\frac{1}{3}}$.
   (ii) Express $4^{\frac{1}{4}}$ in the form 2^k, $k \in \mathbb{Q}$.
   (iii) Find the value of x for which $\left(8^{\frac{1}{3}}\right)\left(4^{\frac{1}{4}}\right) = 2^{4-x}$.

8. (i) Write as a power of 2:
   (a) 8
   (b) $8^{\frac{2}{3}}$.
   (ii) Solve for x the equation $8^{\frac{2}{3}} = \dfrac{2^{3x-4}}{8}$.

9. (i) Write as a power of 3:
   (a) 243
   (b) $\sqrt{27}$
   (ii) Solve for x the equation $3^x = \left(\dfrac{243}{\sqrt{27}}\right)^2$.

10. (i) Write $2^6 - 2^5$ in the form 2^k, where $k \in \mathbb{N}$.
    (ii) Solve for x the equation: $2^{3x-4} = 2^6 - 2^5$.

11. (i) Write $\sqrt{125}$ as a power of 5.
    (ii) Solve for x the equation $\dfrac{5^{2x+1}}{5} = \left(\dfrac{1}{\sqrt{125}}\right)^2$.

12. Solve for p the equation $9^p = \dfrac{1}{\sqrt{3}}$.

13. If $\dfrac{5^2 \times 25^{\frac{1}{2}}}{125^{\frac{2}{3}} \times 5^3} = 5^n$, find n, where $n \in \mathbb{Z}$.

14. Solve the equation $\dfrac{\sqrt[3]{27} \times 3}{9^{\frac{1}{2}} \times 3^4} = 3^n$, where $n \in \mathbb{Z}$.

Section 2E Recurring Decimals

Divide 10 by 3. You get 3.33333333333333…

On the calculator, you see 3.3̇. The dot on top of the second 3 indicates that the 3s go on indefinitely.

Similarly, 3.456745674567… is written as 3.4̇567̇.

These are examples of **recurring decimals**.

Other examples:

Recurring decimal	Written as
3.65656565…	3.6̇5̇
5.494494494…	5.4̇94̇
6.12341234…	6.1̇234̇

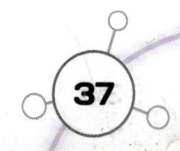

Despite the fact that the decimals never end, we can still write these numbers as fractions.

Example 1

Express 0.3333333… as a rational number.

Solution

Let $x = 0.3333333…$

$\Rightarrow 10x = 3.3333333…$
$\Rightarrow 9x = 3.3333333… - 0.3333333…$
$\Rightarrow 9x = 3$
$\Rightarrow x = \frac{3}{9} = \frac{1}{3}$

Example 2

Express 0.246246246… as a rational number.

Solution

Let $x = 0.246246246…$

$\Rightarrow 1000x = 246.246246246…$
$\Rightarrow 999x = 246.246246246…$
$\qquad\qquad - 0.246246246…$
$\Rightarrow 999x = 246$
$\Rightarrow x = \frac{246}{999}$

We can see that even though there is no limit to the number of decimal places, we can write the number as a fraction **provided the decimals repeat at some stage**. In the next section, we deal with numbers where this does not happen.

Activity 2.4

1. Express 0.22222222… as a rational number.
2. Express 0.66666… as a fraction.
3. Express 0.4545454545… as a rational number.
4. Express 0.237892378923789… as a rational number.
5. Express $5.49\dot{4}$ in the form $\frac{a}{b}$ where $a, b \in \mathbb{Z}$.
6. Express $0.3 2\dot{3}$ in the form $\frac{a}{b}$ where $a, b \in \mathbb{Z}$.
7. Express 1.444444… as a rational number.
8. Can you express 1.414213562… as a rational number? Why? Why is this number different from the previous ones you met in this activity?
9. The following are the first 60 digits of a very familiar number which you have been using for some time. What number is it?
   3.14159265358979323846264338327950288419716939937510582097494…
   Why can't it be written as a rational number?

Section 2F Irrational Numbers

Remember what 'square root' means. When we say that $\sqrt{25} = 5$, we are getting a number which when multiplied by itself gives 25.

We can write a few of the Natural numbers in a table and see their squares.

Natural numbers	1	2	3	4	5	6	7	…
Squares	1	4	9	16	25	36	49	…

Only the Natural numbers on the bottom line of this table have a square root which is a Natural number. They are known as **perfect squares**.

The square roots of all other numbers are not Natural numbers. Examples are $\sqrt{2}, \sqrt{3}, \sqrt{5}$ etc. In fact, these numbers cannot be written as fractions either. They are known as **irrational numbers** for this reason. Irrational numbers like these are also called **surds**.

One of the most famous irrational numbers is $\sqrt{2}$. When we insert $\sqrt{2}$ on a calculator which has a 10-digit display, we get 1.414213562. But these digits are only the start of a never-ending sequence of digits which never shows a pattern.

(Remember that we were able to express numbers with an infinite number of decimal places as fractions **if they had a repeating pattern**. Irrational numbers show no pattern.)

Connections

We find $\sqrt{2}$ appearing in geometry constructions quite often.

Take a square of side 1 unit, for example.
Using the theorem of Pythagoras, we get:

$1^2 + 1^2 = 1 + 1 = 2$

∴ the diagonal is $\sqrt{2}$ units long.

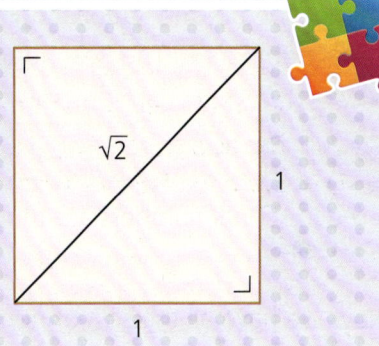

Locating $\sqrt{2}$ on the Number Line

Connections

Even though we cannot write $\sqrt{2}$ precisely, we can still find its location on the number line by using Pythagoras' theorem and our geometry constructions.

- On the number line at number 1, construct a perpendicular line segment of length 1 unit.

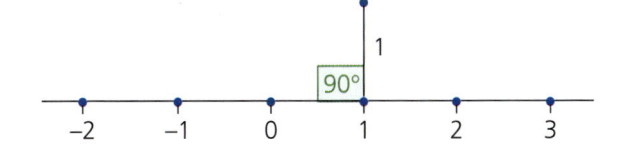

- Complete the right-angled triangle as shown. By our work above with Pythagoras' Theorem, the hypotenuse = $\sqrt{2}$ units.

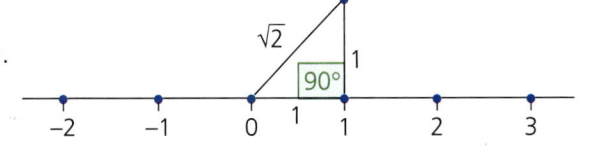

- Using a compass, draw an arc with centre at point 0 and radius = the hypotenuse, to meet the number line. This point is the location of $\sqrt{2}$ on the number line.

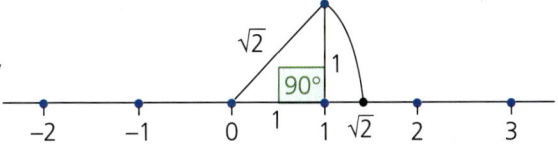

Historical background

The number π is another famous irrational number. You will recall that π is the number you get when you divide the circumference of any circle by its diameter. Even though this number was known for many hundreds of years, it was not until 1767 that it was proved to be irrational by a Swiss mathematician called Lambert.

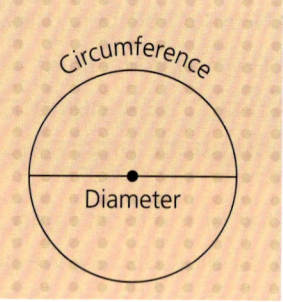

Real Numbers ℝ

When we put the Rational numbers together with the Irrational numbers, we get the set of Real numbers ℝ. The Real numbers completely 'fill up' the number line:

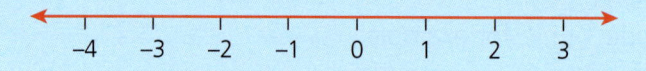

$$-4 \quad -3 \quad -2 \quad -1 \quad 0 \quad 1 \quad 2 \quad 3$$

The Irrational numbers are thus often referred to as ℝ\ℚ.

Now we have all the sets of numbers up to the Real numbers: ℕ, ℤ, ℚ and ℝ.

We can represent them on a Venn diagram like this:

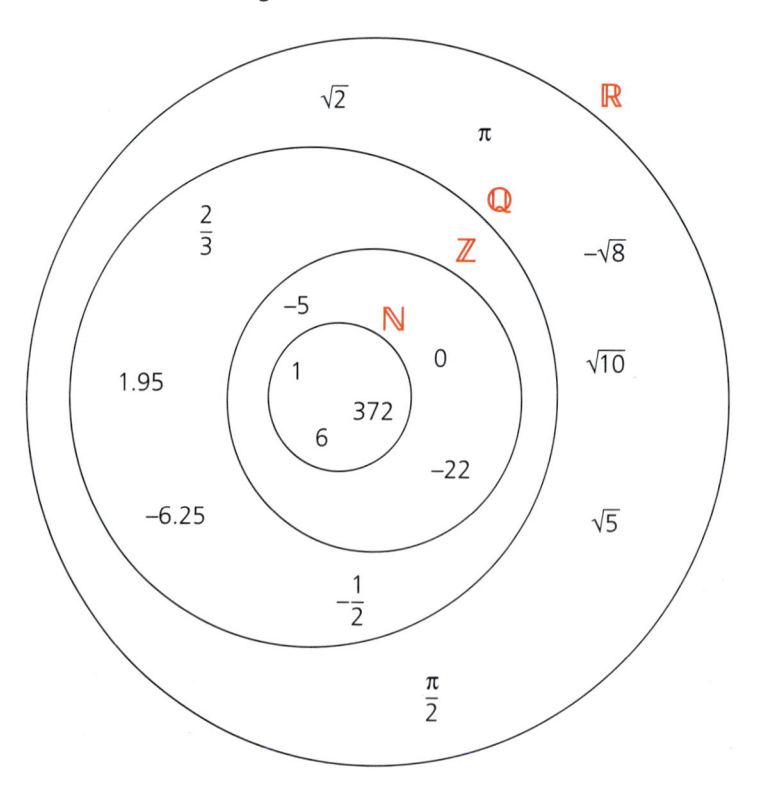

These are just a very small selection of the numbers in these sets.

We can see that ℕ ⊂ ℤ ⊂ ℚ ⊂ ℝ.

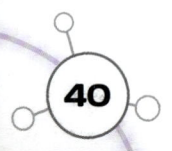

Working with Surds

Remember that $\sqrt{a} = a^{\frac{1}{2}}$, so when we work with surds we are really working with indices, and the same rules apply.

Rules	Examples
$\sqrt{a}\sqrt{a} = a^{\frac{1}{2}} \times a^{\frac{1}{2}} = a^1 = a$	$\sqrt{6}\sqrt{6} = 6^{\frac{1}{2}} \times 6^{\frac{1}{2}} = 6^1 = 6$ $2\sqrt{5} \times 3\sqrt{5} = (2 \times 3) \times 5^{\frac{1}{2}} \times 5^{\frac{1}{2}} = 6 \times 5^1 = 30$
$\sqrt{a}\sqrt{b} = a^{\frac{1}{2}} \times b^{\frac{1}{2}} = (ab)^{\frac{1}{2}} = \sqrt{ab}$	$\sqrt{3}\sqrt{5} = 3^{\frac{1}{2}} \times 5^{\frac{1}{2}} = (3 \times 5)^{\frac{1}{2}} = 15^{\frac{1}{2}} = \sqrt{15}$
$\dfrac{\sqrt{a}}{\sqrt{b}} = \dfrac{a^{\frac{1}{2}}}{b^{\frac{1}{2}}} = \left(\dfrac{a}{b}\right)^{\frac{1}{2}} = \sqrt{\dfrac{a}{b}}$	$\dfrac{\sqrt{15}}{\sqrt{5}} = \sqrt{\dfrac{15}{5}} = \sqrt{3}$
Like terms can be added	$4\sqrt{2} + 5\sqrt{2} - 6\sqrt{2} = 9\sqrt{2} - 6\sqrt{2} = 3\sqrt{2}$
Unlike like terms cannot be added, so $\sqrt{a} + \sqrt{b}$ cannot be simplified, $\sqrt{a} - \sqrt{b}$ cannot be simplified.	$\sqrt{16} + \sqrt{9} \neq \sqrt{25}$ $\sqrt{25} - \sqrt{16} \neq \sqrt{9}$

Example 1

Simplify $3\sqrt{5} + 4\sqrt{5} - 2\sqrt{5}$.

Solution

$3\sqrt{5} + 4\sqrt{5} - 2\sqrt{5}$

$= 7\sqrt{5} - 2\sqrt{5}$

$= 5\sqrt{5}$

Example 2

Simplify $(2\sqrt{3}) \times (4\sqrt{5})$.

Solution

$(2\sqrt{3}) \times (4\sqrt{5})$

$= (2)(4) \times (\sqrt{3})(\sqrt{5})$ ... the associative law for multiplication

$= 8 \times \sqrt{15}$ .... rules of indices

$= 8\sqrt{15}$

We can simplify a surd if one of its factors is a perfect square.

Example 3

Simplify $\sqrt{72} + \sqrt{32}$ using the rules of indices (i.e. calculator not allowed).

Solution

72 has three perfect squares as factors: 4, 9 and 36. Use the biggest: 36.

32 has two perfect squares as factors: 4 and 16. Use the bigger: 16.

$\Rightarrow \sqrt{72} + \sqrt{32}$

$= \sqrt{2 \times 36} + \sqrt{2 \times 16}$

$= \sqrt{2} \times \sqrt{36} + \sqrt{2} \times \sqrt{16}$

$= 6\sqrt{2} + 4\sqrt{2}$

$= 10\sqrt{2}$

Example 4

Simplify $2\sqrt{27} + \dfrac{1}{2}\sqrt{12} - \sqrt{75}$.

Solution

$2\sqrt{27} + \dfrac{1}{2}\sqrt{12} - \sqrt{75}$

$= 2\sqrt{9}\sqrt{3} + \dfrac{1}{2}\sqrt{4}\sqrt{3} - \sqrt{25}\sqrt{3}$

$= 2 \times 3\sqrt{3} + \dfrac{1}{2} \times 2\sqrt{3} - 5\sqrt{3}$

$= 6\sqrt{3} + \sqrt{3} - 5\sqrt{3}$

$= 2\sqrt{3}$

Example 5

Simplify $(3 + \sqrt{5})(4 - 2\sqrt{5})$.

Solution

$(3 + \sqrt{5})(4 - 2\sqrt{5})$
$= 3(4 - 2\sqrt{5}) + \sqrt{5}(4 - 2\sqrt{5})$
$= 12 - 6\sqrt{5} + 4\sqrt{5} - 2(5)$
$= 2 - 2\sqrt{5}$

Example 6

Simplify $\dfrac{-7 + \sqrt{98}}{7}$.

Solution

$\dfrac{-7 + \sqrt{98}}{7}$
$= \dfrac{-7 + \sqrt{49 \times 2}}{7}$
$= \dfrac{-7 + 7\sqrt{2}}{7}$
$= -1 + \sqrt{2}$

Example 7

(i) Write $\dfrac{1}{\sqrt{3}}$ in the form $a\sqrt{3}$, where $a \in \mathbb{Q}$.

(ii) Write $\dfrac{2}{\sqrt{5}}$ in the form $a\sqrt{5}$, where $a \in \mathbb{Q}$.

Solution

(i) $\dfrac{1}{\sqrt{3}} = \dfrac{1}{\sqrt{3}} \times \dfrac{\sqrt{3}}{\sqrt{3}}$
$= \dfrac{\sqrt{3}}{3}$
$= \dfrac{1}{3}\sqrt{3}$

Solution

(ii) $\dfrac{2}{\sqrt{5}} = \dfrac{2}{\sqrt{5}} \times \dfrac{\sqrt{5}}{\sqrt{5}}$
$= \dfrac{2\sqrt{5}}{5}$
$= \dfrac{2}{5}\sqrt{5}$

Example 8

Write $\dfrac{4 + \sqrt{3}}{\sqrt{2}}$ in the form $a\sqrt{b} + c\sqrt{d}$, where $a, c \in \mathbb{Q}$ and $b, d \in \mathbb{N}$.

Solution

$\dfrac{4 + \sqrt{3}}{\sqrt{2}} = \dfrac{4 + \sqrt{3}}{\sqrt{2}} \times \dfrac{\sqrt{2}}{\sqrt{2}}$
$= \dfrac{4\sqrt{2} + \sqrt{6}}{2}$
$= 2\sqrt{2} + \dfrac{1}{2}\sqrt{6}$

Activity 2.5

1 (i) Give two reasons why $-\dfrac{3}{4}$ is not a Natural number.

The diagram represents the sets: Natural numbers $\mathbb{N}$, Integers $\mathbb{Z}$, Rational numbers $\mathbb{Q}$ and Real numbers $\mathbb{R}$.

(ii) Copy the diagram into your copy.

(iii) Insert each of the following numbers in the correct place on the diagram.

$-5, 0, \dfrac{1}{2}, 7, \sqrt{5}, -5.6, 5^{-1}, \pi, \sqrt{2}, \sqrt{9}$

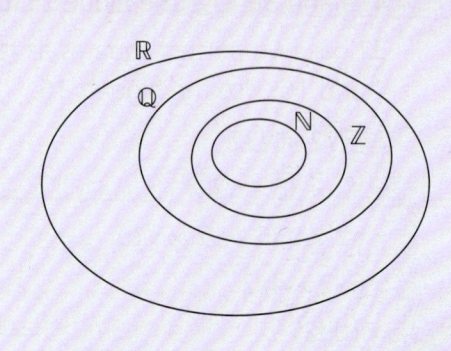

2. The table shows a list of numbers and a list of sets that each number could be an element of. Copy the table into your copy and tick each box opposite the number if the number belongs to that set.

Number	Natural numbers ℕ	Integers ℤ	Rational numbers ℚ	ℝ\ℚ	Real numbers ℝ
4	✓	✓	✓		✓
−77		✓	✓		✓
−1.6			✓		✓
$2\frac{1}{5}$			✓		✓
$\sqrt{4}$	✓	✓	✓		✓
cos 60°			✓		✓
$\frac{\pi}{2}$				✓	✓
$\sqrt{5}$				✓	✓

3. Simplify:
   (i) $2\sqrt{5} + 7\sqrt{5}$
   (ii) $3\sqrt{7} + 7\sqrt{3} + 5\sqrt{7} - 2\sqrt{3}$
   (iii) $2\sqrt{3} \times 5\sqrt{3}$
   (iv) $(-4\sqrt{5})(\sqrt{5})$
   (v) $4\sqrt{7} \times 3\sqrt{2}$
   (vi) $(5\sqrt{2})(-3\sqrt{2})$

4. Simplify:
   (i) $3\sqrt{2} + 10\sqrt{2}$
   (ii) $4\sqrt{6} + 2\sqrt{13} + 5\sqrt{13} - 3\sqrt{6}$
   (iii) $4\sqrt{6} \times 5\sqrt{6}$
   (iv) $(3\sqrt{2})(-\sqrt{5})$
   (v) $-3\sqrt{17} \times 4\sqrt{2}$
   (vi) $(7\sqrt{3})(-5\sqrt{3})$

5. Simplify these surds as far as possible.
   (i) $\sqrt{45}$ (iii) $\sqrt{63}$ (v) $\sqrt{72}$
   (ii) $\sqrt{24}$ (iv) $\sqrt{200}$ (vi) $\sqrt{8}$

6. Simplify:
   (i) $\sqrt{\frac{9}{16}}$
   (ii) $4\sqrt{32}$
   (iii) $\sqrt{80}$
   (iv) $2\sqrt{5} + 3\sqrt{5}$
   (v) $5\sqrt{7} - 2\sqrt{7}$

7. Simplify each of the following as far as possible.
   (i) $\sqrt{75} + \sqrt{48} - \sqrt{12}$
   (ii) $\sqrt{45} + \sqrt{20} - \sqrt{5}$
   (iii) $\sqrt{50} + \sqrt{32} - \sqrt{8}$
   (iv) $\sqrt{28} + \sqrt{63} - \sqrt{7}$

8. In each of the following, find the value of p.
   (i) $\sqrt{48} + \sqrt{75} = p\sqrt{3}$
   (ii) $\sqrt{125} - \sqrt{45} = p\sqrt{5}$
   (iii) $3\sqrt{108} - \sqrt{12} = p\sqrt{3}$
   (iv) $\sqrt{112} - \sqrt{28} = p\sqrt{7}$

9. Simplify each of the following as far as possible.
   (i) $\sqrt{8} \times 6\sqrt{2}$
   (ii) $(-4\sqrt{18})(\sqrt{2})$
   (iii) $3\sqrt{28} \times 3\sqrt{2}$
   (iv) $(3\sqrt{27})(-4\sqrt{12})$
   (v) $(3\sqrt{5})(2\sqrt{7})$

10. Show that $(3\sqrt{5} - 2)(3\sqrt{5} + 2)$ simplifies to a Natural number.

11 Multiply out and simplify as far as possible:
  (i) $(3 + \sqrt{2})(3 - \sqrt{2})$
  (ii) $(7 + \sqrt{5})(7 - \sqrt{5})$
  (iii) $(\sqrt{7} + \sqrt{6})(\sqrt{7} - \sqrt{6})$
  (iv) $(5 + \sqrt{2})^2$

12 The rectangle and square have the same area. The dimensions of both are in cm. The diagrams are not drawn to scale.

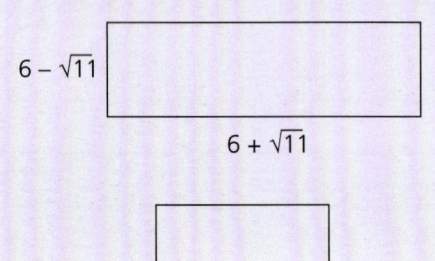

Rectangle: $6 - \sqrt{11}$ by $6 + \sqrt{11}$

(i) Find the area of the rectangle.
(ii) Find the length of one side of the square.

JCHL 2012 Sample Paper

13 Look at the *Formulae and tables* booklet page 13. From the information there, fill in the following table by inserting $\mathbb{Q}$ (for Rational number) or $\mathbb{R}\backslash\mathbb{Q}$ (for Irrational number).

A	30°	45°	60°
cos A			
sin A			
tan A			

14 Simplify $\sqrt{5}(\sqrt{2} + \sqrt{5}) - \sqrt{8}(\sqrt{2} - \sqrt{5})$ without using a calculator. Express your answer in the form $p + q\sqrt{r}$, where $p, q, r \in \mathbb{N}$.

15 Write $\dfrac{\sqrt{3} \times 81}{3^3}$ in the form 3^n where $n \in \mathbb{Q}$.

16 Let $a = \sqrt{5}$.
  (i) Copy the table below into your copy. For each of the numbers in the table below, tick (✓) the correct box to say whether it is rational or irrational. Show all your calculations.

Number	Rational	Irrational
a		
a^{-2}		
$(-a)^2$		
$(a^{-1})^2$		
$a^2 - 7$		

  (ii) Mark the numbers in the table on the number line and label each number clearly.

17 Simplify $\sqrt{3}(2\sqrt{6} - 4\sqrt{3}) - \sqrt{10}(3\sqrt{5} - 2\sqrt{10})$ without using a calculator. Express your answer in the form $a + b\sqrt{2}$, where $a, b \in \mathbb{Z}$.

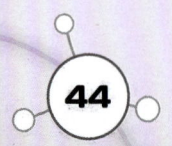

18 Write $\dfrac{1}{\sqrt{2}}$ in the form $a\sqrt{2}$, where $a \in \mathbb{Q}$.

19 Write $\dfrac{2}{\sqrt{3}}$ in the form $a\sqrt{3}$, where $a \in \mathbb{Q}$.

20 Write each of the following in the form $a\sqrt{b} + c\sqrt{d}$, where $a, c \in \mathbb{Q}$ and $b, d \in \mathbb{N}$.

(i) $\dfrac{3 + \sqrt{2}}{\sqrt{3}}$ (ii) $\dfrac{\sqrt{5} - 1}{\sqrt{2}}$ (iii) $\dfrac{5 - \sqrt{3}}{\sqrt{5}}$

Section 2G Scientific Notation

Scientific notation is a special way of writing extremely large or small numbers.

It is commonly used in Astronomy, Science and Engineering.

Numbers in scientific notation are written in the form $a \times 10^n$, where $1 \leq a < 10$ and $n \in \mathbb{Z}$.

For example,

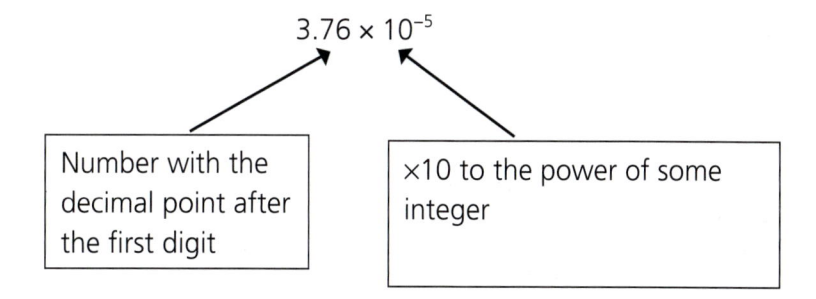

$$3.76 \times 10^{-5}$$

- Number with the decimal point after the first digit
- $\times 10$ to the power of some integer

Example 1

Some tortoises have been known to live more than 150 years, or about 3 850 000 000 seconds. Express this number of seconds in scientific notation.

Solution

$3\,850\,000\,000 = 3.85 \times 10^9$ seconds, since 3.85 would have to be **multiplied** by 10 nine times to get 3 850 000 000.

Example 2

Hair on the human body can grow as fast as 0.000 000 004 3 metres per second.
Express this rate in scientific notation.

Solution

$0.000\,000\,004\,3 = 4.3 \times 10^{-9}$ m/s, since 4.3 would have to be **divided** by 10 nine times to get 0.000 000 004 3.

Example 3

Write the reciprocal of 10 000 in the form 1×10^n, where $n \in \mathbb{Z}$.

Solution

The reciprocal of $10\,000 = \dfrac{1}{10\,000}$

$ = 0.0001$

$ = 1 \times 10^{-4}$

Example 4

Calculate $(4.6 \times 10^8) \times (3.1 \times 10^{-3})$ and give your answer in scientific notation.

Solution

$(4.6 \times 10^8) \times (3.1 \times 10^{-3}) = (4.6)(3.1) \times (10^8)(10^{-3})$ …associative law for multiplication

$\phantom{(4.6 \times 10^8) \times (3.1 \times 10^{-3})\ } = 14.26 \times 10^5$

$\phantom{(4.6 \times 10^8) \times (3.1 \times 10^{-3})\ } = 1.426 \times 10^6$ …we must have $1 \leq a < 10$.

Alternatively, using a calculator:

Type [4] [.] [6] [×10^x] [8] [×] [3] [.] [1] [×10^x] [−] [3] [=]

1426000 will appear on the screen.

Change to scientific notation: 1.426×10^6

Example 5

Calculate $(9.5 \times 10^{-3}) + (2.8 \times 10^{-4})$.

Solution

- Write the numbers in decimal (ordinary) form and add.

  $0.0095 + 0.000\,28$

  $= 0.009\,78$

  Write the answer in scientific notation: 9.78×10^{-3}

- Using a calculator:

  Type [9] [.] [5] [×10^x] [−] [3] [+] [2] [.] [8] [×10^x] [−] [4] [=]

  9.78×10^{-3} will appear on the screen.

Activity 2.6

1. The longest human life recorded was more than 122 years, or about 3 850 000 000 seconds. Express this number of seconds in scientific notation.

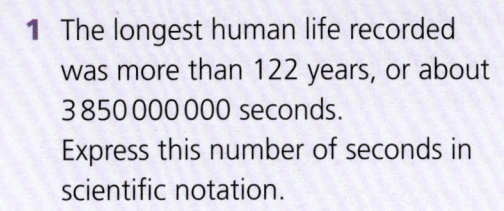

2. Write each of the following values in scientific notation.
   (i) 760
   (ii) 4620
   (iii) 25 000 000
   (iv) 315 000
   (v) 1 075 000 000
   (vi) 63 000 000 000 000

3. The mass of one electron is 9.11×10^{-28} grams. A uranium atom contains 92 electrons. Find the total mass of the electrons in a uranium atom. Express your answer in scientific notation.

4. Write each of the following values in the form $a \times 10^n$, where $1 \leq a < 10$, $n \in \mathbb{Z}$.
   (i) 0.00086
   (ii) 0.00462
   (iii) 27 000 000
   (iv) 0.000 000 326
   (v) 1 077 000 000
   (vi) 0.000 000 078

5. Given that 1 billion is a thousand million, find the sum of €4.7 billion and €600 million.

6. Express each of these as a decimal number.
   (i) 6.3×10^5
   (ii) 9.2×10^{-5}
   (iii) 3.45×10^6
   (iv) 2.9×10^{-4}
   (v) 8.23×10^8
   (vi) 3.3×10^{-6}
   (vii) 1×10^{-3}

7. The amount of gold in the Earth's crust is about 120 000 000 000 000 kilograms. Express this amount in the form $a \times 10^n$, where $1 \leq a < 10$, $n \in \mathbb{Z}$.

8. Write the reciprocal of 100 000 in the form 1×10^n, where $n \in \mathbb{Z}$.

9. Write the reciprocal of 400 000 in the form $a \times 10^n$, where $1 \leq a < 10$, $n \in \mathbb{Z}$.

10. Calculate each of the following and give your answers in scientific notation.
    (i) $8.1 \times 10^3 + 3.2 \times 10^2$
    (ii) $1.8 \times 10^4 - 4.5 \times 10^3$
    (iii) $6.5 \times 10^2 + 3.2 \times 10^2$
    (iv) $(2.2 \times 10^{-2}) - (5 \times 10^{-3})$
    (v) $(3 \times 10^{-3}) + (9 \times 10^{-4})$
    (vi) $(5 \times 10^{-2}) - (7 \times 10^{-6})$

11. Our nearest star (other than the sun) is Alpha Centauri.
    (i) Alpha Centauri is 41 600 000 000 000 000 metres from our sun. Express this distance in kilometres in scientific notation.
    (ii) Alpha Centauri is actually a double star. The two stars that comprise it are 3 500 000 000 metres apart. Express this distance in kilometres in scientific notation.

12. Write the reciprocal of 500 000 in the form 2×10^n, where $n \in \mathbb{Z}$.

13. Calculate each of the following and give your answers in the form $a \times 10^n$, where $1 \leq a < 10$, $n \in \mathbb{Z}$.
    (i) $(4.3 \times 10^3) \times (2 \times 10^4)$
    (ii) $(9 \times 10^{-3}) \times (3 \times 10^1)$
    (iii) $(5.2 \times 10^{-3}) \times (4 \times 10^4)$
    (iv) $(3.3 \times 10^4) \times (3 \times 10^{-4})$

14. Calculate each of the following and give your answers in scientific notation.
    (i) $\dfrac{5 \times 10^5}{2.5 \times 10^2}$
    (ii) $\dfrac{7.4 \times 10^4}{2 \times 10^{-4}}$
    (iii) $\dfrac{8.8 \times 10^{-3}}{1.1 \times 10^{-5}}$
    (iv) $\dfrac{28 \times 10^5}{2 \times 10^{-1}}$

15 Calculate each of the following and express your answers in scientific notation.

(i) $\dfrac{(2 \times 10^4) + (6 \times 10^5)}{(2 \times 10^3)}$

(ii) $\dfrac{(3.5 \times 10^6) - (20 \times 10^4)}{(3 \times 10^4)}$

(iii) $\dfrac{(6.1 \times 10^{-3}) \times (4 \times 10^4)}{(2 \times 10^3)}$

16 Add 1.8×10^6 and 3.5 million. Give your answer in the form $a \times 10^n$, where $1 \leq a < 10$, $n \in \mathbb{Z}$.

17 The diameters of Venus and Saturn are 1.21×10^4 km and 1.21×10^5 km respectively. What is the difference between the diameters of the two planets? Give your answer in the form $a \times 10^n$, where $1 \leq a < 10$, $n \in \mathbb{Z}$.

18 Given that $x = 2 \times 10^{-4}$ and $y = 7 \times 10^{-3}$, evaluate $x + 5y$. Express your answer in the form $a \times 10^n$, where $1 \leq a < 10$, $n \in \mathbb{Z}$.

19 Light travels at a speed of approximately (2.9×10^5) km/s. How many kilometres will light travel in 7 seconds? Express your answer in the form $a \times 10^n$, where $1 \leq a < 10$, $n \in \mathbb{Z}$.

Section 2H Exploring Even, Odd and Prime Numbers

An **even** number is a number which can be divided by 2 without remainder.
The set of even numbers = {2, 4, 6, 8, 10, …}
Thus, every even number = 2 × some number.
If we let n = any number, then every even number is of the form $2n$.

An **odd** number is a number which cannot be divided by 2 without remainder.
The set of odd numbers = {1, 3, 5, 7, 9, …}
Thus, every odd number = (2 × some number) − 1.
If we let n = any number, then every odd number is of the form $(2n - 1)$.
A number of the form $(2n + 1)$ is also odd.

Prime numbers are numbers which have two and only two divisors.
Thus, the prime numbers = {2, 3, 5, 7, 11, 13, 17, 19, 23, …}

Example 1

Prove that the sum of any two even numbers is even.

Solution

Let $2m$ be one even number and let $2n$ be the other even number, where m and n are any two Natural numbers.

Then the sum of these two numbers

$= 2m + 2n$

$= 2(m + n)$ which is a multiple of 2 and thus is even.

Example 2

Prove that the sum of any odd number and any even number is odd.

Solution

Let $2m$ be the even number, where m is any Natural number.

Let $(2n - 1)$ be the odd number, where n is any Natural number.

$$\begin{aligned}\text{Then the sum of these numbers} &= 2m + (2n - 1) \\ &= 2m + 2n - 1 \\ &= 2(m + n) - 1 \\ &= \text{an odd number}\end{aligned}$$

Activity 2.7

1. List all the prime numbers less than 50.

2. Find the prime factors of 72.

3. It is thought that all even numbers greater than 4 can be written as the sum of two odd prime numbers.
   (i) Write down the even numbers from 6 to 16 as the sum of two odd prime numbers (e.g. 6 = 3 + 3).
   (ii) Can you do this for 86?

4. A pair of consecutive prime numbers which differ by 2 are known as 'twin primes'. For example, 3 and 5 are twin primes and so also are 5 and 7. Can you list all the twin primes less than 100?

5. List any five **even** Natural numbers. Verify that each is of the form $2m$, where m is any whole number.

6. List any five **odd** Natural numbers. Verify that each is of the form $2m - 1$, where m is any Natural number.

7. Take any two even Natural numbers and add them. Is your result even or odd? Try this for five other pairs of even Natural numbers. Are the results always even, always odd, or sometimes even and sometimes odd?

8. Prove your answer to question 7.

Hint

> Let $2m$ be one even number and $2n$ be the other even number.

9. Take any two odd whole numbers and add them. Is your result even or odd? Try this for five other pairs of odd whole numbers. Are the results always even, always odd, or sometimes even and sometimes odd?

10. Prove your answer to question 9.

11. Take any two whole numbers, one even the other odd. Add them. Is your result even or odd? Try this for five other pairs of whole numbers, one even the other odd. Are the results always even, always odd, or sometimes even and sometimes odd?

12. Prove your answer to question 11.

13. Now do questions 7, 9 and 11 again, but this time replace the word 'add' with the word 'subtract'. Summarise your findings.

14. Take any two even whole numbers and multiply them. Are the results always even, always odd, or sometimes even and sometimes odd? Can you prove this?

15. Take any two odd whole numbers and multiply them. Are the results always even, always odd, or sometimes even and sometimes odd? Can you prove this?

16. Show by examples that if a is odd, then a^2 is odd. Can you prove this?

17. Take any two Natural numbers, one even the other odd. Multiply them. Is your result even or odd? Try this for five other pairs of Natural numbers, one even the other odd. Are the results always even, always odd, or sometimes even and sometimes odd? Can you prove this?

18. Find two even whole numbers where one is a multiple of the other. Divide the smaller into the bigger. Is the result even or odd? Are the results always the same?

Revision Activity 2

1. (a) The mean distance from the Earth to the Sun is 149 597 871 km. Write this number in the form $a \times 10^n$, where $1 \leq a < 10$ and $n \in \mathbb{Z}$, correct to two significant figures.

   (b) (i) Write each of the numbers below as a decimal correct to two decimal places.

	A	B	C	D	E	F
Number	3.4	$\sqrt{3}$	$\dfrac{187}{63}$	tan 58°	$\dfrac{\pi}{2}$	350%
Decimal number						

   (ii) Mark the numbers in the table on a number line and label each number clearly.

2. (a) Find $\sqrt[3]{139.6}$ correct to three decimal places.

   (b) Find the exact value of $\dfrac{1}{(0.5)^3} - (1.2)^2$.

   (c) Write down the whole number closest to $\sqrt{50} + \tan 72°$.

3. (a) Write 7^{-2} and $81^{\frac{1}{2}}$ without using indices.

   (b) Express 2^{24} in the form $a \times 10^n$, where $1 \leq a < 10$ and $n \in \mathbb{Z}$, correct to three significant figures.

   (c) Show that $\dfrac{(a\sqrt{a})^3}{a^4}$ simplifies to $\sqrt{a}$.

4. Write $\dfrac{\sqrt{3} \times 81}{3^2}$ in the form 3^n where $n \in \mathbb{Q}$.

5. Simplify $\dfrac{2^8 \times 8^{\frac{2}{3}}}{64^{\frac{1}{2}} \times 4^3}$.

   Give your answer in the form 2^n, where $n \in \mathbb{Z}$.

6. Simplify $(\sqrt{6} - 3\sqrt{3})(4\sqrt{3} - 2\sqrt{6})$ without the use of a calculator.

   Express your answer in the form $p\sqrt{2} + q$, where $p, q \in \mathbb{Z}$.

7. Simplify (a) $64^{\frac{3}{2}}$ (b) $64^{\frac{2}{3}}$

8. Solve the equation $\dfrac{2^5 \times 8^{\frac{2}{3}}}{64^{\frac{1}{2}} \times 4^2} = 2^n$, where $n \in \mathbb{N}$.

9. (a) Express $(2^3)(2^3)(2^3)(2^3)$ in the form 2^p where $p \in \mathbb{N}$.

   (b) Express $2^3 + 2^3 + 2^3 + 2^3$ in the form 2^p where $p \in \mathbb{N}$.

10. Express $3^{\frac{1}{2}} + 3^{\frac{1}{2}} + 3^{\frac{1}{2}}$ in the form 3^p where $p \in \mathbb{Q}$.

Exam-style Questions

1. (a) (i) The columns in the table below represent the following sets of numbers: Natural numbers ($\mathbb{N}$), Integers ($\mathbb{Z}$), Rational numbers ($\mathbb{Q}$), Irrational numbers ($\mathbb{R}\backslash\mathbb{Q}$) and Real numbers ($\mathbb{R}$).

   Complete the table by writing either '**Yes**' or '**No**' into each box indicating whether each of the numbers $\sqrt{5}$, 8, –4, $3\frac{1}{2}$, $\frac{3\pi}{4}$ is, or is not, an element of each. (One box has already been filled in. The 'Yes' indicates that the number 8 is an element of the set of Real numbers, $\mathbb{R}$.)

Number/Set	$\mathbb{N}$	$\mathbb{Z}$	$\mathbb{Q}$	$\mathbb{R}\backslash\mathbb{Q}$	$\mathbb{R}$
$\sqrt{5}$					
8					Yes
–4					
$3\frac{1}{2}$					
$\frac{3\pi}{4}$					

   (ii) In the case of $\sqrt{5}$, explain your choice in relation to the set of Irrational numbers ($\mathbb{R}\backslash\mathbb{Q}$) (i.e. give a reason for writing either 'Yes' or 'No').

   (b) Use the properties of surds to show that $\sqrt{98} - \sqrt{18} + \sqrt{2}$ simplifies to $5\sqrt{2}$.

   JCHL 2013 Paper 1

2. (a) Give two reasons why –7.3 is not a Natural number.

   (b) The diagram represents the sets:
   Natural Numbers $\mathbb{N}$
   Integers $\mathbb{Z}$
   Rational Numbers $\mathbb{Q}$
   Real Numbers $\mathbb{R}$

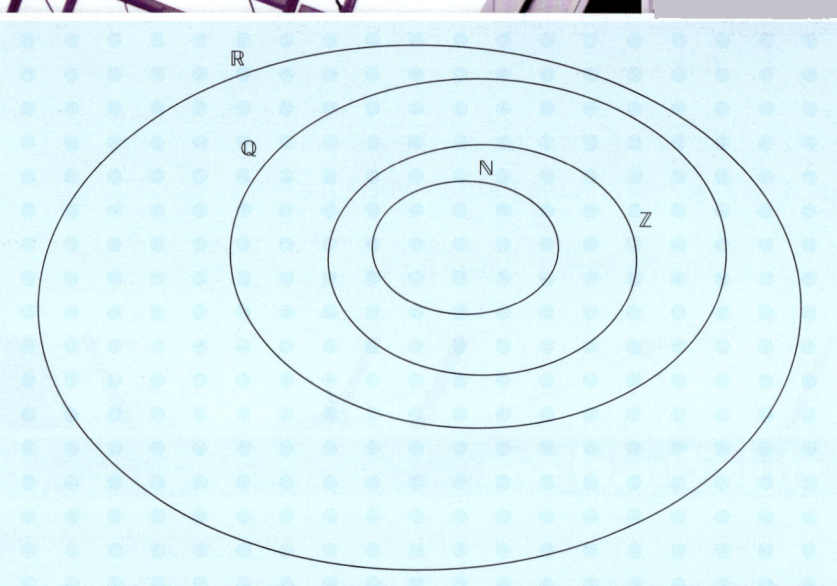

Insert each of the following numbers in the correct place on the diagram.

-8, π, $\frac{1}{3}$, 6, $\sqrt{2}$, -4.5 and 7^{-1}.

JCHL 2012 Paper 1

KEY WORDS AND PHRASES

- Natural number
- Integer
- Rational number
- Irrational number
- Surd
- Real number
- Recurring decimal

Chapter Summary 2

- The set of **Natural numbers** $\mathbb{N} = \{1, 2, 3, 4, 5, \ldots\}$

- The set of **Integers** $\mathbb{Z} = \{\ldots, -4, -3, -2, -1, 0, 1, 2, 3, \ldots\}$

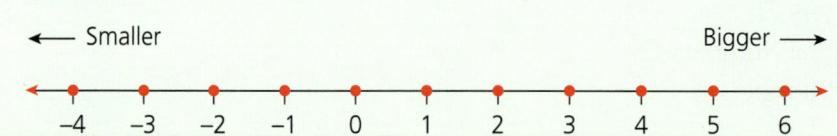

⟵ Smaller   Bigger ⟶

- The **Rational numbers** $\mathbb{Q}$ = the set of all numbers which can be written in the form $\frac{p}{q}$ where p and $q \in \mathbb{Z}$ and $q \neq 0$.
- The set of Irrational numbers $\mathbb{R}\setminus\mathbb{Q}$ = the set of all numbers which cannot be written in the form $\frac{p}{q}$, e.g. π, $\sqrt{2}$, $\sqrt{5}$ etc.
- **Real numbers** $\mathbb{R}$
  When we put the Rational numbers together with the Irrational numbers, we get the set of Real numbers $\mathbb{R}$. The Real numbers 'fill up' the number line completely.
- We cannot divide by zero.
- Rules of indices

Rule 1:	$a^m \times a^n = a^{m+n}$
Rule 2:	$\dfrac{a^m}{a^n} = a^{m-n}$
Rule 3:	$a^0 = 1$
Rule 4:	$(a^m)^n = a^{mn}$
Rule 5:	$a^{-m} = \dfrac{1}{a^m}$
Rule 6:	$a^{\frac{1}{q}} = \sqrt[q]{a}$
Rule 7:	$a^{\frac{p}{q}} = (\sqrt[q]{a})^p$
Rule 8:	$(ab)^m = a^m b^m$
Rule 9:	$\left(\dfrac{a}{b}\right)^m = \dfrac{a^m}{b^m}$

- Operations on surds

$\sqrt{a}\sqrt{a} = a^{\frac{1}{2}} \times a^{\frac{1}{2}} = a^1 = a$
$\sqrt{a}\sqrt{b} = a^{\frac{1}{2}} \times b^{\frac{1}{2}} = (ab)^{\frac{1}{2}} = \sqrt{ab}$
$\dfrac{\sqrt{a}}{\sqrt{b}} = \dfrac{a^{\frac{1}{2}}}{b^{\frac{1}{2}}} = \left(\dfrac{a}{b}\right)^{\frac{1}{2}} = \sqrt{\dfrac{a}{b}}$
Like terms can be added
Unlike like terms cannot be added, so $\sqrt{a} + \sqrt{b}$ cannot be simplified $\sqrt{a} - \sqrt{b}$ cannot be simplified.

Chapter 3

Algebra 1
Expressions

Learning Outcomes

In this chapter, you will learn about:
- Algebraic expressions
- Evaluating expressions
- Simplifying terms
- Dividing terms
- Multiplying terms
- Multiplying expressions including use of brackets and the distributive law
- Factorising:
  - Expressions with a common factor across all terms
  - Expressions where grouping is necessary
  - Quadratic expressions with three terms (trinomials)
  - The difference of two squares
- Dividing expressions

Historical background

The German mathematician Karl Friedrich Gauss is widely acknowledged as one of the three greatest mathematicians of all time. The other two are Newton and Archimedes.

In his first arithmetic class, Gauss' teacher gave the students a task to keep them busy. The problem was to add up all the Natural numbers from 1 to 100. Gauss had the answer almost immediately.

Karl Friedrich Gauss (1777–1855)

What problem-solving strategy did he employ?

Can you work out how he did it? He saw that:

$(100 + 1) = 101$

$(99 + 2) = 101$

$(98 + 3) = 101$ … etc.

Thus the sum = $(101 \times 100) \div 2 = 5050$.

But then, after all, Gauss was a genius!

Section 3A Review

You have already met the following words and phrases in your study of algebra.

Variable:	The letters which stand for unknown numbers in algebra e.g. x, y, z.
Constant:	A term whose value never changes, e.g. 5, -32, $\frac{1}{2}$.
Term:	When a constant and a variable(s) are multiplied together, e.g. $13p$, $3x^2$.
Coefficient:	The constant multiplied by the variable in a term, e.g. in the term $23x^2$, 23 is the coefficient of x^2.
Expression	A set of terms which are added or subtracted, e.g. $5x - 7$ is a linear expression; $3x^2 - 5x + 6$ is a quadratic expression.
Binomial:	An expression with two terms e.g. $(a + b)$.
Trinomial:	An expression with three terms e.g. $x^2 - x + 7$.
Like terms:	Terms with the same variables with the same powers.
Equivalent expressions:	Expressions which can be written in different forms but have the same value e.g. $x^2 + 2x$ and $x^2 + 3x - x$.

Key Points

- Only like terms may be added or subtracted.
- When adding like terms, the powers of the variables do not change.
- Expressions can be multiplied using the Distributive Law.
- The Distributive Law says multiplication is distributive over addition and subtraction.

Example

James has €200.00 savings in his local credit union. He saves €20.00 per week. His savings can be represented by $y = 200 + 20x$, where x is the number of weeks.

(i) What are the constants?
(ii) What do the constants represent?
(iii) What are the variables?
(iv) What do the variables represent?

Solution

(i) The constants are 200 and 20.
(ii) 200 = €200.00 savings. 20 = €20.00 he saves each week.
(iii) The variables are:
   - x (the input/independent variable) and
   - y (the output/dependent variable).
(iv) x represents the number of weeks he has saved.
   y represents his savings in euro.

Activity 3.1

1. Write out the instructions given below in symbols using a variable and constants.

Steps in words	Steps in letters
Think of a number	
Add 4	
Double this answer	
Subtract 3	
Add 7	
Divide by 2	
Subtract the original number	
What is the answer?	

2. An electricity supply company charges for electricity using the formula:

   $C = €(0.18u + 20.00)$, where C is the total cost, u represents the number of units of electricity used and €20.00 is the standing charge.

   (i) Describe in words the cost of electricity to the consumer.
   (ii) Name the variables in this formula.
   (iii) Name the constants in this formula.
   (iv) If Michael uses 500 units of electricity, what is the total cost?

3. The following expressions describe the weekly savings of two people in each of four families.

Moran	Cox	Dunne	Mulligan
Sarah: $10 + 20x$	Tom: $400 - 10x$	Grace: 300	Charlie: $20x$
Robert: $20 + 10x$	Colette: $20 + 19x$	Denis: $-40 + 10x$	Isla: $-50 + 5x$

   Examples: Sarah Moran starts with €10 and is saving €20 per week; Denis Dunne starts with a debt of €40 and is saving €10 per week.

   (i) Find expressions in their simplest form for the combined weekly savings of each family.

   The New Horizons travel company are offering a special deal of a sun holiday for two people for €600.

   (ii) Which family will be the first to save €600?

4. The following patterns are made of matchsticks.

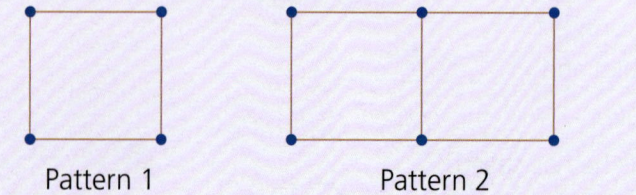

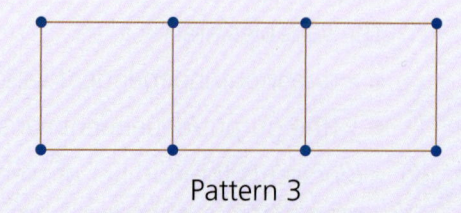

   Pattern 1   Pattern 2   Pattern 3

(i) Draw pattern 4.
(ii) Look at the patterns.
   (a) How many extra matchsticks do you add each time?
   (b) Copy and complete this sentence: 'One rule for the number of matchsticks in a pattern is to start with 4 and add ___ matchsticks for every additional pattern.'
   (c) How many matchsticks will there be in pattern 6?
   (d) How many matchsticks will there be in pattern 10?
   (e) How many matchsticks will there be in pattern 100?
   (f) Can you find a rule for the number of matchsticks if you are given any pattern number?
(iii) Sarah suggested that another rule for the matchsticks is: '3 times the number of the pattern plus 1'. Check this out for the first four patterns. Is it true?
(iv) Peter used 34 matchsticks to make a pattern. Find the number of the pattern.

5 The following table shows the measured heights of two different sunflowers on the day when they were bought and the amount they grew each day afterwards.

Sunflower	A	B
Start height (cm)	12	8
Growth per day (cm)	3	4

(i) Write in words the pattern in the growth of each sunflower.
(ii) Copy and complete these tables for the progress of the sunflowers for the first six days. Take day 0 to be the day of the starting heights.

Time in days	Sunflower A		Change in height (cm)
	Height (cm)	Pattern	
At day 0	12	12	
After day 1	15	12 + 3	+3
After day 2			

CONNECT WITH MATHS 2

Time in days	Sunflower B		Change in height (cm)
	Height (cm)	Pattern	
At day 0	8		
After day 1			+4
After day 2			

(iii) How can you tell from the table that each sunflower has a linear growth rate?

(iv) Copy and complete this sentence:

'Sunflower A is growing at an average rate of _____ per _____.'

(v) Copy and complete this sentence:

'Sunflower B is growing at an average rate of _____ per _____.'

(vi) Copy the axes below and draw two graphs to represent the growth of the sunflowers over the five days. Join the points in each and label the graphs Sunflower A and Sunflower B, respectively.

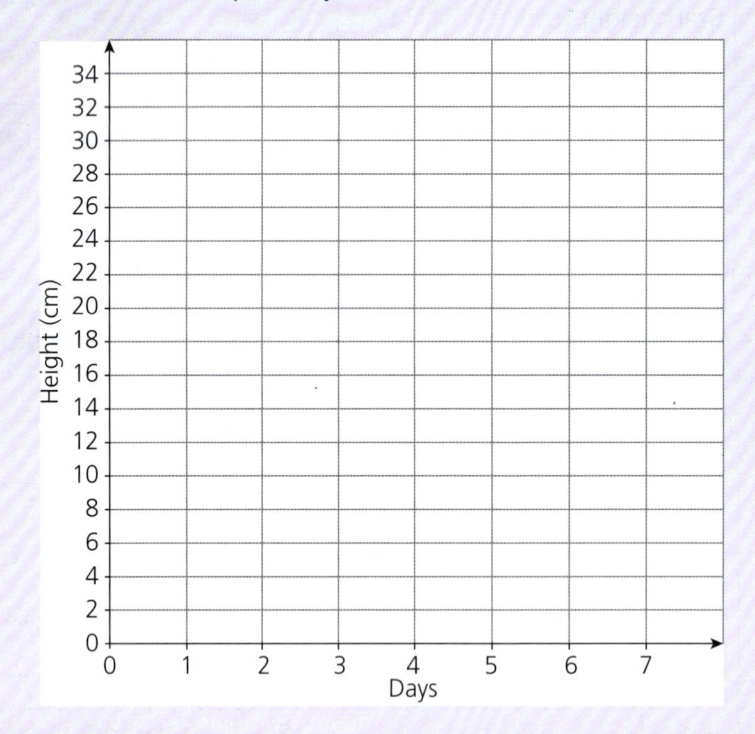

(vii) Express, using symbols, the relationship between the growth of the sunflowers and the number of days since they were bought. Choose your own variables.

(viii) Find the slope of each line. Explain what the slopes mean in this context.

(ix) After how many days were the sunflowers the same height? Where do you see this in the tables? Where do you see this on the graphs?

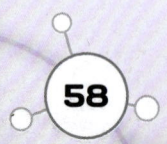

6 $5x + 6$ is a linear expression.

  (i) Write down the coefficient of x.   (ii) What is the constant term?

7 $3x^2 - 4x - 7$ is a quadratic expression.

  (i) Write down the coefficient of x^2 and the coefficient of x.

  (ii) What is the constant term?

8 $3ab - 5ac - 6$ is an algebraic expression.

  (i) Name the variables in the expression.

  (ii) Write down the coefficient of ab and the coefficient of ac.

  (iii) What is the constant term?

9 (i) Copy and complete the diagram below, by writing $3m^2 - 6m + 2$ in ten different ways.
   Note: these are all **equivalent expressions** for $3m^2 - 6m + 2$.

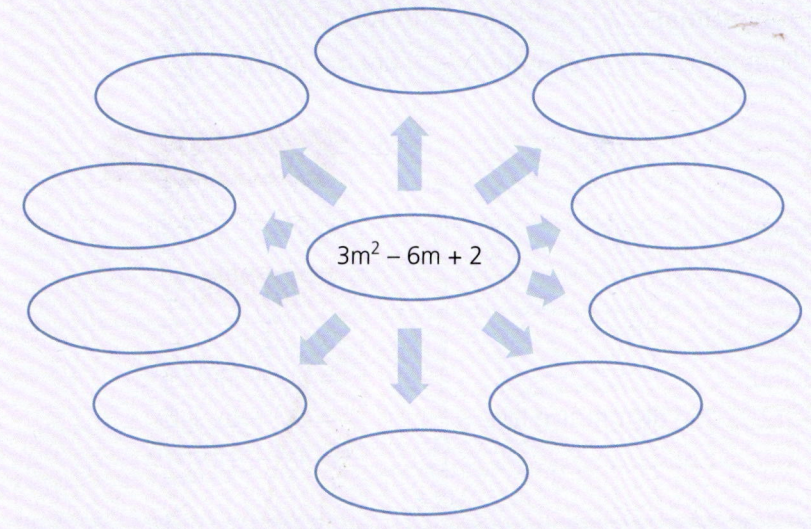

  (ii) Which expression is the most compact?

In questions 10–22, use the distributive law to remove the brackets. Then simplify each expression as far as possible.

10 $5(3x + 2y)$

11 $-2(3a - b)$

12 $7(3 - 2q - r)$

13 $5a(3a - 2b)$

14 $5x - 2(3x - y)$

15 $5 - 2(3x - 2) + 4(5 - x)$

16 $6 + 3(2a - 5) - 7a$

17 $3x(2x - 3y) - x(x + 10y)$

18 $7a(3b - c) - 3b(2a + c)$

19 $x^2(x^3 - x^2 - x - 2)$

20 $4(p + 2q - 5) - (2p - 3q)$

21 $x(3x + 2) - (x^2 - x - 5)$

22 $x^3(x^2 - x) - 3x(x^2 - 2x + 1)$

23 Simplify each of the following.

  (i) $5x^2 - 4x + 8 + 3x^2 + 4x - 7$

  (ii) $a^3 - 4a^2 - 6a + 3a^3 + 6a^2 - a$

  (iii) $-2x(3x + 5) - (6x - 2)$

  (iv) $-5x(2x + 1) - 2(3x + 4)$

24 (i) Copy this diagram into your copy.

  (ii) Find the area of each of the smaller rectangles and hence find the total area in terms of x.

	x^2	$2x$	4
x			
5			

25 Given that $a = x^2 - 2x$ and $b = x^2 + 3x + 4$, write each of the following in terms of x.
  (i) $a + b$ (ii) $a - b$ (iii) $5a - 2b$ (iv) $5a + 2b$

26 Write each of the following in its simplest form.
  (i) $\dfrac{a^5}{a}$
  (ii) $\dfrac{4a^3}{2a^2}$
  (iii) $\dfrac{5a^2b^4}{ab^2}$
  (iv) $\dfrac{8x^5y^2}{12x^3y^3}$
  (v) $\dfrac{4xy^3}{3y}$
  (vi) $\dfrac{16(-a^2)^2}{(-4a)^2}$
  (vii) $\dfrac{3xy}{x} \div \dfrac{6xy}{x^2}$
  (viii) $\dfrac{9(x^2y^3)^2}{xy} \div \dfrac{3x^2y}{2(xy)^3}$

27 Express in its simplest form:
  $2x - [3 - (4 - 3x)] + 6$

28 Express in its simplest form:
  $5a - [4 - (6 - 32a)] - 2$

Section 3B Multiplying Expressions

A **binomial** is an expression with two terms.
For example, $(x + 3)$ and $(2x - 7)$ are binomials.

Example 1

Multiply $(4x + 3)(3x - 4)$.

Solution
$(4x + 3)(3x - 4)$
$= 4x(3x - 4) + 3(3x - 4)$
$= 12x^2 - 16x + 9x - 12$ … the distributive law
$= 12x^2 - 7x - 12$

Example 2

Expand $(2x + 3)^2$.

Solution
$(2x + 3)^2$
$= (2x + 3)(2x + 3)$
$= 4x^2 + 6x + 6x + 9$
$= 4x^2 + 12x + 9$

Example 3

Expand $(ax + b)^2$.

Solution
$(ax + b)^2$
$= (ax + b)(ax + b)$
$= a^2x^2 + abx + abx + b^2$
$= (ax)^2 + 2abx + b^2$

Note: In Examples 2 and 3, there is a clear pattern to be seen when we **square a binomial**:

$(\text{first} + \text{second})^2$
$= (\text{first})^2 + 2(\text{first})(\text{second}) + (\text{second})^2$

If you practise this method, you will find it very convenient and quick.

Example 4

If $(2x + 5)(3x - a) = 6x^2 + 11x - 10$, find the value of a.

Solution
$(2x + 5)(3x - a) = 6x^2 + 11x - 10$
$\Rightarrow 6x^2 - 2ax + 15x - 5a = 6x^2 + 11x - 10$
Equating the constant terms gives
$-5a = -10$
$\Rightarrow a = \dfrac{-10}{-5} = 2$
We can check this by equating the terms with x:
$-2ax + 15x = 11x$
$\Rightarrow -2a + 15 = 11$
$\Rightarrow \qquad -2a = 11 - 15$
$\Rightarrow \qquad -2a = -4$
$\Rightarrow \qquad\quad a = \dfrac{-4}{-2} = 2$ ✓

Activity 3.2

1 Copy and complete the following multiplication arrays. Simplify your answers as far as possible.

(i)
×	2x	−3
5x		
+2		

$(5x + 2)(2x − 3) =$

(iii)
×	−3a	−3
3a		
−3		

$(3a − 3)(−3a − 3) =$

(ii)
×	−4x	−4
5x		
−1		

$(5x − 1)(−4x − 4) =$

(iv)
×	2p	−6
−p		
+5		

$(2p − 6)(−p + 5) =$

In questions 2–14, expand (multiply out) and simplify each expression as far as possible.

2 $(x + 2)(x + 5)$

3 $(a + 4)(a + 6)$

4 $(y − 1)(y − 5)$

5 $(3x − 2)(x + 4)$

6 $(3x − 4)(2x − 5)$

7 $(5p + 1)(2p + 3)$

8 $(5x + 2y)(3x − y)$

9 $(7x − y)(3x + y)$

10 $(5a − 2b)(5a + 2b)$

11 $(x − 1)(x + 3)(2x − 5)$

12 $(x − 2y)(x^2 + 2xy + y^2)$

13 $x(x − 3)(5x − 4)$

14 $(x + 4)(x^2 − x − 1)$

15 Multiply out $(3x − 1)(2x^2 + x − 4)$.

16 If $(3x + 2)(2x + a) = 6x^2 + x − 2$, find the value of a.

17 If $(x − 2)(3x + a) = 3x^2 − 8x + 4$, find a by filling in the array.

×	3x	+a
x	3x²	
−2		

18 If $(x − 3)$ is one factor of $x^2 + x − 12$, find the other factor.

19 Find the area of this rectangle (in terms of x).

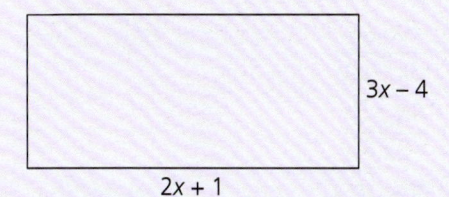

$3x − 4$
$2x + 1$

20 Expand
   (i) $(x + y)^2$
   (ii) $(x − y)^2$

21 Use your answers to question 20 to expand each of the following.
   (i) $(x + 2)^2$
   (ii) $(x − 3)^2$
   (iii) $(a + 4)^2$
   (iv) $(a − 5)^2$
   (v) $(p − 6)^2$
   (vi) $(x + 7)^2$

22 Expand
   (i) $(ax + b)^2$
   (ii) $(ax − b)^2$

23 Use your answers to question 22 to expand each of the following.
   (i) $(3x + 2)^2$
   (ii) $(4x − 1)^2$
   (iii) $(2a − 5)^2$
   (iv) $(4m + 3)^2$
   (v) $(2p − 6)^2$
   (vi) $(2x + 1)^2$

Section 3C Evaluating Expressions

To find the value of an expression for particular value(s) of the variables, **substitute** the value(s) into the variables in the expression.

Example 1

If $p = -5$ and $q = 3$, find the value of the following.

(i) $-5pq$ (ii) $3p^2 - 2p - 8$ (iii) $-q^2 - 4q + 7$ (iv) $\dfrac{-p - 3q}{5p - 2q}$

Solution

(i) $-5pq = -5(-5)(3) = -5(-15) = 75$

(ii) $3p^2 - 2p - 8 = 3(-5)^2 - 2(-5) - 8 = 3(25) + 10 - 8 = 75 + 2 = 77$

(iii) $-q^2 - 4q + 7 = -(3)^2 - 4(3) + 7 = -9 - 12 + 7 = -21 + 7 = -14$

(iv) $\dfrac{-p - 3q}{5p - 2q} = \dfrac{-(-5) - 3(3)}{5(-5) - 2(3)} = \dfrac{5 - 9}{-25 - 6} = \dfrac{-4}{-31} = \dfrac{4}{31}$

Example 2

Find the value of $3x^2 - 5x + \dfrac{4}{x}$ when $x = \dfrac{2}{3}$.

Solution

$3x^2 - 5x + \dfrac{4}{x}$ when $x = \dfrac{2}{3}$

$= 3\left(\dfrac{2}{3}\right)^2 - 5\left(\dfrac{2}{3}\right) + \dfrac{4}{\left(\dfrac{2}{3}\right)}$

$= 3\left(\dfrac{4}{9}\right) - \left(\dfrac{10}{3}\right) + \dfrac{4}{(1)} \times \dfrac{3}{2}$

$= \dfrac{12}{9} - \dfrac{10}{3} + \dfrac{6}{1}$

$= \dfrac{12 - 30 + 54}{9}$ … LCM is 9

$= \dfrac{36}{9}$

$= 4$

Activity 3.3

1 If $x = 3$ and $y = -6$, find the value of the following.

(i) $5x - 2y$
(ii) $-2x - y$
(iii) $-y^2 + 6y$
(iv) $-2y^2 + 2x$
(v) xy
(vi) $(x - 3)^2$
(vii) $y^2 - 6$

2 If $a = 4$ and $b = -3$, find the value of the following.

(i) $5ab$
(ii) $a^2 + 3a + 5$
(iii) $-b^2 - b + 2$
(iv) $\dfrac{-3a - b}{a + b}$

3 If $x = -2$ and $y = -4$, find the value of the following.

(i) $-3xy$
(ii) $x^2 - xy$
(iii) $y^2 - 3y + 5$
(iv) $\dfrac{5x + y}{3x - 2y}$
(v) $\dfrac{4x - 3y}{-2x - y}$
(vi) $\dfrac{3x + 2y}{-x + 2y}$

4 If $m = -1$, $p = -5$ and $q = 3$, find the value of the following.
  (i) mpq
  (ii) $3pq$
  (iii) $2p^3 + 3q^2$
  (iv) $p^3 + q^3$
  (v) $m^3 + m^2 - m$
  (vi) $p^3 - q^3$

5 If $a = -2$, $b = -3$, and $c = -1$, find the value of the following.
  (i) $a^3 - bc$
  (ii) $2a^2c$
  (iii) $2b^2 - 4c^2$
  (iv) $2a - 3b + c$
  (v) $3a^2b^2c^2$
  (vi) $a^2 + b^2 + c^2$

6 Find the value of the following expressions if $x = -4$.
  (i) $3x^2 - 2x + 4$
  (ii) $x^3 - 3x^2 - 4x + 2$
  (iii) $2x^3 - 4x^2 - x + 7$
  (iv) $5 - 4x - 3x^2 - 2x^3$

7 When $x = \frac{1}{3}$, find the value of $\frac{3}{x+1} + \frac{4}{x+5}$.

8 When $x = \frac{1}{2}$, find the value of $\frac{3}{x+2} - \frac{1}{2x+4}$.

9 Given that $y = \sqrt{2x - a}$, find the value of y when $x = 4$ and $a = -1$.

10 Given that $x = 3t - 2$ and $y = \frac{1}{3}t - 4$, express $2x - 3y - 8$ in terms of t, in its simplest form.

11 When $m = \frac{2}{5}$ and $n = \frac{3}{2}$, find the value of $\frac{1}{2m} - \frac{2}{n}$. Write your answer in the form $\frac{a}{b}$, where $a, b \in \mathbb{Z}$.

12 Find the value of $3x^2 - 5x + \frac{4}{x}$, when $x = \frac{2}{3}$.

13 Find the value of $\frac{1}{a-c}$ when $a = 1\frac{1}{2}$ and $c = 2\frac{1}{3}$.

Section 3D Factors

Factors type 1: Expressions where a common factor can be found for all terms

Always look for the highest common factor (HCF) of the expression.

Example 1

Factorise $5x^2y - 15xy^2$.

Solution

$5x^2y - 15xy^2$ ... HCF = $5xy$
$= 5xy(x - 3y)$

Always check to see if the expression is a 'type 1' first.

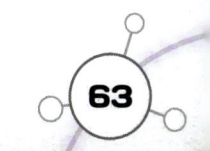

3 Factors type 2: Grouping to get a common factor

Some expressions do not have a common factor for all terms.

This next type usually has four terms ('gang of 4').

Group the terms into pairs which do have common factors.

Example 2

Factorise $px + py - 5x - 5y$.

Solution

$px + py - 5x - 5y$

$= (px + py) + (-5x - 5y)$ ... divide into 2 pairs with common factors

$= p(x + y) - 5(x + y)$ ... factorise the pairs separately (note the sign change)

$= (x + y)(p - 5)$ ... factorise

Check: Work backwards → multiply out the answer

$(x + y)(p - 5) = px - 5x + py - 5y$ ✓

Example 3

Factorise $6c + 12bd - 8d - 9bc$.

Solution

$6c + 12bd - 8d - 9bc$

$= 6c - 8d - 9bc + 12bd$ ... regroup to get pairs with common factors

$= 2(3c - 4d) - 3b(3c - 4d)$ ... note the sign change

$= (3c - 4d)(2 - 3b)$ ... factorise

Check: Work backwards → multiply out the answer

$(3c - 4d)(2 - 3b) = 6c - 9bc - 8d + 12bd$ ✓

Notice that when regrouping, the coefficients of the pairs are in the same ratio, e.g. $6:8 = 9:12$ in Example 3 above. Can you see another way that we could regroup in Example 3?

Activity 3.4

1 Factorise the following expressions.

(i) $5x + 10y$

(ii) $6x - 9y$

(iii) $3p + 15q$

(iv) $x^2 - 5x$

(v) $pq - pm$

(vi) $3xy - 12xz$

(vii) $20a^2 - 15ab$

(viii) $15p^2q^3 - 5p^3q^2$

(ix) $a^3 - a^2 + a$

(x) $5xy^2 - 15x^2y^3 + 10x^2y^4$

2 Factorise the following expressions.

(i) $ax + ay + bx + by$
(ii) $5a + 5b + xa + xb$
(iii) $ap + bp + aq + bq$
(iv) $ax - 3a + bx - 3b$
(v) $a^2 - ab + 4a - 4b$
(vi) $xy + x - y^2 - y$
(vii) $ax + bx - a - b$
(viii) $ax^2 - bx^2 - 3ay + 3by$

3 Factorise the following expressions. You may need to regroup the terms.

(i) $3a - ax + bx - 3b$
(ii) $3x - 15a + 5ab - bx$
(iii) $4c^2 - 3d - 2cd + 6c$
(iv) $ax - 3 - a + 3x$
(v) $2x - kx + ky - 2y$
(vi) $3a - b + 3ab - b^2$
(vii) $3xy - 10x - 10b + 3by$
(viii) $5x^2 - 10xy - 2y + x$
(ix) $6ap - 4b - 12bp + 2a$
(x) $x^2 - ab - bx + ax$

Section 3E More Factors

Factors type 3: Quadratic trinomials

We want to factorise expressions like $x^2 + 4x + 5$ or $6x^2 + 13x + 5$ etc.

Remember that factorising is the opposite of multiplying out.

For example:

$(5x + 3)(2x - 1) = 5x(2x - 1) + 3(2x - 1)$
$\qquad\qquad\qquad = 10x^2 - 5x + 6x - 3$
$\qquad\qquad\qquad = 10x^2 + x - 3$

Hence, the factors of $10x^2 + x - 3$ are $(5x + 3)(2x - 1)$.

This means that the factors for these expressions look like $(ax + b)(cx + d)$ where a, b, c and d are numbers which could be + or –.

Notice that the middle term $(+x)$ in the expression is found by combining the factors of $10x^2$ and -3 (the first and last terms) like this:

$$(5x + 3)(2x - 1)$$

middle term is $(5x)(-1) + (3)(2x) = -5x + 6x = +x$

Example 1

Factorise $6x^2 + 13x + 5$.

Solution

Method 1

Break up the middle term $(+13x)$ into two terms so that we have a 'gang of 4' terms.

To do this, our guide number is $(6)(5) = +30$.

- Find all the factors of +30:

  (30)(1)
  (−30)(−1)
  (15)(2)
  (−15)(−2)
  (3)(10)
  (−3)(−10)
  (5)(6)
  (−5)(−6)

- Only one pair of these factors will add to give the middle coefficient (+13). These are +3 and +10. So we write +13x as (+3x + 10x):

  $6x^2 + 13x + 5 = 6x^2 + 3x + 10x + 5$ … use Type 2 method from here
  $ = 3x(2x + 1) + 5(2x + 1)$
  $ = (2x + 1)(3x + 5)$

  Check: $(2x + 1)(3x + 5) = 6x^2 + 10x + 3x + 5$
  $ = 6x^2 + 13x + 5$ ✓

Method 2

Factorise $6x^2 + 13x + 5$.

Guess and test: We need factors of $6x^2$ to work with factors of +5 (the first and last terms) in order to get +13x in the middle.

Trial 1: $(6x + 5)(x + 1)$ … wrong ✗

Trial 2: $(2x + 5)(3x + 1)$ … wrong ✗

Trial 3: $(2x + 1)(3x + 5)$ … correct ✓

So $6x^2 + 13x + 5 = (2x + 1)(3x + 5)$

Example 2

Factorise $14x^2 − 17x − 6$.

Solution

Method 1

Break up the middle term (−17x) into two terms so that we have a 'gang of 4' terms.

To do this, our guide number is $(14)(−6) = −84$.

- Find all the factors of –84:

$$(84)(-1) \quad (4)(-21)$$
$$(-84)(1) \quad (-4)(21)$$
$$(42)(-2) \quad (6)(-14)$$
$$(-42)(2) \quad (-6)(14)$$
$$(3)(-28) \quad (7)(-12)$$
$$(-3)(28) \quad (-7)(12)$$

- Only one pair of these factors will add to give the middle coefficient (–17). These are +4 and –21. So we write –17x as (+4x – 21x):

$14x^2 - 17x - 6 = 14x^2 - 21x + 4x - 6$ … use Type 2 method from here

$\qquad = 7x(2x - 3) + 2(2x - 3)$

$\qquad = (2x - 3)(7x + 2)$

Check: $(2x - 3)(7x + 2) = 14x^2 + 4x - 21x - 6$

$\qquad = 14x^2 - 17x - 6$ ✓

Method 2

Factorise $14x^2 - 17x - 6$.

Guess and test: We need factors of $14x^2$ to work with factors of –6 (the first and last terms) in order to get –17x in the middle.

Trial 1: $(7x + 6)(2x - 1)$ … wrong ✗

Trial 2: $(7x + 3)(2x - 2)$ … wrong ✗

Trial 3: $(7x + 2)(2x - 3)$ … correct ✓

So $14x^2 - 7x - 6 = (2x - 3)(7x + 2)$

Although method 2 may seem difficult at first, you may find it more efficient with a little practice.

Factors type 4: Difference of two squares

Example 3

Factorise (i) $x^2 - y^2$

(ii) $49m^2 - 9n^2$

Solution

(i) $x^2 - y^2$

$= (x + y)(x - y)$

(ii) $49m^2 - 9n^2$

$= (7m)^2 - (3n)^2$

$= (7m + 3n)(7m - 3n)$

Example 4

Simplify

$(3x - 2)(3x + 2) - (2x + 1)(2x - 1)$.

Solution

$(3x - 2)(3x + 2) - (2x + 1)(2x - 1)$

$= (9x^2 - 4) - (4x^2 - 1)$

$= 9x^2 - 4 - 4x^2 + 1$

$= 5x^2 - 3$

Activity 3.5

Factorise the expressions in questions 1–30.

1. $a^2 + 5a + 6$
2. $x^2 - x - 6$
3. $a^2 - 3a - 88$
4. $m^2 + 11m - 42$
5. $x^2 + 5x - 66$
6. $a^2 - 5a - 66$
7. $5x^2 - 6x + 1$
8. $3x^2 + x - 2$
9. $10x^2 + 11x - 6$
10. $12x^2 - 23x + 10$
11. $6x^2 + x - 35$
12. $11x^2 + 75x - 14$
13. $6x^2 + 7x - 10$
14. $9m^2 - 24m + 16$
15. $25x^2 - 30x + 9$
16. $a^2 - 1$
17. $x^2 - 9$
18. $p^2 - 36$
19. $9m^2 - 1$
20. $25x^2 - 36y^2$
21. $49a^2 - 16b^2$
22. $144x^2 - 9y^2$
23. $169p^2 - 144$
24. $m^2 - 10\,000$
25. $(x + y)^2 - z^2$
26. $(a + b)^2 - 1$
27. $2x^2 - 18$ (3 factors)
28. $(x - 2)^2 - 36y^2$
29. $(3x + 1)^2 - (2x - 1)^2$
30. $101^2 - 99^2$
31. Simplify $(3 - 4x)^2 - (3 - 5x)^2$.
32. Simplify $(7x - 2)(7x + 2) - (5x + 4)(5x - 4)$ and fully factorise the simplified expression.
33. Use factors to simplify $\dfrac{8x^2 - 12x}{4x^2 - 12x + 9}$.
34. Simplify $\dfrac{6x^2 - 17x + 12}{3x - 4}$.
35. Simplify $(2x + a)(4x - 2a) - (3y + a)(6y - 2a)$ and fully factorise the simplified expression.
36. Factorise
    (i) $17y - 5y^2$
    (ii) $6a^2 - 19a + 10$
37. Simplify $(2a - 1)^2 - (a - 1)^2$.

Section 3F Adding and Subtracting Algebraic Fractions

Example 1

Express in its simplest form $\dfrac{3a - 1}{4} - \dfrac{5a + 4}{3} + \dfrac{2a - 7}{6}$.

Solution

The lowest common denominator is 12.

$\dfrac{3a - 1}{4} + \dfrac{5a + 4}{3} - \dfrac{2a - 7}{6} = \dfrac{3(3a - 1) + 4(5a + 4) - 2(2a - 7)}{12}$ … always use brackets in the numerator

$= \dfrac{9a - 3 + 20a + 16 - 4a + 14}{12}$

$= \dfrac{25a + 27}{12}$

Example 2

Write as a single fraction $\dfrac{1}{2x} + \dfrac{5}{4x}$.

Solution

The lowest common denominator is $4x$.

$$\dfrac{1}{2x} + \dfrac{5}{4x}$$
$$= \dfrac{2+5}{4x}$$
$$= \dfrac{7}{4x}$$

Example 3

Express in its simplest form $\dfrac{3}{2x+1} + \dfrac{5}{3x+4}$.

Solution

The lowest common denominator is $(2x+1)(3x+4)$.

$$\dfrac{3}{2x+1} + \dfrac{5}{3x+4} = \dfrac{3(3x+4) + 5(2x+1)}{(2x+1)(3x+4)} \quad \text{… always use brackets}$$
$$= \dfrac{9x + 12 + 10x + 5}{(2x+1)(3x+4)}$$
$$= \dfrac{19x + 17}{(2x+1)(3x+4)}$$

Activity 3.6

Write the expressions in questions 1–15 as single fractions.

1. $\dfrac{5-x}{5} + \dfrac{x-4}{4}$

2. $\dfrac{x+6}{3} + \dfrac{x-4}{5}$

3. $\dfrac{x+4}{2} - \dfrac{x-5}{3} + \dfrac{x}{6}$

4. $\dfrac{2x+5}{3} - \dfrac{3x-2}{5} + \dfrac{2x-1}{15}$

5. $\dfrac{3x-1}{2} - \dfrac{4-x}{5} + (x-3)$

   Hint: Remember that $(x-3) = \dfrac{(x-3)}{1}$

6. $4x - \dfrac{5x-1}{4} + \dfrac{x}{12}$

7. $\dfrac{3p-1}{7} - \dfrac{2p+7}{14} + 7p$

8. $\dfrac{k}{4} + \dfrac{3k-2}{3} - \dfrac{2k-5}{12}$

9. $\dfrac{1}{x} + \dfrac{3}{2x}$

10. $\dfrac{5}{3k} - \dfrac{2}{5k}$

11. $\dfrac{5}{x} + \dfrac{3}{2x+1}$

12. $\dfrac{5}{3x-2} + \dfrac{6}{2x+3}$

13. $\dfrac{3}{3x+1} - \dfrac{1}{2x-4}$

14. $\dfrac{2}{3p-5} - \dfrac{5}{p+1}$

15. $\dfrac{5}{3x+2} - \dfrac{4}{3x-2}$

16. Show that $\dfrac{1}{x-3} - \dfrac{1}{x}$ can be written in the form $\dfrac{p}{x^2 - 3x}$ where $p \in \mathbb{N}$ and find the value of p.

17. Show that $\dfrac{5}{2x-6} + \dfrac{7}{3x-9}$ can be written in the form $\dfrac{k}{6(x-3)}$ where $k \in \mathbb{N}$ and find the value of k.

18. (i) Show that $\dfrac{1}{x-2} = \dfrac{-1}{2-x}$.
    (ii) Write $\dfrac{5}{x-2} + \dfrac{4}{2-x}$ in the form $\dfrac{p}{x-2}$ where $p \in \mathbb{N}$.

19. Write $\dfrac{6}{x-3} + \dfrac{4}{3-x}$ as a single fraction. Verify your answer by letting $x = 10$.

20. Write $\dfrac{3}{x-4} + \dfrac{7}{4-x}$ as a single fraction. Verify your answer by letting $x = 2$.

21. Express as a single fraction $\dfrac{3}{2x+5} + \dfrac{1}{x+5}$.

22. Show that $\dfrac{4}{3x-12} + \dfrac{3}{2x-8}$ can be written in the form $\dfrac{k}{6(x-4)}$ where $k \in \mathbb{N}$ and find the value of k.

Section 3G Long Division

Example 1

Divide $15x^2 + 4x - 32$ by $3x - 4$.

Solution

$$\begin{array}{r} 5x + 8 \\ 3x-4\overline{\smash{)}15x^2 + 4x - 32} \\ \underline{15x^2 - 20x} \\ 24x - 32 \\ \underline{24x - 32} \\ 0 \end{array}$$

Divide $3x$ into $15x^2 \Rightarrow 5x$ on top line (answer)
Multiply $5x$ by $(3x - 4) \Rightarrow 15x^2 - 20x$
Subtract $\Rightarrow 24x$; bring down -32
Divide $3x$ into $24x \Rightarrow +8$ on top line (answer)
Multiply 8 by $(3x - 4) \Rightarrow 24x - 32$
Subtract $\Rightarrow 0$

Answer $= 5x + 8$

Example 2

Divide $x^3 - x^2 - 11x + 15$ by $x - 3$.

Solution

$$\begin{array}{r} x^2 + 2x - 5 \\ x-3\overline{\smash{)}x^3 - x^2 - 11x + 15} \\ \underline{x^3 - 3x^2} \\ 2x^2 - 11x \\ \underline{2x^2 - 6x} \\ -5x + 15 \\ \underline{-5x + 15} \\ 0 \end{array}$$

Divide x into $x^3 \Rightarrow x^2$ on top line (answer)
Multiply x^2 by $(x - 3) \Rightarrow x^3 - 3x^2$
Subtract $\Rightarrow 2x^2$; bring down $-11x$
Divide x into $2x^2 \Rightarrow +2x$ on top line (answer)
Multiply $2x$ by $(x - 3) \Rightarrow 2x^2 - 6x$
Subtract $\Rightarrow -5x$; bring down $+15$
Repeat these 3 steps once more.

Answer $= x^2 + 2x - 5$

Example 3

Divide $6x^3 - 15x + 9$ by $3x - 3$.

Solution

There is no x^2 term in the numerator, so we write the numerator as $6x^3 + 0x^2 - 15x + 9$.

$$
\begin{array}{r}
2x^2 + 2x - 3 \\
3x - 3 \overline{\smash{)}6x^3 + 0x^2 - 15x + 9} \\
\underline{6x^3 - 6x^2} \\
6x^2 - 15x \\
\underline{6x^2 - 6x} \\
-9x + 9 \\
\underline{-9x + 9} \\
0
\end{array}
$$

Divide $3x$ into $6x^3 \Rightarrow 2x^2$ on top line (answer)
Multiply $2x^2$ by $(3x - 3) \Rightarrow 6x^3 - 6x^2$
Subtract $\Rightarrow 6x^2$; bring down $-15x$
Divide $3x$ into $6x^2 \Rightarrow +2x$ on top line (answer)
Multiply $2x$ by $(3x - 3) \Rightarrow 6x^2 - 6x$
Subtract $\Rightarrow -9x$; bring down $+9$
Repeat these 3 steps once more.

Answer $= 2x^2 + 2x - 3$

Activity 3.7

1. Divide
   (i) $x^2 - x - 6$ by $x - 3$
   (ii) $6a^2 + a - 2$ by $2a - 1$
   (iii) $3x^2 - 17x - 28$ by $x - 7$
   (iv) $15p^2 - 7p - 4$ by $5p - 4$
   (v) $6x^2 - 11x - 10$ by $2x - 5$
   (vi) $x^2 - 64$ by $x - 8$
   (vii) $12x^2 + 7xy - 10y^2$ by $3x - 2y$
   (viii) $3 - 10x - 8x^2$ by $1 - 4x$

2. Divide $x^3 - 2x^2 - 24x - 27$ by $(x + 3)$.

3. Divide $2x^3 - 9x^2 - 10x + 25$ by $(x - 5)$.

4. Divide $a^3 - 6a^2 - 12a + 17$ by $(a - 1)$.

5. One factor of $6a^3 + 5a^2 - 25a - 28$ is $(3a + 4)$. Find the other factor.

6. Simplify by division $\dfrac{4p^3 - 4p^2 - 7p - 20}{2p - 5}$.

7. Divide $6k^3 + 7k^2 - 18k + 5$ by $(2k + 5)$.

8. One factor of $2x^3 - 7x^2 + 4x + 3$ is $(2x - 3)$. Find the other factor.

9. The length of one side of a rectangle is $x + 12$. The area of the rectangle is $x^2 + 16x + 48$. Find an expression in x for the other side.

   $x + 12$

   ? | $x^2 + 16x + 48$

10. Simplify by division $\dfrac{3k^3 - 4k - 16}{k - 2}$.

11. $6x^3 - 17x^2 + 2x + 15 = (2x - 3)(ax^2 + bx + c)$ for all values of x. Find the values of a, b and c.

12. (i) Simplify by division $\dfrac{x^3 - 7x^2 + 12x}{x - 4}$.
    (ii) Use factors to check your answer to part (i).

13. Divide $x^3 - 8$ by $x - 2$.

14. Divide $3 - 8x + 3x^2 + 2x^3$ by $(1 - x)$.

Revision Activity 3

1. Factorise fully
   (a) $20xy - 4x^2$
   (b) $5x^2 - 9x - 2$
   (c) $6x^2 - 24y^2$

2. Find the value of $x^2 - 2xy + 3$ when $x = \frac{1}{2}$ and $y = \frac{2}{3}$.

3. Multiply out and simplify
   $(3x - 4)(2x^2 + 5x - 2)$.

4. (a) Factorise $x^2 - ab - bx + ax$.
   (b) Simplify
   $(4x - 2a)(2x + a) - (3y + a)(6y - 2a)$
   and fully factorise the simplified expression.

5. (a) Multiply out $(5x - 2)(3x^2 + x - 6)$.
   (b) Evaluate your answer to part (a) when $x = -1$.

6. Factorise
   (a) $9x^2 - 15x$
   (b) $9x^2 - 24x + 15$
   (c) $3y - 3x - 4xy + 4x^2$

7. Express in its simplest form
   $\frac{5}{x-3} - \frac{3}{x-2}$

8. Simplify $\frac{2p^2 + 4p - 30}{p - 3}$.

9. Express as a single fraction $\frac{x+7}{5} + \frac{3-x}{4}$.

10. Find the value of each expression when $a = -1$, $b = -4$ and $c = 5$.
    (a) $\frac{a^2}{bc}$
    (b) $\frac{a^2 - b}{c + 3}$
    (c) $\frac{a + c}{4bc}$
    (d) $\frac{a + b^3}{b^3 + c}$

Exam-style Questions

1. (a) Express in its simplest form
   $\frac{5-x}{5} + \frac{x-4}{4}$
   (b) Divide $2x^3 + x^2 - 13x + 6$ by $x + 3$.

   JCHL 2013 Paper 1

2. Factorise fully each of the following expressions.
   (a) $5x^3 - 10x^2$
   (b) $4x^2 - 81y^2$
   (c) $a^2 - ab + 3a - 3b$

   JCHL 2012 Paper 1

KEY WORDS AND PHRASES

- Algebra
- Variable
- Factor
- Equivalent expressions
- Indices
- Term
- Coefficient
- Constant
- Expression
- Division
- Distributive Law
- Substitution
- Long division
- Factors
- Factorise
- Common factor
- Quadratic expression
- Linear expression
- Difference of two squares
- Algebraic fractions

Chapter Summary 3

- $5(3x - 2y) = 15x - 10y$ by the Distributive Law.
- $(x + y)^2 = x^2 + 2xy + y^2$
- Factors
    - Type 1: take out the HCF from each term
      e.g. $5x^2y^3 - 10x^3y^2 = 5x^2y^2(y - 2x)$
    - Type 2: group to get a common factor
      e.g. $ax + by + cx + dy = a(x + y) + b(x + y) = (x + y)(a + b)$
    - Type 3: quadratic trinomials
      e.g. $x^2 - x - 6 = (x - 3)(x + 2)$
    - Type 4: difference of two squares
      e.g. $9x^2 - 16y^2 = (3x)^2 - (4y)^2 = (3x + 4y)(3x - 4y)$
- Express two algebraic fractions as one fraction.
- Divide expressions (long division).

Chapter 4

Algebra 2
Linear Equations

Learning Outcomes

In this chapter, you will learn about:
- Solving linear inequalities (review and extension)
- Solving compound linear inequalities
- Using linear inequalities to solve problems

Section 4A Revision: Linear Equations

We have already met linear equations in our study of algebra.

> In an equation, a term or expression is equal (=) to another term or expression. We say that the equation is balanced.

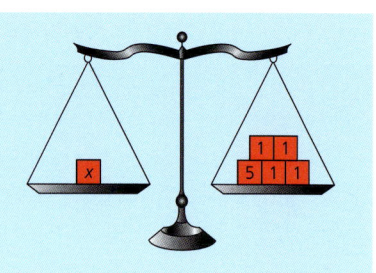

When we solve an equation, we find the value or values of the unknown variable or variables.

To keep an equation balanced, the same operation must be applied to both sides of the equation. This means that:

- If I add a number to one side of an equation, I must add the **same** number to the other side of the equation.
- If I subtract a number from one side of an equation, I must subtract the **same** number from the other side of the equation.
- If I multiply one side of an equation by a number, I must multiply the other side of the equation by the **same** number.
- If I divide one side of an equation by a number, I must divide the other side of the equation by the **same** number.

> A linear equation is any equation of the form $ax + b = 0$ or $y = ax + b$ where $a, b \in \mathbb{R}$.

Example 1

Solve $36k - 13 = 149$.

Solution

$36k - 13 = 149$
$\Rightarrow \quad 36k = 149 + 13$ … add 13 to both sides
$\Rightarrow \quad 36k = 162$
$\quad\quad k = \dfrac{162}{36}$ … divide both sides by 36
$\quad\quad k = 4\dfrac{1}{2}$

Check answer by substituting $k = 4\dfrac{1}{2}$ into original equation:
$$36k - 13 = 149$$
$\Rightarrow 36\left(4\dfrac{1}{2}\right) - 13 = 149$
$\Rightarrow \quad 162 - 13 = 149$
$\Rightarrow \quad\quad 149 = 149 \checkmark$

As LHS = RHS the equation is balanced.

Example 2

Solve $3(n + 4) - 5(n - 1) = 9n + 28$.

Solution

$3(n + 4) - 5(n - 1) = 9n + 28$
$\Rightarrow 3n + 12 - 5n + 5 = 9n + 28$
$\Rightarrow \quad\quad -2n + 17 = 9n + 28$
$\Rightarrow \quad\quad\quad\quad 17 = 9n + 28 + 2n$ … add $2n$ to both sides
$\Rightarrow \quad\quad\quad 17 - 28 = 11n$ … subtract 28 from both sides
$\Rightarrow \quad\quad\quad -\dfrac{11}{11} = n$ … divide both sides by 11
$\Rightarrow \quad\quad\quad\quad -1 = n$

Check answer by substituting $n = -1$ into both sides of the original equation:
LHS: $3(n + 4) - 5(n - 1) = 3(-1 + 4) - 5(-1 - 1) = 3(3) - 5(-2) = 9 + 10 = 19$
RHS: $9n + 28 = 9(-1) + 28 = -9 + 28 = 19 \checkmark$ As LHS = RHS, the equation is balanced.

Example 3

Solve $\dfrac{2}{5}(4y - 7) = 8$.

Solution

$\dfrac{2}{5}(4y - 7) = 8$
$\Rightarrow \dfrac{2(4y - 7)}{5} = 8$
$\Rightarrow 2(4y - 7) = 5(8)$ … multiply both sides by 5
$\Rightarrow 8y - 14 = 40$
$\Rightarrow \quad\quad 8y = 40 + 14$ … add 14 to both sides
$\Rightarrow \quad\quad \dfrac{8y}{8} = \dfrac{54}{8}$ … divide both sides by 8
$\Rightarrow \quad\quad\quad y = 6\dfrac{3}{4}$

Check answer by substituting $y = 6\dfrac{3}{4}$ into the original equation:
$\dfrac{2}{5}\left[4\left(6\dfrac{3}{4}\right) - 7\right] = 8$
$\Rightarrow \dfrac{2}{5}(27 - 7) = 8$
$\Rightarrow \dfrac{2}{5}(20) = 8$
$\Rightarrow \quad\quad 8 = 8 \checkmark$

As LHS = RHS, the equation is balanced.

4 Activity 4.1

Solve the following equations and **verify** your answers.

1. $3x - 7 = 2$
2. $7y - 1 = 13$
3. $5a + 8 = -17$
4. $5x + 12 = 42$
5. $7g + 21 = -14$
6. $2h - 11 = 1 - h$
7. $4t + 3 = 7t + 39$
8. $12z - 1 = 7z + 49$
9. $\dfrac{x + 4}{2} = 3$
10. $\dfrac{4x + 13}{3} = 23$
11. $\dfrac{w + 5}{8} = -3$
12. $\dfrac{3y - 11}{4} = 16$
13. $\dfrac{11s - 2}{7} = -5$
14. $\dfrac{2}{3}(b + 3) = 8$
15. $3(5l - 2) = 9$
16. $7(-2m - 1) - 18 = 3$
17. $2(x - 3) = 3(4 - x)$
18. $4(p - 7) = 5(p + 1)$
19. $2(q + 3) - (q - 2) = 2q - 7$
20. $7(2 + n) - 2(3n + 1) = 10(n + 3)$

Section 4B More Linear Equations with Fractions

The examples below show how to solve linear equations where the coefficients of the variable and the solutions may be rational numbers (elements of $\mathbb{Q}$).

Example 1

Solve $\dfrac{7x}{3} = 6$ for x.

Solution

$\dfrac{7x}{3} = 6$

$\Rightarrow 7x = 3(6)$ … multiply both sides by 3

$\Rightarrow 7x = 18$

$\Rightarrow x = \dfrac{18}{7}$ … divide both sides by 7

Check answer by substituting $x = \dfrac{18}{7}$ into the original equation:

$\dfrac{7\left(\dfrac{18}{7}\right)}{3} = 6 \Rightarrow \dfrac{18}{3} = 6 \Rightarrow 6 = 6$ ✓

As LHS = RHS, the equation is balanced.

Example 2

Solve $\dfrac{2p}{3} - \dfrac{5p}{4} = \dfrac{11}{6}$ for p.

Solution

$\dfrac{2p}{3} - \dfrac{5p}{4} = \dfrac{11}{6}$

$\Rightarrow \dfrac{12(2p)}{3} - \dfrac{12(5p)}{4} = \dfrac{12(11)}{6}$

$\Rightarrow 4(2p) - 3(5p) = 2(11)$ … multiply all terms by the LCM of 3, 4 and 6, i.e. 12

$\Rightarrow 8p - 15p = 22$

$\Rightarrow -7p = 22$

$\Rightarrow p = \dfrac{22}{-7}$ … divide both sides by –7

Check answer by substituting $p = -\frac{22}{7}$ into the original equation:

$$\frac{2\left(-\frac{22}{7}\right)}{3} - \frac{5\left(-\frac{22}{7}\right)}{4} = \frac{11}{6} \Rightarrow \frac{-\frac{44}{7}}{3} + \frac{\frac{110}{7}}{4} = \frac{11}{6} \Rightarrow -\frac{44}{21} + \frac{110}{28} = \frac{11}{6}$$

$$\Rightarrow \frac{154}{84} = \frac{11}{6} \Rightarrow \frac{11}{6} = \frac{11}{6} \checkmark$$

As LHS = RHS, the equation is balanced.

Activity 4.2

Solve the following equations.

1. $\frac{5h}{2} = 3$
2. $\frac{7d}{4} = 5$
3. $\frac{3n}{7} = 2$
4. $\frac{12y}{5} = 7$
5. $\frac{21m}{8} = 9$
6. $\frac{2}{3}x + 4 = 7$
7. $\frac{2c}{9} + 8 = 5$
8. $\frac{3}{5}p - 2 = -7$
9. $\frac{3}{4}v + 2 = 9$
10. $\frac{7}{9}z - 8 = 4$
11. $\frac{2x - 3}{7} = \frac{2}{3}$
12. $\frac{5h + 1}{3} = \frac{4}{5}$
13. $\frac{6m + 7}{8} = \frac{9}{2}$
14. $\frac{3d - 4}{7} = \frac{1}{8}$
15. $\frac{9k + 4}{5} = \frac{6}{11}$
16. $\frac{m + 1}{2} + \frac{2m + 3}{3} = 2$
17. $\frac{2l + 7}{4} + \frac{3l - 5}{2} = \frac{1}{8}$
18. $t - \frac{7t + 3}{9} = \frac{2}{3}$
19. $\frac{1}{5} + \frac{8a - 3}{7} = 3$
20. $\frac{5d - 2}{7} - \frac{9d}{2} = \frac{1}{7}$

Solve the following equations and verify your answers.

21. $\frac{b - 3}{5} - \frac{2b + 7}{2} = \frac{1}{10}$
22. $\frac{1}{3}(2g - 1) + \frac{2}{5}(3 - g) = \frac{2}{3}$
23. $\frac{1}{3}(6f + 1) + \frac{3f - 4}{2} = \frac{1}{6}$
24. $3(c - 2) - \frac{2}{5}(1 - c) = \frac{1}{3}$
25. $\frac{1}{5}(2k + 3) - \frac{7k - 4}{3} = 6$

Section 4C Solving More Problems using Linear Equations

We have already used linear equations to solve problems dealing with everyday situations in our study of algebra. An example of one particular problem is shown below.

Example 1

A triangle *ABC* of perimeter 18 cm has sides of length *l* cm, (*l* + 2) cm and (2*l* – 4) cm.

(i) Write an algebraic equation to represent this information.
(ii) Solve the equation.
(iii) What is the length of each side?
(iv) Substitute your answer to verify your solution.

Triangle ABC with sides: l, l + 2, 2l − 4. Perimeter of ABC = 18

Solution

(i) Perimeter of the triangle =
$$l + (l + 2) + (2l - 4) = 18$$

(ii) $l + (l + 2) + (2l - 4) = 18$
⇒ $4l - 2 = 18$
⇒ $4l = 18 + 2$ … add 2 to both sides
⇒ $l = \dfrac{20}{4} = 5$ … divide both sides by 4

(iii) So the lengths of the sides of the triangle are:
$l = 5$ cm
$l + 2 = 5 + 2 = 7$ cm
$2l - 4 = 2(5) - 4 = 10 - 4 = 6$ cm

(iv) Check answer by substituting $l = 5$ into the original equation:
$l + (l + 2) + (2l - 4) = 18$ ⇒ $5 + (5 + 2) + (2(5) - 4) = 18$
⇒ $5 + (7) + (10 - 4) = 18$ ⇒ $5 + (7) + (6) = 18$
⇒ $18 = 18$ ✓

Example 2

Conor collects 10 cent, 20 cent and 50 cent coins. He saves €13.50.

He saved twice as many 10 cent coins as 50 cent coins, and 4 times as many 20 cent coins as 50 cent coins.

(i) Write an equation in words to represent this information.
(ii) Write a linear equation to represent this information.
(iii) Solve the linear equation.
(iv) How many of each coin did he save?
(v) Check your answer by substituting the values back into the equation.

Solution

(i) Value of 10 cent coins + value of 20 cent coins + value of 50 cent coins = €13.50
= 1350 cent

(ii) Let n = number of 50c coins saved, i.e. 50n cent saved

$\Rightarrow$ 2n = number of 10c coins saved, i.e. 20n cent saved

$\Rightarrow$ 4n = number of 20c coins saved, i.e. 80n cent saved

Total = 50n + 20n + 80n = 1350

(iii) 50n + 20n + 80n = 1350

$\Rightarrow$ 150n = 1350

$\Rightarrow$ $n = \dfrac{1350}{150} = 9$

So he saved nine 50 cent coins = €4.50

(iv) He saved twice as many 10 cent coins as 50 cent coins.

2n = 2(9) = 18 $\qquad\Rightarrow$ He saved eighteen 10 cent coins.

Value = 18(€0.10) = €1.80

He saved four times as many 20 cent coins as 50 cent coins.

4n = 4(9) = 36 $\qquad\Rightarrow$ He saved thirty-six 20 cent coins.

Value = 36(€0.20) = €7.20

(v) Total saved = €1.80 + €7.20 + €4.50 = €13.50

€13.50 = €13.50 ✓

As LHS = RHS, the equation is balanced.

Connections

We can use equations to solve geometry problems.

Example 3

In a parallelogram, one angle is one quarter the size of a larger angle. What sizes are the angles in the parallelogram?

(i) State a property of parallelograms which will help you solve this problem.

(ii) Write a linear equation to represent this information.

(iii) Solve the linear equation.

(iv) Write down the degree measure of both the smaller angle and the larger angle.

(v) Use the theorem stated in part (i) to check/verify your solution.

Solution

(i) In a parallelogram, adjacent angles add to 180° and opposite angles are equal.

(ii) Let A = the smaller angle

$\Rightarrow 4A$ = the larger angle

$\Rightarrow A + 4A = 180$

(iii) $5A = 180$

$\Rightarrow A = \dfrac{180}{5} = 36$

$\Rightarrow 4A = 144$

(iv) Larger angle = 144°

Smaller angle = 36°

(v) Sum of 2 adjacent angles = 180°

$\Rightarrow 144° + 36° = 180°$ ✓

The parallelogram has two angles of size 36° and two angles of size 144°.

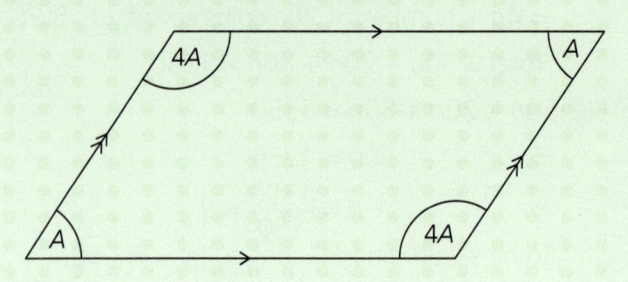

Example 4

Chris travels from Newry to Dublin in 63 minutes. For the first part of his journey he travels a distance at an average speed of 60 km/h. For the second part of the journey he travels $8\frac{1}{2}$ times this distance at an average speed of 120 km/h.

(i) Write an expression for the time taken for each part of the journey.

(ii) Write a linear equation to represent this information.

(iii) Solve the linear equation.

(iv) How far did he travel in the
 (a) first part of his journey
 (b) second part of his journey?

(v) How long did the
 (a) first part of the journey take
 (b) second part of the journey take?

> Time taken = $\dfrac{\text{distance}}{\text{speed}}$

Solution

(i) Let x be the distance travelled at 60 km/h

$\Rightarrow \dfrac{17x}{2}$ = the distance travelled at 120 km/h

Time taken for 1st part of journey = $\dfrac{x}{60}$ hours

Time taken for 2nd part of journey = $\dfrac{\left(\dfrac{17x}{2}\right)}{120} = \dfrac{17x}{240}$ hours

(ii) Total time taken = 63 minutes = $\dfrac{63}{60} = \dfrac{21}{20}$ hours

$\dfrac{x}{60} + \dfrac{17x}{240} = \dfrac{21}{20}$

(iii) $\dfrac{x}{60} + \dfrac{17x}{240} = \dfrac{21}{20}$

$\Rightarrow 240\left(\dfrac{x}{60}\right) + 240\left(\dfrac{17x}{240}\right) = 240\left(\dfrac{21}{20}\right)$ … multiply each side by 240, the LCM

$$\Rightarrow \quad 4x + 17x = 12(21)$$
$$\Rightarrow \quad 21x = 252$$
$$\Rightarrow \quad x = \frac{252}{21} \quad \text{… divide both sides by 21}$$
$$\Rightarrow \quad x = 12$$

(iv) He travelled:
  (a) x km in 1st part of journey = 12 km
  (b) $\frac{17x}{2}$ km in 2nd part of journey = $\frac{17x}{2} = \frac{17(12)}{2}$ = 102 km

(v) (a) Time taken for 1st part of journey = $\frac{x}{60} = \frac{12}{60} = \frac{1}{5}$ hours = 12 minutes
  (b) Time taken for 2nd part of journey = $\frac{17x}{240} = \frac{17(12)}{240}$ = 0.85 hours
    = 0.85 × 60 = 51 minutes

Activity 4.3

1 Write each statement as a linear equation and solve to find the unknown number.
  (i) A number is doubled and 8 is added to the result. The answer is 32. Find the number.
  (ii) If 8 is subtracted from five times a number, the answer is 112. Find the number.
  (iii) A number decreased by 9 is 18. Find the number.
  (iv) The sum of twice a number plus three times the number is 150. What is the number?
  (v) When 14 is added to a number and the result is divided by 3, the answer is 7. What is the number?
  (vi) When 10 is added to twice a number, the result is 40. What is the number?

2 The sum of three consecutive numbers is 126. Find the numbers.

3 The perimeter of the right-angled triangle shown is 12 cm. Find the value of k and the length of each side.

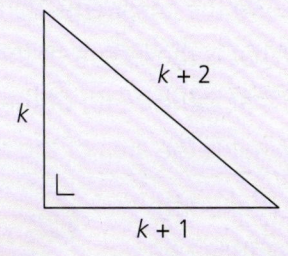

(triangle with sides k, $k+2$, and $k+1$)

4 Jack and Josh ran a race. Jack ran twice as far as Josh in a set amount of time. If the total distance they ran was 12 km, how far did each run?

5 Seán and Sarah share €25.00 between them. If Sarah gets €5 more than Seán, how much money does each get?

6 I spent €x on a pair of shoes and €$(x - 15)$ on a pair of trousers. How much did I spend on each item if the total cost was €95.00?

7 If n is any even number, then n and $n + 2$ are consecutive even numbers (e.g. 2 and 4 are consecutive even numbers). Find two consecutive even numbers if their sum is 194.

8. The perimeter of a triangle is 122 m. The first side is 35 m long, the second side is x m long and the third side is twice as long as the second side. Find the length of the second and third sides.

9. The sum of half Harry's age plus one-third of his age is 50. Find out how old Harry is.

10. If the sum of two consecutive numbers is divided by 5, the answer is 5. Find both numbers.

11. The dimensions of a rectangle are shown in the diagram.

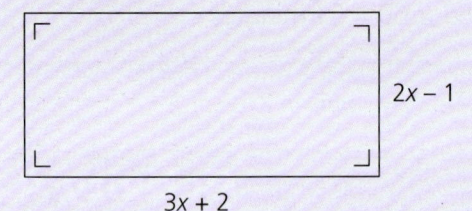

$2x - 1$
$3x + 2$

The perimeter of the rectangle is 32 units.
 (i) Write a linear equation to represent this information.
 (ii) Solve the linear equation.
 (iii) What is the length of the rectangle?
 (iv) What is the width of the rectangle?
 (v) What is the area of the rectangle?

12. Peter is one-fifth of his father's age. Their combined age is 48. 
 (i) Write a linear equation to represent this information.
 (ii) Solve the linear equation.
 (iii) How old is Peter's father?
 (iv) How old is Peter?

13. Joseph has saved a total of €210 made up from €1 and €2 coins. He has 5 times as many €1 coins as €2 coins. 
 (i) Write a linear equation to represent this information.
 (ii) Solve the linear equation.
 (iii) What is the value of the €1 coins saved?
 (iv) What is the value of the €2 coins saved?
 (v) Check your solution.

14. Mary went shopping and bought 3 times as many tins of beans as jars of jam. A tin of beans costs €0.69 and a jar of jam costs €1.50. The total bill was €7.14.  
 (i) Write a linear equation to represent this information.
 (ii) Solve the linear equation.
 (iii) Check your solution.
 (iv) How many jars of jam did Mary buy?
 (v) How many tins of beans did Mary buy?

15. Two angles are supplementary. The larger angle is 30° less than twice the smaller angle.
 (i) What are supplementary angles?
 (ii) Write a linear equation to represent this information.
 (iii) Solve the linear equation.
 (iv) Find the degree measure of the smaller angle.
 (v) Find the degree measure of the larger angle.
 (vi) Use the definition stated in part (i) to verify your solution.

16 Mr Kelly borrowed a sum of money at 10% per year interest. He also borrowed a second sum of money which was €5000 less than the first amount at 6% per year interest. The annual interest charged on the loans totalled €1300. Let x = first amount borrowed.
  (i) Write an expression in x for each amount borrowed.
  (ii) Write a linear equation which represents the information above.
  (iii) Solve the linear equation.
  (iv) How much did he borrow at each rate?
  (v) Check your answers.

17 The length of a rectangle is shown in the diagram.

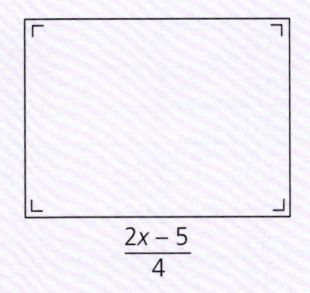

$$\frac{2x-5}{4}$$

The perimeter of the rectangle is $\frac{14x-25}{10}$ units.
  (i) Write a linear equation to represent this information.
  (ii) Solve the linear equation.
  (iii) Express the width of the rectangle in terms of x.

18 In a parallelogram, one angle is two-thirds the degree measure of another angle. The measure of the angles is required.
  (i) Write a property of parallelograms which will help you find the value of the angles in a parallelogram.
  (ii) Write a linear equation to represent this information.
  (iii) Solve the linear equation.
  (iv) What is the degree measure of the larger angle?
  (v) What is the degree measure of the smaller angle?
  (vi) Use the theorem stated in part (i) to verify your solution.

19 In an isosceles triangle, the two equal sides are three-quarters the length of the third side. The perimeter of the triangle is 12.5 units.
  (i) Write a linear equation to represent this information.
  (ii) Solve the linear equation.
  (iii) Calculate the length of each side.
  (iv) Sketch the triangle and label the length of each side.
  (v) Check your solution.

20 Greg travels from Maynooth to Mullingar in 42 minutes. For $\frac{1}{9}$ of the distance he travels at an average speed of 60 km/h. For the rest of the distance he travels at an average speed of 80 km/h.
  (i) Write an expression for the time taken for each part of the journey.
  (ii) Write a linear equation to represent this information.
  (iii) Solve the linear equation.
  (iv) How far did he travel in the
    (a) first part of his journey
    (b) second part of his journey?
  (v) How long did the
    (a) first part of the journey take
    (b) second part of the journey take?

> Time taken = $\frac{\text{distance}}{\text{speed}}$

Revision Activity 4

1. (a) Solve the following linear equations and check your answers.
   (i) $\frac{3}{17}(6c - 1) = 3$
   (ii) $\frac{m-2}{4} = \frac{2-m}{6}$
   (iii) $12 - 7y = -44$
   (iv) $\frac{x-3}{2} - \frac{x+3}{5} = -\frac{10}{3}$

   (b) The larger of two numbers is 14 greater than the smaller number. The smaller number is one-third of the larger number. Find both numbers.

2. Two numbers are consecutive. The sum of the smaller number minus two-thirds of the larger number is 34.
   (a) Write two separate algebraic expressions for each number.
   (b) Write a linear equation to represent this information.
   (c) Solve the linear equation.
   (d) Find the value of both consecutive numbers.
   (e) Verify your answer.

3. The perimeter of a triangle is $\frac{17x}{24}$ units. The lengths of two of the sides are $\frac{3x}{8}$ and $\frac{2x-5}{12}$ units. The length of the third side is required.
   (a) Write a linear equation to represent this information.
   (b) Solve the linear equation to find the length of the third side in terms of x.
   (c) What type of triangle is this? Explain your answer.

4. In a 20-question multiple choice test, 5 marks were awarded for a correct answer and 2 marks were deducted for an incorrect (wrong) answer. James got a total of 51 marks in the test. He attempted all the questions.
   (a) Write a linear equation to represent this information.
   (b) Solve the linear equation.
   (c) How many questions did he get correct?
   (d) How many questions did he get wrong?
   (e) Verify your solution.

5. A taxi driver charges a €2 pick-up charge and €1.10 per km thereafter.
   (a) If a customer is charged €20.70 for a journey of x km, write a linear equation to represent the situation.
   (b) Solve the linear equation to find the number of kilometres the customer travelled.
   (c) Using the linear equation from part (a), find the total taxi fare for the distances shown in the table below.

Distance travelled (km)	Linear equation	Total fare (€)
5		
10		
15		
20		
25		
30		
35		
40		

   (d) Draw a graph to represent the information.
   (e) If a customer travels 33 km, what is the total taxi fare from your graph?

6. A plumber charges €46 per hour and spends on average €18.50 per day on petrol. On a particular day, he earned €234.50 after deducting the cost of his petrol for the day.
   (a) Write a linear equation to represent this information.
   (b) Solve the linear equation to calculate how many hours he worked on this day.
   (c) How much would he earn after deducting the cost of his petrol if he worked 7.5 hours?
   (d) How much would he earn if he worked a total of 37 hours in 5 days, after he deducted the cost of his petrol?

7. Natalie saved €5, €10 and €20 notes during one year to pay for her annual family holiday. At the end of the year, she had saved a total of €2280.

    She saved half as many €5 notes as €20 notes and three-fifths as many €10 notes as €20 notes.

    (a) Write an equation in words to represent this information.
    (b) Write a linear equation to represent this information.
    (c) Solve the linear equation.
    (d) How many of each note did she save?
    (e) Check your answer by substituting the values back into the word equation.

8. Billy planted carrot seedlings in a 3 m by 1.2 m vegetable patch. After two days, one-quarter of the seedlings had been eaten by birds. A week later, one-third of the remaining seedlings had been eaten, leaving 432 seeds approximately (based on planting 6 seeds per 2.54 cm).

    Let x = the number of seedlings Billy planted.

    (a) Write an expression in x which represents the number of seedlings remaining after 2 days.
    (b) Write an expression in x which represents the number of seedlings remaining a week later.
    (c) Write a linear equation to represent the situation after 9 days.
    (d) Solve the equation.
    (e) How many seedlings had been eaten after two days?
    (f) How many seedlings did Billy plant to begin with?

9. There are x cars available to carry a class of students to the cinema. If the students are shared 3 to a car, there is one student left over. If the students are shared 4 to a car, two cars get no students. Find the value of x and the number of students in the class.

Exam-style Questions

1. (a) If $n = 7$ find the value of $2n$ and also the value of $2n + 1$.
   (b) (i) x represents an even number. Explain why $x + 2$ is also an even number.
   (ii) If one-third of the smaller even number is subtracted from half of the larger even number the result is 8. Find the value of x.

   JCHL 2013 Paper 1

2. Solve the following equation.
$$\frac{2x + 5}{3} - \frac{4x - 1}{2} = -\frac{1}{2}$$

   JCHL 2012 Paper 1

KEY WORD

- Linear equation

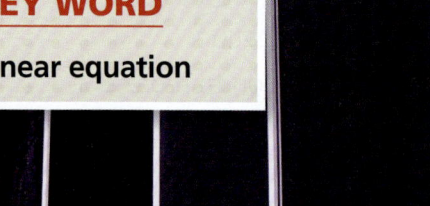

Chapter Summary 4

- When solving a linear equation in one variable/unknown, we need to find the value of the unknown variable (i.e. the letter in the equation).
- In any equation containing only x terms (or another variable) and numbers, we must rearrange the equations as follows:
  $\boxed{x \text{ terms}} = \boxed{\text{numbers}}$ or $\boxed{\text{numbers}} = \boxed{x \text{ terms}}$

Chapter 5

Algebra 3
Linear Inequalities

Learning Outcomes

In this chapter, you will learn about:
- Solving linear inequalities (review and extension)
- Solving compound linear inequalities
- Using linear inequalities to solve problems

Athletes who are serious about their training use a heart-rate monitor to ensure that they are getting the most from their running. They need to ensure that they are working hard enough, but not too hard.

In order to do this, athletes work out what their Maximum Heart Rate (MHR) is.

One formula used to get MHR is $(220 - x)$ where x is the age of the runner. There are other formulae which runners use as well, such as $(205 - 0.5x)$.

Typically, for easy and long runs, an athlete may want to work so that his or her heart-rate stays between 65% and 75% of MHR. To do this, he/she has to work out some simple **inequalities**. We will see how this works in this chapter.

Section 5A Review of Linear Inequalities

This section is a review of the inequalities we worked with in *Connect with Maths 1*.
- We use the following familiar symbols:

    < means less than

    ≤ means less than or equal to

    > means greater than

    ≥ means greater than or equal to

    ∈ means is an element of the set

    ℕ Natural numbers: {1, 2, 3, 4, 5, ...}

    ℤ Integers: {..., −5, −4, −3, −2, −1, 0, 1, 2, 3, 4, 5, ...}

    ℝ Real numbers: these numbers completely 'fill up' the number line.

- A linear **inequality** differs from a linear **equation** in that it may have an infinite number of solutions.

For example:

- $2x = 5$ is a linear equation which has one solution.
- $2x > 5$ and $2x \geq 5$ are linear inequalities which may have many solutions.
- $2x < 5$ or $2x \leq 5$ are linear inequalities which may have many solutions.

Connections

When we are constructing inequalities, we must decide on the type of data which we are dealing with, just as we do with statistical data.

- If the data is continuous, we are working with the set of Real numbers, $\mathbb{R}$.
- If discrete data is involved, then we are usually working with the set $\mathbb{N}$ or $\mathbb{Z}$.

Note

An inequality in which $x \in \mathbb{N}$ or $x \in \mathbb{Z}$ looks like a row of No$\mathbb{Z}$es.

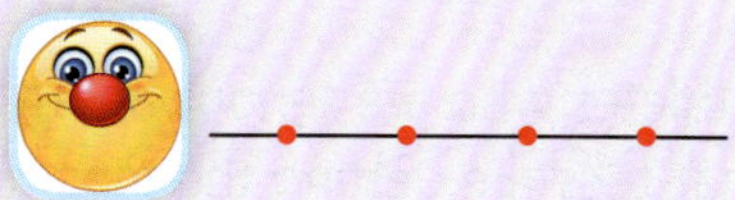

An inequality in which $x \in \mathbb{R}$ looks like a $\mathbb{R}$oad.

The example below reviews how to solve a simple linear inequality.

Example

Graph the solution sets of the following inequalities on the number line.

(i) $8p - 5 \leq 14$, $p \in \mathbb{N}$

(ii) $8p - 5 \leq 14$, $p \in \mathbb{Z}$

(iii) $8p - 5 \leq 14$, $p \in \mathbb{R}$

Solution

(i) $8p - 5 \leq 14$

$\Rightarrow 8p \leq 14 + 5$ ... add 5 to both sides

$\Rightarrow 8p \leq 19$

$\Rightarrow \dfrac{8p}{8} \leq \dfrac{19}{8}$ ... divide both sides by 8

$\Rightarrow p \leq \dfrac{19}{8}$

$p \leq \dfrac{19}{8}$, $p \in \mathbb{N}$. Natural numbers are positive whole numbers excluding 0.

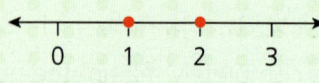

(ii) $p \leq \frac{19}{8}$, $p \in \mathbb{Z}$. Integers are positive and negative whole numbers including 0.

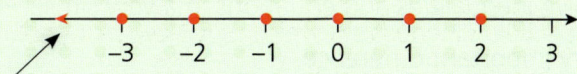

This arrow indicates that the solution set is infinite.

(iii) $p \leq \frac{19}{8}$, $p \in \mathbb{R}$. The Real numbers are all numbers (positive and negative whole numbers, fractions and decimals), so draw a heavy line along the number line.

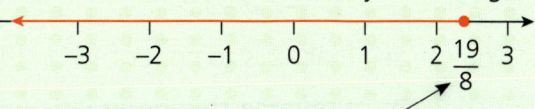

The shaded circle at $\frac{19}{8}$ shows that the number $\frac{19}{8}$ is included.

Activity 5.1

1. Graph on the number line the solution set of $2t - 5 \geq 33$, $t \in \mathbb{R}$.

2. Graph the solution sets of the following inequalities on the number line:
   (i) $4h + 13 < 21$, $h \in \mathbb{N}$
   (ii) $4h + 13 < 21$, $h \in \mathbb{Z}$
   (iii) $4h + 13 < 21$, $h \in \mathbb{R}$.

3. Graph the solution sets of the following inequalities on the number line:
   (i) $2x + 1 \leq 7$, $x \in \mathbb{N}$
   (ii) $2x + 1 \leq 7$, $x \in \mathbb{Z}$
   (iii) $2x + 1 \leq 7$, $x \in \mathbb{R}$.

4. Graph the solution sets of the following inequalities on the number line:
   (i) $11l + 28 > -3l$, $l \in \mathbb{N}$
   (ii) $11l + 28 > -3l$, $l \in \mathbb{Z}$
   (iii) $11l + 28 > -3l$, $l \in \mathbb{R}$.

5. Graph on the number line the solution set of $11q + 14 \leq 36$, $q \in \mathbb{R}$.

6. Graph on the number line the solution set of the inequality $3(2x - 7) - 1 < 4(x - 3) + 6$, $x \in \mathbb{R}$.

7. Graph on the number line the solution set of the inequality $2(p - 7) + 13 > -3(2 + p) + 6$, $p \in \mathbb{N}$.

8. Graph the solution sets of the following inequalities on the number line:
   (i) $4(r - 2) > -5(2r + 1) - 9$, $r \in \mathbb{N}$
   (ii) $4(r - 2) > -5(2r + 1) - 9$, $r \in \mathbb{R}$.

9. Graph on the number line the solution set of $12(m + 1) \geq 7(2 - m) + 6(m + 4)$, $m \in \mathbb{N}$.

10. Graph on the number line the solution set of $4(3w - 1) + 7(w - 4) < 3(2w - 2)$, $w \in \mathbb{R}$.

Section 5B Solving More Inequalities

We have seen that we solve inequalities and equations in a very similar manner.

However, there is one very important difference.

Consider the following example.

We know that 2 < 3 is a correct statement.

Now, if we multiply both sides of this inequality by –1, we get

$$-2 < -3$$

which is a false statement (you can see that –2 is to right of –3 on the number line).

To make the statement correct, we must **reverse the inequality symbol**.

This is true for multiplication or division by any negative number.

> **Key Point**
>
> If we multiply or divide both sides of an inequality by a negative number, we must reverse the inequality symbol.

Example

(i) Solve the inequality $4x \leq 7(2x + 10)$.

Hence, graph the following solution sets on the number line.

(ii) $x \in \mathbb{N}$ (iii) $x \in \mathbb{Z}$ (iv) $x \in \mathbb{R}$

Solution

(i)
$$4x \leq 7(2x + 10)$$
$$\Rightarrow \quad 4x \leq 14x + 70 \quad \text{... expand brackets}$$
$$\Rightarrow \quad 4x - 14x \leq 70 \quad \text{... subtract } 14x \text{ from both sides}$$
$$\Rightarrow \quad -10x \leq 70$$
$$\Rightarrow \quad \frac{-10x}{-10} \geq \frac{70}{-10} \quad \text{... divide both sides by } -10 \text{ and reverse the inequality sign}$$
$$\Rightarrow \quad x \geq -7$$

(ii) $x \geq -7, x \in \mathbb{N}$. Natural numbers are positive whole numbers excluding 0.

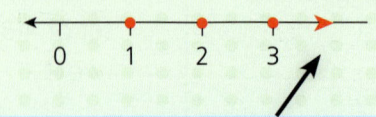

This arrow indicates that the solution set is infinite.

(iii) $x \geq -7, x \in \mathbb{Z}$. Integers are positive and negative whole numbers.

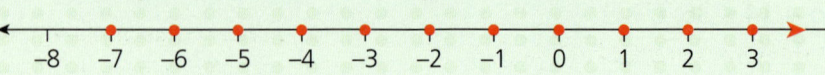

(iv) $x \geq -7$, $x \in \mathbb{R}$. The Real numbers are all numbers, so draw a heavy line along the number line.

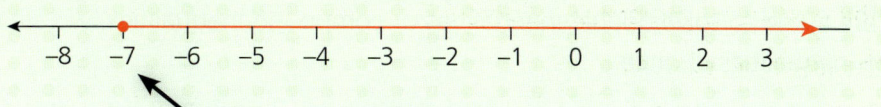

The shaded circle at –7 shows that the number –7 is included.

Activity 5.2

1. (i) Solve the inequality $-7x < 49$.
   (ii) Hence, graph the solution set for $x \in \mathbb{Z}$ on the number line.

2. (i) Solve the inequality $-12b \leq 144$.
   (ii) Hence, graph the solution set for $b \in \mathbb{R}$ on the number line.

3. (i) Solve the inequality $-9c > 81$.
   (ii) Hence, graph the solution set for $c \in \mathbb{Z}$ on the number line.

4. (i) Solve the inequality $4d \geq 5d + 7$.
   (ii) Hence, graph the solution set for $d \in \mathbb{R}$ on the number line.

5. (i) Solve the inequality $2f \geq 3f - 1$.
   (ii) Hence, graph the solution set for $f \in \mathbb{N}$ on the number line.

6. (i) Solve the inequality $7g \geq 1 + 8g$.
   (ii) Hence, graph the solution set for $g \in \mathbb{Z}$ on the number line.

7. (i) Solve the inequality $5h < 6h + 3$.
   (ii) Hence, graph the solution set for $h \in \mathbb{R}$ on the number line.

8. (i) Solve the inequality $13k > 21k - 7$.
   (ii) Hence, graph the solution set for $k \in \mathbb{Z}$ on the number line.

9. (i) Solve the inequality $-2l - 5 > 7$.
   (ii) Hence, graph the solution set for $l \in \mathbb{R}$ on the number line.

10. (i) Solve the inequality $28 - 5n \leq 43$.
    (ii) Hence, graph the solution set for $n \in \mathbb{Z}$ on the number line.

11. (i) Solve the inequality $7 - 3m \leq -5$.
    (ii) Hence, graph the solution set for $m \in \mathbb{N}$ on the number line.

12. (i) Solve the inequality $-3p + 13 \geq -2p - 7$.
    (ii) Hence, graph the solution set for $p \in \mathbb{N}$ on the number line.

13. (i) Solve the inequality $2r - 7 > 9r + 14$.
    (ii) Hence, graph the following solution sets on the number line.
    (a) for $r \in \mathbb{Z}$ (b) for $r \in \mathbb{R}$

14. (i) Solve the inequality $10s + 27 \leq 23s + 1$.
    (ii) Hence, graph the solution set for $s \in \mathbb{N}$ on the number line.

15. (i) Solve the inequality $7t + 3 > -4 + 11t$.
    (ii) Hence, graph the following solution sets on the number line.
    (a) for $t \in \mathbb{N}$
    (b) for $t \in \mathbb{Z}$
    (c) for $t \in \mathbb{R}$

16. (i) Solve the inequality $6y - 7 > 5(3y + 1)$.
    (ii) Hence, graph the following solution sets on the number line.
    (a) for $y \in \mathbb{Z}$ (b) for $y \in \mathbb{R}$

Section 5C Solving Compound Linear Inequalities

When we are asked to solve double inequalities or compound inequalities, we are effectively solving two inequalities at once.

For example, if we want to indicate numbers which are ≥ -3 **and** $\leq +3$ we write $-3 \leq x \leq +3$.

> **Key Point**
>
> It is important to note that we read the inequality from
> - the centre to the left to get the inequality $x \geq -3$, and
> - the centre to the right to get the inequality $x \leq 3$.

Example 1

Graph on the number line the solution set of $-3 \leq x \leq 3$.

(i) for $x \in \mathbb{N}$

(ii) for $x \in \mathbb{Z}$

(iii) for $x \in \mathbb{R}$

Solution

The inequality $-3 \leq x \leq 3$ is a combination of the two inequalities:
$$x \leq 3 \text{ and } x \geq -3.$$

(i) The solution for $x \in \mathbb{N}$ is:

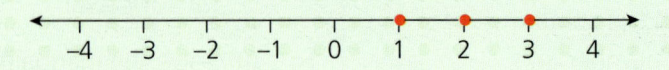

(ii) The solution for $x \in \mathbb{Z}$ is:

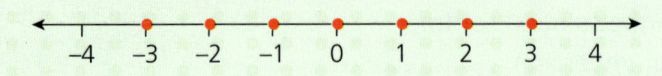

(iii) The solution for $x \in \mathbb{R}$ is:

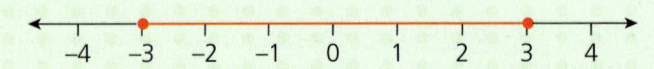

Note:

- The shaded circles at -3 and 3 show that -3 and 3 are included.

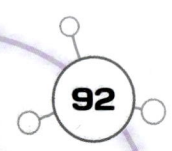

Example 2

(i) Solve the inequality $-4 < 3y + 2 < 11$.

(ii) Graph the solution sets on the number line for the following:

(a) for $y \in \mathbb{N}$ (b) for $y \in \mathbb{Z}$ (c) for $y \in \mathbb{R}$

(iii) List the elements of the set C, where $C = \{y \mid -4 < 3y + 2 < 11, y \in \mathbb{Z}\}$.

Solution

(i) The inequality $-4 < 3y + 2 < 11$ is a combination of the two inequalities:

$3y + 2 < 11$ and $3y + 2 > -4$.

The inequalities can be solved separately or simultaneously.

■ **Solving the inequalities separately**

$3y + 2 < 11$ **and** $3y + 2 > -4$

$\Rightarrow 3y < 11 - 2 \qquad \Rightarrow 3y > -4 - 2$ ... subtract 2 from each side

$\Rightarrow y < \dfrac{9}{3} \qquad \Rightarrow y > -\dfrac{6}{3}$ ... divide each side by 3

$\Rightarrow y < 3$ **and** $\Rightarrow y > -2$

■ **Solving the inequalities simultaneously**

$-4 < 3y + 2 < 11$

$-4 - 2 < 3y + 2 - 2 < 11 - 2$ ... subtract 2 from each part

$\dfrac{-6}{3} < \dfrac{3y}{3} < \dfrac{9}{3}$ ... divide each part by 3

$-2 < y < 3$

So as before $y < 3$ and $y > -2$.

(ii) (a) The solution for $y \in \mathbb{N}$ is:

(b) The solution for $y \in \mathbb{Z}$ is:

(c) The solution for $y \in \mathbb{R}$ is:

The hollow circle at -2 and 3 show that these numbers are <u>not</u> included.

(iii) $C = \{-1, 0, 1, 2\}$

Example 3

Graph on the number line the solution set of the inequality $-7 \leq -x \leq -3$, $x \in \mathbb{N}$.

Solution

$-7 \leq -x \leq -3$

$\Rightarrow \dfrac{-7}{-1} \geq x \geq \dfrac{-3}{-1}$ ... divide each part by -1 and reverse the inequality symbols

$\Rightarrow 7 \geq x \geq 3$

$\Rightarrow 3 \leq x \leq 7$

The solution for $x \in \mathbb{N}$ is:

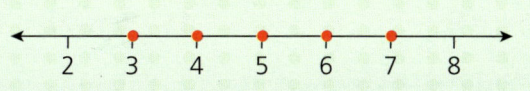

Example 4

(i) Solve the inequality $-7 < \dfrac{-x}{2} < \dfrac{-3}{4}, x \in \mathbb{R}$.

(ii) Graph the solution set on the number line.

Solution

(i) $\quad -7 < \dfrac{-x}{2} < \dfrac{-3}{4}$

$\Rightarrow -28 < -2x < -3 \quad$ ...multiply all sides by 4, the LCD

$\Rightarrow 14 > \quad x > \dfrac{3}{2} \quad$ ... divide all sides by -2 and reverse the inequality symbols

$\Rightarrow \dfrac{3}{2} < \quad x < 14$

(ii) The solution set for $x \in \mathbb{R}$ is

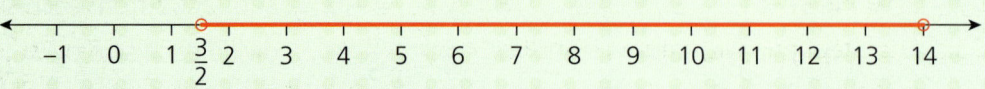

Activity 5.3

1. Write an inequality which is represented by the following graphs.

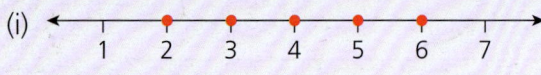

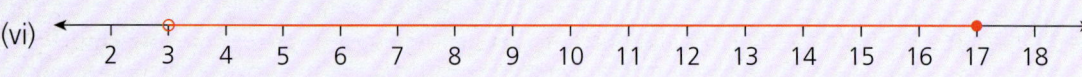

(i), (ii), (iii), (iv), (v), (vi)

Graph the solution sets of the following inequalities on the number line.

2. $3 < y < 5, y \in \mathbb{N}$

3. $-1 < a < 2, a \in \mathbb{Z}$

4. $-7 \leq c \leq 4, c \in \mathbb{R}$

5. $4 \geq d \geq -1, d \in \mathbb{R}$

6. $-2 < x + 1 < 9, x \in \mathbb{Z}$

7. $3 \geq 2h - 7 \geq -5, h \in \mathbb{N}$

8. $-4 \leq 3g + 8 < 17, g \in \mathbb{R}$

9. $9 > 4b + 5 \geq -2, b \in \mathbb{R}$

10. $-7 \leq 5c + 4 \leq 3, c \in \mathbb{R}$

11. $-5 \leq -f \leq -2, f \in \mathbb{N}$

12. $7 \leq -3h \leq 16, h \in \mathbb{Z}$

13. $14 > -7w > 8, w \in \mathbb{R}$

14. $-40 \leq -8b < -17, b \in \mathbb{N}$

15. $3 \geq -2k < -7, k \in \mathbb{R}$

Section 5D Applications of Linear Inequalities

As we saw in the introduction to this chapter, we can use simple linear inequalities in everyday situations.

Example 1

Stephen is a 30-year-old middle-distance runner who uses a heart-rate monitor. To get the most out of his training, Stephen wants to run so that his heart rate stays between 65% and 75% of his Maximum Heart Rate (MHR). He works out his MHR using the formula MHR = 205 − 0.5x, where x stands for the age of the athlete.

  (i) Calculate Stephen's Maximum Heart Rate.
 (ii) Calculate the minimum and maximum heart rates which Stephen wishes to work at.
(iii) Write down an inequality in r to show the range of Stephen's heart rate when he is running.

Solution

  (i) Using the formula, Stephen's MHR = 205 − 0.50x
                                     = 205 − (0.50)(30)
                                     = 205 − 15
                                     = 190 beats per minute

 (ii) Stephen wants his **minimum** heart rate to be 65% of MHR
                                     = 190 × 0.65
                                     = 123.5 beats per minute

   Stephen wants his **maximum** heart rate to be 75% of MHR
                                     = 190 × 0.75
                                     = 142.5 beats per minute

(iii) The range of Stephen's heart rate can be written as $123.5 \le r \le 142.5$

Example 2

Jack has €750 saved in his credit union account. He saves €75 a week from his part-time job. He wishes to save a minimum of €6000 to help pay for his university costs. The maximum amount he will need is €9000.

  (i) Write a compound inequality that represents this information. Let x = the number of weeks he has saved.
 (ii) Solve the compound inequality.
(iii) To save the minimum amount of money, how many weeks must he save?
(iv) To save the maximum amount of money, how many weeks must he save?
 (v) If he starts saving from the summer prior to Transition Year, will he be in a position to save €9000? Explain your answer.

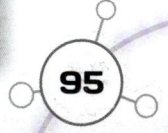

Solution

(i) $\quad 6000 < 750 + 75x \leq 9000$

(ii) $\quad 6000 < 750 + 75x \leq 9000$

$\quad 6000 - 750 < \quad 75x \quad \leq 9000 - 750 \quad$ ... subtract 750 from each part

$\quad\quad 5250 < \quad 75x \quad \leq 8250$

$\quad\quad \dfrac{5250}{75} < \quad x \quad \leq \dfrac{8250}{75} \quad$ ... divide each part by 75

$\quad\quad 70 < \quad x \quad \leq 110$

(iii) Jack must save €75 for 70 weeks to save €6000.

(iv) Jack must save €75 for 110 weeks to save €9000.

(v) Jack should be able to save €9000, as he has approximately 3 years to save which is 156 weeks.

Activity 5.4

1 If $a > b$, copy and complete the following table, indicating whether the statement is true or false.

Statement	True	False
$-a > -b$		
$\dfrac{1}{a} > \dfrac{1}{b}$		
$2a + 3 > 2b + 3$		
$\dfrac{a}{b} < \dfrac{b}{a}$		

2 The recorded temperatures in Ireland on a particular day during the summer of 2013 are shown on the map below.

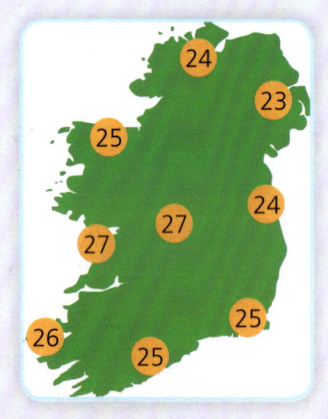

(i) What was the lowest recorded temperature in Ireland on this particular day?

(ii) What was the highest recorded temperature in Ireland on this particular day?

(iii) Represent this information as a compound inequality, where t represents temperature.

(iv) Graph this information on a number line.

3 Movie camera cars are fitted with a crane and a camera to film movies in the movie industry.

The crane's maximum height above the ground is 5.5 m and the minimum height above the ground is 1.2 m. Let h represent height of the crane.

(i) Write a compound inequality that describes the possible heights of the crane.

(ii) Graph this information on a number line. Which number set do you use, $\mathbb{N}$, $\mathbb{Z}$ or $\mathbb{R}$?

4 The Body Mass Index (BMI) range for healthy adults over 20 years of age is between 18.5 and 24.99.

(i) What is the lowest BMI a person can have within this range?

(ii) What is the greatest BMI a person can have within this range?

(iii) Represent this information as a compound inequality, where b represents BMI.

(iv) Graph this information on a number line.

5 Gillian is a 26-year-old half-marathon runner. She wants to run so that her heart rate stays between 85% and 88% of her Maximum Heart Rate (MHR). She works out her MHR using the formula MHR = 220 − x, where x stands for the age of the athlete.

(i) Calculate Gillian's Maximum Heart Rate.

(ii) Calculate the minimum and maximum heart rates which Gillian wishes to work at.

(iii) Write an inequality in x to show the range of Gillian's heart rate when she is running.

6 The normal heart rate ranges from 60 to 100 bpm (beats per minute).

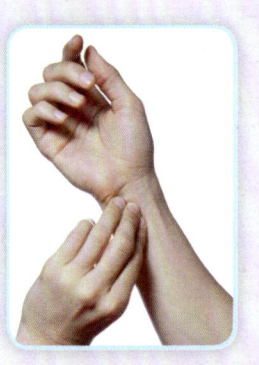

(i) What is the lowest heart rate that a person can have within this range?

(ii) What is the highest heart rate that a person can have within this range?

(iii) Represent this information as a set of inequalities, where h represents heart rate.

(iv) Graph this information on a number line.

7 Motorways in Ireland have a minimum speed limit of 50 km/h and a maximum speed limit of 120 km/h.

(i) Represent this information as a compound inequality, where s represents speed.

(ii) Graph this information on a number line.

8 Normal body temperature ranges between 36.5°C and 37.2°C for a healthy adult.

(i) What is the lowest body temperature a person can have within this range?

(ii) What is the highest body temperature a person can have within this range?

(iii) Represent this information as a set of inequalities, where t represents temperature.

(iv) Graph this information on a number line.

9. In order to become an Air Force Pilot, there are certain height restrictions which must be complied with for safety reasons. They are detailed below.
- Standing height: minimum is 162 cm and maximum is 193 cm.
- Sitting height: minimum is 85 cm and maximum is 100 cm.

(i) Represent the standing height as an inequality.

(ii) Represent the sitting height as an inequality.

(iii) Graph both sets of information on separate number lines.

10. Tolerances are used in manufacturing parts to aid assembly. A cylindrical shaft for a gear-motor has been specified to have a length of 12.5 mm, with a tolerance of ± 0.25 mm. This means the length can be 0.25 mm bigger or 0.25 mm smaller than 12.5 mm.

Shaft

(i) Write a compound inequality to represent this information, letting l represent the length.

(ii) What is the smallest allowable length of the shaft?

(iii) What is the largest allowable length of the shaft?

(iv) Graph this information on a number line.

Revision Activity 5

1. Graph on the number line the solution set of $-2q - 10 \leq 2(q - 1)$, for $q \in \mathbb{Z}$.

2. Graph on the number line the solution set of $2(3 - 7v) \geq v - 5$, for $v \in \mathbb{R}$.

3. Graph on the number line the solution set of $3(w - 2) - 7(3w + 1) \leq 2 - 3w$, for $w \in \mathbb{N}$.

4. (a) Find the solution set of $A: 2x - 7 \geq 5$, $x \in \mathbb{N}$.
   (b) Find the solution set of $B: x - 4 \leq 12$, $x \in \mathbb{N}$.
   (c) Find $A \cap B$, and graph the solution set on a number line.

5. Maria wishes to hire a taxi in Dublin. The taxi hire cost is €4.28 plus €1.22 per km travelled. If Maria has €15 left after her shopping trip, how far in km can she travel in the taxi? Give your answer correct to two decimal places.

6. Graph on the number line the solution set of $-9 \leq 2x - 5 < 7$, $x \in \mathbb{Z}$.

7. Katie wished to spend between €50 and €80 on CDs. She buys x CDs on the internet. Each CD costs €6 and she is charged a one-off shipping cost of €8.
   (a) Write a compound inequality to represent this information.
   (b) Solve the compound inequality.
   (c) What is the minimum number of CDs she might order?
   (d) What is the maximum number of CDs she can order?
   (e) Graph this information on a number line.

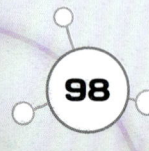

8. A school is holding a fundraiser to raise money for sports equipment. The students sell 15" pizzas for €15, and a local supermarket donates all the ingredients needed. The school needs to raise at least €600 and a maximum of €1000.
   (a) Write a compound inequality to represent this information.
   (b) Solve the compound inequality.
   (c) What is the minimum number of pizzas they need to sell?
   (d) What is the maximum number of pizzas they need to sell?

9. A company manufactures cardboard boxes. They produce cube-shaped boxes in various sizes. The smallest has a surface area of 150 cm² and the largest has a surface area of 6 m².
   (a) Write a compound inequality to represent this information.
   (b) Solve the compound inequality.
   (c) What are the dimensions of the smallest box?
   (d) What are the dimensions of the largest box?

Hint
> The surface area of a cube of side x is $6x^2$.

Exam-style Questions

1. (a) (i) Solve the inequality $-2 \leq 5x + 3 \leq 18$, $x \in \mathbb{R}$.
      (ii) Graph your solution set on the number line.
   (b) (i) Niamh is in a clothes shop and has a voucher which she **must** use. The voucher gives a €10 reduction when more than €35 is spent. She also has €50 cash. Write down an inequality in x to show the range of money she could spend in the shop.
      (ii) Write an inequality in y to show the price range of articles she could buy.

   JCHL 2014 Sample Paper 1

2. (a) Solve the following inequality and show the solution set on the number line.
   $-2 \leq \frac{1}{2}x - 3 < 1$, $x \in \mathbb{N}$.
   (b) Josephine hopes to go to college. She has saved €3000. She will attend college for 32 weeks in her first year. She plans to have at least €800 left at the end of the year.
      (i) If she spends €x each week, write an inequality to represent her spending during the year.
      (ii) Hence, or otherwise, find the maximum amount Josephine can spend each week.

   JCHL 2013 Paper 1

3. For real numbers a, b and c, copy and complete the table below. Indicate whether each statement is always true, never true or sometimes true.

Statement	Always true	Never true	Sometimes true
If $a > b$ and $b > c$, then $a > c$			
If $-a < 4$ and $b < -4$, then $a < b$			
If $a > b$, then $-a > -b$			
If $a > b$ and $b < c$, then $a < c$			
If $3a + 1 > 2$, then $a > 0$			
If $2b - 4 < 3b - 8$, then $b > 4$			
If a and b are both positive and $a < b$, then $\frac{1}{a} < \frac{1}{b}$			

JCHL 2012 Paper 1

KEY WORDS AND PHRASES

- Infinite
- Finite
- Natural numbers
- Integers
- Real numbers
- Element
- Inequality sign
- Inequalities
- Compound inequalities

Chapter Summary 5

Key symbols:

$<$ means less than.
$\leq$ means less than or equal to.
$>$ means greater than.
$\geq$ means greater than or equal to.
$\in$ means is an element of the set.
$\mathbb{N}$ Natural numbers: {1, 2, 3, 4, 5, …}.
$\mathbb{Z}$ Integers: {…, −5, −4, −3, −2, −1, 0, 1, 2, 3, 4, 5, …}.
$\mathbb{R}$ Real numbers: are all the numbers on the number line.

- To multiply or divide a linear inequality by a **negative** number reverse the inequality sign. This means that:
    - $<$ changes to $>$
    - $\leq$ changes to $\geq$
    - $>$ changes to $<$
    - $\geq$ changes to $\leq$

Compound inequalities

- The inequality $-3 \leq x \leq 3$ is a combination of the two inequalities:
  $x \leq 3$ and $x \geq -3$.
- It is important to note that we read the inequality from
    - the centre to the left to get the inequality $x \geq -3$, and
    - the centre to the right to get the inequality $x \leq 3$.

Algebra 4
Simultaneous Equations

Chapter 6

Learning Outcomes

In this chapter, you will learn about:
- Solving simultaneous equations (review and extension)
- Using simultaneous equations to solve problems

Section 6A Review of Simultaneous Equations

In this section, we meet some more challenging examples of simultaneous equations.

Example 1

(i) Solve the following simultaneous equations using an algebraic method:

$$4x - 3y = -1 \quad 7x - 2y = 8$$

(ii) Check your solutions graphically.

Solution

(i) We will use the 'elimination method'.
- Label the equations (1) and (2):

    $4x - 3y = -1$ (1)

    $7x - 2y = 8$ (2)

- Multiply equation (1) by 2 and label as equation (3):

    $8x - 6y = -2$ (3)

- Multiply equation (2) by −3 and label as equation (4):

    $-21x + 6y = -24$ (4)

- Add equations (3) and (4) to eliminate the y terms:

    $8x - 6y = -2$ (3)

    $\underline{-21x + 6y = -24} \quad (4)$

    $-13x \quad\quad = -26$

    $\Rightarrow x \quad = \dfrac{-26}{-13}$ ... divide both sides by −13

    $\Rightarrow x \quad = 2$

- Substitute $x = 2$ into equation (1) to find y:

  $4x - 3y = -1$ (1)

  $\Rightarrow 4(2) - 3y = -1$

  $\Rightarrow 8 - 3y = -1$

  $\Rightarrow -3y = -1 - 8$ ... subtract 8 from both sides

  $\Rightarrow y = \dfrac{-9}{-3}$ ... divide both sides by -3

  $\Rightarrow y = 3$

  Answer: $x = 2$ and $y = 3$

(ii) Find two points for each equation.

Equation 1: $4x - 3y = -1$ (1)

When $x = 0$, $0 - 3y = -1 \Rightarrow -3y = -1 \Rightarrow y = \dfrac{1}{3}$ Point 1 is $\left(0, \dfrac{1}{3}\right)$.

When $y = 0$, $4x - 0 = -1 \Rightarrow 4x = -1 \Rightarrow x = -\dfrac{1}{4}$ Point 2 is $\left(-\dfrac{1}{4}, 0\right)$.

Equation 2: $7x - 2y = 8$ (2)

When $x = 0$, $0 - 2y = 8 \Rightarrow -2y = 8 \Rightarrow y = -4$ Point 1 is $(0, -4)$.

When $y = 0$, $7x + 0 = 8 \Rightarrow 7x = 8 \Rightarrow x = \dfrac{8}{7}$ Point 2 is $\left(\dfrac{8}{7}, 0\right)$.

- Plot the points and draw a graph for each equation, labelling each line.

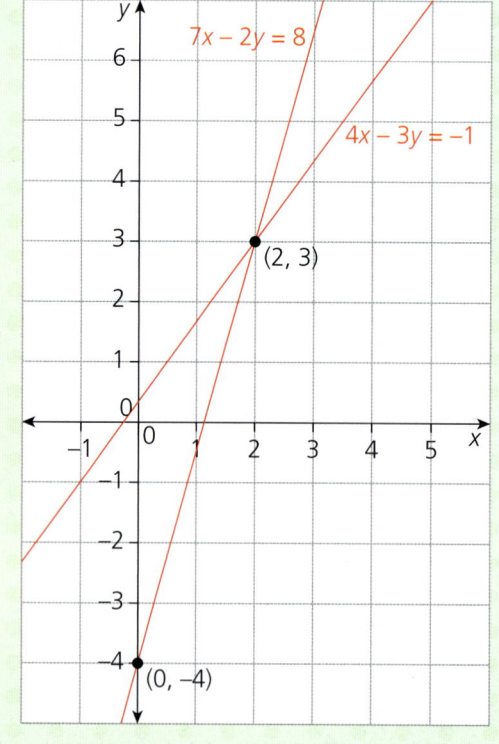

- Find the point of intersection.

  From the graph the two lines cross at the point $(2, 3)$.

  This is the solution, i.e. $x = 2$ and $y = 3$. ✓

Example 2

(i) Solve the following simultaneous equations.
$$2x - \frac{y}{3} = -1$$
$$-6x + 7y = +39$$

(ii) Check your solutions algebraically.

Solution

(i) Label the equations (1) and (2):
$$2x - \frac{y}{3} = -1 \quad (1)$$
$$6x - 7y = -39 \quad (2)$$

- Multiply equation (1) by 3 to eliminate the fraction and label as equation (3):
$$6x - y = -3 \quad (3)$$

- Multiply equation (2) by -1 and label as equation (4):
$$-6x + 7y = 39 \quad (4)$$

- Add equations (3) and (4) to eliminate the x terms:

$$6x - y = -3 \quad (3)$$
$$\underline{-6x + 7y = 39} \quad (4)$$
$$6y = 36$$
$$\Rightarrow y = \frac{36}{6} \quad \text{... divide both sides by 6}$$
$$\Rightarrow y = 6$$

- Substitute $y = 6$ into either equation (1) or (2) to find x:
$$6x - 7y = -39 \quad (2)$$
$$\Rightarrow 6x - 7(6) = -39 \quad \text{... expand brackets}$$
$$\Rightarrow 6x = -39 + 42 \quad \text{... add 42 to both sides}$$
$$\Rightarrow x = \frac{3}{6} \quad \text{... divide both sides by 6}$$
$$\Rightarrow x = \frac{1}{2}$$

Answer: $x = \frac{1}{2}$ and $y = 6$

(ii) Substitute both values back into equation (1) as we did not use this equation to find the solutions originally.
$$2x - \frac{y}{3} = -1 \quad (1)$$
$$\Rightarrow 2\left(\frac{1}{2}\right) - \frac{6}{3} = -1 \quad \text{... substitute } x = \frac{1}{2} \text{ and } y = 6 \text{ into equation (1)}$$
$$\Rightarrow 1 - 2 = -1$$
$$\Rightarrow -1 = -1 \checkmark$$

As the LHS = the RHS, then $x = \frac{1}{2}$ and $y = 6$.

Activity 6.1

For questions 1–5, solve the simultaneous equations
(i) algebraically   (ii) graphically.

1 $x + 2y = 11$
    $3x - 2y = 9$

2 $a + b = 4$
    $2a - 3b = -22$

3 $12m - 5n = -6$
    $7m + 5n = 44$

4 $s - t = -4$
    $2s + 3t = 7$

5 $3x + 5y = 23$
    $-2x - y = 1$

For questions 6–10, solve the simultaneous equations algebraically and check your answers by substitution.

6 $2a - 3b = -13$
    $-a + 4b = 29$

7 $7d = 71 - c$
    $2d + 7c - 27 = 0$

8 $p + 5q = 45$
    $q - p = 3$

9 $9v = -2w + 93$
  $8v + w = 85$

10 $2x = -17 + y$
  $-2y = -23 - 3x$

For questions 11–25,
 (i) Solve the simultaneous equations algebraically.
 (ii) Check your solutions using a suitable method.

11 $a - 4b = 5$
  $\dfrac{a}{2} + b = 1$

12 $3f + 5g = 23$
  $5f + 3g = \dfrac{181}{5}$

13 $5m - 6n = -23$
  $m - n = -\dfrac{19}{5}$

14 $11h - 7k = 0$
  $5h + k - 1 = -\dfrac{31}{77}$

15 $2p + 3q - 7 = -6$
  $p + 5q + 8 = \dfrac{75}{8}$

16 $x + 3y = 9x - 3y = \dfrac{5}{2}$

17 $2x + 3y = -5x - \dfrac{y}{2} = 4$

18 $3s + 4t = -6$
  $2s - \dfrac{t}{2} = \dfrac{7}{3}$

19 $12d - e = -\dfrac{11}{4}$
  $-d + e = \dfrac{11}{12}$

20 $v + 8w = 2$
  $\dfrac{3v}{2} + 7w = \dfrac{29}{8}$

21 $5x - 2y = \dfrac{4}{3}$
  $2x + y = \dfrac{1}{2}$

22 $c + h = 5$
  $\dfrac{4c}{3} - \dfrac{h}{2} = -8$

23 $l + 7m = 12$
  $\dfrac{l}{2} + m = \dfrac{79}{14}$

24 $7r - s = \dfrac{29}{3}$
  $-r + \dfrac{s}{2} = -\dfrac{19}{6}$

25 $\dfrac{3x - 1}{2} - \dfrac{y - 1}{2} = -\dfrac{3}{4}$
  $\dfrac{x + 3}{3} + \dfrac{y + 4}{6} = \dfrac{13}{12}$

Section 6B Applications of Simultaneous Equations

Simultaneous equations can be used to solve real-life problems.

Example 1

Joanne invests €5000. She invests €x in a saving account and €y in a deposit account. The savings account pays her 4% interest per annum and the deposit account pays 6% per annum interest. At the end of the year, she receives a total of €260 interest.

 (i) Write two linear equations to represent this information.
 (ii) Solve the pair of simultaneous equations to find the value of x and y.
 (iii) Check your answers for x and y.
 (iv) How much money did she invest in the savings account?
 (v) How much money did she invest in the deposit account?
 (vi) How much interest did she receive from her savings account?
 (vii) How much interest did she receive from her deposit account?

Solution

(i) The sum of the two values is €5000.
∴ $x + y = 5000$

She receives 4% interest on €x and 6% interest on €y which totals €260.
∴ $\frac{4}{100}x + \frac{6}{100}y = 260$
⇒ $4x + 6y = 26\,000$ ... multiply each side by 100 to eliminate the fractions

(ii) Label the equations (1) and (2):
$x + y = 5000$ (1)
$4x + 6y = 26\,000$ (2)

- Multiply both sides of equation (1) by –4 and label the new equation (3):
$-4x - 4y = -20\,000$ (3)

- Add equations (2) and (3) to eliminate the x terms and solve for y:

$4x + 6y = 26\,000$ (2)
$-4x - 4y = -20\,000$ (3)
―――――――――――
$2y = 6000$
$y = \frac{6000}{2}$ ... divide both sides by 2
$y = 3000$

- Substitute $y = 3000$ into (1):
$x + y = 5000$ (1)
$x + (3000) = 5000$
$x = 5000 - 3000$ ... subtract 3000 from each side
$x = 2000$

(iii) Substitute $x = 2000$ and $y = 3000$ back into the other equation, i.e. (2):
$4x + 6y = 26\,000$ (2)
$4(2000) + 6(3000) = 26\,000$
⇒ $8000 + 18\,000 = 26\,000$
⇒ $26\,000 = 26\,000$ ✓

As LHS = RHS then the solutions are correct.

(iv) Joanne invested €2000 in the savings account.

(v) Joanne invested €3000 in the deposit account.

(vi) Interest on savings account
= 4% of €2000
= 0.04 × €2000
= €80

(vii) Interest on deposit account
= 6% of €3000
= 0.06 × €3000
= €180

Example 2

A family drive from Cork to Dublin, a distance of d km, at an average speed of s km/h in 2.6 hours. On the return journey they travel the same distance but drive on average 20 km/h slower in 3.25 hours due to traffic congestion.

(i) Write a linear equation (in its simplest form) to represent the time taken to travel from
  (a) Cork to Dublin
  (b) Dublin to Cork.

(Hint: Write the linear equations in the form: $ad + bs = c$, where $a, b, c \in \mathbb{Z}$.)

(ii) Solve the pair of simultaneous equations to find the values of d and s.

(iii) Check your answers for d and s.

(iv) Find the distance between Cork and Dublin.

(v) What was the average speed between Cork and Dublin?

(vi) What was the average speed between Dublin and Cork?

Solution

(i) $\dfrac{\text{distance}}{\text{speed}}$ = time taken

(a) Time taken from Cork to Dublin is 2.6 hours.

$$\dfrac{\text{distance}}{\text{speed}} = \text{time taken}$$

$$\dfrac{d}{s} = 2.6$$

$$\dfrac{d}{s} = \dfrac{13}{5} \qquad \text{... write 2.6 as a fraction}$$

$$5d = 13s \qquad \text{... multiply both sides by the LCM } 5s$$

$$5d - 13s = 0 \qquad (1) \qquad \text{... label the equation (1)}$$

(b) Time taken from Dublin to Cork is 3.25 hours. Speed = $s - 20$

$$\dfrac{d}{s-20} = 3.25$$

$$\dfrac{d}{s-20} = \dfrac{13}{4} \qquad \text{... write 3.25 as a fraction}$$

$$4d = 13(s - 20) \qquad \text{... multiply both sides by the LCM } 4(s-20)$$

$$4d = 13s - 260$$

$$4d - 13s = -260 \qquad (2) \qquad \text{... label the equation (2)}$$

(ii) Rewrite the equations (1) and (2):

$5d - 13s = 0 \qquad (1)$

$4d - 13s = -260 \qquad (2)$

Multiply both sides of equation (1) by -1 and label the new equation (3):

$-5d + 13s = 0 \qquad (3)$

Add equations (2) and (3) to eliminate the s terms and solve for d:

$4d - 13s = -260 \qquad (2)$

$\underline{-5d + 13s = 0 \qquad (3)}$

$-d = -260$

$$d = \dfrac{-260}{-1} \qquad \text{... divide both sides by } -1$$

$$d = 260$$

Substitute $d = 260$ into (1):

$5d - 13s = 0 \qquad (1)$

$5(260) - 13s = 0$

$1300 = 13s \qquad \text{... add } 13s \text{ to both sides}$

$\dfrac{1300}{13} = s \qquad \text{... divide both sides by 13}$

$100 = s$

(iii) Substitute $d = 260$ and $s = 100$ back into the other equation, i.e. equation (2).

$4d - 13s = -260 \qquad (2)$

$\Rightarrow 4(260) - 13(100) = -260 \Rightarrow 1040 - 1300 = -260 \qquad \Rightarrow -260 = -260 \checkmark$

As LHS = RHS then the solutions are correct.

(iv) The distance between Cork and Dublin is 260 km.
(v) The average speed between Cork and Dublin was s km/h = 100 km/h.
(vi) The average speed between Dublin and Cork = $(s - 20)$ km/h
$= 100 - 20$ km/h
$= 80$ km/h

Activity 6.2

1 The sum of two numbers is 40. The difference of the two numbers is 4.6.
   (i) Write two linear equations to represent this information.
   (ii) Solve the pair of simultaneous equations to find the values of both numbers.
   (iii) Check your answers.

2 If I double one number, then add a second number, the answer is 50. If I multiply the first number by 7 and subtract half the second number, the answer is 75.
   (i) Write two linear equations to represent this information.
   (ii) Solve the pair of simultaneous equations to find the values of both numbers.
   (iii) Check your answers.

3 If I multiply a number by 4 and subtract half of a second number, the answer is 6.5. If I add 3 to the first number and divide the answer by 2, then subtract one-third of the second number, the answer is 1.5.
   (i) Write two linear equations to represent this information.
   (ii) Solve the pair of simultaneous equations to find the values of the numbers.
   (iii) Check your answers.

4 A musical is being held at the local Arts Centre.
   - The price for 2 adults and 3 concession tickets is €47.50.
   - The price for 1 adult and 2 concession tickets is €27.50.

   (i) Write two linear equations to represent this information.
   (ii) Solve the pair of simultaneous equations to find the price of each type of ticket.
   (iii) Check your answers.

5 Niall invests €25 000. He invests €x in a savings account in Bank A which pays 2% interest per annum. He invests €y in a savings account in Bank B which pays 3% interest per annum. At the end of the year, he receives a total of €650 interest.
   (i) Write two linear equations to represent this information.
   (ii) Solve the pair of simultaneous equations to find the value of x and y.
   (iii) Check your answers for x and y.

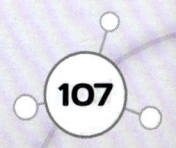

(iv) How much money did he invest in
   (a) Bank A
   (b) Bank B?
(v) How much interest did he receive from
   (a) Bank A
   (b) Bank B?

6 A grocer sells apples and bananas at set prices, irrespective of weight.
- 1 banana and 4 apples cost €2.00.
- 2 bananas and 3 apples cost €1.90.

(i) Write two linear equations to represent this information.
(ii) Solve the pair of simultaneous equations to find the price of a banana and an apple.
(iii) Check your answers.

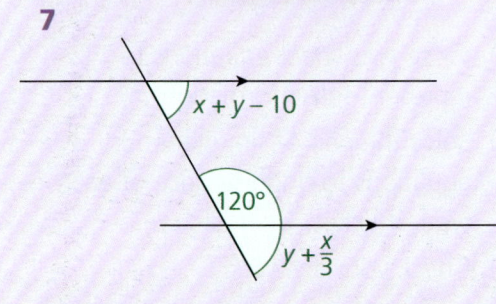

7

(i) What is the degree measure of the angles $(x + y - 10)°$ and $\left(y + \frac{x}{3}\right)°$? Explain your answer using any relevant theorems.
(ii) Write two linear equations to represent this information.
(iii) Solve the pair of simultaneous equations to find the value of x and y.
(iv) Check your answers for x and y.

8 A supermarket sells a certain brand of stir-fry mix and packs of chicken fillets.
- 1 bag of stir-fry mix and 3 packs of chicken fillets costs €12.56.
- 1 bag of stir-fry mix and 2 packs of chicken fillets costs €8.87.

(i) Write two linear equations to represent this information.
(ii) Solve the pair of simultaneous equations to find the price of a bag of stir-fry mix and a pack of chicken fillets.
(iii) Check your answers.

9 A family from Donegal go on holiday to Waterford city. On their journey from Donegal to Waterford, they travel a total distance of d km at an average speed of s km/h, in 4.2 hours. On the return journey the family travel a total distance of d km at an average speed which is 5 km/h more, in 4 hours.

(i) Write a linear equation (in its simplest form) to represent the time taken to travel from
   (a) Waterford to Donegal
   (b) Donegal to Waterford.

Hint
› Write the linear equations in the form: $ad + bs = c$, where $a, b, c \in \mathbb{Z}$.

(ii) Solve the pair of simultaneous equations to find the values of d and s.
(iii) Check your answers for d and s.
(iv) Find the average speed travelled from Donegal to Waterford.
(v) Find the average speed travelled from Waterford to Donegal.

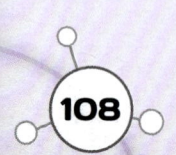

10 The perimeter of a rectangle is 60 cm. The width of the rectangle is one quarter of the length.
  (i) Write two linear equations to represent this information.
  (ii) Solve the pair of simultaneous equations to find the length and the width of the rectangle.
  (iii) Check your answers.
  (iv) Find the area of the rectangle.

11 Timothy invests €31 000 in stocks. He buys €x worth of type A shares and he buys €y worth of type B shares. Share A returns a percentage profit of 11% and share B returns a percentage loss of 4% at the end of the year. He makes an overall profit of €560. 
  (i) Write two linear equations to represent this information.
  (ii) Solve the pair of simultaneous equations to find the values of x and y.
  (iii) Check your answers for x and y.
  (iv) How much money did he invest in
    (a) type A shares
    (b) type B shares?
  (v) How much profit did he make from type A shares?
  (vi) How much loss did he make from type B shares?

12 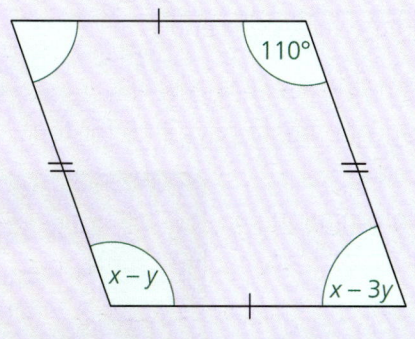
  (i) What is the degree measure of the angle $(x - y)$? Explain your answer using any relevant theorems.
  (ii) What is the degree measure of the angle $(x - 3y)$? Explain your answer using any relevant theorems.
  (iii) Write two linear equations to represent this information.
  (iv) Solve the pair of simultaneous equations to find the values of x and y.
  (v) Check your answers for x and y.

13 A group of friends decide to travel from Burr Point in the Ards Peninsula to Dunmore Head at the tip of the Dingle Peninsula (the most easterly and most westerly point on the island of Ireland). On the first day, they travel two-fifths of the journey $\left(\frac{2d}{5} \text{ km}\right)$ at an average speed of v km/h in 2.75 hours. On the second day, they complete their journey $\left(\frac{3d}{5} \text{ km}\right)$ at an average speed 30 km/h faster than the previous day, in 3.3 hours.

  (i) Write a linear equation (in its simplest form) to represent the time taken to travel
    (a) on day 1
    (b) on day 2.

  > **Hint**
  > Write the linear equations in the form: $ad + bs = c$, where $a, b, c \in \mathbb{Z}$.

  (ii) Solve the pair of simultaneous equations to find the values of d and s.
  (iii) Check your answers for d and s.
  (iv) Find the total distance between Burr Point and Dunmore Head.
  (v) Find the average speed they travelled on
    (a) day 1 (b) day 2.

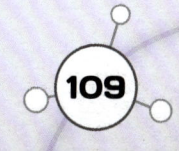

14 Bamboo can grow up to 30 cm a day, depending on the nutrients in the soil, rainfall and sunlight. Bamboo plant A has an initial height of 5 cm and grows at a rate of 22.5 cm per day. Bamboo plant B has an initial height of 20 cm and grows at a rate of 20 cm per day.

(i) Write two linear equations to represent this information, letting h represent the height and d represent the number of days of growth.

(ii) Using an algebraic method find:
  (a) after how many days the bamboo plants are the same height
  (b) what height the bamboo plants are at this point.

(iii) Verify your solutions graphically.

15 Mary wishes to rent an apartment. She has two options:
- Apartment A: Costs €350 a month plus a deposit of €700
- Apartment B: Costs €400 a month plus a deposit of €400.

(i) Write two linear equations to represent this information, letting $R(€)$ represent the total amount spent renting the apartment and m represent the number of months it is rented.

(ii) Using an algebraic method find:
  (a) how many months she needs to stay before apartment A is a better deal
  (b) the total amount she would have spent renting the apartment at this point.

(iii) Verify your solutions graphically.

Revision Activity 6

1 (a) What is the degree measure of the angles $\left(\frac{x}{2} + 2y - 10\right)$ and $(x + y)$? Explain your answer using any relevant theorems.

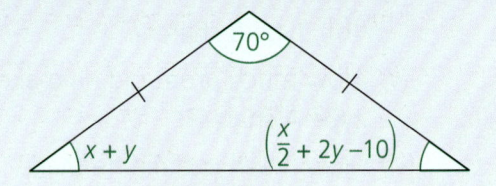

(b) Write two linear equations to represent this information.

(c) Solve the pair of simultaneous equations to find the values of x and y.

(d) Check your answers for x and y.

2 Julie pays €8.10 for two hamburgers and a can of cola. Adam pays €18 for four hamburgers (of the same size) and four cans of cola.

(a) Write two linear equations to represent this information.

(b) Solve the simultaneous equations.

(c) What price is a can of cola?

(d) What price is a hamburger?

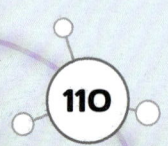

3. Seán works in a local restaurant. He gets paid a basic rate of €x per hour for his contracted 37 hours per week. If he works overtime, he gets paid a higher rate of €y per hour. If Seán works
   - 8 hours overtime, he gets paid €423.65
   - 11 hours overtime, he gets paid €462.50.

   (a) Write two linear equations to represent this information.
   (b) Solve the pair of simultaneous equations, to find
       (i) his basic hourly rate
       (ii) his overtime rate.
   (c) Check your answers.

4. In the English Soccer Championship, no points are awarded for a loss. The table below shows the total number of points received for the teams at the top and the bottom of the league after each had played six games.

Team	Games played	Games won	Games drawn	Games lost	Total points
Top team	6	5	1	0	16
Bottom team	6	1	2	3	5

   (a) If the number of points awarded for a win is x and the number of points awarded for a draw is y, write two linear equations to represent this information.
   (b) Solve the pair of simultaneous equations.
   (c) Find the number of points awarded for
       (i) a win
       (ii) a draw.
   (d) Verify your answers.

5. The perimeter of the top of a rectangular garden table is 8 m. The width of the garden table is one third of the length.
   (a) Write two linear equations to represent this information.
   (b) Solve the pair of simultaneous equations.
   (c) Check your answers algebraically.
   (d) Find the
       (i) width of the table
       (ii) length of the table.
   (e) Find the area of the garden table.

6. A group of 30 students went to a local restaurant for a meal at the end of the school year. They had a choice of two set meals: Meal A costing €6 and Meal B costing €8. A certain number of students bought Meal A and the remainder chose Meal B. The total cost of the meal was €216.
   (a) Write two linear equations to represent this information.
   (b) Solve the simultaneous equations.
   (c) How many students chose Meal A?
   (d) How many students chose Meal B?

CONNECT WITH MATHS 2

7 Martin needs to hire a car for 5 days. He contacts two different car rental companies to get the best value. The information below shows the car rental charges for each company.

	Company A				
Number of days	0	1	2	3	4
Total cost (€)	100	115	130		

	Company B				
Number of days	0	1	2	3	4
Total cost (€)	0	40	80		

(a) Copy and complete the tables for both companies, assuming the patterns continue.
(b) Draw a graph to represent the information for both companies.
(c) After how many days is the cost of the car rental the same?
(d) Which company provides the best value for 5 days car rental?

8 A couple *drive* from Malin Head to Mizen Head, the most northerly and most southerly points on the island of Ireland. They travel a total distance of d km at an average speed of s km/h, in 8.5 hours. On the return journey, the couple *cycle* a different route which is 103 km shorter at an average speed 62 km/h slower, in 35 hours.

(a) Write a linear equation (in its simplest form) to represent the time taken to travel from
  (i) Malin Head to Mizen Head
  (ii) Mizen Head to Malin Head.
(b) Solve the pair of simultaneous equations to find the values of d and s.
(c) Check your answers for d and s.
(d) Find the average speed and the distance travelled by car from Malin Head to Mizen Head.
(e) Find the average speed and the distance travelled by cycle from Mizen Head to Malin Head.

Exam-style Questions

1 A company employs two drivers, John and David. Each has use of a company car and a small van. The company buys €30 worth of Toll Tags for each driver. Each time a vehicle goes through the M50 Toll, a charge will be deducted from the Toll Tags.

John goes through the M50 Toll five times in his car and four times in his small van. He then has €7.90 remaining on his Toll Tags. David goes through the M50 Toll twice in his car and six times in his small van. He then has €8.40 left on his Toll Tags. Calculate how much it costs for a car and for a small van to go through the M50 Toll.

JCHL 2013 Paper 1

2 Consideration is being given to changing the number of points a team gets for a win and also the number of points a team gets for a draw in a soccer league. No points will be awarded for a loss. The table below shows the standing of two teams after six games under the proposed new system.

Team	Played	Won	Drawn	Lost	Points (new system)
Team A	6	2	2	2	12
Team B	6	1	5	0	10

(a) Find the number of points which would be awarded for
   (i) a win
   (ii) a draw under this proposed system.

(b) The current system awards 3 points for a win and 1 point for a draw. Suggest one reason why it might be preferable to change to the system proposed in part (a).

JCHL 2012 Paper 1

KEY WORDS AND PHRASES
- Simultaneous equations
- Solve/verify
- Algebraic
- Graphical

Chapter Summary 6

- A pair of simultaneous equations are two equations which are both true at the same time. The two equations must be solved to find the values of the two unknown variables.
- Simultaneous equations can be solved algebraically or graphically.

Chapter 7

Algebra 5
Quadratic Equations

Learning Outcomes

In this chapter, you will learn about:
- Solving quadratic equations using factors
- Finding a quadratic equation given its roots
- Solving quadratic equations using a formula
- Solving more problems with quadratic equations

Section 7A Solving Quadratic Equations using Factors

As we know, **quadratic** means 'having a highest power of 2'.

In this section, we will do further work on solving quadratic equations such as $2x^2 - 5x - 12 = 0$ or $3x^2 - 5x = 0$.

> **Key Point**
>
> The **zero rule for multiplication:**
> If $(a)(b) = 0$ then either $a = 0$ or $b = 0$.
>
> This rule will enable us to solve quadratic equations. It also means that we always get **two** solutions to a quadratic equation.

Example 1

Solve the equation $(x - 6)(x + 2) = 0$.

Solution

$(x - 6)(x + 2) = 0$

$\Rightarrow$ either $(x - 6) = 0$ or $(x + 2) = 0$ ... zero rule for multiplication

$\Rightarrow x = 6$ or $x = -2$

Example 2

Solve the quadratic equation $3x^2 - 7x = -2$.

Solution

$3x^2 - 7x = -2$

$\Rightarrow \ 3x^2 - 7x + 2 = 0 \quad$ ... we must have 0 on the right-hand side

$\Rightarrow (3x - 1)(x - 2) = 0 \quad$ ... factorise the left-hand side

$\Rightarrow$ either $3x - 1 = 0 \quad$ or $\quad x - 2 = 0 \quad$ ... zero rule for multiplication

$\Rightarrow \qquad\qquad 3x = 1 \quad$ or $\quad x = 2$

$\Rightarrow \qquad\qquad x = \frac{1}{3} \quad$ or $\quad x = 2$

Check answer by substituting $x = \frac{1}{3}$ and $x = 2$ into the original equation:

$3x^2 - 7x + 2 = 0$

When $x = \frac{1}{3} \Rightarrow 3\left(\frac{1}{3}\right)^2 - 7\left(\frac{1}{3}\right) + 2 = 0 \Rightarrow \frac{1}{3} - \frac{7}{3} + 2 = 0 \Rightarrow 0 = 0$ ✓

When $x = 2 \Rightarrow 3(2)^2 - 7(2) + 2 = 0 \Rightarrow 12 - 14 + 2 = 0 \Rightarrow 0 = 0$ ✓

As LHS = RHS for both equations, both solutions are correct.

Connections

There is a direct link between the equation $3x^2 - 7x + 2 = 0$ and the graph of the function $y = 3x^2 - 7x + 2$.

The solution to the equation $3x^2 - 7x + 2 = 0$ can be seen where the graph of $y = 3x^2 - 7x + 2$ crosses the x-axis.

i.e. at $x = \frac{1}{3}$ and $x = 2$.

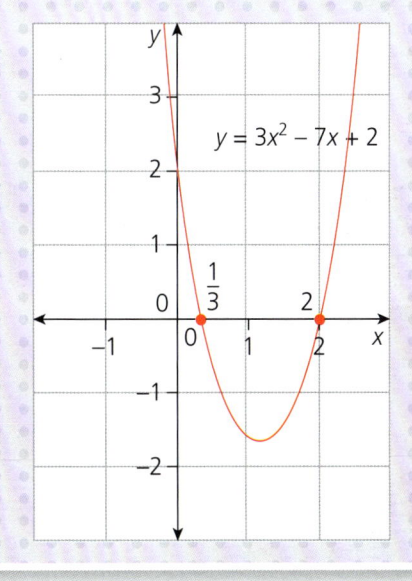

Example 3

Solve the quadratic equation $-5x^2 + 30x = 0$ for x.

Solution

$-5x^2 + 30x = 0$

$\Rightarrow 5x^2 - 30x = 0 \qquad$ ... multiply both sides by -1 so x^2 term is positive

$\Rightarrow 5x(x - 6) = 0 \qquad$ ... factorise the left-hand side

Either $5x = 0$ or $(x - 6) = 0$ ... zero rule for multiplication
$\Rightarrow \quad x = 0$ or $\Rightarrow \quad x = 6$

Check answer by substituting $x = 0$ and $x = 6$ into the original equation.

When $x = 0 \Rightarrow 5(0)^2 - 30(0) = 0 \Rightarrow 0 = 0$ ✓

When $x = 6 \Rightarrow 5(6)^2 - 30(6) = 0 \Rightarrow 180 - 180 = 0 \Rightarrow 0 = 0$ ✓

As LHS = RHS for both equations, both solutions are correct.

Example 4

Solve the quadratic equation $9x^2 - 16 = 0$ for x.

Solution

$9x^2 - 16 = 0$
$\Rightarrow (3x)^2 - (4)^2 = 0$ ... rewrite the LHS as the difference of 2 squares
$\Rightarrow (3x - 4)(3x + 4) = 0$ ... factorise (difference of 2 squares)

Either $(3x - 4) = 0$ or $(3x + 4) = 0$ ... zero rule for multiplication
$\Rightarrow \quad 3x = 4$ or $\Rightarrow \quad 3x = -4$
$\Rightarrow \quad x = \frac{4}{3}$ or $\Rightarrow \quad x = -\frac{4}{3}$

Check answer by substituting $x = \frac{4}{3}$ and $x = -\frac{4}{3}$ into the original equation.

When $x = \frac{4}{3} \Rightarrow 9x^2 - 16 = 0 \Rightarrow 9\left(\frac{4}{3}\right)^2 - 16 = 0 \Rightarrow 0 = 0$ ✓

When $x = -\frac{4}{3} \Rightarrow 9x^2 - 16 = 0 \Rightarrow 9\left(-\frac{4}{3}\right)^2 - 16 = 0 \Rightarrow 0 = 0$ ✓

As LHS = RHS for both equations, both solutions are correct.

Example 5

(i) Solve the quadratic equation $x^2 - x - 6 = 0$.

(ii) Hence, solve the equation $(y - 2)^2 - (y - 2) - 6 = 0$.

Solution

(i) $x^2 - x - 6 = 0$
$\Rightarrow (x - 3)(x + 2) = 0$ ... factorise the left-hand side
$\Rightarrow$ either $x - 3 = 0$ or $x + 2 = 0$ ... zero rule for multiplication
$\Rightarrow \quad x = 3$ or $x = -2$

(ii) The equation $(y - 2)^2 - (y - 2) - 6 = 0$ is exactly the same as $x^2 - x - 6 = 0$ except that x has been replaced everywhere by $(y - 2)$.

We can therefore replace x by $(y - 2)$ in the answers.

$\therefore y - 2 = 3$ or $y - 2 = -2$
$\therefore \quad y = 5$ or $\quad y = 0$

Activity 7.1

1. If you are given that $(a)(b) = 0$, where a, b are Real numbers, what can you conclude about a and b?

2. Write down the roots of these equations.
   (i) $(x-4)(x+3) = 0$
   (ii) $(x+7)(x-3) = 0$
   (iii) $x(x-7) = 0$
   (iv) $(x-5)(x+5) = 0$

In questions 3–20, solve the equation and verify your answers.

3. $x^2 + x - 6 = 0$
4. $x^2 + 8x + 7 = 0$
5. $x^2 + 4x = -3$
6. $x^2 - 6x = -5$
7. $x(x-3) = 18$
8. $36x^2 - 81 = 0$
9. $225x^2 - 169 = 0$
10. $11x^2 - 22x = 0$
11. $(x+2)(x-3) = 6$
12. $35x^2 - 7x = 0$
13. $4x^2 - 25 = 0$
14. $9x^2 - 49 = 0$
15. $4x^2 - 8x = 0$
16. $7x^2 - x = 0$
17. $5x^2 + 6x + 1 = 0$
18. $7x^2 + 10x = -3$
19. $9x^2 + 10x + 1 = 0$
20. $11x^2 + 15x + 4 = 0$

21. (i) Solve the equation $x^2 + 5x - 14 = 0$.
    (ii) Hence, solve the equation $(k-2)^2 + 5(k-2) - 14 = 0$.

22. (i) Solve the equation $3x^2 + 5x = 2$.
    (ii) Hence, solve the equation $3(m-3)^2 + 5(m-3) = 2$.

23. (i) Solve the equation $3p^2 + 14p - 5 = 0$.
    (ii) Hence, solve the equation $3(a+1)^2 + 14(a+1) - 5 = 0$.

24. The diagram shows the graph of the function $y = x^2 - 2x - 3$.

    From the graph, write down the roots of the equation $x^2 - 2x - 3 = 0$.

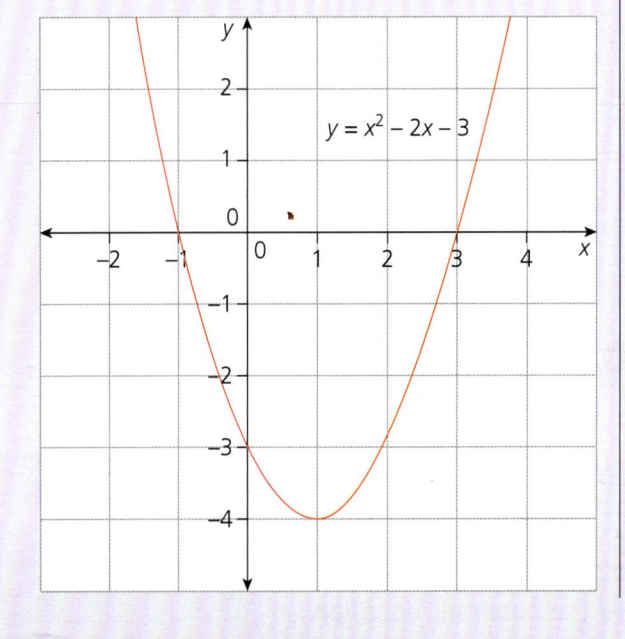

25. The diagram shows the graph of the function $y = 12 - x - x^2$.

    From the graph, write down the roots of the equation $12 - x - x^2 = 0$.

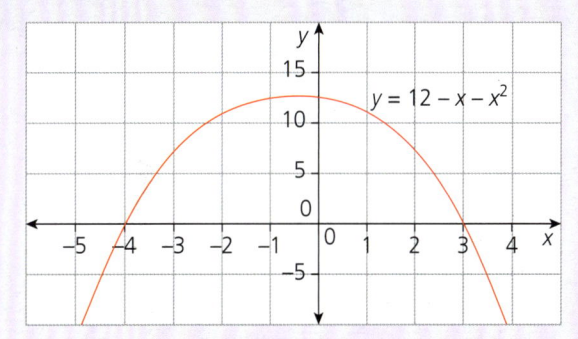

Solve the following equations.

26. $13x^2 - 66x + 5 = 0$
27. $3x^2 - 5x = -2$
28. $4x^2 - 7x + 3 = 0$
29. $6x^2 - 7x + 2 = 0$
30. $10x^2 + 11x - 6 = 0$
31. $9x^2 + 9x - 4 = 0$
32. $8x^2 = 5 - 3x$
33. $13x^2 + 10x - 3 = 0$
34. $-4x^2 - 7x + 2 = 0$
35. $-2x^2 + 7x + 4 = 0$
36. $x^2 + (x+1)^2 = (x+2)^2$

Section 7B Forming a Quadratic Equation given the Roots

Example

(i) Form the quadratic equation with roots 2 and −5.
(ii) Verify your solution.

Solution

(i) Work backwards:

The roots are $x = 2$ and $x = -5$
$\Rightarrow x - 2 = 0$ and $x + 5 = 0$
$\Rightarrow (x - 2)(x + 5) = 0$
$\Rightarrow x^2 + 5x - 2x - 10 = 0$ … multiply out
$\Rightarrow x^2 + 3x - 10 = 0$

(ii) Check answer by substituting $x = 2$ and $x = -5$ into $x^2 + 3x - 10 = 0$.

When $x = 2 \Rightarrow (2)^2 + 3(2) - 10 = 0$
$\Rightarrow 4 + 6 - 10 = 0 \Rightarrow 0 = 0$ ✓
When $x = -5 \Rightarrow (-5)^2 + 3(-5) - 10 = 0$
$\Rightarrow 25 - 15 - 10 = 0 \Rightarrow 0 = 0$ ✓

Activity 7.2

In questions 1–10, form quadratic equations with the given roots.

1. $x = -1$ and $x = 3$
2. $x = 2$ and $x = -3$
3. $x = -2$ and $x = 9$
4. $x = -5$ and $x = -4$
5. $x = 6$ and $x = 7$
6. $x = -4$ and $x = 3$
7. $x = 11$ and $x = -3$
8. $x = -8$ and $x = 10$
9. $x = -4$ and $x = 2$
10. $x = 3$ and $x = -5$

11. The roots of the quadratic equation $ax^2 + bx + c = 0$ are 5 and 9. Find the values of a, b and c.

12. The roots of the quadratic equation $ax^2 + bx + c = 0$ are −12 and 2. Find the values of a, b and c.

13. The roots of the quadratic equation $ax^2 + bx + c = 0$ are −7 and −1. Find the values of a, b and c.

14. The roots of the quadratic equation $x^2 + 6x + c = 0$ are the same. Find the value of c.

15. The roots of the quadratic equation $x^2 - 18x + c = 0$ are the same. Find the value of c.

Section 7C Solving a Quadratic Equation using a Formula

We have solved quadratic equations which can be factorised. However, some quadratic equations cannot be factorised to give roots which are integers or rational numbers.

In such cases, we are often asked to find the roots in surd form or to a number of decimal places. In this situation, we use a formula to solve the quadratic equation.

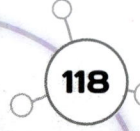

Key Points

To use the formula for solving quadratic equations:
- The quadratic equation must be written in the form $ax^2 + bx + c = 0$.
- The values of a, b and c are substituted into the formula:

$$x = \frac{-b \pm \sqrt{b^2 - 4ac}}{2a}$$

Note that you can also use this formula in cases where factorising is possible.
This formula is on page 20 of the *Formulae and tables* booklet.

Example 1

Solve $2x^2 + 10x + 7 = 0$, correct to two decimal places.

Solution

$2x^2 + 10x + 7 = 0$

Here $a = 2$, $b = 10$ and $c = 7$

$$\therefore x = \frac{-10 \pm \sqrt{10^2 - 4(2)(7)}}{2(2)}$$

$$= \frac{-10 \pm \sqrt{100 - 56}}{4}$$

$$= \frac{-10 \pm \sqrt{44}}{4}$$

$$= \frac{-10 \pm 6.633}{4}$$

$$= \frac{-10 + 6.633}{4} \quad \text{or} \quad \frac{-10 - 6.633}{4}$$

$$= \frac{-3.367}{4} \quad \text{or} \quad \frac{-16.633}{4}$$

$x = -0.84 \quad$ or $\quad x = -4.16$

Connections

Recall what irrational numbers (surds) are. They are numbers like $\sqrt{2}, \sqrt{5}, \sqrt{7}$ etc. which cannot be written as fractions. When we use the formula for solving quadratic equations, we often have to work with surds. Before doing Example 2, make sure that you can simplify surds like $\sqrt{28}$.

Example 2

Solve the equation $t^2 - 2t - 6 = 0$ and write the roots in the form $d \pm \sqrt{e}$ where $d, e \in \mathbb{Z}$.

Solution

$t^2 - 2t - 6$ cannot be factorised.

Solve the quadratic equation $t^2 - 2t - 6 = 0$ using the formula.

$t^2 - 2t - 6 = 0 \Rightarrow 1t^2 - 2t - 6 = 0$

$\therefore a = 1$, $b = -2$ and $c = -6$.

Substitute the values of a, b and c into the formula:

$$t = \frac{-b \pm \sqrt{b^2 - 4ac}}{2a}$$

$$\Rightarrow t = \frac{-(-2) \pm \sqrt{(-2)^2 - 4(1)(-6)}}{2(1)}$$

$$\Rightarrow t = \frac{2 \pm \sqrt{4 + 24}}{2}$$

$$\Rightarrow t = \frac{2 \pm \sqrt{28}}{2} = \frac{2 \pm 2\sqrt{7}}{2} \quad \text{... write the surd } \sqrt{28} \text{ as } 2\sqrt{7}$$

$$\Rightarrow t = \frac{2 + 2\sqrt{7}}{2} \quad \text{or} \quad t = \frac{2 - 2\sqrt{7}}{2}$$

$$\Rightarrow t = 1 + \sqrt{7} \quad \text{or} \quad t = 1 - \sqrt{7}$$

The roots of $t^2 - 2t - 6 = 0$ are $t = 1 \pm \sqrt{7}$.

Activity 7.3

1. (i) Solve the quadratic equation $4x^2 + 4x - 3 = 0$ using factors.
   (ii) Solve the quadratic equation $4x^2 + 4x - 3 = 0$ by using the formula for solving quadratic equations.
   (iii) Check your solutions.

2. (i) Solve the quadratic equation $2x^2 - 3x - 5 = 0$ using factors.
   (ii) Solve the quadratic equation $2x^2 - 3x - 5 = 0$ using the formula for solving quadratic equations.
   (iii) Check your solutions.

3. Solve the equation $2x^2 + 3x - 4 = 0$ correct to three decimal places using the formula for solving quadratic equations.

4. Find the roots of $x^2 + 6x + 3 = 0$ correct to two decimal places.

5. Find the roots of $x^2 - 4x - 2 = 0$ correct to two decimal places.

6. Find the roots of $4n^2 + 7n - 3 = 0$ correct to two decimal places.

7. Solve the equation $x^2 - 4x - 3 = 0$ and give your answers in surd form.

8. Find the roots of the following equations giving your answers in the form $a \pm \sqrt{b}$, where $a, b \in \mathbb{Z}$.
   (i) $x^2 - 2x - 2 = 0$
   (ii) $x^2 - 4x + 1 = 0$
   (iii) $x^2 - 4x - 1 = 0$

9. Solve the equation $t^2 + 2t - 7 = 0$ and write the roots in surd form.

10. Solve the equation $p^2 - 5p - 2 = 0$ and write the roots in surd form.

11. Solve the equation $x^2 - 4x + 2 = 0$ correct to one decimal place.

12. (i) Solve the equation $x^2 - 6x + 4 = 0$ and give your answers in the form $a \pm \sqrt{b}$, where $a, b \in \mathbb{Z}$.
    (ii) Hence, or otherwise, find two values of k for which $(3 + k)^2 - 6(3 + k) + 4 = 0$.
    (iii) Show that the sum of the two values of k is zero.

13. (i) Solve, correct to two decimal places, the equation $x^2 - 4x + 2 = 0$. Express your answer in the form $a \pm b\sqrt{2}$.
    (ii) Use your answer to part (i) to find the two values of p for which $(p - 4)^2 - 4(p - 4) + 2 = 0$.

Section 7D Solving Quadratic Equations with Algebraic Fractions

A quadratic equation can have rational coefficients. Therefore, we need to be able to solve equations of this type.

Example 1

Solve the quadratic equation $\frac{x^2}{2} - \frac{7x}{2} - 9 = 0$. Verify your answer.

Solution

$\frac{x^2}{2} - \frac{7x}{2} - 9 = 0$ ... multiply both sides by 2 to clear the fractions

$\Rightarrow x^2 - 7x - 18 = 0$

$\Rightarrow (x + 2)(x - 9) = 0$

Either $x + 2 = 0$ or $x - 9 = 0$

$\Rightarrow \qquad x = -2$ or $\qquad x = 9$

Check answer by substituting $x = -2$ and $x = 9$ into $x^2 - 7x - 18 = 0$.

When $x = -2 \Rightarrow (-2)^2 - 7(-2) - 18 = 0 \Rightarrow 4 + 14 - 18 = 0 \Rightarrow 0 = 0$ ✓

When $x = 9 \Rightarrow (9)^2 - 7(9) - 18 = 0 \Rightarrow 81 - 63 - 18 = 0 \Rightarrow 0 = 0$ ✓

As LHS = RHS for both equations, both solutions are correct.

Example 2

Solve the equation $\frac{x^2}{3} + 2x - \frac{1}{2} = 0$ correct to two decimal places.

Solution

$\frac{x^2}{3} + 2x - \frac{1}{2} = 0$

$\Rightarrow 2x^2 + 12x - 3 = 0$ ... multiply both sides by 6 (LCM) to eliminate the fractions

Substitute the values $a = 2$, $b = 12$ and $c = -3$ into the formula:

$x = \frac{-b \pm \sqrt{b^2 - 4ac}}{2a}$

$\Rightarrow x = \frac{-(12) \pm \sqrt{(12)^2 - 4(2)(-3)}}{2(2)}$

$\Rightarrow x = \frac{-12 \pm \sqrt{144 + 24}}{4}$

$\Rightarrow x = 0.2404$ or $x = -6.2404$

$\Rightarrow x = 0.24$ or $x = -6.24$ ... write roots to two decimal places

Activity 7.4

Solve each of the quadratic equations below.

1. $\dfrac{x^2}{2} + 2x - \dfrac{21}{2} = 0$
2. $\dfrac{x^2}{6} + \dfrac{11x}{6} = 2$
3. $x^2 - \dfrac{15x}{2} = -9$
4. $\dfrac{x^2 + x}{2} - 2x - 1 = \dfrac{x}{4}$
5. $\dfrac{2x^2}{3} - \dfrac{x^2 + 1}{2} = \dfrac{3 - x - x^2}{6}$
6. $\dfrac{2x^2}{7} - \dfrac{x}{2} = 1$
7. $\dfrac{x^2}{10} - \dfrac{2x}{5} = -\dfrac{1}{5}$
8. $\dfrac{2x^2 + 3}{5} - \dfrac{x + 2}{3} = 2$
9. $\dfrac{6x^2 + x}{4} + \dfrac{8x}{2} = \dfrac{7}{2}$
10. $\dfrac{5x^2 - 1}{6} + \dfrac{x + 7x^2}{2} = \dfrac{1}{3}$

Section 7E Solving Problems using Quadratic Equations

Example

The product of two consecutive Natural numbers is 870.

(i) Write an equation in words to represent this information.
(ii) Represent this information algebraically and solve the equation.
(iii) Find the two consecutive numbers.

Solution

(i) The 1st Natural number multiplied by the 2nd consecutive natural number equals 870.

(ii) Let x = 1st Natural number
$x + 1$ = 2nd Natural number

$\therefore x(x + 1) = 870$
$\Rightarrow x^2 + x - 870 = 0$
$\Rightarrow (x + 30)(x - 29) = 0$
$\Rightarrow \quad (x + 30) = 0 \quad$ or $\quad (x - 29) = 0$
$\Rightarrow \quad x = -30 \quad$ or $\quad x = 29$

(iii) As the numbers both must be Natural numbers, i.e. not negative, then $x = 29$.

$\therefore x = 29$ is the 1st Natural number
$\therefore x + 1 = 29 + 1 = 30$ is the 2nd Natural number.

Note: If you find it hard to factorise a quadratic expression, you can always use the formula if you prefer.

Activity 7.5

1. The product of two consecutive odd natural numbers is 255.
   (i) Write an equation in words to represent this information.
   (ii) Represent this information algebraically and solve the equation.
   (iii) Find the two consecutive odd natural numbers.

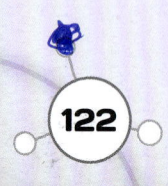

2. The product of two consecutive even numbers is 528.
   (i) Write an equation in words to represent this information.
   (ii) Represent this information algebraically and solve the equation.
   (iii) Find all possible solutions for the two consecutive numbers.

3. The width of a rectangular flower bed is 0.5 m longer than half the length. The total area of the flower bed is 10 m².

   (i) Draw a sketch of the flower bed, labelling the width and length.
   (ii) Write a quadratic equation to represent this information.
   (iii) Solve the quadratic equation.
   (iv) Find the dimensions of the flower bed.

4. The height of a triangular window is 0.5 m shorter than its base. The total area of the window is 1.5 m².
   (i) Write a quadratic equation to represent this information.
   (ii) Solve the quadratic equation.
   (iii) Find the dimensions of the triangular window.
   (iv) Verify your answer.

5. The layout of a 300 m² suburban garden is shown.

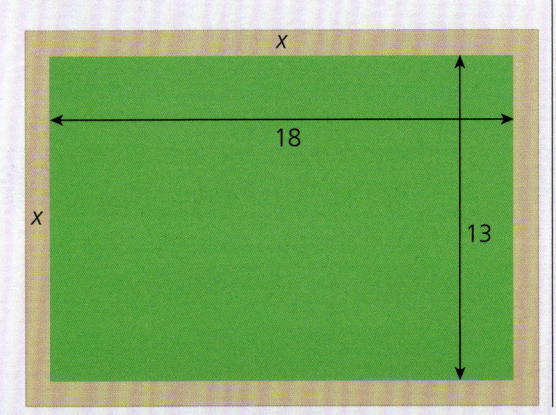

   The inner area represents the lawn. The outer area represents the border which is x m wide.
   (i) Write a quadratic equation to represent this information.
   (ii) Solve the quadratic equation.
   (iii) Find the width of the border.
   (iv) Verify your answer.

6. Maria made a quilt that measures 1.5 m by 2 m. She wants to add a border using 4 m² of material. If she uses all the material and the border is the same width on all four sides:
   (i) Draw a diagram to represent this information.
   (ii) Write a quadratic equation to model this information.
   (iii) Solve the quadratic equation.
   (iv) Find the width of the border.

7. In a right-angled triangle ABC, the hypotenuse [AB] is 8 cm longer than [AC], and [BC] is 7 cm longer than [AC].
   (i) Draw a sketch to represent his information.
   (ii) Using Pythagoras' theorem, write a formula that represents this information and simplify to a quadratic equation.
   (iii) Solve the quadratic equation.
   (iv) Find the lengths of the three sides.
   (v) Verify that the triangle is right-angled.

8. The volume of a box is 2250 cm³. The box has a square bottom of length x cm and a height of 10 cm.
   (i) Show that the volume (V) is represented by the equation $V = 10x^2$.
   (ii) Find the width and length of the box.
   (iii) Check your answer.

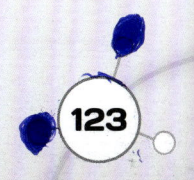

9. The volume of a cylindrical water storage tank is 1692.46 m³. The height of the tank is 11 m.
   (i) Show that the volume (V) is represented by the equation $V = 11\pi r^2$.
   (ii) Find the radius of the water tank, using 3.14 as the value of π.

10. The stopping distance of a car in metres is given by the quadratic equation $d = 0.0056s^2 + 0.14s$, where s is the speed of the car in km/h before applying the brakes.

   (i) What is the stopping distance of a car travelling at 120 km/h?
   (ii) Assuming that a car has an average length of 4 m, how many car lengths does this stopping distance correspond to?
   (iii) What is the maximum speed that a car can travel to be able to stop within 10 car lengths?

Revision Activity 7

1. Solve the following quadratic equations.
   (a) $x^2 - 16x = 0$
   (b) $3x^2 - 27x = 0$
   (c) $2x^2 - 64x = 0$
   (d) $4x^2 = 2x$
   (e) $121x^2 - 49 = 0$
   (f) $4x^2 - 144 = 0$
   (g) $81x^2 = 64$
   (h) $169x^2 = 196$
   (i) $x^2 - 10x + 25 = 0$
   (j) $x^2 - 13x + 36 = 0$
   (k) $x^2 - 5x - 14 = 0$
   (l) $x^2 + x - 56 = 0$

2. Factorise the following quadratic equations, then solve to find the solutions.
   (a) $2x^2 + x - 15 = 0$
   (b) $3x^2 - 11x + 6 = 0$
   (c) $6x^2 + 7x + 2 = 0$
   (d) $4x^2 + 11x + 7 = 0$
   (e) $9x^2 - 9x - 4 = 0$
   (f) $10x^2 - 51x - 22 = 0$
   (g) $14x^2 + 47x - 7 = 0$
   (h) $35x^2 - 8x - 3 = 0$

3. The roots of the quadratic equation $x^2 + 14x + c = 0$ are equal. Find the value of c.

4. Solve the following equation.
   $$\frac{y}{10} - 1 = \frac{12}{5y}$$

5. The square of a number minus 12 equals four times the original number.
   (a) Write a quadratic equation which represents this problem.
   (b) Solve the quadratic equation.
   (c) Find the value of the original number.
   (d) Check your solution.

6. A garden measuring 13 m × 17 m has a pathway laid around it. When the pathway is laid, the total area including the pathway is 320 m². The diagram shows the layout of the garden. The inner area represents the lawn. The outer area represents the path which is x m wide.
   (a) Write a quadratic equation to represent this information.
   (b) Solve the quadratic equation.
   (c) Find the width of the path.
   (d) Check your answer.

Exam-style Questions

1. Solve for x: $3x^2 + 11x = 14$

    JCHL 2013

2. (a) If $n = 7$ find the value of $2n$ and also the value of $2n + 1$.
    (b) (i) x represents an even number. Explain why $x + 2$ is the next even number.
        (ii) If one third of the smaller even number is subtracted from half of the larger even number, the result is 8. Find the value of x.

    JCHL 2013

3. A triangle has a base length of $2x$ cm and a perpendicular height of $(x + 3)$ cm. The area of the triangle is 10 cm². Find the distance x.

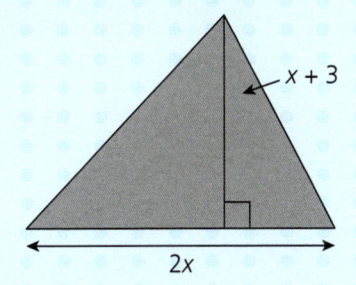

    JCHL 2012

4. Solve each of the following equations.
    (a) $x^2 - 5x - 6 = 0$
    (b) $8x^2 - 14x + 3 = 0$
    (c) $\dfrac{2x + 5}{3} - \dfrac{4x - 1}{2} = -\dfrac{1}{2}$
    (d) Find the roots of the equation $2x^2 - 7x - 6 = 0$. Give your answers correct to two decimal places.

    JCHL 2012

KEY WORDS AND PHRASES

- Roots
- Factors
- Quadratic formula

Chapter Summary 7

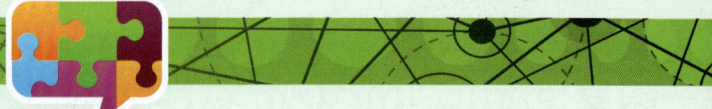

- The zero rule for multiplication: If $(a)(b) = 0$ then either $a = 0$ or $b = 0$.
- Solve equations of the form $ax^2 + bx + c = 0$ by
  - Factorising $ax^2 + bx + c$ if possible
  - Using the formula $x = \dfrac{-b \pm \sqrt{b^2 - 4ac}}{2a}$
- Get a quadratic equation from its roots by working backwards from the roots to the factors of $ax^2 + bx + c$.

Algebra 6
Manipulating Formulae

Chapter 8

Learning Outcomes

In this chapter, you will learn about:
- Manipulating formulae
- Solving problems using manipulation

Section 8A Manipulating Formulae

A **formula** is a statement which connects variables, usually as an equation.

For example, $V = \pi r^2 h$ is a formula which we know very well.
It gives the volume of a cylinder, V, in terms of r, the radius of its base and h, its height.

This formula holds true for every cylinder and may be used in this form to calculate V when given values for r and h.

V is called the **subject** of the formula, since it is on its own on one side of the equation.

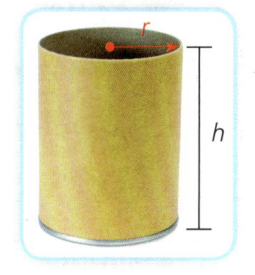

We may want to change the subject of this formula. This means getting one of the other variables on its own on one side. We do this by using the rules of equations that we know very well already:

What we do to one side of an equation, we must do to the other side.

In practice, we do this by removing terms, or part of terms, from one side to the other by performing opposite operations.

Example 1 shows how we use multiplication and division as opposites to change the subject of very simple equations.

Example 1

Make a the subject of each of the following equations.

(i) $4a = n$

(ii) $ma = n$

(iii) $\dfrac{a}{2} = p$

(iv) $\dfrac{a}{m} = p$

CONNECT WITH MATHS 2

Solution

Multiplication and division are opposites. We want *a* on its own on one side only.

(i) $4a = n$ ... *a* is being multiplied by 4
   $\Rightarrow a = \dfrac{n}{4}$ ... divide both sides by 4

(ii) $ma = n$ ... *a* is being multiplied by *m*
   $\Rightarrow a = \dfrac{n}{m}$ ... divide both sides by *m*

(iii) $\dfrac{a}{2} = p$ ... *a* is being divided by 2
   $\Rightarrow a = 2p$ ... multiply both sides by 2

(iv) $\dfrac{a}{m} = p$ ... *a* is being divided by *m*
   $\Rightarrow a = mp$ ... multiply both sides by *m*

The next example shows how we use addition and subtraction as opposites to change the subject of equations.

Example 2

Make *x* the subject of the following equations.

(i) $x + m = p$

(ii) $x - h = k$

Solution

Addition and subtraction are opposites. We want *x* on its own on one side only.

(i) $x + m = p$ ... *m* is being added to *x*
   $\Rightarrow x = p - m$ ... subtract *m* from both sides

(ii) $x - h = k$ ... *h* is being subtracted from *x*
   $\Rightarrow x = k + h$ ... add *h* to both sides

Example 3

Make *a* the subject of the formula $v = u + at$.

Solution

We want *a* on its own on one side only.

$v = u + at$ ... *u* is being added to the term containing *a*

$\Rightarrow v - u = at$ ... subtract *u* from both sides. Now *a* is being multiplied by *t*

$\Rightarrow \dfrac{v - u}{t} = a$ ... divide both sides by *t*

$\Rightarrow a = \dfrac{v - u}{t}$

In Example 4, the variable required is in more than one term.

Example 4

Make k the subject of the following formula.

$akb - 2ck = 7mn$

Solution

We want k on its own on one side only.

$akb - 2ck = 7mn$ ... both terms on the left-hand side contain k
$\Rightarrow k(ab - 2c) = 7mn$ ... factorise k out. Now k is being multiplied by $(ab - 2c)$
$\Rightarrow k = \dfrac{7mn}{ab - 2c}$ ... divide both sides by $(ab - 2c)$

Example 5

Express P as the subject of the formula $A = \dfrac{P - S}{t}$

Solution

We want P on its own on one side only.

$A = \dfrac{P - S}{t}$ ... the term containing P is being divided by t
$\Rightarrow At = P - S$ ... multiply both sides by t. Now S is being subtracted from P
$\Rightarrow At + S = P$ ... add S to both sides
So $P = At + S$

Example 6

Make v the subject of the formula $s = \left(\dfrac{u + v}{2}\right)t$

Solution

We want v on its own on one side only.

$s = \left(\dfrac{u + v}{2}\right)t$ ... the bracket containing v is being multiplied by t
$\Rightarrow \dfrac{s}{t} = \left(\dfrac{u + v}{2}\right)$ ... divide both sides by t. Now the expression containing v is being divided by 2
$\Rightarrow \dfrac{2s}{t} = u + v$ ... multiply both sides by 2. Now u is being added to v
$\Rightarrow \dfrac{2s}{t} - u = v$ ... subtract u from both sides
So $v = \dfrac{2s}{t} - u$

Taking the square root of a number is the opposite of squaring the number, i.e. $\sqrt{a^2} = a$ and $(\sqrt{a})^2 = a$. We need this in the next example.

Example 7

(i) Make b the subject of the formula $\sqrt{a + 4b} = 5c$.

(ii) Make r the subject of the formula $V = \pi r^2$.

Solution

(i) We want b on its own on one side only.

$\sqrt{a + 4b} = 5c$ ... the term with b is under the square root sign

$\Rightarrow (\sqrt{a + 4b})^2 = (5c)^2$ ... square both sides to eliminate the root

$\Rightarrow a + 4b = 25c^2$ ... now a is being added to the term with b

$\Rightarrow 4b = 25c^2 - a$ ... subtract a from both sides. Now b is being multiplied by 4

$\Rightarrow b = \dfrac{25c^2 - a}{4}$ ... divide both sides by 4

(ii) We want r on its own on one side only.

$V = \pi r^2$ ... r^2 is being multiplied by π

$\Rightarrow \dfrac{V}{\pi} = r^2$ ... divide both sides by π. Now r is squared

$\Rightarrow \sqrt{\dfrac{V}{\pi}} = r$ ... take the square root of both sides

So $r = \sqrt{\dfrac{V}{\pi}}$

Example 8

Make L the subject of the formula $T = 2\pi\sqrt{\dfrac{L}{g}}$.

Solution

We want L on its own on one side only.

$T = 2\pi\sqrt{\dfrac{L}{g}}$ ... the term containing L is being multiplied by 2π

$\Rightarrow \dfrac{T}{2\pi} = \sqrt{\dfrac{L}{g}}$ ... divide both sides by 2π. Now L is under a square root sign

$\Rightarrow \left(\dfrac{T}{2\pi}\right)^2 = \dfrac{L}{g}$ ... square both sides. Now L is being divided by g

$\Rightarrow g \times \left(\dfrac{T}{2\pi}\right)^2 = L$ ... multiply both sides by g

So $L = g \times \left(\dfrac{T}{2\pi}\right)^2$

Activity 8.1

1. Rearrange the following equations to make t the subject of the equation.

   (i) $a + t = 2s$
   (ii) $p - t = 5q$
   (iii) $wt = x$
   (iv) $\dfrac{t}{k} = r$
   (v) $\dfrac{f}{t} = gh$
   (vi) $w(t - d) = y$

2. Rearrange the following formulae to make the variable in the brackets the subject of the formula.

   (i) $A = l \times w$ (w)
   (ii) $F = ma$ (a)
   (iii) $T = Fd$ (d)

(iv) $P = \dfrac{F}{A}$ (F)

(v) $W = mg$ (m)

(vi) $P = \dfrac{W}{t}$ (t)

3. Rearrange the following formulae to make x the subject of the formula.

(i) $x^2 = \dfrac{a}{b}$

(ii) $\dfrac{(d-x)}{e} = s - q$

(iii) $\sqrt{(x+g)} = a$

(iv) $\dfrac{x}{2} - d = p$

(v) $rx^2 + qs^2 = y$

(vi) $\dfrac{w}{x^2} + t = s - u$

4. Rearrange the following formulae to make the variable in the brackets the subject of the formula.

(i) $E = mgh$ (h)

(ii) $E = mc^2$ (m)

(iii) $v^2 = u^2 + 2as$ (a)

(iv) $T^2 = \dfrac{4\pi^2 R^3}{GM}$ (M)

(v) $s = ut + \dfrac{1}{2}at^2$ (u)

(vi) $A = \pi r^2$ (r)

(vii) $F = \dfrac{Gm_1 m_2}{d^2}$ (d)

(viii) $V = \dfrac{1}{3}\pi r^2 h$ (r)

(ix) $T = 2\pi\sqrt{\dfrac{l}{g}}$ (g)

5. Rearrange the following formulae to make b the subject of the formula.

(i) $ab - c = bp$

(ii) $u(2 - b) = sb$

(iii) $\dfrac{(b+y)}{c} = 3b$

(iv) $k = \dfrac{(b-w)}{b}$

(v) $\sqrt{\dfrac{b+e}{b}} = c^2$

6. Make l the subject of each of the following formulae.

(i) $\dfrac{yl}{q} = w$

(ii) $p - \dfrac{u}{l} = s$

7. Rearrange the following formulae.

(i) $A = l^2$, to make l the subject

(ii) $T^2 = \dfrac{4\pi^2 R^3}{GM}$, to make R the subject

8. Make w the subject of each of the following formulae.

(i) $2(w - 2) = p - w$

(ii) $\dfrac{5w - p}{w} = bu$

Section 8B Working with Everyday Formulae

This section looks at real-life applications where it is necessary to rearrange a given formula to make another variable the subject.

Example 1

This is the formula used to calculate the **curved surface area** (A) of a cylinder:

$$A = 2\pi rh$$

(i) Rearrange the formula to make r the subject.

(ii) If the curved surface area (A) is 376.8 cm² and the height (h) is 10 cm, find the radius (r) of the cylinder. (Take $\pi = 3.14$)

(iii) Verify your solution.

Solution

(i) We want r on its own on one side.

$A = 2\pi rh$ ... r is being multiplied by $2\pi h$

$\Rightarrow \dfrac{A}{2\pi h} = r$ ... divide both sides by $2\pi h$

(ii) Substitute $A = 376.8$ cm² and $h = 10$ cm into the rearranged formula.

$r = \dfrac{A}{2\pi h}$

$\Rightarrow r = \dfrac{376.8}{2(3.14)(10)}$

$\Rightarrow r = 6$ cm

(iii) Check:

$A = 2\pi rh = 2(3.14)(6)(10) = 376.8$ cm²

The solution is correct.

Example 2

The area of a circular flowerbed is 38.5 m².

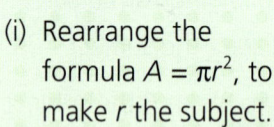

(i) Rearrange the formula $A = \pi r^2$, to make r the subject.

If $\pi = \dfrac{22}{7}$ and $A = 38.5$ m²:

(ii) Find the radius of the flower bed.

(iii) Verify your solution.

Solution

(i) $A = \pi r^2$

$\Rightarrow \dfrac{A}{\pi} = r^2$ ... divide both sides by π

$\Rightarrow \sqrt{\dfrac{A}{\pi}} = r$ ... square root both sides

(ii) Substitute $\pi = \dfrac{22}{7}$ and $A = 38.5$ m² into the formula found in part (i).

$r = \sqrt{\dfrac{A}{\pi}}$

$\Rightarrow r = \sqrt{\dfrac{38.5}{\left(\dfrac{22}{7}\right)}}$

$\Rightarrow r = 3.5$ m

(iii) Check:

$A = \pi r^2 = \left(\dfrac{22}{7}\right)(3.5)^2 = 38.5$ m²

The solution is correct.

Activity 8.2

1 The formula $K = C + 273.15$ is used to calculate degrees Kelvin (°K) where

   C = temperature in degrees Celsius

   K = temperature in degrees Kelvin.

   (i) If C is 37°C, calculate the value of K.

   (ii) Rearrange the formula to make C the subject.

   (iii) If K is 306.15°K, calculate the value of C.

   (iv) Check your solution.

2. The area of a parallelogram is
   $$A = ah$$
   where
   a = base length
   h = perpendicular height.

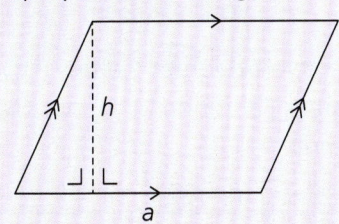

   (i) Rearrange the formula to make h the subject.
   (ii) Rearrange the formula to make a the subject.

   If A is 378 cm² and h is 21 cm,
   (iii) Find the base length (a) of the parallelogram.
   (iv) Check your solution.

3. The area of a triangular window on an A-frame house is given by the formula: 
   $$A = \frac{1}{2}ah$$
   where
   A = area of triangle
   a = base length
   h = perpendicular height.

   (i) Make a the subject of the formula.
   (ii) Find the base length (a) of the triangular window if the perpendicular height (h) is 11 m and the area is 55 m².

4. (i) Rearrange Pythagoras' Theorem:
   $c^2 = a^2 + b^2$, to make b the subject.

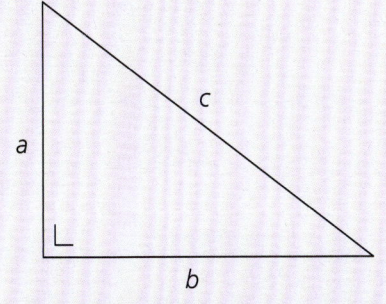

   (ii) Find the length of the side b when $a = 3$ and $c = 5$.
   (iii) Check your solution.

5. If an object is dropped from a height, the formula
   $$v = u + at$$
   gives the velocity after t seconds where
   v = the final speed
   u = the initial speed
   and a = the acceleration due to gravity.

   (i) Rearrange the formula to make u the subject.
   (ii) If v is 35.48 m/s, a is 9.8 m/s² and t is 2.6 s, find the value of u, the initial speed in m/s.
   (iii) Check your solution.

6. Force F required to move a car is given by the formula
   $$F = ma$$
   where
   m is the mass of the car
   and a is the acceleration of the car.

   (i) Rearrange the formula to make m the subject.

   If a Formula 1 car speeds down a track with an acceleration of 0.05 m/s²:

   (ii) Find the value of m if $F = 35$ N. (Ignore units.)
   (iii) Check your solution.

7 The volume of a sphere is given by the formula

$$V = \frac{4}{3}\pi r^3$$

where

　　V = volume of sphere

　　r = radius of sphere.

(i) Rearrange the formula to make r the subject.

(ii) The volume of a Premiership size 5 soccer football is 1843.71 cm³. Assuming the ball is perfectly spherical, find the radius of the ball to one decimal place. (Take π = 3.14)

(iii) Check your solution.

8 The formula used to calculate the voltage in an electrical circuit is

　　$V = IR$

where

　　V = voltage

　　I = current flow (amps)

　　R = resistance.

(i) Rearrange the formula to make R the subject.

(ii) If a 12 volt (V) battery causes 2 amps (I) of current to flow through a light bulb, calculate the resistance (R) of the bulb in ohms.

(iii) Verify your solution.

9 The volume of an ice-cream cone is 314 cm³. The volume of a cone is

$$V = \frac{1}{3}\pi r^2 h$$

where

　　V = volume of a cone

　　h = perpendicular height

　　r = radius.

(i) Rearrange the formula to make r the subject.

(ii) Find the radius of the cone if the height (h) of the cone is 12 cm. (Take π = 3.14)

(iii) Verify your solution.

10 To convert degrees Celsius (°C) to degrees Fahrenheit (°F), we use the formula

$$C = \frac{5}{9}(F - 32)$$

where

　　C = degrees Celsius (°C)

　　F = degrees Fahrenheit (°F).

(i) Rearrange the formula to make F the subject.

(ii) If C is 29°C, calculate the value of F.

(iii) Check your solution.

11 The formula used to calculate density is

$$\rho = \frac{m}{V}$$

where

　　ρ = density

　　m = mass

　　V = volume.

(i) Rearrange the formula to make m the subject.

(ii) Calculate the mass (m) of water if the density of water (ρ) is 1 g/cm³ and the volume of water (V) in a container is 3000 cm³.

(iii) Check your solution.

Revision Activity 8

1. Rearrange the following formulae to make the variable in the brackets the subject.
   (a) $P = \dfrac{F}{A}$ (A)
   (b) $W = mg$ (g)
   (c) $P = \dfrac{W}{t}$ (W)
   (d) $F = \dfrac{Gm_1 m_2}{d^2}$ (m_2)
   (e) $E = mgh$ (h)
   (f) $E = mc^2$ (c)
   (g) $v^2 = u^2 + 2as$ (u)
   (h) $s = ut + \dfrac{1}{2}at^2$ (a)
   (i) $T^2 = \dfrac{4\pi^2 R^3}{GM}$ (R)
   (j) $T = 2\pi\sqrt{\dfrac{l}{g}}$ (l)

2. This is the formula used to calculate the volume of a sphere:
   $$V = \dfrac{4}{3}\pi r^3$$
   where
      V = volume of sphere
      r = radius of sphere.
   (a) Rearrange the formula to make r the subject.

   The volume of the planet Venus is 9.28×10^{11} km³.
   (b) Find the approximate radius of Venus to one decimal place. (Take $\pi = 3.14$)

3. Kinetic energy is the energy associated with the movement of an object. The formula for kinetic energy is:
   $$E = \dfrac{1}{2}mv^2$$
   where
      E = kinetic energy
      m = mass
      v = velocity.
   (a) Rearrange the formula to make v the subject.
   (b) If m is 5 kg and E is 10 joules, calculate the velocity in m/s.
   (c) Check your solution.

4. The total surface area (A) of a baked bean tin is 98π cm².
   (a) Rearrange the formula $A = 2\pi r(h + r)$ to make h the subject.
   (b) If the radius (r) of the tin is 3.5 cm, find the height (h) of the tin.
   (c) Check your solution.

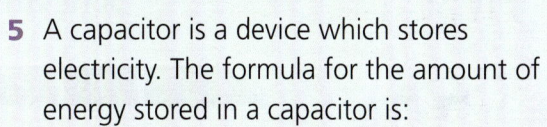

5. A capacitor is a device which stores electricity. The formula for the amount of energy stored in a capacitor is:
   $$W = \dfrac{1}{2}CV^2$$
   where
      W = energy stored
      C = the capacitance
      V = the potential difference. 
   (a) Rearrange the formula to make V the subject.
   (b) Find the potential difference (V) in volts of the capacitor if the capacitance (C) is 10×10^{-6} farads and the energy stored (W) is 0.26 joules.
   (c) Check your solution.

Exam-style Questions

1. The 'Multiplier' is a variable used by economists to measure the effect of an increase in spending in an economy. One version of the Multiplier is $M = \dfrac{1}{S + P}$, where M is the Multiplier, S relates to savings and P relates to imports.

    (a) Calculate the value of M, the Multiplier, if $S = 0.2$ and $P = 0.1$.
    (b) Explain the effect on the size of M if the value of P increases.
    (c) Sometimes the above formula is used to calculate P. Rearrange the formula to make P its subject.

    JCHL 2013

2. A capacitor is a device which stores electricity. The formula $W = \tfrac{1}{2}CV^2$ gives the energy stored in the capacitor, where W is the energy, C is the capacitance and V is the voltage, and standard units are used throughout.

    (a) Find the amount of energy stored in a capacitor when $C = 2500$ and $V = 32$.
    (b) Write V in terms of W and C.

    JCHL 2012

KEY WORDS AND PHRASES

- Manipulate formula
- 'Opposite' operation

Chapter Summary 8

When manipulating formulae or equations, there are two general rules we can follow:

- When you do anything to change one side of a formula, you must do the same on the other side.
- To move or cancel a variable on one side of the formula, you must carry out the 'opposite' operation on both sides of the formula.

If solving a problem when the subject of the formula appears on both sides of the formula:

- Rearrange the formula to bring the subject variable to the LHS and all other variables to the RHS.
- Take out the common factor (i.e. the subject variable!).
- Continue rearranging the formula as normal.

Geometry 1

Chapter 9

Learning Outcomes

In this chapter, you will learn about:

- Theorems 1–6 and 9–10 and 13 (revision)
- The proofs of Theorems 4, 6 and 9
- Construction 3: How to construct a line perpendicular to a line l through a given point not on l
- Using congruent triangles and other methods to carry out proofs
- Theorems 11 and 12
- Construction 7: Division of a line segment into any number of equal segments without measuring it

Why do we study triangles?

One type of building which uses equilateral triangles is the **geodesic dome**. This was patented in 1954 by a remarkable man from America named Buckminster Fuller.

He wanted to build houses as efficiently as possible. He discovered that if a structure with the shape of a sphere was created from triangles, it would have great strength.

The famous geodesic dome in Montreal, Canada.

One of the ways Buckminster Fuller (known as 'Bucky') described the differences in strength between a rectangle and a triangle is that a triangle withstands much greater pressure and is much more rigid – in fact the triangle is twice as strong.

Section 9A Review

This section summarises the geometry we learned about in *Connect with Maths 1*.

Points and Lines

- A **plane** is an **infinite set of points**.
- This is the **line BC**. A line has no beginning or end. We name a line by any two points that it passes through. We could also call this **line CB**.

  We can also name a line by a single lower case letter (as in 'line l').

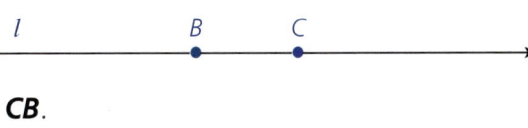

- **Points on the same line are called collinear points.**

  E, G and F are collinear points.

- This is the **ray [BD**. It starts at point B and passes through D on its way to infinity. The ray [BD can also be called the half-line [BD.

  This is ray [QP. It is not the same as ray [PQ.

- This is the **line segment [EF]**. It starts at E and finishes at F. [EF] and [FE] are the same line segment.

  Line segment [GH] is 6 cm long. We write this as |GH| = 6 cm.

- The point where two lines cross is called the **point of intersection** of the two lines.

  In this diagram, S is the point of intersection of lines AB and CD.

  We can write AB ∩ CD = {S}

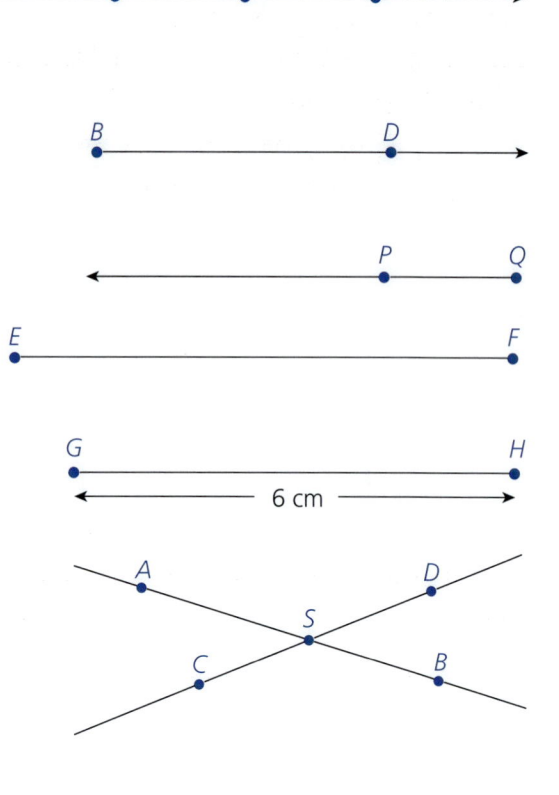

Angles

- Angles can be measured in degrees; |∠PQR| is between 0° and 360° where ∠PQR is any angle.
- The following are the main types of angle. Notice that a right angle has a special symbol.

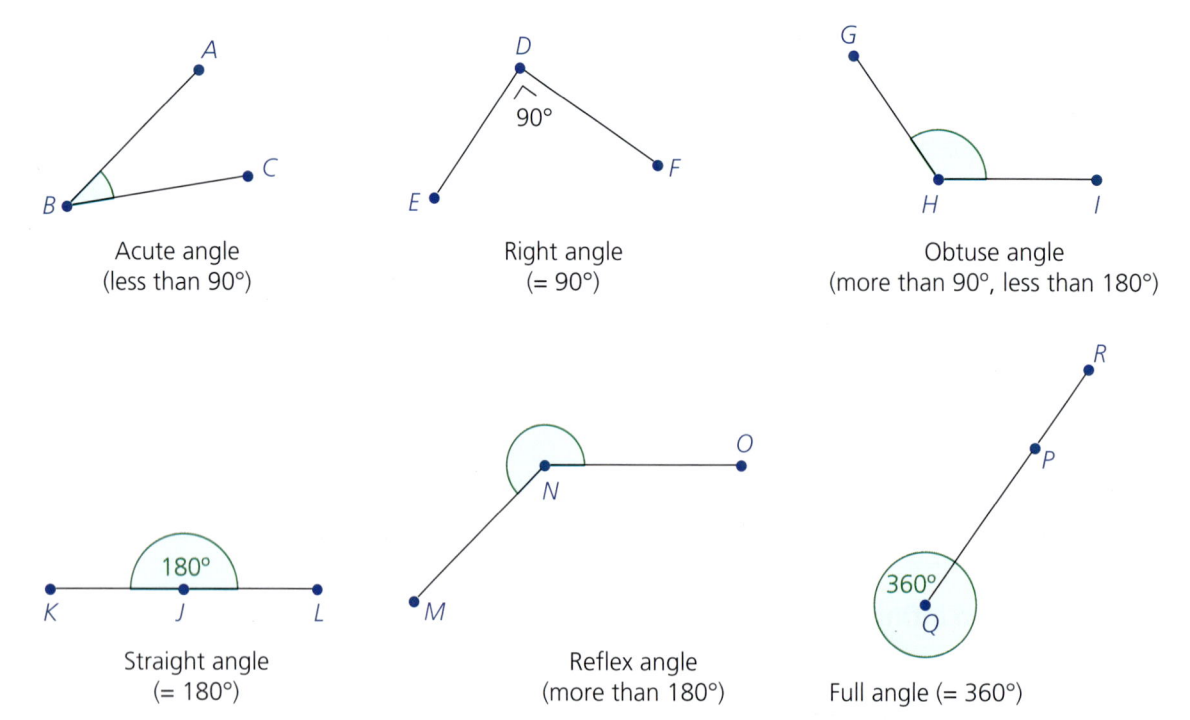

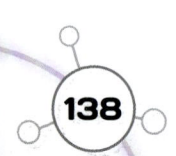

Acute angle (less than 90°)

Right angle (= 90°)

Obtuse angle (more than 90°, less than 180°)

Straight angle (= 180°)

Reflex angle (more than 180°)

Full angle (= 360°)

We sometimes use the term '**ordinary angle**' to mean an angle which is less than 180°. So acute angles or obtuse angles could also be called ordinary angles.

- If $|\angle 1| + |\angle 2| = 180°$, then $\angle 1$ and $\angle 2$ are called **supplementary** angles.

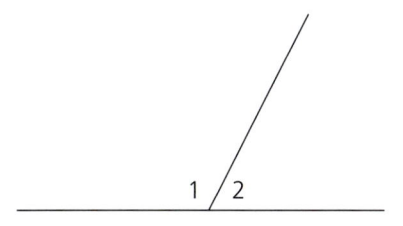

- The pairs of angles directly opposite each other when two lines intersect are called **vertically opposite angles**.

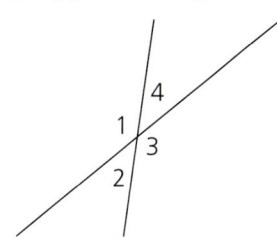

In the diagram there are two such pairs:

$\angle 1$ and $\angle 3$

$\angle 2$ and $\angle 4$.

Parallel Lines and Transversals

A transversal is a line that cuts across two or more lines.

The two parallel lines l and m are both crossed by a transversal t.

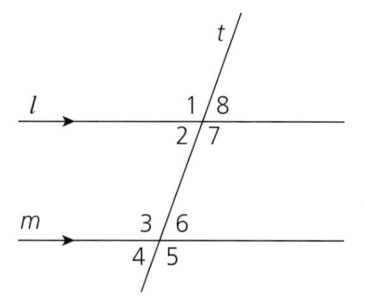

Interior angles

The angles 2, 7, 3 and 6 are between the parallel lines. We call these **interior** angles. There are two on each side of the transversal.

We found that the sum of two **interior angles** on the same side of the transversal is 180°, i.e. $|\angle 2| + |\angle 3| = 180°$ and $|\angle 7| + |\angle 6| = 180°$.

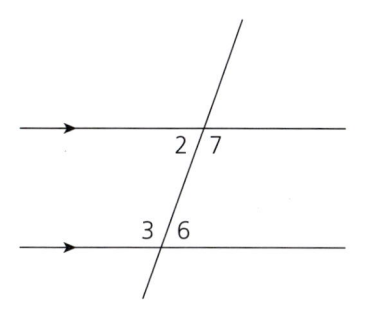

Corresponding angles

Here are all the corresponding angles from the diagram above.

When you see an 'F' shape formed, you have corresponding angles.

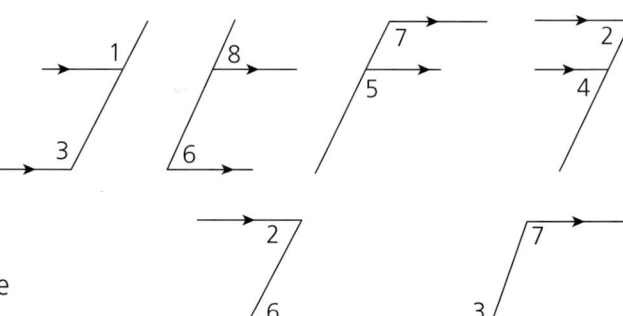

Alternate angles

When you see a 'Z' shape formed, you have alternate angles.

> **Key Point**
>
> Remember: Z shape – alternate angles
> F shape – corresponding angles
> X shape – vertically opposite angles.

Geometry 1

CONNECT WITH MATHS 2

Triangles

- Categories of triangle:
    1. By the number of equal sides:

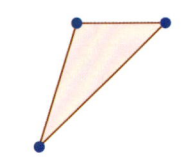

        Scalene (no sides equal) 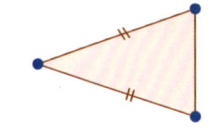   Isosceles (two sides equal) 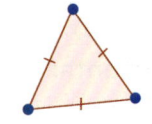   Equilateral (three sides equal)

    2. By the size of the biggest angle:

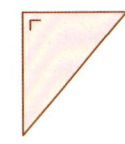

        Right-angled 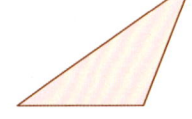   Obtuse-angled 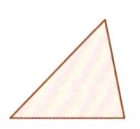   Acute-angled

- The three sides and three angles of a triangle are called its **six parts**. Any one of the angular points of a triangle may be called a **vertex**, and the opposite side is then called the **base**.
- The angle between two sides of a triangle is referred to as the angle **included** by these two sides, or simply, **the included angle**.
- Two triangles which are equal in every respect are called **congruent triangles**.

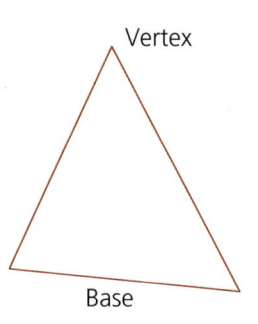

Vertex

Base

Polygons

- A **polygon** is a piece of the plane enclosed by a figure with many sides (a minimum of three, but it could be any number).

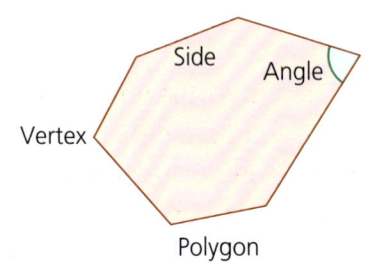

    Side
    Angle
    Vertex
    Polygon

We will be dealing mostly with **convex polygons**, where all the interior angles are ordinary angles.

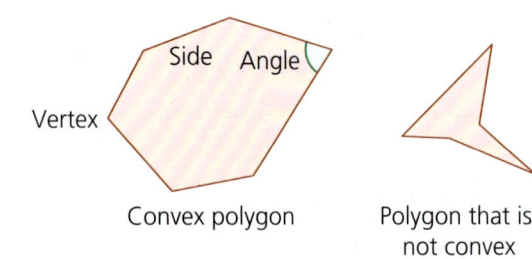

Side   Angle
Vertex

Convex polygon   Polygon that is not convex

- A **regular polygon** has all its sides and angles equal.

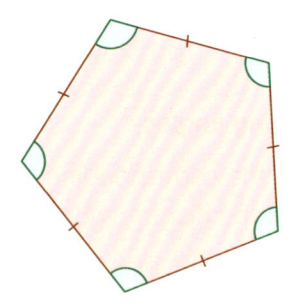

Regular polygon

- A **quadrilateral** is a four-sided polygon.

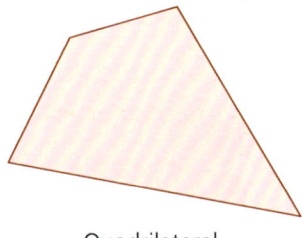

Quadrilateral

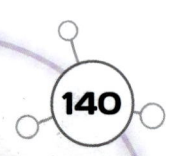

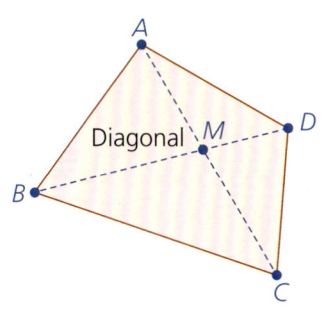

- Every quadrilateral has two **diagonals** which are lines from one vertex to the opposite vertex.

We name a quadrilateral by the letters of its four vertices in cyclical order, either clockwise or anti-clockwise. So this quadrilateral could be called *ABCD* or *BCDA* or *ADCB* etc.

- A **rectangle** is a quadrilateral having right angles at all four vertices.

- A **rhombus** is a quadrilateral having all four sides equal.

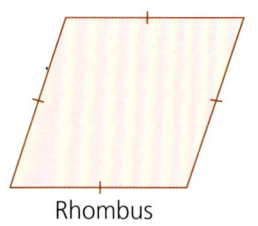

- A **square** is a rectangular rhombus.

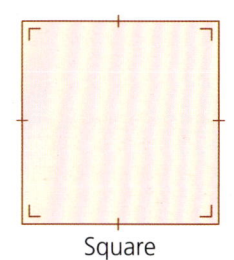

- A **parallelogram** is a quadrilateral for which both pairs of opposite sides are parallel.

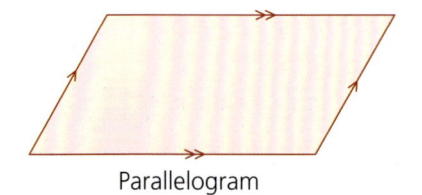

- A **kite** is a quadrilateral that has two adjacent sides of equal length and the other two sides of equal length.

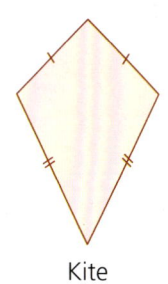

- A **trapezium** is a quadrilateral with two parallel sides.

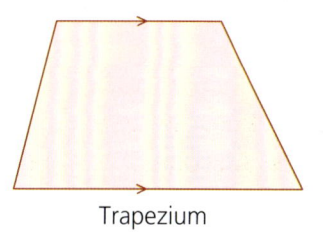

- Other polygons: a **pentagon** has five sides and a **hexagon** has six sides.

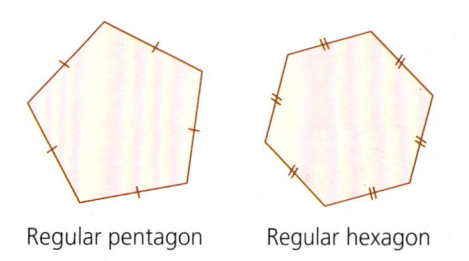

Axioms

- An **axiom** is a mathematical statement which we accept to be true without proof. We need axioms in order to start proving other statements called **theorems**.
- We have five axioms on our course:
  - **Axiom 1 (two points axiom)**: There is exactly one line through any two points.
  - **Axiom 2 (ruler axiom)**:

    (i) $|AB|$ is never negative.
    (ii) $|AB| = |BA|$
    (iii) $|AC| + |CB| = |AB|$

- **Axiom 3 (protractor axiom)**:
    (i) A straight angle has 180°.
    (ii) $|\angle a| = |\angle b| + |\angle c|$

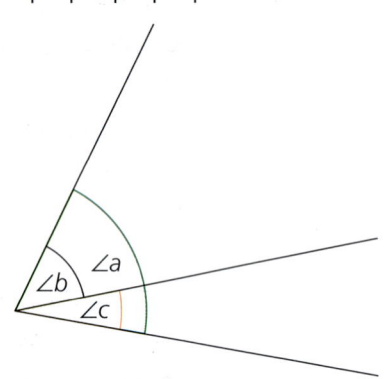

- **Axiom 4**:
    (i) Two triangles are congruent if the three sides of one triangle are equal to the three corresponding sides of the other (**SSS**).
    (ii) Two triangles are congruent if two sides and the included angle of one triangle are equal to the corresponding two sides and included angle of the other (**SAS**).
    (iii) Two triangles are congruent if two angles and the side between them are equal in size (**ASA**).

- **Axiom 5 (axiom of parallels)**: Given any line *l* and a point *P*, there is exactly one line through *P* that is parallel to *l*.

Theorems

- A **theorem** is a statement obtained by logical argument from an axiom (or other theorem).

In *Connect with Maths 1*, we studied the following theorems:

Theorem 1: Vertically opposite angles are equal in measure.

Theorem 2:
(i) In an isosceles triangle, the angles opposite the equal sides are equal.
(ii) Conversely, if two angles in a triangle are equal, then the triangle is isosceles.

Theorem 3:
(i) If a transversal makes equal alternate angles on two lines, then the lines are parallel.
(ii) Conversely, if two lines are parallel, then any transversal will make equal alternate angles with them.

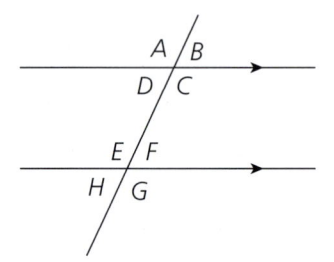

Theorem 4: The angles in any triangle add to 180°.

Theorem 5: Two lines are parallel if and only if for any transversal, corresponding angles are equal.

Theorem 6: Each exterior angle of a triangle is equal to the sum of the two interior opposite angles.

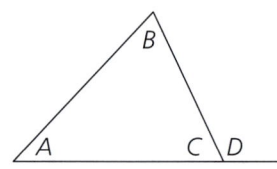

For this triangle, we say that $|\angle A| + |\angle B| = |\angle D|$, where $\angle D$ is the exterior angle and $\angle A$ and $\angle B$ are the interior opposite angles.

Theorem 9: In a parallelogram, opposite sides are equal, and opposite angles are equal.

Theorem 9 (Converse):
(i) If the opposite angles of a convex quadrilateral are equal, then it is a parallelogram.
(ii) If the opposite sides of a convex quadrilateral are equal, then it is a parallelogram.

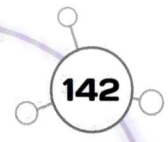

Theorem 10: The diagonals of a parallelogram bisect each other.

Theorem 10 (Converse):

If the diagonals of a quadrilateral bisect one another, then the quadrilateral is a parallelogram.

Theorem 13: If two triangles are similar, then their sides are proportional, in order (and converse).

Theorem 14: Theorem of Pythagoras. The square of the hypotenuse in a right-angled triangle is equal to the sum of the squares of the other two sides.

Theorem 15: (Converse of Pythagoras) If the square of one side of a triangle is the sum of the squares of the other two, then the angle opposite the first side is a right angle.

Proposition 9: If two right-angled triangles have hypotenuse and another side equal in length, respectively, then they are congruent (**RHS**).

Theorem 19:

Corollary 3: Each angle in a semi-circle is a right angle.

Corollary 4: If the angle standing on a chord [BC] at some point of the circle is a right angle, then [BC] is a diameter.

Constructions

In *Connect with Maths 1*, we studied the following constructions:

- **Construction 1:** Use of compass to bisect an angle
- **Construction 2:** Use of compass to draw the perpendicular bisector of a line segment
- **Construction 4:** Line perpendicular to a given line l, passing through a given point on l (two methods: ruler and compass or ruler and set-square)
- **Construction 5:** Line parallel to a given line, through a given point
- **Construction 6:** Division of a line segment into two or three equal segments without measuring it
- **Construction 8:** Line segment of a given length on a given ray
- **Construction 9:** Angle of a given number of degrees with a given ray as one arm
- **Construction 10:** Triangle, given lengths of three sides
- **Construction 11:** Triangle, given SAS data
- **Construction 12:** Triangle, given ASA data
- **Construction 13:** Right-angled triangle, given length of hypotenuse and one other side
- **Construction 14:** Right-angled triangle, given one side and one of the acute angles
- **Construction 15:** Rectangle given side lengths.

Properties of Parallelograms

We now have the following properties of all parallelograms.

- Opposite sides are parallel (the definition of a parallelogram)
- Opposite sides are equal
- Opposite angles are equal
- Adjacent angles add to 180°
- The diagonals bisect each other
- A diagonal divides the parallelogram into two congruent triangles.

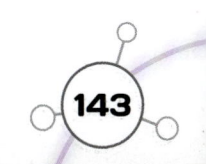

9 Transformations

Axial symmetry

Axial symmetry of an object is the reflection of that object through a line. It is also known as a mirror reflection.

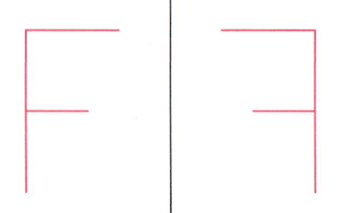

Axis of symmetry

The axis of symmetry of a shape is the line that divides the shape into two symmetrical parts such that each side is the mirror image of the other.

Translation

A translation moves every point in the plane the same distance in the same direction.

Central symmetry

Central symmetry is the reflection of an object through a point.

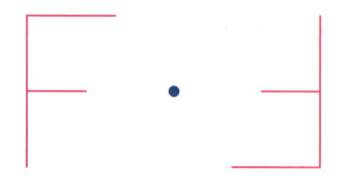

Centre of symmetry

Some shapes are mapped onto themselves under central symmetry in a point. The point P is called the centre of symmetry of the shape.

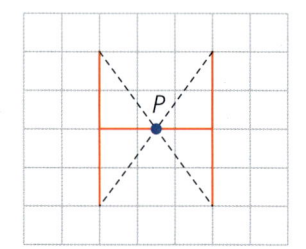

The **orientation** of an object after a transformation is the relative direction in which it is facing.

See how these three transformations change the orientation of an object:

Axial symmetry (back-to-front)	Central symmetry (upside down and back-to-front)	Translation (no change)

Geometry 1

144

CONNECT WITH MATHS 2

Rotation

To '**rotate**' means to move in a circle around (about) a point.

This diagram shows a triangle *ABC* and its image, *A'B'C'*, by an **anti-clockwise** rotation of **90°** about a **point O**.

Every point of the triangle *ABC* turns through the same angle (90° in this case).

This means that $|\angle AOA'| = 90°$, $|\angle BOB'| = 90°$ and $|\angle COC'| = 90°$.

When we want to describe a rotation, we must name three things:

- The **centre of rotation**
- The **angle turned**
- The **direction** (clockwise or anti-clockwise).

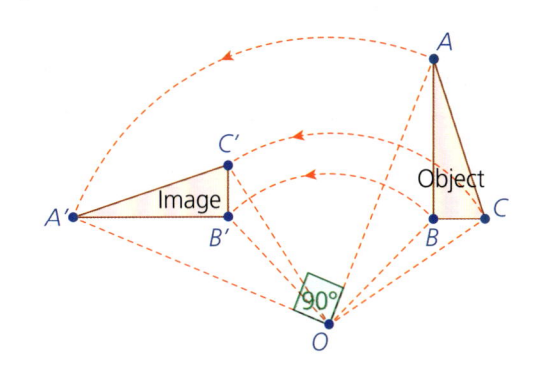

> All of the four transformations (axial symmetry, translation, central symmetry and rotation) preserve length, area and size of angle.

In the next activity, we will revise some of the main ideas we explored in *Connect with Maths 1*.

Activity 9.1

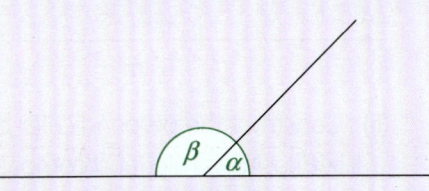

1. (i) What is $|\angle \alpha| + |\angle \beta|$ in the diagram?

   (ii) Copy and complete the following sentence:

   'Angles α and β are known as _____ angles'.

2. The diagram shows two lines intersecting.

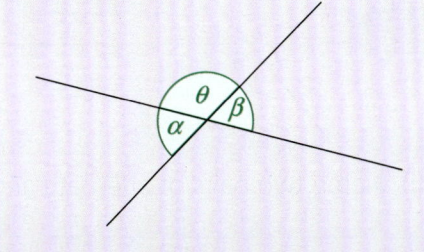

   (i) Copy and complete the following sentence: 'Angles α and β are known as _____ angles'.

   (ii) What is $|\angle \alpha| + |\angle \theta|$?

   (iii) What is $|\angle \theta| + |\angle \beta|$?

   (iv) Prove that $|\angle \alpha| = |\angle \beta|$.

3. Prove that $a + b + c = 360$.

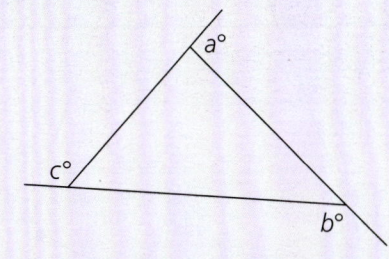

4. Draw separate diagrams to show a scalene triangle, an isosceles triangle and an equilateral triangle. Give a brief description of each.

5 (i) Draw a sketch of the triangle ABC where |AB| = 6 cm, |BC| = 8 cm and |CA| = 7 cm.

(ii) Construct the triangle ABC using a ruler and compass.

6 (i) Draw a sketch of the triangle TUV where |∠TUV| = 47°, |UV| = 8 cm and |∠TVU| = 53°.

(ii) Construct the triangle TUV using a ruler and protractor.

7 (i) Draw a sketch of the triangle PQR where |PQ| = 8 cm, |∠PQR| = 55° and |QR| = 10 cm.

(ii) Construct the triangle PQR using a ruler, compass and protractor.

8 (i) What are congruent triangles?

(ii) Name the three conditions where we can assume that two non-right-angled triangles are congruent.

(iii) Give a reason why each of the following pairs of triangles can be assumed to be congruent.

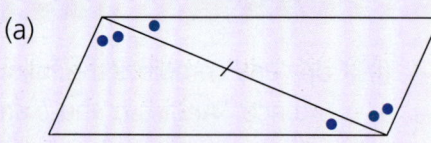

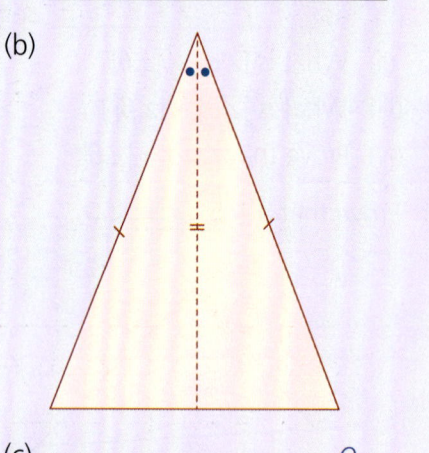

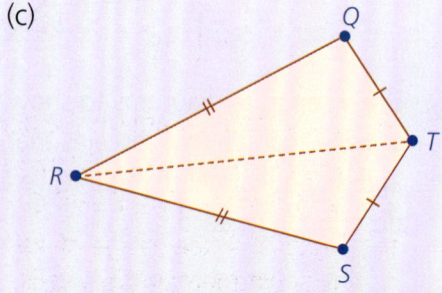

(a)

(b)

(c)

9 (i) Construct an angle ABC where |∠ABC| = 70° using a ruler and protractor.

(ii) Now construct the bisector of ∠ABC using only a ruler and compass. Show all your construction marks.

10 ABC is an isosceles triangle with |AB| = |BC|. BD is the bisector of ∠ABC.

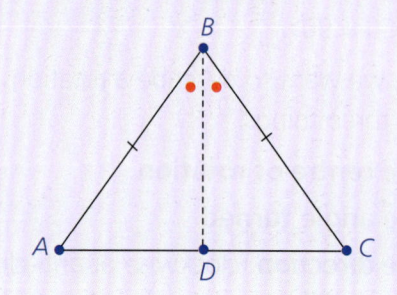

(i) Prove that the triangles ABD and BDC are congruent.

(ii) Hence, prove that |∠BAD| = |∠BCD|.

(iii) State, in your own words, what you have proved about the angles in an isosceles triangle.

(iv) What type of angles are ∠ADB and ∠CDB? Explain your answer.

11 (i) Construct a line segment [AB] such that |AB| = 6 cm.

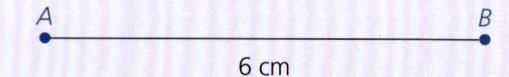

A ———————————— B
           6 cm

(ii) Construct the perpendicular bisector of [AB] using a ruler and compass only.

12 The diagram shows two parallel lines m and n with line t a transversal of them.

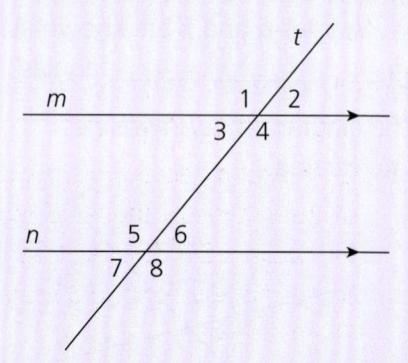

(i) Name two pairs of alternate angles.

(ii) What do you know about these alternate angles?

(iii) Name four pairs of corresponding angles.

(iv) What do you know about these corresponding angles?

(v) Name two pairs of interior angles.

(vi) Given that $|\angle 5| = 130°$, find the size of all the other angles.

13 (i) Draw a rough sketch of the rectangle ABCD, where $|AB| = 6$ cm and $|BC| = 8$ cm.

(ii) Construct the rectangle ABCD accurately.

14 Windows are sometimes made with a pointed arch.

Mary is designing such an arched window.

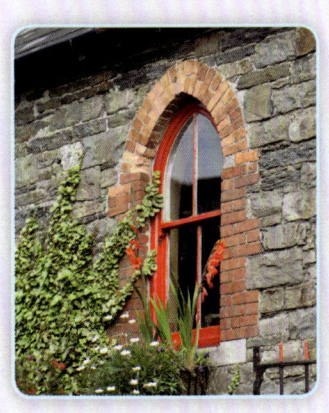

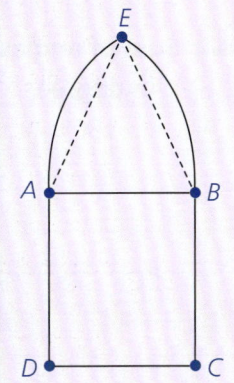

She has drawn an outline of the window as shown in the diagram.

ABCD is a rectangle.

The centre for arc AE is B and the centre for arc EB is A.

$|AD| = 2.5$ m and $|DC| = 1.5$ m.

(i) Show that $|\angle EAB| = 60°$.

(ii) Construct an accurate scale drawing of the outline of the window, using the scale 1 : 25. That is, 1 cm on your diagram should represent 25 cm in reality.

15 (i) Describe, in your own words, what a parallelogram is.

KLMN is a parallelogram. Some angles are marked 1, 2, 3 and 4.

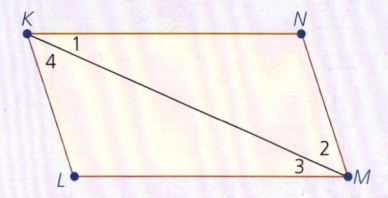

(ii) Name two pairs of alternate angles.

(iii) Prove that the triangles KMN and KLM are congruent.

16 (i) Draw the triangle with vertices A(0, 0), B(3, 5) and C(5, 4) in a co-ordinate plane.

(ii) Draw A'B'C', the image of the triangle ABC, by a rotation of 90° anti-clockwise about A.

(iii) Write down the co-ordinates of A', B' and C'.

(iv) Draw A"B"C", the image of the triangle ABC, by a rotation of 180° about A.

(v) Write down the co-ordinates of A", B" and C".

17 Copy the diagram into your copy and construct the image of the 'T' shape by:

(i) a rotation of 90° anti-clockwise

(ii) a rotation of 180°

(iii) a rotation of 270° anti-clockwise.

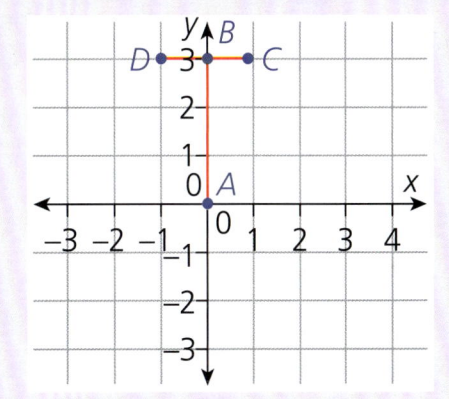

18 (i) Copy the diagram on the next page into your copy. Mark in the co-ordinates of A, B and C.

(ii) Draw PQR, the image of ABC, by axial symmetry in the x-axis.

(iii) Draw XYZ, the image of ABC, by central symmetry in the y-axis.

(iv) What other transformation would give XYZ as the image of ABC?

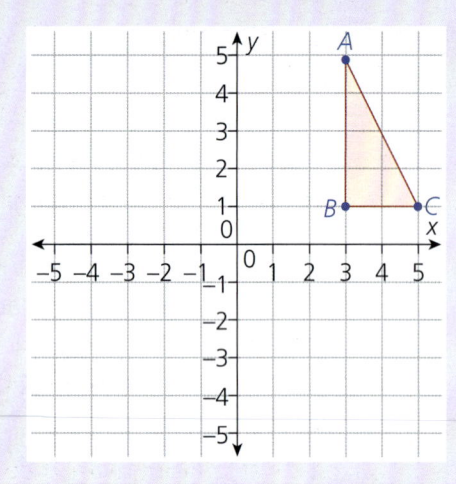

19 Each of the three hands labelled A, B and C shown below is an image of the hand shown in the box on the left under a transformation. For each of A, B and C, state what the transformation is (translation, central symmetry, axial symmetry or rotation) and in the case of a rotation, state the angle and direction.

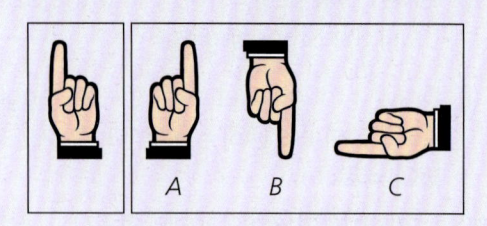

20 (i) Write down the sum of the angles of a triangle in (a) degrees (b) right angles.

(ii) Write down the sum of the angles of a quadrilateral in (a) degrees (b) right angles.

(iii) (a) Copy and complete the following table, to show the sum of the angles of various polygons.

Name of polygon	Number of sides	Sum of angles in degrees	Sum of angles in terms of right angles
triangle	3	180°	2
quadrilateral	4		
pentagon	5		
hexagon	6		
heptagon	7		
octagon	8		

(b) Justify that there is a linear relationship between the number of sides of a polygon and the sum of its angles in terms of right angles.

(c) Draw a graph of this relationship on a copy of the grid.

(d) Derive a formula for the number of right angles in an n-sided polygon.

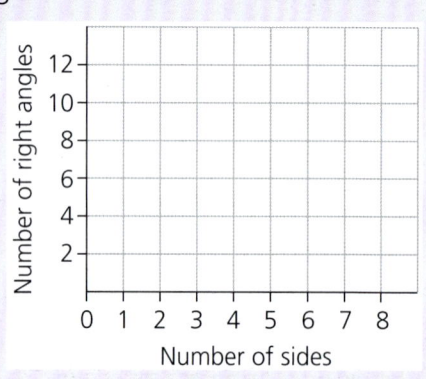

Section 9B Proofs of Theorems 4, 6 and 9

Mathematicians are always seeking to prove statements that they suspect are true. This is the essence of mathematics. They form a **conjecture** (an opinion) and they are pretty sure that it is correct, but they need to **prove** it.

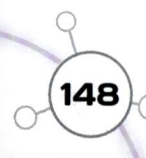

Connections

Not every conjecture turns out to be true. In the Middle Ages, it was believed that the function $f(n) = n^2 + n + 41$ always gave a prime number result whenever n is a number. However, there are numbers n for which $n^2 + n + 41$ is not prime. Can you find the first one?

For example, we are pretty sure that the angles in any triangle add to 180° because we have measured lots of angles in triangles in the past. But we can never do this for every triangle, so we want to prove it is true for every triangle.

The following is how we work towards a **proof**.

1. We have statements which we accept as true to get us started. These statements are known as **axioms**. On our course, we have five axioms. We also have some **definitions**. These axioms and definitions are the foundations of our 'geometry wall'.

2. We prove new statements, called **theorems**, one by one in order, starting with Theorem 1. These theorems are the bricks in the geometry wall. We use our **deductive logic** as the 'mortar' to bond the theorems together.

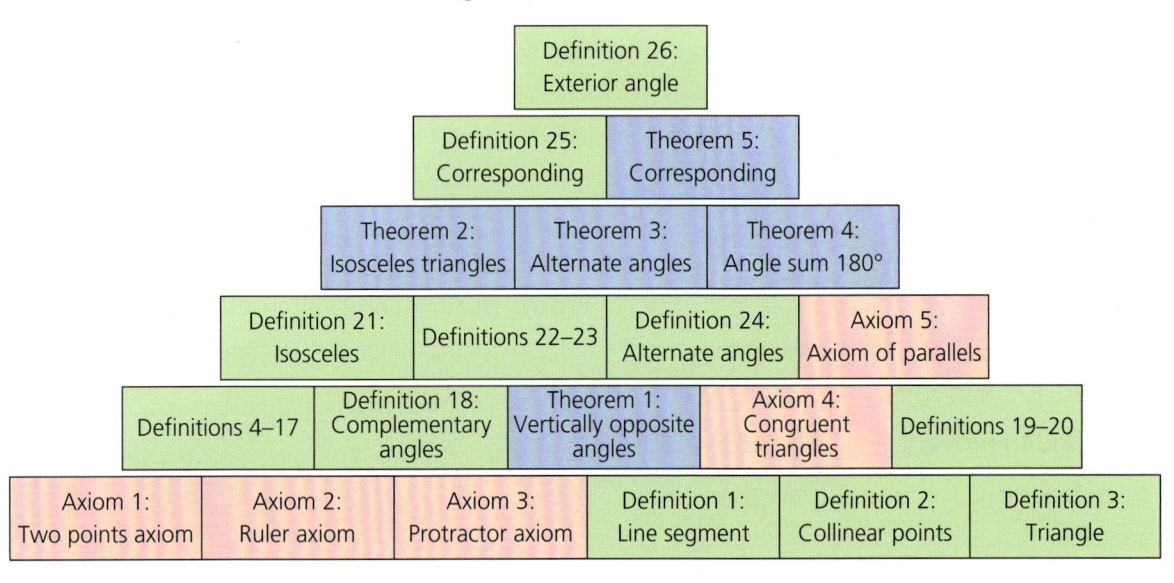

```
                    Definition 26:
                    Exterior angle
              Definition 25:    Theorem 5:
              Corresponding    Corresponding
         Theorem 2:      Theorem 3:       Theorem 4:
     Isosceles triangles  Alternate angles  Angle sum 180°
      Definition 21:                  Definition 24:      Axiom 5:
       Isosceles   Definitions 22–23  Alternate angles  Axiom of parallels
                Definition 18:    Theorem 1:        Axiom 4:
 Definitions 4–17  Complementary  Vertically opposite  Congruent   Definitions 19–20
                     angles         angles          triangles
  Axiom 1:       Axiom 2:       Axiom 3:      Definition 1:   Definition 2:    Definition 3:
Two points axiom  Ruler axiom  Protractor axiom  Line segment   Collinear points    Triangle
```

3. If one statement leads directly to another statement, we say that the first statement **implies** the second statement.
   e.g. The statement 'John is Mary's father' **implies** 'Mary is John's daughter'.
   We use the symbol '⇒' for the word 'implies'.

4. We continue to build up our knowledge using previous theorems.

5. Some theorems have **corollaries**, which are statements which come directly from the theorem, but which are not important enough to be called a theorem.

6. A theorem can have a **converse**, which is the statement read backwards.

   e.g. Theorem 2: In an isosceles triangle, the angles opposite the equal sides are equal.
   Converse of Theorem 2: If two angles are equal, then the triangle is isosceles.

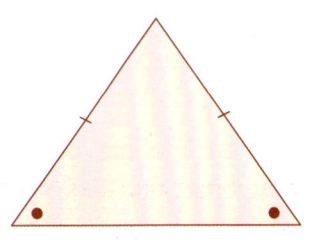

7. The converse of a statement is not always true. For example:

   Statement: If Rex is a dog,
   then Rex is a mammal. (True)

   Converse: If Rex is a mammal,
   then Rex is a dog. (False)

We have five formal proofs to learn in our course: Theorems 4, 6, 9, 14 and 19.

However, we have learned some informally already. For example in Activity 9.1 we proved Theorems 1 and 2.

The following is the formal proof of Theorem 4. Notice the steps required:

- The statement of the theorem
- Diagram
- Given (what you know about the situation)
- Required to prove
- Construction (if necessary)
- Proof.

THEOREM 4 (formal proof required)

The angles in any triangle add to 180°.

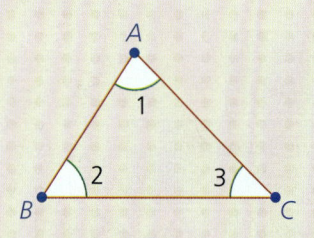

Given: Any triangle ABC with angles marked 1, 2 and 3.

Required to prove: $|\angle 1| + |\angle 2| + |\angle 3| = 180°$.

Construction: Through A draw the line $DE \parallel BC$.

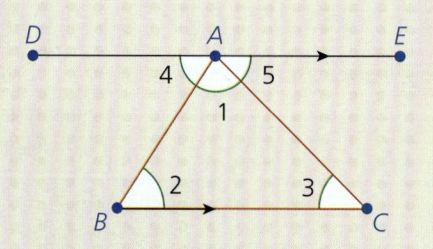

Proof: $|\angle 2| = |\angle 4|$ ... alternate angles
$|\angle 3| = |\angle 5|$ ... alternate angles
$\Rightarrow |\angle 2| + |\angle 3| = |\angle 4| + |\angle 5|$
$\Rightarrow |\angle 1| + |\angle 2| + |\angle 3| = |\angle 1| + |\angle 4| + |\angle 5|$
$= 180°$
$\Rightarrow |\angle 1| + |\angle 2| + |\angle 3| = 180°$ ... QED

Note: QED stands for the Latin words 'quod erat demonstrandum' which means 'which was required to be shown'. We put this at the end of a proof to signal that we have completed it.

The word 'show' in a question generally means 'prove'.

We can now prove Theorems 6 and 9.

THEOREM 6 (formal proof required)

Each exterior angle of a triangle equals the sum of the two interior opposite angles.

Given: Triangle ABC with $[BC]$ extended to D. The angles marked 1, 2, 3 and 4 are as shown in the diagram.

Required to prove: $|\angle 4| = |\angle 1| + |\angle 2|$

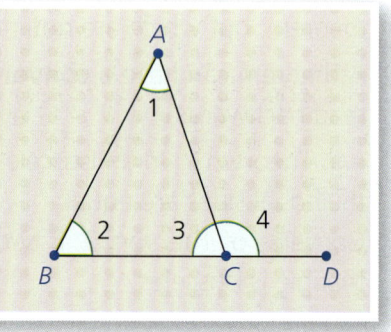

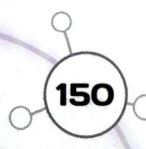

Proof: $|\angle 1| + |\angle 2| + |\angle 3| = 180°$ ... Theorem 4

$|\angle 4| + |\angle 3| = 180°$ ... supplementary angles

$\Rightarrow |\angle 1| + |\angle 2| + |\angle 3| = |\angle 4| + |\angle 3|$

$\Rightarrow |\angle 1| + |\angle 2| = |\angle 4|$ ... subtract $|\angle 3|$ from each side ... QED

THEOREM 9 (formal proof required)

In a parallelogram, opposite sides are equal and opposite angles are equal.

Given: A parallelogram *ABCD*.

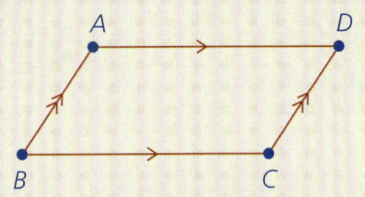

Required to prove: (i) $|AB| = |CD|$ and $|AD| = |BC|$

(ii) $|\angle ABC| = |\angle ADC|$ and $|\angle BAD| = |\angle BCD|$

Construction: Join *AC*. Mark in angles 1, 2, 3 and 4.

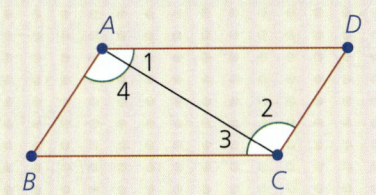

Proof: In the two triangles *ADC* and *ABC*

$|\angle 1| = |\angle 3|$ ... alternate angles

$|AC| = |AC|$ ... common side

$|\angle 2| = |\angle 4|$ ... alternate angles

$\Rightarrow$ triangles *ADC* and *ABC* are congruent by ASA

$\Rightarrow |AB| = |CD|$ and $|AD| = |BC|$ and $|\angle ADC| = |\angle ABC|$

By adding equal angles, we also get $|\angle BAD| = |\angle BCD|$ ... QED

COROLLARY TO THEOREM 9

A diagonal divides a parallelogram into two congruent triangles.

Proof: In the proof of the theorem we proved that triangles *ADC* and *ABC* are congruent by *ASA*. ... QED

THEOREM 9 (CONVERSE)

(i) If the opposite angles of a convex quadrilateral are equal, then it is a parallelogram.

(ii) If the opposite sides of a convex quadrilateral are equal, then it is a parallelogram.

Activity 9.2

1 In each of the following diagrams, ABCD is a parallelogram. Find the angles α, β and γ in each case.

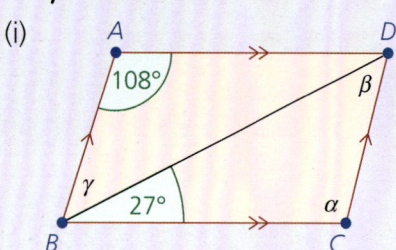

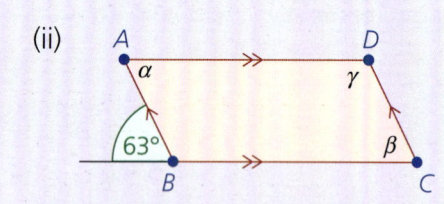

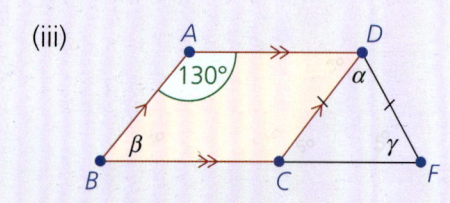

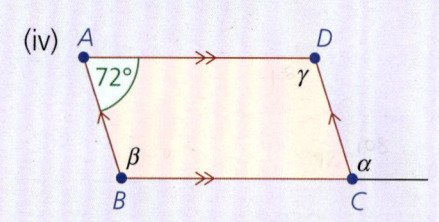

(i)

(ii)

(iii)

(iv)

2 The diagram shows a parallelogram and one exterior angle. Find the value of x and the value of y.

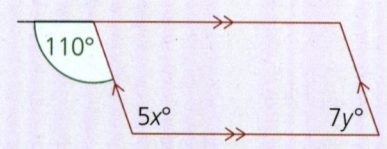

3 ABCD is a parallelogram with its diagonals intersecting at E. Some angles are marked 1, 2, 3 and 4.

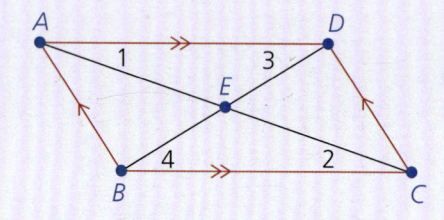

(i) Prove that the triangles ADE and EBC are congruent.

(ii) Hence, show that $|AE| = |EC|$ and that $|BE| = |ED|$.

(iii) State, in your own words, the theorem that you have just proved.

4 STUV is a parallelogram where $|SV| = 2 \times |ST|$. M is the mid-point of $[TU]$. Angles 1 to 9 are marked.

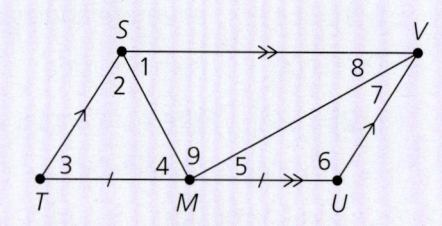

(i) Name another line segment which has length equal to $|SV|$.

(ii) Name three line segments which have length equal to $|ST|$.

(iii) Name two isosceles triangles in the diagram.

(iv) Name four pairs of equal angles, giving a reason in each case.

(v) Prove that SM bisects $\angle TSV$.

(vi) Does MV bisect $\angle SVU$? Give a reason for your answer.

(vii) Prove that $|\angle SMV| = 90°$.

5 (i) Prove that the three angles of a triangle sum to 180°.

(ii) In the diagram, *BE* is the bisector of ∠*ABC*. *D* is any point on *BE*.
DY ⊥ *AB* and *DZ* ⊥ *BC*.

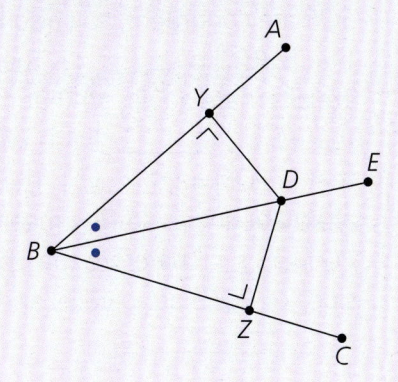

(a) Prove that the triangles *BYD* and *BDZ* are congruent.

(b) Hence, prove that |*DY*| = |*DZ*|.

(c) What have you proved about the relationship between any point on the bisector of an angle and the arms of the angle?

6 *ABC* is an isosceles triangle with |*AB*| = |*AC*|. |∠*ABC*| = 59° and *CD* ⊥ *AB*.

Show that |∠*BAC*| = 2 × |∠*DCB*|.

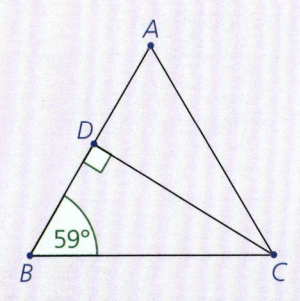

7 The diagram shows an isosceles triangle *PQR*, with |*PQ*| = |*PR*|. *MN* is parallel to *PQ*.

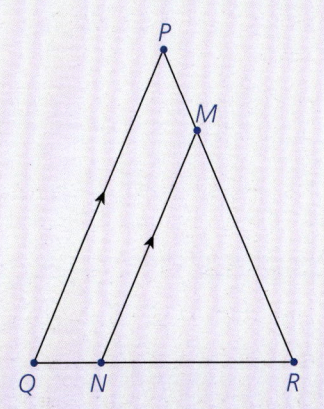

(i) Name three pairs of equal angles, giving a reason in each case.

(ii) Prove that the triangle *MNR* is isosceles.

8 (i) Explain the words axiom, theorem, converse and corollary.

(ii) Prove that opposite sides and opposite angles of a parallelogram are equal.

(iii) The diagram shows a parallelogram *ABCD* with diagonal [*AC*].

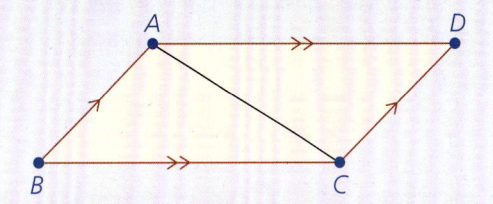

Prove that the diagonal divides the parallelogram into two congruent triangles.

(iv) Show by a diagram that the converse of the statement in part (iii) is not true, i.e. show that if a diagonal of a quadrilateral divides it into two congruent triangles, it does not mean that the quadrilateral has to be a parallelogram.

9 The diagram shows a quadrilateral with four sides of equal length. The mid-points of two of its sides are joined with a straight line.

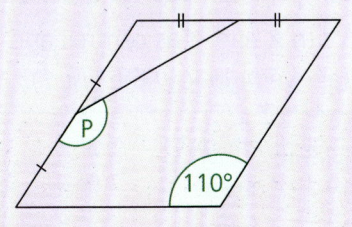

Calculate the size of angle *P*. Show how you worked out your answer.

10. The quadrilateral *PQRS* has its opposite sides equal. That is, |*PS*| = |*QR*| and |*PQ*| = |*SR*|. We want to prove that *PQRS* is a parallelogram.

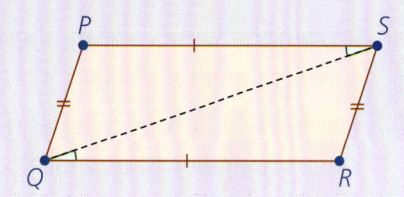

   (i) Draw the triangles *PQS* and *QRS* separately.
   (ii) Mark in all the parts in each that are equal with similar markings.
   (iii) Prove that the triangles *PQS* and *SQR* are congruent.
   (iv) Copy and complete the following statement:

   'I know that the triangles *PQS* and *SQR* are congruent, so I also know that |∠*PSQ*| = |∠_____|. These are alternate angles so that means that *PS* ∥ _____. I also know that |∠*PQS*| = |∠_____|. These are alternate angles so that means that *PQ* ∥ _____. Therefore the opposite sides of *PQRS* are parallel and so it is a _____.'

Section 9C Constructions 3 and 4

In this section, we look at how to construct a line perpendicular to a given line through a given point.

This construction was already shown in *Connect with Maths 1*.

Construction 4

To construct a line perpendicular to a given line *l*, through a point **on** *l*.

Method

1. With *P* as centre and any radius, draw two arcs intersecting the line *l* at *X* and *Y*.

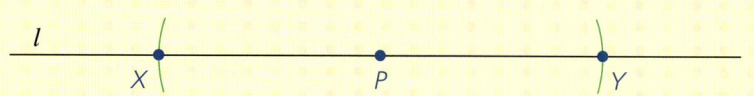

2. Set your compass to draw an arc longer than |*PX*|.

3. With *X* and *Y* as centres and the same radius, draw two more arcs intersecting at *Q* (above or below the line *l*).

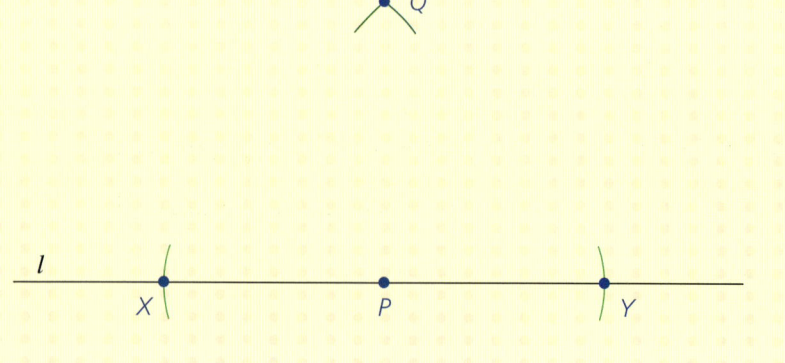

4. Join Q to P. The line QP is perpendicular to *l*.

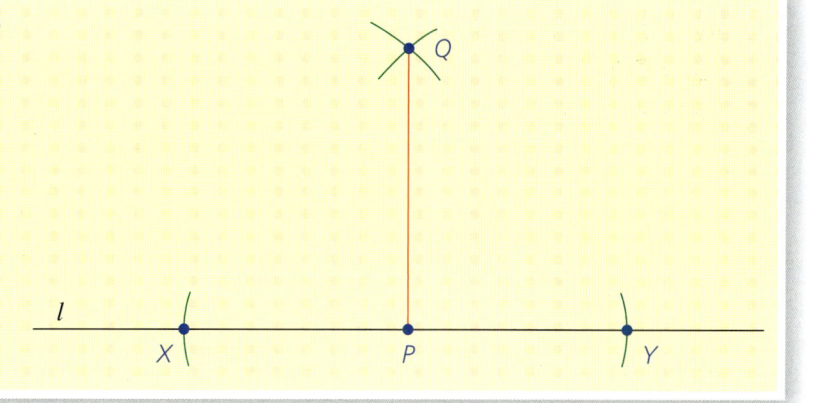

You can also use a set-square and straight-edge to perform the above construction.
We now look at the following construction which is for Higher Level only.

Construction 3

To construct a line perpendicular to a given line *l*, through a point **not on** *l*.

Method 1: Using a straight-edge and set-square

1. Given a line *l* and point P not on *l*. (P could be above or below *l*.)

2. Place the straight-edge (or ruler) along line *l* and place the set-square on the straight-edge.

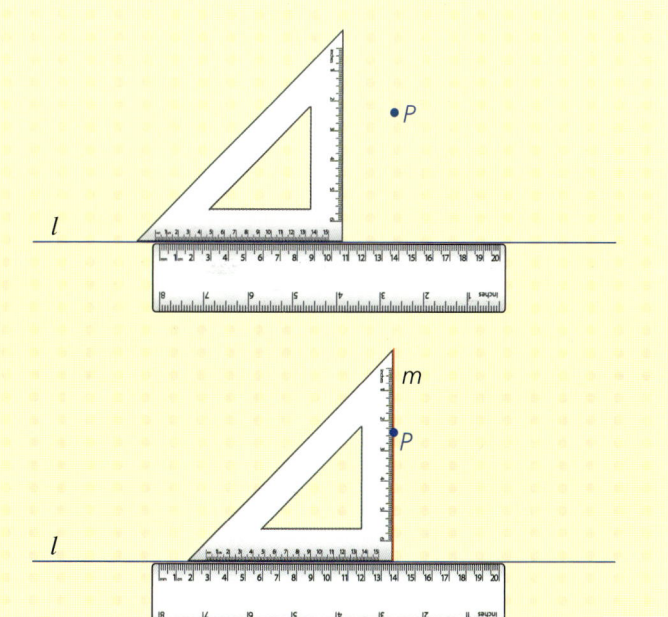

3. Move the set-square along the straight-edge until it just reaches the point P. Draw the line *m* through P using the edge of the set-square.

m is the required line perpendicular to *l* through point P.

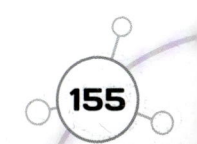

Method 2: Using a straight-edge and compass

1. Given a line *l* and point *P* not on *l*.
   (*P* could be above or below *l*.)

2. Using *P* as centre and any radius, draw two arcs to cut *l* at *R* and *S*.

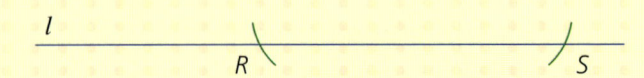

3. Using *R* as centre and the same radius, draw an arc on the opposite side of *l* to *P*. Using *S* as centre and the same radius, draw another arc to intersect the first arc at *Q*.

4. Join *PQ*.

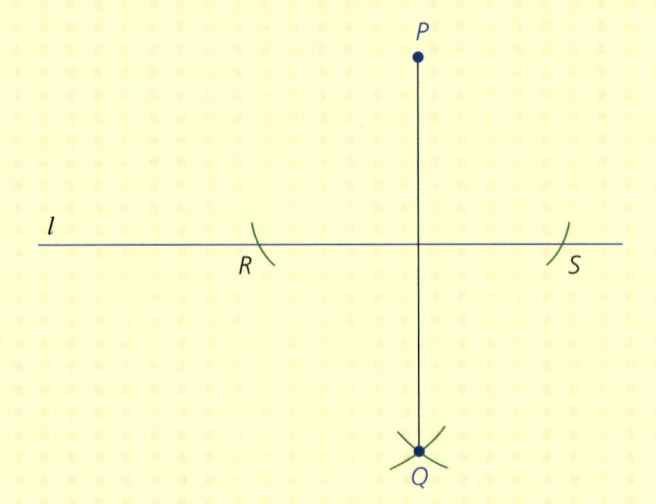

PQ is then the required perpendicular to *l*.

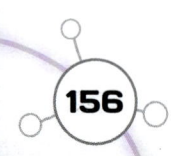

Activity 9.3

In questions 1–4, copy the diagram into your copy and construct the line segment [PQ] perpendicular to AB using only a straight-edge and compasses.

1.

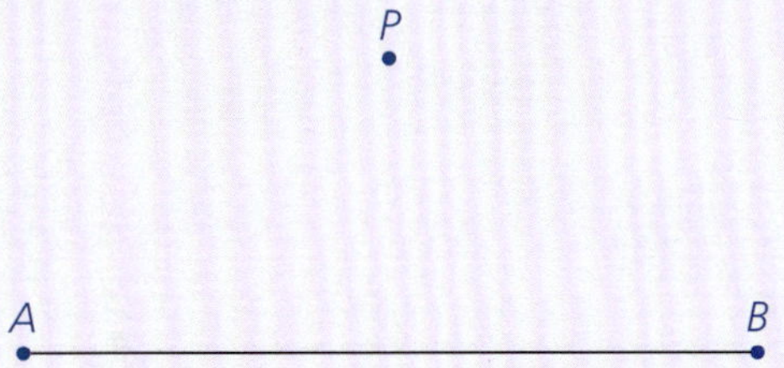

2.

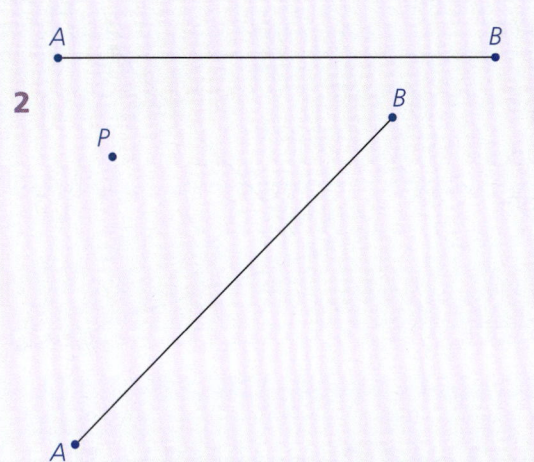

3.

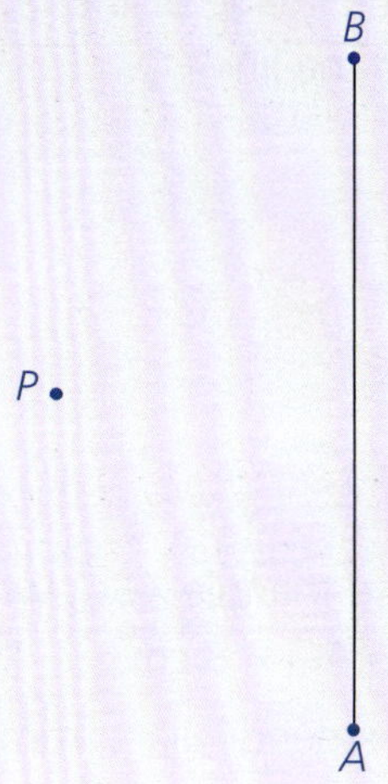

4.

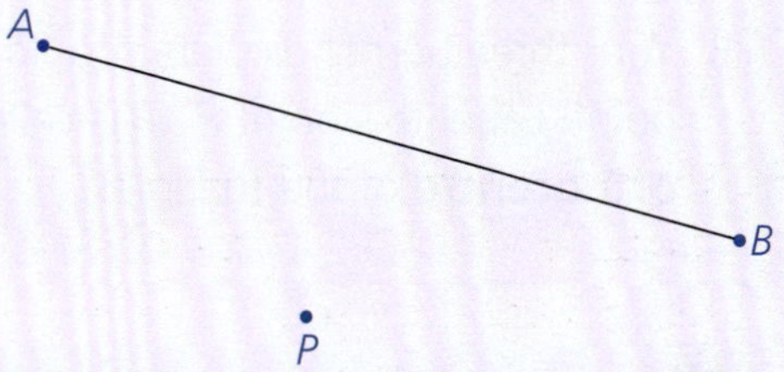

5. Repeat the constructions in questions 1–4 above, using a straight-edge and set-square.

6. The point P ∈ AB. 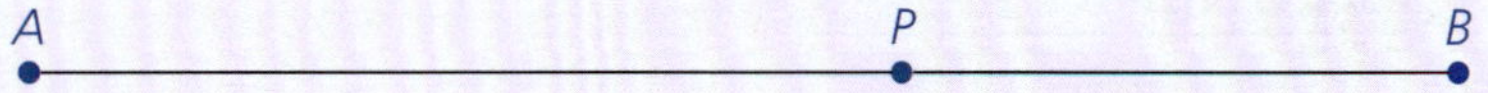
   (i) Copy the diagram into your copy.
   (ii) Draw a line perpendicular to AB through P.

7. (i) Copy the diagram into your copy.
   (ii) Construct perpendiculars from the points D, C and E onto AB using a straight-edge and set-square.
   (iii) Use the construction in part (ii) to construct the image of the triangle DEC by axial symmetry in the line AB.

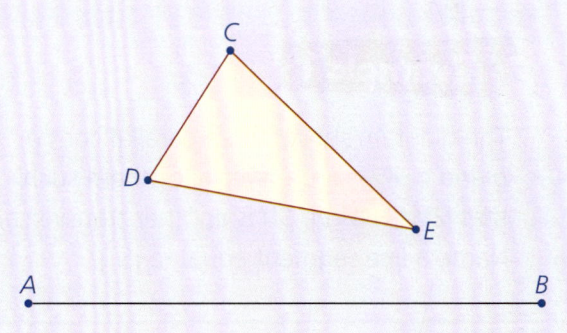

8. (i) Copy the diagram into your copy.
   (ii) Construct perpendiculars from the points D, C and E onto AB using a straight-edge and set-square.
   (iii) Use the construction in part (ii) to construct the image of the triangle DEC by axial symmetry in the line AB.

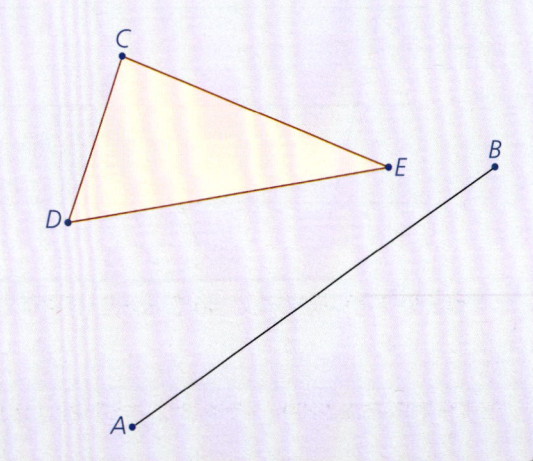

9. (i) Copy the diagram into your copy.
   (ii) Construct the image of the 'F' shape by axial symmetry in the line PQ.

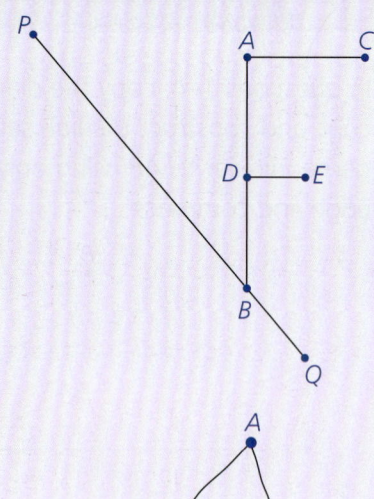

10. (i) Construct the triangle ABC, where |AB| = 6 cm, |BC| = 7 cm, |AC| = 8 cm.
    (ii) Construct perpendiculars from each of the vertices of the triangle onto the opposite sides.
    (iii) Your three perpendiculars should meet at one point. Label this point P. (P is called the **orthocentre** of the triangle.)

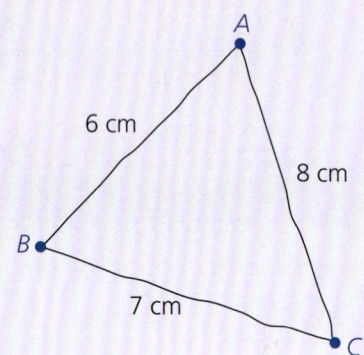

Section 9D Theorems 11, 12 and 13 and Construction 7

THEOREM 11

If three parallel lines cut off equal segments on some transversal line, then they will cut off equal segments on some other transversal.

Example 1

The diagram shows three parallel lines a, b and c. ZV is a transversal of them such that |ZW| = |WV|. SU is another transversal. Name a line segment equal to |ST|.

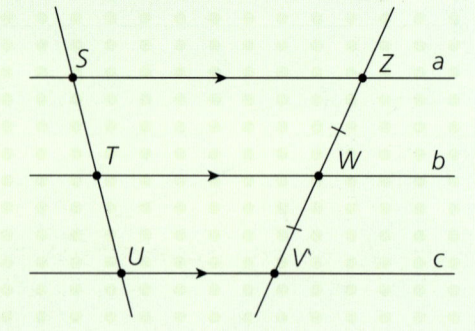

Solution

The three parallel lines a, b and c cut off equal intercepts on transversal ZV

∴ they cut equal intercepts off the transversal SU.

∴ |ST| = |TU|

THEOREM 12

Let ABC be a triangle. If a line DE is parallel to BC and cuts $[AB]$ in the ratio $m:n$, then it also cuts $[AC]$ in the same ratio.

i.e. $|AD|:|DB| = |AE|:|EC|$

We can write this as $\dfrac{|AD|}{|DB|} = \dfrac{|AE|}{|EC|}$ i.e. $\dfrac{\text{Top}}{\text{Bottom}} = \dfrac{\text{Top}}{\text{Bottom}}$.

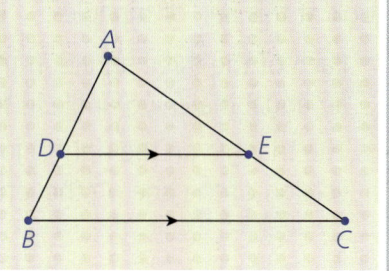

Key Points

In the above diagram, it is also true that:

- $\dfrac{|AD|}{|AB|} = \dfrac{|AE|}{|AC|}$ i.e $\dfrac{\text{Top}}{\text{Whole}} = \dfrac{\text{Top}}{\text{Whole}}$

- $\dfrac{|AB|}{|DB|} = \dfrac{|AC|}{|EC|}$ i.e $\dfrac{\text{Whole}}{\text{Bottom}} = \dfrac{\text{Whole}}{\text{Bottom}}$

Example 2

In the diagram, $DE \parallel BC$. Find x.

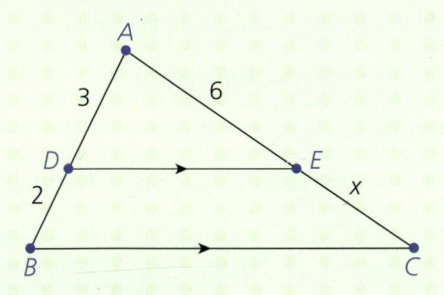

Solution

$\dfrac{|AD|}{|DB|} = \dfrac{|AE|}{|EC|}$ ... Theorem 12

$\Rightarrow \dfrac{3}{2} = \dfrac{6}{x}$

$\Rightarrow 3(x) = 6(2)$

$\Rightarrow 3x = 12$

$\Rightarrow x = 4$

Example 3

In the diagram, $ST \parallel QR$. Find x.

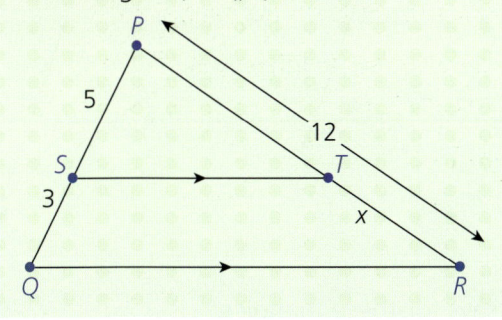

Solution

$\dfrac{|PR|}{|TR|} = \dfrac{|PQ|}{|SQ|}$ ... Theorem 12

$\Rightarrow \dfrac{12}{x} = \dfrac{5+3}{3}$

$\Rightarrow 8(x) = 12(3)$

$\Rightarrow 8x = 36$

$\Rightarrow x = \dfrac{36}{8} = \dfrac{9}{2}$

THEOREM 12 (CONVERSE)

Let ABC be a triangle. If a line l cuts the sides AB and AC in the same ratio, then it is parallel to BC.

Similar Triangles (Revision)

Look at this pair of triangles.

- Each of the three angles in triangle *PQR* has an equal matching angle in triangle *STV*.
- The triangle on the right is just a larger version of the one on the left.

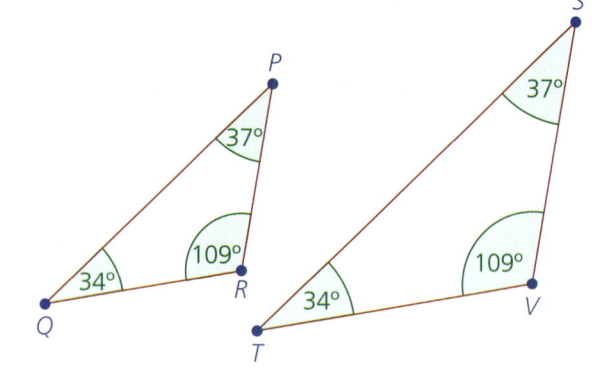

These triangles are called **equiangular** triangles or **similar** triangles.

Corresponding sides are the sides which match in each triangle. For example, in the example above, [*PQ*] corresponds to [*ST*].

We now revisit Theorem 13 which we studied in *Connect with Maths 1*.

THEOREM 13

If two triangles are similar, their sides are proportional, in order.

THEOREM 13 (CONVERSE)

If the sides of two triangles are in proportion, then the two triangles are similar.

Example 4

ABC and *PQR* are similar triangles.
Find the value of *x*.

Solution

First identify the corresponding sides. The corresponding sides are opposite the equal angles.

Hence:

- [*AB*] in △*ABC* corresponds to [*PQ*] in △*PQR*
- [*BC*] in △*ABC* corresponds to [*QR*] in △*PQR*

Start with the side marked *x*.

$\frac{|PQ|}{|AB|} = \frac{|QR|}{|BC|}$ … this is what Theorem 13 says for these triangles

$\Rightarrow \frac{x}{3} = \frac{7.5}{5}$

$\Rightarrow 5x = 3(7.5)$

$\Rightarrow x = \frac{22.5}{5} = 4.5$

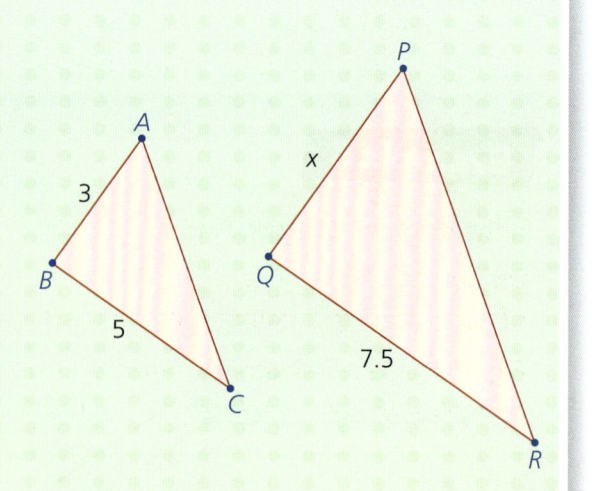

Example 5

In the triangle ABC, $|\angle BAC| = 90°$ and $AD \perp BC$.

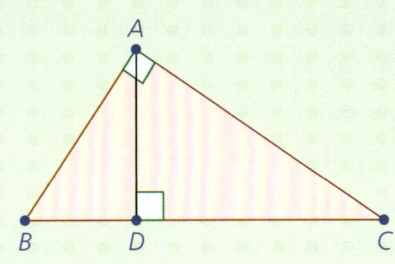

(i) Prove that triangles ABC and ADC are similar.

(ii) Hence prove that $|BC| \times |DC| = |AC|^2$.

Solution

(i) Draw the two triangles ABC and ADC separately.

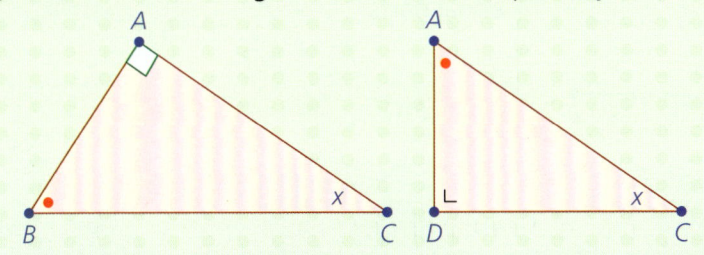

Both the triangles ADC and ABC have a right angle and $\angle C$.

∴ the 3rd angles in each triangle are equal … Theorem 4

∴ ADC and ABC are similar triangles.

(ii) ∴ $\dfrac{|AC|}{|DC|} = \dfrac{|BC|}{|AC|}$ … Theorem 13

$\Rightarrow |AC|^2 = |BC|.|DC|$ … cross-multiply … QED

Construction 7

Division of a line segment into any number of equal segments without measuring it.

E.g. to divide a line into four equal segments without measuring it.

Method

Step 1: Draw a line segment [AB].

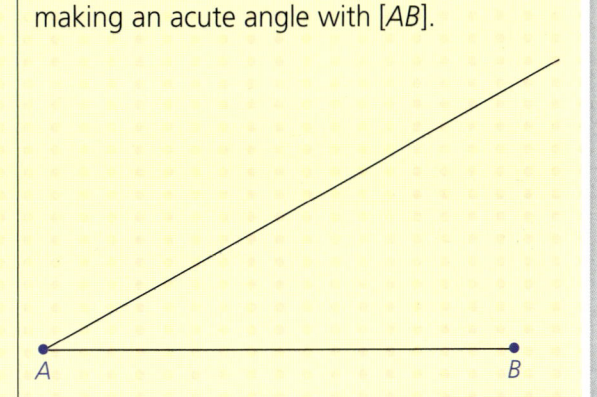

Step 2: Draw a ray from the point A making an acute angle with [AB].

Step 3: With *A* as centre and any radius, draw an arc crossing the ray at *P*.

With *P* as centre and the same radius, draw a second arc crossing the ray at *Q*.

With *Q* as centre and the same radius, draw a third arc crossing the ray at *R*.

With *R* as centre and the same radius, draw a fourth arc crossing the ray at *S*.

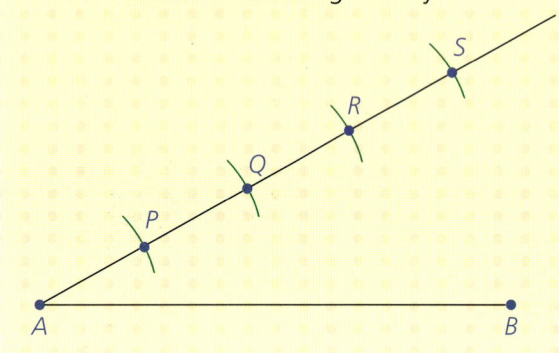

Step 4: Join *B* to *S*.

Use a set-square and ruler to draw [RK], [QL] and [PM] parallel to SB.

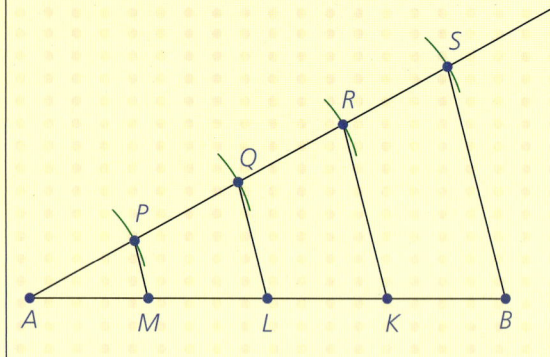

[AB] is now divided into four equal parts.

Activity 9.4

1 In each of these diagrams, lines *a*, *b* and *c* are parallel.
Find the value of *x* in each. Explain your answers.

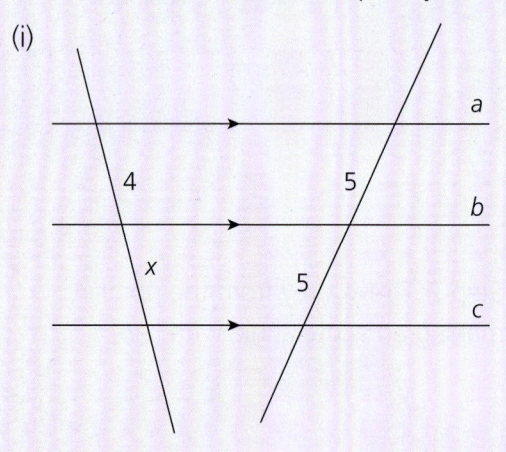

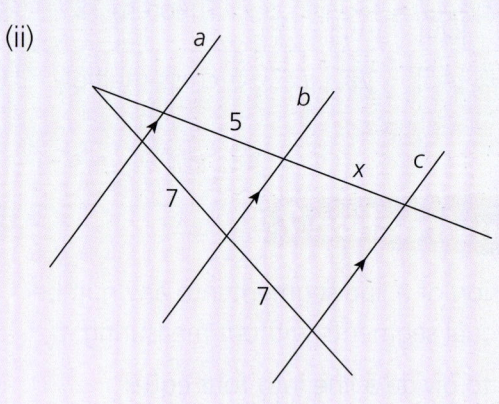

(i) (ii)

2 The diagram shows a street map. Russell Street, Farrell Street and Elizabeth Street are all parallel to each other. How far is it from Elizabeth Street to Russell Street? Explain your answer.

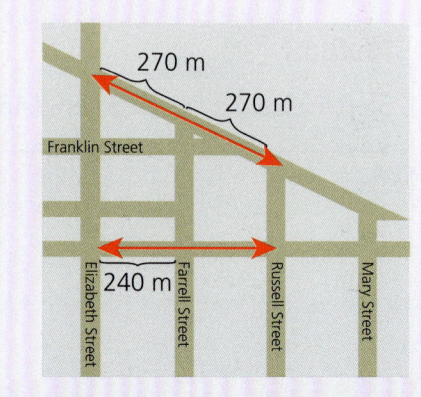

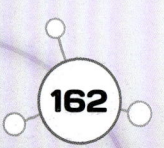

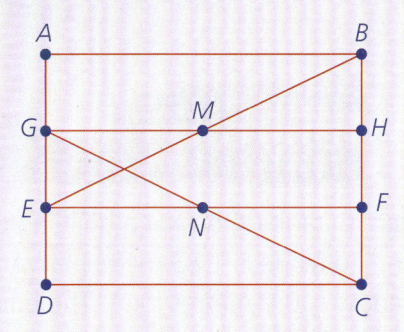

3 Peter is designing a new iron gate and has drawn this sketch of it. The gate is to be 2 metres wide and 1.8 metres high. The horizontal bars are to be an equal distance apart.

(i) Copy the diagram into your copy and mark in the dimensions.
(ii) Name five line segments equal to |AG|.
(iii) Name a line segment equal to |BM|. Explain your answer.
(iv) Name a line segment equal to |GN|. Explain your answer.
(v) Fill in the length |AE| on your diagram.
(vi) Calculate the length of [EB] correct to two decimal places.
(vii) Calculate the total length of iron needed to make the gate.

4 Find the value of x for the following pairs of similar triangles correct to two decimal places.

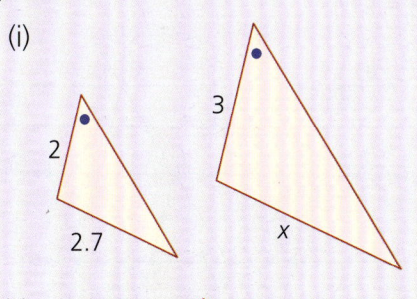

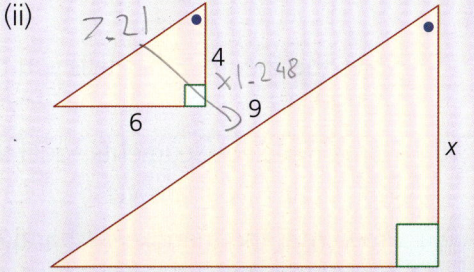

(i)

(ii)

5 Find the value of x in each of these diagrams.

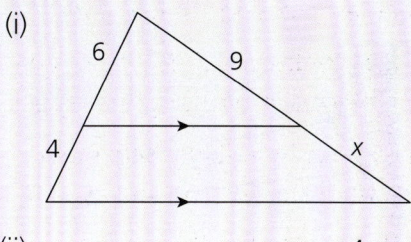

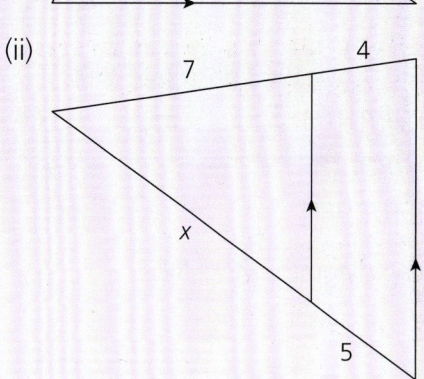

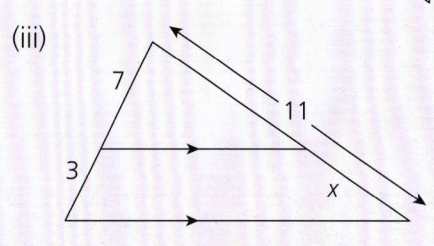

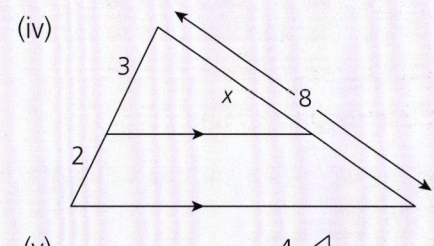

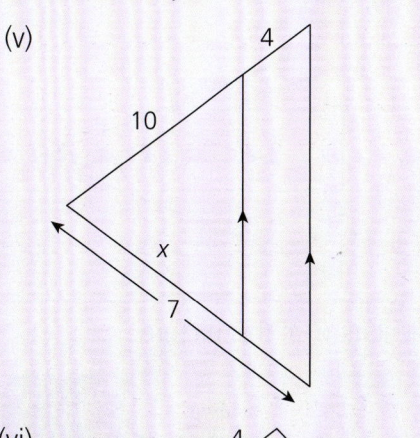

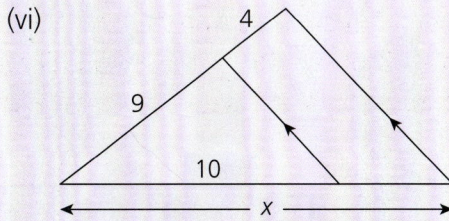

(i)
(ii)
(iii)
(iv)
(v)
(vi)

6 In the diagram, $ST \parallel QR$.
$|PS|:|SQ| = 5:3$.

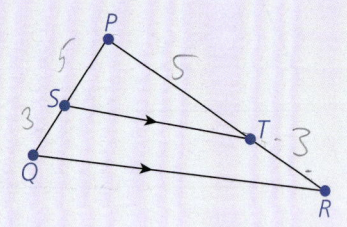

Write down the following ratios.
(i) $|PT|:|TR|$
(ii) $|PQ|:|PS|$
(iii) $|TR|:|PR|$

7 In the diagram, $MN \parallel BC$.

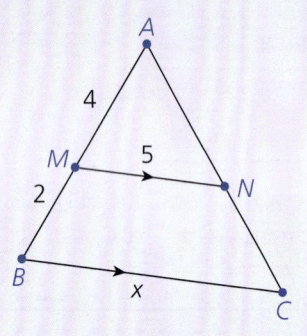

(i) Show that the triangles AMN and ABC are similar.
(ii) Use this fact to find x.

8 Find the value of x and the value of y in this diagram.

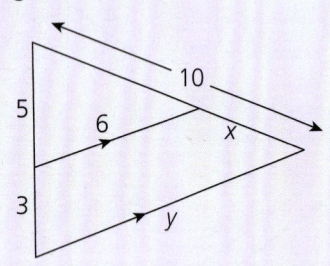

9 Calculate w in this picture.

10 Calculate the height of the geyser.

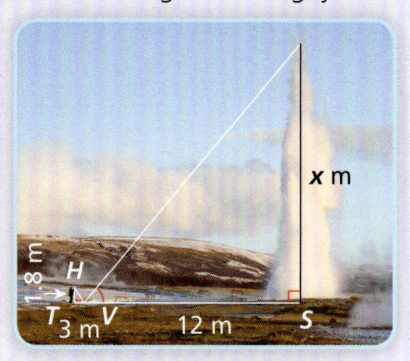

11 Ryan is standing beside a building on a sunny day. He is 1.83 metres tall. His shadow is 0.9 metres long. The building casts a shadow which is 6.5 m long.
(i) Draw two triangles to show this.
(ii) Explain how this information can be used to find the height of the building.
(iii) Find the height of the building correct to one decimal place.

12 In the diagram, $HM \parallel GB$ and $MN \parallel BC$.

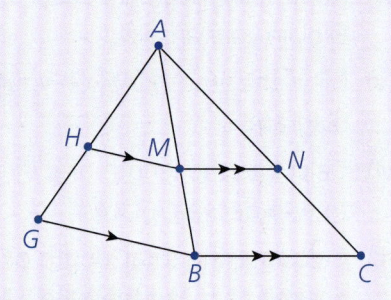

Prove that $HN \parallel GC$.

13 In the diagram, the three lines a, b and c are parallel. Also $KW \parallel LM$, $KW \parallel TV$ and $|KL| = |LN|$.

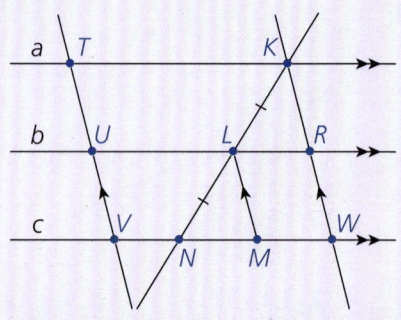

(i) State the theorem that tells you that $|TU| = |UV|$.
(ii) Name three line segments equal to $|KR|$. Explain your answers.
(iii) Prove that the triangles KLR and LMN are congruent.

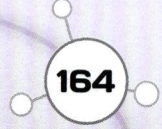

14 In this diagram, DC is parallel to AB. AC and BD intersect at E.

   (i) Prove that triangles DEC and AEB are similar.
   (ii) Hence, prove that $|DC| \times |EB| = |AB| \times |DE|$.

   $|DC| = 3$ cm, $|AE| = 6$ cm and $|AB| = 8$ cm.

   (iii) Find $|EC|$ correct to one decimal place.

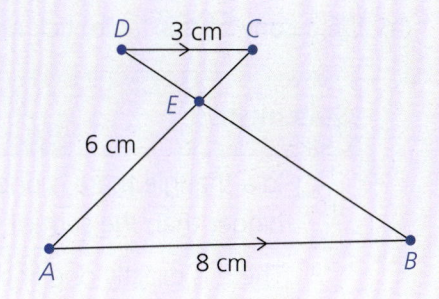

15 In the triangle ABC, $|\angle BAC| = 90°$ and $AD \perp BC$.

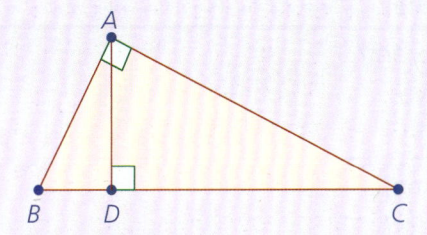

Using similar triangles, prove that $|BD| \times |BC| = |BA|^2$.

Hint

> Draw the triangles out separately and mark in all the equal angles.

16 ABC is a triangle and DE is parallel to BC.
$|AD| = 2$, $|DB| = 3$ and $|AE| = 3$.

   (i) Find $|EC|$.
   (ii) Given that $|\angle BAC| = 90°$, show that area of $\triangle ADE$: area of $BDEC = 4 : 21$.

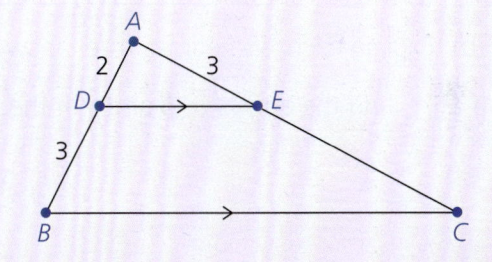

17 In the triangle ABC, $|\angle BAC| = 90°$ and $AD \perp BC$.

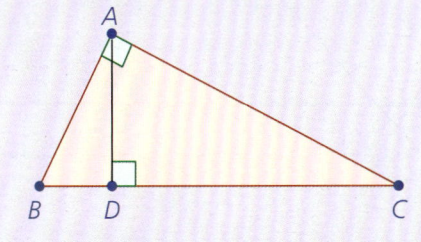

   (i) Prove that the triangles ADC and ABC are similar.
   (ii) Write down one ratio equal to $\dfrac{|AC|}{|AB|}$.
   (iii) If $|AC| = 2 \times |AB|$ and $|AD| = 4$, find the value of $|DC|$.

Revision Activity 9

1. (a) On a copy of this table, tick one box for each of the statements.

	Statement	Always true	Sometimes true	Never true
(i)	In a triangle there is one angle which is bigger than the sum of the other two angles			
(ii)	There is exactly one line through any two given points			
(iii)	A parallelogram has a centre of symmetry			
(iv)	Two triangles are congruent if two sides and an angle of one triangle are equal to two sides and an angle of the other			
(v)	Given any line l and a point P, there is more than one line through P that is parallel to l			
(vi)	A right-angled triangle is also isosceles			
(vii)	A diagonal divides a parallelogram into two congruent triangles			
(viii)	The diagonals of a rectangle which is not a square are perpendicular			
(ix)	If the diagonals of a quadrilateral are perpendicular, then it is a square			

(b) Explain each 'sometimes true' answer using diagrams.

2. If $l_1 \parallel l_2$ find the angles α, β and γ in the diagram.

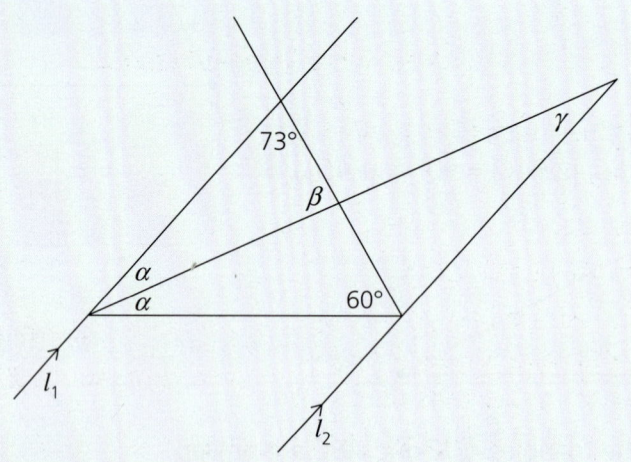

3. (a) The diagram shows a regular hexagon. Copy the diagram and draw in all its axes of symmetry.

   (b) [BE] and [AD] intersect at O.
   What is the measure of the angle of the rotation about O which maps E onto A?

   (c) Describe two transformations which map [ED] onto [AB].

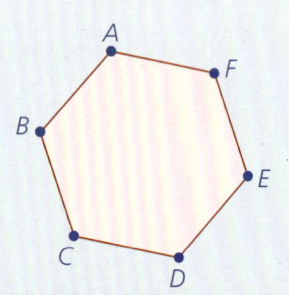

4 Each of the diagrams A, B, C and D shows the object in Figure 1 and its image under a transformation. For each of A, B, C and D, state the transformation(s) (translation, axial symmetry, central symmetry or rotation) that will map the object onto that image. In the case of a rotation, state the angle and direction.

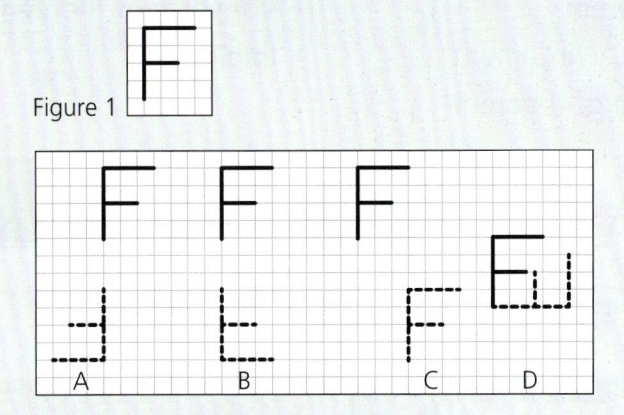

Figure 1

Exam-style Questions

1 Darragh is using a compass and straight-edge to bisect the angle ∠ABC. His construction lines are shown on the diagram using dotted lines. His points D, E and F are labelled.

   (a) Darragh says that |DF| = |EF|. Explain why he is correct.

   (b) Draw in the line segments [DF] and [EF].

   Now prove, using congruent triangles, that the line BF bisects ∠ABC.

   JCHL 2014 Sample Paper 2

2 ABC is an isosceles triangle with |AB| = |AC|.

   [BA] is produced to D.

   AE is parallel to BC.

   (a) Prove that [AE bisects ∠DAC.

   (b) Would the result in part (a) still apply if |AB| and |AC| were not equal?
   Give a reason for your answer.

   JCHL 2011 Paper 2

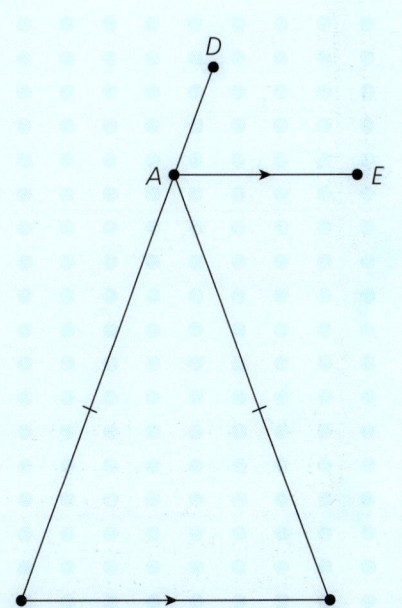

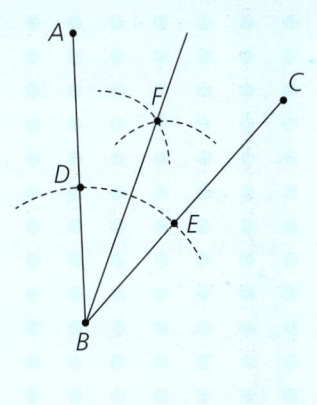

KEY WORDS AND PHRASES

- Axiom
- Theorem
- Logical argument
- Proof of theorem
- Corollary
- Converse of theorem
- Implies

Chapter Summary 9

- **Construction 3:** To construct a line perpendicular to a given line l, through a point not on l.
- **Theorem 11**

   If three parallel lines cut off equal segments on some transversal line, then they will cut off equal segments on some other transversal.
- **Theorem 12**

   Let ABC be a triangle. If a line l is parallel to BC and cuts $[AB]$ in the ratio $m:n$, then it also cuts $[AC]$ in the same ratio.
- **Construction 7:** Division of a line segment into any number of equal segments without measuring it.

Chapter 10

Geometry 2

Learning Outcomes

In this chapter, you will learn about:
- The theorem of Pythagoras
- The proof of the theorem of Pythagoras
- Theorem 19: The properties of angles in circles

You will need...

- a pencil
- a ruler
- a geometry set

Section 10A Right-angled Triangles

By now, you are familiar with the theorem known as Pythagoras' Theorem. It tells us a rather surprising thing about right-angled triangles, which you probably would not arrive at without being told. It is so important that there have even been songs written about it!

The longest side in a right-angled triangle is referred to as the **hypotenuse**.

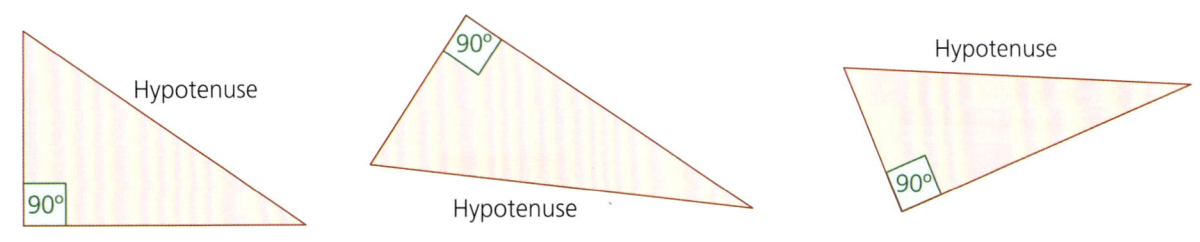

The hypotenuse is the side opposite the right angle.

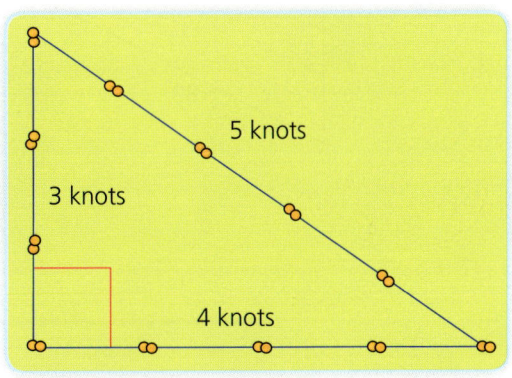

Ancient Egyptian square tool

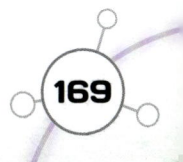

THEOREM 14: THE THEOREM OF PYTHAGORAS

In a right-angled triangle, the square of the hypotenuse is the sum of the squares of the other two sides.

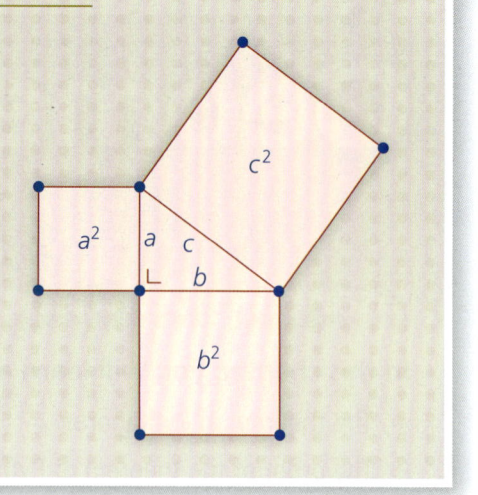

This is the way it appears in the *Formulae and tables* booklet:

$$c^2 = a^2 + b^2$$

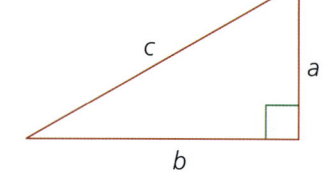

THEOREM 15: THE CONVERSE OF PYTHAGORAS' THEOREM

If the square of one side of a triangle is equal to the sum of the squares of the other two sides, then the angle opposite the first side is a right angle.

Example 1

Use the theorem of Pythagoras to check whether this triangle is right-angled.

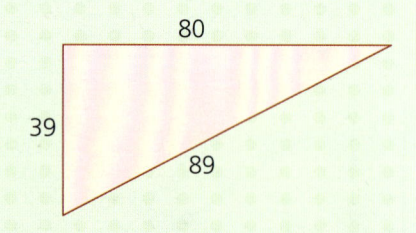

(Triangle with sides 39, 80, 89)

Solution

Look for the longest side: it is 89.

Check to see if
(Longest side)^2 = sum of squares of the other two sides

Is $89^2 = 39^2 + 80^2$?

$7921 = 1521 + 6400$

$7921 = 7921$ ✓

$\Rightarrow$ it is a right-angled triangle.

Example 2

Use the theorem of Pythagoras to check whether this triangle is right-angled.

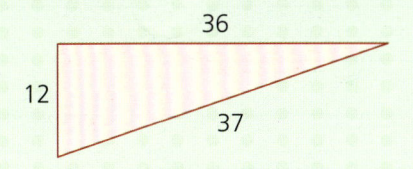

[Triangle with sides 12, 36, 37]

Solution

Look for the longest side: it is 37.

Check to see if
(Longest side)^2 = sum of squares of the other two sides

Is $37^2 = 36^2 + 12^2$?

$1369 = 1296 + 144$

$1369 = 1440$ ✗

$\Rightarrow$ it is **not** a right-angled triangle.

Example 3

Given any two integers p and q ($p > q$), it is possible to form three numbers a, b and c where:

$a = p^2 - q^2$, $b = 2pq$, $c = p^2 + q^2$

These three numbers a, b and c are then known as **Pythagorean triples**.

(i) For $p = 8$ and $q = 6$, calculate a, b and c.

(ii) If a, b and c are the lengths of a triangle, show that the triangle is right-angled.

Solution

(i) For $p = 8$ and $q = 6$:

$a = p^2 - q^2 = 8^2 - 6^2 = 64 - 36 = 28$
$b = 2pq = 2(8)(6) = 96$
$c = p^2 + q^2 = 8^2 + 6^2 = 64 + 36 = 100$

(ii) $c^2 = 100^2 = 10\,000$

$a^2 + b^2 = 28^2 + 96^2 = 784 + 9216$
$\qquad\qquad\quad = 10\,000$

$\therefore c^2 = a^2 + b^2$

$\Rightarrow$ the triangle is right-angled.

Class Activity

As we saw before, a set of three integers a, b and c where $a^2 = b^2 + c^2$ is called a **Pythagorean triple.**

For example, {3, 4, 5} is a Pythagorean triple, since $5^2 = 3^2 + 4^2$.

How many Pythagorean triples are there?

(i) Working in pairs, copy and complete this table.

	Triple	Is the longest^2 = sum of squares of other two?	Pythagorean triple?
Original	3, 4, 5	$3^2 + 4^2 = 5^2$ $9 + 16 = 25$ ✓	Yes
Multiply original by 2	6, 8, 10	$6^2 + 8^2 = 10^2$	

	Triple	Is the longest² = sum of squares of other two?	Pythagorean triple?
Multiply original by 3			
Multiply original by 4			
Multiply original by 5			
Multiply original by 6	18, 24, 30		
Multiply original by 7			

(ii) How many Pythagorean triples do you think there are?

(iii) Copy this table and make up three new Pythagorean triples for each set below.

Original Pythagorean triple	Three new Pythagorean triples from these
5, 12, 13	
8, 15, 17	
7, 24, 25	

Historical note

As you can see from the last activity, we can get many values for x, y and z which satisfy the equation $x^2 + y^2 = z^2$.

In 1637, Pierre de Fermat, was looking for solutions to the equation $x^3 + y^3 = z^3$.

This equation only differs from the previous equation by the fact that each power of 2 has been replaced by a power of 3. However, Fermat could not find any solutions to this new equation.

Pierre de Fermat 1601–65

In fact, amazingly, there are no values of x, y and z which satisfy the equation $x^3 + y^3 = z^3$.

Indeed, there are no solutions to the equation $x^4 + y^4 = z^4$ either, or any equation $x^n + y^n = z^n$ where n is any integer greater than 2.

Fermat claimed to have proved this, but said that the margin of the page he was writing on was too narrow to write it in and his proof was never found. Thus it became known as **Fermat's Last Theorem**.

Andrew Wiles 1953–

For over 300 years mathematicians tried to prove or disprove Fermat's Last Theorem. It was finally proved to be true by Andrew Wiles, an English mathematician, in 1995. His proof is 400 pages long!

PYTHAGORAS' THEOREM (formal proof required)

The square on the hypotenuse of a right-angled triangle is equal to the sum of the squares on the other two sides.

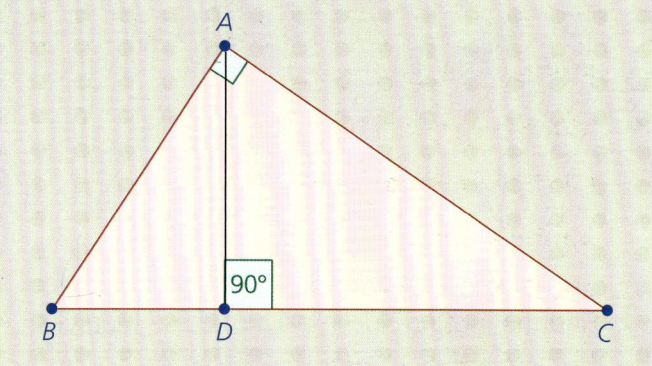

Given: Right-angled triangle ABC with $|\angle BAC| = 90°$.
Required to prove: $|BC|^2 = |AB|^2 + |AC|^2$
Construction: Draw $AD \perp BC$.
Proof: Draw the three triangles in the diagram separately.

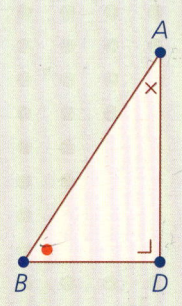

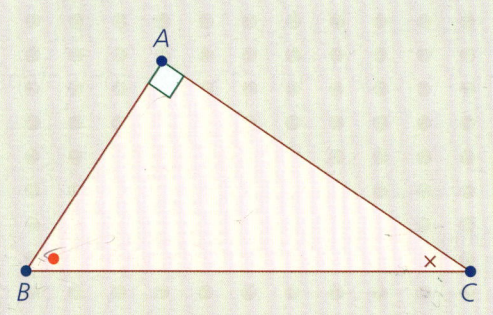

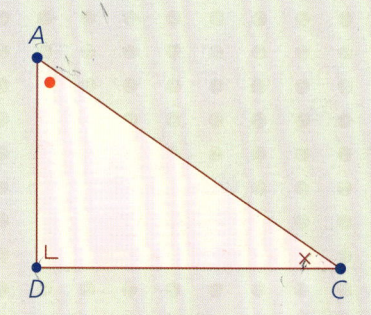

Both the triangles ABD and ABC have a right angle and $\angle B$.

∴ the 3rd angles in each triangle are equal … Theorem 4

∴ ABD and ABC are similar triangles.

∴ $\dfrac{|AB|}{|BC|} = \dfrac{|BD|}{|AB|}$ … Theorem 13

$\Rightarrow |AB|^2 = |BC| \cdot |BD|$ … equation (1)

Both the triangles ADC and ABC have a right angle and $\angle C$.

∴ the 3rd angles in each triangle are equal … Theorem 4

∴ ADC and ABC are similar triangles.

∴ $\dfrac{|AC|}{|BC|} = \dfrac{|DC|}{|AC|}$

$\Rightarrow |AC|^2 = |BC| \cdot |DC|$ … equation (2)

Adding equations (1) and (2), we get

$|AB|^2 + |AC|^2 = |BC| \cdot |BD| + |BC| \cdot |DC|$
$= |BC|(|BD| + |DC|)$
$= |BC| \cdot |BC|$
$= |BC|^2$ … QED

Activity 10.1

1. Write down Pythagoras' theorem for each of these triangles.

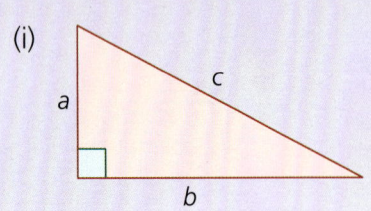

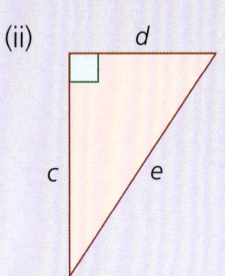

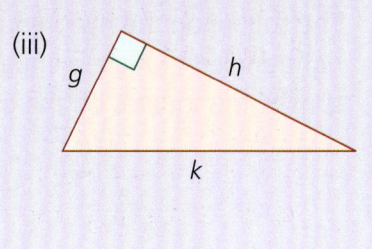

    (i)   (ii)   (iii)

2. Find the missing side in each of these triangles.

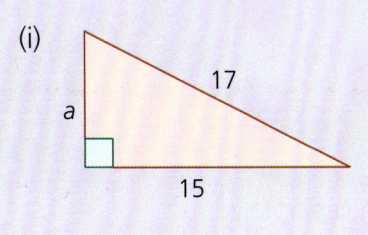

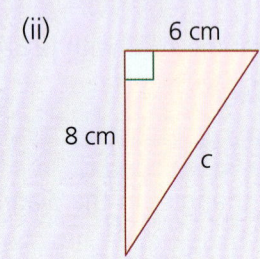

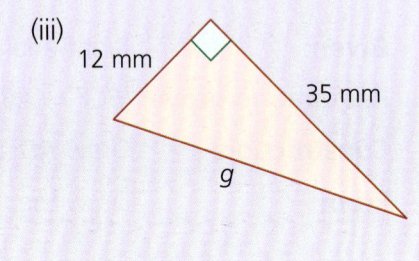

    (i)   (ii)   (iii)

3. The diagram shows a ramp which is to be constructed over some steps.

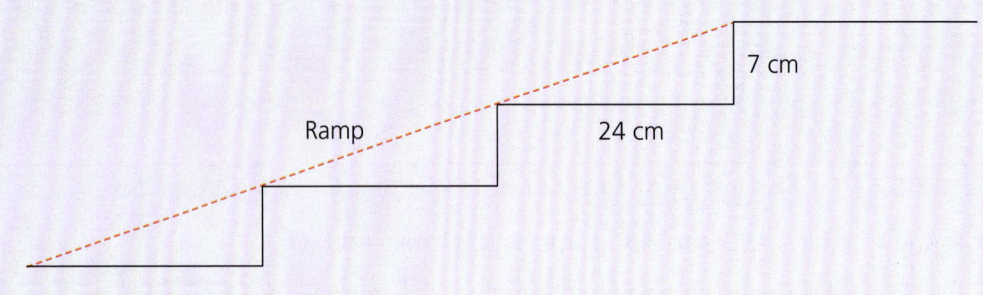

    (i) Find the length of the ramp.
    (ii) What is the slope of the ramp?

4. The pitch at Croke Park is 144.5 m long and 88 m wide. Find the distance between the corner flags on opposite sides of the pitch (i.e. the diagonal). Give your answer correct to one decimal place.

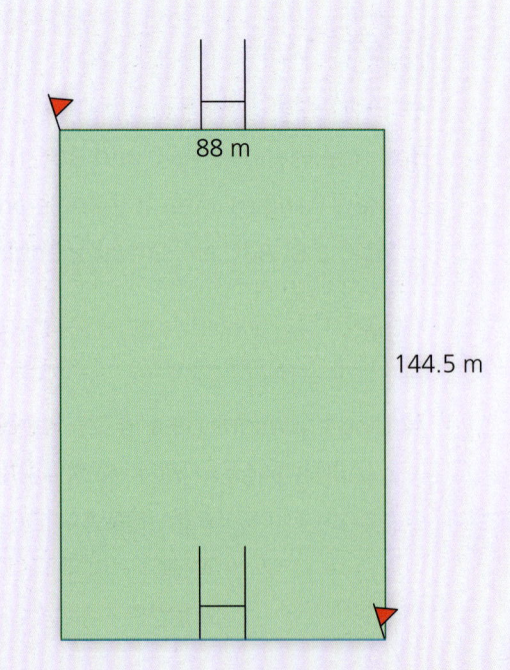

5. Tommy is a builder. He is constructing a roof which is to be supported by two parallel walls. In order to get started, he needs to find a point Q on one wall which is directly across from the point P on the other wall.

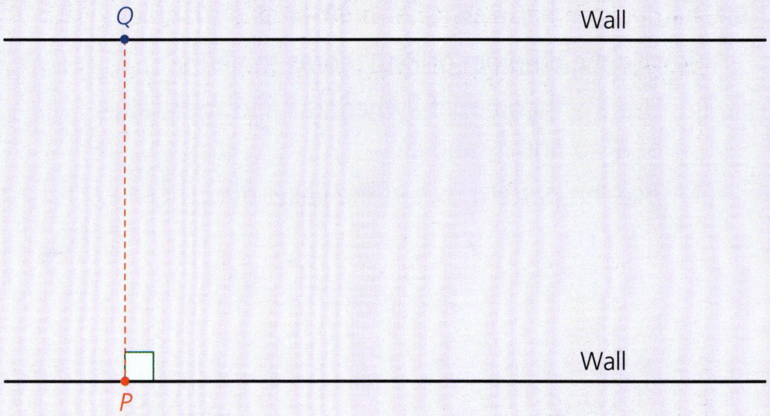

   Show how Tommy might use the theorem of Pythagoras to find the point Q.

6. If $p^2 - q^2$, $2pq$ and $p^2 + q^2$ are the lengths of the sides of a triangle, show that the triangle is right-angled.

7. In the game of rugby, a player may be required to kick the ball from the ground over the bar between the goalposts (the 'H' shape in the diagram below).

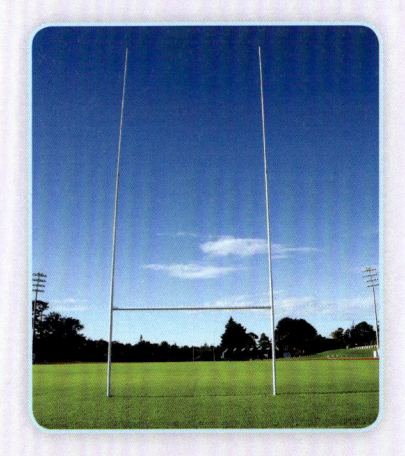

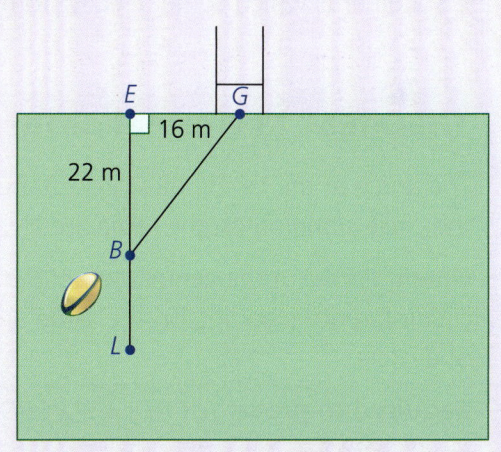

   Jonathan is the team kicker and he aims to kick the ball over the bar and between the posts from the point B in the diagram. |EG| = 16 m, |EB| = 22 m and |∠GEB| = 90°.

   (i) How far is the ball from the goalposts (i.e. |BG| in the diagram)?

   (ii) The rules of the game indicate that, for certain kicks, you must choose a point along the line EL to kick the ball at the posts. If you were Jonathan, would you choose the point B? What measurements would help you in your decision?

   (iii) To be sure to clear the bar of the goalposts, Jonathan must be able to kick the ball at least 10 metres beyond the posts. If his maximum length of kick is 55 metres, what is the maximum distance that he can be from the point E if the ball is on the line EL?

8. The diagram shows a cube of side 4 m.

   (i) Calculate |GC|, a diagonal of the base of the cube.

   (ii) Calculate |EC|, an internal diagonal of the cube.

   Give your answers in surd form.

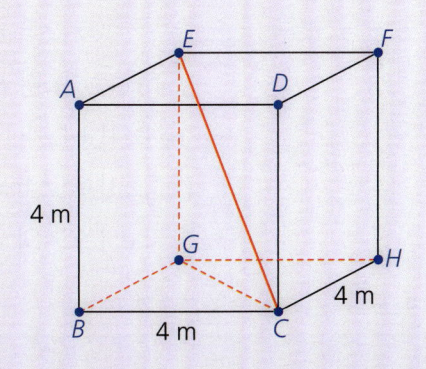

9 The diagram has a series of right-angled triangles.
   (i)   Use the theorem of Pythagoras to find a^2.
   (ii) Use the theorem of Pythagoras and your value of a^2 to find b^2 and c^2.
   (iii) Use this pattern to find the value of d.

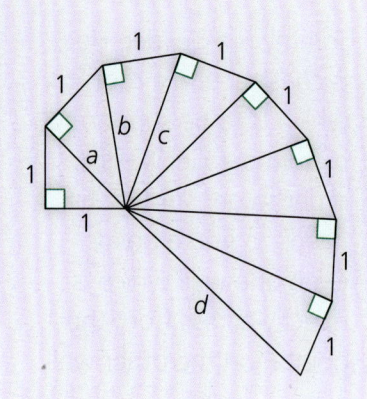

Section 10B Angles in Circles

This section deals with angles in circles and the relationships between them.

First, we prove a new theorem. This theorem has four **corollaries** that go with it. Corollaries are statements which come directly from a theorem and can be proved.

THEOREM 19 (formal proof required)

The angle at the centre of a circle standing on a given arc is twice the angle at any point of the circle standing on the same arc.

Given: $\angle CAD$ at the centre and $\angle CBD$ at the circumference standing on the same arc CD of a circle.

Required to prove: $|\angle CAD| = 2|\angle CBD|$

Construction: Join B to A and produce (extend) to E. Label angles as shown.

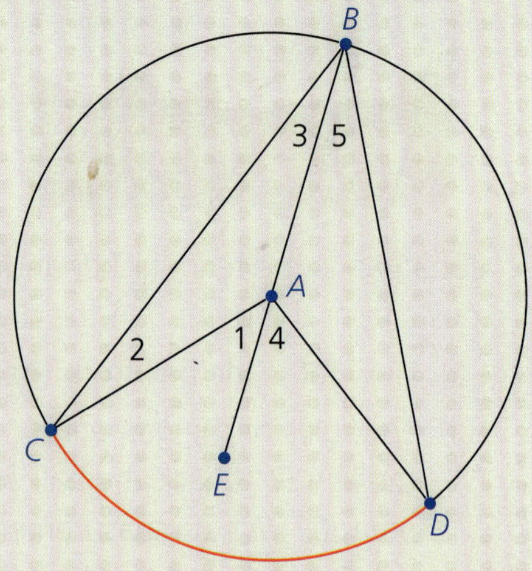

Proof: $[AB]$ and $[AC]$ are radii of the circle

$\Rightarrow |AB| = |AC|$

$\Rightarrow$ triangle ACB is isosceles

$\Rightarrow \quad |\angle 2| = |\angle 3| \qquad \ldots$ Theorem 2

$\Rightarrow |\angle 2| + |\angle 3| = 2|\angle 3|$

Also, exterior angle $|\angle 1| = |\angle 2| + |\angle 3| \qquad \ldots$ Theorem 6

$\Rightarrow |\angle 1| = 2|\angle 3|$

Similarly, $|\angle 4| = 2|\angle 5|$

$\Rightarrow |\angle 1| + |\angle 4| = 2|\angle 3| + 2|\angle 5| \qquad \ldots$ by addition

i.e. $|\angle 1| + |\angle 4| = 2[\,|\angle 3| + |\angle 5|\,]$

i.e. $|\angle CAD| = 2|\angle CBD| \qquad \ldots$ QED

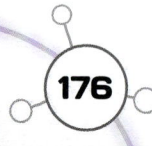

COROLLARY 1 OF THEOREM 19

All angles at points of a circle standing on the same arc are equal.

Given: ∠ABC and ∠ADC at a circle standing on the same arc AC of the circle.

Required to prove: |∠1| = |∠2|

Proof:

|∠3| = 2|∠1|

|∠3| = 2|∠2|

⇒ |∠1| = |∠2| … QED

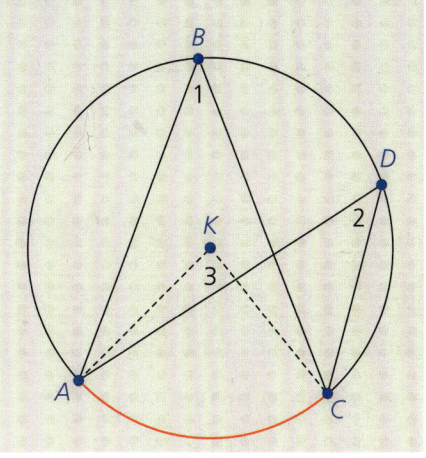

COROLLARY 2 OF THEOREM 19

Each angle in a semi-circle is a right angle.

Required to prove: |∠PQR| = 90°

Proof:

Let PR be a diameter of circle with centre O.

|∠POR| = 180°   … straight angle

|∠POR| = 2|∠PQR| … Theorem 19

⇒ |∠PQR| = 90°   … QED

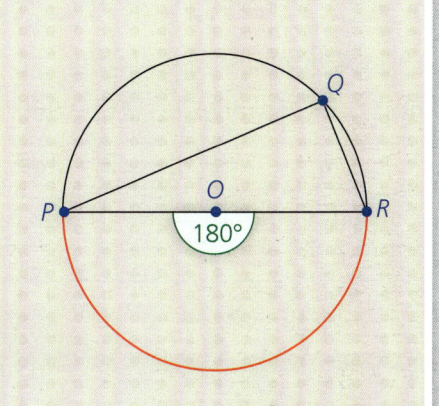

COROLLARY 3 OF THEOREM 19

If the angle standing on a chord [PR] at some point of the circle is a right angle, then [PR] is a diameter.

Given: Right angle ∠PQR standing on a chord [PR] of a circle of centre O.

Required to prove: [PR] is a diameter of the circle.

Proof:

|∠PQR| = 90°   … given

⇒ |∠POR| = 180°

⇒ ∠POR is a straight angle

⇒ [PR] is a diameter   … QED

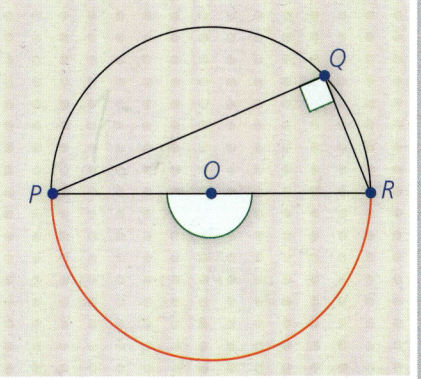

A **cyclic quadrilateral** is a quadrilateral whose four vertices are on a circle.

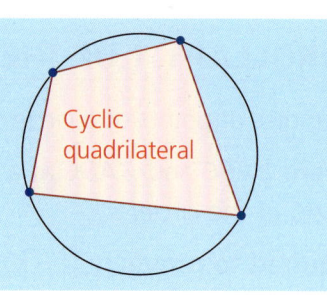

Cyclic quadrilateral

COROLLARY 4 OF THEOREM 19

If *ABCD* is a cyclic quadrilateral, then opposite angles sum to 180°.

Given: Cyclic quadrilateral *ABCD* in a circle of centre *K*.

Required to prove:

$|\angle BAD| + |\angle BCD| = 180°$

$|\angle ABC| + |\angle ADC| = 180°$

Proof:

$|\angle AKC| = 2|\angle 1|$ ... Theorem 19

Also, reflex $|\angle AKC| = 2|\angle 2|$ ... Theorem 19

But $|\angle AKC|$ + reflex $|\angle AKC| = 360°$ ... full revolution

$\Rightarrow |\angle 1| + |\angle 2| = 180°$

Similarly, it may be shown that $|\angle BAD| + |\angle BCD| = 180°$ ... QED

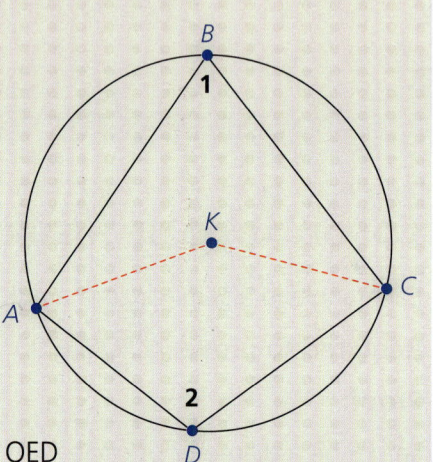

Activity 10.2

In this activity, the letters in the angles refer to the size of the angle in degrees.

1 Find the angle α in each of the following diagrams. The centre of each circle is *C*.

(i) 120°

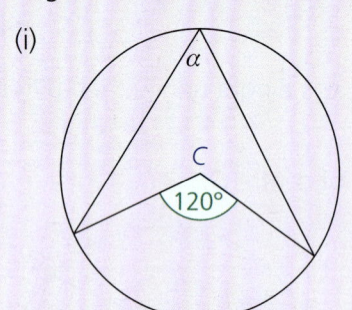

(ii) 110°

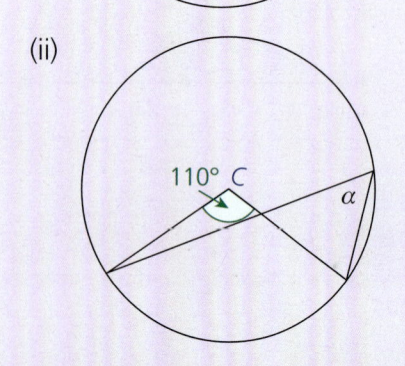

(iii) 68°

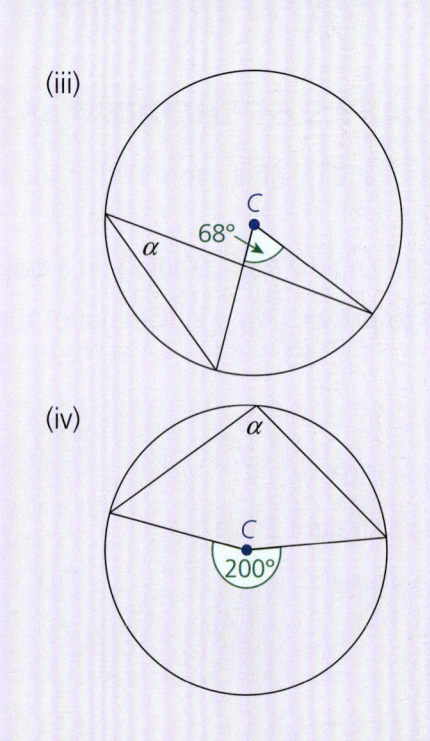

(iv) 200°

(v) [circle with angle α at top, central angle 180° at C]

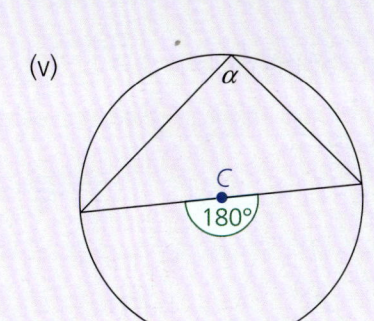

(vi) [circle with central angle 140° at C, and angle α]

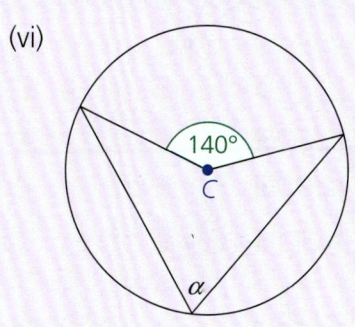

(vii) [circle with angle 102° at C, and angle α]

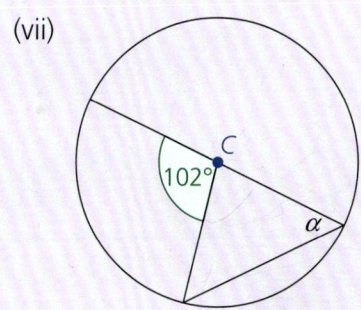

(viii) [circle with angle 120° at C, and angle α]

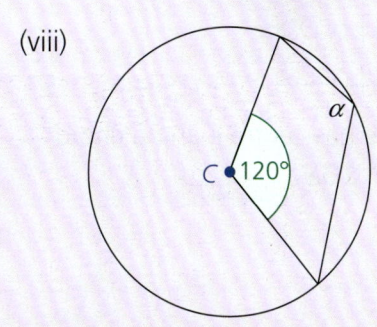

2 The circle in the diagram has A as its centre.
   (i) Write down the value of α.
   (ii) Write down the value of β.
   (iii) What can you conclude about α and β?

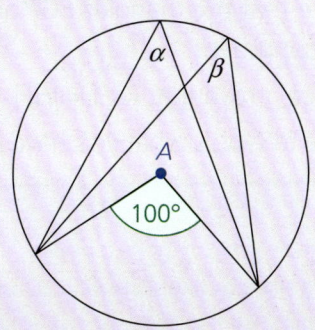

[circle with angles α and β at top, A as centre, angle 100°]

3 The centre of the circle is C.
   (i) What type of quadrilateral is BDEF?
   (ii) Find the value of α.
   (iii) Write down the value of β.
   (iv) Write down the value of angle θ.
   (v) What is the value of α + θ?

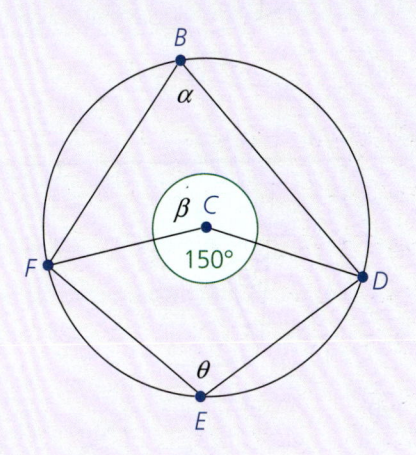

[circle with points B, F, D, E; angle α at B, β at C, 150° at C, θ at E]

4 Find the value of θ in each of the following. The centre of each circle is C.

   (i) [circle with angle θ and 75° at top, C centre]

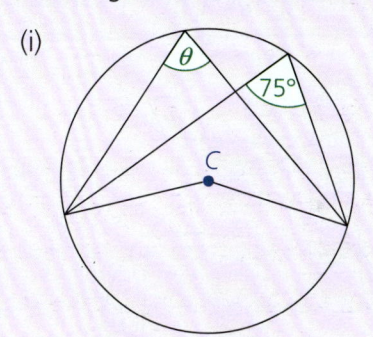

   (ii) [circle with C centre, 50° and θ angles]

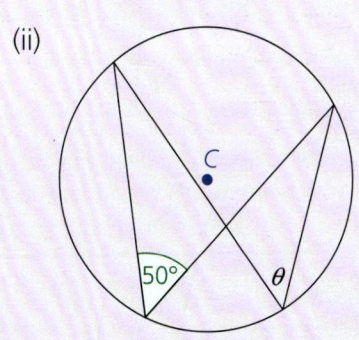

   (iii) [circle with θ at top, C centre, 50° at bottom]

179

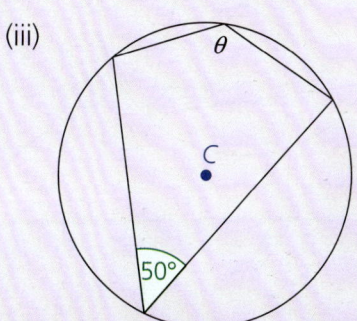

(iv)

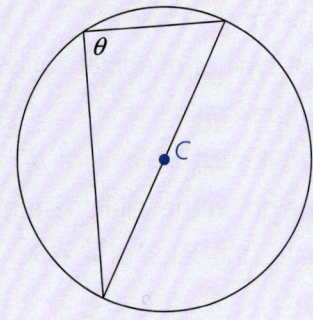

(v)

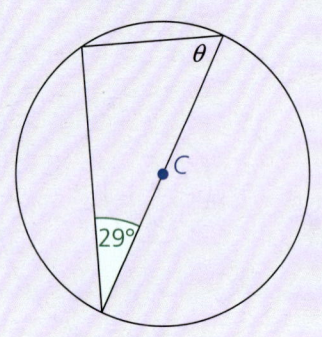

(vi)

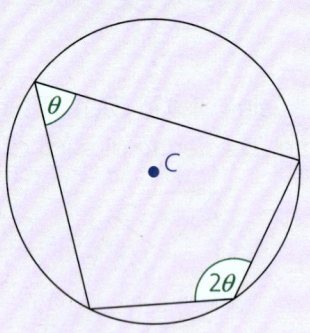

(vii)

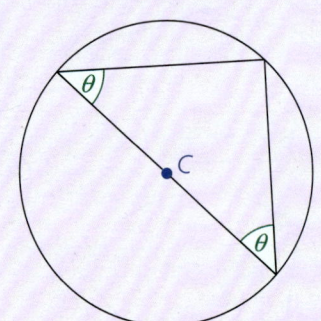

(viii)

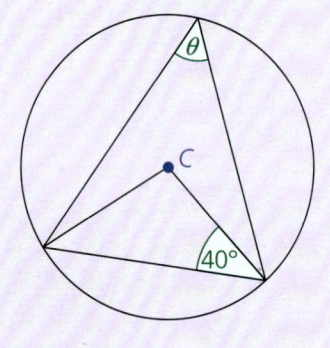

5 The centre of the circle is O.

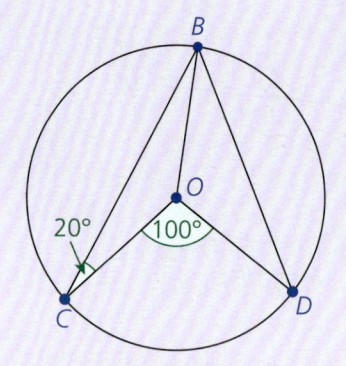

(i) Find $|\angle COB|$.
(ii) Find $|\angle ODB|$.

6 The centre of the circle is O.

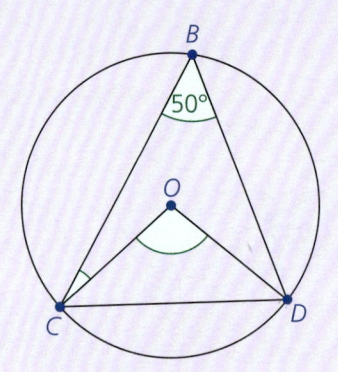

(i) Find $|\angle COD|$.
(ii) Find $|\angle OCD|$.

7 The circle has centre E and a chord [GH]. EP ⊥ GH.

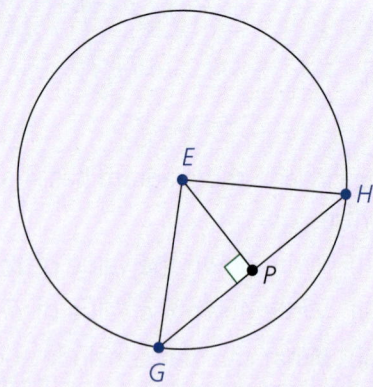

(i) Prove that the triangles EGP and EPH are congruent.
(ii) Hence, prove that $|GP| = |HP|$.
(iii) State in words what you have proved.

8. K is the centre of the circle and $|PM| = |MN|$. $|\angle PQN| = 70°$.
   Find:
   (i) $|\angle QPN|$
   (ii) $|\angle QPM|$

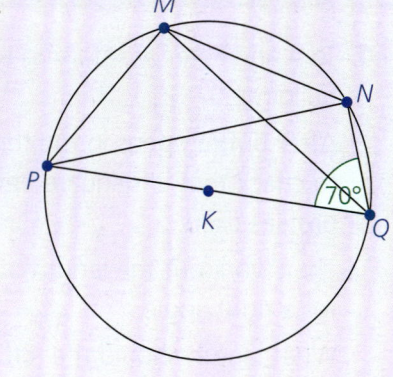

9. $ABCD$ is a parallelogram
   The points A, B and C lie on the circle which cuts $[AD]$ at P. The line CP meets the line BA at Q.
   Prove that $|CD| = |CP|$.

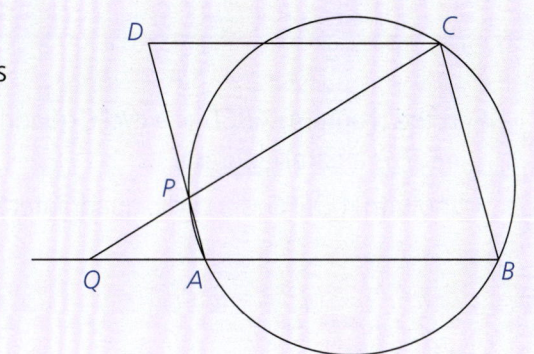

10. (i) Prove that the two triangles STP and QTR are similar.
    (ii) Prove that $|ST| \times |TR| = |QT| \times |TP|$.

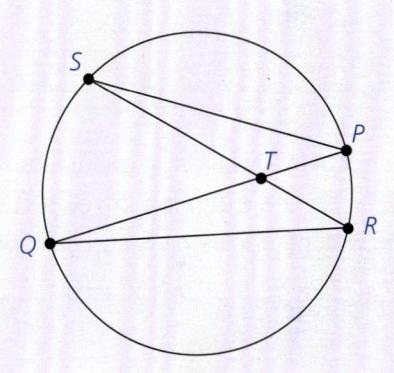

11. The angles indicated in the diagram are equal.
    Prove that $[KN]$ is a diameter of the circle.

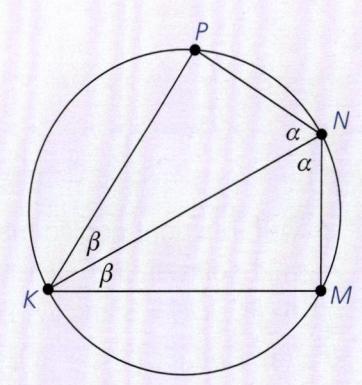

12. $ACBD$ is a quadrilateral. $|AC| = |AB| = |AD|$.
    $|\angle CAD| = 121°$.
    Calculate $|\angle CBD|$ and explain your reasoning.

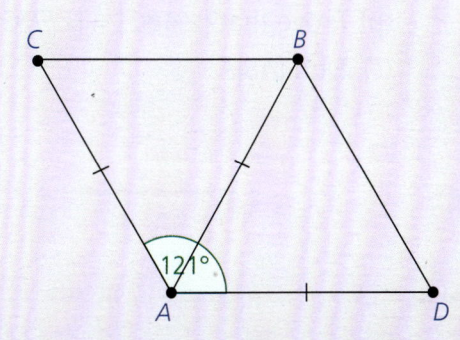

Revision Activity 10

1. Tom and Peter are starting to construct an L-shaped building.

   After putting pegs in the three main corners, they want to check that it is square before getting the rest of the profiles fixed.

   They work out the length of the red dotted line to check for a right angle.

   What length should the red dotted line be?

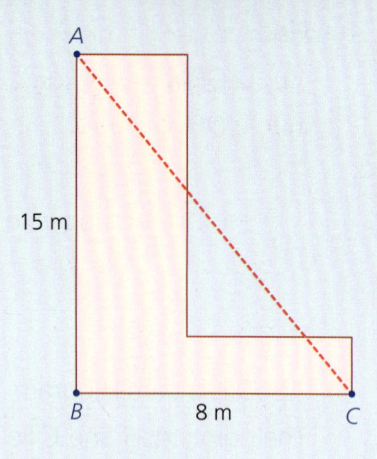

2. In the diagram, ABCD is a cyclic quadrilateral and ABCF is a parallelogram.

   Show that DEFG is a cyclic quadrilateral.

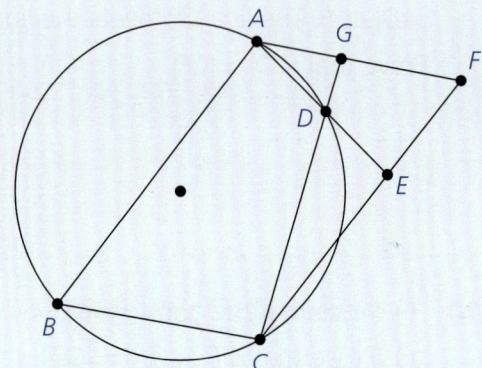

3. ABCD is a cyclic quadrilateral. The opposite sides, when extended, meet at P and Q, as shown.

   The angles α, β, and γ are as shown.

   Prove that $\beta + \gamma = 180° - 2\alpha$.

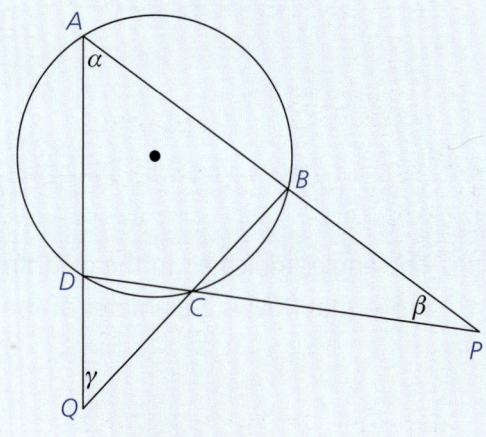

4. ABC is a right-angled triangle. E is the mid-point of [BC]. DE is perpendicular to BC. |DE| = 3 and |DC| = 5.

   (a) Find |EC|.
   (b) Prove that |∠ABC| = |∠EDC|.
   (c) Find |AB|.

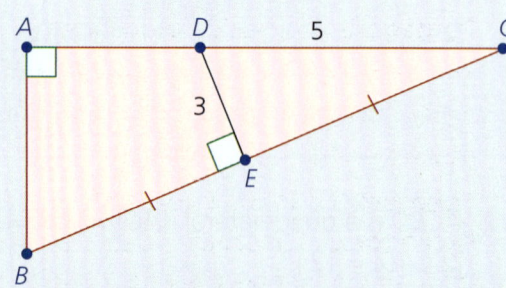

Exam-style Questions

1. Given any two positive integers m and n ($n > m$), it is possible to form three numbers a, b and c where:
$$a = n^2 - m^2, \ b = 2nm, \ c = n^2 + m^2$$
These three numbers a, b and c are then known as a 'Pythagorean triple'.

   (a) For $m = 3$ and $n = 5$, calculate a, b and c.

   (b) If the values of a, b and c from part (a) are the lengths of the sides of a triangle, show that the triangle is right-angled.

   (c) If $n^2 - m^2$, $2nm$ and $n^2 + m^2$ are the lengths of the sides of a triangle, show that the triangle is right-angled.

   JCHL 2014 Sample Paper 1

2. A, B, C and D are four points on a circle as shown.
   $[AD]$ bisects $\angle BAC$.

   P is the point of intersection of AD and BC.

   (a) Show that $\triangle ADB$ and $\triangle APC$ are similar.

   (b) Show that $|AC| \times |BD| = |AD| \times |PC|$.

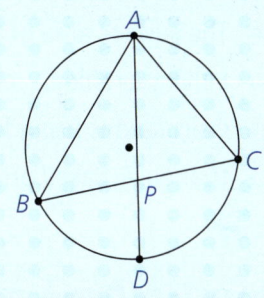

   JCHL 2014 Sample Paper 2

KEY WORDS AND PHRASES
- Hypotenuse
- Pythagoras' Theorem
- Pythagorean triple
- Cyclic quadrilateral

Chapter Summary 10

- **Theorem 14: The theorem of Pythagoras** (formal proof required)
  The square on the hypotenuse of a right-angled triangle is equal to the sum of the squares on the other two sides.

- **Theorem 15: The converse of Pythagoras' Theorem**
  If the square of one side of a triangle is equal to the sum of the squares of the other two sides, then the angle opposite the first side is a right angle.

- **Theorem 19** (formal proof required)
  The angle at the centre of a circle standing on a given arc is twice the angle at any point of the circle standing on the same arc.

- **Corollary 1 of Theorem 19**
  All angles at points of a circle standing on the same arc are equal.

- **Corollary 2 of Theorem 19**
  Each angle in a semi-circle is a right angle.

- **Corollary 3 of Theorem 19**
  If the angle standing on a chord $[PR]$ at some point of the circle is a right angle, then $[PR]$ is a diameter.

- **Corollary 4 of Theorem 19**
  If $ABCD$ is a cyclic quadrilateral, then opposite angles sum to 180°.

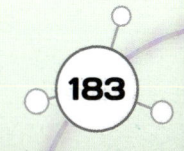

Chapter 11: Applied Measure

Learning Outcomes

In this chapter, you will learn about:

- Area and perimeter of various shapes (review and extension)
- The nets of prisms, cylinders and cones
- The surface area of triangular-based prisms, cylinders and cones
- Solving problems relating to the curved surface area of cylinders, cones and spheres
- Calculations using formulae for the volume of rectangular solids, cylinders, cones, triangular-based prisms, spheres and combinations of these

Section 11A Area and Perimeter of a Triangle

In this section, we will build on our knowledge of perimeter and area of different shapes which we met in *Connect with Maths 1*.

Key Points

The formulae for the perimeter and area of various shapes are summarised below.

- **Square**
  Area = length × length
  Perimeter = 4 × length
  $= 4l$

- **Rectangle**
  Area = length × width
  Perimeter = 2(length) + 2(width)
  $= 2l + 2w$

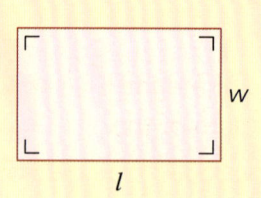

- **Triangle**
  Area = $\frac{1}{2}$ × base × perpendicular height
  $= \frac{1}{2} \times b \times h$
  Perimeter = sum of all three sides

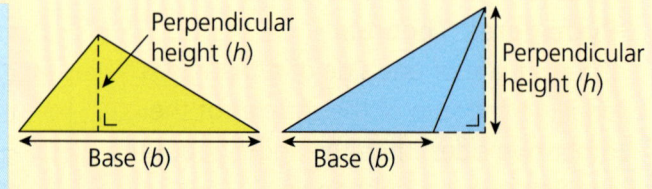

The formulae for a triangle are on page 9 of the *Formulae and tables* booklet.

Connections

We need to use our knowledge of geometry theorems in this section, especially that which relates to congruent triangles.

In the isosceles triangle ABC shown, |AB| = |AC|.

[AD] is drawn perpendicular to [BC].

The triangles ABD and ADC are congruent (RHS).

Hence |BD| = |DC|.

We will use this information in the following examples.

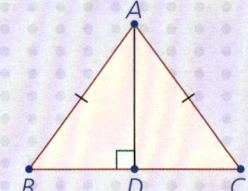

Example 1

ABC is an isosceles triangle with |AB| = |AC| = 10 cm and |BC| = 12 cm.

(i) Find h, the perpendicular height of the triangle ABC.

(ii) Find the area of ABC.

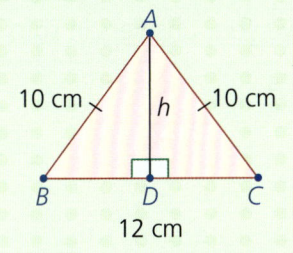

Solution

(i) The triangles ABD and ADC are congruent (RHS).

Hence |BD| = |DC| = 6 cm.

Using the theorem of Pythagoras on triangle ADC, we have

$h^2 + 6^2 = 10^2$

$\Rightarrow h^2 = 10^2 - 6^2$

$\Rightarrow h^2 = 100 - 36 = 64$

$\Rightarrow h = \sqrt{64} = 8$ cm

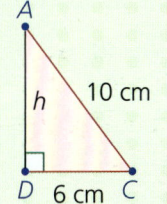

(ii) Area of triangle ABC

$= \dfrac{1}{2} \times$ base $\times$ perpendicular height

$= \dfrac{1}{2} \times 12 \times 8 = 48$ cm^2

Example 2

ABC is an equilateral triangle of side length 8 cm.

Find the area of triangle ABC in surd form.

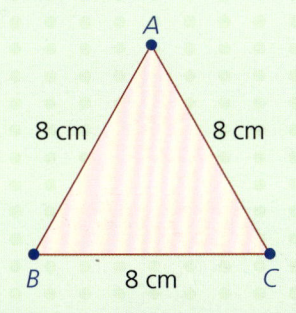

Solution

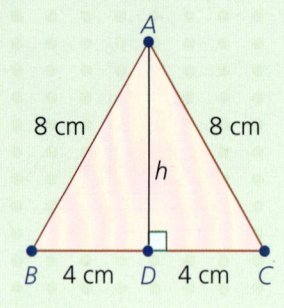

Draw [AD] ⊥ [BC].

The triangles ABD and ADC are congruent (RHS).

Hence |BD| = |DC| = 4 cm.

Using the theorem of Pythagoras on triangle ADC, we have

$h^2 + 4^2 = 8^2$

$\Rightarrow h^2 = 8^2 - 4^2$

$\Rightarrow h^2 = 64 - 16 = 48$

$\Rightarrow h = \sqrt{48} = 4\sqrt{3}$ cm

Area of triangle ABC

$= \frac{1}{2} \times$ base $\times$ perpendicular height

$= \frac{1}{2} \times 8 \times 4\sqrt{3} = 16\sqrt{3}$ cm²

Activity 11.1

1 Find the area of each of the following isosceles triangles.

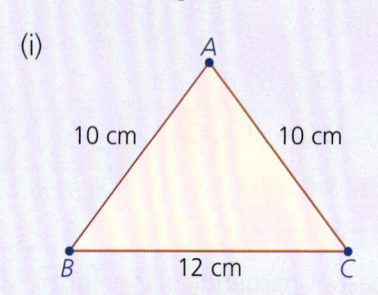

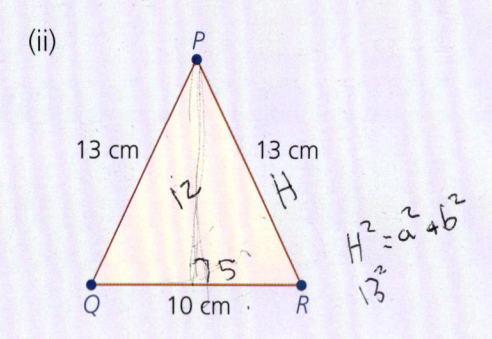

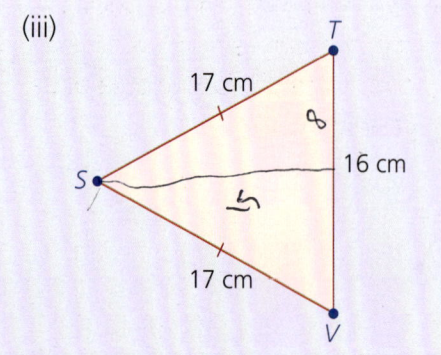

(i) Triangle ABC with AB = AC = 10 cm, BC = 12 cm.

(ii) Triangle PQR with PQ = PR = 13 cm, QR = 10 cm.

(iii) Triangle STV with ST = SV = 17 cm, TV = 16 cm.

2 Find the area of the following equilateral triangles. Give your answers in surd form.

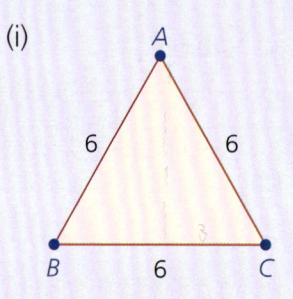

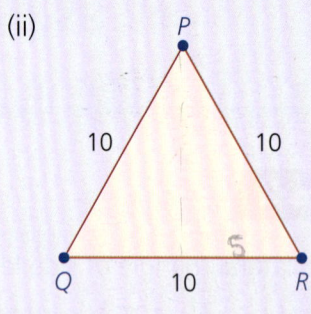

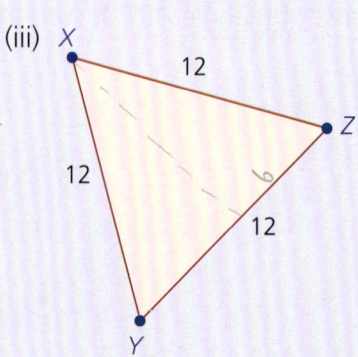

(i) Triangle ABC with sides 6.

(ii) Triangle PQR with sides 10.

(iii) Triangle XYZ with sides 12.

3 Find the area of the following right-angled triangles.

(i) Triangle PQR with P, Q, R: PQ = 3, QR = 4, PR = 5, right angle at Q.

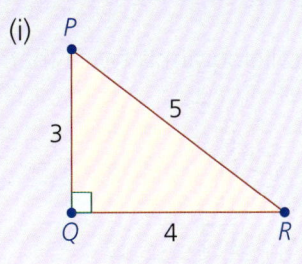

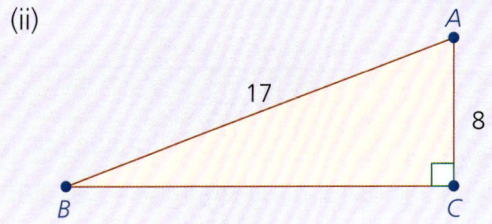

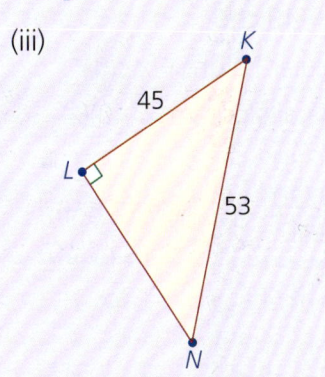

(ii) Triangle ABC with AB = 17, AC = 8, right angle at C.

(iii) Triangle KLN with KL = 45, KN = 53, right angle at L.

4 For each of the following triangles find:
   (i) the area of the triangle to the nearest cm²
   (ii) the perimeter of the triangle, to the nearest cm where appropriate.

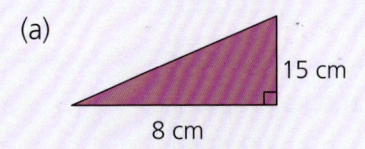

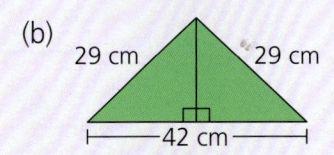

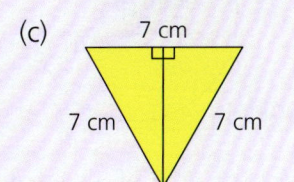

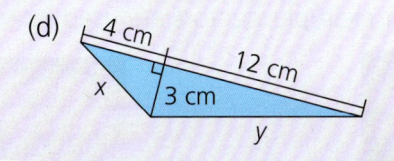

(a) Right-angled triangle with legs 8 cm and 15 cm.

(b) Triangle with two sides 29 cm, 29 cm and base 42 cm.

(c) Triangle with sides 7 cm, 7 cm, 7 cm.

(d) Triangle with sides 4 cm, 3 cm, 12 cm, labelled x and y.

5 ABCD is a parallelogram with diagonal [AC]. |BC| = 6 and |AB| = 4. The perpendicular height = 3.

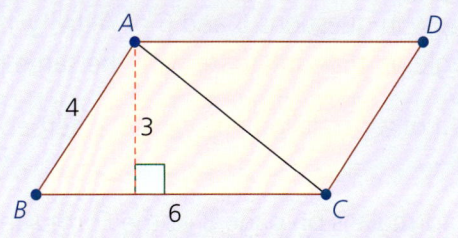

(AB = 4, perpendicular height = 3, BC = 6)

(i) Find the area of triangle ABC.
(ii) Prove that the triangles ABC and ADC are congruent.
(iii) How does the area of ABCD compare to the area of the triangle ABC?
(iv) Write down the area of parallelogram ABCD.

6 KLMQ is a parallelogram with diagonal [KM]. |KQ| = 7 and |QM| = 12. The perpendicular height = 6.

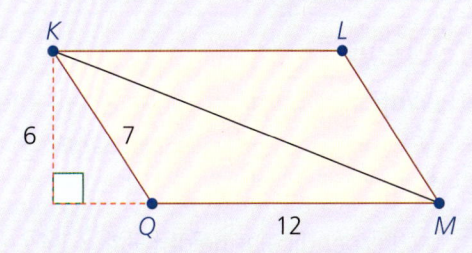

(KQ = 7, perpendicular height = 6, QM = 12)

(i) Find the area of triangle KQM.
(ii) Show that the triangles KQM and KLM are congruent.
(iii) How does the area of KLMQ compare to the area of the triangle KQM?
(iv) Write down the area of parallelogram KLMQ.
(v) From your work in this question and also in question 5, can you give a formula for the area of a parallelogram?

Applied Measure

11

Section 11B Parallelograms and Circles

The Area of a Parallelogram

We saw in questions 5 and 6 of Activity 11.1 that the area of a parallelogram is twice that of a triangle on the same base with the same perpendicular height.

> Area of a parallelogram = base × perpendicular height
> $= a \times h$

This formula is on page 8 of the *Formulae and tables* booklet.

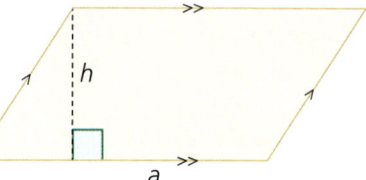

Example 1

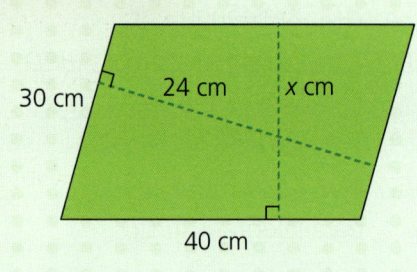

(i) Find the area of this parallelogram.
(ii) Hence or otherwise, find the value of the perpendicular height, x.

Solution

(i) Write down the information we know:
- Area of a parallelogram = ah
- Base = a = 30 cm
- Perpendicular height = h = 24 cm

Area = $30 \times 24 = 720$ cm²

(ii) Write down the information we know:
- Area of a parallelogram = 720 cm²
- Base = a = 40 cm
- Perpendicular height = x cm
- Area of parallelogram = $(40)(x)$

$\Rightarrow 40x = 720$
$\Rightarrow x = \dfrac{720}{40}$ ... divide both sides by 40
$\Rightarrow x = 18$ cm

Arcs and Sectors of Circles

In *Connect with Maths 1*, we worked with the circle (disc) and its properties.

Key Points

- **Circle**

> Circumference of a circle = $2\pi r$
> Area of a circle = πr^2

These formulae are on page 9 of the *Formulae and tables* booklet.

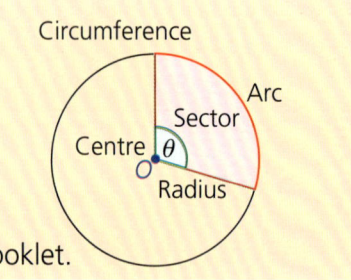

In some situations, it is necessary to work out the perimeter and/or the area of a **sector** of a circle instead of the circumference/area of a full circle. For example, sectors are used in:

- Pie charts
- Window design
- Garden design

Connections

Sectors and arcs are fractions of discs and circles. Therefore, we can use our knowledge of ratio and proportion when working with these, as we see in the next example.

Example 2

A circle of radius 7 cm is shown. Sector OBA of the circle and the arc AB are also shown. $|\angle BOA| = 90°$.

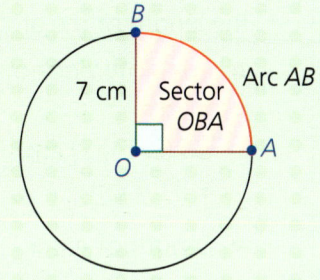

(i) Find the area of the circle, taking π as $\frac{22}{7}$.

(ii) Find the area of the sector OBA.

(iii) Find the circumference of the circle.

(iv) Find the length of the arc AB.

Solution

(i) The area of the circle = πr^2
$= \frac{22}{7}(7)(7)$
$= 154 \text{ cm}^2$

(ii) We use our knowledge of ratio and proportion to find the area of the sector OBA from the area of the circle.

The sector OBA has an angle of 90°. As 90° is $\frac{1}{4}$ of 360° (a full circle), the area of the sector OBA is $\frac{1}{4}$ of the area of the circle.

$= \frac{1}{4} \times 154$

$= 38.5 \text{ cm}^2$

(iii) The circumference of the circle
$= 2\pi r$
$= 2 \times \frac{22}{7} \times 7$
$= 44 \text{ cm}$

(iv) Using equal ratios, the length of the arc $AB = \frac{1}{4}$ of the circumference of the circle.

$\therefore$ length of arc $AB = \frac{1}{4} \times 44 = 11 \text{ cm}$

Notice that in the above example, we use $\frac{1}{4}$ of the circle measurements to get the sector and arc measurements, since the sector angle of 90° as a fraction of a full circle $= \frac{90}{360} = \frac{1}{4}$.

This gives us formulae to calculate the length of an arc and the area of a sector of a circle, when the angle θ is measured in degrees.

Key Points

- **Sector of a circle**

  Length of arc $= \frac{\theta}{360°} \times 2\pi r$

  Area of a sector $= \frac{\theta}{360°} \times \pi r^2$

These formulae are on page 9 of the *Formulae and tables* booklet.

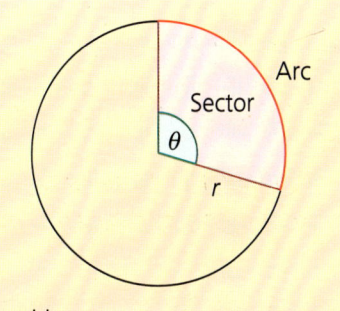

CONNECT WITH MATHS 2

Example 3

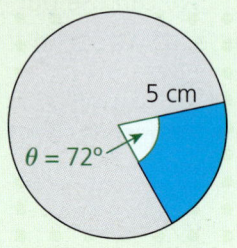

(i) Find the area of this circle.
(ii) Find the area of the sector shaded blue.
(iii) What is the ratio of the circumference of the full circle to the length of the arc of the sector shaded blue?
[Let $\pi = 3.14$]

Solution

(i) Area of circle = πr^2
$= (3.14)(5)^2$
$= 78.5 \text{ cm}^2$

(ii) Write down the information we know:
- Area of a sector = $\frac{\theta}{360} \times \pi r^2$
- Radius = 5 cm
- Angle $\theta = 72°$

- Area of the sector = $\frac{\theta}{360} \times \pi r^2$
$= \frac{72}{360} \times (3.14)(5)^2$
$= \frac{72}{360} \times 78.5$
$= 15.7 \text{ cm}^2$

(iii) Find the circumference of the circle and the length of the arc, then find the ratio.

- Circumference of the circle
$= 2\pi r$
$= 2(3.14)(5) \text{ cm}$
$= 31.4 \text{ cm}$

- Length of arc = $\frac{\theta}{360°} \times 2\pi r$
$= \frac{72}{360} \times 31.4$
$= 6.28 \text{ cm}$

- Ratio
Circumference of circle : Length of arc
$= 31.4 : 6.28$ … divide both by 6.28
$= 5 : 1$

Activity 11.2

1 Find the area of each of the parallelograms.

(i) 22 m, 13 m

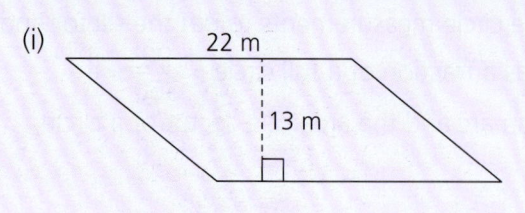

(ii) 26 cm, 30 cm

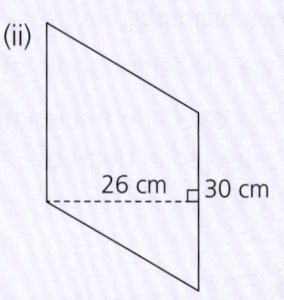

2 Using the information given on each parallelogram, find the missing values in each.

(i) 28, 22, b, 19.25

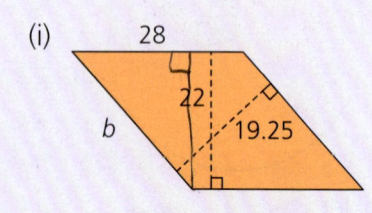

(ii) 15, 20, h, 13

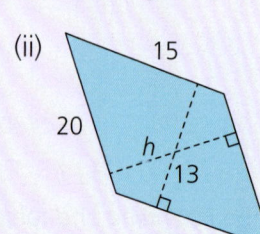

(iii) b, 12, 15, 17

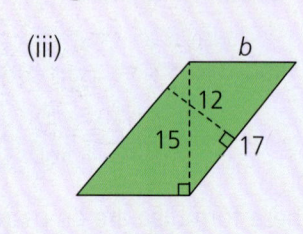

3 Find the area of each of the following shapes. Let π = 3.14 where appropriate.

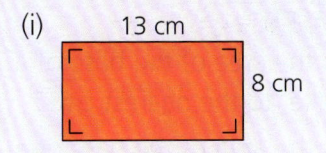

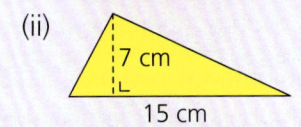

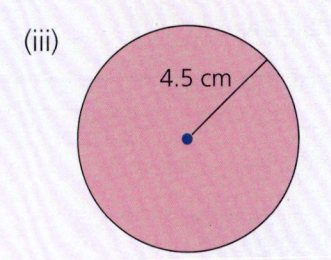

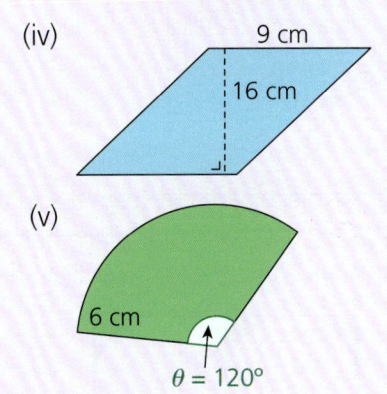

(i) 13 cm, 8 cm

(ii) 7 cm, 15 cm

(iii) 4.5 cm

(iv) 9 cm, 16 cm

(v) 6 cm, θ = 120°

(iii) 5.5 cm

(iv) 12 cm, θ = 36°

(v) 9.4 cm, θ = 90°

(vi) 1.5 m, θ = 240°

4 For each of the following shapes, find:
(a) the outer perimeter
(b) the area enclosed.

Where necessary, give your answer correct to two decimal places.

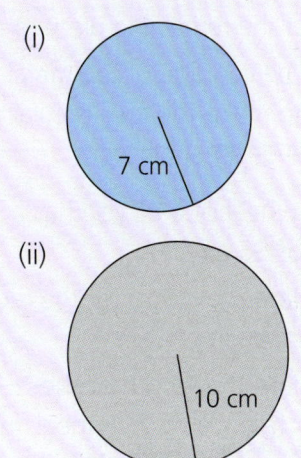

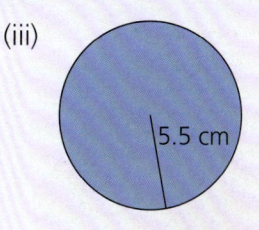

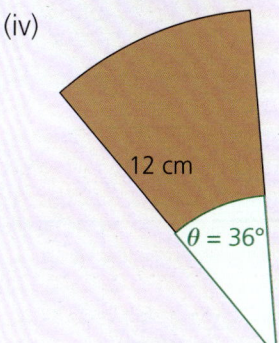

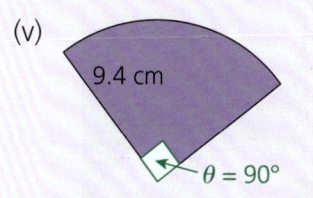

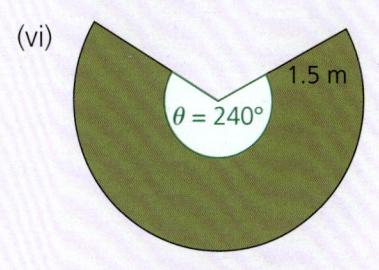

(i) 7 cm

(ii) 10 cm

5 For each of the following shapes, find:
(a) the perimeter
(b) the area, correct to one decimal place.

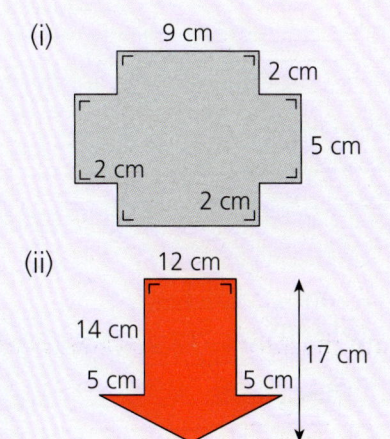

(i) 9 cm, 2 cm, 5 cm, 2 cm, 2 cm

(ii) 12 cm, 14 cm, 5 cm, 5 cm, 17 cm

(iii)

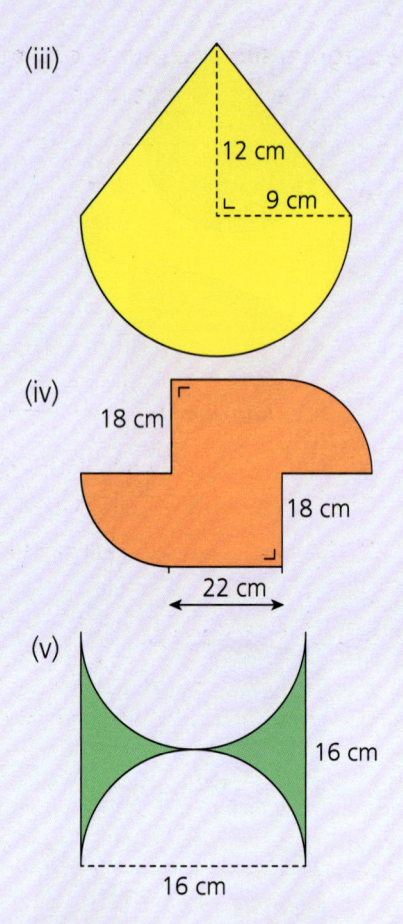

12 cm
9 cm

(iv)
18 cm
18 cm
22 cm

(v)
16 cm
16 cm

6 Find the value of the variables in each of the following shapes, given the area of the shape in each case.

(i)
w
Area 112 cm²
14 cm

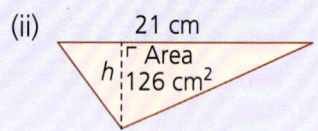

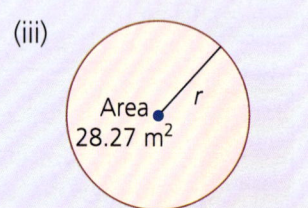

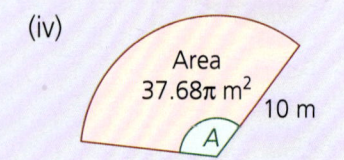

(ii)
21 cm
Area 126 cm²
h

(iii)
Area 28.27 m²
r

(iv)
Area 37.68π m²
10 m
A

7 A small chocolate cake has diameter 15 cm. A large chocolate cake has diameter 20 cm.

(i) What is the area of the base of a small cake, to the nearest cm²?

(ii) What is the area of the base of a large cake, to the nearest cm²?

(iii) What is the difference in area between the bases of 2 large cakes and 3 small cakes?

8 Find the area of this shape.

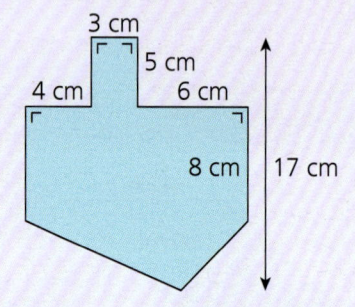

3 cm
5 cm
4 cm
6 cm
8 cm
17 cm

9 Four circular pieces are cut from a square piece of metal. Each circular piece has a radius of 5 cm.

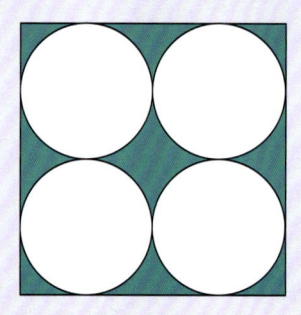

(i) Find, in cm² to two decimal places, the area of the remaining piece of metal.

(ii) What percentage of the metal was used to make the four circular pieces, to two decimal places?

10 The front wheel of a bicycle has a diameter of 56 cm.

(i) Calculate the length of the radius of the wheel, in cm.

(ii) Calculate the length of the circumference of the wheel, in cm. Take π as $\frac{22}{7}$.

(iii) How far does the bicycle travel when the wheel makes 250 complete turns? Give your answer in metres.

11 Pat designed the garden shown below for a pre-school.

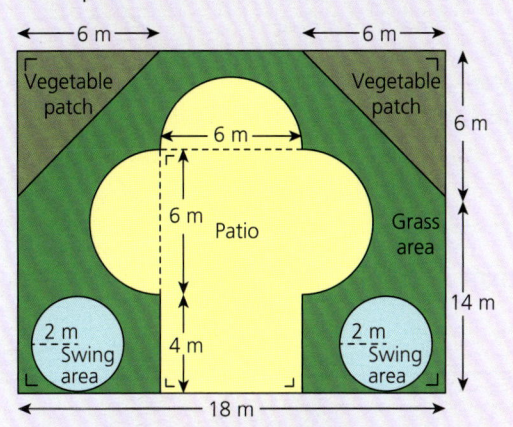

(i) What is the total area of the garden?
(ii) What is the total area of the two vegetable patches?
(iii) Find the area of the patio, correct to the nearest m².
(iv) What is the area of the grass region of the garden?
(v) What percentage of the garden is not grass? Give your answer to the nearest percent.

12 The diagram shows a parallelogram with several shapes drawn inside it.

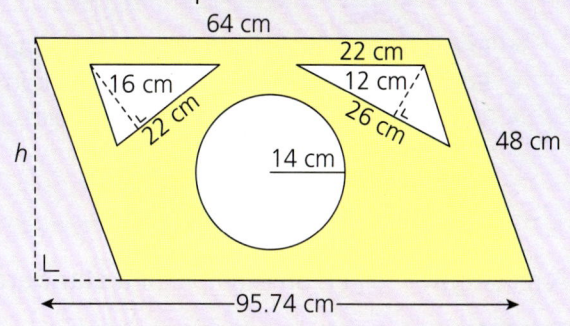

(i) Find the perpendicular height of the parallelogram, to two decimal places.
(ii) Find the area of the region shaded yellow.
(iii) What percentage of the parallelogram is not shaded? Give your answer to the nearest percent.

Section 11C Prisms

We meet prisms in everyday situations. Here are some examples.

> **Key Points**
>
> A **prism** is a 3-dimensional figure where:
> - the bases (or ends of the object) are the same shape and size
> - the bases are parallel to one another
> - the sides of the object form parallelograms.

When we describe prisms, we generally mention three key properties.

We will use a triangular-based prism to explain each of these properties.

CONNECT WITH MATHS 2

Key Points

- **Faces** are the individual flat surfaces of an object.
- **Edges** are the line segments that join two vertices.
- **Vertices** (singular: **vertex**) are any points where two or more edges meet.

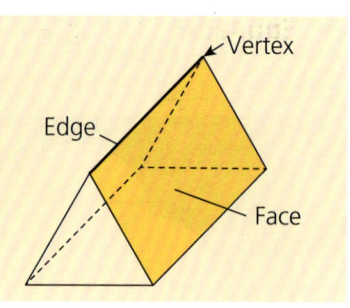

A rectangular solid is an example of a **standard prism**.

Other examples of standard prisms are shown here.

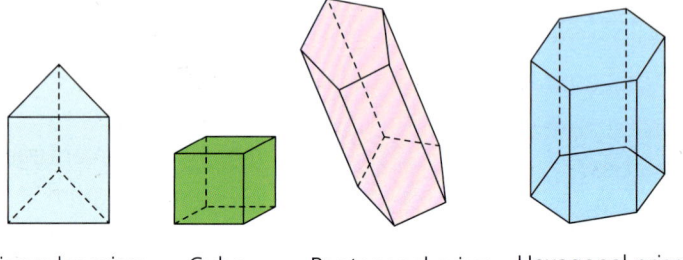

Triangular prism   Cube   Pentagonal prism   Hexagonal prism

Other prisms that we will meet are called **irregular shaped prisms**. They differ from standard prisms in that they are made from a combination of two or more standard shaped prisms. Here are some examples of irregular shaped prisms.

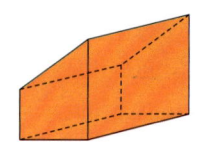

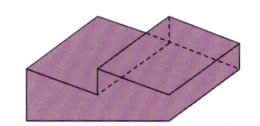

The following is a range of prisms along with a sample net for each.

■ Right-angled triangular-based prism		
	We can see that the cross-section or base of this prism is a right-angled triangle.	

■ Isosceles triangular-based prism		
	We can see that the cross-section or base of this prism is an isosceles triangle.	

Equilateral triangular-based prism

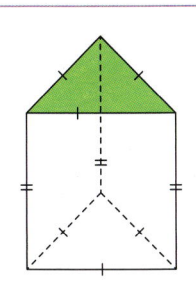

We can see that the cross-section or base of this prism is an equilateral triangle.

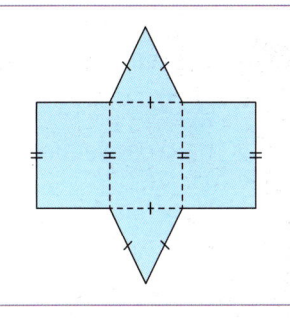

Rectangular prism

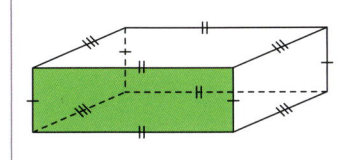

All six sides are flat, all angles are right angles and all of the faces are rectangles. It is also known as a **cuboid**.

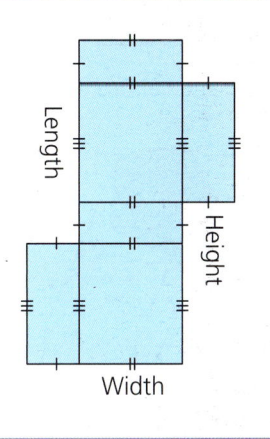

Cube

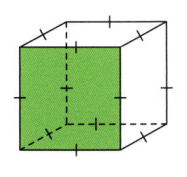

A cube has six identical square faces. It is also known as a **regular hexahedron**.

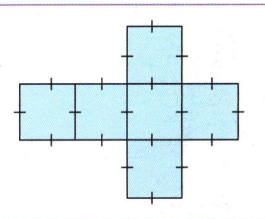

Pentagonal prism

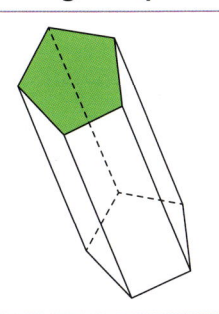

This prism has a pentagon-shaped cross-section. It has two pentagon bases and five rectangular sides.

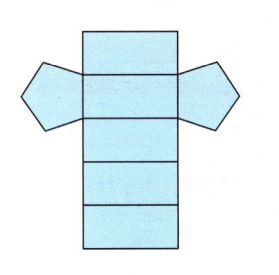

Hexagonal prism

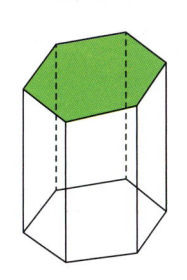

This prism has a hexagon cross-section. It has two hexagon bases and six rectangular sides.

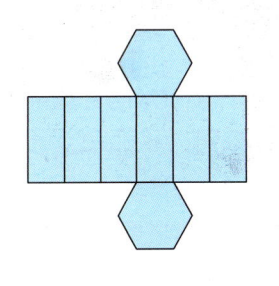

11 Volume of Prisms

To find the **volume** of any prism, we must find the area of the **cross-section** (or **base**) of the prism and multiply it by the height or depth of the prism.

The cross-sections of different regular and irregular prisms are shown. The green highlighted side is the cross-section.

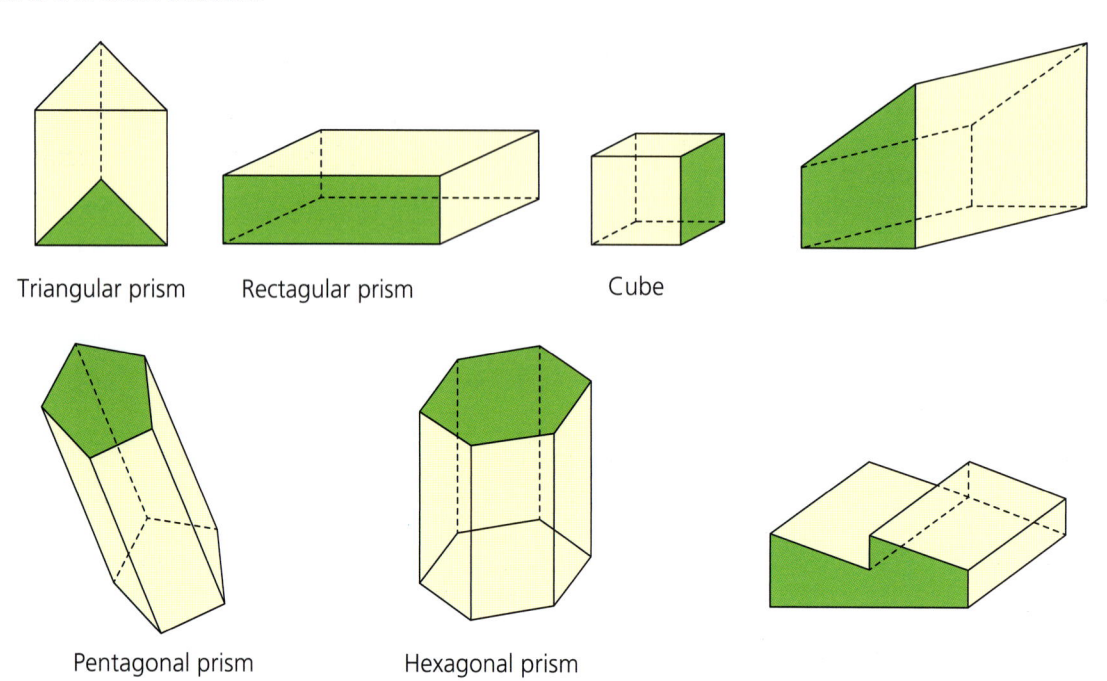

Triangular prism   Rectagular prism   Cube

Pentagonal prism   Hexagonal prism

> **Key Point**
>
> Volume of a prism = area of the cross-section × height/depth of the prism

Example 1

The images show (i) a regular prism and (ii) an irregular prism.

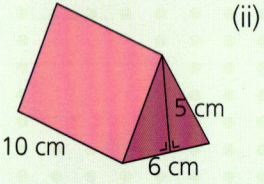

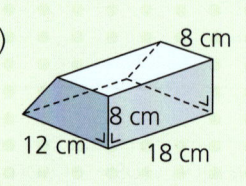

(i) 10 cm, 5 cm, 6 cm

(ii) 8 cm, 8 cm, 12 cm, 18 cm

(a) Draw a sketch of the cross-section of each of the prisms above.
(b) Hence, find the volume of each prism.

Solution

(i) (a) Cross-section of the prism

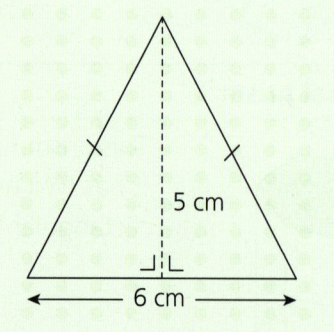

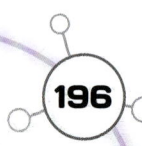

Triangle with equal sides, height 5 cm, base 6 cm

(b) Area of cross-section
= Area of a triangle
= $\frac{1}{2} \times b \times h$
= $\frac{1}{2} \times 6 \times 5 = 15$ cm²

Volume of the prism = area of the cross-section × depth of the prism
= 15 cm² × 10 cm = 150 cm³

(ii) (a) Cross-section of the prism

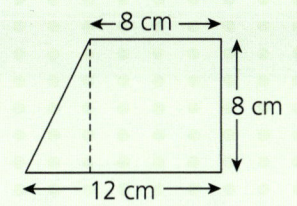

(b) Area of cross-section
= Area of triangle + Area of square
= $\left(\frac{1}{2} \times b \times h\right) + (l \times l)$
= $\left(\frac{1}{2} \times 4 \times 8\right) + (8 \times 8)$
= 16 + 64 = 80 cm²

Volume of the prism
= area of the cross-section × depth of the prism
= 80 cm² × 18 cm
= 1440 cm³

Total Surface Area (TSA) of a Prism

We have already met the **total surface area** of rectangular solids. We used the net of a solid to assist in finding the total surface area of the solid.

The **total surface area** (TSA) of any prism can be found using the same method.

Key Point

The TSA of a prism is the sum of all the areas of the faces for a given prism.

Example 2

(i) Draw a net of the surface of this prism.

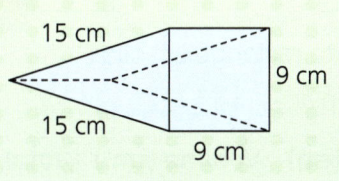

(ii) Find the total surface area of the prism, correct to one decimal place.

Solution

(i) Net for the prism

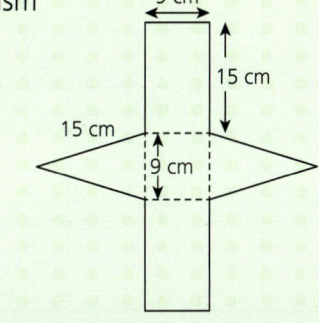

(ii) Form a right-angled triangle to find the perpendicular height of the prism base.

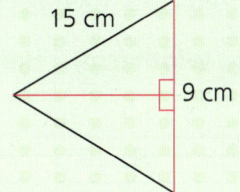

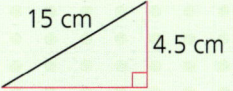

Pythagoras' Theorem:
$c^2 = a^2 + b^2$
$\Rightarrow 15^2 = 4.5^2 + b^2$
$\Rightarrow 225 = 20.25 + b^2$

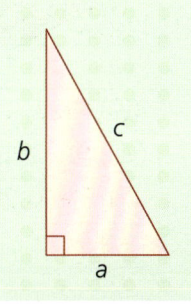

CONNECT WITH MATHS 2

$$\Rightarrow 225 - 20.25 = b^2 \quad \text{... subtract 20.25 from both sides}$$
$$\Rightarrow 204.75 = b^2$$
$$\Rightarrow \sqrt{204.75} = b \quad \text{... square root both sides}$$
$$\Rightarrow 14.309... = b$$
$$\Rightarrow b = 14.3 \text{ cm (one decimal place)}$$

Total surface area = 2(area of a triangular face) + 2(area of a rectangular face) + (area of the square face)

Total surface area
$$= 2\left(\frac{1}{2} \times 14.3 \times 9\right) + 2(15 \times 9) + (9 \times 9)$$
$$= 128.7 + 270 + 81$$
$$= 479.7 \text{ cm}^2$$

Activity 11.3

1 For the rectangular solid shown, find:
  (i) the total surface area
  (ii) the volume
  (iii) the capacity in litres.

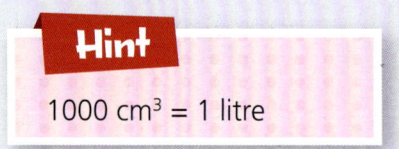

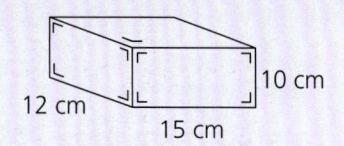

Hint
$1000 \text{ cm}^3 = 1$ litre

2 State which of the nets below (A, B, C or D) is a net for the rectangular solid shown. Explain your answer.

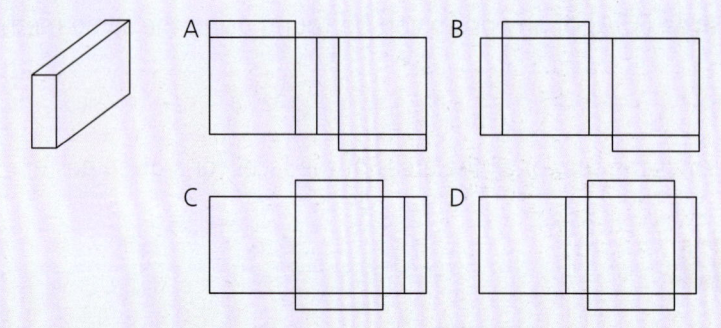

3 Copy and complete the table which relates to rectangular solids.
Give your answers correct to three decimal places.

	Length (cm)	Width (cm)	Height (cm)	Volume (cm³)	Total surface area (cm²)
(i)	6	5.5	7		
(ii)	12.5	9	9		
(iii)	60	70	80		
(iv)	1.2	1.6	1.8		
(v)	$\frac{1}{2}$	$\frac{3}{4}$	$\frac{2}{3}$		
(vi)	15		17	4080	
(vii)		3.4	5.8	90.712	
(viii)	13	8		832	
(ix)	26		20		3662
(x)		22.6	11.7		2826.94

4 Find the capacity of each of the following rectangular water tanks. Give your answers in litres correct to two decimal places.

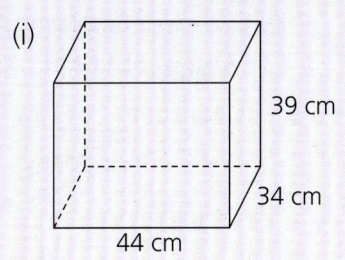

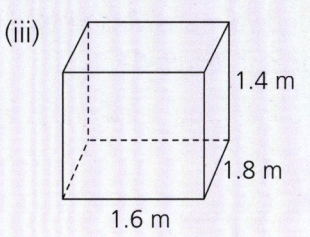

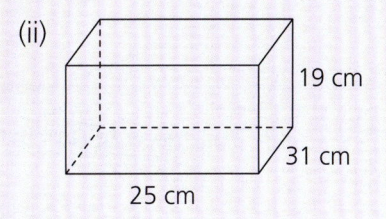

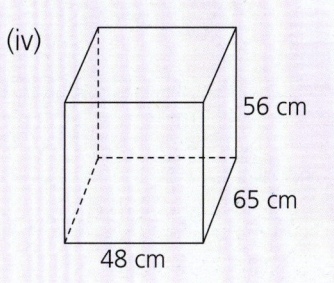

(i) 44 cm × 34 cm × 39 cm

(ii) 25 cm × 31 cm × 19 cm

(iii) 1.6 m × 1.8 m × 1.4 m

(iv) 48 cm × 65 cm × 56 cm

5 For each of these prisms:
(a) draw a sketch of the cross-section
(b) find the cross-sectional area
(c) find the volume of the prism
(d) find the total surface area of the prism.

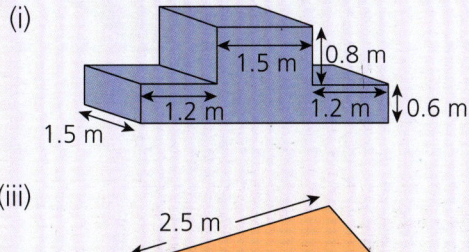

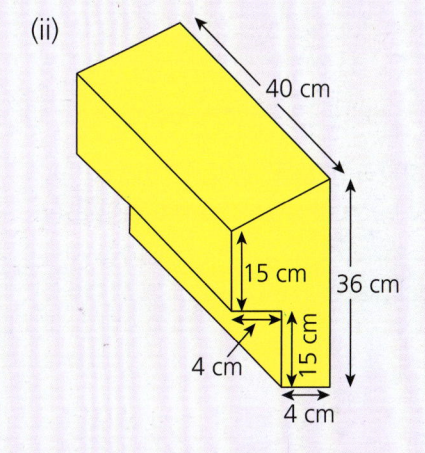

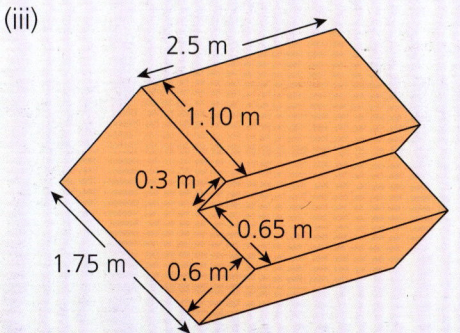

(i) 1.5 m, 1.2 m, 1.2 m, 0.8 m, 0.6 m, 1.5 m

(ii) 40 cm, 36 cm, 15 cm, 15 cm, 4 cm, 4 cm

(iii) 2.5 m, 1.10 m, 0.3 m, 0.65 m, 0.6 m, 1.75 m

6 (i) Copy and complete the table for each prism listed.

Prism base	Number of sides	Number of edges	Number of vertices
(a) Cube			
(b) Rectangular solid			
(c) Triangular prism			
(d) Pentagonal prism			
(e) Hexagonal prism			

(ii) Draw a sketch of the cross-section of each prism in part (i).

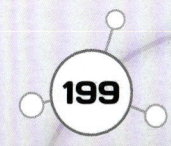

7 Find (a) the volume and (b) the surface area of each of these triangular-based prisms. Round your answers to two decimal places if required.

(i) 12 cm, 4 cm, 4 cm, 4 cm

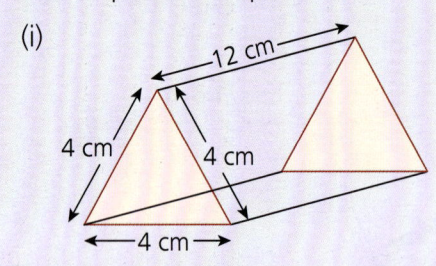

(ii) 41 cm, 41 cm, 80 cm, 70 cm

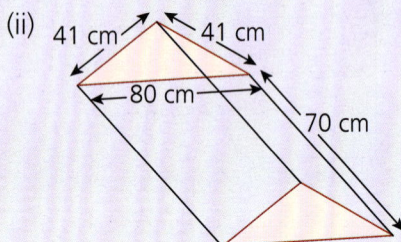

(iii) 13 cm, 7 m, 25 m

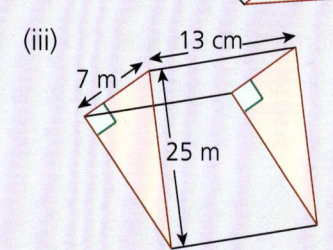

8 Find (a) the volume and (b) the surface area of each of these triangular-based prisms. Round your answers to two decimal places if required.

(i) 24 cm, 37 cm, 35 cm

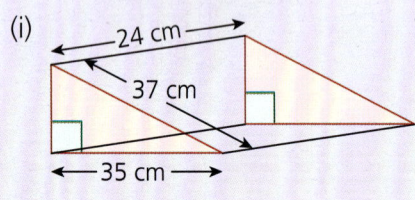

(ii) 12 m, 9 m, 9 m, 9 m

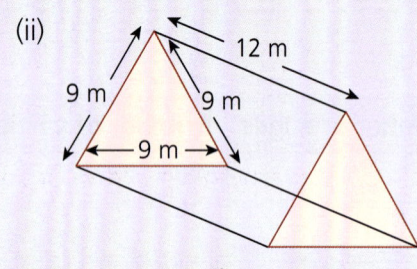

(iii) 109 cm, 109 cm, 80 cm, 120 cm

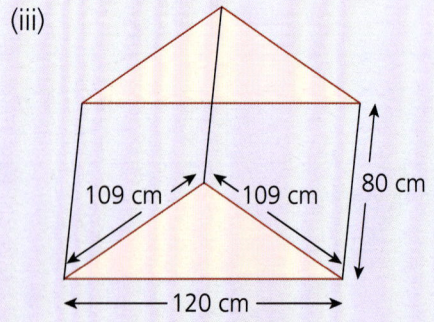

9 For each of these prisms, find the value of the missing side. Round your answers to two decimal places if required.

(i) Volume = 9.625 m³
    x m, Area 2.75 m²

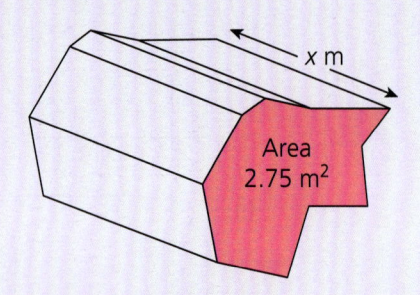

(ii) Volume = 6604 cm³
    x cm, Area 254 cm²

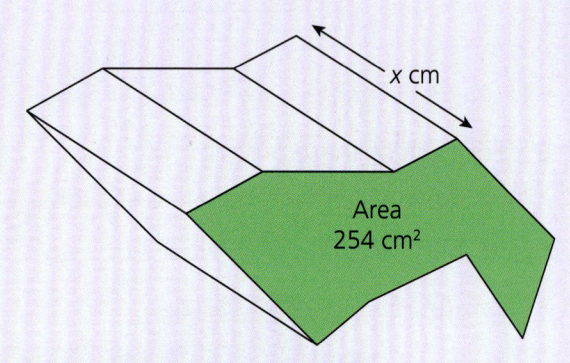

(iii) Volume = 30 240 cm³
    x cm, Area 1728 cm²

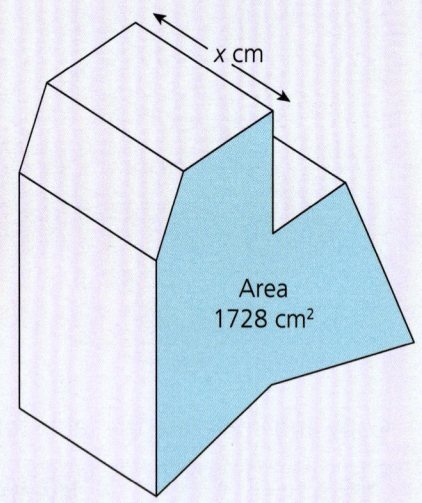

10 A 7-sided prism has the numbers 1, 2, 3, 4, 5, 6 and 7 written on each side. The diagram shows a net of this prism.

Draw a sketch of the net into your copy and number each face such that no two consecutive numbered faces touch when the net is formed into a prism.

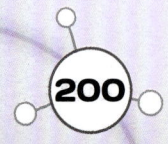

11 When this net is formed into a polygonal prism, which sides are opposite each other?

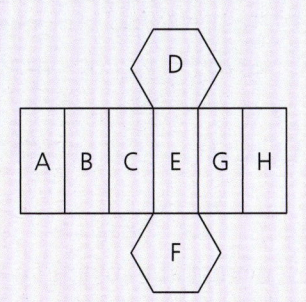

12 The diagram is a net for an 8-sided prism.

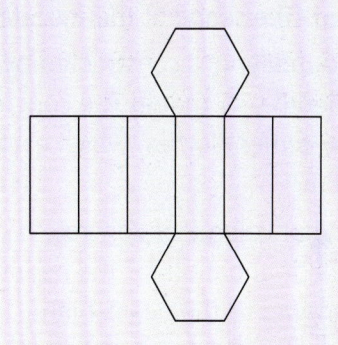

Draw a sketch of the net into your copy and number each face such that no two consecutive numbered faces touch when the net is formed into a prism.

13 State which of the nets below (A, B, C or D) is an **incorrect** net for this object.

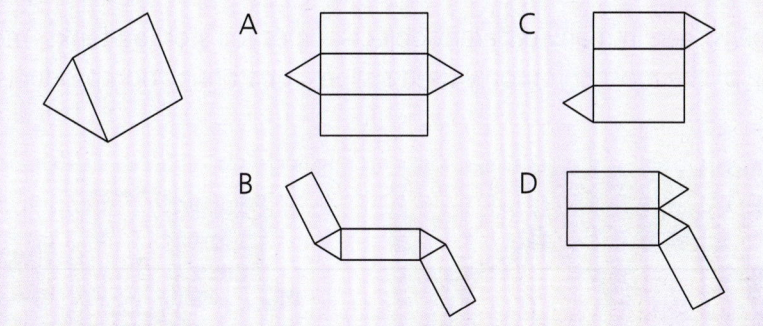

14 State which of the nets below (A, B, C, D or E) are the **correct** nets for this object.

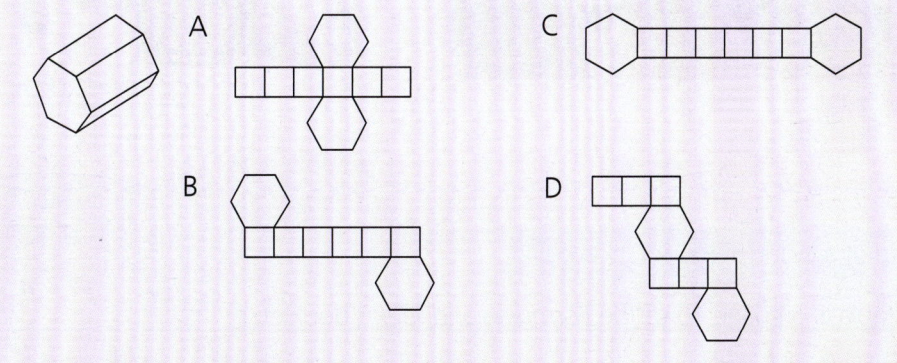

15 A company sells a range of fruit juice. One of the products is a rectangular carton of apple juice which has the dimensions 12 cm by 5 cm by 33 cm.
  (i) Sketch a net of the apple juice carton.
  (ii) Find the volume of apple juice in the carton.

The volume of one carton of apple juice is equivalent to five smaller cartons which have a square base of length 6 cm.
  (iii) Find the volume of this smaller carton.
  (iv) Find the height of this smaller carton.

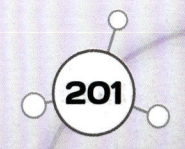

16 The foundation of a new building is about to be poured. The shape of the foundation is shown.

The foundation is constructed by pouring concrete to a depth of 1 metre. The concrete is delivered to site by cement lorries, which each have a capacity of 10 m³.

(i) What volume of concrete is required to lay the foundation for the new building? Give your answer to the nearest litre.

(ii) If the foundation was filled to a depth of 2 metres, what is the minimum number of trips each driver would have to make, assuming there are three drivers and they all do the same number of trips?

Section 11D Cylinders

The cylinder shape is seen in many different objects: pipes, oil storage tanks, medicine capsules, etc. Also, it is one of the most commonly used shapes for storing food products, typically in a tin can.

Key Point

Volume of a cylinder = $\pi \times r^2 \times h$

The formula is on page 10 of the *Formulae and tables* booklet.

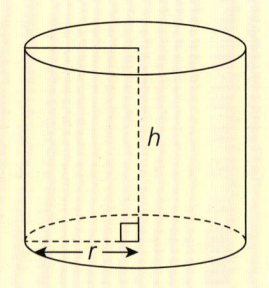

Note: A cylinder is **not a prism**.

In a prism, the bases or ends are the same size and shape, are parallel to each other, and *the sides of the figure form parallelograms*.

As the side of a cylinder is curved, it cannot form a parallelogram because there are no straight lines.

Net of a Cylinder

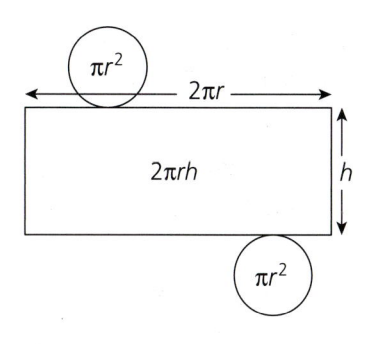

- A cylinder has two congruent (equal) circles.
- The curved surface makes a rectangle when it is flattened out.
- The length of two of the sides of the rectangle is equal to the circumference of the circle formed at the top and bottom of the cylinder ($2\pi r$).
- The length of the other two sides in the rectangle is equal to the height of the cylinder (h).

Surface Area of a Cylinder

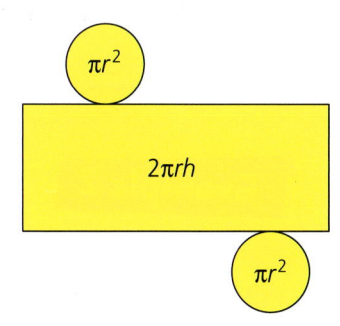

The curved surface area is the area of the curved part of the cylinder. In the net it is the rectangular section, so to find its area we multiply length × width = $2\pi r \times h = 2\pi rh$.

Curved surface area of a cylinder = $2\pi rh$

The **total surface area** of a cylinder is seen from the net as the area of the rectangle plus two circles.

Total surface area of a cylinder = $2\pi rh + 2\pi r^2$
$= 2\pi r(h + r)$

Example 1

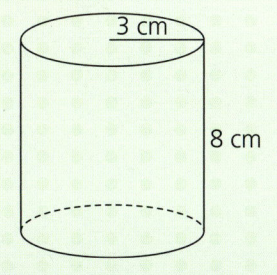

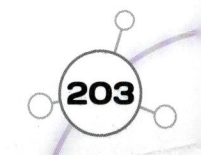

The diagram shows a cylinder of height 8 cm and base radius 3 cm.

(i) Find the volume of the cylinder, in terms of π.
(ii) Calculate the total surface area of the cylinder, using $\pi = 3.14$.
(iii) Find the dimensions of the smallest rectangular box that could contain this cylinder.

Solution

Given $r = 3$ cm, $h = 8$ cm

(i) Volume = $\pi \times r^2 \times h$
$= \pi \times 3^2 \times 8$
$= 72\pi$ cm^3

(ii) Total surface area (TSA) = $2\pi rh + 2\pi r^2$
$= 2\pi(3)(8) + 2\pi(3)^2$
$= 48\pi + 18\pi$
$= 66\pi$ cm^2
$= 66(3.14)$
$= 207.24$ cm^2

(iii) - Smallest height of the box = height of cylinder
$$= 8 \text{ cm}$$
- Smallest width of the box = width of the cylinder
Width of the box = diameter of circle $\Rightarrow d = 2r$
$$= 2(3) = 6 \text{ cm}$$

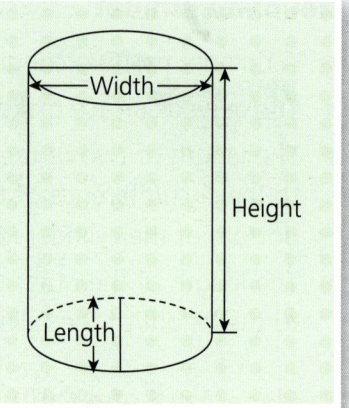

Example 2

The radii of two cylinders are in the ratio $2:1$ and their heights are in the ratio $2:3$. What is the ratio of the volumes of the two cylinders?

Solution

We are given the ratios that link both the radius and the height.
- Let x be a factor of the radii and let y be a factor of the height for both cylinders.
  - Radii ratio = $2:1$, so $2x$ and x are the radii.
  - Height ratio = $2:3$, so $2y$ and $3y$ are the heights.
- Draw a sketch of the two cylinders and label all known dimensions.

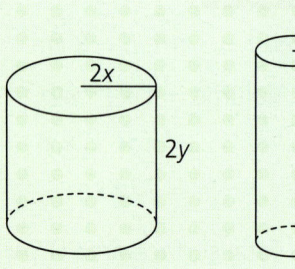

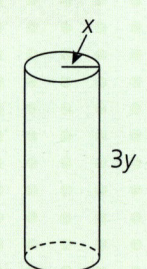

Cylinder 1 Cylinder 2

Volume of cylinder 1 $= \pi r^2 h = \pi (2x)^2 (2y) = 8\pi x^2 y$

Volume of cylinder 2 $= \pi r^2 h = \pi (x)^2 (3y) = 3\pi x^2 y$

Ratio

Volume of cylinder 1 : Volume of cylinder 2
$= 8\pi x^2 y : 3\pi x^2 y$ ... divide both parts of the ratio by $\pi x^2 y$
$= 8 : 3$

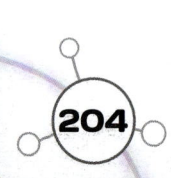

Activity 11.4

1. The table gives some data relating to cylinders. Copy and complete the table.
   Give all answers correct to two decimal places.

	π	Height	Radius	Volume	Total surface area
(i)	3.14	6 cm	2 cm		
(ii)	π	5 m	5 m		
(iii)	22/7	28 cm	21 cm		
(iv)	22/7	7 cm		1985.5 cm³	
(v)	π		8.4 m		368π m²
(vi)	3.14	1.4 m		89.019 m³	
(vii)	π		30 cm		6672.5 cm²
(viii)	π		66 mm	104 544π mm³	
(ix)	22/7		7 cm		748 cm²
(x)	3.14		32 cm	176 844.8 cm³	
(xi)	3.14		5.5 cm		500.83 cm²
(xii)	3.14		35 cm	1099 cm³	

2. How many cylindrical glasses can be filled from a full cylindrical jug, when they have the following measurements?
   - Jug: radius 6 cm, height 30 cm
   - Glass: radius 2 cm, height 5 cm

3. Draw a net of this cylinder, showing all dimensions clearly.

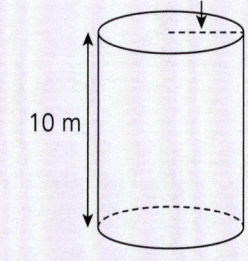

4. A company selling tinned fruit offers a 3-pack deal for tinned pineapples.
   (i) If a new label is designed for the curved area of the tin, what size will each label be? Give your answer correct to one decimal place.
   (ii) What is the capacity of one tin? Give your answer correct to two decimal places.

   The company decides to package the three tins in a rectangular box.

   (iii) What are the dimensions of the smallest box that can enclose the three tins? Give each dimension correct to one decimal place.

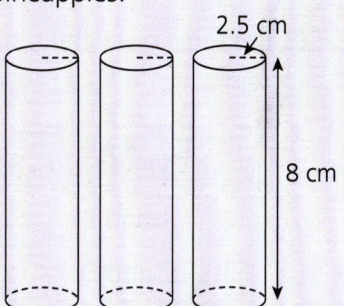

5 A soup tin in the form of a cylinder has a diameter of 7 cm and a height of 10 cm. The cylinder is constructed from pieces of metal cut from a thin sheet measuring 23 cm by 18 cm.

(i) Which one of the four diagrams, A, B, C or D could represent the sheet of metal from which the cylinder has been cut? Give a reason for your choice.

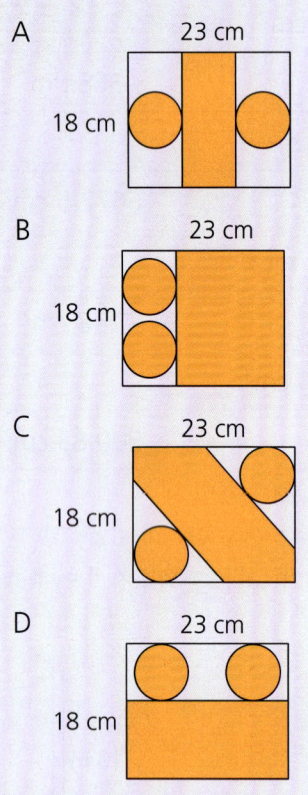

A 23 cm, 18 cm

B 23 cm, 18 cm

C 23 cm, 18 cm

D 23 cm, 18 cm

(ii) Find the area of metal which remains after the pieces have been cut out.

JCHL 2012 Phase 2

6 The table gives the ratio of radii and heights for different pairs of cylinders.

	Cylinders	Radii	Height
(i)	A and B	2 : 5	7 : 6
(ii)	C and D	3 : 8	7 : 3
(iii)	E and F	1 : 4	4 : 1
(iv)	G and H	11 : 15	17 : 13

For each pair of cylinders, find the ratio of their volumes.

7 The diagram shows a water-storage tank which a farmer uses in an outbuilding. It is a cylinder of diameter 2.7 m and height 1.8 m.

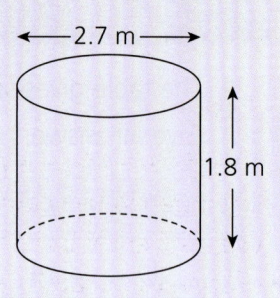

The farmer wants to buy a new tank to increase the volume of water he can store. He can either increase the diameter by 1 metre or increase the height by 1 metre.

(i) What is the difference, in litres, between the volume obtained by increasing the diameter by 1 m and the volume obtained by increasing the height by 1 m?

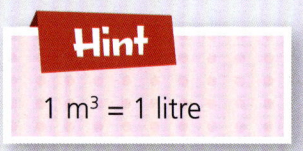

Hint
$1 \text{ m}^3 = 1$ litre

(ii) He chooses the tank that maximises the volume, and he wants to insulate the tank by wrapping insulation around the sides. The insulation comes in rolls 23.25 m long and 1.8 m wide. How many layers of insulation can he wrap around the new tank if he uses a complete roll?

8 A cylinder of height h having a base of radius $\sqrt{2}$ is placed inside another cylinder also of height h as in the diagram.

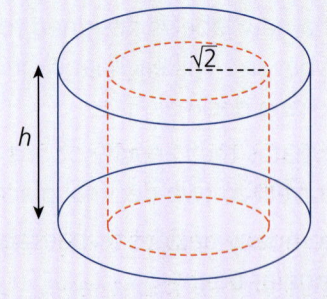

If the space between the two cylinders is to have a volume equal to the volume of the inner cylinder, calculate the radius of the base of the outer cylinder.

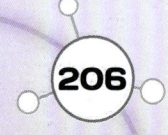

Section 11E Spheres and Hemispheres

Spheres

The **sphere** shape is a very common shape as everyone who is interested in ball games will know. Many of the sports we play use a spherical ball of some sort. There are also many examples of spheres in nature, such as bubbles. The Earth is not quite a sphere, though it is often thought of as such.

A sphere is a very efficient shape when used as a container; the surface area can contain the maximum amount of volume possible compared with any other shape.

Key Points

A sphere will always have the following characteristics:
- All points on the surface are the same distance from the centre (radius).
- It is perfectly symmetrical.
- There are no edges or corners.
- The formula for calculating the surface area is:

  Surface area of a sphere = $4\pi r^2$

- The formula for calculating the volume is:

  Volume of a sphere = $\frac{4}{3}\pi r^3$

These formulae are on page 10 of the *Formulae and tables* booklet.

Example 1

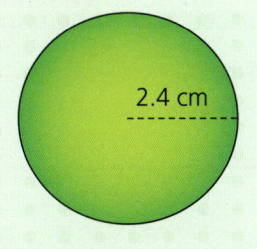

The diagram shows a sphere of radius 2.4 cm. Find:
(i) the surface area of the sphere
(ii) the volume of the sphere.
Give your answers in terms of π.

Solution

Given radius = 2.4 cm

(i) Surface area = $4 \times \pi \times r^2$
$= 4 \times \pi \times (2.4)^2$
$= 4 \times \pi \times 5.76$
$= 23.04\pi$ cm²

(ii) Volume = $\frac{4}{3} \times \pi \times r^3$
$= \frac{4}{3} \times \pi \times (2.4)^3$
$= \frac{4}{3} \times \pi \times 13.824$
$= 18.432\pi$ cm³

11 Hemispheres

The hemisphere is the shape which is exactly half a sphere.

Our most common usage of the term hemisphere is when we make reference to the two hemispheres of the Earth: the Northern and Southern Hemispheres. The equator divides these two hemispheres.

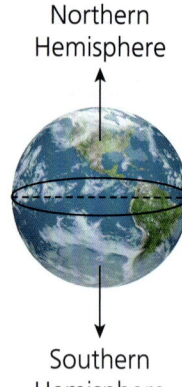

Key Points

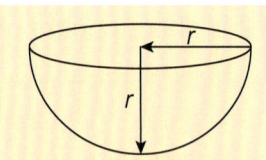

- The surface of a hemisphere has a curved part and a flat part in the shape of a circle.
- The formula for calculating the **volume** is:

$$\text{Volume of a hemisphere} = \frac{1}{2}\left(\frac{4}{3} \times \pi \times r^3\right) = \frac{2}{3}\pi r^3$$

- The formula for calculating the **total surface area** is:

$$\text{Surface area of a hemisphere} = \frac{1}{2}(4\pi r^2) + \pi r^2 = 2(\pi r^2) + (\pi r^2) = 3\pi r^2$$

- The volume and surface area of a hemisphere are **not** in the *Formulae and tables* booklet, but may be found by adapting the formulae for a sphere.

Example 2

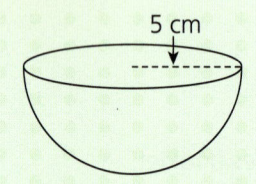

The diagram shows a hemisphere of radius 5 cm.

(i) Find the volume of the hemisphere correct to two decimal places.
(ii) Find the surface area of the hemisphere.
Use $\pi = 3.14$.

Solution

(i) Volume of hemisphere $= \frac{2}{3} \times \pi \times r^3$
$= \frac{2}{3} \times (3.14) \times (5)^3$
$= 261.666666$ cm^3
$= 261.67$ cm^3 correct to two decimal places

(ii) Total surface area of hemisphere
$= 3 \times \pi \times r^2$
$= 3 \times (3.14) \times (5)^2$
$= 235.5$ cm^2

Combined Shapes

Our next step in exploring applied measure is where we combine the solid shapes we have already encountered to make new shapes. A compound shape is composed of regular solid shapes.

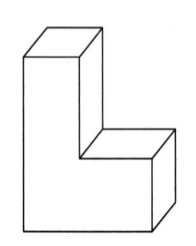

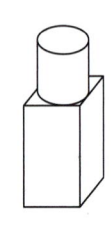

CONNECT WITH MATHS 2

Compound shapes can be seen in commemorative objects such as plaques and monuments.

Key Points

To find the volume of a compound shape we must:
- Break up the compound shape into multiple regular shapes.
- Use the volume formula for each regular shape to calculate the volume of that shape.
- Add or subtract the volume of each portion to get the total volume of the compound shape.

Example 3

A perfume bottle of height 21 cm is shown. It consists of a cylinder with radius 2 cm and height 5 cm and a rectangular portion with base 5 cm by 7 cm.
Find the volume of the bottle, correct to the nearest cm³.

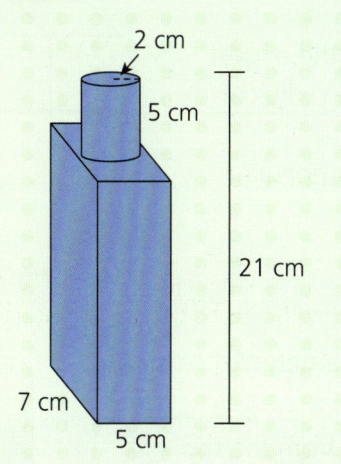

Solution

- Split the bottle into standard 3D shapes.
- Cylinder portion:
  Volume = $\pi r^2 h$
  = (3.14)(2)²(5)
  = 62.8 cm³ 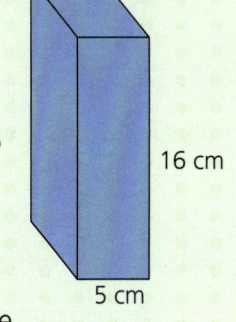 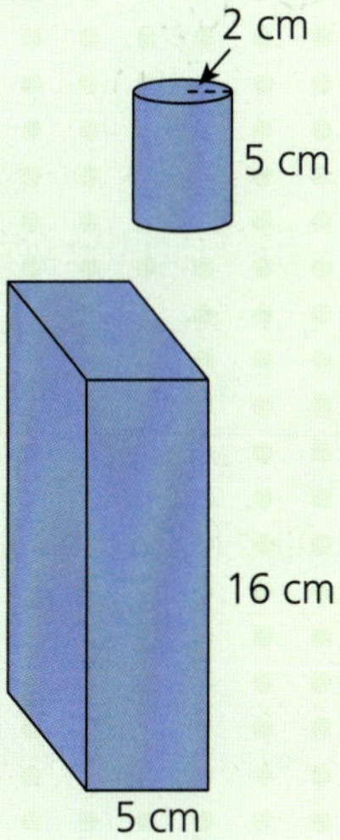
- Cuboid portion:
  Volume = lwh
  = 5 × 7 × 16
  = 560 cm³
- Total volume of bottle
  = 62.8 cm³ + 560 cm³ = 622.8 cm³

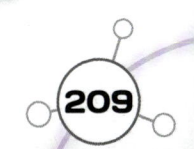

Activity 11.5

1. The table gives some data relating to spheres. Copy and complete the table.
   Unless otherwise specified, give all answers correct to three decimal places.

	π	Radius	Volume	Curved surface area
(i)	3.14	7 m		
(ii)	$\frac{22}{7}$			25.872 cm²
(iii)	3.14			383.328 m²
(iv)	Use the calculator value for π	3.5 cm		
(v)	Use the calculator value for π	15 cm		
(vi)	$\frac{22}{7}$		21 214.286 cm³	

2. A 'student of the year' award consists of a cylindrical base with a hemisphere on top.
   The radius of the cylinder and hemisphere is 3 cm. 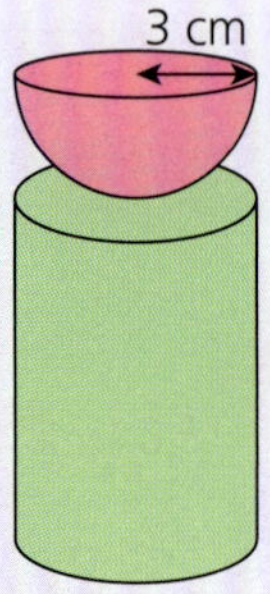
   (i) Find the volume of the hemisphere, correct to two decimal places.
   (ii) If the total volume of the award is 282.60 cm³, what is the height of the cylindrical portion of the award to the nearest cm?
   (iii) What is the total height of the award?

3. A time capsule is constructed of a cylindrical section and two hemispherical ends.
   The length of the cylindrical section is 85 cm and the radius is 28 cm. 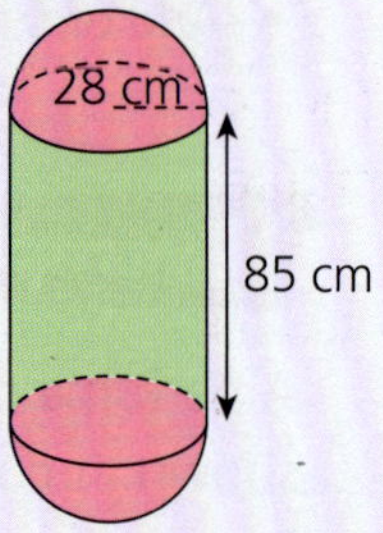
   (i) Find the surface area of the capsule in cm². Give your answer correct to two significant figures.
   (ii) Find the volume of the capsule in m³. Give your answer correct to two decimal places.

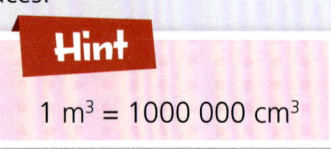

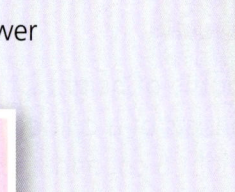

   Hint
   1 m³ = 1 000 000 cm³

4. A sculptor buys four wooden blocks with the dimensions shown. 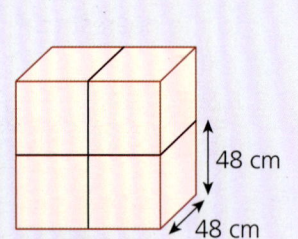
   (i) Find the volume of one of the wooden blocks.
   (ii) The sculptor needs to turn the four blocks into the largest four spheres he can for a sculpture. What is the radius of the largest sphere the sculptor can make?
   (iii) The volume of the sculpture must be under 160 000 cm³ to meet the requirements of the display. Will the sculpture meet the requirement?
   (iv) By how much was the sculptor under or over the limit in cm³?

5. (i) A solid metal cylinder has height 20 cm and diameter 14 cm. Find its curved surface area in terms of π.
   (ii) A hemisphere with diameter 14 cm is removed from the top of this cylinder, as shown.
   Find the total surface area of the remaining solid in terms of π.

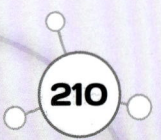

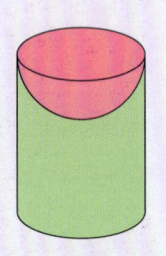

6 A golf club sells golf balls in packs of three. Each ball has radius 4.5 cm. The balls are packaged so that they fit exactly into a cylindrical tube, as shown.

   (i) Find, in terms of π, the volume of one golf ball.

   (ii) Find, in terms of π, the volume of the air in the cylindrical tube.

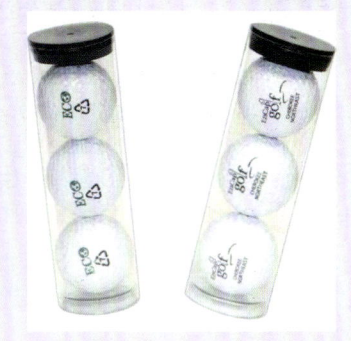

7 An ornament is carved from a rectangular block of wood which has a square base and a height of 24 cm. The ornament consists of two identical spheres and two identical cubes as illustrated. The diameter of each sphere is equal to the length of the side of each cube. The ornament has the same width as the original block.

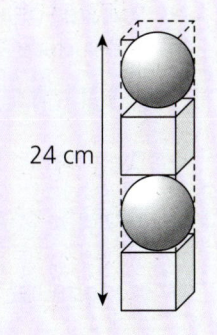

   (i) Find the side length of each cube.

   (ii) Find the volume of the ornament, correct to two decimal places.

   (iii) To make the ornament, what percentage of the original block of wood is carved away?

JCHL 2012 Phase 2

Section 11F Cones

The cone shape is most commonly associated with ice cream or traffic cones but also occurs in nature.

Key Points

- The perpendicular height of the cone is labelled **h**.
- The radius of the circle at the base is labelled **r**.
- The **slant height** of the cone is labelled **l**.

The cones we will be working with are **right circular cones** where the vertex is directly above the centre of the circular base.

Since the lines l, h and r form a right-angled triangle we can use Pythagoras' Theorem if necessary to calculate one of these lengths.

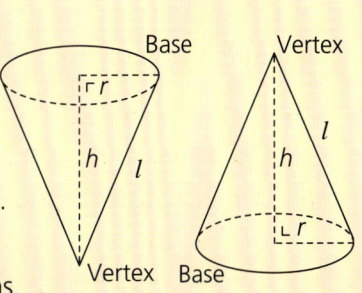

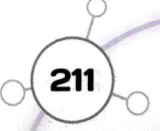

- The curved surface of a cone makes a sector of a circle when it is flattened out. (The curved surface is also known as the **lateral surface**.)
- The base of the cone is a circle.
- The **vertex** (also called the apex) is the tip point of the cone.
- To calculate the total surface area we use the formula:

   Total surface area of a cone = area of circle + surface area of lateral surface

- The area of a circle is given by $\pi \times r^2$
- The surface area of the lateral surface equals $\pi \times r \times l$

   Total surface area of a cone = $(\pi \times r^2) + (\pi \times r \times l) = \pi r^2 + \pi r l$

- The formula for calculating the volume is:

   Volume of a cone = $\frac{1}{3} \times \pi \times r^2 \times h = \frac{1}{3}\pi r^2 h$

These formulae are on page 10 of the *Formulae and tables* booklet.

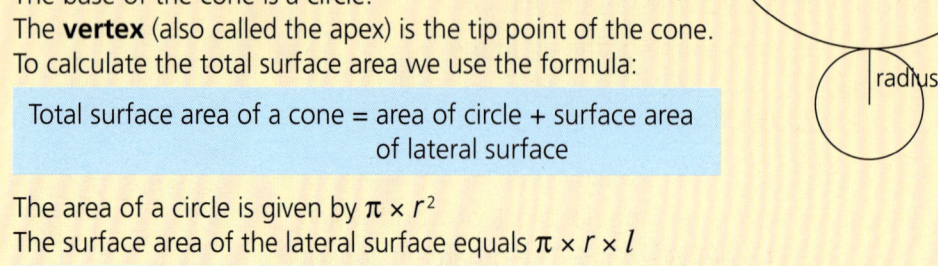

Example 1

For the cone shown, find:
  (i) the slant height
  (ii) the total surface area in terms of π
  (iii) the volume in terms of π.

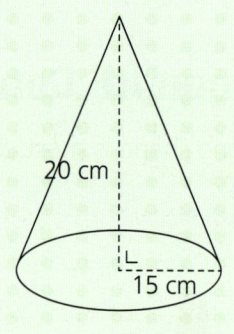

Solution

(i) Using Pythagoras' Theorem,
$$h^2 + r^2 = l^2$$
$$\Rightarrow 20^2 + 15^2 = l^2$$
$$\Rightarrow 400 + 225 = l^2$$
$$\Rightarrow 625 = l^2$$
$$\Rightarrow \sqrt{625} = l$$
$$\Rightarrow 25 \text{ cm} = l$$
$$\therefore l = 25 \text{ cm}$$

(ii) Total surface area
$$= (\pi \times r^2) + (\pi \times r \times l)$$
$$= (\pi)(15)^2 + (\pi)(15)(25)$$
$$= (\pi)(225) + (\pi)(375)$$
$$= 600\pi \text{ cm}^2$$

(iii) Volume = $\frac{1}{3} \times \pi \times r^2 \times h$
$$= \frac{1}{3}\pi(15)^2(20)$$
$$= 1500\pi \text{ cm}^3$$

Example 2

The radii of two cones are in the ratio $3:5$ and their heights are in the ratio $7:6$. What is the ratio of the volumes of the two cones?

Solution

As we are given the ratio that links the radius and the height, let x = a factor of the radii and let y = a factor of the height for both cones.

Radii ratio = $3:5$, so let **$3x$ and $5x$ be the radii**.

Height ratio = $7:6$, so let **$7y$ and $6y$ be the heights**.

Draw a sketch of the two cones and label them.

Volume of cone 1 $= \frac{1}{3}\pi r^2 h = \frac{1}{3}\pi(3x)^2(7y) = 21\pi x^2 y$

Volume of cone 2 $= \frac{1}{3}\pi r^2 h = \frac{1}{3}\pi(5x)^2(6y) = 50\pi x^2 y$

Ratio

Volume of cone 1 : Volume of cone 2
$\Rightarrow 21\pi x^2 y : 50\pi x^2 y$ ... divide both sides by $\pi x^2 y$
$\Rightarrow 21 : 50$

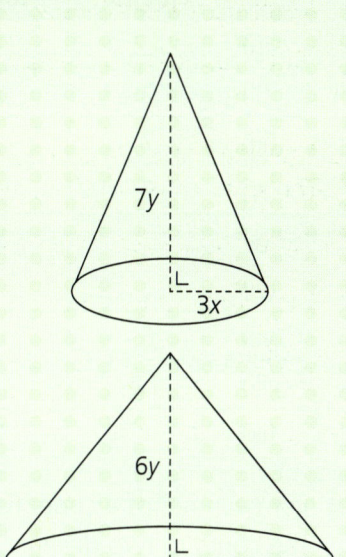

Example 3

A grain silo consists of a cylinder on top of an inverted cone.

The height of the cylindrical part is 10 m and the length of its radius is 2 m. The slant height of the cone is 2.5 m.

Show that the volume of the silo is 42π m³.

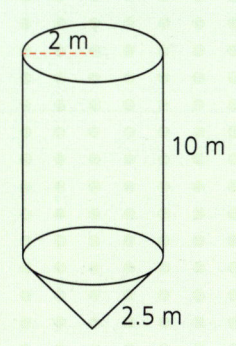

Solution

- **Cone**

  The cone has the same base radius as the cylinder = 2 m.

  Find its perpendicular height first.
  Use the theorem of Pythagoras:
  $h^2 = 2.5^2 - 2^2$
  $= 6.25 - 4$
  $= 2.25$
  $\Rightarrow h = \sqrt{2.25} = 1.5$ m

  Volume of cone $= \frac{1}{3}\pi r^2 h$
  $= \frac{1}{3}\pi(2)^2(1.5)$
  $= 2\pi$ m³

- **Cylinder**

  Volume $= \pi r^2 h$
  $= \pi(2)^2(10)$
  $= 40\pi$ m³

  Total volume $= 40\pi + 2\pi = 42\pi$ m³

Activity 11.6

1. The table gives some data relating to cones. Copy and complete the table.
   Using π = calculator value, give all answers correct to two decimal places.

	Height	Radius	Volume	Total surface area
(i)	12	4		
(ii)	2	6		
(iii)	7	3		
(iv)	9		763.40	
(v)		15	2356.19	
(vi)		3		113.04
(vii)	6		157	
(viii)	12		1809.58	
(ix)		18		8138.88

2. For each net of a cone, find (a) the volume of the cone and (b) the total surface area of the cone, to two decimal places. Let π = calculator value.

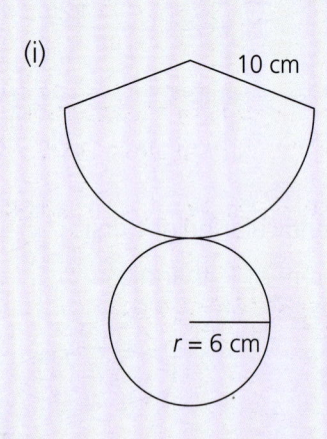

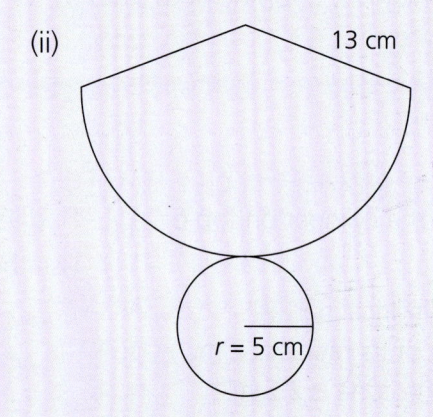

   (i) 10 cm, r = 6 cm

   (ii) 13 cm, r = 5 cm

3. The diagram shows a grain storage silo which consists of a cylinder with radius of 2.2 m and height of 6 metres and a cone with a perpendicular height of 1.5 m attached.
   (i) What is the slant height of the cone, correct to one decimal place?
   (ii) What is the maximum capacity of the grain storage silo, correct to two decimal places?
   (iii) Calculate the percentage of grain which is stored in the cone portion of the silo (give your answer correct to the nearest percent).

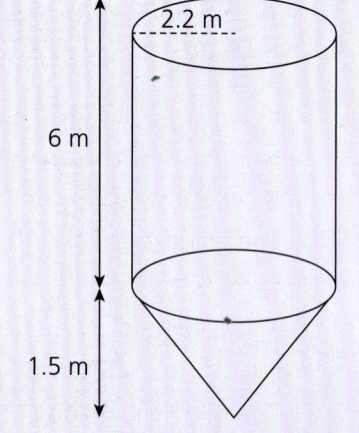

4. A cone has radius $2R$ and height $6R$.
   (i) Find its volume in terms of π and R.

   The cone fits exactly into a rectangular box.
   (ii) Find the length, width and height of the box in terms of π and R.
   (iii) Find the volume of this box in terms of π.

5 The diagram shows a cone centred on top of a rectangular solid.

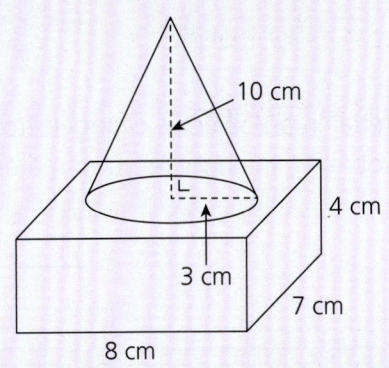

Calculate the volume of the complete shape, correct to two decimal places.

6 The diagram shows a cone surmounted on a cylinder with the given dimensions.

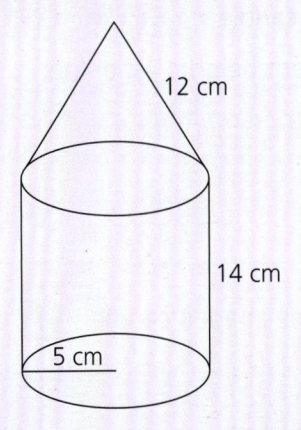

Calculate:
 (i) the volume of the complete shape
 (ii) the total surface area of the shape.
Give both answers to two decimal places.

7 There are three cones (A, B and C) in a line. Cone A has a radius of 3 cm and a height of 10 cm. The volume of cone B : the volume of cone A = 5 : 2.
The volume of cone B : the volume of cone C = 5 : 3.
Calculate the volume of the three cones in terms of π.

8 The table shows the ratios of the radii and heights of different pairs of cones.

	Cones	Radii	Height
(i)	A and B	2 : 3	4 : 6
(ii)	C and D	10 : 15	1 : 3
(iii)	E and F	6 : 4	4 : 6
(iv)	G and H	13 : 7	17 : 5

Find the ratio of the volumes for each pair of cones.

9 The diagram shows a cone A with a cone B cut out of it.

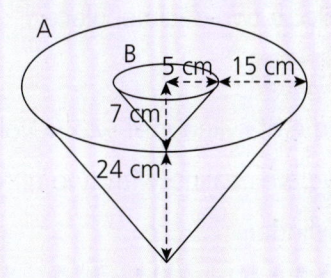

Calculate the volume of the resulting shape, correct to two decimal places.

10 A solid metal hemisphere has a radius of 12 cm.

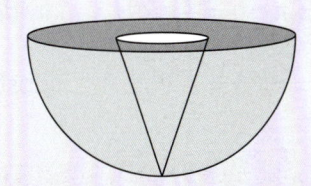

(i) Calculate the volume of the hemisphere. Give your answer in terms of π.

A solid cone of radius 4 cm and height 12 cm is cut from the hemisphere.

(ii) Calculate the volume of the cone. Give your answer in terms of π.

The remaining metal in the hemisphere is melted down and recast into cones of the same dimensions as the cone above.

(iii) How many cones can be formed from the remaining metal?

JCHL 2013 Paper 2

Section 11G Problem Solving Involving a Range of 3D Shapes

Equal Volumes

In this section, we will examine situations where the material in an object is changed from one shape to another. This process is highlighted when you examine how recycled material is reformed for reuse.

Example 1

A cylinder of wax with radius 10 cm and height 30 cm was melted down and moulded into a cone-shaped candle with a height of 45 cm. Find the radius of the candle to two decimal places.

Solution

Volume of cylinder of wax = Volume of the cone-shaped candle

As we are dealing with two different radii and two different heights, label the:

- Cylinder

  Radius = r, height = h

- Cone

  Radius = R, height = H

Hence, put volume of the cylinder = volume of the cone-shaped candle

$\Rightarrow \pi r^2 h = \frac{1}{3}\pi R^2 H$ ... divide both sides by π

$\Rightarrow r^2 h = \frac{1}{3} R^2 H$ ... substitute all known values into the equation

$\Rightarrow (10)^2(30) = \frac{1}{3} R^2 (45)$

$\Rightarrow 3000 = 15 R^2$ ... divide both sides by 15

$\Rightarrow \frac{3000}{15} = R^2$

$\Rightarrow \sqrt{200} = R$ ... find the square root of both sides

$\Rightarrow 14.14 = R$

The radius of the cone is 14.14 cm to two decimal places.

Displaced Liquids

Another method of measuring the volume of an object is to use Archimedes' Principle, which was first proved over 2200 years ago. Archimedes' Principle states that the volume of an object is equal to the volume of water displaced if the object is immersed in a container of water.

This is the method Archimedes used to find the general formulae for the volume of a sphere and the volume of a cone.

Example 2

A cylinder with a radius of 8 cm is partially filled with water. A solid cone with a radius of 6 cm and a height of 6 cm is fully immersed in the water, causing the surface of the water to rise. Calculate the increase in the height of water in the cylinder.

Solution

Let the increase in the height of water in the cylinder be equal to H.

We can say that:

Volume of rise in water in the cylinder = Volume of the cone immersed

$\pi \times r^2 \times H = \frac{1}{3} \times \pi \times r^2 \times h$ ... divide both sides by π

$(8)^2 \times H = \frac{1}{3} \times (6)^2 \times (6)$ ... substitute in all known values

$64H = 72$ ... divide both sides by 64

$H = 1.125$

The increase in the height of the water in the cylinder is 1.125 cm.

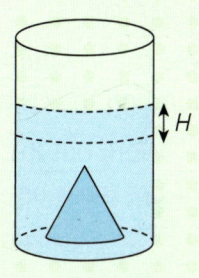

Flow Rate

In some cases, we must examine problems where a container of liquid is filled or emptied from another source. When a liquid flows from one container into another, there is a measurable flow rate.

Flow rate is the amount of fluid flowing in a given time. It is calculated using the formula:

> Flow rate = speed × cross-sectional area

Using the information about the flow rate may allow us to calculate the volume of a container without knowing all the specific details of the container.

In this section, we will focus only on liquids flowing through cylindrical pipes or tubes.

Example 3

Water from a private well moves through a 4 cm diameter cylindrical pipe at a speed of 25 cm/s.

John starts to fill a large rectangular fish tank from the tap. The tank has a base of 50 cm by 30 cm. After 2 minutes, what is the depth of the water in the fish tank? Let $\pi = 3.14$.

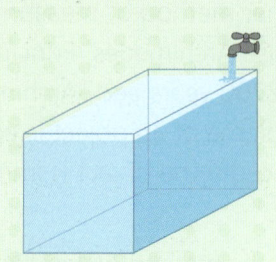

Solution

First, work out the flow rate of water passing through the cylindrical pipe in one second.

The speed is 25 cm/s.

$r = 2$ cm

Flow rate in the cylindrical pipe
= cross-sectional area × speed
= $\pi \times r^2 \times$ speed
= $(3.14) \times (2)^2 \times 25$
= 314 cm³/s

We can say that 314 cm³ of water passes through the cylindrical pipe every second.

- Work out the total number of seconds the tap is on.

    2 minutes = 120 seconds

- Calculate the volume of water that passes through the pipe in 2 minutes.

    314 × 120 = 37 680 cm³

- Work out the depth of the water in the rectangular tank.

    Let the depth of the water in the cuboid be represented by H.

    Volume of rise in water in the cuboid = Volume of water through the tap in 2 minutes

    $l \times w \times h = 37\,680$
    $(50)(30)(H) = 37\,680$
    $1500(H) = 37\,680$ ... divide both sides by 1500
    $H = 25.12$

    The depth of the water in the tank after 2 minutes is 25.12 cm.

Activity 11.7

1. A rectangular block of wax has dimensions $l = 1.6$ m, $w = 0.8$ m and $h = 1.2$ m. The block is melted down and turned into small cubes of side length 40 cm. How many cubes can be made from this block of wax?

2. A sphere of copper with radius 9 cm is melted down and turned into a cone-shaped ornament with radius = 6 cm. Find the height of the cone-shaped ornament.

3. A cone of metal with a height of 15 cm is melted down and turned into spheres of radius 8 cm. Find the volume of each sphere, correct to three decimal places.

4. A cylinder of lead with a radius of 18 cm and a height of 12 cm is melted down and turned into a cone with a radius of 24 cm. Find the height of the cone, correct to three decimal places.

5. A cylinder with radius 10 cm is partially filled with water. A cone of radius 6 cm and height 6 cm is fully immersed in the water which causes the water to rise by H cm.
   Calculate this increase in height.

6. A cylinder with radius 10 cm is partially filled with water. Six spheres of radius 3 cm are fully immersed in the water which causes the water to rise by H cm.
   Calculate the increase in height correct to one decimal place.

7. A cylinder with radius 12 cm is partially filled with water. A cone of radius 4.5 cm is fully immersed in the water which causes the water to rise by 3.5 cm.
   Calculate the height of the cone correct to three decimal places.

8. A cylinder with radius 6 cm is filled with water and a sphere of radius 3 cm is fully immersed in the water. This sphere is then removed.
   Calculate the drop in height, H cm, after the sphere has been removed.

9. A cone with radius 15 cm and height 20 cm is filled with water. A cylinder with a radius of 10 cm and a height of 5 cm is then fully immersed into the water-filled cone. If this cylinder is removed, what percentage of the cone is now filled with water? Give your answer to two decimal places.

10. A tank of water is connected to a smart pump via a pipe. The pipe has a radius of 2.5 cm and the tank's dimensions are: width = 1 m, length = 2 m and height = 1 m. The pump turns on automatically when the height of the water falls to 10% of the full height of the cylinder and the pump turns off when the height of the water is at 90% of the tank. When the pump is turned on the water flows through the pipe at a speed of 20 cm/s.
    (i) What is the volume of water in the tank at the 10% minimum limit?
    (ii) What is the volume of the water in the tank when it reaches the 90% maximum limit?
    (iii) What volume of water is pumped through the pipe in one second (the flow rate)?
    (iv) How long does it take the pump to fill the tank to the 90% level, to the nearest minute?

11. Water moves through a cylindrical pipe of diameter 3 cm at a speed of 14 cm/s.
    (i) What volume of water flows through the cylindrical pipe in 1 second (the flow rate)?
    (ii) If a cylindrical container has a radius of 8 cm and a height of 24 cm, find the time taken to fill the container, correct to three decimal places.

Revision Activity 11

1. The diagram shows the gable-end wall of a garage.
   (a) Find the total area of the gable-end wall.
   The cost of 5 litres of paint is €26.50.
   5 litres of this paint will cover an area of 33 m².
   (b) Find the cost of painting the gable-end wall with this paint.

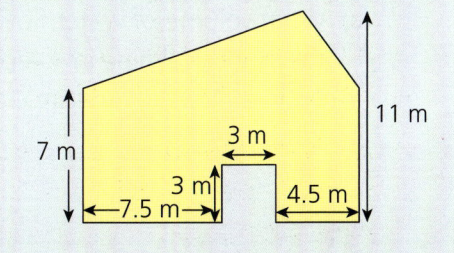

2. Find (a) the volume and (b) the surface area of the triangular-based prism shown. Give your answers correct to two decimal places.

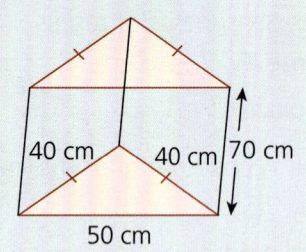

40 cm, 40 cm, 70 cm, 50 cm

3. When this net is formed into a hexagonal prism, which sides are opposite each other?

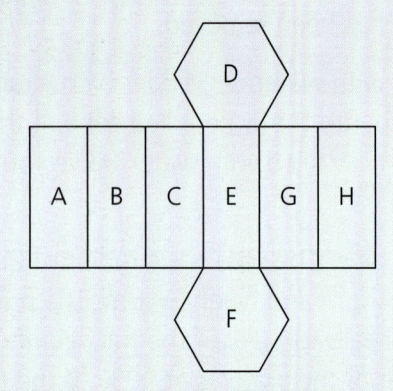

(net with hexagons D and F, and rectangles A, B, C, E, G, H)

4. A cylinder made from bronze with a height of 28 cm is melted down and turned into a cone with radius 20 cm and height 15 cm.

Find the radius of the cylinder, to two decimal places.

5. A cylinder with radius 10 cm is filled with water, then a sphere of radius 4.5 cm is fully immersed in the water.

Calculate the rise in height, H cm, after the sphere was added. Give your answer correct to two decimal places.

6. Water moves through a cylindrical pipe of diameter 6 cm at a speed of 32 cm/s.

(a) What volume of water flows through the cylindrical pipe in 1 second (the flow rate), to two decimal places?

(b) If a cuboid-shaped container has a base of 65 cm by 55 cm, find the height of the water in the container if the water flows from the cylindrical pipe into the container for 45 seconds. Write your answer correct to three decimal places.

7. A rectangular container has length 36 cm and height 18 cm. The volume of the container is 15 552 cm³.

(a) Find the width of the rectangular container in cm.

(b) Find the total surface area of the closed container in cm².

This container is used to ship cube-shaped boxes of side 4 cm.

(c) How many of these cubes can fit into the rectangular container?

This container is also used to ship boxes containing spherical balls of radius 3 cm.

(d) How many of these balls can fit into the container?

8. A hot water tank is in the shape of a hemisphere on top of a cylinder as shown.

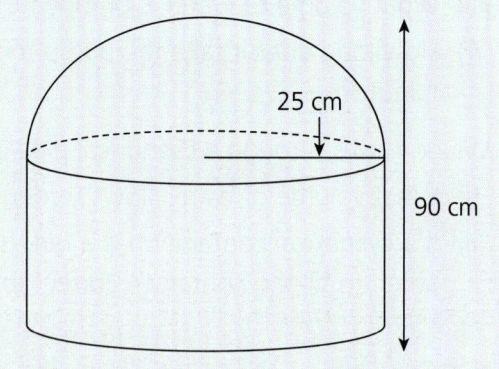

25 cm, 90 cm

The hemisphere has a radius of 25 cm and the container has a height of 90 cm. Find the volume of the container in litres, giving your answer correct to the nearest litre.

Hint

1 litre = 1000 cm³

Exam-style Questions

1. Liam's garden is in the shape of a square. It has four equal right-angled triangular lawns and a smaller square patio in the centre, as shown.
   (a) Find the length of the hypotenuse of one of the right-angled triangular lawns.
   (b) Find the area of one of the triangular lawns.
   (c) Find the area of the square patio in the middle.
   (d) The patio is to be paved with rectangular flagstones of length 80 cm and width 50 cm. Calculate the number of flagstones Liam needs to buy to cover the patio, allowing an extra 20% for waste.

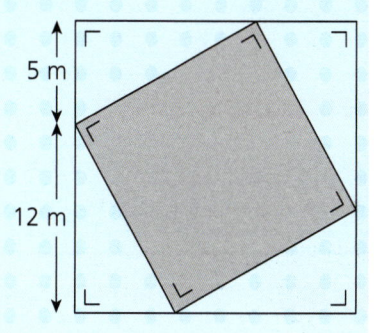

   JCHL 2013 Phase 3

2. The dimensions of two solid cylinders are shown in the diagrams.
   (a) Calculate the ratio of the curved surface area of the smaller cylinder to the curved surface area of the larger cylinder.
   (b) Calculate the ratio of the volume of the smaller cylinder to the volume of the larger cylinder.

   JCHL 2012

3. A triangle has a base length of $2x$ cm and a perpendicular height of $(x + 3)$ cm.
   The area of the triangle is 10 cm². Find the distance x.

   JCHL 2012

KEY WORDS AND PHRASES

- Rectangular solid
- Cube
- Capacity
- Volume
- Litre
- Curved surface area
- Total surface area
- Prism
- Faces, vertices and edges
- Cross-section of prism
- Triangular-based prism
- Rectangular prism
- Hexagonal prism
- Cylinder
- Comparison ratios
- Sphere
- Hemisphere
- Right circular cone
- Net of a cone
- Slant height of a cone
- Lateral surface of cone
- Vertex
- Equal volumes
- Displaced liquids
- Flow rate

Applied Measure

Chapter Summary 11

- Area of a parallelogram = base × perpendicular height = $a \times h$

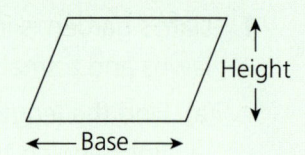

Rectangular Solids
- Total surface area = $2(l \times w) + 2(l \times h) + 2(w \times h)$
- Volume = length (l) × width (w) × height (h)

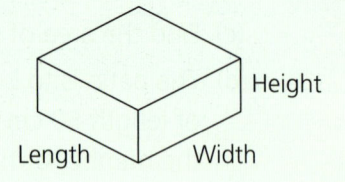

Prisms
- A prism is a 3-dimensional figure where:
  - the bases (or ends of the object) are the same shape and size
  - the bases are parallel to one another
  - the sides form parallelograms.

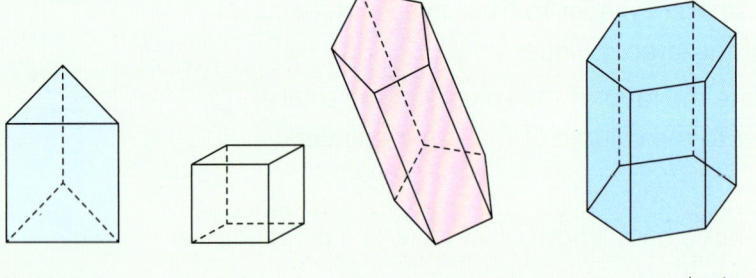

Triangular prism   Cube   Pentagonal prism   Hexagonal prism

- Volume of a prism = area of the cross-section × height of the prism
- Total Surface Area (TSA) of a prism is the sum of the areas of all the faces of the prism.

Cylinders
- Volume = $\pi \times r^2 \times h$
- Curved surface area = $2\pi rh$
- Total surface area = $2\pi rh + 2\pi r^2$

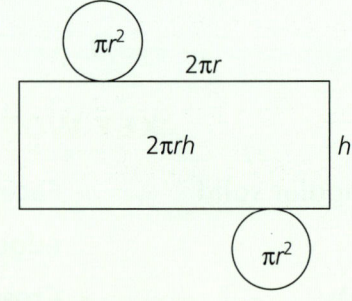

Cylinder net

Spheres and Hemispheres
- Surface area of a sphere = $4 \times \pi \times r^2$
- Volume of a sphere = $\frac{4}{3} \times \pi \times r^3$

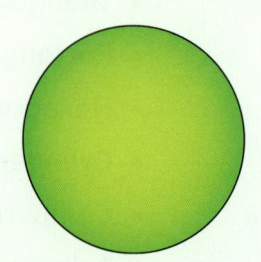

- Volume of a hemisphere = $\frac{1}{2}\left(\frac{4}{3} \times \pi \times r^3\right) = \frac{2}{3} \times \pi \times r^3$
- Surface area of a hemisphere = $3\pi \times r^2$

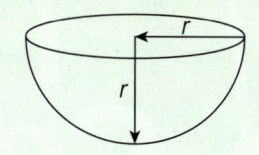

Cones

- Surface area of the base = $\pi \times r^2$
- Surface area of the lateral surface = $\pi \times r \times l$
- Total surface area of a cone = $(\pi \times r^2) + (\pi \times r \times l)$
- Volume of a cone = $\frac{1}{3} \times \pi \times r^2 \times h$

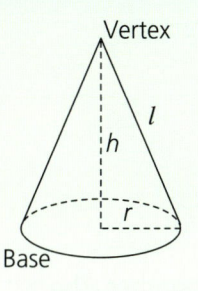

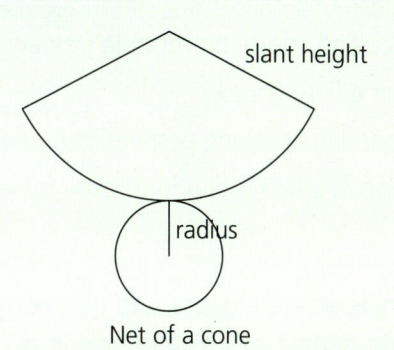

Net of a cone

Compound Shapes

When dealing with a compound shape, we follow these steps:
- Break up the compound shape into regular shapes.
- Use the volume formula for each regular shape to calculate the volume of that shape.
- Add or subtract the volume of each portion to get the total volume of the compound shape.

Flow Rate

Where a liquid flows from one container into another, this means that there is a measurable flow rate.

Flow rate is the amount of fluid flowing in a given time.

Flow rate = speed × cross-sectional area

Chapter 12

Co-ordinate Geometry

Learning Outcomes

In this chapter, you will learn about:
- The distance and mid-point formula (review)
- The slope of a line (review)
- Slopes of parallel lines and perpendicular lines
- The equation of a line in the form $ax + by + c = 0$

Co-ordinate geometry is where algebra and geometry come together. The creation of co-ordinate geometry was a hugely important development. Due to its applications in all areas of science, it is regarded as the mother of all modern applied mathematics.

René Descartes (1596–1650), inventor of co-ordinate geometry

Section 12A Distance and Mid-point Between Two Points

> **Key Point**
>
> When working with co-ordinate geometry, it is very important to draw a diagram. Diagrams help us to understand what is required in a question and also can be used to check whether an answer is reasonable or not.

Distance Between Two Points

The formula for the distance between two points is arrived at by using the theorem of Pythagoras. The formula must work for any pair of points. That is, the points must be **variable**, so we use variables for the co-ordinates. We usually let these points be called (x_1, y_1) and (x_2, y_2).

Example 1

Find the distance from $P(x_1, y_1)$ to $Q(x_2, y_2)$.

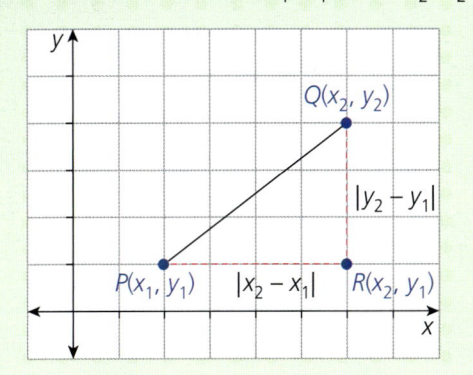

Solution

Draw $[PQ]$. Then locate a point R so that PQR is a right-angled triangle.

$|QR| = |y_2 - y_1|$ units
$|PR| = |x_2 - x_1|$ units

Now we can use Pythagoras' Theorem to find $|PQ|$.

$|PQ|^2 = |PR|^2 + |QR|^2$
$ = |x_2 - x_1|^2 + |y_2 - y_1|^2$
$\Rightarrow |PQ| = \sqrt{|x_2 - x_1|^2 + |y_2 - y_1|^2}$ units

Distance formula

The distance $|PQ|$ from $P(x_1, y_1)$ to $Q(x_2, y_2) = \sqrt{|x_2 - x_1|^2 + |y_2 - y_1|^2}$

This formula is given in the *Formulae and tables* booklet, page 18.

Example 2

Find the distance between $A(-2, 5)$ and $B(7, -3)$. Leave your answer in surd form.

Solution

Let $A(-2, 5) = (x_1, y_1)$ and $B(7, -3) = (x_2, y_2)$
Distance $= \sqrt{(x_2 - x_1)^2 + (y_2 - y_1)^2}$
$ = \sqrt{(7 - (-2))^2 + (-3 - 5)^2}$
$ = \sqrt{(7 + 2)^2 + (-8)^2}$
$ = \sqrt{(9)^2 + (-8)^2}$
$ = \sqrt{81 + 64}$
$ = \sqrt{145}$ units

Mid-Point Between Two Points

The mid-point between $P(x_1, y_1)$ and $Q(x_2, y_2)$ is $\left(\dfrac{x_1 + x_2}{2}, \dfrac{y_1 + y_2}{2}\right)$.

This formula is given in the *Formulae and tables* booklet, page 18.

You may find it easier to remember the mid-point as (the mean of the *x*'s, the mean of the *y*'s).

Example 3

Find the mid-point M between $A(-2, -2)$ and $B(5, 3)$.

Solution

Let $A(-2, -2) = (x_1, y_1)$ and $B(5, 3) = (x_2, y_2)$

$M = \left(\dfrac{-2 + 5}{2}, \dfrac{-2 + 3}{2}\right) = \left(\dfrac{3}{2}, \dfrac{1}{2}\right)$

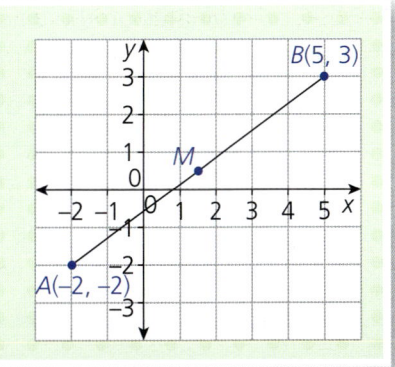

12 Activity 12.1

Co-ordinate Geometry

1 Look carefully at the diagram.

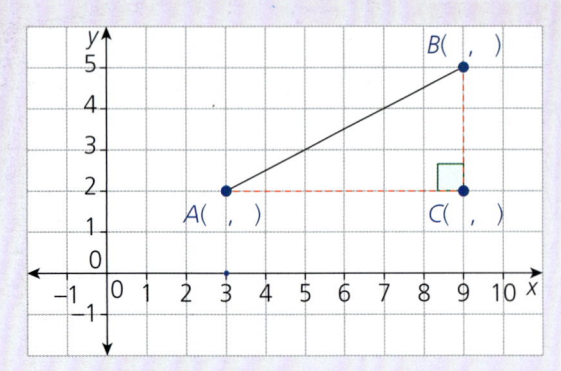

(i) Copy the diagram into your copy. Fill in the co-ordinates of A, B and C.

(ii) Write down $|AC|$ and $|BC|$.

(iii) Use the theorem of Pythagoras to find the hypotenuse of the triangle ABC.

(iv) Use the distance formula to find $|AB|$.

2 Copy the diagram into your copy.

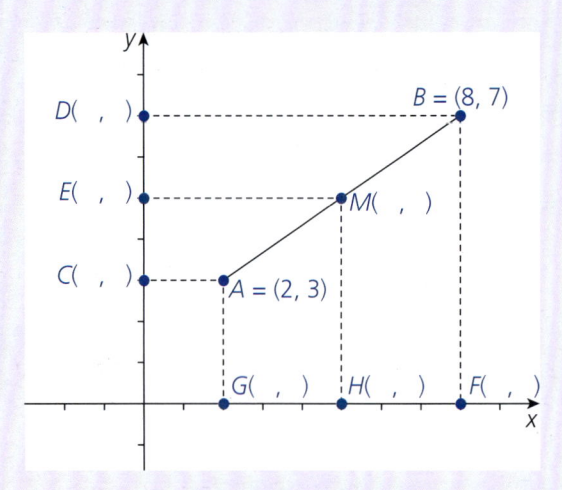

(i) Fill in the co-ordinates of points D, C, G and F.

(ii) E is the mid-point [DC]. Fill in its co-ordinates on the diagram.

(iii) H is the mid-point [GF]. Fill in its co-ordinates on the diagram.

(iv) Use the co-ordinates of E and H to fill in the co-ordinates of M, the mid-point of [AB].

(v) Write, in your own words, the formula for getting the co-ordinates of the mid-point between two points.

3 A(−2, 3) and B(5, 6) are two points.

(i) Show these points in the co-ordinate plane.

(ii) Calculate $|AB|$.

(iii) Find M, the mid-point of [AB].

(iv) Verify that M is the mid-point of [AB] by showing that $|AM| = |MB|$.

4 The triangle PQR has co-ordinates (−5, 3), (1, 6) and (4, 0) respectively.

(i) Show these points on a co-ordinate plane.

(ii) Use the distance formula to show that PQR is an isosceles triangle which is also right-angled.

5 A(8, 1), B(1, 6) and C(−4, −1) are three points in the plane.

(i) Show these points on a co-ordinate plane.

(ii) Use the distance formula to find out if the triangle ABC is isosceles.

6 P(0, 4), Q(3, 2) and R(9, −2) are three points.

(i) Show these points in the co-ordinate plane.

(ii) Use the distance formula to show that these points are collinear.

7 A(−1, 5) and B(−3, 2) are two points.

(i) Draw the line segment [AB] in the co-ordinate plane.

(ii) Draw [A'B'], the image of [AB] by reflection in the y-axis.

(iii) Find $|AB|$ and $|A'B'|$.

(iv) From your answer to part (iii), what observation can be made about reflection of this line segment in the y-axis?

8 PQRS is a quadrilateral in the co-ordinate plane as shown on the next page.

(i) Write down the co-ordinates of P, Q, R and S.

(ii) Used the mid-point formula to check whether the diagonals bisect each other.

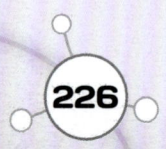

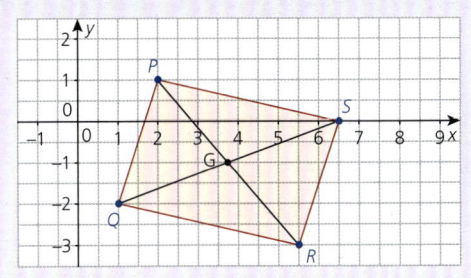

(iii) Is *PQRS* a parallelogram? Justify your answer.

9. The diagram shows the path of two ships which left a harbour at 12.00 noon and are each travelling at steady speeds. The *x*-axis represents the East–West direction and the origin is the harbour. The units are kilometres.

   At 2.00 pm ship 1 is at location *A* and ship 2 is at location *B*.

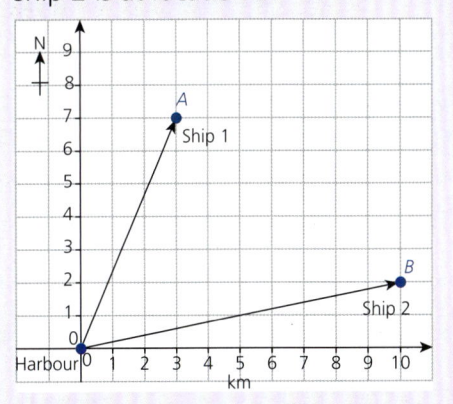

   (i) Find the distance that each ship has travelled by 2.00 pm correct to two decimal places.
   (ii) Find the steady speed of each ship correct to two decimal places.
   (Hint: This is not a distance–time graph, so the slope is not relevant to speed here.)
   (iii) How far apart are the ships at 2.00 pm? Give your answer correct to two decimal places.
   (iv) Find the co-ordinates of the location which is half-way between the ships at 2.00 pm.

10. The diagram represents two roads running perpendicular to each other with the origin as their intersection. The *x*-axis represents the East–West direction. The units are metres.
    At a certain time, Michael is 60 metres west of the intersection and heading east at a steady speed of 4 m/s. At the same time, Clodagh is 40 metres south of the junction and going north at a steady speed of 2 m/s.
    (Give all distances correct to two decimal places.)

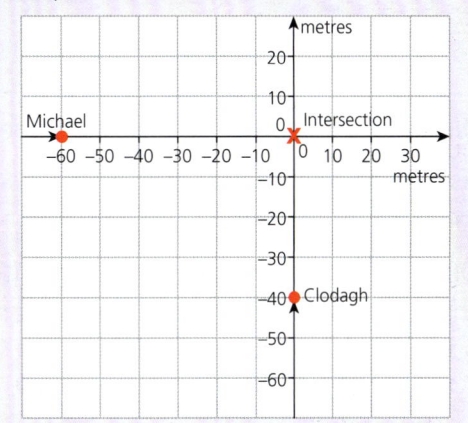

    (i) What is the distance between Michael and Clodagh at the start?
    (ii) Find the co-ordinates of the location which is half-way between them.
    (iii) What are their locations after 10 seconds?
    (iv) How far apart are they after 10 seconds?
    (v) How far is Michael from the intersection at the time that Clodagh is at the intersection?

11. *ABC* is a triangle in the co-ordinate plane.

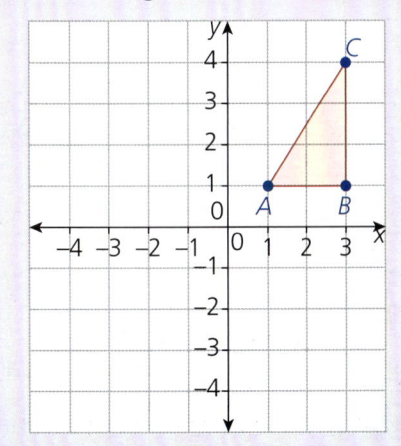

    Copy the diagram into your copy. On your diagram, draw the image of the triangle *ABC* by:

    (i) axial symmetry in the *x*-axis
    (ii) axial symmetry in the *y*-axis
    (iii) central symmetry in the origin.

Section 12B Slope of a Line

The slope of a line is measured as $\frac{\text{rise}}{\text{run}}$.

- Lines with + slopes go up from left to right: 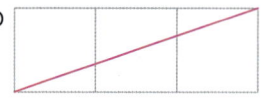
- Lines with – slopes go down from left to right:

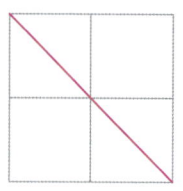

We can use a formula to calculate slope.

As with all formulae we use two points with variable co-ordinates: $P(x_1, y_1)$ and $Q(x_2, y_2)$.

On the diagram, we can see that the rise is the change in the y co-ordinates $= y_2 - y_1$ and the run is the change in the x co-ordinates $= x_2 - x_1$.

Put $\frac{\text{rise}}{\text{run}}$ to get this formula:

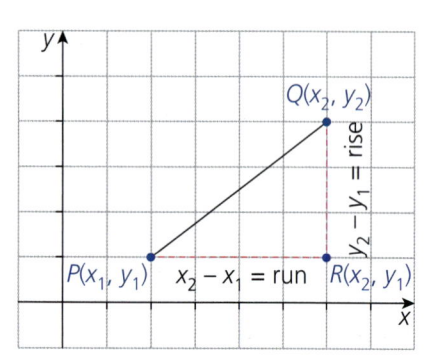

Slope formula
The slope of the line through $P(x_1, y_1)$ and $Q(x_2, y_2) = \dfrac{y_2 - y_1}{x_2 - x_1}$

This formula is given in the *Formulae and tables* booklet, page 18.
The letter m is used to denote the slope in formulae.

Example 1

Find the slope of the line which passes through $A(-3, -1)$ and $B(4, 5)$.

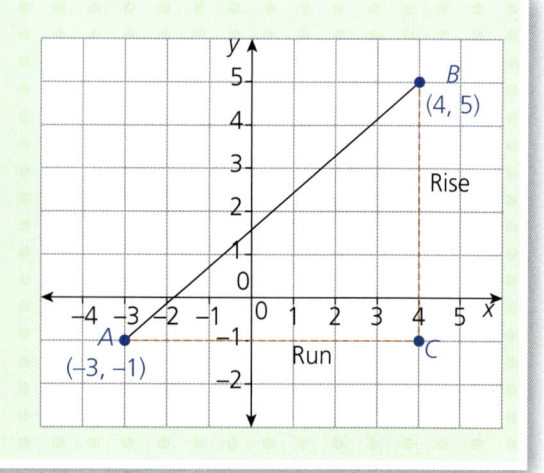

Solution

Let $A(-3, -1) = (x_1, y_1)$ and $B(4, 5) = (x_2, y_2)$

The slope of $AB = \dfrac{y_2 - y_1}{x_2 - x_1} = \dfrac{5 - (-1)}{4 - (-3)} = \dfrac{6}{7}$

Parallel Lines

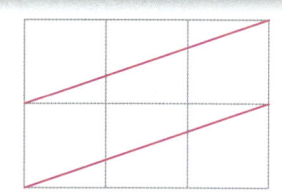

It is easy to see that two lines with equal slopes are parallel.

If l is a line with slope m_1 and p is a line with slope m_2, and l is parallel to p, then $m_1 = m_2$.

Key Point

$l \parallel p \Rightarrow m_1 = m_2$

The opposite is also true: if $m_1 = m_2$ then the lines are parallel, i.e. $l \parallel p$.

Perpendicular Lines

The relationship between the slopes of perpendicular lines is not obvious.

Look carefully at the example in the diagram.

$P(0, 0)$, $A(-3, 4)$ and $B(4, 3)$ are points.

The triangles ADP and BPE are congruent because each has a right angle included between sides 3 and 4 units long (SAS).

Thus the angles in each triangle are equal as marked on the diagram.

Thus, since $\alpha + \beta = 90°$, we have $|\angle APB| = 90°$ and so $AP \perp PB$.

Now look at the slopes of AP and PB.

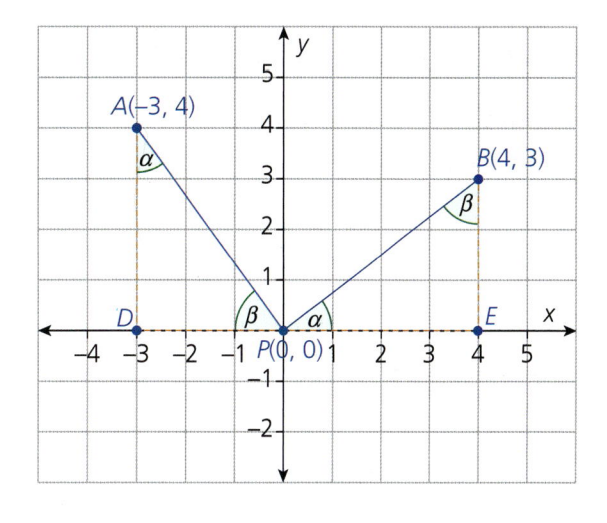

The slope of $PB = m_1 = \dfrac{3}{4}$

The slope of $AP = m_2 = -\dfrac{4}{3}$

If l is a line with slope m_1 and p is a line with slope m_2 and $l \perp p$, then $(m_1)(m_2) = -1$

To get a slope perpendicular to a given slope, turn the slope upside down and change the sign.

Key Point

$l \perp p \Rightarrow (m_1)(m_2) = -1$

The opposite is also true:
If $(m_1)(m_2) = -1$, then the lines are perpendicular, i.e. $l \perp p$.

The slopes of all perpendicular lines behave like this.

Example 2

$A(1, 5)$ and $B(-3, 2)$ are two points in the plane.
(i) Find the slope of a line which is parallel to AB.
(ii) Find the slope of a line which is perpendicular to AB.

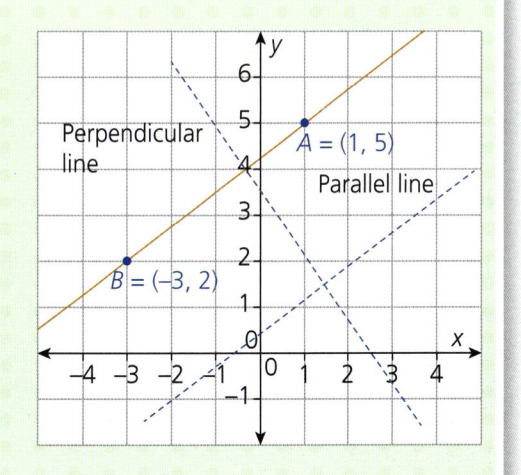

Solution

(i) Let $A(1, 5) = (x_1, y_1)$ and $B(-3, 2) = (x_2, y_2)$

Slope of $AB = \dfrac{y_2 - y_1}{x_2 - x_1} = \dfrac{2 - 5}{-3 - 1} = \dfrac{-3}{-4} = \dfrac{3}{4}$

Slope of any line parallel to $AB = \dfrac{3}{4}$

(ii) Slope of any line perpendicular to $AB = -\dfrac{4}{3}$

Connections

Connection to trigonometry:

The slope of a line = $\frac{\text{rise}}{\text{run}}$.

In the diagram, the line makes an angle θ with the +x-axis.

Hence $\tan \theta = \frac{\text{opposite}}{\text{adjacent}} = \frac{\text{rise}}{\text{run}}$

i.e. $\tan \theta$ = the slope of the line.

Hence, we have the following rule:

> The slope of a line = $\tan \theta$ where θ is the angle which the line makes with the +x-axis.

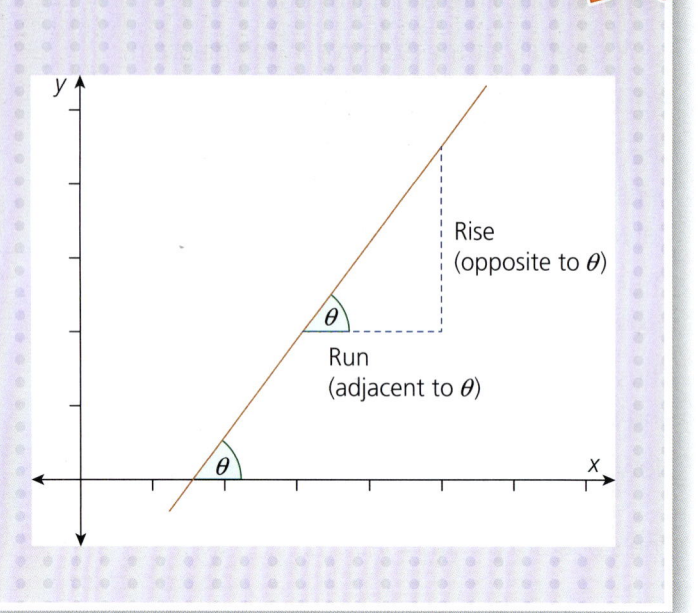

Example 3

Find the slope of the line AB in this diagram.

Solution

AB makes an angle of 45° with the +x-axis

$\Rightarrow$ the slope = $\tan 45° = 1$

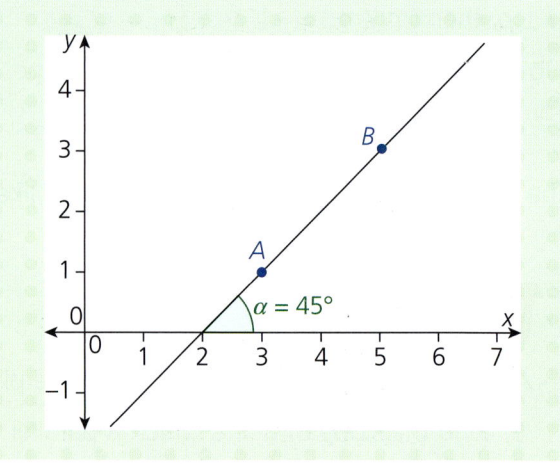

Note: We cannot measure the slope of a vertical line.

This is because the run = 0 for a vertical line. When we put $\frac{\text{rise}}{\text{run}}$, we would have to divide by zero, which we know we cannot do.

So we say that the slope of a vertical line is undefined.

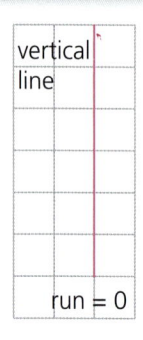

Activity 12.2

1 Copy and complete this table.

Slope of line k	Slope of line parallel to k	Slope of line perpendicular to k
$\frac{2}{3}$		
$\frac{5}{2}$		
$-\frac{3}{7}$		
$-\frac{1}{3}$		
4		
$-\frac{1}{6}$		
1		
−1		

2 $A(-1, 2)$, $B(3, 4)$ and $C(4, -8)$ are three points.
  (i) Plot these points in the co-ordinate plane.
  (ii) Prove that $AB \perp AC$.

3 $A(1, -1)$, $B(5, 3)$, $C(1, 7)$ and $D(-3, 3)$ are the vertices of a quadrilateral.
  (i) Draw the quadrilateral in a co-ordinate plane.
  (ii) Prove that opposite sides of the quadrilateral are parallel. What type of quadrilateral has this property?
  (iii) Prove that adjacent sides of ABCD are perpendicular. With this extra property, what type of quadrilateral is ABCD?

4 FGHD is a quadrilateral as shown.

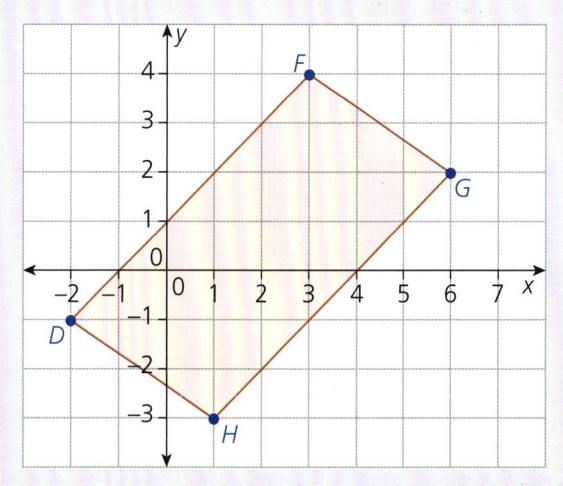

  (i) Write down the co-ordinates of F, G, H and D.
  (ii) Prove that FGHD is a parallelogram.

5. The diagram shows a quadrilateral *ABCD*.

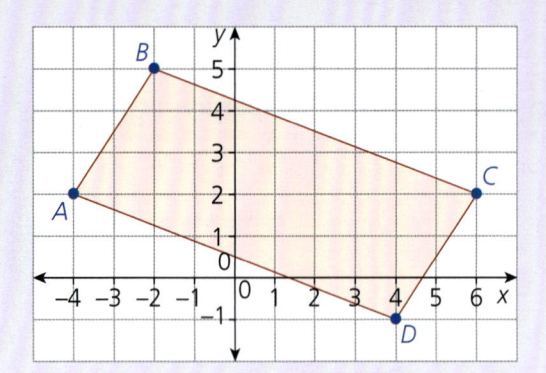

   (i) Prove that one pair of opposite sides are equal in length and are parallel.

   (ii) Can you now conclude that *ABCD* is a parallelogram?

6. Find the slope of the line *p* in the diagram. Give your answer in surd (square root) form.

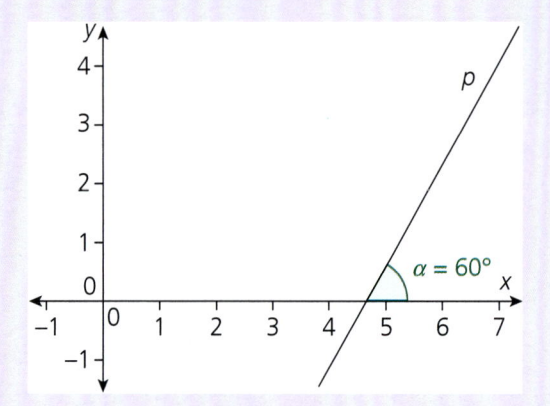

7. Look at the diagram.

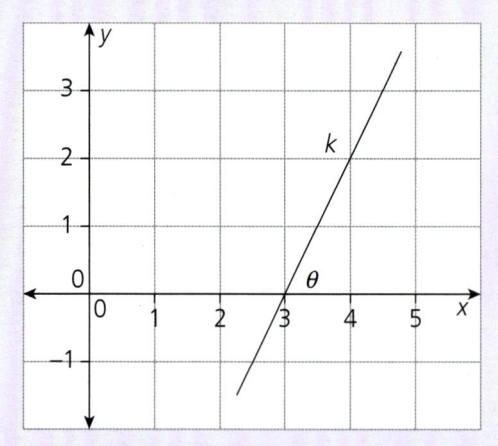

   (i) Write down the slope of line *k*.

   (ii) What is θ, the angle which the line *k* makes with the +*x*-axis? Give your answer to the nearest degree.

8. The picture shows a roadway sign (in Irish and English) on a road in Slane, Co. Meath. It indicates that the road will have a slope downwards of 10% for the next 500 metres.

   (i) Express 10% as a fraction.

   (ii) On squared paper, draw a line which has a slope of 10%.

   (iii) Imagine a car or lorry driving down a road with the same slope. Why does the sign instruct drivers to use crawl gear?

9. In the right-angled triangle *CEF*, one of the acute angles is three times as large as the other acute angle.

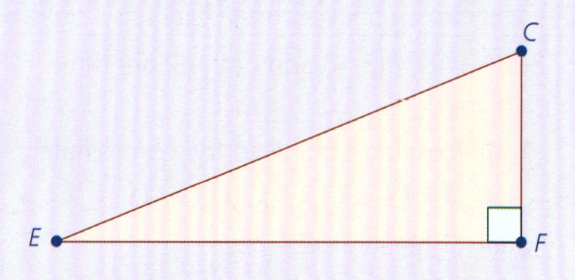

   (i) Find the measures of the two acute angles in the triangle.

   (ii) The triangle in part (i) is placed on a co-ordinate diagram. The base [*EF*] is parallel to the *x*-axis.

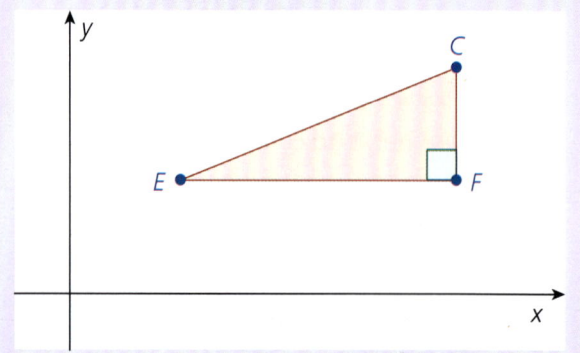

   Find the slope of *EC*. Give your answer correct to three decimal places.

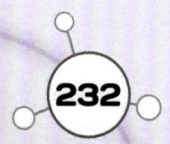

Section 12C The Equation of a Line

The equation of the line which passes through (0, c) and has slope m is $y = mx + c$.

This formula is given in the *Formulae and tables* booklet, page 18.

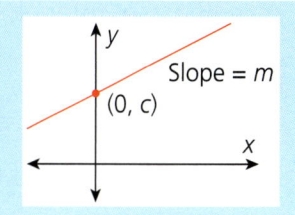

Example 1

A line l passes through the point (0, −2) and has a slope $= \frac{1}{2}$.

Find the equation of the line in the form $y = mx + c$.

Solution

Formula: $y = mx + c$ has slope m and point (0, c)

$m =$ slope $= \frac{1}{2}$

(0, −2) is (0, c) so $c = -2$

Equation of l is $y = \frac{1}{2}x - 2$

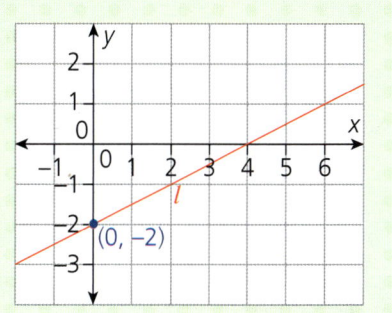

The Equation of a Line in the Form $ax + by + c = 0$

There is only one line which has a given slope and passes through a given point.

For example, there is **only one line** k in the plane that passes through (1, 3) and has a slope = 2.

The slope of a line is the same all along the line, so if we pick **any point** (x, y) on the line k, then the slope of the line $= \frac{y-3}{x-1}$.

The slope of this line also = 2

∴ we have the equation $\frac{y-3}{x-1} = 2$ which can be simplified:

⇒ $\quad y - 3 = 2(x - 1)$

⇒ $\quad y - 3 = 2x - 2$

⇒ $2x - y + 1 = 0$ … this is what the equation of a line often looks like.

The equation of the line PQ which passes through (x_1, y_1) and has slope m is $y - y_1 = m(x - x_1)$.

This formula is given in the *Formulae and tables* booklet, page 18.

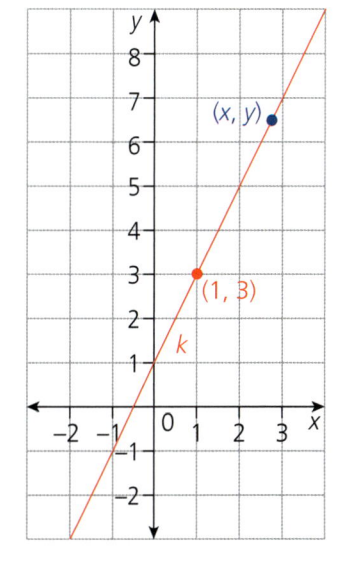

To use this formula, we need two pieces of information:

- one point on the line
- the slope of the line.

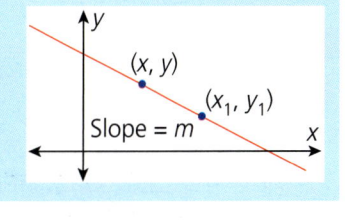

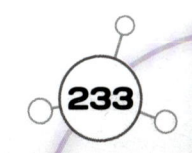

CONNECT WITH MATHS 2

Example 2

A line l passes through the point $(-3, 2)$ and has a slope $= \frac{3}{4}$. Find the equation of the line.

Solution

Use the formula $y - y_1 = m(x - x_1)$

The point (x_1, y_1) here is $(-3, 2)$, so $x_1 = -3$ and $y_1 = 2$.

$m = \frac{3}{4}$

Apply the formula:

$$y - 2 = \frac{3}{4}(x + 3)$$

$\Rightarrow \quad 4y - 8 = 3x + 9$ ... multiply both sides by 4

$\Rightarrow -3x + 4y - 8 - 9 = 0$

$\Rightarrow \quad -3x + 4y - 17 = 0 \quad \text{or} \quad 3x - 4y + 17 = 0$

Equation of l is $3x - 4y + 17 = 0$.

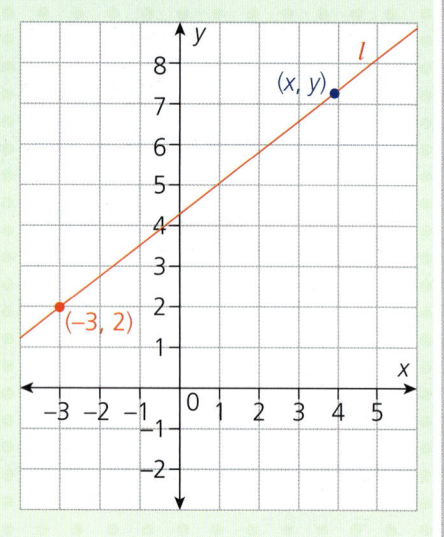

Example 3

A line l passes through the points $(-2, 2)$ and $(1, -5)$. Find the equation of the line.

Solution

First we need to get the slope:

slope $= \dfrac{y_2 - y_1}{x_2 - x_1} = \dfrac{-5 - 2}{1 + 2} = -\dfrac{7}{3}$

Use the formula: $y - y_1 = m(x - x_1)$

We can use either of the points.

Use $(1, -5)$, so $x_1 = 1$ and $y_1 = -5$

$m = -\dfrac{7}{3}$

Apply the formula:

$$y + 5 = -\frac{7}{3}(x - 1)$$

$\Rightarrow \quad 3y + 15 = -7x + 7$ ... multiply both sides by 3

$\Rightarrow 7x + 3y + 15 - 7 = 0$

$\Rightarrow \quad 7x + 3y + 8 = 0$ is the equation of the line.

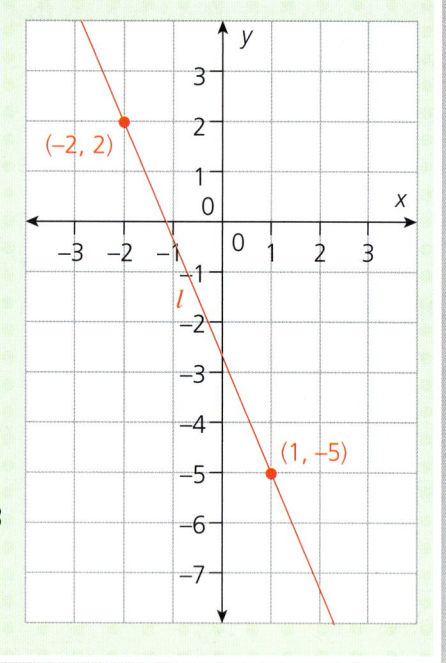

> **Key Point**
>
> Think of the equation of a line as a **rule** which every point on the line obeys; if a point is on the line, its co-ordinates will satisfy the equation of the line.

> **Key Point**
>
> When you are given the **equation** of a line, always try to imagine what its **graph** looks like.

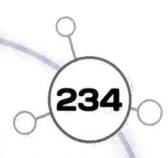

How to Draw a Line Given its Equation

To draw a line, we need two points on the line. **Any two points will do**, but we are often interested in the points where a line crosses the axes.

The points on the x-axis and the y-axis have special properties.

- Every point on the x-axis has a y co-ordinate = 0.

  Thus $y = 0$ is the equation of the x-axis.

- To find the point where a line crosses the x-axis, let $y = 0$ and find x. The point is $(x, 0)$.

- Every point on the y-axis has an x co-ordinate = 0.

  Thus $x = 0$ is the equation of the y-axis.

- To find the point where a line crosses the y-axis, let $x = 0$ and find y. The point is $(0, y)$.

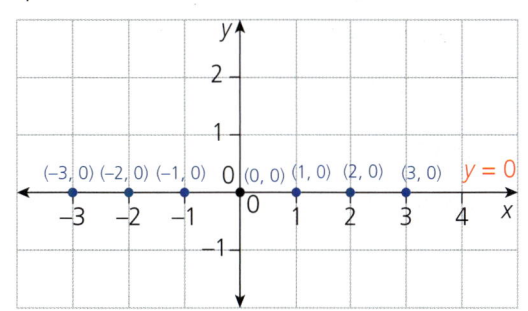

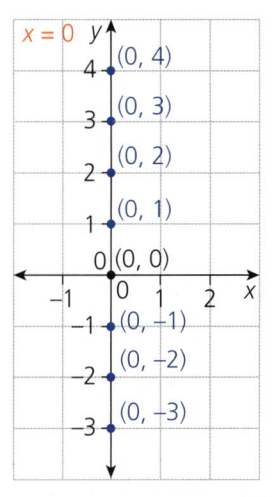

Example 4

(i) Find the points where the line $3x + 2y = 12$ cuts the x-axis and the y-axis.

(ii) Hence, sketch the line in the co-ordinate plane.

(iii) Is $(2, 4)$ on this line?

Solution

(i) Let $y = 0$

$\therefore 3x + 2(0) = 12$

$\therefore 3x = 12$

$\therefore x = 4$

Crosses x-axis at $(4, 0)$

Let $x = 0$

$\therefore 3(0) + 2y = 12$

$\therefore 2y = 12$

$\therefore y = 6$

Crosses y-axis at $(0, 6)$

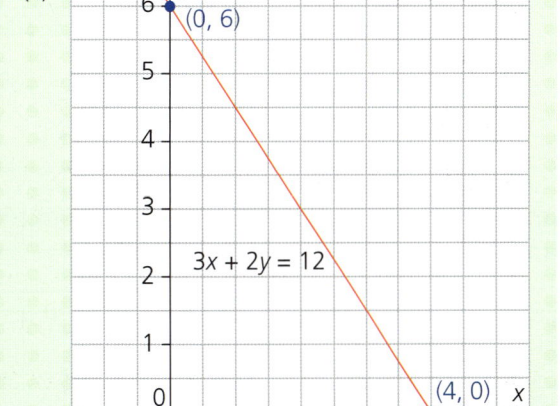

(iii) Substitute $(2, 4)$ into the equation

$3x + 2y = 12$

$3(2) + 2(4) = 6 + 8 = 14 \neq 12$

$\therefore (2, 4)$ is not on this line.

(A look at the graph confirms this.)

Example 5

Sketch the line $x = 2y$.

Solution

Find two points on the line:

Let $x = 0$

$\therefore\ 0 = 2y$

$\therefore\ y = 0$

$\therefore$ Point $(0, 0)$ is on the line.

Let $x = 4$

$\therefore\ 4 = 2y$

$\therefore\ y = 2$

$\therefore$ Point $(4, 2)$ is on the line.

This is the line:

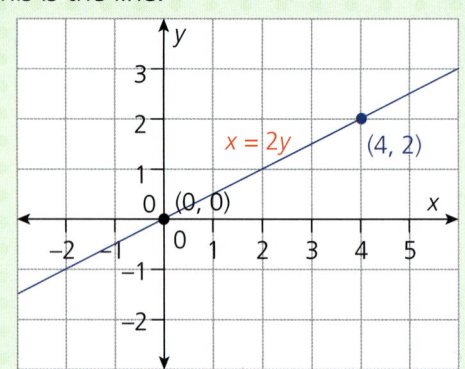

> Every line with an equation of the form $y = mx$ passes through the origin. These lines have a slope $= m$.

Example 6

Sketch the line $y = -3$.

Solution

The line $y = -3$ is made up of all the points which have a y co-ordinate of -3.

For example: $(0, -3)$, $(1, -3)$, $(2, -3)$, $(-1, -3)$, $(-\frac{1}{4}, -3)$, etc.

This is line:

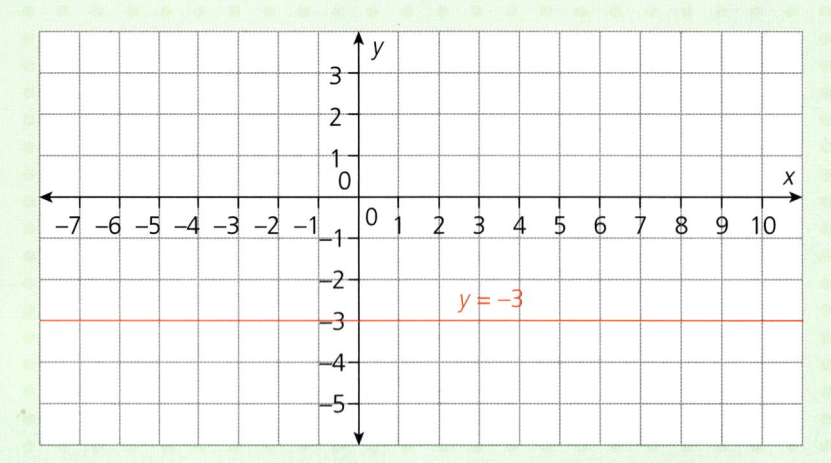

> Every line with an equation of the form $y = b$ is parallel to the x-axis. These lines are horizontal and so each of them has a slope $= 0$.

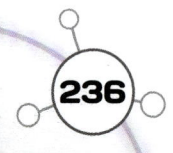

Example 7

Sketch the line $x = 2$.

Solution

The line $x = 2$ is made up of all the points which have an x co-ordinate of 2.

For example: $(2, 0)$, $(2, 1)$, $(2, 2)$, $(2, -1)$, $\left(2, -\frac{1}{2}\right)$, etc.

This is the line:

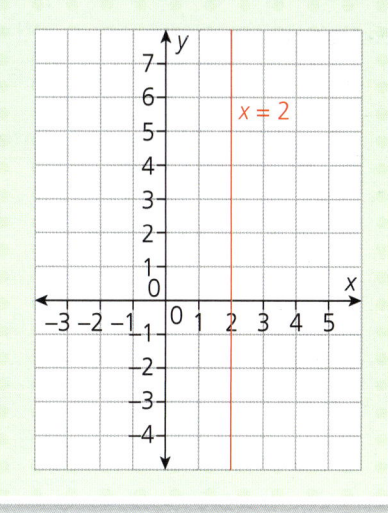

Every line of the form $x = a$ is parallel to the y-axis. These lines are vertical and so have an undefined slope.

Activity 12.3

1. Which one of the following graphs shows the line $y = \frac{1}{2}x + 3$? Explain your choice.

A

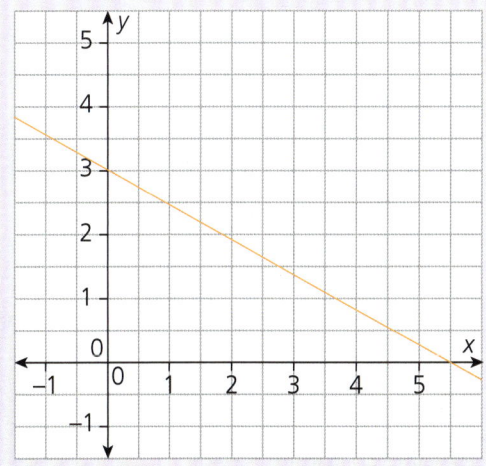

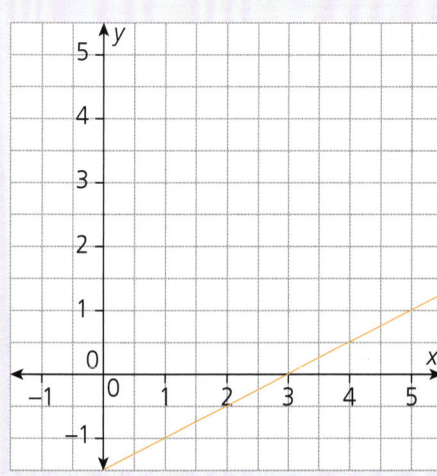

B

C

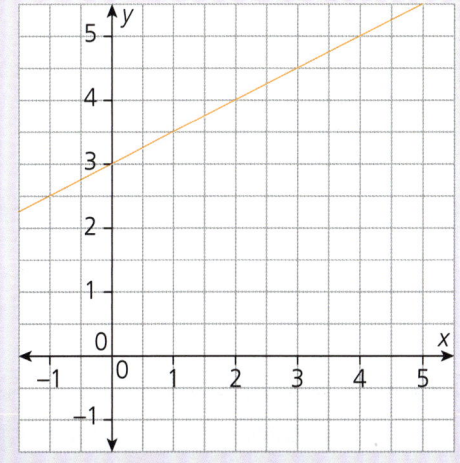

D

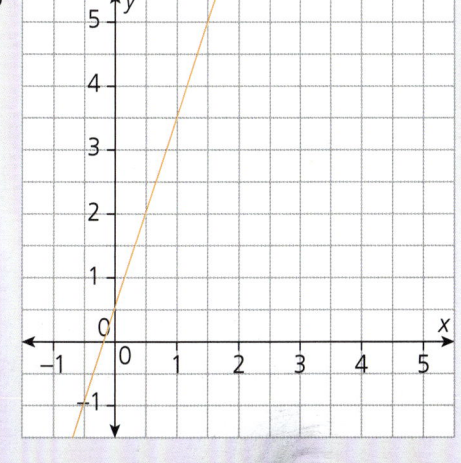

2 Write the equation of each of the following lines in the form $y = mx + c$. Then write each equation in the form $ax + by + c = 0$ where $a, b, c \in \mathbb{Z}$.

	Line	Slope	y-intercept
(i)	p	$\frac{2}{3}$	(0, –1)
(ii)	q	–1	(0, 5)
(iii)	r	2	(0, 0)
(iv)	s	5	(0, –30)
(v)	t	$-\frac{1}{3}$	(5, –6)

3 The table gives the equations of five lines.

Line 1	$y = 2x - 5$
Line 2	$y = -2x + 5$
Line 3	$y = 6x + 15$
Line 4	$y = 2x + 10$
Line 5	$y = \frac{1}{2}x - 5$

(i) Which line has the greatest slope? Give a reason for your answer.

(ii) Which lines are parallel? Give a reason for your answer. Draw a sketch of these two lines in a co-ordinate plane.

(iii) Which lines are perpendicular? Give a reason for your answer. Draw a sketch of these two lines in a co-ordinate plane.

(iv) The table shows some values of x and y for the equation of one of the lines. Which equation do they satisfy?

x	y
6	–2
8	–1
20	5

(v) There is one value of x which will give the same value of y for Line 1 as it will for Line 3. Find, using algebra, this value of x and the corresponding value of y.

(vi) Verify your answer to part (v) above.

4 The line k has a slope of $\frac{1}{3}$ and passes through the point (2, –3).
(i) Draw a sketch of the line.
(ii) Write the equation of k in the form $ax + by + c = 0$ where $a, b, c \in \mathbb{Z}$.

5 (i) Draw a sketch of each of the following lines.

Line	Slope	Point on the line
A	$\frac{1}{3}$	(–1, 4)
B	2	(3, –2)
C	–1	(1, 5)
D	Undefined	(5, 10)
E	$-\frac{1}{4}$	(–2, 3)
F	0	(1, 2)

(ii) Write the equation of each line in the form $ax + by + c = 0$ where $a, b, c \in \mathbb{Z}$.

6 (i) Sketch the line $3x - 2y = 6$ in the Cartesian (co-ordinate) plane.
(ii) Is (2, –1) on the line?

7 (i) Sketch the line $4x + y = 2$ in the Cartesian (co-ordinate) plane.
(ii) Is (1, –2) on the line?

8 Sketch the line $x = y$ in the co-ordinate plane.

9 Plot these lines in the same co-ordinate plane (label each line):
$x = 3, y = 0, x = -4, y = -3$.

10 $A(3, -2)$, $B(1, 4)$ and $C(-2, 1)$ are three points.
(i) Plot these points in the Cartesian plane.
(ii) Find the slope of AB.
(iii) Find the equation of the line k which passes through C and is parallel to AB.

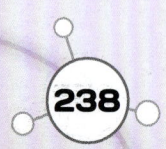

11 $P(-3, -2)$, $Q(-1, 4)$ and $R(2, 1)$ are three points.
   (i) Plot these points in the Cartesian plane.
   (ii) Find the slope of PQ.
   (iii) Find the equation of the line l which passes through R and is perpendicular to PQ.

Section 12D Finding the Slope of a Line from its Equation

We need to be able to read the slope of a line from its equation. This is easy if the equation is in the form $y = mx + c$. In this case, the slope is the coefficient of the x term.

When the equation is in the form $ax + by + c = 0$ (the standard form of the equation), we have to change it to the form $y = mx + c$.

Example 1

Find the slope of the line $3x + 2y + 6 = 0$.

Solution

$3x + 2y + 6 = 0$
$\Rightarrow 2y = -3x - 6$
$\Rightarrow y = -\dfrac{3}{2}x - 3$
$\Rightarrow$ slope $m = -\dfrac{3}{2}$ ... coefficient of x

Key Point

Notice that the slope of $3x + 2y + 6 = 0$ is $\dfrac{-3}{2}$ (the negative of the coefficient of the x term divided by the coefficient of the y term).
We can use this fact if the equation is in the form $ax + by + c = 0$:

The slope of $ax + by + c = 0$ is $\dfrac{-a}{b}$

Example 2

Find the slope of the line $5x - 3y + 7 = 0$.

Solution

Method 1

$5x - 3y + 7 = 0$
$\Rightarrow -3y = -5x - 7$
$\Rightarrow y = \dfrac{-5}{-3}x - \dfrac{7}{-3}$
$\Rightarrow y = \dfrac{5}{3}x + \dfrac{7}{3}$
$\Rightarrow$ slope $m = \dfrac{5}{3}$

Method 2

$5x - 3y + 7 = 0$ is of the form
$ax + by + c = 0$
$a = 5$ and $b = -3$
slope $= \dfrac{-a}{b} = \dfrac{-5}{-3} = \dfrac{5}{3}$

Example 3

State whether the lines $k: 3x - 4y + 6 = 0$ and $p: 4x + 3y - 5 = 0$ are
(i) parallel (ii) perpendicular or (iii) neither parallel nor perpendicular.

Solution

Find the slopes of the lines k and p and compare them.

$k: 3x - 4y + 6 = 0 \qquad$ Slope of $k = m_1 = \dfrac{-a}{b} = \dfrac{-3}{-4} = \dfrac{3}{4}$

$p: 4x + 3y - 5 = 0 \qquad$ Slope of $p = m_2 = \dfrac{-a}{b} = -\dfrac{4}{3}$

$(m_1)(m_2) = \dfrac{3}{4} \times -\dfrac{4}{3} = -1 \Rightarrow$ the lines k and p are perpendicular.

Example 4

(i) Write down the equations of three lines which are parallel to
$k: 4x - y + 5 = 0$.

(ii) Write down the equations of three lines which are perpendicular to
$p: 2x + 5y - 6 = 0$.

Solution

(i) $4x - y + 5 = 0$ is **parallel** to any line with the same ratio of x coefficient to y coefficient.
Three such lines are: $4x - y + 3 = 0; \qquad 4x - y + 10 = 0; \qquad 4x - y + 50 = 0$.

(ii) $2x + 5y - 6 = 0$ is **perpendicular** to any line with the coefficients of the x and y terms switched and one sign changed.
Three such lines are: $5x - 2y + 3 = 0; \qquad 5x - 2y + 6 = 0; \qquad -5x + 2y + 22 = 0$.

Activity 12.4

1. The line p has the equation $2x + 3y + 6 = 0$.
   (i) Write the equation in the form $y = mx + c$.
   (ii) Write down the slope of p.

2. Find the slopes of the following lines.
   (i) $y = 3x + 7$
   (ii) $y = \dfrac{1}{2}x - 20$
   (iii) $2x + y = 12$
   (iv) $3x - 2y + 4 = 0$
   (v) $x - 4y = 0$
   (vi) $y = 2$
   (vii) $2x - 7y = 15$
   (viii) $x = 3$
   (ix) $2x = 4y + 7$
   (x) $y + 3x - 2 = 0$

3. $3x - 2y + 12 = 0$ is the equation of a line k.
   (i) Find the slope of this line.
   (ii) Write down the equation of a line which is parallel to k.
   (iii) Write down the equation of a line which is perpendicular to k.

4. Write down the equations of three lines which are parallel to $2x - y + 3 = 0$.

5. Write down the equations of three lines which are perpendicular to $3x + 4y - 6 = 0$.

6. For each of the following pairs of lines, say whether they are (a) parallel, (b) perpendicular, (c) neither parallel nor perpendicular.
   (i) $2x - 3y + 12 = 0$ and $3x - 2y + 11 = 0$
   (ii) $2x - 5y + 10 = 0$ and $2x - 5y - 2 = 0$
   (iii) $x - y + 3 = 0$ and $y + x - 1 = 0$
   (iv) $x - 2 = 0$ and $x + 3 = 0$
   (v) $y = 0$ and $y - 5 = 0$
   (vi) $y = 0$ and $x = 0$
   (vii) $5x - 2y + 12 = 0$ and $5x + 2y + 1 = 0$

7. In the diagram, the lines p, q and r are parallel to the x-axis and the line n is parallel to the y-axis.

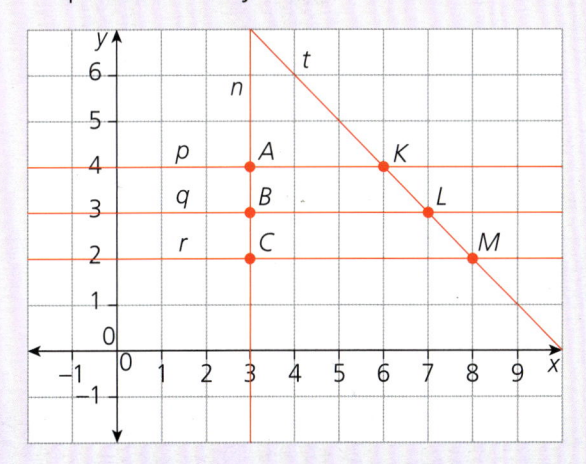

   (i) Write down the equations of the lines p, q, r and n.
   (ii) Write down the co-ordinates of A, B and C and verify that $|AB| = |BC|$.

   The line t is a transversal of the lines p, q and r and contains the points K, L and M.
   (iii) Use a theorem to explain how we know that $|KL| = |LM|$.
   (iv) Use the distance formula to verify that $|KL| = |LM|$.

8. In the co-ordinate diagram shown, the lines p and q are parallel, and so are the lines m and n.

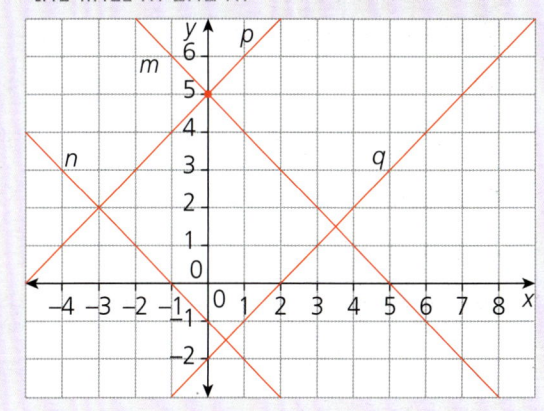

   The equations of the four lines are given in the table.

Equation	Line
$x + y = -1$	n
$x - y = -5$	p
$x + y = 5$	m
$x + y = 2$	q

   Copy and complete the table by matching the lines to their equations.

9. The equation of the line k is $5x - 2y = 6$.
   (i) Find the slope of k.
   (ii) Find the equation of the line p which is perpendicular to k and contains the point $(-2, 5)$. Give your answer in the form $ax + by + c = 0$.

10. Find the equation of the line which is parallel to $3x - 2y = 5$ and which contains the point $(3, -4)$.

11. Find the equation of the line which is perpendicular to the line $4x + y = 10$ and which contains the point $(-1, 2)$.

12. Find the equation of the line which is parallel to $x = 3y$ and which contains the point $(1, 0)$.

13. Find the equation of the line which is perpendicular to $3x - 2y = 5$ and which contains the point $(2, 2)$.

Section 12E Intersection of Lines

Example 1

(i) Find the point where the line $y = 2x + 1$ intersects the line $y = x + 3$.

(ii) Draw the lines in the co-ordinate plane.

Solution

(i) At the point of intersection,

$y = 2x + 1$ and $y = x + 3$ (simultaneously)

∴ at this point, $2x + 1 = x + 3$

$\Rightarrow \quad 2x - x = 3 - 1$

$\Rightarrow \quad x = 2$ ... the x co-ordinate

Substitute $x = 2$ into one of the equations:

$y = x + 3$

$\Rightarrow y = 2 + 3 = 5$ ... the y co-ordinate

The lines intersect at $(2, 5)$.

(ii) 3 points on $y = 2x + 1$ are $(0, 1)$, $(1, 3)$ and $(2, 5)$.

3 points on $y = x + 3$ are $(0, 3)$, $(1, 4)$ and $(2, 5)$.

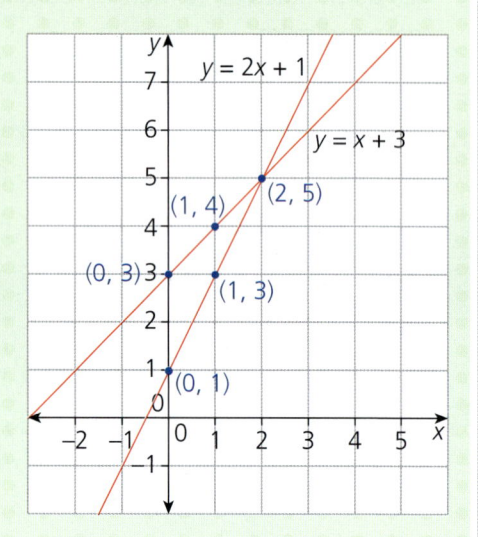

Example 2

(i) Sketch the lines l: $2x + y = 6$ and n: $x - 2y = -2$.

(ii) Find $l \cap n$, their point of intersection.

Solution

(i) To sketch the line l, we need two points on $2x + y = 6$

If $x = 0$, then $y = 6$ ∴ $(0, 6) \in l$

If $y = 0$, then $2x = 6 \Rightarrow x = 3$ ∴ $(3, 0) \in l$

To sketch the line n, we need two points on $x - 2y = -2$

If $x = 0$, then $-2y = -2$

$\Rightarrow y = 1$ ∴ $(0, 1) \in n$

If $y = 0$, then $x = -2$ ∴ $(-2, 0) \in n$

We can now sketch the two lines:

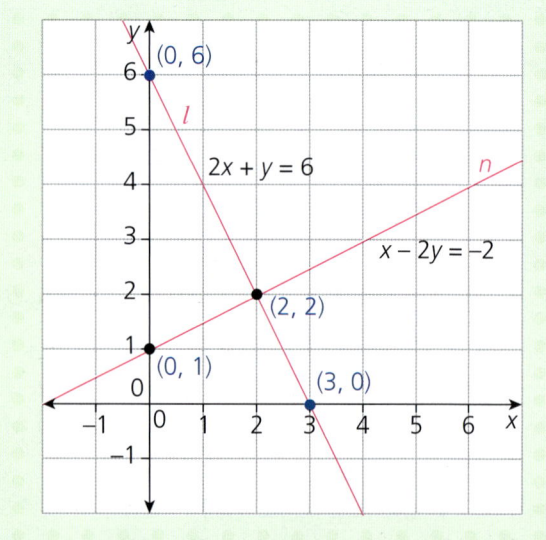

(ii) The graph suggests that $(2, 2)$ is the point of intersection, but we must use algebra to be sure. We solve the simultaneous equations:

$2x + y = 6$

$x - 2y = -2$

We can use one of two methods:

Method 1
Elimination method

$2x + y = 6 \quad \ldots (1)$
$x - 2y = -2 \quad \ldots (2)$
$\Rightarrow 4x + 2y = 12 \quad \ldots$ multiply (1) by 2

$\Rightarrow \quad 5x = 10 \quad \ldots$ add to eliminate y
$\Rightarrow \quad x = 2$

Using equation (1) substitute 2 for x
$\Rightarrow 2(2) + y = 6$
$\Rightarrow \quad y = 6 - 4$
$\Rightarrow \quad y = 2$
$\Rightarrow (2, 2)$ is confirmed as the point of intersection.

Check:
Substitute (2, 2) into $2x + y = 6$
$\Rightarrow 2(2) + 2 = 6 \checkmark$
Substitute (2, 2) into $x - 2y = -2$
$\Rightarrow 2 - 2(2) = -2 \checkmark$

Method 2
Substitution method

$2x + y = 6 \quad \ldots (1)$
$x - 2y = -2 \quad \ldots (2)$
Rewrite (1): $y = (6 - 2x)$
Substitute $(6 - 2x)$ into (2):
$\Rightarrow x - 2(6 - 2x) = -2$
$\Rightarrow x - 12 + 4x = -2$
$\Rightarrow \quad 5x = -2 + 12$
$\Rightarrow \quad 5x = 10$
$\Rightarrow \quad x = 2$

$y = (6 - 2x) \Rightarrow y = 6 - 4 \Rightarrow y = 2$
$\Rightarrow (2, 2)$ is confirmed as the point of intersection.

You may find the substitution method easier if the coefficient on one of the variables in an equation is 1.

Activity 12.5

1. Two lines in the plane are $l: 2x + y = 3$ and $p: x - y = 9$.
   (i) Find two points on each line and draw the lines in the co-ordinate plane.
   (ii) Find $l \cap p$ as accurately as you can from your graph.
   (iii) Find $l \cap p$ algebraically.

2. Two lines in the plane are $p: 3x + 2y = 6$ and $q: 2x - 3y = 4$.
   (i) Find two points on each line and draw the lines in the co-ordinate plane.
   (ii) Find $p \cap q$ as accurately as you can from your graph.
   (iii) Find $p \cap q$ algebraically.
   (iv) What is the relationship between lines p and q?

In questions 3–7, sketch each of the pairs of lines, p and q, and find their point of intersection by solving as simultaneous equations.

3. $p: x + y = 6$
   $q: x - y = 2$

4. $p: x = 3$
   $q: x + 3y = 9$

5. $p: x = y$
   $q: 3x - y = 9$

6. $p: x + y = 0$
   $q: 2x + y = -4$

7. $p: 3x - 2y = 11$
   $q: 2x + 3y = 3$

8 The equations $2x + 2y - 7 = 0$ and $x + y + 3 = 0$ represent lines in the plane.

Explain what happens through algebra and with a diagram when you try to find the point of intersection of these two lines.

9 The equations $x + 2y + 3 = 0$ and $2x + 4y + 6 = 0$ represent lines in the plane.

Explain what happens through algebra and with a diagram when you try to find the point of intersection of these two lines.

Revision Activity 12

1 (a) Plot the following points in a co-ordinate plane.

A	B	C	D	E
(–2, 0)	(3, 0)	(6, –3)	(1, –3)	(0, 3)

(b) Calculate the mid-point of [EC].
(c) Find the slope of BC.
(d) Write down the equation of BC in the form $y = mx + c$.
(e) Find the slope of AD.
(f) Write the equation of the line AD in the form $ax + by + c = 0$.
(g) What type of quadrilateral is ABCD? Justify your answer.
(h) Say whether the triangles ABC and ADC are congruent. Give a reason for your answer.
(i) What is the ratio of the area of the triangle ABC to the area of the quadrilateral ABCD? Justify your answer.

2 $A(3, –2)$ and $B(–4, 5)$ are two points.
(a) Find |AB|. Express your answer as a surd.
(b) Find the mid-point of [AB].
(c) Find the slope of AB.
(d) Find the equation of AB.

3 (a) Find the equation of the line l which passes through $(3, –1)$ and has slope $= \frac{2}{3}$.
(b) Draw a sketch of l.

4 Find the slope of line k in surd form.
Hence, write down the equation of line k in the form $y = mx + c$.

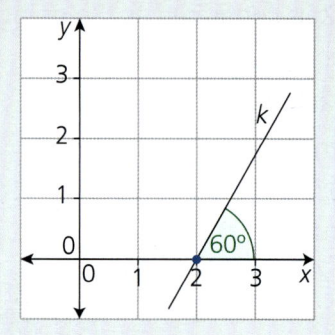

5 The equation of the line q is $3x - 2y = 6$.
(a) Find the slope of q.
(b) Find the equation of the line m which is perpendicular to q and contains the point $(1, –3)$. Give your answer in the form $ax + by + c = 0$.

6 The quadrilateral ABCD is shown in the diagram.

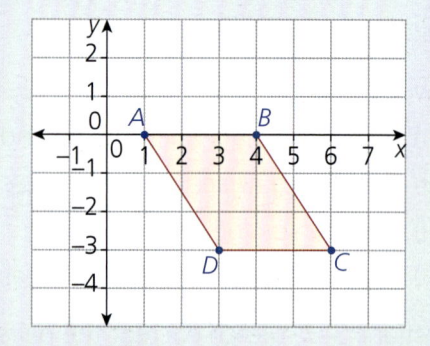

(a) Show that ABCD is a parallelogram.
(b) Find the equations of the lines containing the two diagonals [AC] and [BD].
(c) Find the point of intersection of the diagonals.

7. (a) l is the line $3x + 2y + 18 = 0$. Find the slope of l.
   (b) The line k is perpendicular to l and cuts the x-axis at the point $(7, 0)$. Find the equation of line k.
   (c) Find the point of intersection of the lines k and l.

8. The map shows part of a town. Distances are measured (in kilometres) horizontally and vertically from the Train Station and shown in co-ordinate form.
   (a) First Street and Second Street run from east to west. Write down the equations of First Street and Second Street.
   (b) Fifth Avenue runs from north to south. Write down the equation of Fifth Avenue.
   (c) Transverse Road runs through $(0, 6)$ and $(4, 0)$. Find its equation.
   (d) State, in your own words, a theorem which explains why $|TU| = |UV|$.
   (e) Verify that $|TU| = |UV|$.

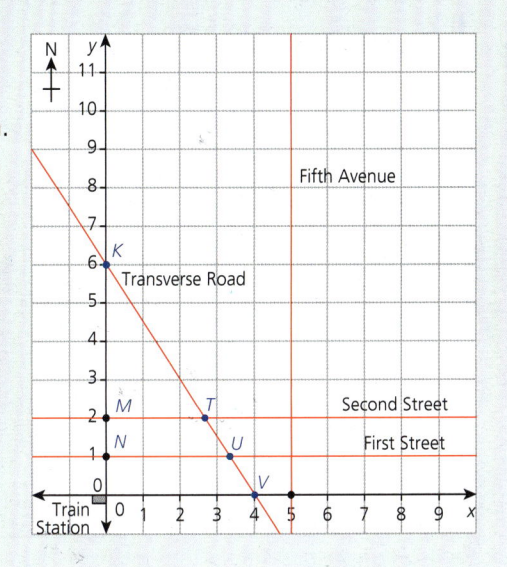

9. The diagram shows a ship's path. It has passed through location P which is 30 km due west of a lighthouse at L. It has also passed through location Q.

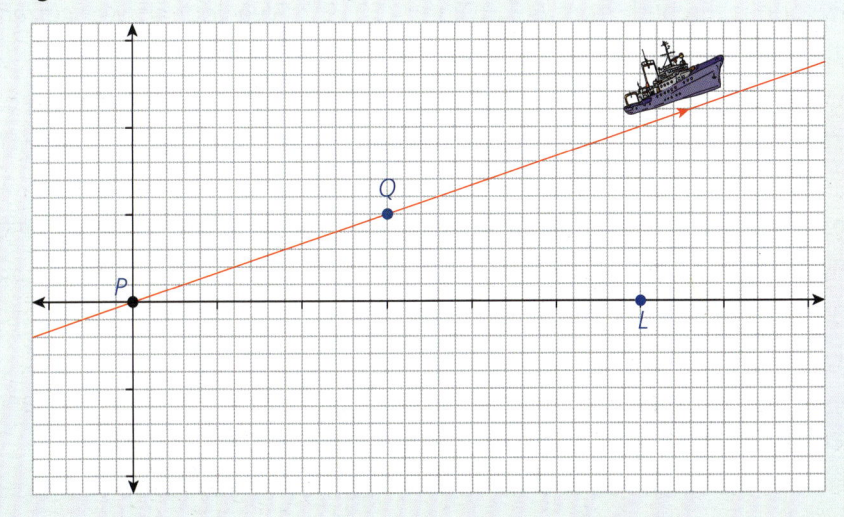

   (a) Copy the diagram and draw in a set of co-ordinates that takes the point P as the origin, the line east–west through P as the x-axis and kilometres as units.
   (b) Fill in the co-ordinates of Q and L on your diagram.
   (c) Find the distance from Q to the lighthouse correct to three decimal places.
   (d) Find the equation of the line along which the ship is moving.
   (e) Show by calculation that the ship also passes through location $(36, 12)$.
   (f) Construct accurately the point R on the ship's path which is closest to the lighthouse. Show all your construction lines clearly.
   (g) Write in the co-ordinates of R as accurately as you can and find its distance from the lighthouse.
   (h) Find the direction in which the ship is travelling.

Exam-style Question

1 The map below shows part of a town containing a park and some streets. Distances are measured (in kilometres) horizontally and vertically from the Town Hall and shown in co-ordinate form.

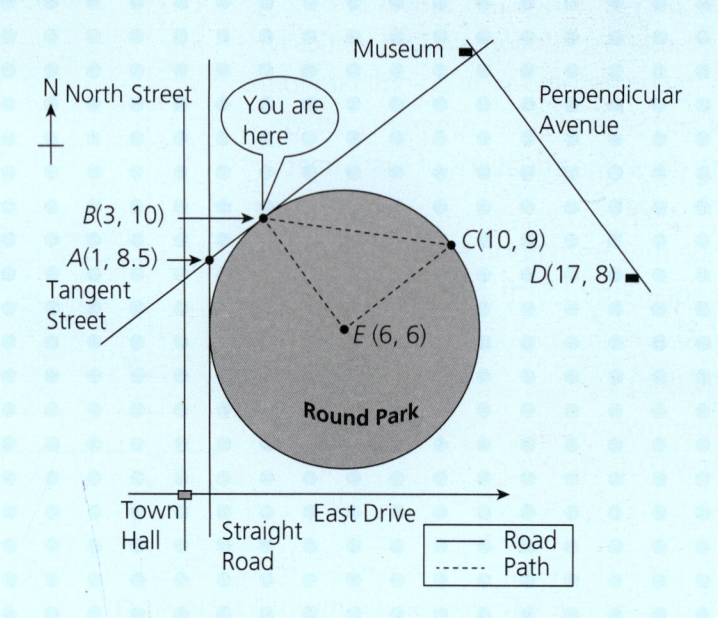

(a) How long is the path from $B(3, 10)$ to $C(10, 9)$? Give your answer correct to three significant figures.

(b) $E(6, 6)$ is the centre of Round Park. How much shorter is it to walk directly from B to C rather than to take the path to E and then on to C? Give your answer correct to the nearest km.

(c) The points $A(1, 8.5)$ and $B(3, 10)$ are on Tangent Street. Find the equation of Tangent Street.

(d) Perpendicular Avenue is perpendicular to Tangent Street and passes through $D(17, 8)$. Find its equation.

(e) The museum is located at the intersection of Tangent Street and Perpendicular Avenue. Find the co-ordinates of the museum.

(f) John is at the Town Hall and wants to go to the museum. Give one possible route he might take and calculate the total distance he must travel if he takes that route.

JCHL 2011 Paper 2

KEY WORDS AND PHRASES

- Co-ordinate geometry
- Length of line segment
- Distance between points
- Mid-point
- Slope
- Equation of a line
- Intersection of lines

Chapter Summary 12

- Distance formula: The distance $|PQ|$ from $P(x_1, y_1)$ to $Q(x_2, y_2) = \sqrt{|x_2-x_1|^2 + |y_2-y_1|^2}$
- The mid-point between $P(x_1, y_1)$ and $Q(x_2, y_2)$ is $\left(\dfrac{x_1 + x_2}{2}, \dfrac{y_1 + y_2}{2}\right)$
- Slope formula: The slope of the line through $P(x_1, y_1)$ and $Q(x_2, y_2) = \dfrac{y_2 - y_1}{x_2 - x_1}$
- $l \parallel p \Rightarrow m_1 = m_2$
- $l \perp p \Rightarrow (m_1)(m_2) = -1$
- The slope of a horizantal line $= 0$.
- The slope of a vertical line is undefined.
- The equation of the line which passes through $(0, c)$ and has slope m is $y = mx + c$.
- The equation of the line which passes through (x_1, y_1) and has slope m is $y - y_1 = m(x - x_1)$.
- The slope of $ax + by + c = 0$ is $\dfrac{-a}{b}$.

Co-ordinate Geometry

Chapter 13: Probability

Learning Outcomes

In this chapter, you will learn about:
- Counting and probability (review)
- Using binary/counting methods to solve problems involving successive random events where only two possible outcomes apply to each event
- The use of set theory to discuss outcomes and experiments

The Birthday Paradox

Imagine that there are 365 people in a room. It is possible that each one of them has a different birthday. Now if there were just 23 people in a room, what do you think the chances are that at least two of them have the same birthday?

You might be surprised to learn that there is a 50–50 chance of this happening with just 23 people in a room. Furthermore, if you have 47 people in a room there is a 95% chance that at least two of them will have the same birthday. This is known as the **Birthday Paradox** and is just one example of how working with probabilities can sometimes give surprising results.

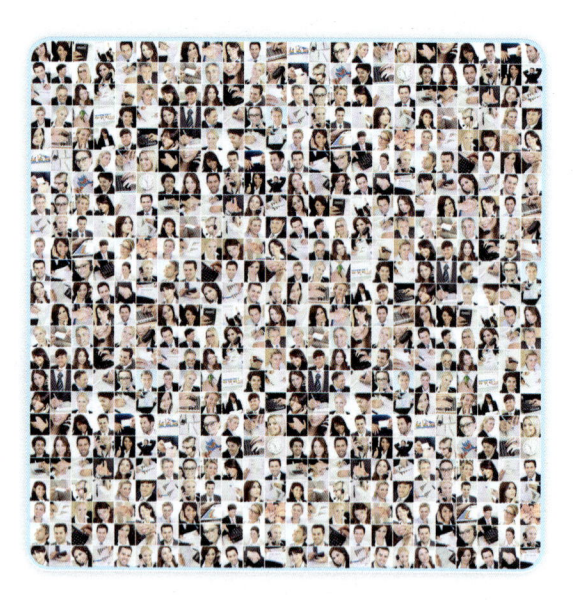

Section 13A Review of Probability

These are some of the important ideas that we have learned previously.

1. The Fundamental Principle of Counting:
   If one event has m possible outcomes and a second event has n possible outcomes, then the total number of outcomes is $m \times n$.
2. Probability deals with uncertainty and measures the likelihood of an event.

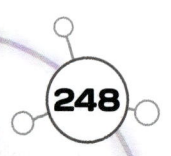

3. The probability scale goes from 0 to 1.

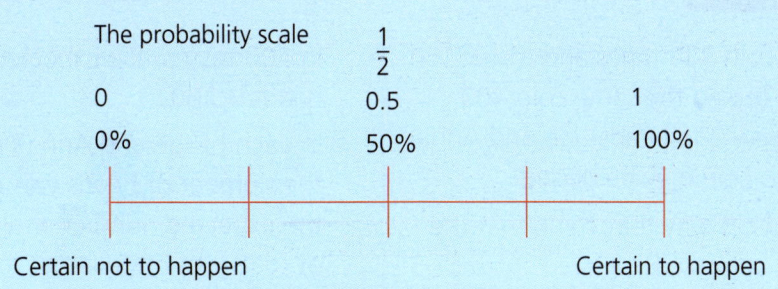

The probability scale

```
0           1/2          1
0%         0.5         100%
           50%
Certain not to happen    Certain to happen
```

4. Relative frequency = $\dfrac{\text{number of times an event occurs in a trial}}{\text{total number of trials}}$.

5. As the number of trials increases, the relative frequency leads to better estimates of the probability of an event.

   In other words, theoretical probability is relative frequency over a very large number of trials.

6. For equally likely outcomes:

   Probability of an event $[P(E)]$ = $\dfrac{\text{number of favourable outcomes}}{\text{total number of possible outcomes}}$.

7. Expected frequency = probability × the number of trials.

8. Probability of an event not happening = 1 − probability that it will happen.

Key Points

- The probability P of any event must satisfy the inequality $0 \leq P \leq 1$. Any probability answer greater than 1 must be incorrect.
- The sum of the probabilities of all the outcomes of an experiment is 1.

The following worked examples will help to revise these topics.

Example 1

(i) When you roll a die, which number is most likely to come up?

(ii) If you roll a die 720 times, how many fives would you expect to get?

Solution

(i) All numbers are equally likely.

(ii) You would expect to get a five in about $\dfrac{1}{6}$ of the throws.

Expected frequency = probability × the number of trials

$= 720 \times \dfrac{1}{6}$

$= 120$ fives

Example 2

The probability that Tom scores a goal in a match is $\dfrac{2}{3}$. What is the probability that Tom does not score?

Solution

Either Tom scores a goal or he does not score,

so $P(\text{score}) + P(\text{no score}) = 1$

$\Rightarrow \quad P(\text{no score}) = 1 - P(\text{score})$

$= 1 - \dfrac{2}{3}$

$= \dfrac{1}{3}$

Example 3

Joe tossed a coin 300 times and threw 164 heads. Anna tossed the same coin 400 times and threw 235 heads. Joe and Anna think that this coin may be biased.

(i) Give a reason why they think that the coin may be biased.
(ii) Isabella used all the above data and calculated that an estimate of the probability of throwing a head with this coin is 0.57. Show how Isabella might have calculated this probability.

Solution

(i) The probability of throwing a head with a fair coin = $\frac{1}{2}$.

Therefore in 300 tosses of a coin we expect $\left(300 \times \frac{1}{2}\right) = 150$ heads.

In 400 tosses, the expected number of heads = 200.

In each of Joe and Anna's experiments, the number of heads was greater than the expected number and the number of trials was quite large, so the coin might be biased. We would need a larger number of trials to say this with more confidence.

(ii) Isabella's calculations:

Total number of trials = 300 + 400 = 700
Total number of heads = 164 + 235 = 399

Relative frequency of getting a head
= $\frac{399}{700}$ = 0.57

Using Relative Frequency to Estimate Probabilities

We have learned that we can use relative frequency to estimate the probability of an event. Example 4, which follows, has more searching questions.

Example 4

The colours of 500 cars that pass a particular set of traffic lights during a two-hour period are recorded by a group of students.

Colour	Frequency	Relative frequency	Daily frequency (see part (v))
Red	70		
Blue	100		
Yellow	45		
White	55		
Black			
Silver	140		
Total	500		

(i) Calculate the number of black cars and write it into the table.
(ii) Calculate the relative frequency of each colour and write these into the table.

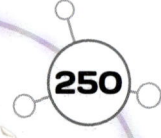

(iii) Suggest a method to check that your relative frequency calculations are correct. Perform this check.

(iv) What is the probability that the next car to pass the lights is red?

(v) Use the information to estimate the frequency of each colour if 2400 cars pass the lights in a full day. Write this information into the table.

(vi) The data collected by the students is not a random sample of the cars passing throughout the day. Do you think that this makes your estimates in part (v) unreliable? Give a reason for your answer.

JCHL 2011 Paper 2

Solution

(i) $500 - (70 + 100 + 45 + 55 + 140) = 500 - 410$
$= 90$ black cars

(ii)

Colour	Frequency	Relative frequency	Daily frequency (see part (v))
Red	70	$\frac{70}{500} = 0.14$	336
Blue	100	$\frac{100}{500} = 0.2$	480
Yellow	45	$\frac{45}{500} = 0.09$	216
White	55	$\frac{55}{500} = 0.11$	264
Black	90	$\frac{90}{500} = 0.18$	432
Silver	140	$\frac{140}{500} = 0.28$	672
Total	500	$\frac{500}{500} = 1$	2400

(iii) The sum of the relative frequencies should be 1
or The percentages should sum to 100%.
Check: $0.14 + 0.2 + 0.09 + 0.11 + 0.18 + 0.28 = 1$ ✓

(iv) $\frac{70}{500} = 0.14 = 14\%$

(v) Frequency of each colour:

Red: $\frac{70}{500} \times 2400 = 336$ White: $\frac{55}{500} \times 2400 = 264$

Blue: $\frac{100}{500} \times 2400 = 480$ Black: $\frac{90}{500} \times 2400 = 432$

Yellow: $\frac{45}{500} \times 2400 = 216$ Silver: $\frac{140}{500} \times 2400 = 672$

(vi) No. A test is reliable if repeated runs of the test would give the same results. There is no reason to say that if this test was run again it would be different because of the sample not being random. The colour of a vehicle is random and running the test at different times of the day or on different days would not necessarily make the test any more reliable.

Activity 13.1

1. (i) Use one of the following to describe each one of the statements below.

   Certain;   Very likely;   Likely;
   Evens chance;   Unlikely;
   Very unlikely;   Impossible

   A: I will win the Lotto this week.

   B: I will be in school on the next school day after tomorrow.

   C: It will rain on at least one day in November.

   D: The next baby born in Ireland will be a boy.

   E: The next time I roll a die, a seven will be the outcome.

   (ii) Show each of the above on a probability scale.

2. If you toss a coin 1000 times, how many times would you expect it to land:
   (i) heads up   (iii) on its edge?
   (ii) tails up

3. Find the probability that it will not rain tomorrow, if the probability that it will rain tomorrow is:
   (i) $\frac{1}{2}$
   (ii) $\frac{3}{4}$
   (iii) 0.7
   (iv) 20%

4. Grace plays chess with her friends. Based on previous matches, the probability that Grace beats Linda is 0.6 and the probability that she beats Michael is 0.4.
   (i) What is the probability that Linda beats Grace?
   (ii) What is the probability that Michael beats Grace?

5. Emer has a three-course lunch at a restaurant. She selects a starter, a main course and a dessert from the menu below.

Starter	**Main course**	**Dessert**
Soup	Roast chicken	Fruit salad
Melon	Baked cod	Apple crumble
Smoked salmon	Roast beef	Ice cream
Green salad	Vegetarian lasagne	Cheesecake
	Hamburger	

   (i) Write one three-course lunch that Emer could select.

   (ii) How many different selections for a three-course lunch can Emer make?

   Assuming that each selection is equally likely, what is the probability that she selects:

   (iii) soup for her starter

   (iv) a green salad, roast beef and fruit salad for her three-course lunch?

6. (i) (a) What is the probability of an event that will never happen?
   (b) What is the probability of an event that is certain to happen?
   (c) What is the probability of an event that has an evens chance of happening?

   (ii) In an experiment, a standard fair die is tossed. In the context of that experiment, give one example of each of the following.

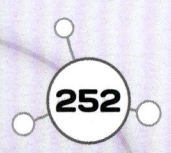

(a) an event that has an evens chance of happening
(b) an event that will never happen
(c) an event that is certain to happen.

7 A plastic toy is in the shape of a hemisphere. When it falls on the ground, there are two possible outcomes: it can land with the flat side facing down or with the flat side facing up. Two groups of students (Group X and Group Y) are trying to find the probability that it will land with the flat side down.

(i) Explain why, even though there are just two outcomes, the answer is not necessarily equal to $\frac{1}{2}$.

(ii) In their experiment, Group X dropped the toy 50 times. From this, they estimated that the probability that the toy lands flat side down is 0.68. Group Y dropped the toy 300 times and estimated that it lands flat side down with probability 0.74.

   (a) Which group's estimate is likely to be better, and why?
   (b) How many times did the toy land flat side up for Group Y?
   (c) Using the data from the two groups, what is the best estimate of the probability that the toy lands flat side down?

8 A bag contains 32 beads of which 12 are red, 15 are blue and 5 are white.

A bead is taken at random from the bag. What is the probability that the colour of the bead is:
(i) blue
(ii) red or white?

9 One letter is chosen at random from the letters of the word MISSISSIPPI.
(i) Find the probability that the letter chosen is S.
(ii) Find the probability that the letter chosen is a consonant.

10 To travel to work, Jack can walk or travel by bus or travel by car with a friend. To return home, he can walk or travel by bus.
(i) In how many different ways can Jack travel to and from work on any one day?
(ii) List all the different ways.

11 A meeting is attended by 18 men and 24 women. Of the men, 13 are married and the others are single. Of the women, 15 are married and the others are single.
(i) A person is picked at random. What is the probability that this person is a man?
(ii) A person is picked at random. What is the probability that this person is married?
(iii) A man is picked at random. What is the probability that he is single?
(iv) A woman is picked at random. What is the probability that she is married?

12 Anete writes down the date as 09082014. She then selects one of the digits at random.
(i) What is the probability that Anete selects the 8?
(ii) What is the probability that Anete selects a prime number?

13 A letter is picked at random from a newspaper. The table shows the probabilities of choosing the vowels.

Vowel	A	E	I	O	U
Probability	0.05	0.14	0.06	0.09	0.02

What is the probability that a vowel is not picked?

14 Three cards, numbered 2, 3 and 4 respectively, are shuffled and placed in a row with the numbers visible.
   (i) Write down all the possible arrangements of the digits.
   (ii) Find the probability that the numbers shown are in the order 2, 4, 3.
   (iii) Find the probability that the middle digit is 3.

15 Eight teams take part in a basketball competition. The teams are divided into two pools. Teams A, B, C and D are in Pool 1, while teams P, Q, R and S are in Pool 2.

In the final, the winning team from Pool 1 plays the winning team from Pool 2. Each team is equally likely to be the winner from its pool.
   (i) How many different team pairings are possible for the final?
   (ii) What is the probability that team D plays team R in the final?
   (iii) What is the probability that team A plays in the final?
   (iv) What is the probability that team C does not play in the final?

16 In Tom's bookcase there are 96 books. He categorises them as fiction or general and they are either hardback or paperback.

	Hardback	Paperback
Fiction	17	37
General	30	12

Tom picks one book at random from the bookcase.
Find the probability that the book selected is:
   (i) a hardback book of fiction
   (ii) a hardback book
   (iii) a general paperback
   (iv) not a paperback book of fiction.

17 Primrose Hill Post-Primary School has 760 students: 410 girls and 350 boys. The school has a Junior Cycle and a Senior Cycle.
   (i) Copy and complete the following table to show the numbers of boys and girls at each level in the school.

	Girls	Boys
Junior Cycle	220	
Senior Cycle		155

   (ii) A student is picked at random. What is the probability that the student is a boy?
   (iii) A student is picked at random. What is the probability that the student is in Junior Cycle?
   (iv) A senior student is picked at random. What is the probability that the student is a boy?
   (v) A girl is picked at random. What is the probability that she is in Senior Cycle?

18 (i) What is the probability of getting a 6 when a fair die is tossed?

A fair die is tossed 1000 times. The results are partially recorded in the table.

Number on die	1	2	3	4	5	6
Frequency	166	159	180		165	151
Relative frequency						

   (ii) Copy the table and calculate the number of times a 4 appeared.
   (iii) Calculate the relative frequency of each outcome and write it into the table.
   (iv) Give a possible reason for the difference in value between the relative frequency for 6 in the table and your answer to part (i).

19 A spinner has four unequal sections: blue, yellow, white and brown.
    The probability that the spinner will land on blue = 0.3. 108
    The probability that the spinner will land on yellow = 0.2. 72
    The probability that the spinner will land on white is the same as the probability that it will land on brown. 90 + 90
    (i) Calculate the probability that the spinner will land on brown. Justify your answer.
    (ii) Construct this spinner accurately, showing all angle sizes clearly.

20 A spinner has four unequal sections: red, black, pink and grey.
    The probability that the spinner will land on red is 0.1 [P(red) = 0.1].
    The probability that the spinner will land on black is 0.15 [P(black) = 0.15].
    The probability that the spinner will land on pink is the same as the probability that it will land on grey.
    Calculate the probability that the spinner will land on grey. Justify your answer.

Section 13B Combining Two Events

When dealing with the probabilities for two events, we need to be able to identify the set of all the possible outcomes (this is called the **sample space**).

We can use several methods to do this:

(i) by systematic listing   (ii) using a two-way table   (iii) using a tree diagram.

Example 1

A fair coin is tossed twice. Show all the possible outcomes.

Solution

Method 1

Systematic listing: (H, H), (H, T), (T, H), (T, T).

Method 2

Two-way table:

		Second coin	
		Head (H)	Tail (T)
First coin	Head (H)	H, H	H, T
	Tail (T)	T, H	T, T

We can see the 4 possible outcomes in the table: (H, H), (H, T), (T, H), (T, T).

Method 3

Tree-diagram

First toss   Second toss   Outcome

- H → H (Head, Head)
- H → T (Head, Tail)
- T → H (Tail, Head)
- T → T (Tail, Tail)

Again, we see the four possible outcomes: (H, H), (H, T), (T, H) and (T, T).

Mutually Exclusive Events

Two events are **mutually exclusive** if the two events cannot happen or take place at the same time.

For example, when tossing a coin, the events 'heads' and 'tails' are mutually exclusive because they cannot both happen at the same time.

Example 2

State whether the following pairs of events are mutually exclusive.

(i) E: a die is rolled and shows a 4.
F: a die is rolled and shows an odd number.

(ii) G: picking a student from a class who plays hurling.
H: picking a student from a class who plays soccer.

Solution

(i) It is not possible to show a 4 and an odd number at the same time, so these are mutually exclusive events.

(ii) It is possible for a student to play hurling and soccer, so these events are not mutually exclusive.

> **Key Point**
>
> If E and F are **mutually exclusive** events then $P(E \text{ or } F) = P(E) + P(F)$.

Example 3

A card is picked at random from a pack of playing cards. Find the probability that the card is a Heart or the Jack of Clubs.

Solution

E = the event that a Heart card is picked

$P(E) = \dfrac{13}{52} = \dfrac{1}{4}$

F = the event that the Jack of Clubs is picked

$P(F) = \dfrac{1}{52}$

E and F are mutually exclusive events as a card cannot be a Heart and be the Jack of Clubs at the same time.

$\therefore P(E \text{ or } F) = P(E) + P(F)$

$= \dfrac{1}{4} + \dfrac{1}{52}$

$= \dfrac{13}{52} + \dfrac{1}{52}$

$= \dfrac{14}{52}$

$= \dfrac{7}{26}$

Independent Events

Two events are **independent** if one event happening has no effect on the probability of the other happening.

For example: E = event of getting a 6 in one roll of a fair die

F = event of getting a head in one toss of a fair coin

These are independent events as one event happening has no effect on the other.

Note that $P(E) = \frac{1}{6}$ and $P(F) = \frac{1}{2}$.

If we use a two-way diagram, we can see the 12 possible outcomes of rolling a die and tossing a coin.

		Die					
		1	2	3	4	5	6
Coin	Head	(H, 1)	(H, 2)	(H, 3)	(H, 4)	(H, 5)	(H, 6)
	Tail	(T, 1)	(T, 2)	(T, 3)	(T, 4)	(T, 5)	(T, 6)

Thus $P(E \text{ and } F) = \frac{1}{12}$ which is the same as $\frac{1}{6} \times \frac{1}{2}$.

We can see that $P(E \text{ and } F) = P(E) \times P(F)$.

> **Key Point**
>
> The multiplication rule for independent events:
> If E and F are **independent** events then $P(E \text{ and } F) = P(E) \times P(F)$.

Example 4

A coin is tossed twice.

(i) If event E is the first toss shows a head and event F is the second toss shows a tail, are these events independent?

(ii) Find $P(E \text{ and } F)$.

Solution

(i) These are independent events as the outcome of the first toss has no effect on the outcome of the second.

(ii) $P(E) = \frac{1}{2}$ and $P(F) = \frac{1}{2}$

$\Rightarrow P(E \text{ and } F) = P(E) \times P(F)$

$= \frac{1}{2} \times \frac{1}{2} = \frac{1}{4}$

Finding Probabilities with Tree Diagrams

Tree diagrams can be used to find the probabilities for two independent events, even when the outcomes are not equally likely.

Example 5

The probability that Michelle is late for school on any day is 0.2.

Find the probability that on two consecutive days she is:

(i) never late   (ii) late just once.

Solution

The probability that Michelle is late for school on any day is 0.2

∴ the probability that Michelle is not late on any day = 1 − 0.2 = 0.8.

Use a tree diagram:

(i) The probability that Michelle is never late is on the bottom set of branches:

P(not late, not late) = 0.8 × 0.8
= 0.64

(ii) The probability that Michelle is late just once is found from the two middle sets of branches.
We add these probabilities:

P(late, not late) + P(not late, late)
= 0.16 + 0.16 = 0.32

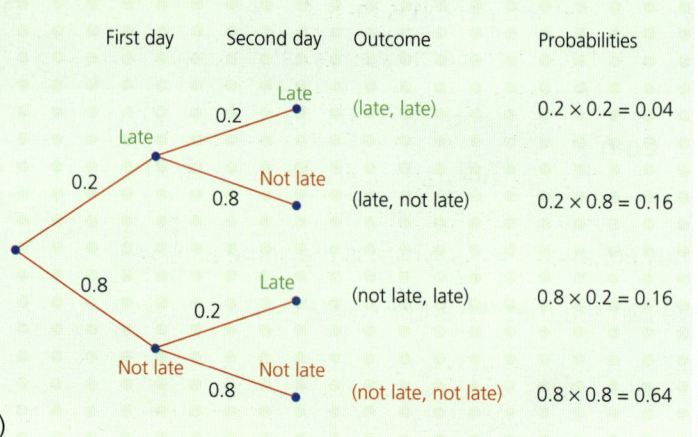

First day	Second day	Outcome	Probabilities
Late 0.2	Late 0.2	(late, late)	0.2 × 0.2 = 0.04
	Not late 0.8	(late, not late)	0.2 × 0.8 = 0.16
Not late 0.8	Late 0.2	(not late, late)	0.8 × 0.2 = 0.16
	Not late 0.8	(not late, not late)	0.8 × 0.8 = 0.64

Key Point

When using tree diagrams, we always **multiply along the branches** to get the probabilities of combined events.

Activity 13.2

1. (i) Use each of the following methods to show all the possible outcomes when two fair coins are tossed.
   - (a) Systematic listing
   - (b) A two-way diagram
   - (c) A tree diagram

   (ii) Two fair coins are tossed. What is the probability of getting two heads?

   (iii) Two fair coins are tossed 800 times. How often would you expect to get two heads?

   (iv) In a class exercise, two coins are tossed 30 times. Two heads are recorded on 18 of these occasions. If this exercise was repeated, is it likely that two heads would again be recorded 18 times? Explain your reasoning.

   (v) Lucy tosses a coin repeatedly. She records eight heads in successive throws. How likely is it that the next toss will be a head? Choose from the following answers, giving your reason:
   Extremely unlikely; Fairly unlikely; 50–50 chance; Fairly likely; Almost certain.

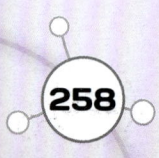

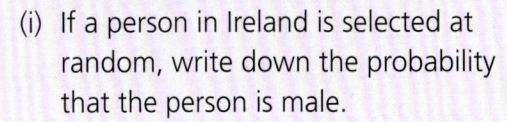

2. The 2011 Census of Ireland shows that the number of males living in Ireland is about the same as the number of females.

   (i) If a person in Ireland is selected at random, write down the probability that the person is male.

   (ii) Three people are chosen at random. We are interested in whether they are male or female. Copy and complete the tree diagram to show the eight equally likely outcomes.

   (iii) Hence, copy and complete the table of probabilities below.

Three males	Two males, one female	One male, two females	Three females
$\frac{1}{8}$			

   (iv) Examine this statement carefully: 'If you pick three people at random, it's **more likely than not** that you'll get two males and one female.' Is this statement correct? Justify your answer using the answers to part (iii).

3. A game is played by spinning two unbiased spinners and adding the numbers. Each spinner is divided into equal sections. Players get a prize if they get a total of 7.

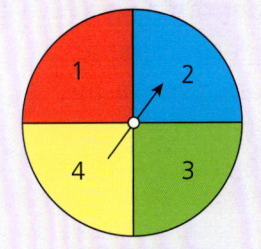

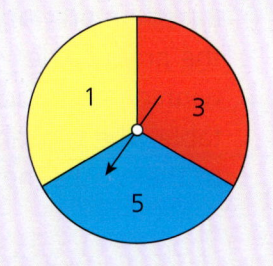

   (i) Draw a two-way table to show all the possible outcomes.

   (ii) James plays the game once. Find the probability that he will get a score of 3.

   (iii) Find the probability that James wins a prize.

   (iv) Which of the following best describes James's chances of winning a prize?

   Extremely unlikely; Not very likely; Evens chance; Very likely; Dead certainty.

   (v) James would like to investigate whether the first spinner is really fair after all. Describe how he could find the true probability of getting each of the numbers 1 to 4 with that spinner.

4. Zach and Chloe are students of a large school who are experimenting with probability. One morning before class, they decide to guess whether the next three students to arrive will be a boy or a girl.

   (i) Zach says that these outcomes are equally likely. Chloe says they are not. What information about the students in the school would you need to decide which of them is correct?

   (ii) Use a tree diagram to write out the sample space (i.e. the set of all possible outcomes). For example, in your diagram, use BGB to stand for the outcome Boy, Girl, Boy.

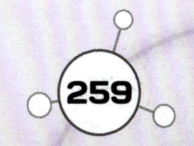

(iii) If the outcomes are equally likely, what is the probability that the three students will be two boys followed by a girl?

(iv) Chloe bets that there will be at least one girl among the next three students. What is the probability that Chloe is correct, assuming all outcomes are equally likely?

(v) Zach bets that the next three students will be either two girls and a boy or three girls. What is the probability that Zach is correct, assuming all outcomes are equally likely?

5 An unbiased spinner has five equal sectors: two coloured yellow and three coloured blue.

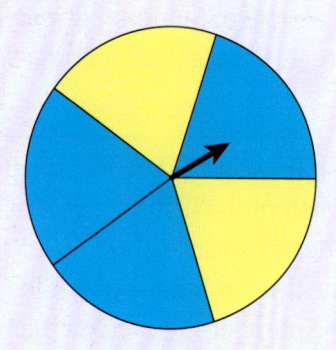

(i) Find the probability that the pointer stops on blue for one spin of the spinner.

(ii) Use a tree diagram to list all the possible outcomes of three successive spins of the spinner.

6 Three coins are tossed. Each coin gives either a head (H) or a tail (T).

(i) Use a tree diagram to write out the sample space (i.e. list all the possible outcomes).

(ii) Find the probability that the result is three heads.

(iii) Find the probability that the result includes at most one head.

(iv) Find the probability that the number of heads is two or more.

7 Two spinners, each with four equal segments numbered 1 to 4, are spun.

(i) Using a list, table, tree diagram, or otherwise, show all the possible outcomes.

(ii) If the spinner is fair, what is the probability of getting two threes?

(iii) Vesna thinks that one of the spinners is not fair. Describe an experiment that she could do to find out whether the spinner is fair.

8 A calculator is set up to show the numbers **1** and **7** at random.

A number is shown every time the EXE key is pressed.

The EXE key is pressed 3 times.

What is the probability that:

(i) the number **1** is shown each time

(ii) the same number is shown each time?

NCCA Pre-Junior Cert 2011

9 Aaron and Billy are running in a 800 m race followed later by a 1500 m race. Based on previous performances, the probabilities of each of them winning each race are given in the table. The probability that neither of them wins the 800 m race is also given.

	Aaron	Billy	Neither
800 m race	$\frac{1}{5}$	$\frac{2}{5}$	$\frac{2}{5}$
1500 m race	$\frac{1}{4}$	$\frac{1}{3}$	

(i) Copy and complete the table.

(ii) Copy the tree diagram below. Complete the list of possible outcomes. For example, (A, A) represents the outcome that Aaron wins the first race and the second race. Write in the probability of each outcome.

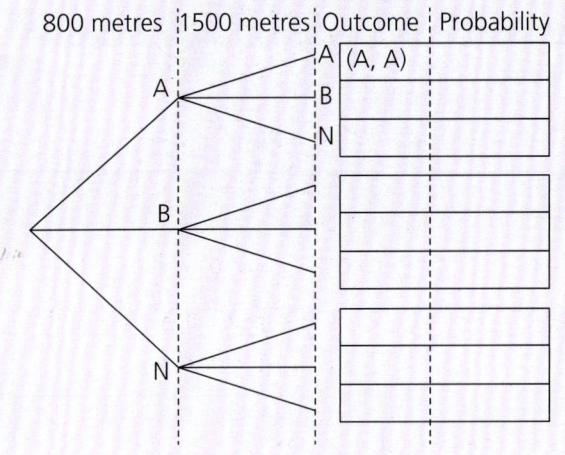

(iii) What is the probability that Aaron and Billy win a race each?

10. The diagram shows two spinners. The first spinner has four equal segments numbered 1, 2, 3 and 4. The second spinner has three equal segments labelled A, B and C.

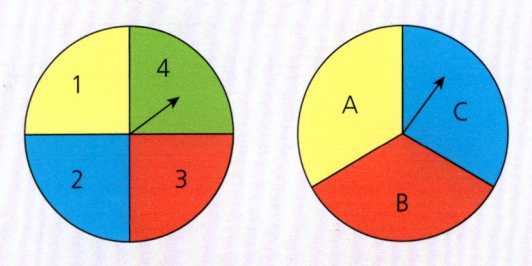

A game consists of spinning the two spinners and noting the result on each. For example, the outcome shown is (4, C).
(i) List all the possible outcomes.
(ii) Find the probability that the outcome is (3, B).
(iii) Find the probability that the outcome is an even number with the letter A.
(iv) Find the probability that C is in the outcome.

11. These two spinners are part of a game. A player gets to spin each spinner once. A prize is won only if both spinners point to blue after each has been spun once.

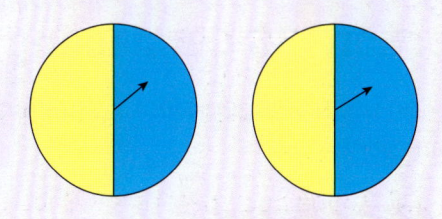

Ben thinks that he has a 50–50 chance of winning.

Chloe thinks that the probability of her winning is $\frac{1}{3}$, since, she says, 'There are three outcomes: (yellow, yellow), (yellow, blue) and (blue, blue).'

(i) Is Ben correct?
(ii) Is Chloe correct?

Explain your reasoning with diagrams.

12. Ava and Ryan are taking part in a quiz. They are asked a particular question and are unsure of the answer.

The probability that Ava will get the answer correct = 0.8.

The probability that Ryan will get the answer correct = 0.7.

(i) Construct a probability tree diagram to show all the possible outcomes.
(ii) What is the probability that at least one of them answers correctly?
(iii) What is the probability that neither of them answers correctly?

13. Suppose that every child that is born has an equal chance of being a boy or a girl.
(i) Write out the sample space for the situation where a mother has two children.
(ii) What is the probability that a randomly chosen mother of two children would have two girls?
(iii) What is the probability that this mother of two children would have two boys?
(iv) What is the probability that this mother of two children would have one boy and one girl?

NCCA Student Resources 2009

Section 13C Connecting Probability with Sets

We can use sets to represent a situation and make it easier to work out the probability of an event.

Example

A group of 100 students were surveyed to find out whether they drank tea (T), coffee (C) or a soft drink (D) at any time in the previous week.

24 had not drunk any of the three.

51 drank tea or coffee but not a soft drink.

41 drank tea.

20 drank at least two of the three.

8 drank tea and a soft drink but not coffee.

9 drank a soft drink and coffee.

4 drank all three.

(i) Copy and represent the above information on the Venn diagram.

(ii) Find the probability that a student chosen at random from the group had drunk tea or coffee.

(iii) Find the probability that a student chosen at random from the group had drunk tea and coffee but not a soft drink.

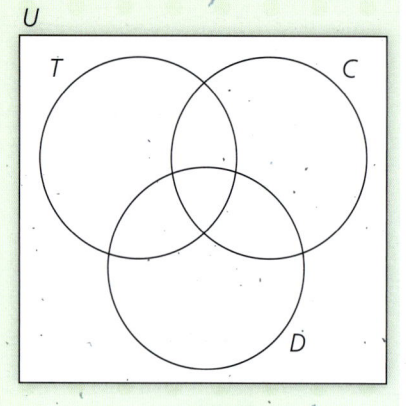

JCHL 2013 Sample Paper

Solution

(i) U [100]

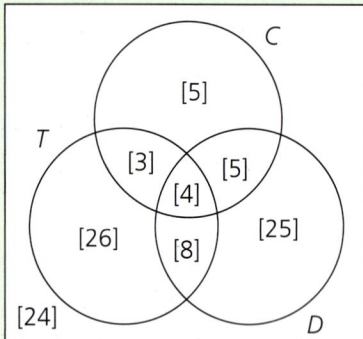

T [26], T∩C [3], C [5], T∩C∩D [4], C∩D [5], T∩D [8], D [25], outside [24]

(ii) Number who had drunk tea or coffee = 26 + 3 + 5 + 8 + 4 + 5 = 51

Total number of students = 100

Probability = $\dfrac{51}{100}$.

(iii) Number who had drunk tea and coffee but not a soft drink = 3

Total number of students = 100

Probability = $\dfrac{3}{100}$.

Activity 13.3

1 The sets in the Venn diagram represent the students in a class of 28 students who study Spanish and French.

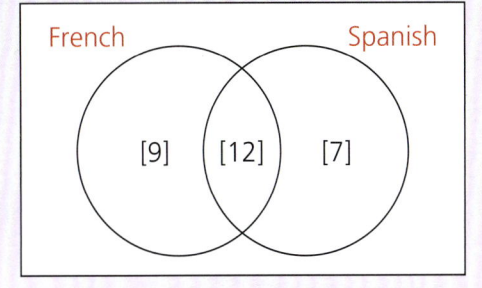

U [28]

French — [9] [12] [7] — Spanish

(i) How many students study both Spanish and French?

A student is picked at random from the class.

(ii) Find the probability that the student studies both Spanish and French.

(iii) Find the probability that the student studies Spanish but not French.

2 In this Venn diagram, the universal set is a normal deck of 52 playing cards. The two sets shown represent Spades and picture cards (Kings, Queens and Jacks).

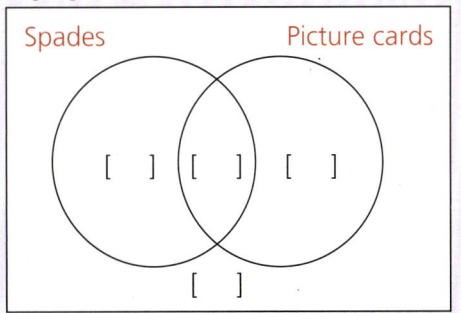

U [52]

Spades — [ ] [ ] [ ] — Picture cards

[ ]

(i) Copy the Venn diagram and show the number of elements in each region.

(ii) (a) A card is drawn at random from a pack of 52 cards. Find the probability that the card drawn is a Spade that is not a picture card.

(b) A card is drawn at random from a pack of 52 cards. Find the probability that the card drawn is a Spade or a picture card.

(c) A card is drawn at random from a pack of 52 cards. It is not replaced. A second card is drawn at random. Find the probability that neither card drawn is a Spade or a picture card.

3 35 people coming back from America were asked if they had visited New York, Boston or San Francisco. The results were:

20 had visited New York.

13 had visited Boston.

16 had visited San Francisco.

7 had been to all three cities.

3 had been to both New York and San Francisco, but not Boston.

1 had been to both New York and Boston, but not San Francisco.

8 had been to Boston and San Francisco.

(i) Display this information on a Venn diagram.

(ii) If one person is chosen at random from the group, what is the probability that the person had not visited any of the three cities?

(iii) If one person is chosen at random from the group, what is the probability that the person had visited New York only?

(iv) If one person is chosen at random from the group, what is the probability that the person had visited Boston or New York?

4 A leisure centre has 180 members. The weights room is used by 107 members, while the swimming pool is used by 124 members. 24 members do not use either of these facilities in the centre.

(i) Draw a Venn diagram to represent this information.

(ii) What is the probability that a member picked at random uses both the weights room and the swimming pool?

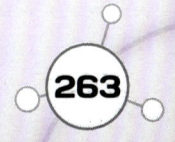

(iii) What is the probability that a member picked at random uses the swimming pool only?

5 80 Third Year students responded to a survey about their travels in Europe.

30 had been to France,

26 had been to Spain,

and 28 had travelled to Germany.

12 had travelled to both France and Spain,

8 had travelled to both Germany and Spain,

while x had travelled to France and Germany only.

4 students had been to all three countries.

Twice as many had never travelled to any of these destinations as had travelled to France and Germany only.

(i) Represent this information on a Venn diagram.

(ii) Find the value of x.

(iii) If a student is picked at random from the whole group, what is the probability that the student had been to all three countries?

(iv) If a student is picked at random from the whole group, what is the probability that the student had been to France only?

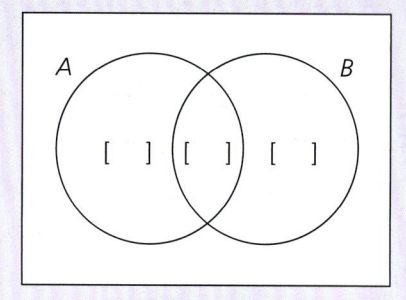

6 Two events A and B are such that $P(A) = 0.6$, $P(B) = 0.4$ and $P(A \cap B) = 0.2$.

(i) Copy and complete this Venn diagram for the above probabilities.

(ii) Use your diagram to find $P(A \cup B)$.

7 A group of Third Year students did a survey of all 120 students in their year to find out how many had accounts on social media sites Facebook and Twitter. The results were:

- Of the 120 students, 65 had accounts on Facebook.
- Of those with accounts on Facebook, 25 also had accounts on Twitter.
- There were 35 students who did not have an account on either site.

(i) Represent this information on a Venn diagram.

(ii) What is the probability that a student chosen at random (from all those surveyed) will have an account on Facebook?

(iii) What is the probability that a student chosen at random from those with an account on Facebook will also have an account on Twitter?

(iv) What is the probability that a student chosen at random from those with an account on Twitter will also have an account on Facebook?

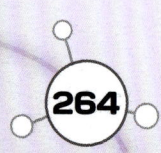

8 In a survey, 54 people were asked which political party they had voted for in the last three elections. The results were:

30 had voted for the Conservatives.

22 had voted for the Liberals.

22 had voted for the Republicans.

12 had voted for the Conservatives and the Liberals.

9 had voted for the Liberals and the Republicans.

8 had voted for the Conservatives and the Republicans.

5 had voted for all three parties.

(i) Represent this information in a Venn diagram.

(ii) If one person is chosen at random, what is the probability that the person chosen did not vote in any of the three elections?

(iii) If one person is chosen at random, what is the probability that the person chosen voted for at least two different parties?

(iv) If one person is chosen at random, what is the probability that the person chosen voted for the same party in all three elections?

JCHL 2013 Paper 2

Revision Activity 13

1 A, B, C, D and E represent the probabilities of certain events occurring.

(a) Write the probability of each of the events listed in a copy of the table below.

Event		Probability
A Club is selected in a random draw from a pack of playing cards	A	
A tossed fair coin shows a tail on landing	B	
The sun will rise in the east tomorrow	C	
May will follow directly after June	D	
A randomly selected person was born on a Thursday	E	

(b) Place each of the letters A, B, C, D and E at its correct position on a copy of the probability scale below.

0 ———————————————————— 1

JCHL 2012 Paper 2

2. The faces of one cube are marked with the odd numbers 1, 3, 5, 7, 9 and 11.
The faces of another cube are marked with the even numbers 2, 4, 6, 8, 10 and 12.
The cubes are rolled and the scores are added.

(a) Copy and complete the following table to show all the possible scores.

		\multicolumn{6}{c}{First cube}
		1	3	5	7	9	11
Second cube	2	3					
	4						
	6				13		
	8		11				
	10						
	12						23

(b) What is the highest possible score?
(c) What is the probability of getting the highest score?
(d) What is the probability of scoring an even number?

3. There are four main blood groups: group O, group A, group B and group AB. The blood in each group is further classed as either rhesus positive (+) or rhesus negative (−).
The percentage of a population in each blood group is given in the table.

Blood group	\multicolumn{2}{c}{O}	\multicolumn{2}{c}{A}	\multicolumn{2}{c}{B}	\multicolumn{2}{c}{AB}
Rhesus positive (+) or rhesus negative (−)	O$^+$	O$^-$	A$^+$	A$^-$	B$^+$	B$^-$	AB$^+$	AB$^-$
Percentage	8	47	5	26	2	9	1	2

(a) (i) Find the percentage of the population in blood group O.

(ii) Find the percentage of the population with rhesus positive blood.

(b) The table below has statements about a person's blood group. A person is picked at random from the population. In each case, find the probability that the statement is true for that person.

Statement	Probability
Is in blood group A$^+$	
Is in blood group AB	
Is in blood group A or B	
Has blood which is rhesus negative	
Is not in blood group O	

(c) Over a period, 8000 people donate blood at a clinic. How many of these would you expect to donate each of the following blood types, according to the percentages given in the table?

   (i) type AB blood

   (ii) rhesus negative blood

   (iii) rhesus positive blood.

4 In a class of students, there are 12 boys and 16 girls. Three of the boys wear glasses and four of the girls wear glasses.

A student is picked at random from the class.

(a) What is the probability that the student is a boy?

(b) What is the probability that the student wears glasses?

(c) What is the probability that the student is a boy who wears glasses?

A girl is picked at random from the class.

(d) What is the probability that she wears glasses?

5 Lily and David were both born in the same week (Monday to Sunday inclusive). Assuming that a baby is equally likely to be born on any day of the week, what is the probability that:

(a) Lily was born on Saturday

(b) Lily was born on Saturday and David was born on Tuesday

(c) Lily and David were both born on Sunday?

6 Tickets for a raffle are placed in a box. The box contains 15 blue tickets and 10 red tickets. Tickets are drawn at random from the box and they are not replaced. What is the probability that:

(a) the first ticket drawn is red

(b) the first ticket drawn and the second ticket drawn are both red

(c) the first ticket drawn is red and the second ticket drawn is blue?

7 In an experiment, a standard die is tossed 600 times. The results are partially recorded in the table.

Number on die	1	2	3	4	5	6
Frequency	92	101	115	98		105

(a) Calculate the number of times that a 5 appeared. Copy and complete the table.

(b) After looking at the results, Anne claims that the die is unbiased (fair). Do you agree with her? Give a reason for your answer.

(c) If this die is tossed 300 times, how many times would you expect to get an even number based on the data in the table? Give a reason for your answer.

JCHL 2014 Sample Paper 2

8 A fair circular spinner consists of three equal sectors. Two are coloured blue and one is coloured white.

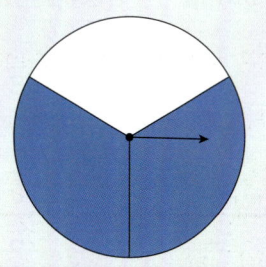

The spinner is spun and a fair coin is tossed.

(a) What is the probability of the spinner landing on a blue sector?

(b) Find the probability of getting white and a head.

(c) Find the probability of getting blue and a tail.

Exam-style Questions

1 The arrows represent the different routes that a skier can take when skiing down a mountain. The circles on the diagram represent different points on the routes.

   (a) When leaving any particular point on the mountain, a skier is equally likely to choose any of the available routes from that point. Fill in the boxes in the diagram which represent the probability that the skier will take that route.

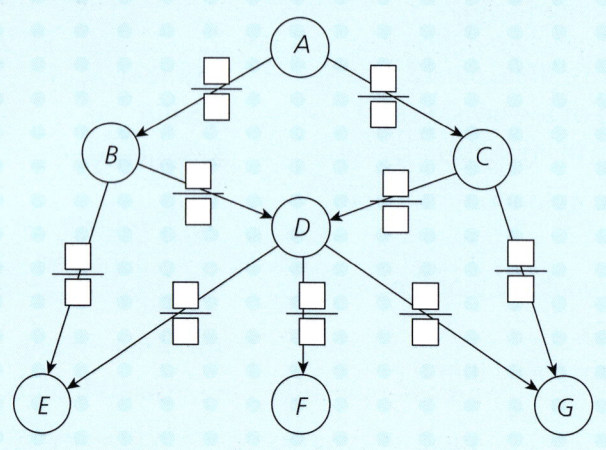

   (b) (i) If the skier starts at point A, in how many different ways can the skier reach the point E?

   (ii) If the skier starts at point A, find the probability that the skier will reach the point E.

   JCHL 2013 Paper 2

2 The percentage distribution of blood groups in the Irish population is given in the table below. The table also gives information about which types of blood can be safely used when people need to be given blood during an operation.

Blood group	Percentage in Irish population	Blood groups to which transfusions can be safely given	Blood groups from which transfusions can be safely received
O−	8	All	O−
O+	47	O+, AB+, A+, B+	O+ and O−
A−	5	A−, A+, AB+, AB−	A− and O−
A+	26	A+ and AB+	A+, O−, O+, A−
B−	2	B−, B+, AB−, AB+	B− and O−
B+	9	B+ and AB+	B+, B−, O−, O+
AB−	1	AB− and AB+	AB−, O−, A−, B−
AB+	2	AB+	All

Source: Irish Blood Transfusion Service

(a) If an Irish person is chosen at random, what is the probability that person will have blood group AB–?

(b) Mary has blood group B–. If a person is chosen at random from the population, what is the probability that Mary could safely receive blood from that person?

(c) Aaron has blood group O+ and donates blood. What is the probability that his blood can be given to a person randomly chosen from the population?

(d) The Irish Blood Transfusion Service recently asked that people with blood group O– should give blood as regularly as possible. Give a reason why this might be the case.

JCHL 2011 Paper 2

KEY WORDS AND PHRASES

- Mutually exclusive events
- Independent events
- Tree diagram
- Systematic list

Chapter Summary 13

- The Fundamental Principle of Counting:

  If one event has m possible outcomes and a second event has n possible outcomes, then the total number of outcomes is $m \times n$.

- For equally likely outcomes:

  Probability of an event $[P(E)] = \dfrac{\text{number of favourable outcomes}}{\text{total number of possible outcomes}}$

- Expected frequency = probability × the number of trials.
- Probability of an event not happening = 1 – probability that it will happen.
- We can identify the set of all the possible outcomes (the sample space).
    - by systematic listing
    - using a two-way table
    - using a tree diagram.
- Two events are mutually exclusive if the two events cannot happen or take place at the same time.
    - If E and F are mutually exclusive events then $P(E \text{ or } F) = P(E) + P(F)$.

- Two events are independent if one event happening has no effect on the probability of the other happening.
  - If E and F are independent events, $P(E \text{ and } F) = P(E) \times P(F)$.
- When using tree diagrams, we always multiply along the branches to get the probabilities of combined events.
- We can use sets to represent a situation and make it easier to work out the probability of an event.

Statistics

Chapter 14

Learning Outcomes

In this chapter, you will learn about:
- The nature of statistics (review)
- Selecting a sample from a population (simple random sample)
- The importance of representativeness so as to avoid biased samples
- Outliers
- Sampling variability and its implications
- Evaluating reliability of data and data sources
- The use of back-to-back stem and leaf plots to display data
- Quartiles and interquartile range
- Mean of a grouped frequency distribution

A statistician solves problems using real data.

Florence Nightingale, the 'Lady with the Lamp', who is famous for her work as a nurse in caring for the wounded in the Crimean War, was also known as 'the passionate statistician'.

She created graphs, which are often described as roses or coxcombs (although she did not refer to them as such), to highlight that the death toll from diseases was greater than the death toll from wounds in the Crimean War. One of her original graphs is shown here.

Florence Nightingale (1820–1910)

'Diagram of the Causes of Mortality in the Army of the East'

The data is plotted by month in 30-degree wedges where each wedge in the diagram represents a month from April 1854 to March 1855.

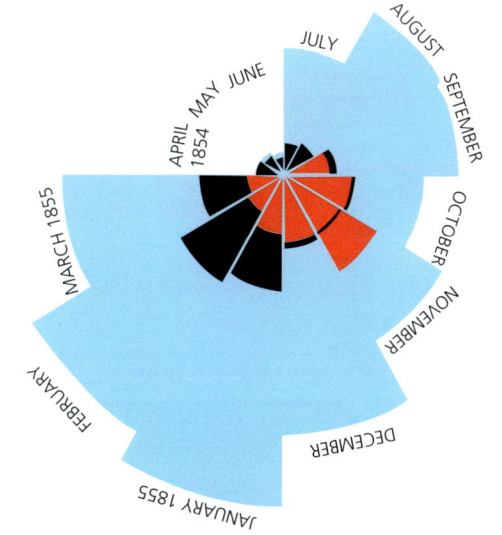

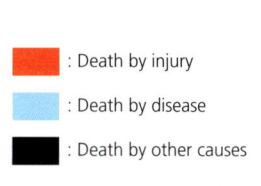

- Death by injury
- Death by disease
- Death by other causes

Nightingale realised that soldiers were dying needlessly from malnutrition, poor sanitation, and lack of activity and her graph shows this very clearly.

She strove to improve living conditions for the wounded troops, and kept meticulous records of the death toll in the hospitals as evidence of the importance of patient welfare.

Section 14A Review

Statistics involves the exploration of and use of patterns and relationships in data.

Statistics is required because of **variation** which exists among people and in the world around us and it allows us to look for patterns in that variation.

The Central Statistics Office was established in 1949 as Ireland's national statistical office (www.cso.ie) to provide information which is vital for future planning.

Data is used in order to answer questions and solve problems in the real world. The **data handling cycle** in the diagram shows how we proceed in solving problems using data.

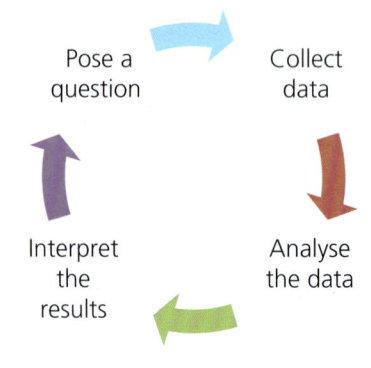

Data we collect ourselves is called **primary data**.

Data we use which has already been collected by someone else is called **secondary data**, i.e. data which exists in books, journals, the Internet etc.

We can use **secondary data from international students** through the random data selector from *CensusAtSchool*: http://rds.censusatschool.org.uk/

Types of Data

How we analyse data depends on the type of data.

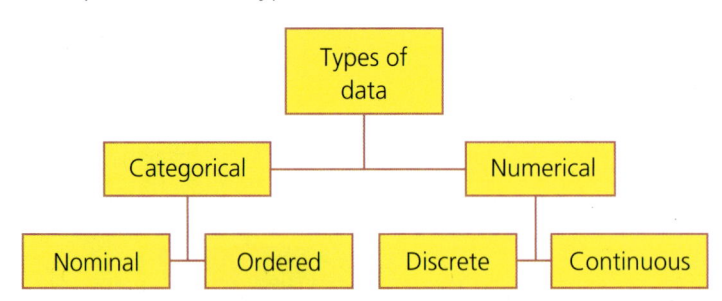

- **Discrete numeric data** have gaps between the possible values, e.g. 1, 2, 3, 4, … or shoe sizes 4, $4\frac{1}{2}$, 5, $5\frac{1}{2}$, 6, …
- **Continuous numeric** data can take on any value between two given real number values and result from measurement, e.g. the speed of a car could be 82.345 197… km per h. In practice of course, measurements can only be recorded correct to a certain number of decimal places.

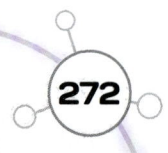

- A **variable** is something whose value we can measure for each person in a population and its value can vary from person to person. The height of students is an example of a variable. When we use a **spreadsheet**, each row contains the data for one person and each column contains the data for a different variable.
- An **outlier** in a dataset is an item of data which lies far away from the overall pattern of the rest of the data. In this **dot plot** of temperatures, we can see that 33°C is an outlier.

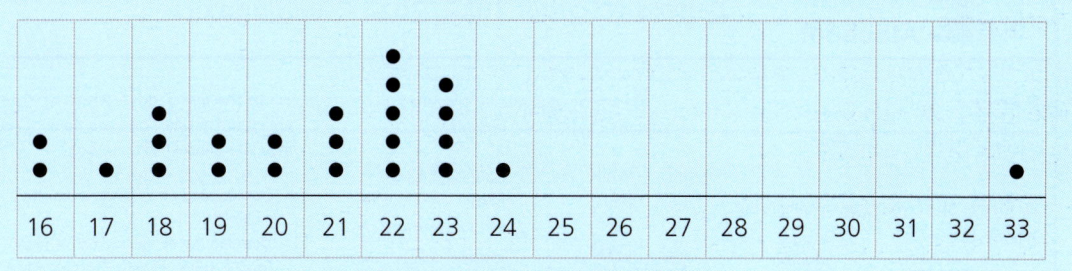

Outliers can occur for a variety of reasons. They can be errors or genuine observations. Outliers should always be investigated. A student height which is ten times the average height must be an error in the placing of the decimal point. If you include the income of a premier league football player in an income distribution, be prepared to see an outlier which is genuine.

Being a Statistically Aware Consumer

When evaluating information from a survey or opinion poll carried out by someone else, consider:

- Who carried out the survey?
- What was the population?
- How was the sample selected?
- How large was the sample?
- What was the response rate?
- How were the subjects contacted?
- When was the survey conducted?
- What were the exact questions asked?

We also need to consider variation (apart from natural variation) which is due to measurement error and input error, i.e. data being recorded incorrectly.

Always question the logic, the numbers, the sources and the procedures used to generate the statistics when evaluating statistical claims.

Activity 14.1

1. What is primary data? Give an example.
2. What is secondary data? Give an example.
3. What type of data is produced by each question in the 2012/2013 *CensusAtSchool* Questionnaire shown below?

CensusAtSchool 2012/2013 Questionnaire

1. Are you:
   ☐ Female   ☐ Male

2. Please state your age in completed years:
   ☐☐☐ years

3. Which hand do you write with?
   ☐ Right
   ☐ Left
   ☐ Either (ambidextrous)

4. a) In how many languages can you hold an everyday conversation?
   ☐☐☐

4. b) Specify these languages in the order you speak them best:
   ☐☐☐
   ☐☐☐
   ☐☐☐

4. c) Is there a language you would like to learn that is not currently available in your school?
   ☐ Yes   ☐ No
   If yes, please specify:
   ....

5. Complete the following measurements, answer to the nearest tenth of a cm:
   Height ....cm
   Length of right foot ....cm
   Open arm span ....cm
   Circumference of your wrist ....cm
   Open hand span of the hand you write with ....cm

6. Write down a two digit number.
   ☐☐

7. a) How do you usually travel to school? (Select one answer)
   ☐ Walk   ☐ Rail/Dart/Luas
   ☐ Bus   ☐ Boat
   ☐ Car   ☐ Other (please
   ☐ Cycle   specify ....)

7. b) How long does it usually take you to travel to school? (Answer to the nearest minute)
   ☐☐☐ minutes

8. a) What is the weight of your school bag today? (Answer to one decimal place.)
   School bag weight ....kg

8. b) How do you carry your school bag?
   ☐ On two shoulders (e.g. backpack)
   ☐ On one shoulder
   ☐ In my hand
   ☐ On wheels
   ☐ Other (please specify: ....)

9. Do you play a musical instrument?
   ☐ Yes   ☐ No
   If yes, please state your MAIN musical instrument.
   ....

10. Which of the following do you have? (You may tick more than one)
    ☐ A TV in your bedroom
    ☐ Your own MP3 player e.g. iPod
    ☐ Access to the Internet from your mobile phone
    ☐ Your own Facebook page
    ☐ Your own Twitter page
    ☐ Your own Bebo page
    ☐ Skype on a computer at home
    ☐ A game console at home e.g. PlayStation, Xbox, Nintendo
    ☐ None of these

11. In the last 7 days, which of these online activities have you done? (You may tick more than one box)
    ☐ Downloaded or listened online to music
    ☐ Downloaded or viewed online video (eg Youtube, iPlayer, Netflix, etc.)
    ☐ Played online game(s)
    ☐ Kept in touch with friends (e.g. through instant messaging, Facebook, Bebo, etc.)
    ☐ Researched topics related to school work
    ☐ Have been online but did none of the above activities
    ☐ Have not been online in the last seven days

12. a) What is the natural colour of your hair?
    ☐ Light Brown   ☐ Black
    ☐ Dark Brown   ☐ Red
    ☐ Blonde   ☐ Other

12. b) Is your hair dyed now?
    ☐ Yes   ☐ No

12. c) How long is it since your last haircut?
    ☐☐☐ weeks

12. d) How much did you spend on that haircut?
    ☐ €0 - €9.99   ☐ €30 - €39.99
    ☐ €10 - €19.99   ☐ €40 - €49.99
    ☐ €20 - €29.99   ☐ €50 or more

13. If you could take part in the Olympics, in which sport would you like to represent Ireland?
    ☐ Archery   ☐ Modern pentathlon
    ☐ Athletics   ☐ Rowing
    ☐ Badminton   ☐ Sailing
    ☐ Basketball   ☐ Shooting
    ☐ Boxing   ☐ Swimming
    ☐ Canoeing   ☐ Synchronized swimming
    ☐ Cycling   ☐ Table tennis
    ☐ Diving   ☐ Taekwondo
    ☐ Equestrian   ☐ Tennis
    ☐ Fencing   ☐ Triathlon
    ☐ Field Hockey   ☐ Volleyball
    ☐ Football   ☐ Water polo
    ☐ Gymnastics   ☐ Weightlifting
    ☐ Handball
    ☐ Judo

This resource is from the *CensusAtSchool* project at www.censusatschool.ie

4. State whether the following data is (a) categorical nominal, (b) categorical ordered, (c) numerical discrete or (d) numerical continuous.
   (i) Speed of a jet plane
   (ii) Religious denomination
   (iii) Number of people who voted Labour in the last election
   (iv) Air temperature
   (v) Breeds of cattle
   (vi) Number of points scored in a hurling match
   (vii) Number of people attending a concert hall
   (viii) The types of breakfast cereal in a local shop
   (ix) The birth months of students in a class.

5. Write a question which will yield each of the following types of data.
   (i) categorical nominal
   (ii) categorical ordered
   (iii) numerical discrete
   (iv) numerical continuous

6. Your teacher has asked you to carry out a statistical investigation.
   (i) What are the main steps in carrying out a statistical investigation?
   (ii) Describe a statistical investigation you could carry out using the above steps.

7. As a statistically aware consumer, evaluate the following statements.
   (i) A new advertisement for John and Jerry's ice cream introduced in late May of last year resulted in a 40% increase in ice cream sales for the following three months. Hence, the advertisement was effective.
   (ii) The more churches in a city, the more crime there is in the city.
   (iii) Most car drivers have fewer than the average number of car accidents.
   (iv) A newspaper headline tells us that eating a particular type of food increases our risk of getting a certain disease by 20%. Should we be alarmed if we eat that food?
   (v) The violent crime rate is on the increase.
   (vi) On average, 1 in every 15 Europeans is totally illiterate.
   (vii) A politician is reputed to have said 'Our aim is to have all students achieve above average marks in mathematics in the Junior Cert.'

Section 14B Collecting Data: Sampling

A **population** is the entire group, of size N, of people, animals or objects about which we want information.
A **unit** is any individual member of the population.
A **census** occurs when every member of the population has data collected about them.
A **sample** of size n is a subset of a population from which we actually collect information. When $n = N$, we have a **census**.

A sample should be **representative of the population** it is chosen from, i.e. it should have approximately the same variations we would see in the population.

Sample data are collected and summarised in order to give us insights into the population.

Sampling is carried out in situations where a census would be too expensive, would take too long or would be impractical. For example, one cannot test the lifetimes of all batteries produced. In similar cases, where measurement destroys the units being tested, a census is not feasible.

How big should a sample be? There is no magic number which tells us how large a sample should be to allow us to make inferences about the population. A large random sample will include a lot of people with lots of variation, whereas a small sample will not have the same degree of variation. For political polls, 1000 people is considered to be a big enough sample size regardless of the population size.

In **market research**, people's opinions are sampled in order to get an idea of the views of the whole population.

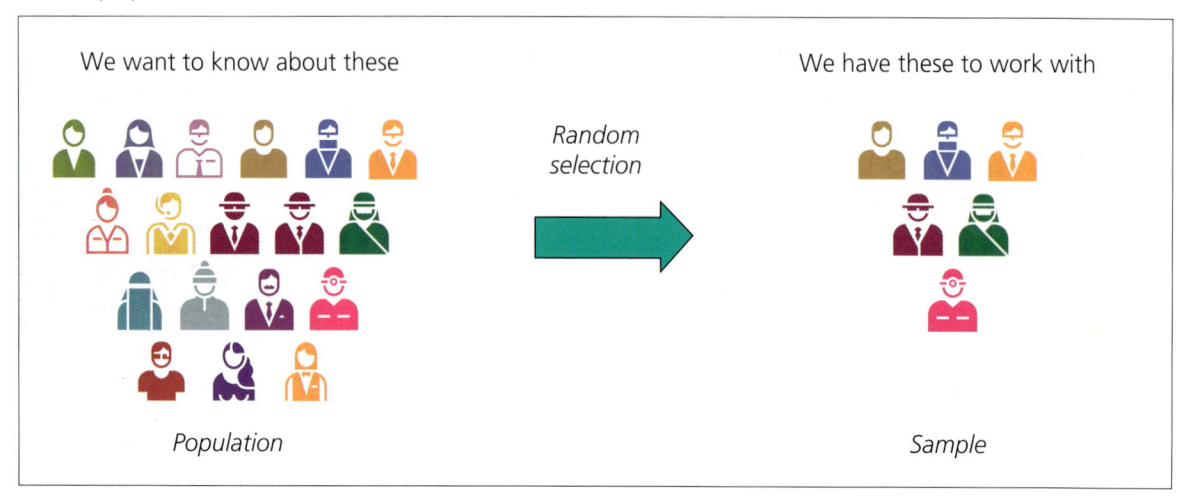

A **sampling frame** is a list of the units/individuals from which a sample is drawn.

If the population we are interested in is all the students in a school, then the sampling frame would be the roll book. Ideally the sampling frame includes the whole population. The register of electors is a sampling frame. It should contain the population of all those eligible to vote, but this is not always the case.

A **distribution** is a list of the values that a **variable** takes. It shows the variation in these values.

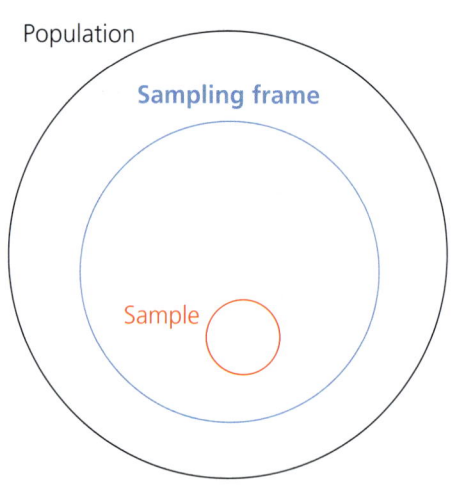

Reliability: In everyday life, when we say that someone or something is reliable, we mean that a person or thing can be depended upon time after time.

A measurement is considered to be **reliable** when repeated measurements by anyone on the same unit of the population give the same result.

e.g. If you weigh yourself a number of times in succession using the same scales, you should get approximately the same result. If you do, the measurement is reliable. Sometimes we take repeated measurements on the same person and then take the average of these measurements to improve reliability.

A **statistic** is some value, e.g. an average, which we are interested in calculating for the **sample**, e.g. the mean height of a sample of students or the percentage who travel to school by car. If we look at a different sample, we might get a different value of the statistic. The fact that a statistic can vary from sample to sample is known as **sampling variability**. We use the **sample statistic** as an estimate of the value for the population.

Simple Random Sampling

To enable us to make generalisations about a population from a sample, sampling should be **random**. Random sampling does not mean that we can just pick anyone for the sample.

In a **random sample**, each unit in the population has an equal chance of being selected.

In **simple random sampling**, each unit of the population has an equal chance of being selected and each sample of a particular size has an equal chance of being chosen.

To produce a simple random sample, you need two things:

- a list of the units in the population
- a source of random numbers.

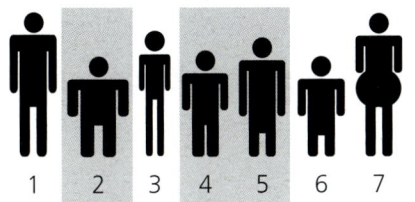

- Assign numbers
- Generate random selections

Example

Select a simple random sample from a class of 30 students.

Solution

The **population** is the class of 30 students.

Let's decide on a sample of size 5.

(We chose this size as it is convenient for calculating several values of the mean and we have limited time.)

RanInt#(1,30)

Method 1

- Assign a number from 1 to 30 to each student.
- Use a calculator to generate five different random integers from 1 to 30.
- The students who have been assigned those randomly generated integers form the sample.

Method 2

- Put the numbers 1 to 30 into a container, mix them up, and choose five different random numbers in succession.
- Each time we choose a number, we should replace it in the container.
- The students with those integers assigned to them in the list make up the random sample.

When we use a large sample size, **random sampling** will approximate a representative sample.

A Random Sample which is not a Simple Random Sample

If, in a school which has an equal number of male and female students, we decide to flip a coin to decide whether a sample will be from the males or the females, then every student has an equal chance of selection. If the coin comes up heads, we select 20 male students at random and if it comes up tails, we select 20 female students at random. Even though every student has an equal chance of being selected, every sample of 20 has not an equal chance of selection as the sample consists of one gender only.

Bias in Sampling

> Whenever a sample overestimates or underestimates whatever we are trying to measure for the population, then that sample is **biased**.
>
> Bias in sampling occurs when a particular group is **excluded**, **under-represented** or **over-represented** in the sample.

For example:

- If a sample survey about a whole-school issue is completed by only First Year students, the sample is biased because all other class groups are excluded.
- Self-selection of sample members, i.e. volunteers, can cause those with strong opinions about the survey issues to be over-represented, e.g. when asking people to phone in their opinions on a particular subject to a radio show, people who are free to ring in at that time of day, those with a particular interest in the topic and those who are not shy about speaking in public will be over-represented.
- Low response rates, e.g. people who do not fill in responses to questionnaires sent through the post, can cause a sample to be biased.

Other examples of bias are:

- Dishonest answers to survey questions, e.g. sometimes people are dishonest when asked their age or how much they earn.
- Wording of survey questions, the order in which questions are asked, the type of options offered and whether or not the question is open to misinterpretation, e.g. Are you tall?
- The sample size is too small, e.g. a sample of 10 people from the population of a country is asked which brand of dog food they prefer for their dog.

Activity 14.2

1. (i) What is meant by a simple random sample?
   An airline wishes to take a simple random sample of the 300 passengers on one of its flights from San Francisco to Tokyo.
   (ii) Identify the population and the sampling frame.
   (iii) Explain how a simple random sample can be generated in this case.
   (iv) A suggestion is made to instead randomly select a seat position (e.g. right window) and survey all the passengers sitting in those seats. Explain why this will not give a simple random sample.

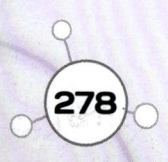

2 A magazine is interested in the percentage of its readers who favour an online-only version of the magazine instead of the printed version. A random sample of 300 readers from the subscription list respond to a question asking them for their preference and 200 of the respondents are in favour of introducing the online-only version. Identify:
  (i) the population
  (ii) the sampling frame
  (iii) the variable measured
  (iv) the sample
  (v) what the magazine wishes to estimate about the population of interest
  (vi) the value of the statistic.
  (vii) Do you think that the statistic measured is a good estimate of the opinions of all readers?

3 There are 80 people at a meeting. Describe how you would take a simple random sample of 20 people from this group.

4 A population consists of four items, A, B, C and D. List all the different simple random samples of size 2 which can be selected from this population.

5 In a lottery draw, the six winning numbers are randomly generated from a defined range of numbers (e.g. 1 to 45). Assuming that the draw is fair:
  (i) What type of sampling is used? Explain your answer.
  (ii) The balls for some lotto draws have different colours. Assume that the following process of selection occurs.

A colour is first randomly chosen. Assume the colour red is randomly chosen. Six red balls are then chosen at random. Is this simple random sampling? Justify your answer.

6 The following data were collected as a simple random sample of the ages of students who were members of a tennis club:
14, 16, 15, 17, 13
The mean of the population
  (i) is 15   (iii) is 16.1581
  (ii) is 16   (iv) could be any value.
Which is the correct answer?

7 The Gardai Síochana wants to know how Dublin inner-city residents feel about the police service. A questionnaire with several questions about the police is prepared. A sample of 500 mailing addresses in the inner-city areas is chosen, and a Garda is sent to each address to administer the questionnaire to an adult living there.
  (i) Identify the population, variables measured and the sample.
  (ii) Describe the potential bias.

8 (i) What is meant by the term 'bias' as applied to sampling?
  (ii) Which of the following sampling methods is most likely to produce bias?
    1: A simple random sample of size $n = 50$
    2: A volunteer sample of size $n = 500$
    Explain your answer.

9 The time on a clock is consistently five minutes fast. Is the measurement
  (i) reliable
  (ii) biased?

10 What advice would you give to someone who wishes to conduct a survey in your school on student opinions about the school canteen?

11 The following questionnaire seeks to gather data on attitudes to sport.

> Q1. How sporty are you?
> Q2. Are attitudes to sport in your household influenced by matriarchal or patriarchal undertones?
> Q3. How often do members of your household go to the gym?
> Q4. Given that participation in sport keeps teenagers from being involved in underage drinking and undesirable behaviour, do you agree with budgetary cuts which will reduce the number of sporting facilities?
> Q5. Do you think women are better at sport than men?

(i) Write a critical comment about each question.
(ii) Write five questions that would be clear and suitable for the above survey.

12 Describe why the following examples could lead to biased samples.

(i) We want to estimate how many students watch romantic comedies in a co-educational school with 1000 students. Suppose we take a random sample of 50 students and ask if they watch romantic comedies. All in the sample happen to be girls. (This is unlikely but possible.)

(ii) A survey is carried out on the radio asking people to phone in their opinions on reducing the length of the school holidays.

(iii) A sample of 1000 members of the public are randomly selected to take part in a survey. Only 200 people respond.

(iv) A survey question asks: 'Do you think, following recent acts of vandalism in your town, that young people should be required to do community service during the summer holidays?'

Section 14C Estimating the Population Mean

Suppose we wanted an **estimate** of the mean height of a population of 15-year-old students. We would use a **simple random sample** of 15-year-old students to estimate the mean height. The mean height of the sample would be unlikely to be the same as the mean height of the population but we would expect it to be close if our sample was randomly chosen from the population and if the sample was of a suitable size. To illustrate this, we will use a small population of 30 students.

Table showing heights of 30 fifteen-year-olds: the numbers in the shaded columns are the numbers assigned to each student.

	Height (cm)		Height (cm)		Height (cm)		Height (cm)		Height (cm)		Height (cm)
1	165	6	157	11	161	16	172	21	170	26	155
2	165	7	153	12	152	17	165	22	174	27	160
3	166	8	150	13	161	18	157	23	174	28	172
4	168	9	179	14	144	19	174	24	164	29	156
5	180	10	157	15	174	20	159	25	152	30	163

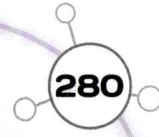

The **population mean = 163.3 cm** (Verify this value using your calculator.)

We will generate 10 random samples of size 5, using **simple random sampling** and find the mean of each sample. We will compare those means to each other and to the population mean.

One set of 10 random samples is shown below. Generate your own set.

	Height (cm)	Height (cm)	Height (cm)	Height (cm)	Height (cm)	Sample mean (cm)
Sample 1	174	153	164	172	161	164.8
Sample 2	157	180	172	165	159	166.6
Sample 3	164	166	157	161	174	164.4
Sample 4	161	157	156	174	179	165.4
Sample 5	152	168	166	174	150	162
Sample 6	157	152	166	150	165	158
Sample 7	172	165	172	179	161	169.8
Sample 8	174	164	150	174	159	164.2
Sample 9	157	174	160	163	168	164.4
Sample 10	174	166	174	157	152	164.6
Mean of the sample means (cm)						164.42

We can see **sampling variability** in the values of the mean but most values are close to the population mean.

- Most of the sample means are close to the population mean.
- In real life, we estimate the population mean using the mean of just one sample. So it is very important that this sample is representative of the population.

(Note: There are 142 506 possible samples of size 5 which we can take from a population of 30 units!)

Activity 14.3

1. Do you expect the mean of a sample to be equal to the maximum or minimum values in the population? Explain.

2. Since the sample size is always smaller than the size of the population, the sample mean
    (i) must be smaller than the population mean
    (ii) must be larger than the population mean
    (iii) must be equal to the population mean
    (iv) can be smaller, larger or equal to the population mean.
    Choose the correct answer.

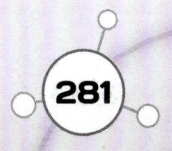

3 The table below shows the heights of a population of 30 fifteen-year-old students.

Height (cm)	Height (cm)	Height (cm)	Height (cm)	Height (cm)	Height (cm)
165	157	161	172	170	155
165	153	152	165	174	160
166	150	161	157	174	172
168	179	144	174	164	156
180	157	174	159	152	163

(i) Use the above table to take ten simple random samples of size 5. Make a table to show all the samples.
(ii) Calculate the mean of each sample of five heights.
(iii) How do all the sample means compare to each other?
(iv) Compare the sample means to the population mean.
(v) Compare the mean of the sample means to the population mean.

Section 14D Numerical Analysis of Data

Numbers calculated from data that are used to summarise the data are referred to as **summary statistics** or **descriptive statistics**.

The two most useful questions to ask to help you to summarise a set of data are:

(i) What is a typical or average value, i.e. a **measure of central tendency**?
(ii) How widely '**spread**' are the numbers?

Measures of Central Tendency

> The **mode** is the most frequent value or category.
> The centre of a **categorical dataset** is always described by the mode.

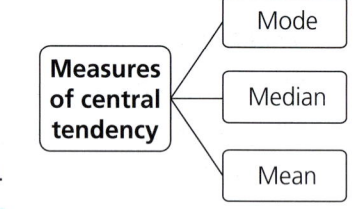

The modal women's shoe size is the size worn by the most women.

> The **median** is the number that divides the **ordered** data in half.

Before finding the **median**, the data must be put in order from the smallest to the largest value. It is the middle value. 50% of the ordered data lies below the median and the other 50% lies above the median. The median is not affected by unusually large or unusually small data values.

> The **mean** is the sum of all the values divided by the total number of values in the dataset. It represents the '**fair share**' value of the data.

> The median and mean are used with **numerical data** only.

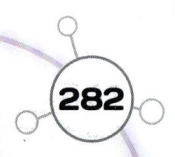

In the *Formulae and tables* booklet (Statistics and Probability) page 33, the **mean μ of a population** is defined as:

$$\mu = \frac{\Sigma x}{n} \text{ from a list of } n \text{ numbers}$$

$$\mu = \frac{\Sigma fx}{\Sigma f} \text{ from a frequency table}$$

where μ = the population mean; Σ means 'the sum of'; f = frequency.

The **mean of a sample** is denoted by $\bar{x}$.

The **mean** takes into account all the data values. Hence, the mean can give a distorted measure of the centre of the distribution due to unusually large or small values.

Mean of a Grouped Frequency Distribution

When we have continuous data, we often group the data into **intervals**. We need to be able to find the mean of such a grouped frequency distribution.

Example 1

The weights in kg of a sample of 19 first year male university students are as follows.

62, 64, 70, 80, 62, 64, 70, 64, 71, 112, 70, 66, 71, 75, 65, 73, 66, 70, 72

(i) Calculate the mean of the data.

(ii) Fill in the grouped frequency table.

Weights (kg)	60–65	65–70	70–75	75–80	80–85	85–90
Frequency						

Weights (kg)	90–95	95–100	100–105	105–110	110–115
Frequency					

60–65 means: 60 kg ≤ weight < 65 kg

(iii) Using the **mid-interval value**, calculate the mean of the grouped frequency distribution.

> The mid-interval value is the mean of the two extreme values of the interval. The mid-interval value for the interval 60–65 = (60 + 65) ÷ 2 = 62.5.

(iv) Why is the mean of the grouped frequency distribution not equal to the mean of the raw data?

(v) In which interval of the grouped frequency distribution does the median lie?

Solution

(i) Mean = (62 + 64 + 70 + 80 + 62 + 64 + 70 + 64 + 71 + 112 + 70 + 66 + 71 + 75 + 65 + 73 + 66 + 70 + 72) ÷ 19 = 70.9 kg

(ii)

Weights (kg)	60–65	65–70	70–75	75–80	80–85	85–90
Frequency	5	3	8	1	1	0

Weights (kg)	90–95	95–100	100–105	105–110	110–115
Frequency	0	0	0	0	1

(iii) $\bar{x} = \dfrac{(62.5)(5) + (67.5)(3) + (72.5)(8) + (77.5)(1) + (82.5)(1) + (112.5)(1)}{19} = 71.97$ kg

(iv) The mean of a grouped frequency distribution assumes that each value in an interval is equal to the mid-interval value, which is not the case.

(v) The median is the 10th data item which lies in the interval 70–75 kg.

Activity 14.4

1 The following table refers to the ages of 70 guests at a wedding.

Age (in years)	0–20	20–40	40–60	60–80
Number of guests	5	18	21	26

40–60 years means: 40 years ≤ age < 60 years

(i) Using mid-interval values, estimate the mean age of the guests to the nearest year.
(ii) What percentage of the guests were over 40 years old?
(iii) What is the greatest number of guests who could have been over 65?
(iv) What is the smallest number of guests who could have been over 65? Explain.

2 The heights in centimetres of 60 randomly selected female students aged 16 years are given in the table.

Height (cm)	150–155	155–160	160–165	165–170	170–175	175–180
Frequency	2	9	14	20	11	4

150–155 cm means: 150 cm ≤ height < 155 cm

(i) Draw a histogram of the data and describe the shape of the distribution.
(ii) What is the modal interval?
(iii) In which interval does the median lie?
(iv) Calculate the mean height to the nearest centimetre using the mid-interval values.
(v) Under what circumstances could this be exactly equal to the actual mean of the raw data?

3. There are 30 students in a class. On Friday, each student present in the class is asked how many days they had been absent that week. The results are recorded in the table below.

Number of days absent	None	One	Two	Three	Four	Five
Number of students	12	3	4	1	2	0

(i) How many students were absent on Friday?

(ii) On the following Monday, all of the students were present in class and the table was updated to include the entire class. Which number from the above table could not have changed? Give a reason for your answer.

(iii) A pie chart is drawn for the actual data collected on Monday. The number of degrees for each sector is shown in the table below. Use this data to calculate the mean number of absences per student for the previous week correct to one place of decimals.

Number of days absent	None	One	Two	Three	Four	Five
Number of students						
Number of degrees	144°	60°	84°	36°	24°	12°

(iv) The total number of days that were missed during the week depends on the answers given by the students who were absent on Friday. Draw and complete tables to show the largest and smallest possible number of days which could have been missed by these students.

(v) Complete a table to show another possible number of days missed by these students.

(vi) For the table you have completed for part (v), construct a pie chart of the data.

4. Twenty people enrolled in a weight loss programme. Their weights in kilograms before the programme were:
129, 153, 86, 77, 94, 124, 103, 76, 89, 83, 98, 86, 107, 128, 78, 82, 94, 79, 115, 104.

(i) Order the data from smallest to largest.

(ii) Fill in a grouped frequency table for the data starting at 75 kg using intervals of 10 kg.

(iii) Estimate the mean of the data, correct to the nearest kilogram, using mid-interval values from the grouped frequency table in part (ii).

(iv) If each person on the weight loss programme lost 4 kg after six weeks, what would the mean weight of the group be after the six weeks? Guess first and then verify your answer.

(v) If each person on the weight loss programme lost y kg after six weeks, what would the mean weight of the group be after the six weeks?

5. The following table shows the distribution of the amounts spent by a number of people in a restaurant.

Amount spent	€0–€16	€16–€32	€32–€48	€48–€64	€64–€80
Number of customers	2	9	x	11	5

€32–€48 means: €32 ≤ amount spent < €48

(i) Taking the mid-interval values, the estimate of the mean amount spent by the customers was €43.20. How many people spent between €32 and €48?

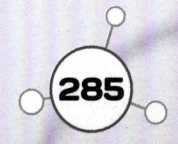

(ii) What percentage of the customers spent less than €64?

(iii) If each of the customers had spent €2 more, use the mean estimated in part (i) to find the estimate of the new mean amount spent by the customers. Use two methods.

6 The table shows the distances travelled by seven paper airplanes after they were thrown.

Airplane	A	B	C	D	E	F	G
Distance (cm)	188	200	250	30	380	330	302

(i) Find the median of the data.

(ii) Find the mean of the data.

(iii) Airplane D is thrown again and the distance it travels is measured and recorded in place of the original measurement. The median of the data remains unchanged and the mean is now equal to the median. How far did airplane D travel the second time?

(iv) What is the minimum distance that airplane D would need to have travelled in order for the median to have changed?

JCHL 2013 Sample Paper 2

7 The grouped frequency table below refers to the marks obtained by 80 students in a test. Note that in this case the intervals are not equal.

Marks	0–40	40–55	55–70	70–100
Number of students	12	20	25	23

40–55 marks means: 40 ≤ mark < 55

(i) What percentage of students obtained 55 marks or higher?

(ii) In what interval does the median lie?

(iii) Using mid-interval values, estimate the mean mark for the class to the nearest integer.

8 Below is a list of the ages in years of 44 people who signed up for an aerobics class.

27	17	21	34	42	19	40	39	22	45	29	22	30	39
60	24	25	38	29	30	28	21	53	58	24	61	28	31
35	18	22	27	47	30	34	62	48	54	19	20	23	24
52	49												

(i) Use the data to copy and complete the grouped frequency table.

Age in years	15–20	20–25	25–30	30–35	35–40	40–45	45–50	50–55	55–60	60–65
Tally										
Frequency										
Relative frequency (%)										

15–20 means 15 years or more but less than 20 years

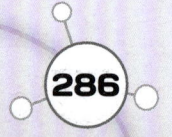

(ii) What is the modal interval?

(iii) What percentage of the participants are over 60 years of age?

(iv) Calculate the mean using (a) the raw data, (b) the mid-interval values.

(v) Draw a histogram of the data using relative frequency on the y-axis.

(vi) When might it be especially useful to put relative frequency on the y-axis?

9 The salaries, in €, of the different employees working in a call centre are listed below.

22 000	16 500	38 000	26 500	15 000	21 000	15 500	46 000
42 000	9 500	32 000	27 000	33 000	36 000	24 000	37 000
65 000	37 000	24 500	23 500	28 000	52 000	33 000	25 000
23 000	16 500	35 000	25 000	33 000	20 000	19 500	16 000

(i) Use this data to copy and complete the grouped frequency table below.

Salary (€1000)	0–10	10–20	20–30	30–40	40–50	50–60	60–70
No. of employees							

10–20 means €10 000 or more but less than €20 000

(ii) Using mid-interval values find the mean salary of the employees.

(iii) (a) Outline another method which could have been used to calculate the mean salary.

(b) Which method is more accurate? Explain your answer.

JCHL 2013 Paper 2

Measures of Spread of the Data

We have previously met the **range** as a measure of spread of numeric data.

Range = maximum value − minimum value

When data values are evenly spread, the range is a good measure of spread. When the dataset contains data values which are unusually high or unusually low compared to the rest of the data, we can use another measure of spread called the **interquartile range**.

First, we need to identify numbers called **quartiles**.
Quartiles (Q_1, Q_2, Q_3) are numbers that separate **ordered numerical data** into four groups each containing (as closely as possible) equal numbers of values.

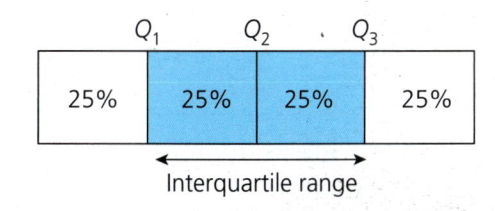

The **second quartile (Q_2)** is the median.
The **lower quartile (Q_1)** is the number that is one quarter of the way through the ordered dataset from the lower end. We can also think of Q_1 as the median of the lower half of the data.

The **upper quartile** (Q_3) is the number that is one quarter of the way through the ordered dataset from the upper end (or three-quarters of the way from the lower end). We can also think of Q_3 as the median of the upper half of the data.

> The **interquartile range** (**IQR**) = $Q_3 - Q_1$ is the range of the middle 50% of the data. It is a measure of spread which is not influenced by unusually large or unusually small values of the data, unlike the range.

When the median is used as the measure of centre for data, the interquartile range is often used as the measure of spread.

Finding Quartiles and the Interquartile Range

Example 2

(Using an **odd** sample size)

The estimates, in order, for the number of seconds in a minute, given by 9 students are 63, 63, 65, 71, 72, 76, 78, 82 and 106 seconds.

(i) What is the range of the data?
(ii) Is the range a good measure of the spread of the data? Explain.
(iii) Find the median, quartiles and interquartile range.
(iv) What does the interquartile range tell you?

Solution

(i) The **range** = 106 − 63 = 43 seconds.

(ii) The range is not a good measure of the spread of this data since the data is not evenly spread. The range uses only the two extreme values of the data and one of those is unusually large, giving an over-estimate of the spread of the data.

(iii) The data are first ordered: 63, 63, 65, 71, 72, 76, 78, 82, 106
The **median** = 72 seconds (the middle value which is the 5th data item).

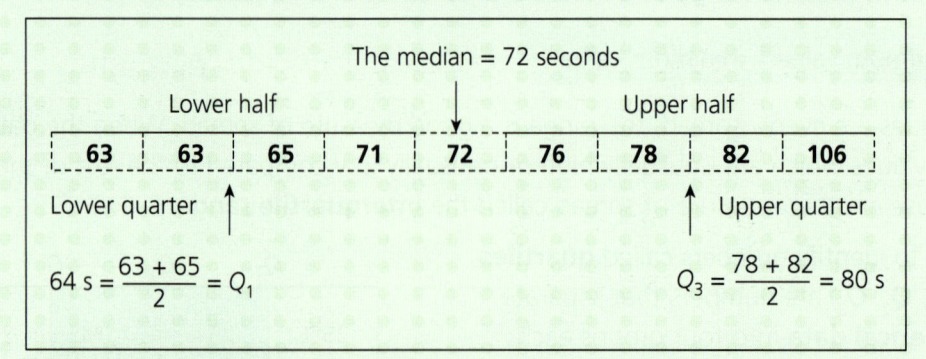

```
                    The median = 72 seconds
                             ↓
      Lower half                    Upper half
  63 | 63 | 65 | 71 | 72 | 76 | 78 | 82 | 106
Lower quarter  ↑                ↑  Upper quarter

64 s = (63 + 65)/2 = Q_1            Q_3 = (78 + 82)/2 = 80 s
```

$64\text{ s} = \dfrac{63 + 65}{2} = Q_1 \qquad\qquad Q_3 = \dfrac{78 + 82}{2} = 80\text{ s}$

The **lower quartile** Q_1 = 64 seconds, is the 'median of the lower half of the data' (excluding the median of all the data).

The **upper quartile** Q_3 = 80 seconds, is the 'median of the upper half of the data' (excluding the median of all the data).

The **interquartile range** = $Q_3 - Q_1$ = 80 − 64 = 16 seconds.

(iv) The interquartile range gives the spread of the middle 50% of the ordered data.

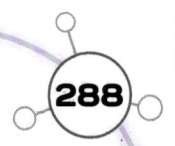

Example 3

(Using an **even** sample size)

Suppose another student added her estimate of 57 seconds to the data for Example 1. The estimates for the number of seconds in a minute given by 10 students are now 63, 63, 65, 71, 72, 76, 78, 82, 106 and 57 seconds.

(i) What is the range of the data?
(ii) Find the median, quartiles and interquartile range.

Solution

(i) The **range** = 106 − 57 = 49 seconds.
(ii) The data are first ordered: 57, 63, 63, 65, 71, 72, 76, 78, 82, 106
The **median** = 71.5 seconds (the average of the 5th and 6th data values)

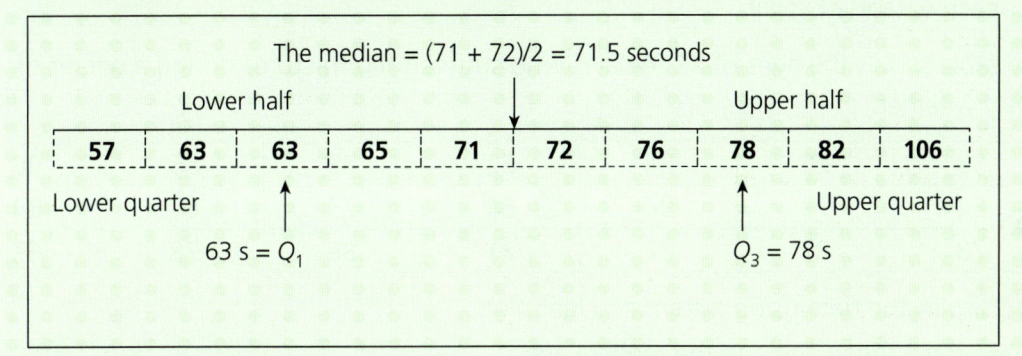

```
                    The median = (71 + 72)/2 = 71.5 seconds
             Lower half                    |          Upper half
    | 57 | 63 | 63 | 65 | 71 | 72 | 76 | 78 | 82 | 106 |
Lower quarter    ↑                              ↑         Upper quarter
              63 s = Q₁                      Q₃ = 78 s
```

The **lower quartile** Q_1 = 63 seconds, is the 'median of the lower half of the data' (excluding the median of all the data).
The **upper quartile** Q_3 = 78 seconds, is the 'median of the upper half of the data' (excluding the median of all the data).
The **interquartile range** = $Q_3 - Q_1$ = 78 − 63 = 15 seconds.

The Five-number Summary

A reasonably complete description of the centre and spread of numerical data is the **five-number summary**, i.e. the minimum, the lower quartile Q_1, the median Q_2, the upper quartile Q_3, and the maximum.

Using the data from Example 2:
57, 63, 63, 65, 71, 72, 76, 78, 82, 106 seconds

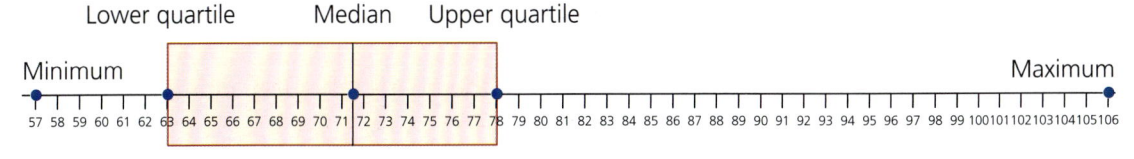

We can show the five-number summary with a box around the interquartile range.

In summary:

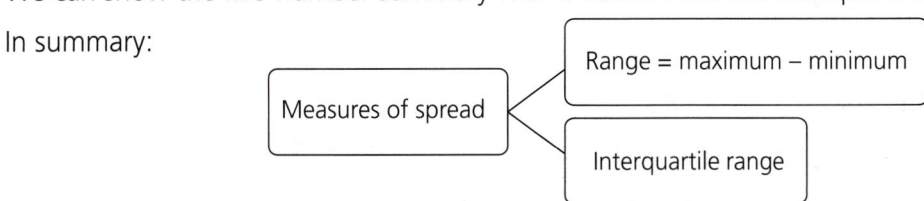

Measures of spread
- Range = maximum − minimum
- Interquartile range

Activity 14.5

1. Two groups of people are asked to estimate how much money they have in their wallets to the nearest euro.

   Group 1 (€): 22, 34, 19, 5, 1, 46, 23, 34, 22, 22, 34, 91, 33

   Group 2 (€): 13, 5, 19, 14, 23, 7, 11, 18, 16, 21, 24

   (i) Find the mode(s), median and mean for both datasets.

   (ii) Which measure of centre, the mean or the median, do you think is best for each dataset? Explain.

   (iii) Find the range for both datasets.

   (iv) Find the lower quartile, upper quartile and interquartile range for both datasets. Give your answers correct to the nearest euro.

   (v) Which measure of spread, the range or the interquartile range, do you think is best for each dataset? Explain.

2. The table shows the ages of 21 females who suffered hip fractures during a period of frosty weather.

53	76	84	62	78	85	98
84	73	94	84	73	87	84
73	87	82	71	86	78	67

   (i) Display the data using a stem and leaf plot.

   (ii) Find the mean age and the median age.

   (iii) What is the relationship between the mean age and the median age? Why do you think this is the case?

   (iv) Find the range of ages in the data.

   (v) Find the lower quartile, upper quartile and the interquartile range for the data.

   (vi) Which measure of spread, the range or the interquartile range, do you think best describes the data? Explain your answer.

3. Thirty students were asked on the *CensusAtSchool* questionnaire 'How long does it usually take you to travel to school? Answer to the nearest minute.'

   The data, in minutes, given by the students is shown in the table.

20	5	40	5	15	10	20	15	20	20
15	15	30	35	23	8	15	10	15	10
13	8	4	35	15	5	15	5	10	25

   (i) Display the data using a stem and leaf plot.

   (ii) Find the mean time taken to travel to school (to the nearest minute) and the median time.

   (iii) What is the relationship between the mean time and the median time? Why do you think this is the case?

   (iv) Find the range of times in the data.

   (v) Find the lower quartile, upper quartile and the interquartile range for the data.

   (vi) What is the percentage of students in the interquartile range of times?

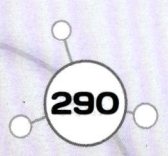

4. Twenty students were asked to rate a TV programme on a scale of 1–10. The scores they gave are shown below.

   Scores from group 1:

5	6	7	7	8	9	6	8	9	6
7	5	6	8	6	6	7	8	9	7

   Another group of 20 students were asked to rate the same TV programme. Their scores are shown in the table below.

   Scores from group 2:

4	7	10	5	9	8	6	10	10	5
5	7	6	6	8	5	4	7	9	9

   Compare the distributions of scores from the two groups by
   (i) comparing their means and their medians
   (ii) comparing their ranges and interquartile ranges
   (iii) using a suitable graphical representation.

5. Three groups of 10 students in a Third Year class were investigating how the number of jelly beans in a bag varies for three different brands of jelly beans.

   Each student counted the number of jelly beans in a bag of brand A or B or C. Their results are recorded in the table.

Group 1 (Brand A)				
23	25	25	26	26
32	32	33	34	35
Group 2 (Brand B)				
17	22	22	24	24
29	29	29	29	29
Group 3 (Brand C)				
25	25	25	26	26
29	29	30	30	31

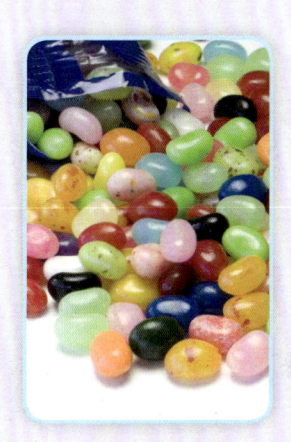

   (i) Display the data in a way which allows you to describe and compare the data for each brand.
   (ii) If you were to buy a bag of jelly beans, which brand would you buy? Give a reason for your answer based on the data provided in the tables. In your explanations, you should refer to the **mean** number of jelly beans per bag and the **range** or spread of the number of jelly beans per bag.

   JCHL 2014 Sample Paper 2

6. In a *CensusAtSchool* questionnaire, students were asked to state how many soft drinks they had consumed in the previous two days.

   The data below is a random sample of 50 students from the 7211 students who responded, selected using the Random Data Selector on www.censusatschool.ie.

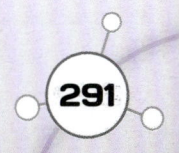

6	7	7	0	5	0	1	6	4	1
0	2	5	1	3	0	0	3	1	0
1	2	0	1	2	2	0	11	2	0
1	0	0	4	0	5	0	3	11	1
1	1	0	2	4	2	1	19	0	1

(i) What is the type of data in the dataset?
(ii) Set up a frequency table for the data. Use a tally row.
(iii) What is the range of the data?
(iv) What percentage of the students consumed less than four soft drinks in the previous two days?
(v) Display the data using a line plot.
(vi) If there are any outliers in the data, list them.
(vii) Looking at the line plot, what do you expect the relationship to be between the mean and the median? Justify your answer.
(viii) By finding the mean and the median of the data, confirm your answer to part (vii).
(ix) Find the interquartile range for this data.

Section 14E Graphical Analysis of Data

You have met the following types of graphical analysis of data in *Connect with Maths 1*.

Line plot (sometimes called dot plot)
Number of cars sold

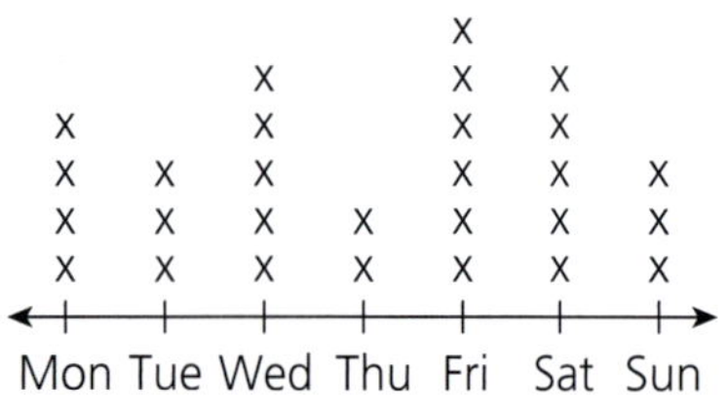

Bar chart

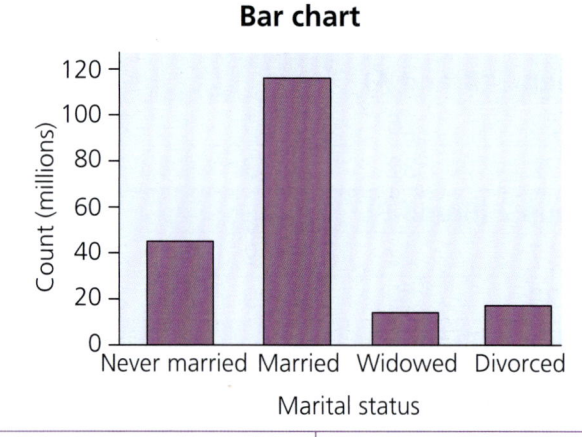

Pie chart
Types of cars owned by a group
- BMW M5
- BMW M3
- Viper GTS-R
- Corvette Z06

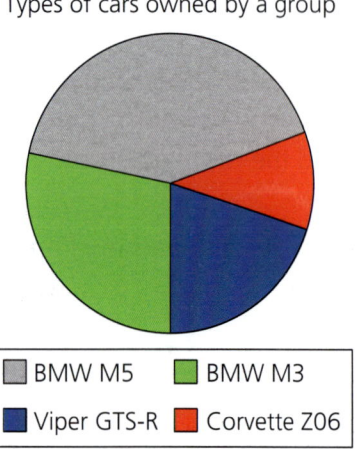

Histogram
Class scores for final exam

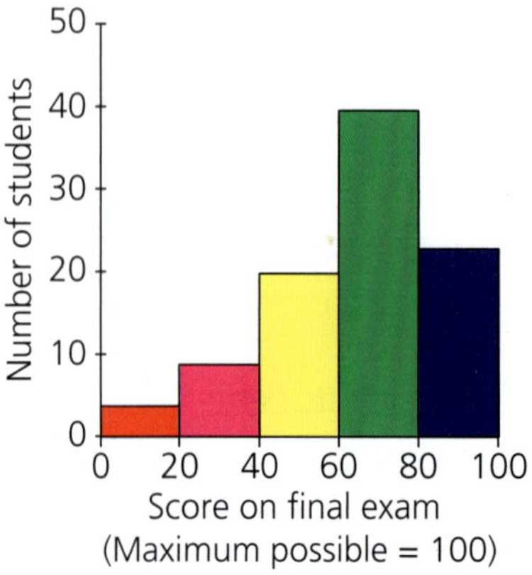

Stem and leaf plot
Ages of people at a meeting

1	9
2	2 5 6 7 8 9
3	0 4 6 7
4	2 3 4 6 8 9
5	2 3 5 7 8
6	2

Key: 1|9 means 19 years

The type of graph we use to display data is determined by the type of data as shown below.

Type of data	Line plot	Bar chart	Frequency table	Histogram	Pie chart	Stem plot
Categorical	✓	✓	✓		✓	
Discrete numerical	✓	✓	✓		✓	✓
Continuous numerical	✓		✓	✓		✓

We will extend our graphical representations to back-to-back stem and leaf plots later on in this chapter.

Shape of a Distribution

We have considered the **centre** and **spread** of data distributions and now we will consider the **shape** of a distribution of numerical data. We can look at the shape of a distribution of numerical data using a **line plot**, a **stem and leaf plot** and a **histogram**.

Symmetrical Distributions

Distributions such as the ones shown below are **symmetrical**. In real life, perfect symmetry for distributions is rare but distributions can approximate this shape. The upper and lower halves are mirror images of each other.

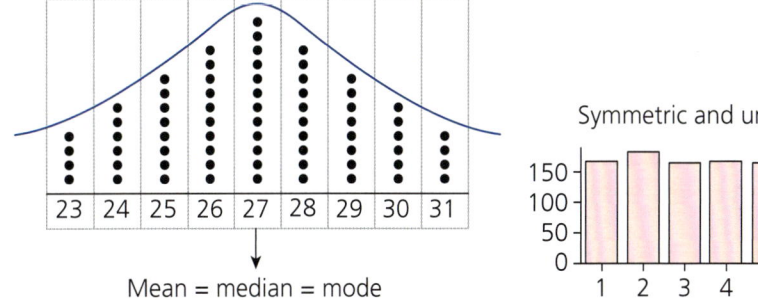

Normal Distributions

Datasets consisting of for instance, heights, weights, lengths of bones and so on, for adults of the same species and sex tend to follow a **normal distribution**.

Most units in the population are clumped around the mean with numbers of individuals decreasing the further values are from the mean in either direction.

The graph of a normal distribution is bell-shaped and symmetrical.

Skewed Right

The following is a dot plot based on the number of soft drinks consumed by a sample of 50 students in the previous two days. If we imagine that we are 'throwing a rope' over the data, the curve of the rope over the data can be used to approximate the general shape as shown on the line plot below.

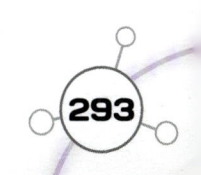

Soft drinks consumed by 50 students in the previous two days

Median = 1   Mean = 2.6   Number of soft drinks consumed

Skewed Left

The distribution of marks in a test are shown below using a histogram and a stem and leaf plot, showing a 'tail' to the left. We describe this shape of distribution as **negatively skewed** or **skewed left**.

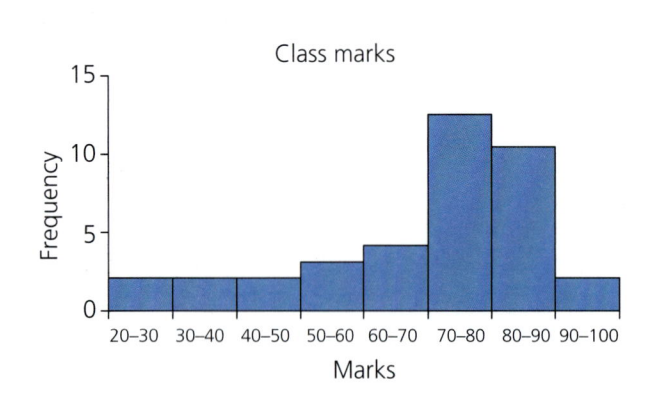

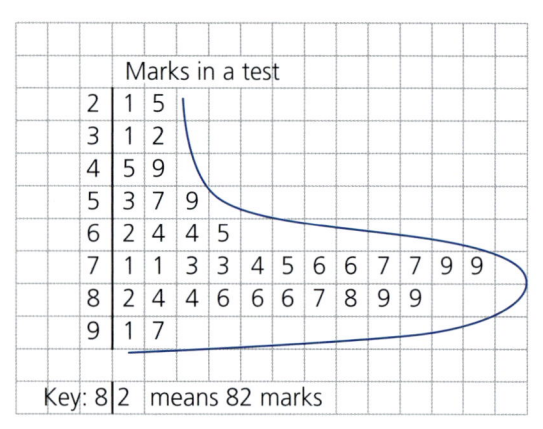

Class marks

Marks in a test										
2	1	5								
3	1	2								
4	5	9								
5	3	7	9							
6	2	4	4	5						
7	1	1	3	3	4	5	6	6	7	7	9	9
8	2	4	4	6	6	6	7	8	9	9
9	1	7								

Key: 8|2 means 82 marks

In summary:

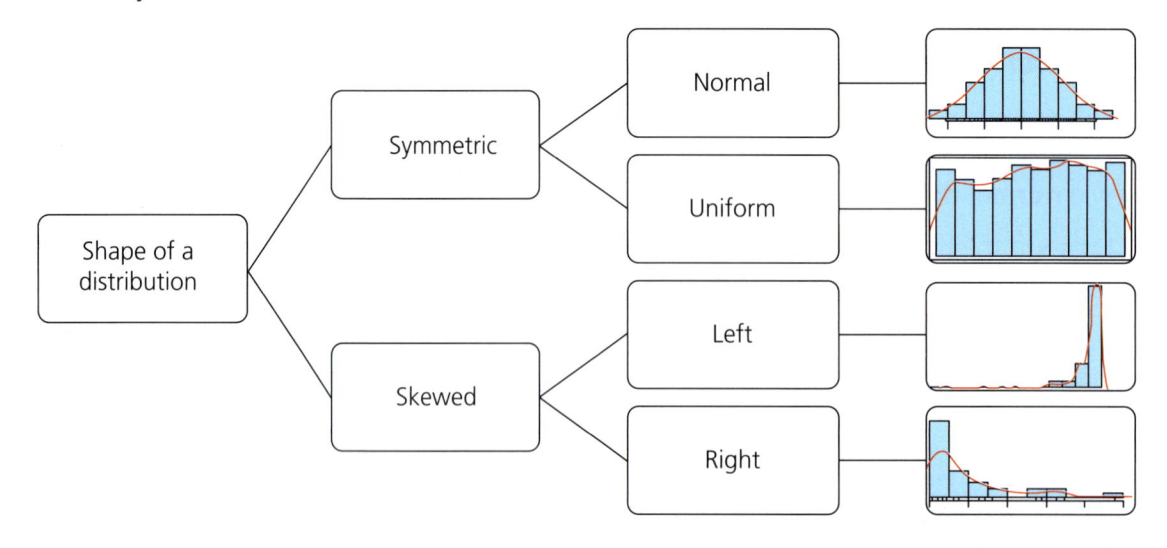

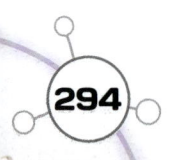

Shape of a distribution
- Symmetric
  - Normal
  - Uniform
- Skewed
  - Left
  - Right

Activity 14.6

1 For the stem and leaf display of data shown:
  (i) State whether or not the data is approximately symmetrical, approximately bell-shaped, skewed left or skewed right.
  (ii) Identify any outliers.
  (iii) Calculate the mean and the median. Compare the mean and median values.

	Heights of females						
15	8	8					
16	2	4	4	5	6	6	8
17	0	1	2	3	3	4	
18	0	0	1				

Key: 16 | 2   means 162 cm

2 The distribution of weights of a sample of male students is shown.
  (i) Describe the shape of the data distribution.
  (ii) Identify clusters or gaps if they exist.
  (iii) Identify any outliers.

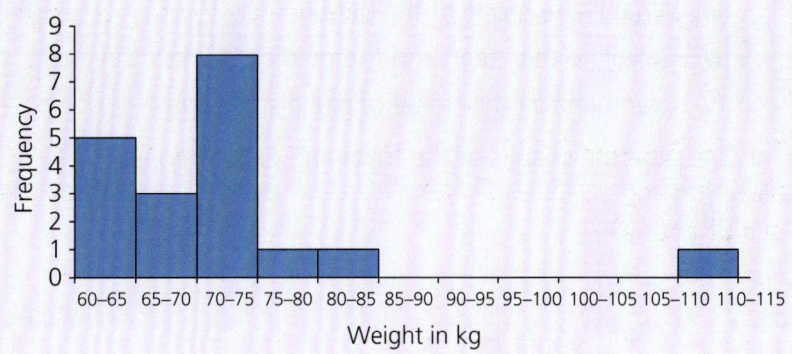

60–65 means: 60 kg ≤ weight < 65 kg

3 A randomly selected group of drivers were asked to give their average maximum driving speed in km/h. The responses are shown in the table.

Speed (km/h)	70	80	90	100	110	120	130
Frequency	1	2	2	5	8	9	3

  (i) How many drivers were in the sample?
  (ii) Draw a suitable graphical representation to display the data.
  (iii) Describe the shape of the data distribution.
  (iv) Given the shape of the data distribution, do you expect the mean to be greater than, less than or equal to the median?
  (v) Verify your answer to part (iv) by calculating the mean and the median.

4 Thirty people live in an apartment building. Their ages are shown in the table.

54	30	45	35	38	40	35	45	35	37
48	46	48	40	48	47	48	46	47	46
39	47	46	34	37	47	39	45	36	40

  (i) Represent the data using a line plot.
  (ii) Comment on the existence of any clusters, gaps or outliers in the group.
  (iii) What is the mode of the data?
  (iv) Calculate the mean and the median ages.
  (v) What is the relationship between the mean and the median? Why do you think this is so? Use the line plot to help answer this question.

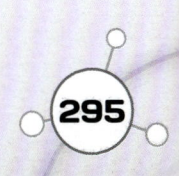

5 The following data shows the marks for the summer test achieved by a class of Science students.

65	65	62	49	66	63	60	65	65	64
68	68	67	66	58	64	64	63	64	66
67	60	68	58	69	71	63	65	66	48

(i) Represent the data using a line plot.
(ii) Comment on the existence of any clusters, gaps or outliers in the group.
(iii) What is the mode of the data?
(iv) Calculate the mean and the median marks.
(v) Comment on the shape of the distribution.

6 Describe the shapes of the following distributions.

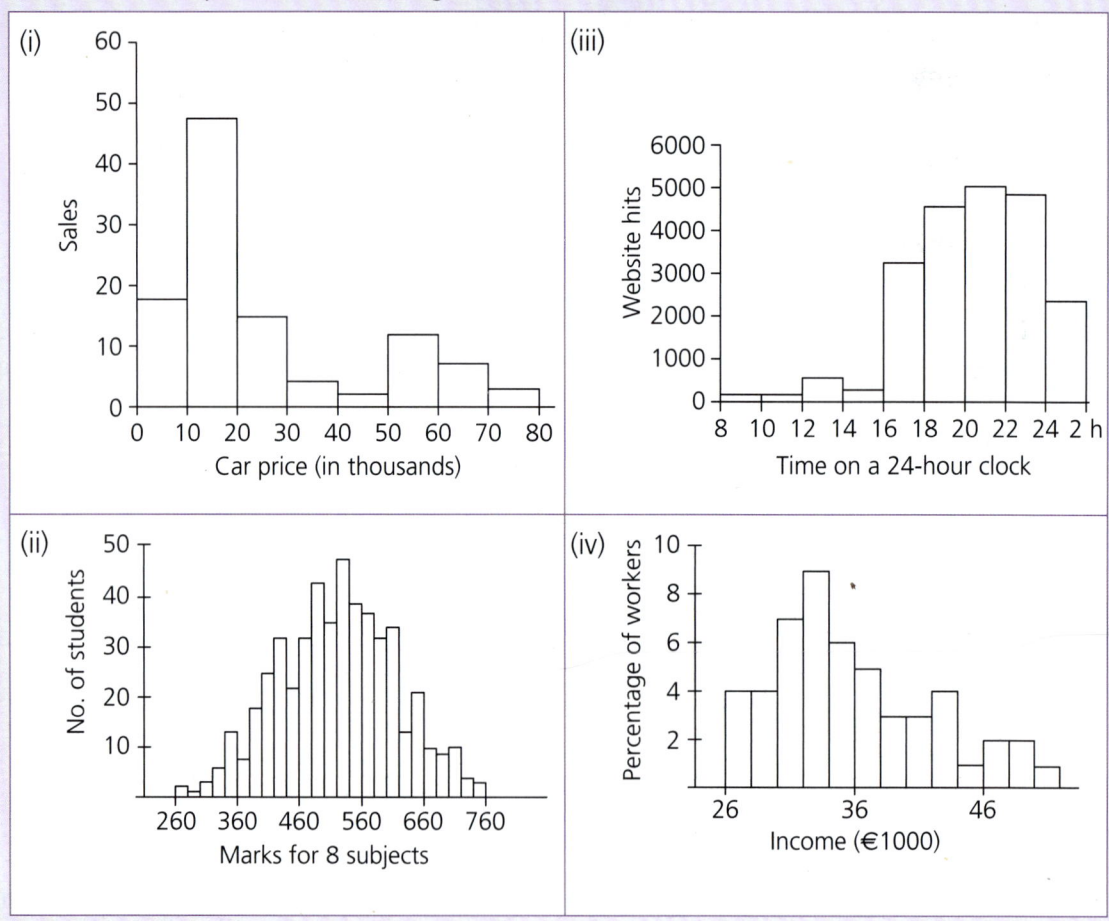

Back-to-back Stem and Leaf Plots

We can read the minimum, lower quartile, median, upper quartile and the maximum values directly from a stem and leaf plot. We can also see the shape of a distribution from a stem and leaf plot and we do not lose the detail of the data as happens when we use a histogram.

Stem and leaf plots are a good way to **compare** two related datasets.
The way we do this is to place the stem and leaf plots **back-to-back**.

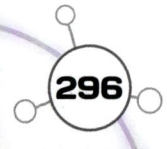

Example

The pulse rates in beats per minute (bpm) of a group of participants in an aerobics class are taken before and after exercise.

Rate before (bpm)	53	61	79	72	50	58	64	67	59	66	60	52	67	76	66
Rate after (bpm)	64	82	67	84	72	59	92	62	71	68	74	71	74	89	78

(i) Draw a back-to-back stem and leaf plot to display the data before and after exercise.

(ii) Looking at the stem and leaf plots, how do the pulse rates compare before and after exercise?

(iii) Describe the shape of the distributions before and after exercise.

(iv) Find the maximum, minimum and range of the data before exercise and after exercise.

(v) Use the back-to-back stem and leaf plot to compare the medians before and after exercise.

(vi) Use the stem and leaf plots to find the interquartile ranges before exercise and after exercise.

(vii) Do you think it is reasonable to say that pulse rates were greater after than before the exercise? Justify your answer.

Solution

(i)

					Leaves ordered					
	Pulse rate before exercise					Pulse rate after exercise				
		9	8	3	2	0	5	9			
7	7	6	6	4	1	0	6	2	4	7	8
				9	6	2	7	1	1	2	4	4	8
							8	2	4	9		
							9	2				
					Key:	8	2	means 82 bpm			
						2	7	means 72 bpm			

(ii) The pulse rates have shifted upwards after exercise. They were clustered between 50 and 80 bpm before exercise and now they are clustered between 60 and 90 bpm. They are also more spread out after exercise than before exercise.

(iii) Before exercise, the values are clustered towards the lower values with a slight tail in the positive direction, i.e. towards the higher values. After exercise, the shape is approximately symmetrical and bell-shaped.

(iv) Before exercise: minimum = 50 bpm; maximum = 79 bpm; range = 29 bpm
After exercise: minimum = 59 bpm; maximum = 92 bpm; range = 33 bpm

(v) Median before exercise = value of the 8th data point = 64 bpm
Median after exercise = value of the 8th data point = 72 bpm

> (vi) Before: $Q_1 = 58$ bpm, $Q_3 = 67$ bpm, interquartile range $= Q_3 - Q_1 = 9$ bpm
> After: $Q_1 = 67$ bpm, $Q_3 = 82$ bpm, interquartile range $= Q_3 - Q_1 = 15$ bpm
> (vii) Yes, in general pulse rates were greater after than before the exercise.
> Both the maxima and minima rates are greater after exercise.
> The median is greater after exercise. The mean before exercise = 63 bpm and the mean after exercise is 74 bpm which is greater.

Activity 14.7

1 A teacher records the marks from the same test for two different class groups, class A and class B.

Class A	58	62	65	70	71	75	75	75	78	78	80	80	82	84	85	91	96	98	99
Class B	61	53	54	75	99	98	98	96	78	57	90	75	93	51	75	96	99	59	95

(i) Compare the modes, medians and means for both class groups.

(ii) Given the measures of central tendency only without the raw data, what conclusion might you draw about the two distributions?

(iii) Draw a back-to-back stem and leaf plot to compare the two classes' test marks.

(iv) Compare the two classes based on the graphical representations for each class.

(v) Compare the two sets of class results using range and interquartile range.

2 A stem and leaf plot can be used to show the distribution of the ages (in years) of guests at two different parties.

			John's party					Sorcha's party						
						0	0	0	1	5	7			
						1	2	2	3					
		9	9	9	8	8	2	5	7	7	8			
5	4	3	3	1	1	3	3	4	4	4	5	5	6	7	8
					0	4	0							
						5	3	5	5	6	7	8	8	8	9
						6	5	6	6					
						7	2	3						
						8	5	5						
						9	2							
					Key:	7	2	means 72 years						

(i) Write one sentence to compare the distribution of the ages of people at each party using initial impressions of the plot.

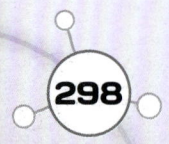

(ii) How many people attended each party?
(iii) Write down the minimum age, maximum age and range of ages for both parties.
(iv) Make a suggestion as to what people were celebrating for each party.
(v) Describe the shape of both distributions of ages.
(vi) Find the measures of central tendency, mode, median and mean, of those attending both parties.
(vii) Compare the spread of the middle 50% of each distribution.

3 A full class of students is given a test in Statistics. Following the test (**Test 1**), the teacher revises the test material with the students. She then gives them another test which is similar to the first test to see if the students have improved their marks based on the revision.

The test results for the second test (**Test 2**) are given in this table.

83	86	79	43	58	38	69	58	57	100
86	35	62	97	82	78	46	77	77	100
98	98	83	37	58	45	68	49	59	100

(i) Copy and complete the back-to-back stem and leaf plot showing the results for Test 2.

Test 2							Test 1				
						0	5	7			
						1	8				
						2	2	3	6		
						3	4	7	8		
						4	4				
						5	1	1	2	3	5	8
						6	2	4	4		
						7	1	8	8	9	
						8	2	3	8	8	9
						9	4	6			
						10	0				
				Key:	9	4	means 94 marks				

(ii) Was anyone absent for the second test? Explain.
(iii) Find the maximum, minimum, range, median, mean and interquartile range for both tests.
(iv) Do the results indicate that marks have improved in Test 2 from Test 1? Justify your answer.
(v) The teacher is wondering what proportion of the students improved in the second test. Can she find this using the stem and leaf plot?

4 Students measured the heights in metres of two different churches in their town using a clinometer. The following data was collected.

Church A: estimated heights (m)

53	65	87	35	39
40	53	60	59	42
46	55	57	78	57
65	74	65	82	48
48				

Church B: estimated heights (m)

49	38	84	58	52
40	47	49	48	48
40	50	54	56	52
39	58	56	55	39
43	48			

When they measured the height of church A, it was their first time using the clinometer and they measured the height of church B on the following days.

(i) How many students were in the class on the first and second days?

(ii) Draw a back-to-back stem and leaf plot to compare the distributions of the two datasets.

(iii) Looking at the stem and leaf plot, how would you describe the height of 84 m as an estimate for the height of church B?

(iv) State one difference between the two distributions.

(v) Compare the range and interquartile range of the estimated heights for both churches.

(vi) Do the answers to part (v) indicate to you that students have improved, in general, in their use of the clinometer?

(vii) What is the mean of the estimated heights of church A?

(viii) Given that the actual height of church A is 62 m, calculate the difference between the mean of the estimated heights and the actual height, which we will refer to as the 'error'.

(ix) The percentage error in the estimated height is the error as a percentage of the actual value. Calculate the percentage error for the mean of the estimated heights of church A, correct to one decimal place.

5 The weights in kg of babies born on each day of the week in a certain hospital to mothers who smoke and mothers who do not smoke are given in the table.

	Monday	Tuesday	Wednesday	Thursday	Friday	Saturday	Sunday
Smoker	2.5	1.9	2.9	4.3	3.7	2.3	3.4
	2.7	3.1	2.8	3.4	2.5	2.8	3.2
	3	3.7					
Non-smoker	2.4	2.9	3.3	3.7	3.8	3.6	3.4
		3.2	4.2	3.1	2.9	4.1	3.6
			4.1	5		2.3	

(i) Use a back-to-back stem and leaf plot to display the data.

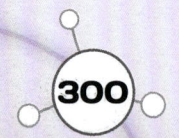

(ii) Describe the distribution of the data for the weights of the babies born to mothers who **smoke**, by making one statement about each of the following characteristics of the distribution: shape, central tendency and spread.

(iii) Describe the distribution of the data for the weights of the babies born to mothers who **do not smoke**, by making one statement about each of the following characteristics of the distribution: shape, central tendency and spread.

6 Refer to the data in question 5: 
  (i) 'Heavier babies are born to mothers who do not smoke.' Comment on this statement, taking the data into account. Support your answer with reference to the following.
    (a) Comparison of the medians and means of the two datasets
    (b) Comparison of the maxima and minima range of the two datasets
  (ii) Just because there are differences between the weights of the babies in the two datasets, does this mean that the difference is due only to whether or not the mothers smoke?
  What other factors do you think could affect the weights of newborn babies besides the fact that the mother smokes or does not smoke?
  (iii) In choosing a sample of mothers to test the claim that 'heavier babies are born to mothers who do not smoke', how would a researcher take account of the other factors referred to in part (ii)?

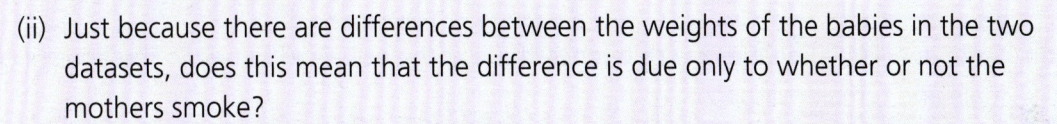

7 A quality controller arranged to have a random sample of walnuts measured and then tasted. The tasters were asked to classify the walnuts as either sweet or sour.

The lengths of the walnuts which were classified as **sour** are given below in mm:

65, 67, 75, 73, 71, 83, 55, 82, 87, 74, 69, 88, 75, 63

The lengths of the walnuts which were classified as **sweet** are given below in mm:

32, 56, 76, 73, 59, 75, 67, 68, 85, 63, 63, 46, 101, 70, 73, 72, 82

  (i) Draw a suitable graphical representation to compare the distribution of lengths of this sample of sweet and sour walnuts.
  (ii) Find the median length for each of the sets of data.
  (iii) Explain what you mean by interquartile range. Compare the spread of each of the sets of data using range and interquartile range.
  (iv) Which measure of spread do you think is most useful in this case? Explain.
  (v) What appears to be similar and what appears to be different about the lengths of sweet and sour walnuts based on this sample?

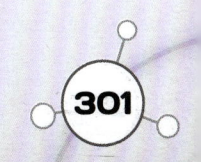

8. The ages of the Academy Award winners for best male actor and best female actor (at the time they won the award) from 1992 to 2011 are as follows.

Male actor	54	52	37	38	32	45	60	46	40	36	47	29	43	37	38	45	50	48	60	50
Female actor	42	29	33	36	45	49	39	26	25	33	35	35	28	30	29	61	32	33	45	29

(i) Represent the data on a back-to-back stem and leaf plot.

	Male actors				Female actors		
				2			
				3			
				4			
				5			
				6			
				Key:			

(ii) State one similarity and one difference that can be observed between the ages of the male and female winners.

(iii) Mary says 'The female winners were younger than the male winners.' Investigate this statement in relation to:
   (a) the mean age of the male winners and mean age of the female winners
   (b) the median age of the male winners and the median age of the female winners.

(iv) Find the interquartile ranges of the ages of the male winners and of the female winners.

JCHL 2012 Paper 2

Revision Activity 14

1. The runtimes of the 1980s best film Oscar nominations are shown in the histogram.

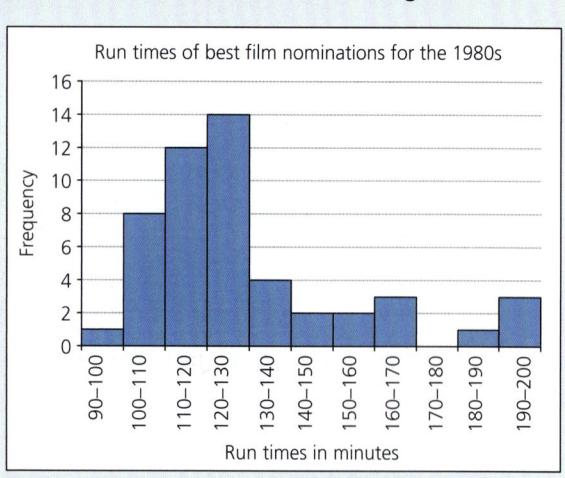

(a) How many films were nominated for best film as shown in the histogram for this period?
(b) What are the minimum and maximum runtime intervals?

(c) Describe the shape of the distribution. Explain your answer.
(d) Using the histogram, make a table showing the frequency for each runtime interval.
(e) What is the modal runtime interval?
(f) Estimate the mean runtime using mid-interval values.
(g) Which interval contains the median runtime interval?
(h) Describe what the histogram tells you about the runtimes of these films.

2 The table shows the results of a school survey into favourite types of music.

Music type	Pop	Rock	Classical	Other
Number of students	50	25	4	16

(a) Draw a pie chart to illustrate this information, showing clearly how you calculate the size of each angle.
(b) What other graphical representations could you use to display this data?
(c) Use one of the graphical representations you suggested in part (b) to display the data.
(d) Comment on the usefulness of both graphical representations in this case. Under what circumstances would one of them be better than the other?

3 The number of students attending primary and second level schools in Ireland in 2010 is illustrated in the pie charts below.

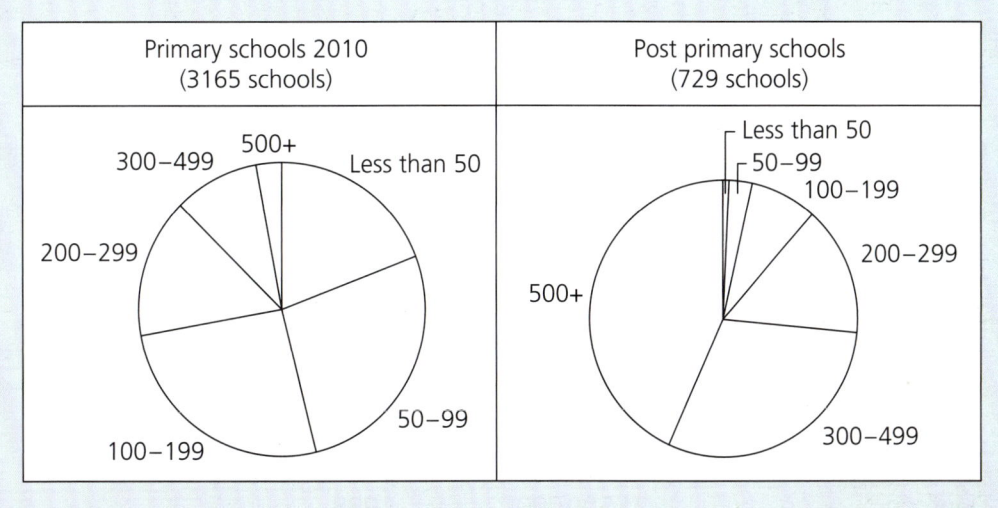

(a) The angle in the slice for primary schools with between 100 and 199 pupils is 93.725°. Calculate the number of schools in this category.
(b) Mary claims that the charts show that there is roughly the same number of post primary schools as primary shools in the 200–299 range. Do you agree with Mary? Give a reason for your answer based on the data in the charts.

JCHL 2014 Sample Paper

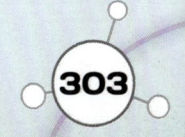

4 Data on the type of broadband connection used by enterprises in Ireland for 2008 and 2009 is contained in the table below.

	2008	2009
	%	%
Broadband connection	84	84
By type of connection		
DSL [< 2Mb/s]	31	29
DSL [> 2Mb/s]	41	45
Other fixed connection	31	20
Mobile broadband	24	27

Source: Central Statistical Office

(a) Display the data in a way that allows you to compare the data for the two years.
(b) Identify any trends that you think are shown by the data.

JCHL 2011 Paper 2

5 Below is a list of record-breaking transfer fees for soccer players, measured in pounds sterling.

Player	Transfer fee (£)	Year
Gareth Bale	85 000 000	2013
Cristiano Ronaldo	80 000 000	2009
Kaka	56 000 000	2009
Zinedine Zidane	46 000 000	2001
Luis Figo	37 000 000	2000
Hernan Crespo	35 500 000	2000
Christian Vieri	32 000 000	1999
Denilson	21 500 000	1998
Ronaldo	19 500 000	1997
Alan Shearer	15 000 000	1996
Gianluigi Lentini	13 000 000	1992

(a) Use a suitable graphical representation to display the data.
(b) What is the range of the data?
(c) What is the percentage increase (to the nearest %) in the record for Cristiano Ronaldo compared with that for Gianluigi Lentini?
(d) What is the mean of the record transfer fees in the table?

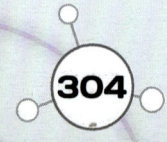

6 Thirty randomly selected students were surveyed to find the number of times they had bought lunch in the school canteen during the previous week.

The following results were obtained.

2	3	1	2	2	3	2	1	2	3
4	4	5	5	4	3	3	2	2	2
3	2	3	4	4	4	4	2	3	3

(a) Organise the data using a frequency table.
(b) Construct a pie chart, bar chart and line plot to display the data.
(c) Comment on whether or not you think one of the graphical displays is better than the others.
(d) What does the data tell you about the eating habits of the students in the sample?
(e) Can you apply the conclusions to the population of students in the school?

7 The All-Ireland Poc Fada Hurling and Camogie Championships is an annual tournament testing the skills of Ireland's best hurlers and Camogie players. *Poc Fada* is the Irish for 'long puck'. Competitors in the senior final must puc a ball (sliotar) with a hurley over a course measuring 5 kilometres in mountainous terrain in County Louth. The winner is the competitor who achieves this with the least number of pucs.

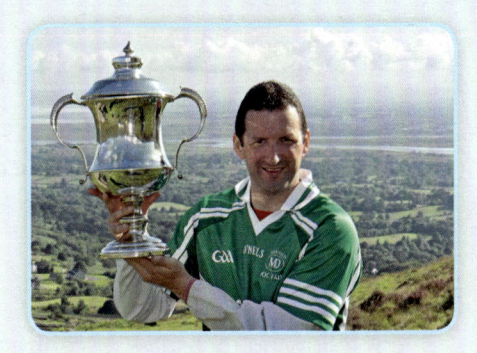

The number of pucs needed to complete the course in 2011 and 2012 are shown in the table.

| **2011** | 54 | 58 | 60 | 54 | 61 | 58 | 50 | 63 | 54 | 60 | 57 | 60 | 61 | 58 |
| **2012** | 54 | 50 | 47 | 48 | 39 | 48 | 46 | 49 | 46 | 47 | 49 | 49 | | |

(a) How many competitors took part in 2011 and 2012?
(b) What was the winning score for each of the years 2011 and 2012?
(c) Draw a back-to-back stem and leaf diagram to compare the results for both years.
(d) Use your diagram to identify the median number of pucs in each case.
(e) Use another measure of central tendency to compare the two sets of results.
(f) How would you compare the results for 2012 with the results for 2011?
(g) Give two possible reasons for the differences between the results in 2011 and 2012.

8 The following three questions are taken from *CensusAtSchool* questionnaires.

Q1. 'How important do you think the Census is to Education?'
(The students answered using a sliding scale from 1 to 1000.)

Q2. 'How tall are you without shoes? (Answer in centimetres)'

Q3. 'What is your best time on the interactive question?'
(This was a 'reaction-time' type of question.)

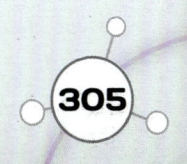

The histograms below show the distribution of the responses from a random sample of 100 Irish students.

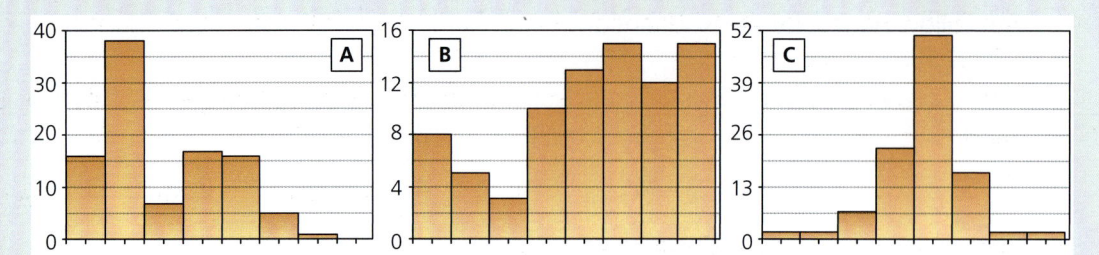

(a) Match each histogram to either of Q1, Q2 or Q3. Explain your choice.

(b) Describe the shape of each histogram.

9 Ten students submitted their Design portfolios which were marked out of 40.
The marks they obtained were:

37   34   34   34   29   27   27   10   4   28

(a) For these marks find
  (i) the mode   (ii) the median   (iii) the mean.

(b) Comment on your results.

(c) An external moderator reduced all the marks by 3. Find the mode, median and mean of the moderated marks.

10 A clerk entering salary data into a company spreadsheet accidentally put an extra '0' in the boss's salary, listing it as €2 000 000 instead of €200 000. Explain how this error will affect the following measures of centre for the company payroll: (a) the median, (b) the mean.

11 The following back-to-back stem and leaf plot shows the ages of all the Oscar winners for best supporting actress and best supporting actor.

Ages of best supporting actors		Ages of best supporting actresses
	1	0 1
	1	6
0	2	3 4 4 4
9 8 7	2	5 7 8 8 8 8 9 9 9
4 3 2 1	3	0 0 0 0 1 2 3 3 3 3 4 4 4 4
9 9 8 8 7 7 6 6 5	3	5 5 5 5 5 8 9 9 9 9 9
4 4 4 4 3 3 2 1 1 0 0 0	4	0 1 1 1 2 2 3 4 4 4 4 5 5 5 5 5
9 9 8 7 7 7 7 6 6 6 6 6 6 6 5 5	4	6 6 7 8
4 4 3 3 2 1	5	0 3
9 7 7 6 6 5	5	6 6 9
4 3 3 3 3 1	6	1 2 4
7 7 6 1	6	5 5
3 2 1 0 0	7	0 1 2
9 7 7 7	7	
2 0	8	
	8	

Key: 3|6 means 36 years

(a) Describe the shape of the distribution of the ages of (i) the actors, (ii) the actresses.

(b) How many actors and actresses are shown in the back-to-back stem and leaf plot?

(c) What is the range of ages shown in the plot for (i) the actors, (ii) the actresses?

(d) What is the median age and the interquartile range of ages for the actors?

(e) What is the median age and the interquartile range of ages for the actresses?

(f) Would you agree that the age at which best supporting actors win an Oscar tends to be older than the age at which best supporting actresses tend to win an Oscar? Justify your answer.

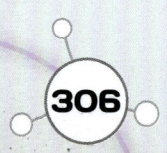

12. On June 6, 2013, the *Guardian* newspaper published a list of the top 50 British and Irish Lions from the last 125 years, selected by a panel of judges. The Welsh player Gareth Edwards was named as the greatest Lion in history with the Irish player Willie John McBride coming second.

    The number of players chosen from each country for the top 50 players is shown in the table below.

Country	Ireland	England	Scotland	Wales
Number of players in the top 50	9	16	9	16

    (a) The following pie chart displays the data. Comment on how well it represents the data.

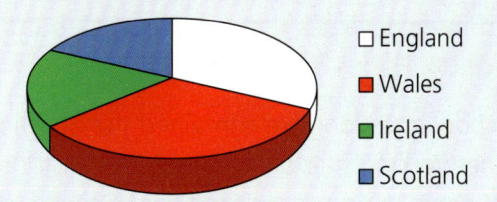

    (b) Suggest alternative ways of displaying the data. Display the data using a suitable graphical representation.

13. The Central Bank of Ireland has initiated a National Payments Plan, an initiative which focuses on a range of measures to promote electronic payments and reduce Ireland's very high usage of cash and cheques.

    The results of a survey on payment usage in Ireland in January 2011 gave the following results.

Cheques	Cash	Laser/Debit card	Credit card	Direct debit
2	60	20	14	4

    (a) Draw a suitable graphical representation to display the data in the table.

    (b) The following question was asked of a sample of Irish people in a survey about payment usage. 'If cheques were removed as a means of payment, what level of difficulty would this present to you in your personal circumstances? Please use a scale where 1 is no difficulty and 5 is extremely difficult.' The data collected for this question is shown in the chart.

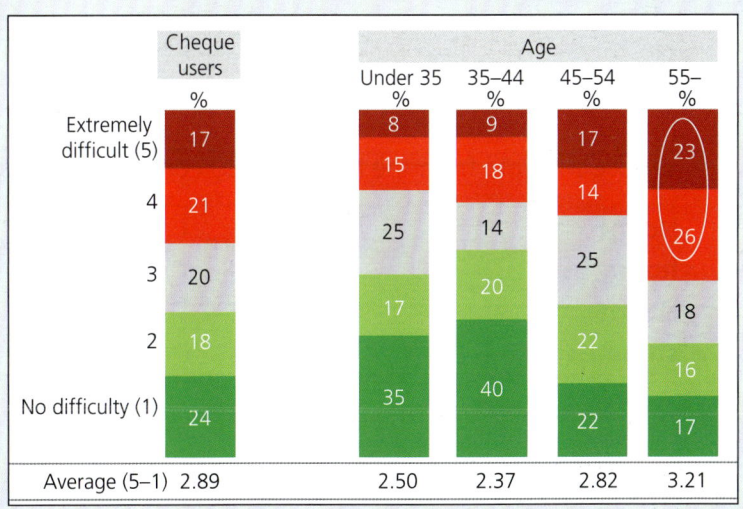

    What percentage of all cheque users state that the removal of cheques would cause substantial difficulty?

    (c) Discuss how the removal of cheques would affect the under-35 age group compared to the over-55 age group.

14 First Year students were asked how much pocket money they spent in a certain week. The results are shown in the frequency distribution table.

Amount of pocket money in €	0–5	5–10	10–15	15–20	20–25
Number of students	5	21	14	x	6

5–10 means €5 or more but less than €10

Taking mid-interval values, it was found that the mean amount of pocket money spent in that week was €11.13.

(a) Find the value of x.

(b) Draw a histogram to illustrate this information.

(c) Verify using the mid-interval values that the mean amount of pocket money spent was €11.13.

15 The phase 9 *CensusAtSchool* questionnaire contained the question 'Approximately how long do you spend on social networking sites each week?' The histogram below illustrates the answers given by 100 students, randomly selected from those who completed the survey.

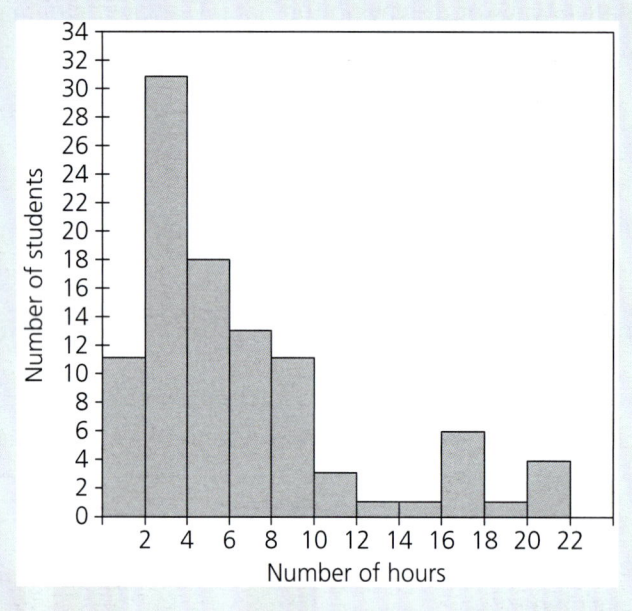

(a) Use the data from the histogram to complete the frequency table below.

No. of hours	0–2	2–4	4–6	6–8	8–10	10–12	12–14	14–16	16–18	18–20	20–22
No. of students											

2–4 means 2 hours or more but less than 4 hours

(b) What is the modal interval?

(c) Taking mid-interval values, find the mean amount of time spent on social networking sites.

(d) John is conducting a survey on computer usage by students at his school. His questionnaire asks the same question. He plans to carry out his survey by asking the question to twenty first year boys on the Monday after the mid-term break. Give two reasons why the results from John's question might not be as representative as those in the histogram.

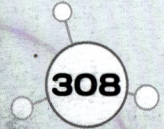

JCHL 2014 Sample Paper

Exam-style Questions

1. The ages of the 30 people who took part in an aerobics class are as follows:

18	24	32	37	9	13	22	41	51	49
15	42	37	58	48	53	27	54	42	24
33	48	56	17	61	37	63	45	20	39

   The ages of the 30 people who took part in a swimming class are as follows:

16	22	29	7	36	45	12	38	52	13
33	41	24	35	51	8	47	22	14	24
42	62	15	24	23	31	53	36	48	18

   (a) Represent this data on a back-to-back stem and leaf diagram.

   (b) Use your diagram to identify the median in each case.

   (c) What other measure of central tendency could have been used when examining this data?

   (d) Based on the data, make one observation about the ages of the two groups.

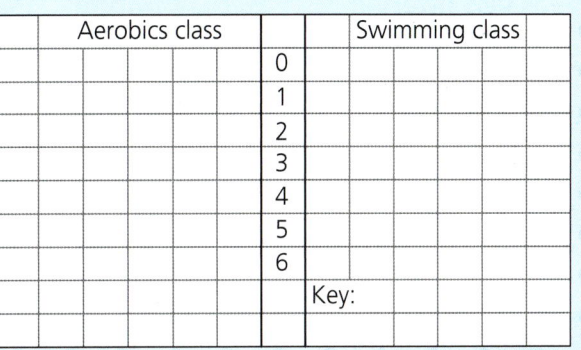

   JCHL 2013 Paper 2

2. In total, 7150 second level school students from 216 schools completed the 2011/2012 phase 11 *CensusAtSchool* questionnaire. The questionnaire contained a question relating to where students keep their mobile phones while sleeping.

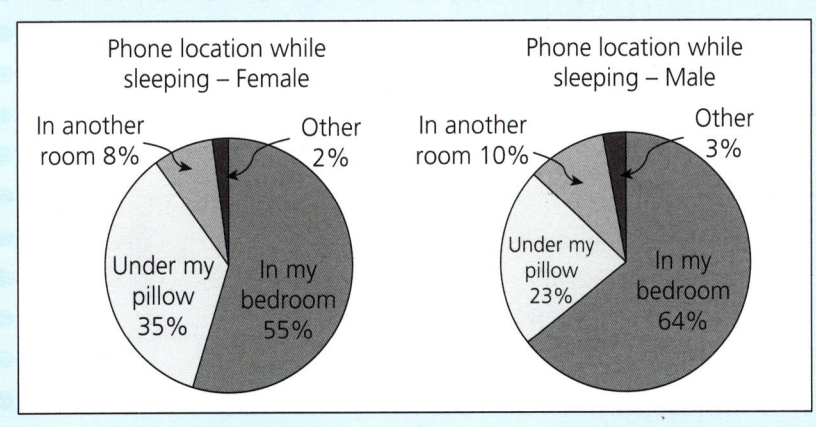

   Phone location while sleeping – Female
   - In another room 8%
   - Other 2%
   - Under my pillow 35%
   - In my bedroom 55%

   Phone location while sleeping – Male
   - In another room 10%
   - Other 3%
   - Under my pillow 23%
   - In my bedroom 64%

   (a) Given that this question was answered by 4171 girls and 2979 boys, calculate how many female students kept their mobile phones under their pillows.

   (b) Calculate the overall percentage of students who kept their mobile phones under their pillows.

   (c) A new pie chart is to be drawn showing the mobile phone location for all students. Calculate the measure of the angle that would represent the students who kept their mobile phones under their pillows.

   JCHL 2013 Paper 2

14 Statistics

KEY WORDS AND PHRASES

- Average
- Bar chart
- Bias
- Categorical data (nominal)
- Categorical data (ordinal)
- Class interval
- Cluster of data
- Data
- Data handling cycle
- Dataset
- Descriptive statistics (summary statistics)
- Distribution
- Five-number summary
- Frequency
- Frequency table
- Histogram
- Interquartile range
- Mean
- Measure of central tendency
- Measure of spread
- Median
- Mode
- Line plot (dot plot)
- Numerical data (continuous)
- Numerical data (discrete)
- Normal distribution
- Outcome
- Outlier
- Pie chart
- Population
- Quartiles
- Random sample
- Range
- Relative frequency
- Sample
- Sample size
- Statistic
- Simple random sample
- Skewness
- Skewed positively (right)
- Skewed negatively (left)
- Stem and leaf plot
- Symmetric distribution
- Variable

Chapter Summary 14

- Statistics is about **variation**. The **data handling cycle** shows how we proceed in solving problems using data.
- A **census** is when we collect data on the entire population.
- We often make **inferences** about the population based on **random samples**.
- Samples must be **representative** of the population in order to be useful.
- **Biased samples** over or underestimate what we are trying to measure for the population.

Pose a question → Collect data → Analyse the data → Interpret the results →

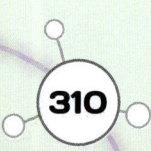

- The **type of data** we collect determines the type of analysis we can perform on it.

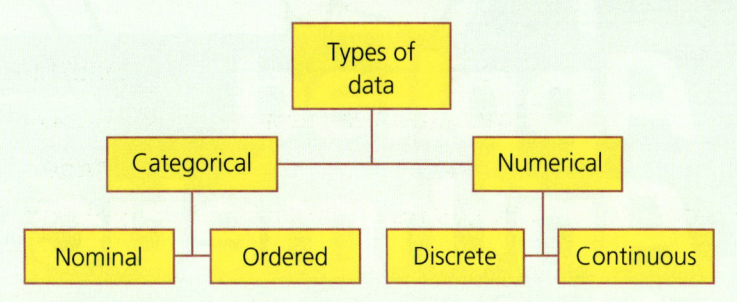

```
                    Types of
                     data
              ┌────────┴────────┐
         Categorical         Numerical
         ┌───┴───┐          ┌────┴────┐
      Nominal  Ordered   Discrete  Continuous
```

- We can perform **numerical** and **graphical analysis** of data.
- Numerical analysis involves
    - **Measures of central tendency**, i.e. mode (for categorical and numerical data), median and mean (for numerical data only)
    - **Measures of spread**, i.e. range and interquartile range, are for numerical data only.
- The type of graphical analysis and the types of data suited to each type of graph is summarised in the table.

Type of data	Line plot	Bar chart	Frequency table	Histogram	Pie chart	Stem plot
Categorical	✓	✓	✓		✓	
Discrete numerical	✓	✓	✓		✓	✓
Continuous numerical	✓		✓	✓		✓

- Histograms and stem and leaf plots involve grouped data.
- If we wish to compare datasets graphically, we can use back-to-back stem and leaf plots.

Chapter 15

Applied Arithmetic

Learning Outcomes

In this chapter, you will learn about:
- Solving problems that involve:
  - Cost price
  - Selling price
  - Profit and loss
  - Mark-up (profit as a percentage of the cost price)
  - Margin (profit as a percentage of the selling price)
- Solving problems that involve compound interest
- Solving problems that involve income tax and net pay (including other deductions)

Section 15A Percentage Profit and Loss

In *Connect with Maths 1*, we solved problems involving percentage profit or loss. Knowing whether a business makes a profit or loss is very important for the long-term success of any business.

Key Points

Recall:
- If the cost price is less than the selling price, there is a profit:
  Profit = Selling price − Cost price = positive amount.
- If the cost price is more than the selling price, there is a loss:
  Loss = Cost price − Selling price = positive amount.
- The **percentage profit or loss** formulae are:

$$\% \text{ Profit} = \frac{\text{Profit amount}}{\text{Cost price}} \times 100$$

$$\% \text{ Loss} = \frac{\text{Loss amount}}{\text{Cost price}} \times 100$$

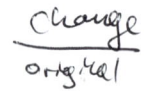

Example 1

(i) An armchair was bought at a cost price of €120 and was sold for €170. Find the % profit, to 2 decimal places.

(ii) A guitar was bought at a cost price of €150 and was sold for €105. Find the % loss.

Solution

(i) Cost price of armchair = €120 and selling price of armchair = €170. 
- Find the profit.
  - Profit = Selling price − Cost price
  - Profit = €170 − €120 = €50
- % Profit = $\dfrac{\text{Profit amount}}{\text{Cost price}} \times 100 = \dfrac{50}{120} \times 100 = 41.67\%$

(ii) Cost price of guitar = €150 and selling price of guitar = €105. 
- Find the loss.
  - Loss = Cost price − Selling price
  - Loss = €150 − €105 = €45
- % Loss = $\dfrac{\text{Loss amount}}{\text{Cost price}} \times 100 = \dfrac{45}{150} \times 100 = 30\%$

Mark-up and Margin

In business situations, we generally wish to make a profit on all the products we sell. However, in some situations, a business may record a loss on product(s).

The following situations can affect the profit made by a business:

- 'Sales' when products are marked down in price
- Discounts for employees
- A 'loss leader', where a company makes a decision to sell a product at a loss to generate sales for other products
- The launch of a new product
- Inventory shrinkage due to water or fire damage
- Selling an older version of a product, when a new product line is launched.

Key Points

We can use **mark-up or margin** to analyse a company's ability to make a profit or not.

- **Mark-up**
  Mark-up is the profit as a percentage (%) of the **cost price**.

$$\text{Mark-up} = \dfrac{\text{Profit}}{\text{Cost price}} \times 100$$

- **Margin**
  Margin is the profit as a percentage (%) of the **selling price**.

$$\text{Margin} = \dfrac{\text{Profit}}{\text{Selling price}} \times 100$$

Example 2

Caroline imports handheld tied flowers at a cost of €25 per bunch. She sells the flowers for €40 per bunch.

(i) Calculate the profit Caroline makes on each bunch of flowers.
(ii) Calculate the mark-up.
(iii) Calculate the margin.
(iv) What do you notice about the value of the margin compared with the mark-up?
Can you explain why this is the case?

Solution

(i) Cost price = €25 and
Selling price = €40
Profit = €40 − €25
= €15

(ii) Mark-up = $\dfrac{\text{Profit}}{\text{Cost price}} \times 100$

= $\dfrac{15}{25} \times 100$

= 60%

(iii) Margin = $\dfrac{\text{Profit}}{\text{Selling price}} \times 100$

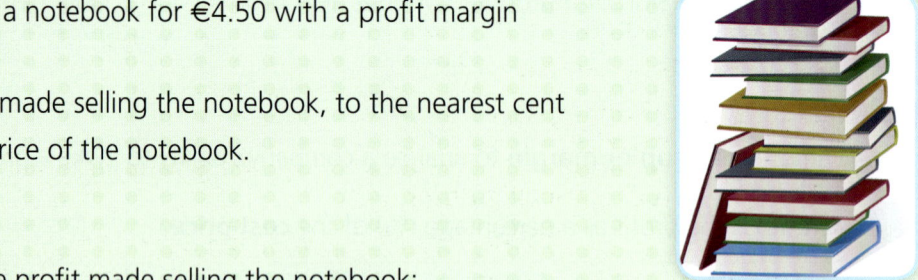

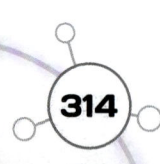

= $\dfrac{15}{40} \times 100$

= 37.5%

(iv) The mark-up is greater than the margin because a profit was made. As a result

$\dfrac{\text{Profit}}{\text{Cost price}} > \dfrac{\text{Profit}}{\text{Selling price}}$

In this case, the ratios are:

$\dfrac{15}{25} > \dfrac{15}{40} \Rightarrow \dfrac{3}{5} > \dfrac{3}{8}$

Example 3

A retailer sells a notebook for €4.50 with a profit margin of 33%. Find:

(i) the profit made selling the notebook, to the nearest cent
(ii) the cost price of the notebook.

Solution

(i) To find the profit made selling the notebook:
- Write down all the information we know:
  Selling price = €4.50
  Margin = 33%
- Substitute the known values into the formula and calculate the profit.

Margin = $\dfrac{\text{Profit}}{\text{Selling price}} \times 100$

$$\Rightarrow \quad 33 = \frac{\text{Profit}}{4.50} \times 100$$

$$\Rightarrow \quad \frac{33}{100} = \frac{\text{Profit}}{4.50} \quad \text{... divide both sides by 100}$$

$$\Rightarrow \quad 4.5 \times 0.33 = \text{Profit} \quad \text{... multiply both sides by 4.5}$$

$$\Rightarrow \quad 1.485 = \text{Profit}$$

The profit made on the notebook is €1.49, to the nearest cent.

(ii) Cost price = Selling price − Profit
 = €4.50 − €1.49
 = €3.01

Example 4

A hardware store buys wooden picnic tables at a cost price of €140 each.

Find the selling price of one table if it is sold with:

(i) a 32% mark-up

(ii) a 32% margin, correct to the nearest cent.

Solution

(i) 32% mark-up

Cost price = €140
Mark-up = 32%
Let p = Profit.

- Substitute the known values into the formula and calculate the Profit.

$$\text{Mark-up} = \frac{\text{Profit}}{\text{Cost price}} \times 100$$

$$32 = \frac{p}{140} \times 100 \quad \text{... multiply both sides by 140}$$

$$32(140) = p \times 100 \quad \text{... divide both sides by 100}$$

$$\frac{32(140)}{100} = p$$

€44.80 = p = Profit

- Calculate the selling price of one picnic table.

∴ Selling price = Cost price + Profit
 = €140 + €44.80
 = €184.80

(ii) 32% margin

Cost price = €140
Margin = 32%
Let P = Profit.

- Substitute the known values into the formula and calculate the profit.

$$\text{Margin} = \frac{\text{Profit}}{\text{Selling price}} \times 100$$

$$32 = \frac{P}{184.80} \times 100 \quad \text{... multiply both sides by 184.80}$$

$$32(184.80) = P(100) \quad \text{... divide both sides by 100}$$

$$\frac{32(184.80)}{100} = P$$

59.136 = P

€59.14 = P = Profit

- Selling price = Cost price + Profit
 = €140 + €59.14
 = €199.14

Activity 15.1

1. The table shows the cost price and selling price for a number of different-sized beds.
   Calculate the percentage profit for each bed.

	Item	Cost price	Selling price
(i)	Single bed	€275.00	€330.00
(ii)	Double bed	€460.00	€529.00
(iii)	King-size bed	€680.00	€850.00

2. Find the selling price of each of the following items based on the cost price and the percentage profit or loss given.

	Item	Cost price	% Profit/loss
(i)	Frying pan	€45.00	15% profit
(ii)	Food mixer	€96.00	18% profit
(iii)	Vegetable strainer	€8.00	10% loss

3. Find the cost price of each of the following items based on the selling price and the percentage profit given, correct to the nearest cent.

	Item	Selling price	% Profit
(i)	Laptop	€520.00	10
(ii)	External hard drive	€120.00	16
(iii)	Computer mouse	€11.00	20

4. In the case of each of (i), (ii) and (iii) in the table, calculate the:
   (a) profit
   (b) mark-up
   (c) margin.

   Write all answers correct to two decimal places.

	Cost price (€)	Selling price (€)
(i)	10.00	12.50
(ii)	6.00	7.20
(iii)	45.00	63.00

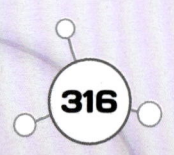

5. Calculate the cost price of each of the following products to the nearest cent.

	Product	Selling price (€)	Margin
(i)	DVD	19.99	30%
(ii)	Computer game	49.99	35%
(iii)	Headphones	150.00	60%

6. Calculate the selling price of each of the following products to the nearest cent.

	Item	Cost price (€)	Mark-up
(i)	Shirt	12	15%
(ii)	Jumper	15	20%
(iii)	Jeans	49	30%

7. A coffee machine has a cost price of €444.31. The mark-up is 17.5%.
   (i) Calculate the selling price of the coffee machine, to the nearest cent.
   (ii) Calculate the margin for the coffee machine, correct to the nearest percentage.
   (iii) What do you notice about the value of the mark-up compared with the margin? Can you explain why this is the case?

8. A 40″ LED Freeview 3D television is sold at €899.99. The margin is 42%.
   (i) Calculate the cost price of the television, to the nearest cent.
   (ii) Calculate the mark-up, correct to two decimal places.

9. A top-of-the-range electronic tablet is sold for €609.53. 
   (i) If the margin is 59%, find the cost price of the tablet to the nearest cent.
   (ii) Calculate the mark-up, correct to the nearest percentage.

10. Milk is bought from a farmer at 34 cent per litre. The milk is subsequently sold at an average price of €1.20 per litre. Calculate:
    (i) the profit per litre
    (ii) the mark-up
    (iii) the margin.
    (iv) What do you notice about the value of the mark-up compared with the margin? Can you explain why this is the case?

11. A new car is sold for €19 000. 
    (i) If the dealer's mark-up is 7%, calculate the cost price of the car from the manufacturer to the nearest euro.
    (ii) Find the cost price of the car, if the mark-up is 15% to the nearest euro.

12 A meat factory buys beef from a farmer for €4 per kilogram. The beef is subsequently sold by a butcher at an average price of €15 per kilogram. Calculate:

   (i) the profit per kg   (ii) the mark-up   (iii) the margin to the nearest %.

13 A jeweller buys gold rings at a cost price of €210 each. Calculate the selling price of a ring, correct to the nearest cent, if it is sold with a:

   (i) 34% mark-up   (ii) 34% margin.

14 A toy store buys children's bikes for €76. Calculate the selling price of one bike if it is sold with a:

   (i) 28% mark-up

   (ii) 28% margin, correct to the nearest cent.

Section 15B Compound Interest

In *Connect with Maths 1*, we solved problems involving basic compound interest up to 3 years.

> **Key Points**
>
> **Recall:**
> The **compound interest formula** states:
>
> $F = P(1 + i)^t$ … see page 30 of the *Formulae and Tables booklet*
>
> where F = final amount including interest
> P = principal amount invested
> i = annual interest rate (as a decimal)
> t = time in years.
>
> This formula assumes that compounding happens once a year.

Annual Percentage Rate (APR) and Annual Equivalent Rate (AER)

When dealing with **loan and credit agreement** calculations, we refer to the **Annual Percentage Rate (APR)**. This is the interest rate paid to the financial institution.

When dealing with **savings and investments** we refer to the **Annual Equivalent Rate (AER)**. This is the interest rate paid by the financial institution.

Example 1

Maeve gets a loan of €9000 to buy a car. The interest rate available on this loan is 10.9% APR. She has arranged to pay back the loan as follows.

- Pay €2000 at end of year 1.
- Pay another €2000 at end of year 2.
- Pay the remainder at end of the 3rd year.

(i) What amount will Maeve have to pay at the end of the 3rd year?

(ii) Calculate the interest paid.

Solution

(i) Work out the total amount paid for the loan after 3 years:

	Principal (P) (€)	Rate of interest (i) as a decimal	Amount (F) at end of year (€) $F = P(1+i)^t$	Loan repayment (€)
Year 1	9000	0.109	$(9000 \times 1.109)^1 = 9981$	2000
Year 2	9981 − 2000 = 7981	0.109	$(7981 \times 1.109)^1 = 8850.93$	2000
Year 3	8850.93 − 2000 = 6850.93	0.109	$(6850.93 \times 1.109)^1 = 7597.68$	

Alternatively, we can work out the solution using the following method:
- Amount owed at end of year 1:   €9000 × 1.109 = €9981
- Loan repayment at end of year 1:   = €2000
- Total loan owed at start of 2nd year: €9981 − €2000 = €7981
- Amount owed at end of year 2:   €7981 × 1.109 = €8850.93
- Loan repayment at end of year 2:   = €2000
- Total loan owed at start of 3rd year: €8850.93 − €2000 = €6850.93
- Amount owed at end of year 3:   €6850.93 × 1.109 = €7597.68

(ii) Maeve will have to pay €7597.68 + €4000 = €11 597.68 in total over the 3 years.
Total amount paid − loan amount = total interest paid on loan
⇒ €11 597.68 − €9000 = €2597.68
Maeve has to pay €2597.68 interest.

Example 2

Julie invested some money at an interest rate of 7% AER for 4 years. At the end of the 4 years, the final investment was worth €1966.19. Calculate the principal amount that Julie invested to the nearest euro.

Solution

- Label all variables given in the question.
    - $F = €1966.19$
    - $P = ?$
    - $i = 7\% = 0.07$
    - $t = 4$

- Rearrange the compound interest formula to make P the subject of the formula.

    $F = P(1+i)^t$ ... divide both sides by $(1+i)^t$

    $\Rightarrow \dfrac{F}{(1+i)^t} = P$

- Substitute all known values into this formula to solve for the principal amount.

$$\frac{F}{(1+i)^t} = P$$

$$\frac{1966.19}{(1.07)^4} = P$$

$1499.996937 = P$ ... round to the nearest euro

€1500 = P

Julie invested €1500 at the start of the investment.

Example 3

Ben invested €3800 for 1 year and received €4085 at the end of the year. Calculate the interest rate that Ben received on his investment.

Solution

Method 1

- Interest earned = Final amount − Principal amount
  = €4085 − €3800
  = €285

- Interest rate ($r\%$)

$$= \frac{\text{Interest amount}}{\text{Principal amount}} \times \frac{100}{1}$$

$$= \frac{285}{3800} \times \frac{100}{1}$$

$$= 7.5\%$$

Method 2 (Unitary method)

€3800 = 100%

$€1 = \frac{100}{3800}\%$

$€4085 = \left(\frac{100 \times 4085}{3800}\right)\%$

= 107.5%

⇒ $r = 7.5\%$

Activity 15.2

1. €12 500 was invested in a savings account for 3 years.

   (i) Copy and complete the table using the interest rates and annual withdrawals shown. Round all final amounts to the nearest cent.

Year	Principal amount (P) in euro	Interest rate as a percentage %	Interest rate (i) as a decimal	Final amount (F) in euro	Amount of money withdrawn at the end of the year (€)
1	12 500	7.5			1000
2		6.7			650
3		6.2			

   (ii) What was the value of the investment at the end of the 3rd year?

2

	Amount invested	AER (%)	Period of investment
(i)	€60	4%	3
(ii)	€175	3%	6
(iii)	€2500	5%	7
(iv)	€17 300	7%	4
(v)	€138 900	9.5%	5
(vi)	€1 080 200	12.5%	2

(a) Calculate the total amount of each investment given in the table.

(b) Calculate the amount of interest earned on each investment.

3 Calculate the final amount, to the nearest cent, for each situation below.

  (i) A principal investment of €500 invested in a savings account at 6% APR for 5 years

  (ii) A principal investment of €1500 invested for 3 years at 8.9% APR

  (iii) A principal investment of €5000 invested for 10 years at 12% APR

4 A car costs €26 500 new. The value of the car depreciates by 10% in year 1, 8% in year 2 and 7% in year 3.

  (i) Calculate the value of the car at the end of year 1.

  (ii) Calculate the value of the car at the end of year 2.

  (iii) Calculate the value of the car at the end of year 3.

5 Adam invests €7000 in shares for 4 years.

  ■ For the first 2 years his shares increase in value by 8% per annum.

  ■ In the 3rd year his shares depreciate in value by 4%.

  ■ In the 4th year his shares make a loss of 2%.

  (i) Calculate the value of the shares after the first 2 years.

  (ii) Calculate the value of the shares at the end of the 3rd year.

  (iii) Calculate the value of the shares at the end of the 4th year.

6 Jonathan invests €3000 for 3 years with the condition that he cannot withdraw any money until the end of the 3rd year. The interest rate for each year is shown in the table.

Year	AER
1	6%
2	4%
3	2.5%

Calculate the value of the investment after 3 years.

7 Ciara invests €2000 for 6 years with the condition that she cannot withdraw any money until the end of the 6th year.

The interest rate for each year is shown in the table.

Year	AER
1 & 2	4%
3 & 4	3.5%
5 & 6	2%

Calculate the value of the investment after 6 years.

8 A production machine was bought at a cost of €257 000. If the machine depreciated at a rate of 12% in the first year and a rate of 10% in the second year, calculate the value of the machine after two years.

9 A car was bought new for €32 800. At the end of the first year, the car had depreciated by 18%.

(i) Calculate the value of the car at the end of the first year.

At the end of the second year, the car was sold for €23 130.

(ii) Calculate the depreciation rate (%) of the car for the second year, correct to the nearest percentage.

10 Eibhlinn's house depreciated by 8% over a two-year period.

(i) At the end of this two-year period, the house was worth €203 136. Calculate the original value of the house.

Eibhlinn sold the house a year later for a price of €192 979.

(ii) Calculate the total depreciation rate (%) of the house, as a percentage of the original value of the house.

11 Find the interest rate for each case in the table, correct to the nearest percentage.

	Investment amount	Final amount	No. of years
(i)	€26 800	€33 834.38	4
(ii)	€9100	€11 463.38	3
(iii)	€210 000	€281 027.37	5

12 Find the value of the principal amount in each of the following cases, correct to the nearest euro.

	Investment amount at end	AER	No. of years
(i)	€1102.5	5%	2
(ii)	€3156.19	6%	3
(iii)	€5512.50	5%	2
(iv)	€72 081.30	12.5%	5

13 Scott and his wife invested a certain amount of money in the bank at an interest rate of 6% AER for 4 years. If the final investment was worth €1966.19, calculate the principal amount invested.

14 Mia invested €x at an interest rate of 5.5% AER for 5 years. At the end of the 5 years, the value of the investment was €8560.59. Calculate the principal amount invested by Mia.

15 €4000 was invested for 2 years at r% compound interest. A tax of 20% was deducted each year from the interest gained. At the end of the first year, the investment amounted to €4135, after tax was deducted.

(i) Calculate the rate of interest r%.

(ii) Find the amount of the investment to the nearest % at the end of 2 years, after tax has been deducted.

Section 15C Income Tax

In *Connect with Maths 1*, we solved basic income tax and net income problems. These problems were based on the Irish income tax system where the standard rate of tax of 20% was applied to all gross pay.

Key Points

Recall:

Words	Meaning
Wage	A **wage** is the amount of money an employee is paid based on the number of hours they work.
Salary	A **salary** is the amount of money an employee is paid regardless of the number of hours they work.
Gross salary/ Gross pay	Income before deductions is called **gross salary** or **gross pay**.
Gross tax	**Gross tax** is the amount of tax owed to the Government before tax credits are deducted.
Tax credits	A tax credit is a sum deducted from the gross tax that a person pays.
Tax payable	**Tax payable** is also called tax due. It is calculated using the formula: **Tax payable = Gross tax − Tax credits**
Net income	Net income is also called net pay or take-home pay. It is calculated using the formula: **Net income = Gross salary − Tax payable**

Standard Rate Cut-Off Point (SRCOP)

Two rates of income tax apply in Ireland:

- The standard rate which applies to the lower part of income up to a certain level
- The higher rate which applies to income above this level.

The Standard Rate Cut-Off Point (SRCOP) is the amount of income up to which a person pays tax at the standard rate.

The lower rate of tax is 20% and the higher rate is 41%. The standard rate cut-off point for a single person is €32 800 (2014 figures).

For example, a single person earning €45 000 will pay:

- 20% tax on the first €32 800; and
- 41% on the remainder, i.e. €45 000 − €32 800 = €12 200.

Visually, this information can be represented as:

The example below shows how to calculate the net pay for a couple who earn more than the standard rate cut-off point.

Example 1

A couple earn a total of €87 000 per annum. The standard rate cut-off point is €65 600 and their tax credits total €3300.

(i) Calculate the gross tax for the year by completing the table below.

Tax rate	Amount charged at this rate	Gross tax due
Standard rate of tax @ 20%	€65 600	
Higher rate of tax @ 41% on balance		
Gross tax due		

(ii) Calculate the tax payable for the year.
(iii) Calculate their net income for the year.

Solution

(i) The gross tax is calculated as shown.

Tax rate	Amount charged at this rate	Gross tax due
Standard rate of tax @ 20%	€65 600	€65 600 × 20% = €65 600 × 0.2 = €13 120
Higher rate of tax @ 41% on balance	Balance: €87 000 − €65 600 = €21 400	€21 400 × 41% = €21 400 × 0.41 = €8774
Gross tax due		€13 120 + €8774 = €21 894

(ii) Tax payable = Gross tax − tax credits
= €21 894 − €3300 = €18 594

(ii) Net income/pay = Gross pay − Tax payable
= €87 000 − €18 594
= €68 406

Statutory and Non-statutory Deductions

In reality, PAYE (Pay As You Earn) workers pay other statutory and non-statutory deductions which are deducted from their pay slip.

Statutory deductions are monies deducted from a person's gross income that have to be paid to the State.

Statutory deductions include:

- **PAYE** stands for Pay As You Earn and is used to pay for public services, i.e. healthcare, education, gardaí, infrastructure, etc. PAYE is a tax charged on gross income at a standard rate of 20% and at a higher rate of 41% on the balance.

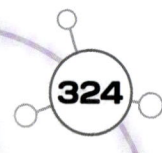

- **PRSI** stands for Pay Related Social Insurance. A PRSI contribution is paid by employers and employees (normally 4% for Class A1 workers) towards social welfare benefits, State old age pensions and a National Training Fund levy.
- **USC** stands for Universal Social Charge and replaced the health and income levies from 2011. These charges cover employees for various social welfare benefits and medical benefits. USC is charged at three different rates for PAYE workers: 2%, 4% and 7%.
- The 2014 rates for PAYE, PRSI and USC in Ireland are listed in the table.

Deduction	Single person	Single/Widowed or a surviving civil partner qualifying for one-parent family tax credit	Married couple or in civil partnership with 2 incomes	Married couple or in civil partnership with 1 income
PAYE (Pay As You Earn)	Personal tax credits of €1650 **Income tax rate:** 20% on first €32 800; 41% on the balance	Personal tax credits of €1650 **Income tax rate:** 20% on first €36 800; 41% on the balance	Tax credits of €3300 **Income tax rate:** 20% on the first €65 600; 41% on the balance	Tax credits of €3300 **Income tax rate:** 20% on the first €41 800; 41% on the balance
PRSI (Pay Related Social Insurance)	Class A1 PRSI is charged at 4% when you earn more than €352 per week, €1525.33 per month or €18 304 per annum			

	Rate	Income band
USC (Universal Social Charge)	2%	Up to €10 036
	4%	Between €10 036 and €16 016 (€5980)
	7%	Greater than €16 016
	Note: An individual earning less than €10 036 will not pay USC.	

Non-statutory deductions are deductions from a person's gross income that are voluntary.

Non-statutory deductions include:
- Union fees
- Private health insurance
- Private pension schemes
- Saving accounts.

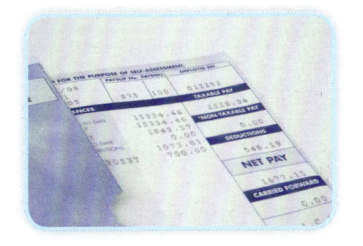

Example 2

Peter earns €50 500. He pays PAYE, PRSI and USC statutory deductions on his gross pay. He also pays a non-statutory deduction of €980 per annum on private health insurance.

(i) Find his PAYE/gross tax for the year by completing the table below.

PAYE rate	Amount charged at this rate	PAYE due
Standard rate of tax @ 20%	€32 800	
Higher rate of tax @ 41% on balance		
Total PAYE due		

(ii) Find the tax payable for the year, if his tax credits are €1650.

(iii) Find his PRSI for the year by completing the table below.

PRSI rate	Amount charged at this rate	PRSI due
4% on gross income over €18 304		

(iv) Find his USC for the year, by completing the table below.

USC rate	Amount charged at this rate	USC due
2% up to €10 036	€10 036	
4% on next €5980	€5980	
7% on balance		
Total USC due		

(v) Calculate the total deductions for the year.

(vi) Calculate Peter's net income for the year.

Solution

(i) PAYE/gross tax is charged at 20% for the first €32 800 earned and 41% on the balance.

PAYE rate	Amount charged at this rate	PAYE due
Standard rate of tax @ 20%	€32 800	€32 800 × 20% = €32 800 × 0.2 = €6560
Higher rate of tax @ 41% on balance	Balance: €50 500 − €32 800 = €17 700	€17 700 × 41% = €17 700 × 0.41 = €7257
	Total PAYE due	= €6560 + €7257 = €13 817

(ii) Tax payable = Gross tax − Tax credits = €13 817 − €1650 = €12 167

(iii) PRSI charges:

PRSI rate	Amount charged at this rate	PRSI due
4% on gross income over €18 304	€50 500 − €18 304 = €32 196	€32 196 × 4% = €32 196 × 0.04 = €1287.84

(iv) USC charges:

USC rate	Amount charged at this rate	USC due
2% up to €10 036	€10 036	€10 036 × 2% = €10 036 × 0.02 = €200.72
4% on next €5980	€5980	€5980 × 4% = €5980 × 0.04 = €239.20
7% on balance	Balance: €50 500 − €16 016 = €34 484	€34 484 × 7% = €34 484 × 0.07 = €2413.88
Total USC due		€200.72 + €239.20 + €2413.88 = €2853.80

(v) Total deductions = Tax payable + PRSI + USC + Health insurance policy
 = €12 167 + €1287.84 + €2853.80 + €980 = €17 288.64

(vi) Net income = €50 500 − €17 288.64 = €33 211.36

Example 3

Eileen pays €14 432 gross tax on her PAYE contribution. Her tax credits amount to €1650 and her SRCOP is €32 800. The standard rate of tax is 20% and the higher rate of tax is 41%.

(i) Calculate her gross salary from her gross tax.
(ii) Calculate the tax payable for her PAYE contribution.
(iii) Calculate her PRSI contribution if she is a Class A1 PRSI worker (4% of gross salary).
(vi) Calculate her USC contributions.
(v) Calculate her net income.

Solution

(i) Let €x = amount charged at 41% tax

(€32 800 @ 20%) + (€x @ 41%) = Gross tax

$\Rightarrow$ (€32 800 × 0.2) + (€x × 0.41) = €14 432

$\Rightarrow$ €6560 + 0.41x = €14 432 .... expand brackets

$\Rightarrow$ 0.41x = €14 432 − €6560 .... subtract €6560

$\Rightarrow$ $x = \dfrac{€7872}{0.41}$ .... divide by 0.41

$\Rightarrow$ x = €19 200

Gross salary = €32 800 + €19 200 = €52 000

(ii) Tax Payable = Gross tax on PAYE − tax credits = €14 432 − €1650 = €12 782

(iii) PRSI = (Gross salary − €18 304) × 4%
      = (€52 000 − €18 304) × 0.04
      = €33 696 × 0.04
      = €1347.84

(iv)

USC rate	Amount charged at this rate	USC due
2% up to €10 036	€10 036	€10 036 × 2% = €10 036 × 0.02 = €200.72
4% on next €5980	€5980	€5980 × 4% = €5980 × 0.04 = €239.20
7% on balance	Balance: €52 000 − €16 016 = €35 984	€35 984 × 7% = €35 984 × 0.07 = €2518.88
Total USC due		€200.72 + €239.20 + €2518.88 = €2958.80

(v) Net income
    €52 000 − €12 782 − €1347.84 − €2958.80
    = €34 911.36

Activity 15.3

When dealing with money in this section, we always round answers to the nearest cent, i.e. two decimal places.

Use the following table to help answer the questions below, if necessary.

Tax rate	Amount charged at this rate	Gross tax due
Standard rate of tax @ 20%		
Higher rate of tax @ 41% on balance		
Gross tax due		

1. A married couple with one income earn a total of €1450 per week. The standard rate cut-off point is €1262 and their tax credits total €63.46 per week.

   (i) Calculate the gross tax per week.
   (ii) Calculate the tax payable per week.
   (iii) Calculate the net income per week.
   (iv) Calculate the couple's net income for the year.

2 For each of the situations described in the table:
  (i) calculate the gross tax for the year
  (ii) calculate the tax payable for the year
  (iii) calculate the net income for the year.

Scenario	Income details
A	Niamh is a solicitor who earns a total of €93 000 per annum. She is the sole earner of a married couple. Her standard rate cut-off point is €41 800 and her tax credits total €3300.
B	A farmer earns a total of €47 000 per annum. He is the sole earner of a married couple. The standard rate cut-off point is €41 800 and his tax credits total €3300.
C	A couple have a combined earning of €72 000. Their standard rate cut-off point is €65 600 and their tax credits total €3300.

3 For each of the situations described in the table:
  (i) calculate the gross tax per week/month
  (ii) calculate the tax payable per week/month
  (iii) calculate the net income per week/month.

Scenario	Income details
A	John's weekly wage is €570 and he has tax credits of €31.73. His standard rate cut-off point is €630.77 per week.
B	A carpenter earns a total of €3800 per month. The standard rate cut-off point is €3483.33 and his tax credits total €275 per month.
C	A couple have a combined earning of €5990 per month and tax credits of €275. They have a standard rate cut-off point of €5466.67.

4 Siobhán has tax credits of €1650. She pays €7000 income tax. Her standard rate cut-off point is €32 800. The standard rate of tax is 20% and the higher rate is 41%.
  (i) Calculate the total amount of her income charged at the higher rate of 41%. Give your answer to the nearest cent.
  (ii) Calculate her gross income.

5 A woman pays income tax of €11 000 and her tax credits are €3300. She is the sole earner of a married couple. Her standard rate cut-off point is €41 800. The standard rate of tax is 20% and the higher rate is 41%.
  (i) Calculate the total amount of her income charged at the higher rate of tax. Give your answer to the nearest cent.
  (ii) Calculate her salary before any deductions.

6 Orla has a standard rate cut-off point of €32 800 and tax credits of €1650 for the year. She has a gross income of €34 650 for the year. The standard rate of income tax is 20% and the higher rate is 41%.
  (i) What is Orla's net income for the year?
  (ii) Orla's net income changes to €29 379. What is Orla's new gross income for the year?

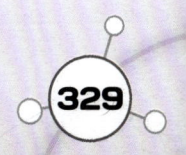

7. Martin's gross income is €38 000 and his gross income tax amounts to €8692. The standard rate cut-off point is €32 800. The standard rate of tax is 20% and the higher rate is 41%. His take-home pay is €30 958.

   (i) What are Martin's tax credits for the year?

   Martin gets an increase in gross pay such that his gross income tax amounts to €10 455.

   (ii) Calculate Martin's new gross income.

   (iii) What is Martin's new take-home pay for the year?

8. Kathy has a gross income of €75 000. The standard rate of tax is 20% and the higher rate is 41%. The SRCOP is €36 800 and she has a tax credit of €1650.

   (i) What is Kathy's net tax for the year?

   (ii) What is Kathy's take-home pay for the year?

   Kathy's take-home pay increases to €57 404.

   (iii) Calculate Kathy's new gross income.

Use the following tables as a guide in questions 9 to 13.

PRSI rate	Amount charged at this rate	PRSI due
4% on gross income over €18 304		

USC rate	Amount charged at this rate	USC due
2% up to €10 036	€10 036	
4% on next €5980	€5980	
7% on balance		
	Total USC due	

9. Calculate how much PRSI and USC each of the following people pays per year.

   (i) Susan is a part-time hairdresser who earns €18 000 per year.

   (ii) Clare is a receptionist who earns €26 000 per year.

   (iii) Mark is an engineer who earns €59 000 per year.

   (iv) Conor is an accountant who earns €87 000 per year.

10. Peter earns €57 350. He pays PAYE, PRSI and USC statutory deductions on his gross pay. His pay is subject to a non-statutory deduction of €1350 per annum on private health insurance. PAYE is charged at standard 20% on his standard rate cut-off point of €32 800 and the remainder of his income is charged at 41%.

    (i) Find his PAYE/gross tax for the year.

    (ii) Find the tax payable for the year, if his tax credits are €1650.

    (iii) Find his PRSI for the year, by copying and completing the PRSI table given above.

    (iv) Find his USC for the year, by copying and completing the USC table given above.

    (v) Calculate the total deductions for the year.

    (vi) Calculate Peter's net income for the year.

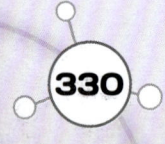

11. Frank and his wife have a combined gross income of €93 000. There are PAYE, PRSI and USC statutory deductions on their gross pay. Their pay is also subject to a non-statutory deduction of €760 per annum on union fees. PAYE is charged at 20% on their standard rate cut-off point of €65 600 and the remainder of their income is charged at 41%.

   (i) Calculate their PAYE/gross tax for the year.
   (ii) Calculate their tax payable for the year, if their tax credits are €3300.
   (iii) Calculate their PRSI for the year, by copying and completing the PRSI table given previously.
   (iv) Calculate their USC for the year, by copying and completing the USC table given previously.
   (v) Calculate the total deductions for the year.
   (vi) Calculate their net income for the year.

12. A man earns €1230 per week. He pays PAYE, PRSI and USC statutory deductions on his gross pay. His pay is subject to a non-statutory deduction of €28 per week on private health insurance. PAYE is charged at a standard rate of 20% on his SRCOP of €630.77 and the remainder of his income is charged at 41%.

    (i) Find his PAYE/gross tax for the week.
    (ii) Find the tax payable for the week, if his tax credits are €31.73 per week.
    (iii) Find his PRSI for the week.
    (iv) Find his USC for the week.
    (v) Calculate the total deductions for the week.
    (vi) Calculate the net income for the week.
    (vii) Based on your calculations, how much does the man earn in a year?

13. Tommy is a married man and the only earner in the home. He earns €6200 per month. He pays PAYE, PRSI and USC statutory deductions on his gross pay. His pay is subject to deductions of €150 per month on private health insurance and €230 per month on a saving scheme. Income tax is charged at 20% on his standard rate cut-off point of €3483.33 per month and the remainder of his income is charged at 41%.

    (i) Calculate his PAYE/gross tax for the month.
    (ii) Calculate the tax payable for the month, if his tax credits are €275 per month.
    (iii) Calculate his PRSI for the month.
    (iv) Calculate his USC for the month.
    (v) Calculate the total deductions for the month.
    (vi) Calculate Tommy's net income for the month.

14. Karen pays €14 068 gross tax on her PAYE contribution. She is a single parent so her tax credits amount to €1650 and her SRCOP is €36 800. The standard rate of tax is 20% and the higher rate of tax is 41%.

    (i) Calculate her gross salary from her gross tax.
    (ii) Calculate the tax payable for her PAYE contribution.
    (iii) Calculate her PRSI contribution if she is a Class A1 PRSI worker.
    (iv) Calculate her USC contributions.
    (v) Calculate her net income.

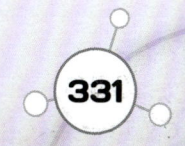

15 Paul pays €21 238 gross tax on his PAYE contribution. His tax credits amount to €1650 and his SRCOP is €32 800. He also pays €850 per year on private health insurance which is deducted from his pay. The standard rate of tax is 20% and the higher rate of tax is 41%.

(i) Calculate his gross salary.

(ii) Calculate his take-home pay after all deductions are made.

Revision Activity 15

1. (a) What is profit (reference cost and selling price)?
   (b) What is loss (reference cost and selling price)?
   (c) How do you calculate % profit?
   (d) How do you calculate % loss?
   (e) What is the difference between mark-up and margin?

2. A shop buys a set of branded suitcases for €150. They resell the suitcases for €225. Calculate the:
   (a) % profit
   (b) Margin
   (c) Mark-up.
   (d) What do you notice about the value of the margin compared with the mark-up? Can you explain why this is the case?

3. A retailer sells two litres of car engine antifreeze and coolant concentrate for €19.49. There is a 50% profit margin on this product.
   (a) Calculate the actual cost price of the antifreeze and coolant concentrate, to the nearest cent.
   (b) Calculate the mark-up on the antifreeze and coolant concentrate.

4. Oscar borrows €10 000 for three years at 6% per annum compound interest.
   He repays €2700 at the end of each of the first two years.

   (a) How much must he repay at the end of the third year to clear his loan?

   He extends the duration of the loan to 5 years. Hence, he pays off the remainder of the loan in equal instalments at the end of the 4th and 5th years. The rate remains at 6% per annum compound interest.

   (b) How much would he need to repay, at the end of each year, to clear his loan at the end of 5 years? Give your answer correct to the nearest cent.
   (c) What was the total amount of interest Oscar paid for this loan?

   Hint
   > Calculate the interest paid per year.

5. €12 000 was invested for 2 years. The interest rate for the first year was 4%.
   (a) Calculate the amount of the investment at the end of the first year.
   At the end of the second year the investment amounted to €13 228.80.
   (b) Calculate the interest rate for the second year.

6. Dermot has €5000 and would like to invest it for two years. A special savings account offers a rate of 3% for the first year and a higher rate for the second year, if the money is retained in the account. Tax of 33% will be deducted each year from the interest earned.

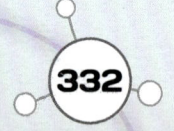

(a) How much will the investment be worth at the end of one year, after tax is deducted?

(b) Dermot calculates that, after tax has been deducted, his investment will be worth about €5268 at the end of the second year. Calculate the rate of interest for the second year.

JCHL 2014 Sample Paper

7 Siobhán and her husband have a combined income of €57 500 between them and tax credits of €3300. Their standard rate cut-off point is €65 600, the standard rate of tax is 20% and higher rate is 41%.

(a) Calculate the net tax payable.

(b) Calculate their net income.

8 A woman pays income tax of €11 000 and her tax credits are €3300, as she is the sole earner of a married couple. Her standard rate cut-off point is €41 800, the standard rate of tax is 20% and higher rate is 41%.

(a) Calculate the total amount of her income charged at the higher rate of tax. Give your answer to the nearest cent.

(b) Calculate her salary before any deductions.

9 The standard rate of income tax is 20% and the higher rate is 41% for both Matthew and his brother.

Matthew has tax credits of €1650 for the year and a standard rate cut-off point of €32 800. His gross income for the year is €37 500.

(a) Calculate the total tax payable by Matthew for the year.

Matthew's brother James has tax credits of €3300 for the year and a standard rate cut-off point of €41 800. His gross tax for the year is €12 542. As he is married and is the sole earner, his tax credits are twice as much as Matthew's.

(b) Calculate James' gross income.

(c) What is James' take-home pay?

Exam-style Questions

1 The minimum wage per hour for different categories of workers is shown in the table. By law the under-18 minimum wage is set at 70% of the minimum wage for an experienced adult worker.

Category	Min. wage per hour
Experienced adult worker	€8.65
Aged under 18	€6.06
Over 18 in first year from date of first employment	€6.92
Over 18 in second year of first employment	€7.79
Source: www.citizensinformation.ie	

(a) Verify that this is true for the rates shown in the table.

(b) The government has decided that it is going to reduce all minimum wage rates by 6%. Calculate the new minimum wage for an experienced adult worker, correct to two decimal places, after this reduction.

(c) John is an experienced adult worker. After the reduction, he says 'If the minimum wage were to be increased by 6%, then I would be back earning €8.65 per hour.' Is John's statement correct? Explain your answer.

JCHL 2013

2 The USC (Universal Social Charge) is calculated on gross income. The rates of the USC are:
- 2% on the first €10 036 of gross annual income
- 4% on the next €5980
- 7% on the balance.

(a) Niamh earned €45 000 in 2011. Find her USC for that year.

The table shows a selection of the tax credits available in Ireland in 2011.

Individual's tax credits	Tax credit 2011
Single person	€1650
Married or civil partner	€3300
Widowed or surviving civil partner	€2190
Home carer	€810
PAYE	€1650
One-parent family	€1650

(b) Niamh is a single person who is a PAYE worker. Calculate her total tax credits for 2011.

(c) The standard rate of tax is 20% and the higher rate is 41%. The standard rate cut-off point for a single person is €32 800. Calculate Niamh's tax bill for 2011.

(d) Calculate Niamh's net pay for the year, after tax and USC are paid.

JCHL 2012

KEY WORDS AND PHRASES

- Selling price
- Cost price
- Profit
- Loss
- Percentage profit
- Percentage loss
- Mark-up
- Margin
- Wage
- Salary
- Gross pay/salary/income
- Gross tax
- Tax credits
- Compound interest
- Depreciation
- APR (Annual Percentage Rate)
- AER (Annual Equivalent Rate)
- Standard rate of tax
- Higher rate of tax
- Pay As You Earn (PAYE)
- Standard Rate Cut-Off Point (SRCOP)
- Tax payable/tax due
- Universal Social Charge (USC)
- Pay Related Social Insurance (PRSI)
- Statutory deductions
- Non-statutory deductions
- Net income/pay or take-home pay

Chapter Summary 15

Profit and Loss

- The **percentage profit or loss** formulae are:

$$\% \text{ Profit} = \frac{\text{Profit amount}}{\text{Cost price}} \times 100$$

$$\% \text{ Loss} = \frac{\text{Loss amount}}{\text{Cost price}} \times 100$$

Mark-up

Mark-up is the profit as a percentage (%) of the **cost price**.

$$\text{Mark-up} = \frac{\text{Profit}}{\text{Cost price}} \times 100$$

Margin

Margin is the profit as a percentage (%) of the **selling price**.

$$\text{Margin} = \frac{\text{Profit}}{\text{Selling Price}} \times 100$$

Compound Interest

- The compound interest formula states:

$F = P(1 + i)^t$ …found on page 30 of the *Formulae and Tables* booklet

Income Tax

Gross pay is taxed at two different rates:

- **the 'standard rate' of 20%** which is applied to all earnings up to the standard rate cut-off point of €32 800; and
- **the 'higher rate' of 41%** applied to the balance of the gross pay.
- PRSI and USC are deducted from gross pay.

Chapter 16

Functions

Learning Outcomes

In this chapter, you will learn about:
- Linear and quadratic functions
- Applications of linear and quadratic functions
- Exponential functions and their applications
- Transformations of functions

Section 16A Quadratic Functions

A **function** is a special relation in which no two couples have the same first element.

On an arrow diagram, we have a function if **exactly one** arrow leaves each element of the input set A.

- The **domain** of a function is the set which has all the inputs, e.g. in this example the domain = $\{-2, -1, 0, 1, 2\}$.
- The **codomain** is the set which contains all the **possible** outputs, e.g. in this example the codomain = $\{0, 1, 2, 3, 4\}$.
- The **range** is the set of **actual** outputs, e.g. in this example the range = $\{0, 1, 4\}$.

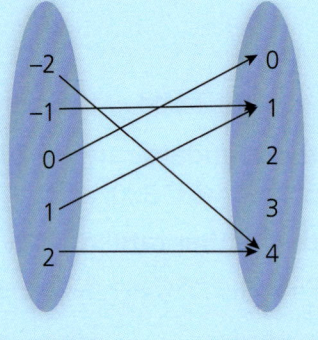

Inputs (x's)   Outputs (y's)

We generally label functions using letters. As the word function begins with the letter f, that letter is commonly used to refer to functions. However, if we have more than one function in a question, then we also use other letters, e.g. g, h, k, etc. Words are also used to name functions.

Functions can be referred to using the following notation:

$f(x) =$ pronounced 'f of x'

$f: x \to$ pronounced 'f such that x is mapped onto'

$y =$

So the function: $f(x) = 2x^2 - 3x + 6$ can also be written as

$$f: x \to 2x^2 - 3x + 6$$

or $y = 2x^2 - 3x + 6$

This section will help to revise quadratic functions which we have met already. We will also look at quadratic functions of the form $f(x) = ax^2 + bx + c$ where $a < 0$.

In Example 1, we look at the function $f(x) = x^2$, which is the simplest quadratic function.

Example 1

(i) Graph the function
   $f: x \to x^2$ in the domain $-3 \leq x \leq 3$, $x \in \mathbb{R}$.

(ii) Find the range of values of x for which $f(x)$ is increasing.

(iii) Find the range of values of x for which $f(x)$ is decreasing.

(iv) Find the minimum point of the graph.

(v) Find the minimum value of $y = f(x)$.

(vi) Write down the equation of the axis of symmetry of the graph.

Solution

(i) Make an input/output table.

Input: x	Output: $y = f(x)$	Couples
−3	$(−3)^2 = 9$	(−3, 9)
−2	$(−2)^2 = 4$	(−2, 4)
−1	$(−1)^2 = 1$	(−1, 1)
0	$(0)^2 = 0$	(0, 0)
1	$(1)^2 = 1$	(1, 1)
2	$(2)^2 = 4$	(2, 4)
3	$(3)^2 = 9$	(3, 9)

Draw the graph.

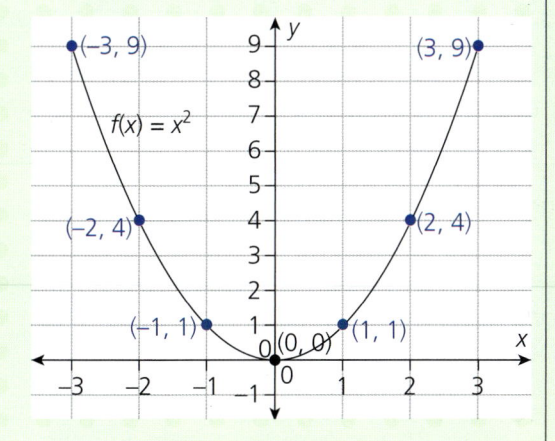

(ii) The function (y-value) is increasing if the graph (y-value) is rising as you read from **left to right**. The function is increasing for $x > 0$.

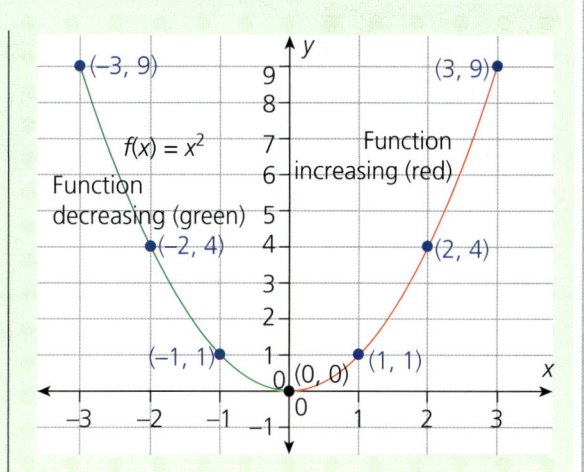

(iii) The function (y-value) is decreasing if the graph is 'falling' as you read from **left to right**.

The function $f(x)$ is decreasing for $x < 0$.

(iv) The minimum point on the graph is (0, 0).

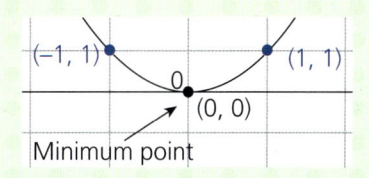

(v) The minimum value of $y = f(x) = 0$.

(vi) To find the axis of symmetry, draw a vertical line through the minimum point of the graph.

The axis of symmetry for $f(x) = x^2$ is the y-axis, i.e. the line $x = 0$.

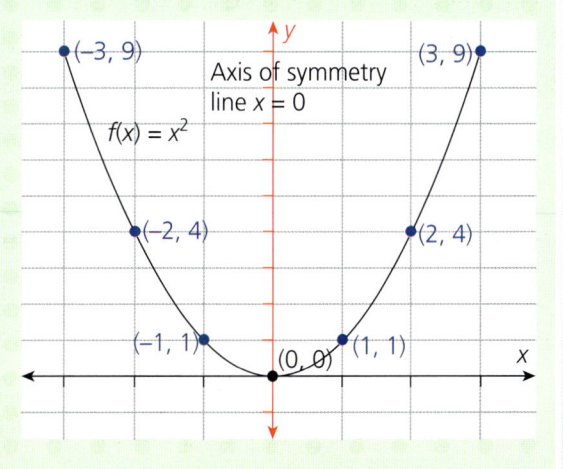

The shape of this graph is known as a **parabola**. Parabolas are seen in many everyday objects such as the reflectors of car headlights, satellite dishes, etc.

Example 2

(i) Graph the function $g: x \to -x^2$ in the domain $-3 \leq x \leq 3$.
(ii) Compare and contrast this graph with the graph of $f(x) = x^2$.
(iii) Find the maximum point of the graph.
(iv) Find the maximum value of the function (i.e. the maximum y-value).
(v) Find the range of values of x for which $f(x)$ is increasing.
(vi) Find the range of values of x for which $f(x)$ is decreasing.
(vii) Write down the equation of the axis of symmetry of the graph.

Solution

(i) Make an input/output table.

Input: x	Output: $y = g(x)$	Couples
−3	$-(-3)^2 = -9$	(−3, −9)
−2	$-(-2)^2 = -4$	(−2, −4)
−1	$-(-1)^2 = -1$	(−1, −1)
0	$(0)^2 = 0$	(0, 0)
1	$-(1)^2 = -1$	(1, −1)
2	$-(2)^2 = -4$	(2, −4)
3	$-(3)^2 = -9$	(3, −9)

Draw the graph.

(ii) This graph of $g(x) = -x^2$ is the image of the graph of $f(x) = x^2$ by axial symmetry in the x-axis. It is also a parabola. It has a maximum point.

(iii) The maximum point of the graph is (0, 0).

(iv) The maximum value of the function (maximum y-value) is 0.

(v) The function $g(x)$ is increasing for $x < 0$.

(vi) The function $g(x)$ is decreasing for $x > 0$.

(vii) The axis of symmetry for $g(x) = -x^2$ is the y-axis. i.e. the line $x = 0$.

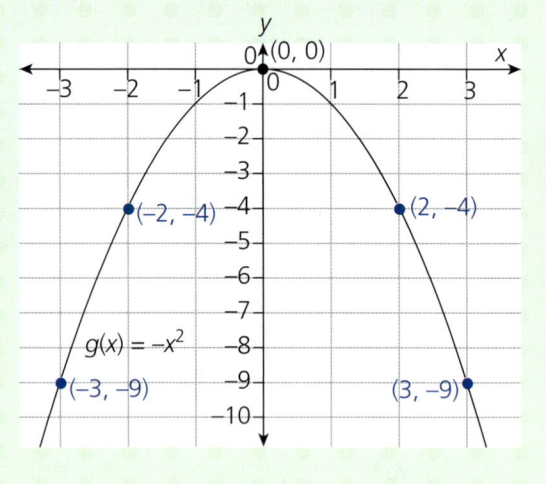

Note from Examples 1 and 2 how the coefficient of x^2 determines the shape of the graph.

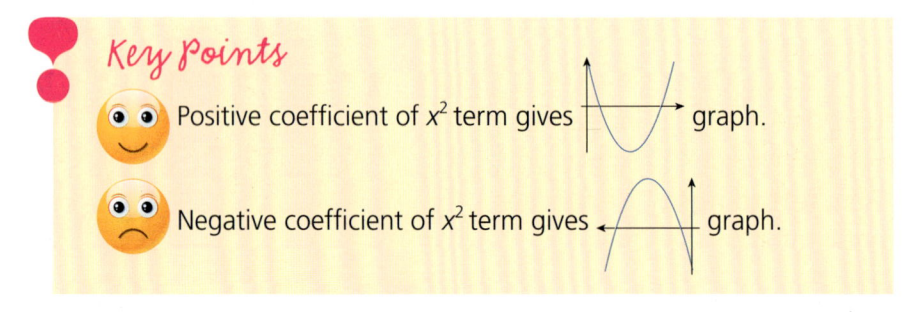

Key Points

Positive coefficient of x^2 term gives ⋃ graph.

Negative coefficient of x^2 term gives ⋂ graph.

Example 3

(i) Graph the function $h: x \to 4 + 3x - 2x^2$ in the domain $-2 \leq x \leq 4$, $x \in \mathbb{R}$.

Use your graph to estimate:

(ii) $h(3.5)$

(iii) the values of x for which $h(x) = -3$

(iv) the roots of the equation $4 + 3x - 2x^2 = 0$

(v) the range of values of x for which $h(x) > 0$.

Solution

(i) Make an input/output table.

Input: x	Function: $4 + 3x - 2x^2$	Output: $y = h(x)$	Couples
−2	$4 + 3(-2) - 2(-2)^2$	−10	(−2, −10)
−1	$4 + 3(-1) - 2(-1)^2$	−1	(−1, −1)
0	$4 + 3(0) - 2(0)^2$	4	(0, 4)
1	$4 + 3(1) - 2(1)^2$	5	(1, 5)
2	$4 + 3(2) - 2(2)^2$	2	(2, 2)
3	$4 + 3(3) - 2(3)^2$	−5	(3, −5)
4	$4 + 3(4) - 2(4)^2$	−16	(4, −16)

Draw the graph.

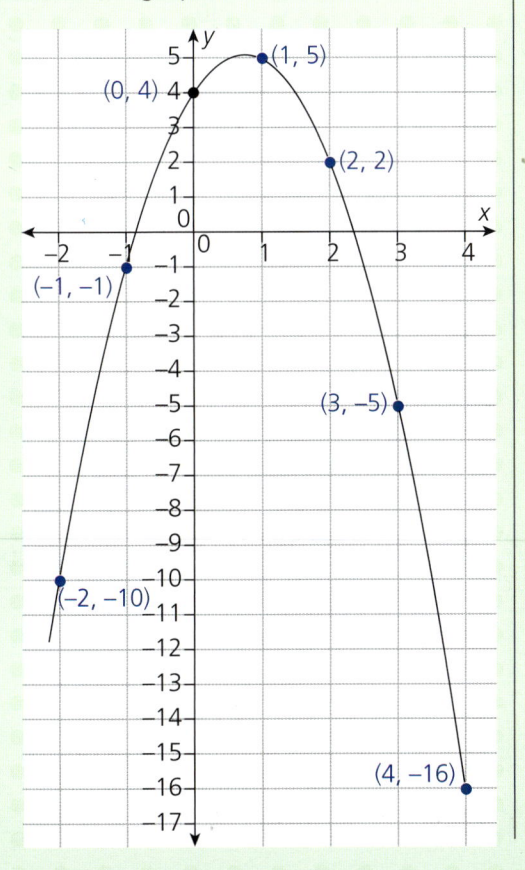

(ii) $h(3.5)$ = the **value of y** when $x = 3.5$.
- Go to 3.5 on the x-axis.
- Draw a vertical line to meet the graph.
- Follow horizontally to meet the y-axis.

$h(3.5) = -10$

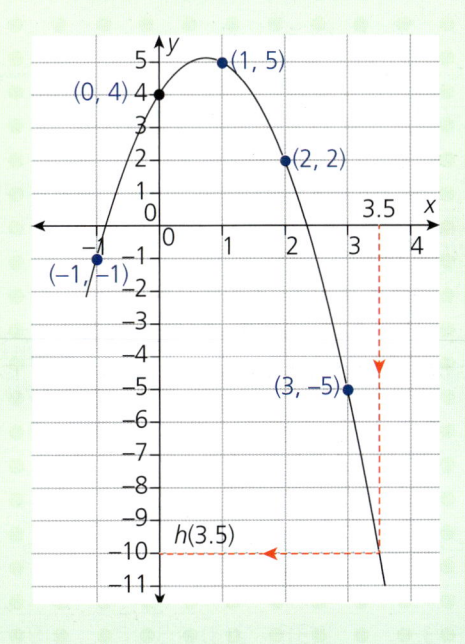

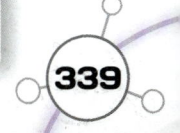

(iii) $h(x) = -3$ means that $y = -3$.

We are looking for the **values of x** which give a y-value of -3.
- Find the points where the line $y = -3$ meets the graph.
- Draw vertical lines on each side to meet the x-axis.
- Read the x values.

$h(x) = -3$ for $x = -1.25$ and 2.8.

(iv) The x-values that give a y-value of zero are the 'roots' of the equation.

The roots of the equation $h(x) = 4 + 3x - 2x^2 = 0$ are found where the graph intersects the x-axis.

The roots are -0.9 and 2.4 approx.

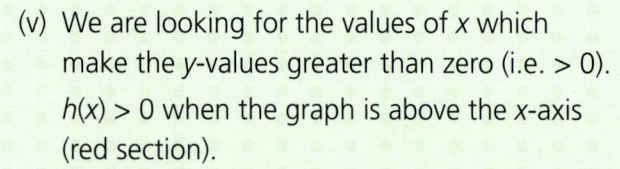

(v) We are looking for the values of x which make the y-values greater than zero (i.e. > 0).

$h(x) > 0$ when the graph is above the x-axis (red section).

The range of values of x is $-0.9 < x < 2.4$.

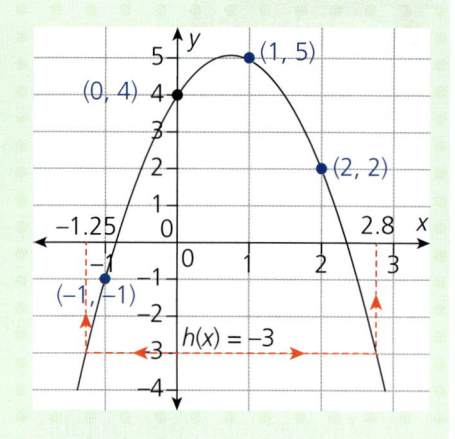

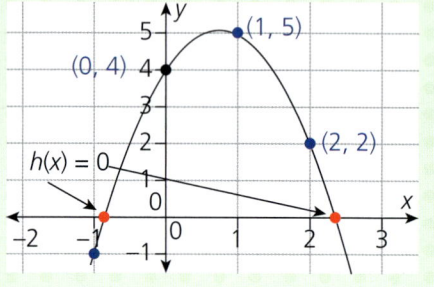

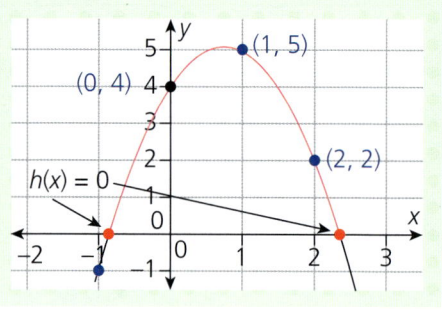

Example 4

(i) Using the same axes and scales, draw the graphs of

$f: x \to 2x^2 - 2x - 3$

$g: x \to 2 - 3x$

in the domain $-2 \leq x \leq 3$, $x \in \mathbb{R}$.

(ii) Use your graphs to estimate the values of x for which $f(x) = g(x)$.

Solution

(i) Make input/output tables.

Input: x	$f(x) = 2x^2 - 2x - 3$	Output: $y = f(x)$
-2	$2(-2)^2 - 2(-2) - 3$	9
-1	$2(-1)^2 - 2(-1) - 3$	1
0	$2(0)^2 - 2(0) - 3$	-3
1	$2(1)^2 - 2(1) - 3$	-3
2	$2(2)^2 - 2(2) - 3$	1
3	$2(3)^2 - 2(3) - 3$	9

Input: x	$g(x): 2 - 3x$	Output: $y = g(x)$
-2	$2 - 3(-2)$	8
0	$2 - 3(0)$	2
3	$2 - 3(3)$	-7

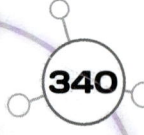

Draw the graphs.

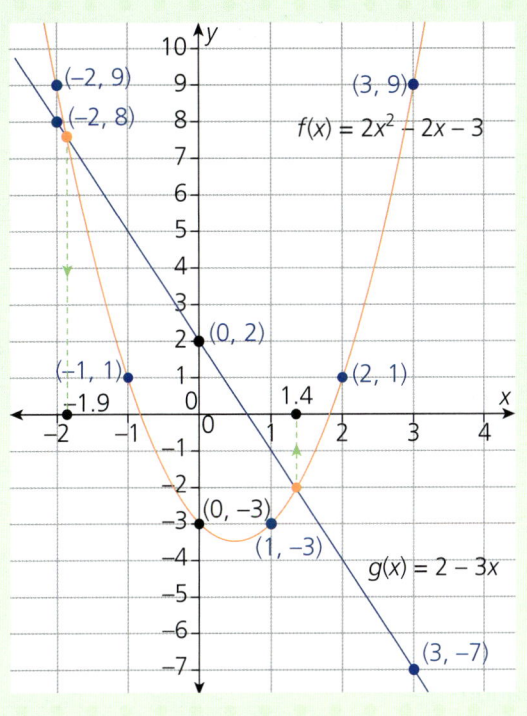

(ii) We want the values of x which give the same y-value for each function. f(x) = g(x) at the points where the graphs intersect. The x-values are −1.9 and 1.4 approx.

Example 5

Part of the quadratic function $y = x^2 + ax + b$ where $a, b \in \mathbb{Z}$ is shown.

The points $P(4, 6)$ and $Q(2, -2)$ are on the curve.

(i) Use the given points to form two equations in a and b.

(ii) Solve your equations to find the value of a and the value of b.

(iii) Write down the co-ordinates of the points where the curve crosses the y-axis.

(iv) Find the points where the curve crosses the x-axis. Give your answers correct to one place of decimals.

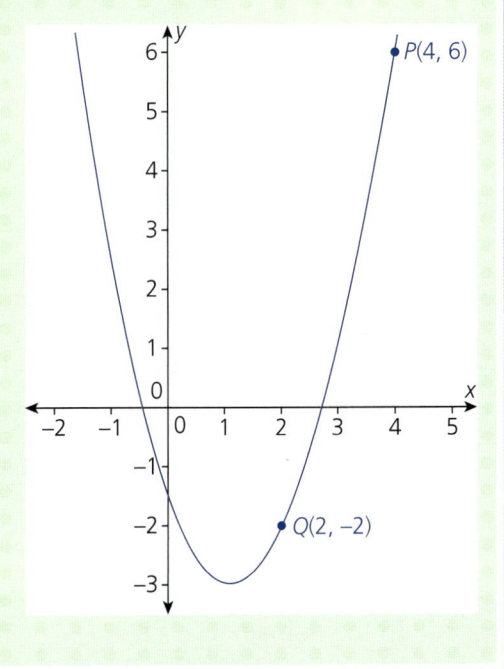

Solution

(i) $y = x^2 + ax + b$

$(4, 6) \in$ the curve

$\Rightarrow \quad 6 = (4)^2 + 4a + b$

$\Rightarrow \quad 6 = 16 + 4a + b$

$\Rightarrow 4a + b = -10 \ldots$ equation 1

$(2, -2) \in$ the curve

$\Rightarrow \quad -2 = (2)^2 + 2a + b$

$\Rightarrow \quad -2 = 4 + 2a + b$

$\Rightarrow -2a - b = 6 \ldots$ equation 2

(ii) Solve:

$4a + b = -10$

$-2a - b = 6$

Add $\Rightarrow 2a = -4$

$\Rightarrow a = -2$

Substitute into equation 1:

$4a + b = -10$

$\Rightarrow 4(-2) + b = -10$

$\Rightarrow \quad b = -10 + 8$

$\Rightarrow \quad b = -2$

Thus the function is $y = x^2 - 2x - 2$.

(iii) The curve crosses the y-axis where $x = 0$

$\Rightarrow y = 0 - 0 - 2 = -2$

i.e. at the point $(0, -2)$

(iv) The curve crosses the x-axis where $y = 0$

$\Rightarrow x^2 - 2x - 2 = 0$

Use the formula $x = \dfrac{-b \pm \sqrt{b^2 - 4ac}}{2a}$

$\Rightarrow x = \dfrac{+2 \pm \sqrt{(-2)^2 - 4(1)(-2)}}{2}$

$\Rightarrow x = \dfrac{+2 \pm \sqrt{4 + 8}}{2}$

$\Rightarrow x = \dfrac{+2 \pm \sqrt{12}}{2}$

$x = 2.73$ or -0.73 correct to two decimal places

$\Rightarrow$ the co-ordinates are $(2.73, 0)$ and $(-0.73, 0)$.

Activity 16.1

1 Let f be the function $f: x \to x^2 + 2x$.
  (i) Find the value of $f(5)$.
  (ii) Find the value of $f(2) - f(-2)$.
  (iii) Express $f(t)$ and $f(t + 1)$ in terms of t.
  (iv) Find the value of t for which $f(t) = f(t + 1)$.

2 $f: x \to 3x + k$ and $g: x \to 4x^2 - k$ are two functions defined on $\mathbb{R}$, where $k \in \mathbb{Z}$.
  (i) If $f(2) = 4$, find the value of k.
  (ii) Find the two values of x for which $f(x) + g(x) = 0$.

3 (i) Graph the function $f: x \to 10 + 2x - 2x^2$ in the domain $-3 \leq x \leq 3$.
  (ii) Find the maximum point of the graph.
  (iii) Find the range of values of x for which $f(x)$ is increasing.
  (iv) Find the range of values of x for which $f(x)$ is decreasing.
  (v) Draw in the axis of symmetry of the graph and write down its equation.

4 (i) Graph the function $f: x \to -2x^2 + 7x - 1$ in the domain $-2 \leq x \leq 4$, $x \in \mathbb{R}$.

Use your graph to estimate:
  (ii) $f(2.5)$
  (iii) the values of x for which $f(x) = 2.5$
  (iv) the roots of the equation $-2x^2 + 7x - 1 = 0$
  (v) the range of values of x for which $f(x) > 0$.

5. Part of the graph of the quadratic function $y = x^2 + bx + c$ where b and $c \in \mathbb{Z}$, is shown.

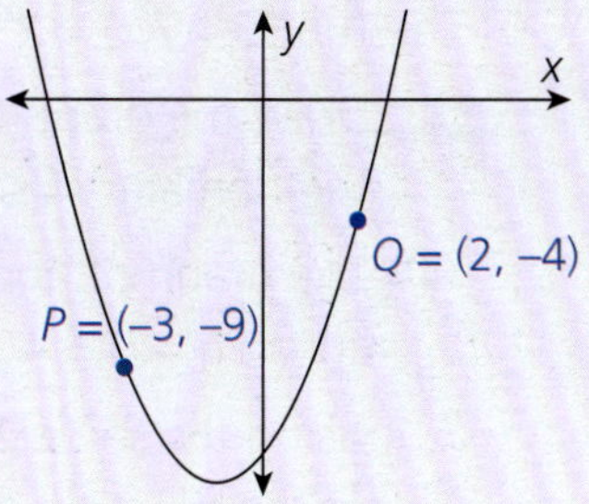

   The points $P(-3, -9)$ and $Q(2, -4)$ are on the curve.
   (i) Use the given points to form two equations in b and c.
   (ii) Solve your equations to find the value of b and the value of c.
   (iii) Write down the co-ordinates of the point where the curve intersects the y-axis.
   (iv) Find the points where the curve crosses the x-axis.
       Give your answers correct to one place of decimals.

6. Part of the graph of the quadratic function $y = ax^2 + bx + c$ where a, b and $c \in \mathbb{Z}$, is shown.

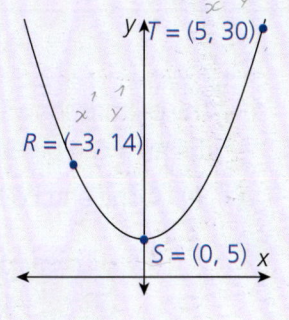

   The points $R(-3, 14)$, $S(0, 5)$, $T(5, 30)$ are on the curve.
   (i) What is the value of c in the equation of the function?
   (ii) Form two equations in a and b.
   (iii) Solve your equations to find the value of a and the value of b.

7. The following couples belong to a function: {(−4, −4), (−3, −9), (−2, −12), (−1, −13), (0, −12), (1, −9), (2, −4), (3, 3), (4, 12)}.
   (i) Using patterns of first and second differences, show that the above couples satisfy the equation of a quadratic function $f(x)$.
   (ii) What is the value of c in the equation $f(x) = ax^2 + bx + c$?
   (iii) Find the equation of the function.

8. (i) Three functions $f(x)$, $g(x)$ and $h(x)$ are defined as follows:
   $f(x) = 2x^2 + 5x - 3$, $g(x) = x^2 - 4x + 4$, $h(x) = x^2 - 3x$.
   (a) Solve $f(x) = 0$.   (b) Solve $g(x) = 0$.   (c) Solve $h(x) = 0$.

   (ii) The table shows the sketches of six different functions. Three of the sketches belong to the three functions from part (i).

   Decide which of the graphs belong to functions $f(x)$, $g(x)$ and $h(x)$.

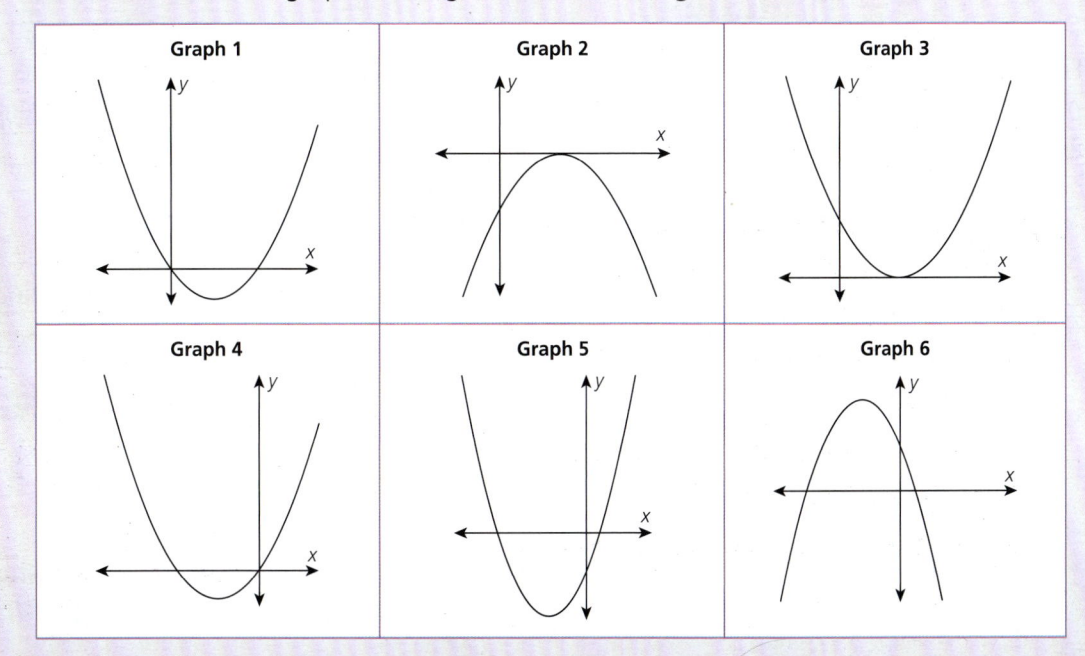

9. The function $f(x) = x^2 + x - 6$.
   (i) Draw the graph of the function $f(x)$ in the domain $-4 \leq x \leq 4$.
   (ii) The graph of another function $g(x)$ is linear. $g(-2) = 10$ and $g(3) = 0$. Using the same axes, draw the graph of the function g.
   (iii) Use the graphs to find the values of x for which $f(x) = g(x)$.

10. (i) Using the same axes, draw the graphs of
    $f: x \to 5 - 3x - 2x^2$
    $g: x \to -2x - 1$
    in the domain $-3 \leq x \leq 2$, $x \in \mathbb{R}$.
    (ii) Use your graphs to estimate:
    (a) the maximum value of $f(x)$
    (b) the values of x for which $f(x) = g(x)$
    (c) the range of values of x for which $f(x) \geq g(x)$.

11. The picture shows the top section of the Spanish Arch in Galway city. George wants to see if the arch can be described by a function. He puts a co-ordinate grid over the arch as shown.
    (i) Copy and complete the table to show the value of y for each of the given values of x.

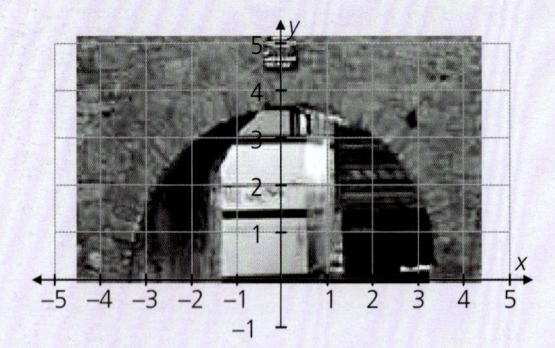

x	y
−3	
−2	
−1	
0	
1	
2	
3	

   (ii) Is it possible to represent this section of the Spanish Arch by a quadratic function? Give a reason for your answer.

JCHL 2014 Sample Paper 1

Section 16B Applications of Linear and Quadratic Functions

Functions can be used to model many real-life applications. We can use models to make predictions and for optimisation. The points where a graph intercepts the axes and maximum and minimum points are very important in applications.

Example 1

A farmer wishes to use 100 metres of fencing to enclose a rectangular section of land. What is the biggest area that he can enclose?

Class Discussion

What problem-solving strategy could you use here?

Before reading the solution, try 'guess and test'. Try out different possible lengths for the sides of the rectangle and see what you come up with.

Solution

The farmer can try different lengths for the rectangle and he will get different areas each time. Thus the area enclosed depends on the length of the rectangle.

We say that **the area is a function of the length**.

Let x be the length of the rectangle.
Let y be the width of the rectangle.
Then the perimeter $= 2x + 2y = 100$
$$\Rightarrow \quad x + y = 50$$
$$\Rightarrow \quad y = 50 - x$$

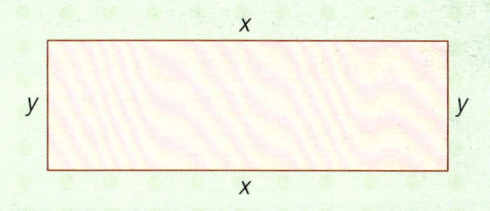

Thus, the area (A) of the rectangle = length × width
$$= x(50 - x)$$
$$= 50x - x^2$$

Now we have the area (A) as a function of the length (x).

We can write this in function notation as $A(x) = 50x - x^2$.

We can draw the graph of this function and use it to estimate the value which will give us the maximum area.

Make an input/output table.

Input: x (metres)	$A(x) = 50x - x^2$	Output: $y = A(x)$ (m²)
0	$50(0) - 0^2$	0
10	$50(10) - 10^2$	400
20	$50(20) - 20^2$	600
30	$50(30) - 30^2$	600
40	$50(40) - 40^2$	400
50	$50(50) - 50^2$	0

Draw the graph.

The graph has a maximum point at (25, 625) … this point is estimated from the graph.

The greatest area is 625 m² which is obtained when the length is 25 m.

That is, the rectangle with the greatest area is actually a square.

Alternatively: The roots of the equation $f(x) = 0$ are $x = 0$ and $x = 50$. Therefore the axis of symmetry of the graph is the line $x = 25$. This line passes through the maximum point of the graph.

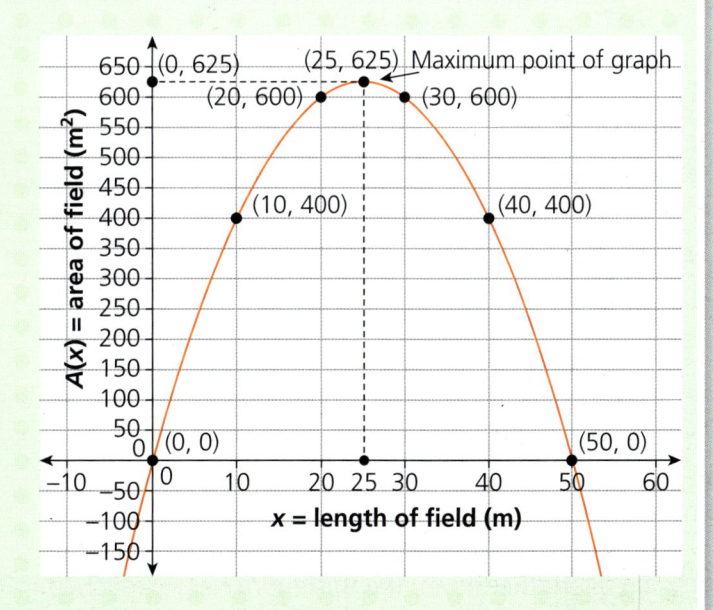

Substituting $x = 25$ into the equation $y = 50x - x^2$ gives $y = 625$.

Example 2

The height, y metres, of a golf ball above ground level x seconds after it is hit, is represented by the function

$$f : x \to 6x - x^2, x \in \mathbb{R}.$$

(i) Draw the graph of f for $0 \leq x \leq 6$, $x \in \mathbb{R}$.

Use your graph:

(ii) to find the maximum height reached by the golf ball

(iii) to estimate the number of seconds the golf ball was more than 3 metres above the ground.

Solution

(i) Draw an input/output table:

Input (x)	Output ($6x - x^2$)	Couples
0	$6(0) - (0)^2 = 0$	(0, 0)
1	$6(1) - (1)^2 = 5$	(1, 5)
2	$6(2) - (2)^2 = 8$	(2, 8)
3	$6(3) - (3)^2 = 9$	(3, 9)
4	$6(4) - (4)^2 = 8$	(4, 8)
5	$6(5) - (5)^2 = 5$	(5, 5)
6	$6(6) - (6)^2 = 0$	(6, 0)

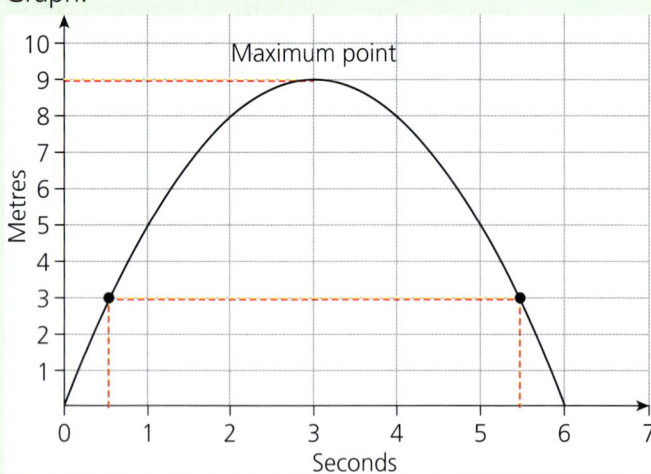

Graph:

(ii) From the graph, the maximum height reached = 9 m.

(iii) The ball was more than 3 metres above the ground from 0.5 seconds to 5.5 seconds approx., i.e. for 5 seconds.

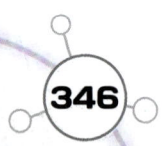

Activity 16.2

1. A rectangular site, with one side facing the road, is to be fenced off.

   The side facing the road, which does not require fencing, is l m in length.

   The sides perpendicular to the road are x m in length.

   The length of fencing that will be used to enclose the rest of the site is 140 m.

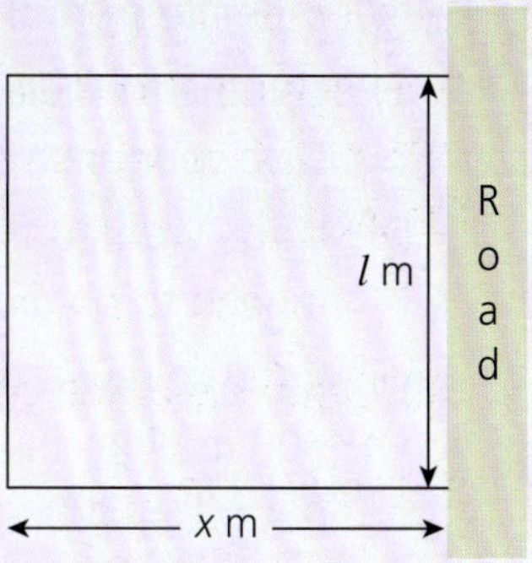

   (i) Write an expression in terms of x, for the length (l) of the side facing the road.

   (ii) (a) Show that the area of the site, in m², is $-2x^2 + 140x$.

   (b) Let f be the function $f: x \to -2x^2 + 140x$. Evaluate $f(x)$ when x = 0, 10, 20, 30, 40, 50, 60, 70.

   Hence, draw the graph of f for $0 \leq x \leq 70$, $x \in \mathbb{R}$.

   (iii) Use your graph from part (ii) to estimate:

   (a) the maximum possible area of the site

   (b) the area of the site when the road frontage (l) is 30 m long.

   JCHL 2014 Sample Paper

2. The formula for the height, y metres, of a ball above ground level, x seconds after it is fired vertically into the air, is given by:

   $f(x) = y = 35x - 5x^2$.

   (i) Draw the graph of f for $0 \leq x \leq 7$, $x \in \mathbb{R}$.

   (ii) Use your graph to estimate:

   (a) the maximum height reached by the ball

   (b) the height of the ball after 5.5 seconds

   (c) the two times that the ball is 20 metres above the ground.

3. A company manufactures rectangular wooden frames for framing photographs. One particular frame has inside dimensions of 10 cm by 15 cm.

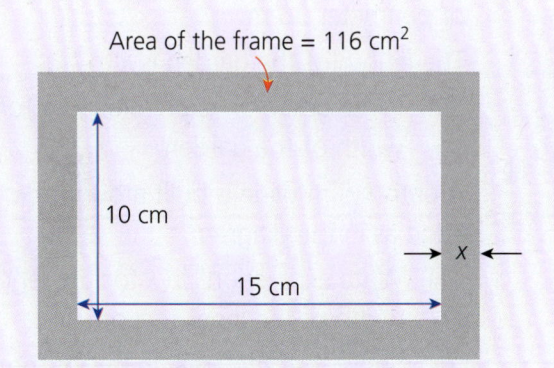

   (i) Find the width, x cm, of wood in the frame which will make the area of the frame itself equal to 116 cm².

   (ii) Explain how the value of x could be estimated from a graph.

   (iii) Estimate the value of x using a graph.

4. A coin is dropped from a height of 50 m. Its height above the ground varies with time. The function representing how its height, in metres, changes with time is

   $h = f(t) = 50 - 5t^2$ where t is measured in seconds.

   (i) Use a table to show the height above the ground for the first four seconds after the coin is dropped.

   (ii) Estimate from the table when the coin hits the ground.

(iii) Plot a graph of height versus time for the first four seconds after the coin is dropped.
(iv) Estimate from the graph when the coin hits the ground.
(v) Use the formula for height to verify your estimates of when the coin hits the ground. Give your answer correct to two decimal places.
(vi) If you wanted the coin to hit the ground after three seconds, from what height would it need to be dropped?
(vii) If the coin was dropped from the top of the Eiffel Tower, which is approximately 300 m high, the function representing how height changes with time would be $h = g(t) = 300 - 5t^2$. How long would it take the coin to fall to the ground when dropped from the top of the Eiffel Tower? Give your answer correct to two decimal places.

5 The height of a rocket t seconds after it has been launched is given by $h = f(t) = -5t^2 + 90t$.

(i) What is the height of the rocket above ground when it is launched?
(ii) Copy and complete the following table for the height of the rocket above ground from the time it is launched.
(iii) How long after the launch does it take the rocket to fall back to ground?
(iv) Draw a graph of the height versus time since launch.
(v) Using the graph, estimate the time at which the rocket is at its greatest height.
(vi) Calculate the greatest height reached by the rocket.

Time elapsed since launch (s)	Height above ground (m)
0	
2	
4	
6	
8	
10	
12	
14	
16	
18	

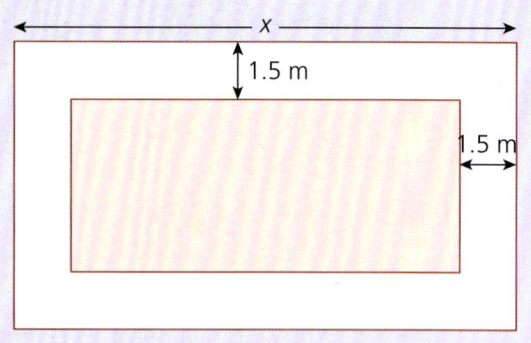

6 The diagram shows a rectangular garden of perimeter 36 m.

The length of the garden is x m.

(i) Write down an expression in x for the width of the garden.

A path 1.5 m wide is built around the garden's edge as in the diagram.

(ii) Write expressions in x for the length and width of the inner section.
(iii) Show that the area, in m², of the inner section is $-x^2 + 18x - 45$.

The area of the inner section is represented by the function:
$f : x \to -x^2 + 18x - 45$.

(iv) Draw the graph of f for $3 \leq x \leq 15$, $x \in \mathbb{R}$.
(v) Find the maximum possible area of the inner section.

7. The price for a tour decreases by €20 for every additional person who buys a ticket to go on the tour. The price per ticket is €520 before anyone signs up.

   Let n be the number of tickets sold.

   (i) What is the cost of a ticket for the tour if five people sign up to go on the tour?

   (ii) What is the cost of a ticket for the tour if n people sign up to go on the tour?

   (iii) Revenue equals the number of tickets sold multiplied by the price per ticket.

   If n people sign up to go on the tour, write in terms of n, the total revenue collected by the tour company.

   (iv) Copy and complete the following table showing the relationship between the number of people n, and the revenue, R.

   (v) What does the negative answer mean in the table for $n = 30$?

   (vi) Draw a graph for the revenue function $R(n)$ using the table in part (iv).

   (vii) For what numbers of people signing up for the tour will the revenue be zero? Estimate from the graph first and then find the answer algebraically.

n	R (€)
0	
5	
10	
15	
20	
25	
30	

   (viii) Using the graph, find the value of n which will maximise the value of R.

   (ix) What is the maximum revenue possible under the given conditions?

8. Two identical cylindrical tanks, A and B, have a height of 100 cm. At a particular instant, the water in tank A is 15 cm high and the height of water is increasing at a steady rate of 10 cm every 5 seconds. At the same time the height of water in tank B is 100 cm and the height of water is decreasing at 10 cm every 5 seconds.

   (i) Draw up a table showing the height of water in each tank at 5 second intervals, until tank A is almost full and tank B is empty.

   (ii) Based on the table, is the relationship between time and height a linear relationship? Justify your answer.

   (iii) Calculate the rate of change of height with time for the water in each tank.

   (iv) For each tank, using the same axes and scales, draw the graph to represent the height of water in the tank.

   (v) Explain what the co-ordinates (50, 0) for tank B mean in the context of the question.

   (vi) For each tank, write down a formula which gives the height of water in the tank at any given time. State clearly the meaning of any letters used in your formulae.

   (vii) Estimate, from your graphs, when the height of water is the same in both tanks and what that height is.

   (viii) Verify your answer to part (vii) using your formulae from part (vi).

9. A stadium has seating capacity for 13 000 spectators. Tickets for an event must be purchased in advance. When the ticket price for a regular event is €25, the expected attendance at the event is 8500 people. Market research suggests that for every €1 that the ticket price is reduced, the expected attendance would increase by 500 people.

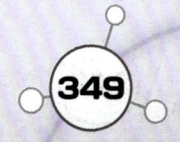

(i) Copy and complete the table for the expected increase in attendance and the expected total attendance given the reduction in ticket price from €25 shown in the first column.

Ticket price (€)	Expected increase in attendance	Expected total attendance (n)
24	(1)(500)	8500 + (1)(500) = 9000
23		
22		
21		
20		
…	…	…
x		

(ii) If n people attend the event, what is the total income generated from ticket sales, given that each ticket costs €x? Write this equation in terms of x.
(iii) What ticket prices would yield zero income?
(iv) Sketch the graph of the relationship between ticket price and income.
(v) What ticket price would yield maximum income? Calculate this income.
(vi) What would the ticket price be if the organisers wished to fill the stadium?
(vii) What is the difference between the income generated using the answer to part (v) and the income generated at a ticket price which would fill the stadium?
(viii) Could the organisers charge €10 per ticket given the expected attendance and the effect of reducing the ticket price? Explain.

Section 16C Exponential Functions

Katie was asking for pocket money. She said, 'For pocket money, I would like just 3 cent right now, 6 cent tomorrow, 12 cent the next day, 24 cent the next day and so on, doubling each day for the 30 days of next month. Surely that's not too much to ask?'

Is this a good deal for Katie or is it a good deal for her parents?

Katie wants to get the following amounts in cent:

3 + 3(2) + 3(2)(2) + 3(2)(2)(2) + … for thirty-one days

= 3 + 3(2) + 3(2)^2 + 3(2)^3 + 3(2)^4 + … + 3(2)^{30}

This relationship between the number of days and the amount of pocket money is an example of an **exponential function**.

In the above example, the function $f(x) = 3(2^x)$ gives the amount of pocket money each day where x is the number of days that have passed since to first day (day 0).

> **Key Point**
>
> In an exponential function, **the variable is in the exponent** (index).

Example 1 will tell us whether this is a good idea for Katie.

Example 1

(i) Make a table of values for the function $f(x) = 3(2^x)$ for $0 \leq x \leq 5$, $x \in \mathbb{Z}$.

(ii) How can you tell from the table that the graph of f is not a straight line?

(iii) Use these values to plot the graph of $f(x) = 3(2^x)$.

(iv) Where does the curve intercept the y-axis?

(v) As x increases, is y increasing or decreasing?

(vi) Evaluate $3(2^x)$ for $x = 10, 20$ and 30 using your calculator.

Solution

(i)

x	$f(x) = 3(2^x)$	Couples
0	$2^0 = 3$	(0, 3)
1	$2^1 = 6$	(1, 6)
2	$2^2 = 12$	(2, 12)
3	$2^3 = 24$	(3, 24)
4	$2^4 = 48$	(4, 48)
5	$2^5 = 96$	(5, 96)

(ii) The differences in the output values for consecutive values of x are not constant, so the graph is not a straight line.

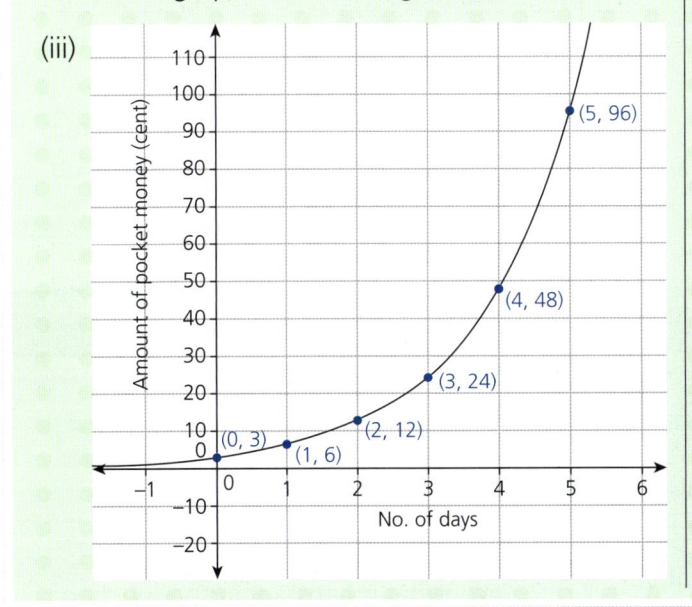

(iv) The y-intercept = 3, i.e. the curve crosses the y-axis at (0, 3).

(v) As x increases, y is increasing very quickly.

(vi) $3(2^{10}) = 3072$
$3(2^{20}) = 3\,145\,728$
$3(2^{30}) = 3\,221\,225\,472$

(iii) [Graph showing exponential curve with points (0, 3), (1, 6), (2, 12), (3, 24), (4, 48), (5, 96); x-axis labelled "No. of days", y-axis labelled "Amount of pocket money (cent)"]

- You can see that the graph in Example 1 'zooms' upwards. This is what all **exponential** graphs look like.
- The graph in Example 1 shows what Katie's pocket money would be for the first five days because $3(2^x)$ is the graph of a 'doubling' function.
- The point (5, 96) on the graph indicates that Katie would get 96 cent on the 5th day. This seems reasonable enough.
- Now see what she would get on the 10th, 20th and 30th days (the answers to Example 1 part (vi)).

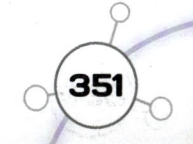

CONNECT WITH MATHS 2

Katie would have to be given

- 3072 cent = €30.72 on the 10th day
- 3 145 728 cent = €31 457.28 on the 20th day
- 3 221 225 472 cent = €32 212 254.72 on the 30th day!

Now we can see what people mean when they say that something is **growing exponentially**.

2^x is just one example of an exponential function; other examples are 3^x, 4^x or a^x where $a \in \mathbb{R}$.

Example 2

For $f(x) = 2^x$:

(i) What is the base?
(ii) What is the exponent (index)?
(iii) What is varying in the function?
(iv) What is constant in the function?
(v) What is the domain (the possible inputs for x)?
(vi) For what values of x is 2^x negative?
(vii) What is the range of f?
(viii) What happens to the output as x decreases?
(ix) Is an output of 0 possible?

Solution

(i) The base = 2
(ii) The exponent = x
(iii) x is varying.
(iv) 2 (the base) is constant.
(v) The domain is $\mathbb{R}$, the set of real numbers.
(vi) There are no values of x for which 2^x is negative.
(vii) The range is the set of positive real numbers
(viii) As x decreases, the output (y-values) gets smaller and smaller.
(ix) An output of 0 is impossible. There is no value of x which will make $2^x = 0$.

Activity 16.3

1 (i) Make a table of values for the function $f(x) = 3^x$ for $0 \le x \le 4$, $x \in \mathbb{Z}$.
(ii) How can you tell from the table that the graph of f is not a straight line?
(iii) Use these values to plot the graph of $f(x) = 3^x$.
(iv) What is the y-intercept of the graph?
(v) As x increases, is y increasing or decreasing?
(vi) Evaluate 3^x for x = 10, 20 and 30 using your calculator. Why does the calculator show the value of 3^{30} differently?

2 For $f(x) = 3^x$:
(i) What is the base?
(ii) What is the exponent (index)?
(iii) What is varying in the function?
(iv) What is constant in the function?
(v) What is the domain (the possible inputs for x)?
(vi) For what values of x is 3^x negative?
(vii) What is the range of f?
(viii) What happens to the output as x decreases?
(ix) Is an output of 0 possible?

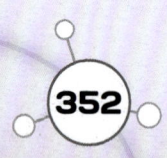

3. (i) Make a table of values for the function $f(x) = 2(3^x)$ for $0 \le x \le 3$.
   (ii) Use these values to plot the graph of $f(x) = 2(3^x)$.
   (iii) Where does the curve intercept the y-axis?
   (iv) Evaluate $2(3^x)$ for $x = 10$ and 20 using your calculator.

4. (i) Draw the graphs of $f(x) = x^2$ and $g(x) = 2^x$, $0 \le x \le 3$, $x \in \mathbb{R}$, using the same axes.
   (ii) Use your graphs to solve the equation $x^2 = 2^x$.

5. A cell divides itself into two every day. The number of cells C after D days is given by the function $C = 2^D$.
   (i) Draw a graph of the function for $0 \le D \le 6$.
   (ii) Use your calculator to find the number of cells after 18 days.

6. In an experiment, the number of bacteria B found in a sample after m minutes is given by the formula:
   $B = 50(3)^{0.04m}$.
   (i) Find the number of bacteria in the sample at the start of the experiment.
   (ii) Find the number of bacteria in the sample after 3 hours.

7. Part of the graph of $f(x) = ka^x$ is shown.

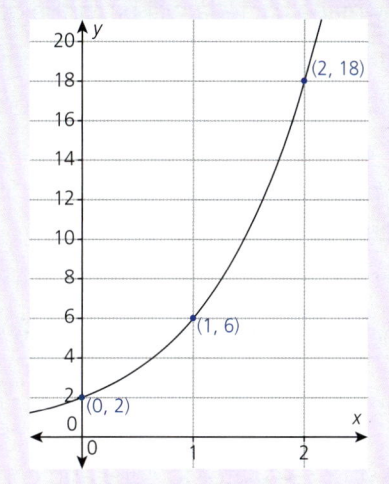

   (i) Find the value of k and the value of a.
   (ii) Hence, find $f(7)$.

8. The graphs of four functions are shown below. The graphs are labelled A, B, C and D. The four functions are listed in the table. Match the graphs to the functions, by putting the correct letter beside each one in a copy of the table.

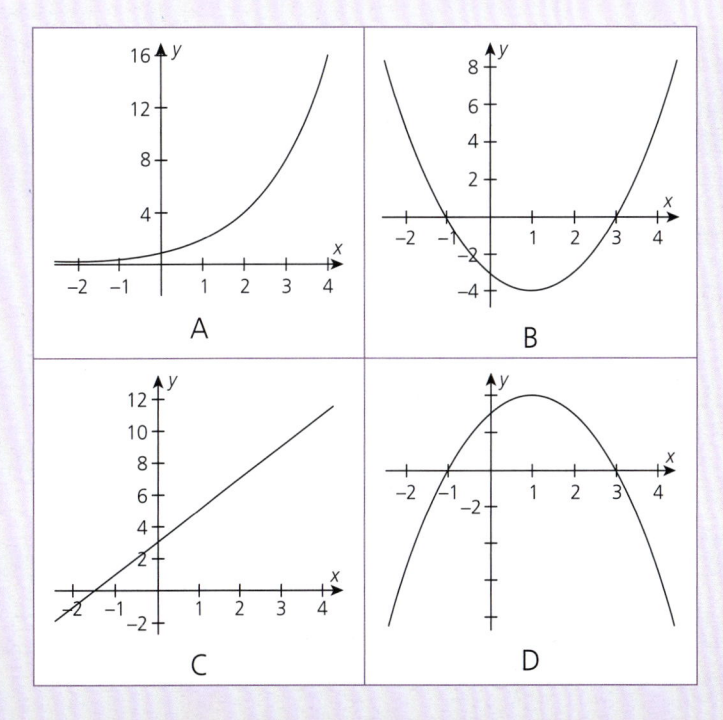

Function	Graph
$f(x) = 2x + 3$	
$g(x) = (x - 3)(x + 1)$	
$h(x) = 2^x$	
$j(x) = 3 + 2x - x^2$	

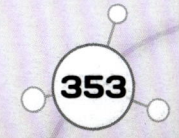

9 The number of bacteria in a Petri dish is growing approximately exponentially. Initially, there were 4 bacteria in the dish.

The table shows the approximate number of bacteria in the dish from the time when counting started, at the end of each hour for a period of 4 hours.

Time elapsed t (hours)	0	1	2	3	4
Number of bacteria $N = f(t)$	4	12	36	108	324

(i) Using the function $f(t) = ab^t$ to model the growth of the bacteria, what are the values of a and b?

(ii) How many bacteria will be in the dish after 24 hours?

(iii) Write the answer to part (ii) correct to two significant figures.

(iv) Write the answer to part (iii) in words.

(v) Use your calculator to help you to estimate how long in hours it would take for the number of bacteria to reach 250 000. Give your answer correct to three decimal places.

(vi) Why might the exponential growth of an organism not continue indefinitely?

10 Two functions f and g are defined for $x \in \mathbb{R}$ as follows:

$$f \mapsto (3^x)$$
$$g \mapsto -4x^2 + 20x + 5$$

(i) Use your calculator to copy and complete the table below. Use your table to draw the graphs of f and g for $0 \le x \le 4$.

x	0	0.5	1	1.5	2	2.5	3	3.5	4
$f(x)$									
$g(x)$									

(ii) Use the graphs to estimate the value of x for which $f(x) = g(x)$.

(iii) Let k be a number such that $(3^k) = 8$.
Use your graph to estimate the value of k. Use your calculator to estimate the value of k to two decimal places.

(iv) Estimate $g(k)$ from the graph.

Section 16D Transformations of Linear and Quadratic Functions

Linear Functions

Example 1 looks at graphs of functions of the form $f(x) = ax$, where $a \in \mathbb{Z}$, $x \in \mathbb{R}$.

Example 1

(i) Draw the graphs of the functions $f(x) = 1x$, $g(x) = 2x$ and $h(x) = 3x$, in the domain $-3 \leq x \leq 3$, using the same axes.

(ii) Compare and contrast the three graphs you have plotted.

(iii) The graphs are of the form $f(x) = ax$. What effect does varying a have on the graphs?

(iv) What would you expect $p(x) = 7x$ to look like?

Solution

(i) Make an input/output table for each graph.

x	f(x) = x
−3	3
0	0
3	3

x	g(x) = 2x
−3	−6
0	0
3	6

x	h(x) = 3x
−3	−9
0	0
3	9

Draw the graphs.

(ii) All three graphs:
- are lines of the form $y = mx$, where m = the slope
- have **positive** slopes
- pass through the point (0, 0) and therefore represent proportional relationships.

The graphs differ in that $g(x) = 2x$ has a slope twice that of $f(x) = x$, and $h(x) = 3x$ has a slope three times that of $f(x) = x$.

(iii) Since a is the slope of each graph, as a increases, the slope (rate of change) increases.

(iv) The graph of $p(x) = 7x$ will be a line through the point (0, 0) with a slope = 7.

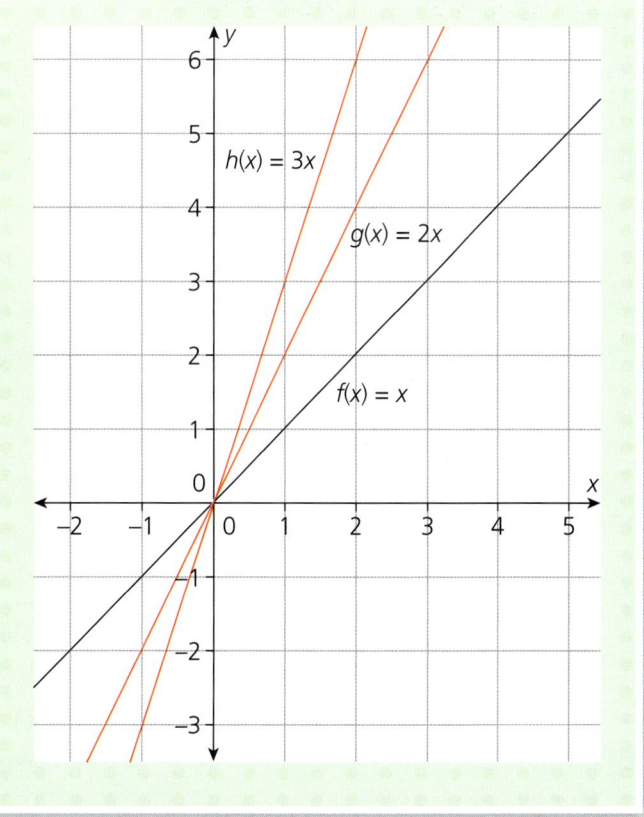

Example 2 looks at graphs of functions of the form $f(x) = ax + b$, where $a, b \in \mathbb{Z}$, $x \in \mathbb{R}$.

Example 2

(i) Draw the graphs of the functions $g(x) = x$, $h(x) = x + 1$, $k(x) = x + 3$ and $l(x) = x - 2$, in the domain $-3 \leq x \leq 3$, using the same axes.

(ii) Compare and contrast the four graphs you have plotted.

(iii) The graphs are of the form $f(x) = ax + b$. What effect does varying b have on the graphs?

(iv) Where do the graphs cut the y-axis?

(v) What would you expect $f(x) = x + 6$ to look like?

Solution

(i) Make an input/output table for each graph.

x	g(x) = x
−3	−3
0	0
3	3

x	h(x) = x + 1
−3	−2
0	1
3	4

x	k(x) = x + 3
−3	0
0	3
3	6

x	l(x) = x − 2
−3	−5
0	−2
3	1

Draw the graphs.

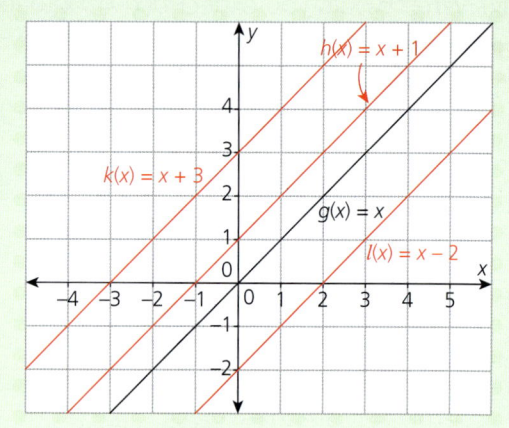

(ii) The graphs are lines which are parallel with positive slope.

- The graph of $h(x) = x + 1$ is the image of the graph of $g(x)$ by a translation of 1 unit up the y-axis.
- The graph of $k(x) = x + 3$ is the image of the graph of $g(x)$ by a translation of 3 units up the y-axis.
- The graph of $l(x) = x - 2$ is the image of the graph of $g(x)$ by a translation of 2 units down the y-axis.

(iii) Varying b has the effect of translating the line.

(iv) The graphs all cut the y-axis at the point b, i.e. $(0, b)$.

(v) The graph of the function $f(x) = x + 6$ is a line parallel to $g(x)$ and it intercepts the y-axis at $(0, 6)$.

Quadratic Functions

Example 3 looks at graphs of functions of the form $f(x) = ax^2$, where $a \in \mathbb{N}$, $x \in \mathbb{R}$.

Example 3

(i) Graph the functions $g(x) = x^2$, $h(x) = 2x^2$, $k(x) = 3x^2$, in the domain $-3 \leq x \leq 3$, using the same axes.

(ii) Compare and contrast the three graphs you have plotted.

(iii) The graphs are of the form $f(x) = ax^2$. What effect does varying a have on the shape of the graphs?

(iv) What would you expect $l(x) = 7x^2$ to look like?

Solution

(i) Draw an input/output table for each function.

x	$g(x) = x^2$
−3	9
−2	4
−1	1
0	0
1	1
2	4
3	9

x	$h(x) = 2x^2$
−3	18
−2	8
−1	2
0	0
1	2
2	8
3	18

x	$k(x) = 3x^2$
−3	27
−2	12
−1	3
0	0
1	3
2	12
3	27

Draw the graphs.

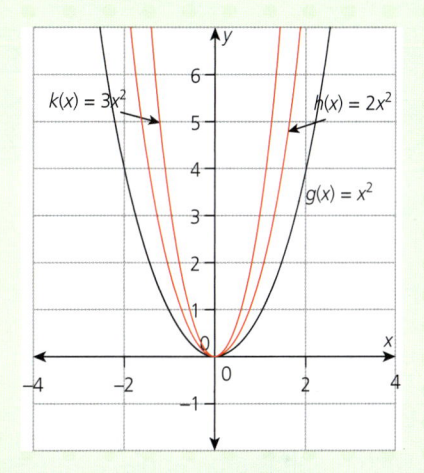

(ii) Each graph is a parabola, all are symmetrical about the y-axis, have $y > 0$ for all $x \in \mathbb{R}$ and all have the same minimum point (0, 0).

The rate of change of $y = 3x^2$ is greater than the rate of change of $y = 2x^2$ which is greater than the rate of change of $y = x^2$.

(iii) Varying a varies the rate of change of the function. For $a > 0$, the bigger the value of a the 'narrower' the graph of the function.

(iv) $l(x) = 7x^2$ is a parabola, symmetrical about the y-axis, has $y > 0$ for all $x \in \mathbb{R}$ and has a minimum point of (0, 0). The rate of change of y with respect to x for $y = 7x^2$ is seven times greater than the rate of change of y with respect to x for $y = x^2$. Hence, the graph of $y = 7x^2$ is 'narrower' than the graph of $y = x^2$.

16 Functions

Example 4 looks at graphs of functions of the form $f(x) = x^2 + c$, where $c \in \mathbb{Z}$, $x \in \mathbb{R}$.

Example 4

(i) Graph the functions $g(x) = x^2$, $h(x) = x^2 + 3$, $k(x) = x^2 - 2$, in the domain $-3 \leq x \leq 3$, using the same axes.

(ii) Compare and contrast the three graphs you have plotted.

(iii) The graphs are of the form $f(x) = x^2 + c$. What effect does varying c have on the shape of the graphs?

(iv) What would you expect $f(x) = x^2 + 8$ to look like?

(v) What would you expect $n(x) = x^2 - 3$ to look like?

Solution

(i) Draw an input/output table for each function.

x	$g(x) = x^2$
−3	9
−2	4
−1	1
0	0
1	1
2	4
3	9

x	$h(x) = x^2 + 3$
−3	12
−2	7
−1	4
0	3
1	4
2	7
3	12

x	$k(x) = x^2 - 2$
−3	7
−2	2
−1	−1
0	−2
1	−1
2	2
3	7

Draw the graphs.

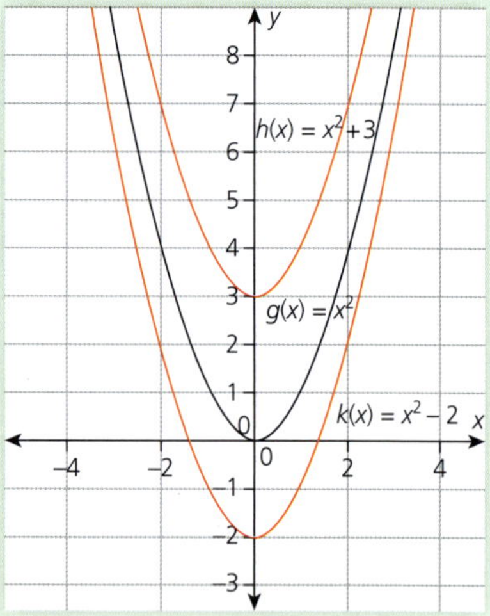

(ii) Each graph is a parabola, all are symmetrical about the y-axis, and have **the same rate of change** at each x value.

The minimum point of each graph is different.

(iii) Varying c shifts the graph of $y = x^2$ vertically. In other words, the graph of $y = x^2 + c$ is translated c units vertically with respect to the graph of $y = x^2$.

(iv) $f(x) = x^2 + 8$ is a parabola, symmetrical about the y-axis, and has a minimum point of (0, 8).

The rate of change of y with respect to x for $y = x^2 + 8$ is the same as the rate of change of y with respect to x for $y = x^2$.

The graph of $y = x^2 + 8$ is the image of the graph of $y = x^2$ by a vertical translation of 8 units upwards.

(v) $n(x) = x^2 - 3$ is a parabola, symmetrical about the y-axis, and has a minimum point of (0, −3).

The rate of change of y with respect to x for $y = x^2 - 3$ is the same as the rate of change of y with respect to x for $y = x^2$.

The graph of $y = x^2 - 3$ is the image of the graph of $y = x^2$ by a vertical translation of 3 units downwards.

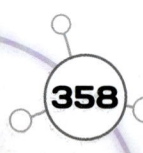

Examples 5 and 6 look at graphs of functions of the form $f(x) = (x + a)^2 + b$.

Example 5

(i) Graph the functions $g(x) = x^2$, $h(x) = (x - 2)^2$, $k(x) = (x + 3)^2$ in the domain $-5 \leq x \leq 5$, using the same axes.

(ii) Compare and contrast the three graphs you have plotted.

(iii) Copy and complete this table.

Function	Minimum point of the graph	Equation of the axis of symmetry
$g(x) = x^2$	(0, 0)	$x = 0$ (y-axis)
$h(x) = (x - 2)^2$		
$k(x) = (x + 3)^2$		

(iv) What would you expect $l(x) = (x - 5)^2$ to look like?

Solution

(i) Draw an input/output table for each function.

x	$g(x) = x^2$
−5	25
−4	16
−3	9
−2	4
−1	1
0	0
1	1
2	4
3	9
4	16
5	25

x	$h(x) = (x - 2)^2$
−5	49
−4	36
−3	25
−2	16
−1	9
0	4
1	1
2	0
3	1
4	4
5	9

x	$k(x) = (x + 3)^2$
−5	4
−4	1
−3	0
−2	1
−1	4
0	9
1	16
2	25
3	36
4	49
5	64

Draw the graphs.

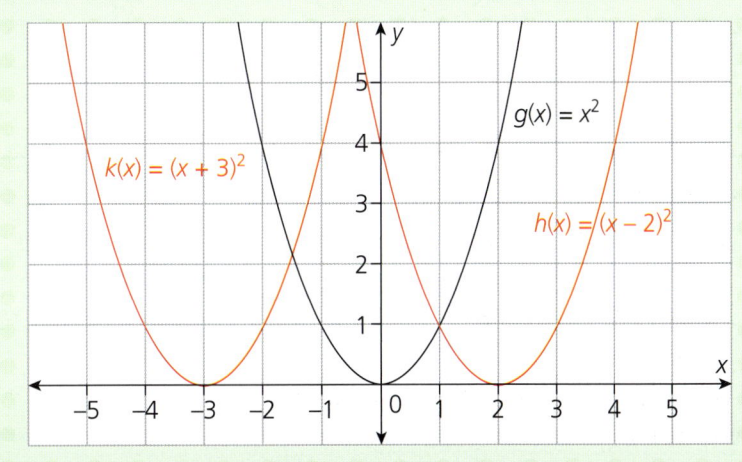

Functions

CONNECT WITH MATHS 2

(ii) The graph of $h(x) = (x - 2)^2$ is the image of $g(x) = x^2$ by a translation of 2 units to the right. The graph of $k(x) = (x + 3)^2$ is the image of $g(x) = x^2$ by a translation of 3 units to the left.

(iii)

Function	Minimum point of the graph	Equation of the axis of symmetry
$g(x) = x^2$	(0, 0)	$x = 0$ (y-axis)
$h(x) = (x - 2)^2$	(2, 0)	$x = 2$
$k(x) = (x + 3)^2$	(-3, 0)	$x = -3$

(iv) The graph of $h(x) = (x - 5)^2$ is a parabola which is the image of $g(x) = x^2$ by a translation of 5 units to the right. Its minimum point is (5, 0) and its axis of symmetry is the line $x = 5$.

Example 6

(i) Graph the functions $g(x) = x^2$, $h(x) = (x - 2)^2$, $k(x) = (x - 2)^2 + 3$ in the domain $-3 \leq x \leq 6$, using the same axes.

(ii) Compare and contrast the three graphs you have plotted.

(iii) Copy and complete this table.

Function	Minimum point of the graph	Equation of the axis of symmetry
$g(x) = x^2$	(0, 0)	$x = 0$ (y-axis)
$h(x) = (x - 2)^2$		
$k(x) = (x - 2)^2 + 3$		

(iv) What would you expect $l(x) = (x - 3)^2 - 5$ to look like?

Solution

(i) Draw an input/output table for each function.

x	$g(x) = x^2$
-3	9
-2	4
-1	1
0	0
1	1
2	4
3	9
4	16
5	25
6	36

x	$h(x) = (x - 2)^2$
-3	25
-2	16
-1	9
0	4
1	1
2	0
3	1
4	4
5	9
6	16

x	$k(x) = (x - 2)^2 + 3$
-3	28
-2	19
-1	12
0	7
1	4
2	3
3	4
4	7
5	12
6	19

Draw the graphs.

(ii) The graph of $h(x) = (x - 2)^2$ is the image of $g(x) = x^2$ by a translation of 2 units to the right.

The graph of $k(x) = (x - 2)^2 + 3$ is the image of $h(x)$ by a translation of 3 units vertically upwards.

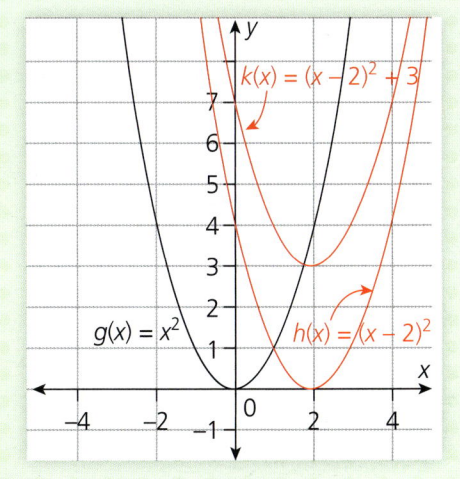

(iii)

Function	Minimum point of the graph	Equation of the axis of symmetry
$g(x) = x^2$	(0, 0)	$x = 0$ (y-axis)
$h(x) = (x - 2)^2$	(2, 0)	$x = 2$
$k(x) = (x - 2)^2 + 3$	(2, 3)	$x = 2$

(iv) The graph of $l(x) = (x - 3)^2 - 5$ is the image of $g(x) = x^2$ by a translation of 3 units to the right followed by a translation of 5 units vertically downwards. Its minimum point is $(3, -5)$ and its axis of symmetry is the line $x = 3$.

Activity 16.4

1. The following functions are of the form $f(x) = ax$, where $a \in \mathbb{Z}, x \in \mathbb{R}$:

   $p(x) = -1x$, $q(x) = -2x$ and $r(x) = -3x$.

   (i) Graph each function in the domain $-3 \leq x \leq 3$, using the same axes.

   (ii) Compare and contrast the three graphs you have plotted.

   (iii) What would you expect $t(x) = -7x$ to look like?

2. The following functions are of the form $f(x) = ax + b$, where $a, b \in \mathbb{Z}, x \in \mathbb{R}$:

   $g(x) = -2x$, $h(x) = -2x - 2$, $k(x) = -2x - 4$ and $l(x) = -2x - 5$.

   (i) Graph each function in the domain $-3 \leq x \leq 3$, using the same axes.

   (ii) Compare and contrast the four graphs you have plotted.

   (iii) Where do the graphs cut the y-axis (when $x = 0$)?

   (iv) What would you expect $f(x) = -2x + 2$ to look like?

3. The following functions are of the form $f(x) = ax^2$, where $a \in \mathbb{N}, x \in \mathbb{R}$.

   (i) Graph the functions $g(x) = x^2$, $h(x) = 3x^2$, $k(x) = 4x^2$ in the domain $-3 \leq x \leq 3$, using the same axes.

   (ii) Compare and contrast the three graphs you have plotted.

   (iii) What effect does varying a have on the shape of the graphs?

   (iv) What would you expect $p(x) = 5x^2$ to look like?

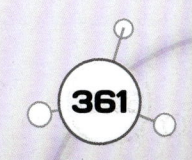

4 The following functions are of the form $f(x) = x^2 + c$, where $c \in \mathbb{Z}$, $x \in \mathbb{R}$.
   (i) Graph the functions $g(x) = x^2$, $h(x) = x^2 + 1$, $k(x) = x^2 - 3$, in the domain $-3 \leq x \leq 3$, using the same axes.
   (ii) Compare and contrast the three graphs you have plotted.
   (iii) What effect does varying c have on the shape of the graphs?
   (iv) What would you expect $p(x) = x^2 + 5$ to look like?
   (v) What would you expect $n(x) = x^2 - 5$ to look like?

5 (i) Graph the functions $g(x) = x^2$, $h(x) = (x - 1)^2$, $k(x) = (x + 2)^2$ in the domain $-5 \leq x \leq 5$, using the same axes.
   (ii) Compare and contrast the three graphs you have plotted.
   (iii) Copy and complete this table.

Function	Minimum point of the graph	Equation of the axis of symmetry
$g(x) = x^2$	(0, 0)	$x = 0$ (y-axis)
$h(x) = (x - 1)^2$		
$k(x) = (x + 2)^2$		

   (iv) What would you expect $l(x) = (x - 4)^2$ to look like?

6 (i) Graph the functions $g(x) = x^2$, $h(x) = (x + 1)^2$, $k(x) = (x + 1)^2 + 2$ in the domain $-3 \leq x \leq 6$, using the same axes.
   (ii) Compare and contrast the three graphs you have plotted.
   (iii) Copy and complete this table.

Function	Minimum point of the graph	Equation of the axis of symmetry
$g(x) = x^2$	(0, 0)	$x = 0$ (y-axis)
$h(x) = (x + 1)^2$		
$k(x) = (x + 1)^2 + 2$		

   (iv) What would you expect $l(x) = (x + 1)^2 - 4$ to look like?

7 Use the patterns emerging from your work so far to copy and complete this table.

Function	Minimum point of the graph	Equation of the axis of symmetry
$g(x) = x^2$	(0, 0)	$x = 0$ (y-axis)
$h(x) = (x + 2)^2$		
$k(x) = (x + 2)^2 + 2$		
$p(x) = (x - 5)^2$		
$q(x) = (x - 5)^2 + 4$		
$r(x) = (x - 1)^2 - 6$		
$t(x) = (x + 3)^2 + 2$		

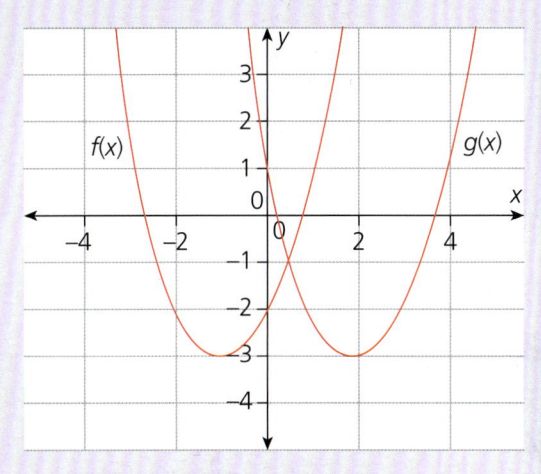

8 The graphs of two functions f and g are shown below.

The functions are $(x - 2)^2 - 3$ and $(x + 1)^2 - 3$. Identify clearly which is f and which is g.

9 (i) If $(x - k)^2 - 4 = x^2 - 6x + 5$ for all x and $k \in \mathbb{N}$, find the value of k.

(ii) Hence, write down:

(a) the co-ordinates of the minimum point

(b) the equation of the axis of symmetry of the function $f: x \to x^2 - 6x + 5$.

10 (i) If $(x + h)^2 + 3 = x^2 + 4x + 7$ for all x and $h \in \mathbb{N}$, find the value of h.

(ii) Hence, write down:

(a) the co-ordinates of the minimum point

(b) the equation of the axis of symmetry of the function $f: x \to x^2 + 4x + 7$.

Revision Activity 16

1 Let f be the function $f: x \to x^2 + bx + c$, $x \in \mathbb{R}$, and $b, c \in \mathbb{Z}$.

The graph of f cuts the x-axis at the points where $x = -3$ and $x = 2$.

(a) Find the value of b and the value of c.

(b) Find the value of x for which $f(x) = f(x + 2)$.

2 The graphs of six functions are shown. The graphs are labelled A to F.

The six functions are listed in the table following the graphs.

(a) Match the graphs to the functions.

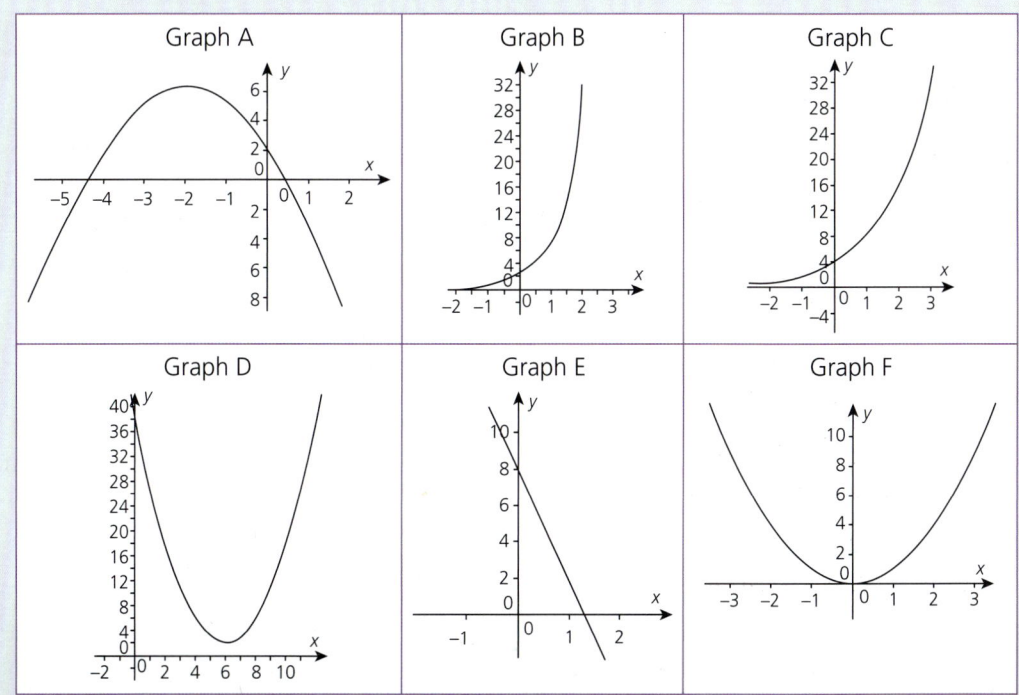

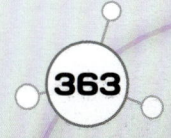

Function	Graph
$f(x) = 4(2^x)$	
$g(x) = 2(4^x)$	
$k(x) = -(x + 2)^2 + 6$	
$mx = (x - 6)^2 + 2$	
$n(x) = x^2$	
$f(x) = -6x + 8$	

(b) Explain how you decided on your answers.

3 Two functions f and g are defined for $x \in \mathbb{R}$ as follows.
$$f \mapsto 2(3^x)$$
$$g \mapsto -5x^2 + 20x - 4$$

(a) Copy and complete the table and use it to draw the graphs of f and g for $0 \leq x \leq 4$.

x	0	0.5	1	1.5	2	2.5	3	3.5	4
f(x)									
g(x)									

(b) Use the graphs to estimate the values of x for which $f(x) = g(x)$.

(c) Let k be a number such that $2(3^k) = 8$.

Use your graph to estimate the value of k. Use your calculator to estimate the value of k to two decimals places.

(d) Estimate $g(k)$ from the graph.

4 Fruit flies can multiply very fast. Starting with 20 fruit flies in a large jar with lots of food, the number of fruit flies in the jar was counted every three days for a number of weeks. The table shows the results.

Time (days)	0	3	6	9	12	15	18	21	24	27	30
Number of fruit flies	20	23	28	34	40	48	57	67	80	95	113

(a) Verify that the relationship between time and the number of fruit flies in the jar is
   (i) not linear, (ii) not quadratic but is approximately exponential.

(b) If this pattern continued, how many fruit flies would be in the jar after
   (i) 36 days, (ii) 72 days?

(c) Could this pattern of growth continue indefinitely? Explain your answer.

5 A manufacturing company models its total cost in euro for producing x items using the cost function $C(x) = 500 + 90x$. It models the total revenue in euro from the sales of the x items using the revenue function $R(x) = 150x - x^2$. The company expects to sell all the items it produces.

(a) The company produced 50 items on one day. Find the production cost and total revenue for the 50 items.

(b) What do the answers to part (a) tell you about the profit on the day in question?

Hint
> Profit = revenue − costs

(c) Write a general expression for the profit made by the company when it produces x items.

(d) What is the situation regarding profit if the company produces no items?

(e) What number of items produced will yield zero profit?

(f) Sketch a graph of the profit function.

(g) What number of items should be produced to give maximum profit?

Hint
> Use the axis of symmetry of the graph.

(h) What is the maximum profit?

6 A tennis ball is thrown upwards from the top of a 10 m high building. Its height in metres above the ground t seconds after it is thrown up is given by
$h = f(t) = -5t^2 + 20t + 10$.

(a) Copy and complete the table for the height of the tennis ball above ground.

Time (seconds)	Height above ground (metres)
0	
1	
2	
3	
4	
5	

(b) Estimate from the table the time it takes to fall back to ground level.

(c) Verify your answer to part (b) and find a more accurate answer using algebra.

(d) Draw a graph of height of the tennis ball versus time.

(e) Estimate the time at which the tennis ball is at its maximum height.

(f) At what time will the ball be at the same height as the building from which it was thrown on its way to the ground?

(g) What is a realistic domain for the function given the context?

(h) What is the range of the function for this context?

Exam-style Questions

1. Part of the quadratic function $y = x^2 + ax + b$ where $a, b \in \mathbb{Z}$ is shown.

    The points $R(2, 3)$ and $S(-5, -4)$ are on the curve.

    (a) Use the given points to form two equations in a and b.

    (b) Solve your equations to find the value of a and the value of b.

    (c) Write down the co-ordinates of the point where the curve crosses the y-axis.

    (d) Find the points where the curve crosses the x-axis. Give your answers correct to one place of decimals.

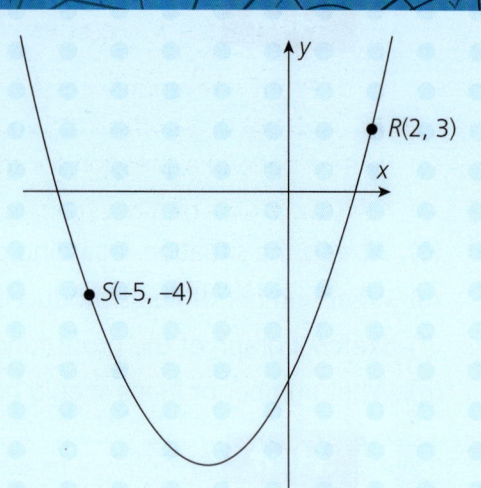

    JCHL 2013 Sample Paper 1

2. Let f be the function $f: x \mapsto x^2 - 3x + 12$. Let g be the function $g: x \mapsto 2^{x-1}$.
    Show that $f(4) = g(5)$.

    JCHL 2013 Sample Paper 1

3. The graphs of two functions f and g are shown on the grid. The functions are:

    $f(x) = (x + 2)^2 - 4$

    $g(x) = (x - 3)^2 - 4$

    (a) Match the graphs to the functions by putting $f(x)$ or $g(x)$ beside the corresponding graphs on a copy of the grid.

    (b) Write down the roots of $f(x)$ and the roots of $g(x)$.

    (c) Sketch the graph of $h: x \mapsto (x - 1)^2 - 4$ on your grid.

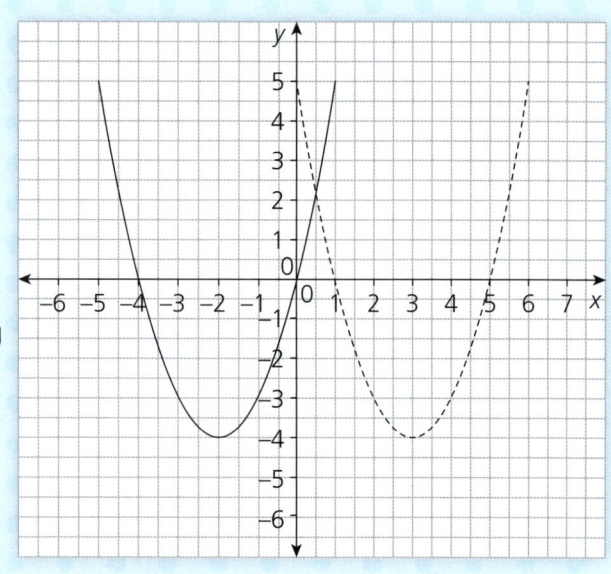

    (d) If $(x - h)^2 - 2 = x^2 - 10x + 23$, $h \in \mathbb{N}$, find the value of h.

    (e) Write down the equation of the axis of symmetry of the graph of the function $f: x \mapsto x^2 - 10x + 23$.

    JCHL 2013 Sample Paper 1

4. Investigate whether the pattern in the table is linear, quadratic or exponential. Explain your conclusion.

Term 1	Term 2	Term 3	Term 4	Term 5
$2a - b + 2c$	$8a - 2b + 2c$	$18a - 3b + 2c$	$32a - 4b + 2c$	$50a - 5b + 2c$

    JCHL 2013 Paper 2

5 (a) Three functions, $f(x)$, $g(x)$ and $h(x)$, are defined as follows:
$f(x) = 2x^2 + x - 6$, $g(x) = x^2 - 6x + 9$ and $h(x) = x^2 - 2x$.
Solve $f(x) = 0$. Solve $g(x) = 0$. Solve $h(x) = 0$.

(b) Sketches of six different functions are shown. Three of the sketches belong to the three functions from part (a).

Match each of $f(x)$, $g(x)$, $h(x)$ with the correct sketch.

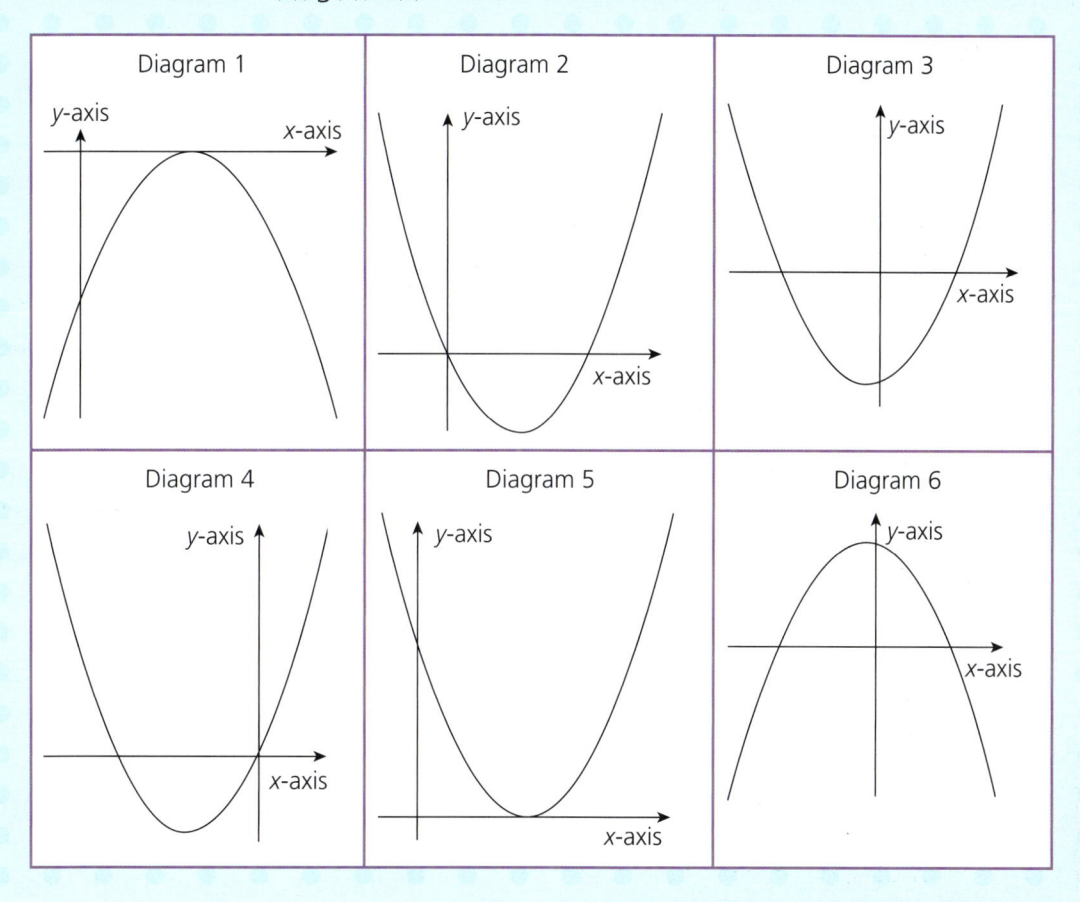

Diagram 1

Diagram 2

Diagram 3

Diagram 4

Diagram 5

Diagram 6

JCHL 2013 Paper 2

KEY WORDS AND PHRASES

- **Linear function**
- **Quadratic function**
- **Exponential function**

Chapter Summary 16

Functions

A function is a special relation in which no two couples have the same first element.

On an arrow diagram, we have a function if exactly one arrow leaves each element of the input set A.

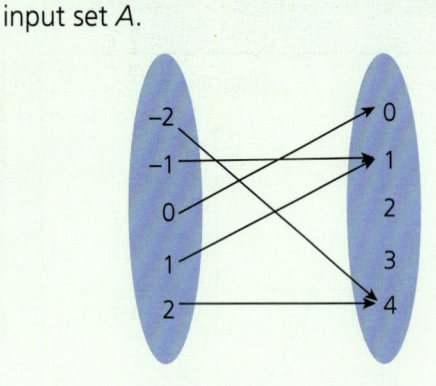

Inputs (x's)　　Outputs (y's)

- The domain of a function is the set which has all the inputs.
- The codomain is the set which contains all the possible outputs.
- The range is the set of actual outputs.
- The function $f(x) = 2x^2 - 3x + 6$ can also be written as:

$$f: x \to 2x^2 - 3x + 6 \text{ or}$$
$$y = 2x^2 - 3x + 6$$

- Graphs of quadratic functions:
  - Positive coefficient of x^2 term gives graph: 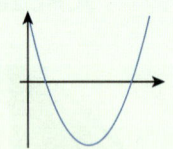
  - Negative coefficient of x^2 term gives graph:

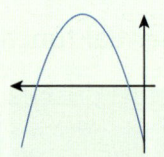

- Graphs of exponential functions 'zoom' to infinity.

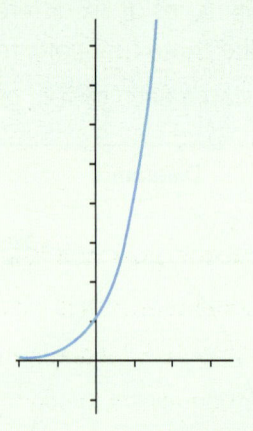

- Transformation of functions (examples)
  - The graph of $g(x) = 2x$ has a slope twice that of $f(x) = x$, and the graph of $h(x) = 3x$ has a slope three times that of $f(x) = x$.
  - The graph of $k(x) = x + 3$ is the image of the graph of $f(x) = x$ by a translation of 3 units up the y-axis.
    The graph of $l(x) = x - 2$ is the image of the graph of $f(x) = x$ by a translation of 2 units down the y-axis.
  - The rate of change of y with respect to x for $y = 7x^2$ is seven times greater than the rate of change of y with respect to x for $y = x^2$. Hence the graph of $y = 7x^2$ is 'narrower' than the graph of $y = x^2$.
  - The rate of change of y with respect to x for $y = x^2 + 8$ is the same as the rate of change of y with respect to x for $y = x^2$ when plotted on the same axes and scales. The graph of $y = x^2 + 8$ is the image of the graph of $y = x^2$ by a vertical translation of 8 units upwards.

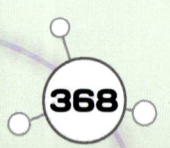

Trigonometry

Chapter 17

Learning Outcomes

In this chapter, you will learn about:
- The trigonometric ratios: sine, cosine and tangent
- Angle measure in degrees, minutes and seconds
- Using trigonometry to solve problems

Imagine that you are an engineer and you want to construct a tunnel under a mountain. You want two teams of workers to start at different ends and to meet somewhere under the mountain.

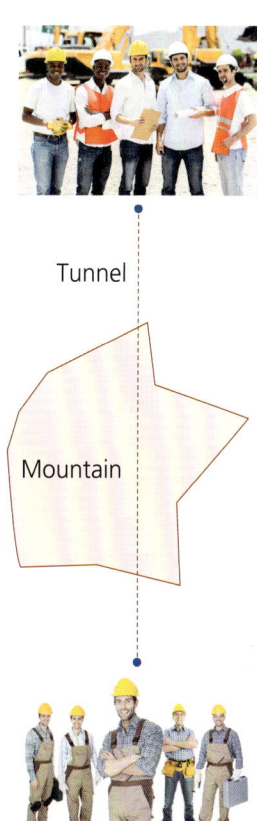

The teams cannot see each other. How do you ensure that the teams meet?

This problem was solved by Heron, a Greek mathematician who lived around 50 AD. His solution shows the power of simple geometry and trigonometry. Can you figure out how this might be done? You already have all the knowledge you need to do it.

We will see how this problem is solved later in this chapter.

Section 17A Sine, Cosine and Tangent

We have already met three trigonometrical ratios called sine, cosine and tangent:

$$\sin A = \frac{\text{Opposite}}{\text{Hypotenuse}}$$

$$\cos A = \frac{\text{Adjacent}}{\text{Hypotenuse}}$$

$$\tan A = \frac{\text{Opposite}}{\text{Adjacent}}$$

Perhaps you remember these by saying 'SOH-CAH-TOA'.

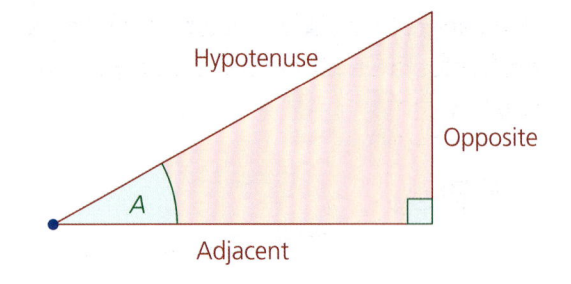

Key Point

- Remember that these ratios apply to **right-angled triangles only**.

Connections

These ratios are also called **trigonometric functions** because for any angle A:

- there is only one value for $\sin A$
- there is only one value for $\cos A$
- there is only one value for $\tan A$.

Angle of Elevation and Angle of Depression

In this diagram, a person in a low position is looking up at an object.

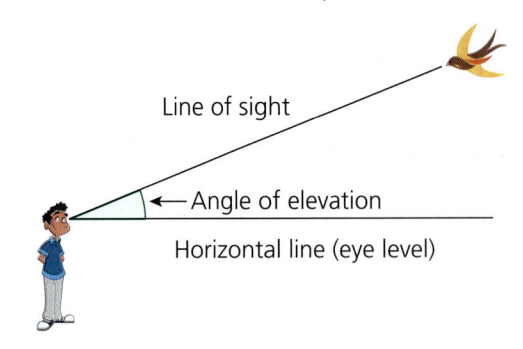

The angle between his line of sight and the horizontal line is called the **angle of elevation**.

In this diagram, a person is looking down at an object in a lower position.

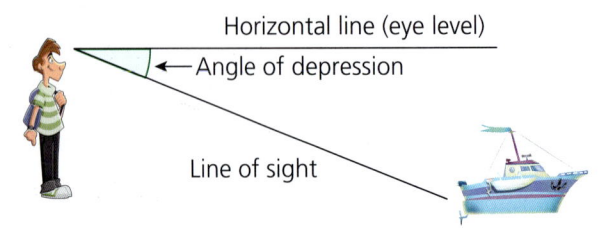

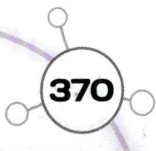

The angle between his line of sight and the horizontal line is called the **angle of depression**.

A **clinometer** or **theodolite** is used to measure angles of elevation and depression. You can make a simple clinometer using a protractor, a pen tube, some string and a small weight.

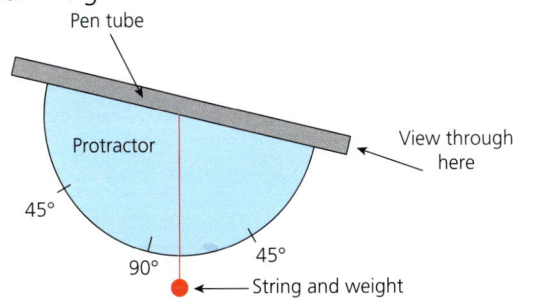

To measure distance, you can use a long measuring tape or a trundle wheel.

Example 1

Find the length of the side marked x in this triangle.

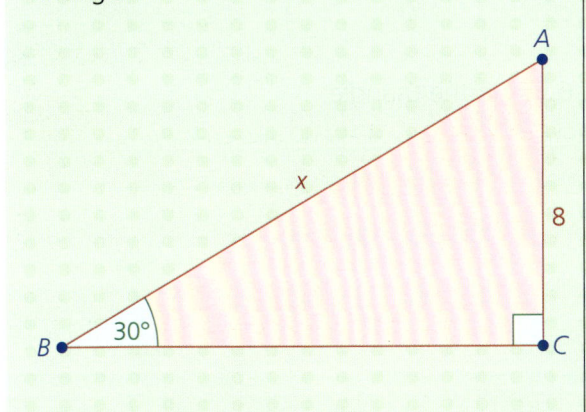

Solution

We always start by identifying the angle concerned.

The angle concerned is 30°.

8 is OPPOSITE this angle.

The other side is the HYPOTENUSE which $= x$

The ratio that connects OPP and HYP is sine.

$$\Rightarrow \sin 30° = \frac{\text{OPP}}{\text{HYP}} = \frac{8}{x}$$

$$\Rightarrow x \sin 30° = 8$$

$$\Rightarrow x = \frac{8}{\sin 30°}$$

$$\Rightarrow x = 16$$

Example 2

Find the angle β in this diagram, correct to two decimal places.

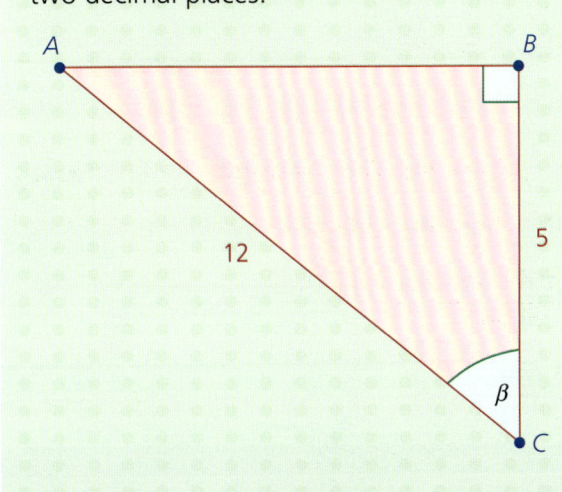

Solution

The angle concerned is β.

The side 5 = adjacent and 12 = hypotenuse.

cos is the ratio that connects ADJ and HYP.

$$\cos \beta = \frac{\text{ADJ}}{\text{HYP}} = \frac{5}{12} = 0.416666\ldots$$

We need to ask: 'What is the angle whose cos $= 0.416666\ldots$?'

This is found on the calculator by pressing

[SHIFT] [cos] 0.416666 [=]

So $\beta = \cos^{-1}(0.416666) = 65.37568°$

$= 65.38°$ to two decimal places.

Example 3

A lifeguard is sitting on a tower 10.5 metres high. He is watching a swimmer in the sea at an angle of depression of 26.57°.

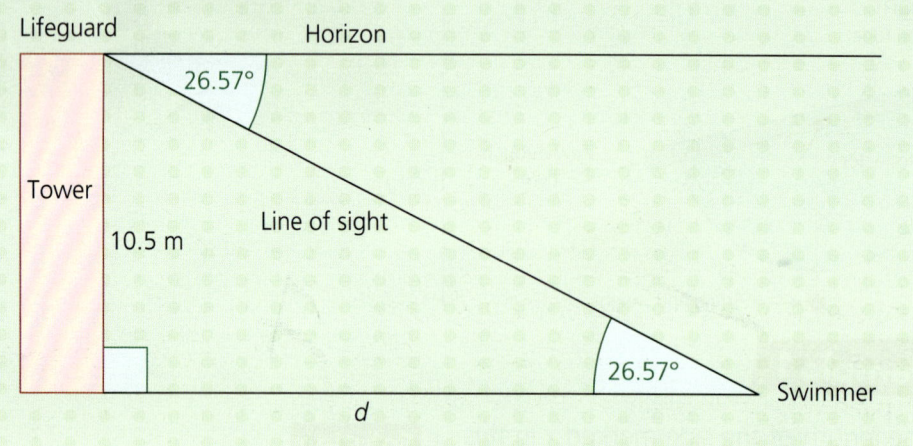

How far is the swimmer from the tower (correct to three decimal places)?

Solution

Use equal alternate angles to get the angle 26.57° in the triangle.

$$\Rightarrow \tan 26.57° = \frac{\text{OPP}}{\text{ADJ}} = \frac{10.5}{d}$$

$$\Rightarrow d \tan 26.57° = 10.5$$

$$\Rightarrow d = \frac{10.5}{\tan 26.57°}$$

$$\Rightarrow d = 20.995 \text{ m}$$

Example 4

(i) Construct an angle A such that $\tan A = \frac{4}{5}$ (draw a rough sketch first).

(ii) Hence, find (a) $\sin A$ and (b) $\cos A$ in surd form.

Solution

(i) $\tan A = \frac{\text{opposite}}{\text{adjacent}}$

Construct a right-angled triangle with base 5 units and height 4 units.

(ii) Find the hypotenuse h:

$h^2 = 4^2 + 5^2$

$\Rightarrow h^2 = 41$

$\Rightarrow h = \sqrt{41}$

$\Rightarrow$ (a) $\sin A = \frac{\text{OPP}}{\text{HYP}} = \frac{4}{\sqrt{41}}$

(b) $\cos A = \frac{\text{ADJ}}{\text{HYP}} = \frac{5}{\sqrt{41}}$

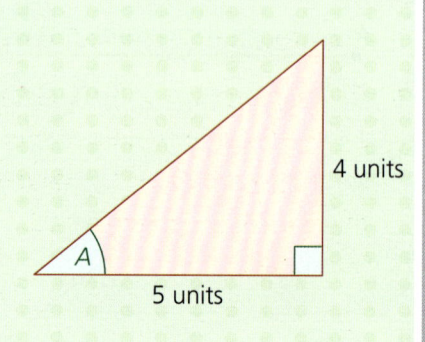

Activity 17.1

1. (i) Use the theorem of Pythagoras to find the hypotenuse in this triangle.

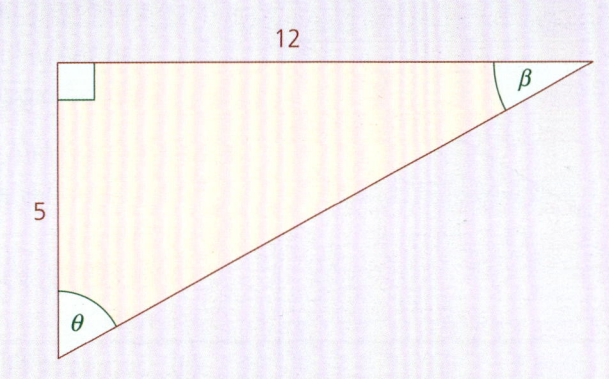

   (ii) Use the diagram to write the following ratios.
      (a) $\sin \beta$ (b) $\cos \beta$ (c) $\tan \beta$ (d) $\sin \theta$ (e) $\cos \theta$ (f) $\tan \theta$

   (iii) Explain why some of the answers in part (ii) are the same.

2. (i) Find the following ratios from this right-angled triangle.
      (a) $\sin A$
      (b) $\cos B$
      (c) $\sin B$
      (d) $\cos A$

   (ii) Write down the ratios for $\tan A$ and $\tan B$. How are they related?

3. Which of the following equals $|AC|$?
   (i) $6 \sin 30°$
   (ii) $6 \tan 30°$
   (iii) $6 \cos 30°$
   (iv) $\tan 30°$

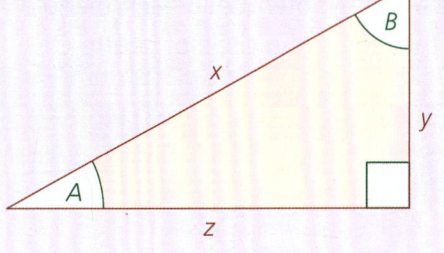

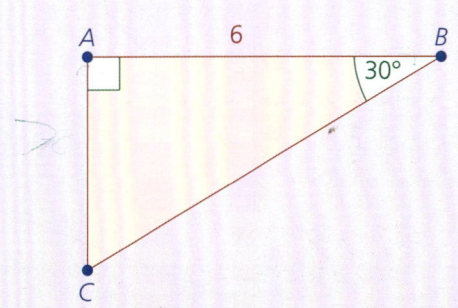

4. (i) Construct a right-angled triangle containing an angle A such that $\sin A = 0.7$.
   (ii) From your triangle, find $\cos A$ in surd form.

5. Construct a right-angled triangle containing an angle B where $\tan B = \dfrac{4}{5}$.

6. The diagram shows a crane 8 m long supported on a block 2.5 m high.
   Find the length h of the steel wire when the crane is at an angle of 37° to the horizontal.

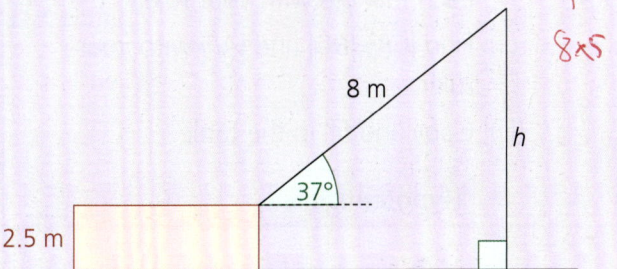

7 Which of the following statements are correct for this right-angled triangle?

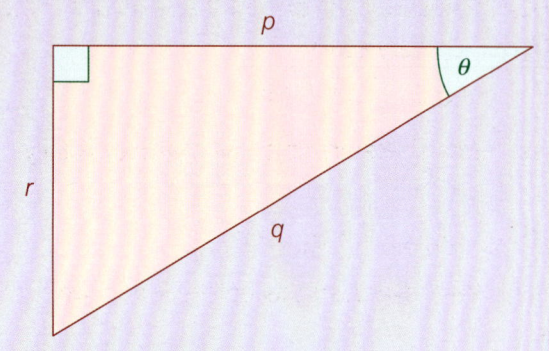

(i) $r = p \cos \theta$
(ii) $r = p \tan \theta$
(iii) $q = p \sin \theta$
(iv) $p = q \cos \theta$

8 The diagram shows three right-angled triangles. The hypotenuse in each triangle equals the radius of a circle of centre O.

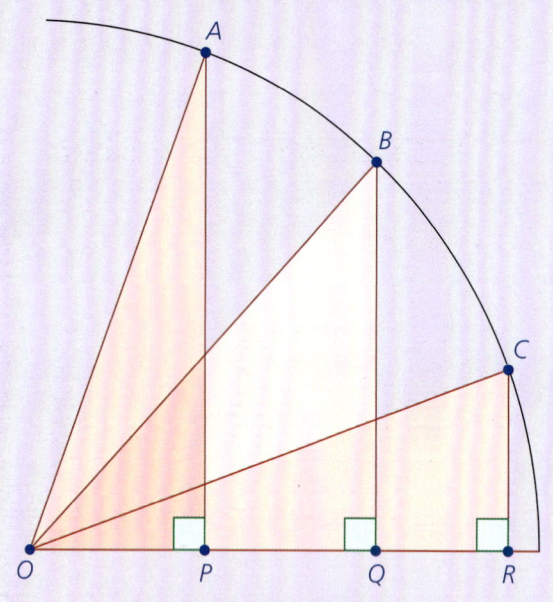

(i) Find the length of the hypotenuse of each triangle with your ruler.
(ii) Find |CR|, |BQ| and |AP| with your ruler.
(iii) Copy and fill in the table.

Hypotenuse =	
|CR| =	$\sin \angle COR = \dfrac{|CR|}{|OC|} =$
|BQ| =	$\sin \angle BOQ =$
|AP| =	$\sin \angle AOP =$

(iv) What can you conclude about the value of the sine of an angle as the angle gets bigger?
(v) Can the value of the sine of an angle ever be bigger than 1?

9 See the diagram for question 8 above. This question is about the cosine function.

(i) Find |OR|, |OQ| and |OP| with your ruler.
(ii) Copy and fill in the table below.

Hypotenuse =	
|OR| =	$\cos \angle COR = \dfrac{|OR|}{|OC|} =$
|OQ| =	$\cos \angle BOQ =$
|OP| =	$\cos \angle AOP =$

(iii) What can you conclude about the cosine of an angle as the angle gets bigger?
(iv) Can the cosine of an angle ever be bigger than 1?

10 See the diagram for question 8 above. This question is about the tangent function.

(i) Copy and fill in the table.

Side lengths	tan values
|CR| = |OR| =	$\tan \angle COR = \dfrac{|CR|}{|OR|} =$
|BQ| = |OQ| =	$\tan \angle BOQ =$
|AP| = |OP| =	$\tan \angle AOP =$

(ii) What can you conclude about the value of the tangent of an angle as the angle gets bigger?
(iii) Can the tangent of an angle ever be bigger than 1?

Section 17B Degrees, Minutes and Seconds

As we know, there are 360° in a circle. This is probably because the ancient Babylonians loved the number 360: it has 24 factors, so it can be divided up very easily.

A degree can be divided into 60 parts called minutes. We write 1° = 60′.

A minute can be subdivided into 60 parts called seconds. These are so small that we usually ignore them.

For example, 34 degrees 42 minutes 14 seconds is written as 34° 42′ 14″.

On the calculator, the button we use is labelled [°′″]. We have used this before when we worked with hours, minutes and seconds of time.

To enter 54° 37′ on a calculator, press 54 [°′″] 37 [°′″] and then press [=].

To enter tan 49° 52′, press [tan] 49 [°′″] 52 [°′″] [=]. The answer 1.186 136 92 will appear on the screen. You may be required to write this correct to a number of decimal places.

Key Point

We will be measuring angles in degrees, but angles are often measured in units called radians. Make sure that your calculator is in **degree mode**.

Example 1

(i) Convert 35.7° to degrees and minutes.
(ii) Convert 56° 27′ to decimal degrees.

Solution

(i) 35.7° (this is decimal degrees)
On the calculator, press 35.7 [°′″] [=].
35° 42′ 0″ appears on the screen.
This is 35 degrees, 42 minutes and zero seconds.
Answer = 35° 42′

(ii) 56° 27′
On the calculator, press 56 [°′″] 27 [°′″] [=] [S⇔D] [S⇔D].
56.45 appears on the screen.
Answer = 56.45°

Example 2

(i) Find sin 37° 56′ correct to four decimal places.
(ii) If cos A = 0.4567, find angle A correct to the nearest minute.

Solution

(i) sin 37° 56′
On the calculator, press
[sin] 37 [°′″] 56 [°′″] [=].
Answer = 0.614 744 166 6
     = 0.6147 correct to four decimal places.

(ii) cos A = 0.4567 ⇒ A = cos^{-1}(0.4567)
On the calculator, press
[SHIFT] [cos] 0.4567 [=].
62.825 631 33 appears. This is the answer in decimal form.
Press [°′″] once. 62° 49′ 32.27″ appears.
Answer = 62° 50′ to the nearest minute.

Example 3

Find the third angle in the triangle ABC. Give your answer in degrees and minutes.

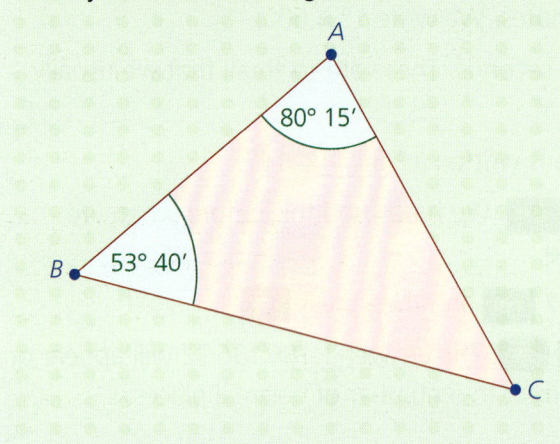

Triangle ABC with angle A = 80° 15′, angle B = 53° 40′.

Solution

|∠ACB| = 180° − (53° 40′ + 80° 15′)

Press

180 [°′″] − (53 [°′″] 40 [°′″] + 80 [°′″] 15 [°′″])

The answer 46° 5′ 0″ appears on the screen.

Answer: 46° 5′

Activity 17.2

Make sure that your calculator is in **degree mode** before starting this activity.

1. Convert the following angles to degrees and minutes, correct to the nearest minute.
   (i) 15.75°
   (ii) 35.5°
   (iii) 86.25°
   (iv) 45.4°
   (v) 33.33°
   (vi) 41.22°

2. Convert the following angles to decimal degrees, correct to one decimal place.
   (i) 17° 42′
   (ii) 49° 56′
   (iii) 22° 22′
   (iv) 82° 16′
   (v) 3° 36′
   (vi) 85° 24′

3. Calculate the following additions and subtractions. Give your answers in degrees and minutes.
   (i) 24° 56′ + 39° 42′
   (ii) 52° 11′ − 19° 53′
   (iii) 62° 44′ − 7° 52′
   (iv) 13° 13′ + 18° 37′
   (v) 81° 16′ − 3° 3′
   (vi) 45° 19′ + 24° 31′
   (vii) 22° 14′ − 14° 31′
   (viii) 63° 19′ + 22° 11′

4. Use your calculator to evaluate the following trigonometric ratios correct to four decimal places.
   (i) sin 32° 14′
   (ii) tan 46° 15′
   (iii) cos 86° 28′
   (iv) tan 16° 16′
   (v) cos 26° 52′
   (vi) sin 34° 53′
   (vii) tan 44° 36′
   (viii) sin 48° 12′

5. Two angles in a triangle measure 27° 52′ and 54° 43′. Find the third angle.

6. Two angles in an isosceles triangle both measure 46° 32′. Find the third angle.

7 Find the measure of the angles marked with a letter in the following diagrams. Give your answers in degrees and minutes correct to the nearest minute.

(i) [Triangle with angles 109° 39', 38° 36', and A]

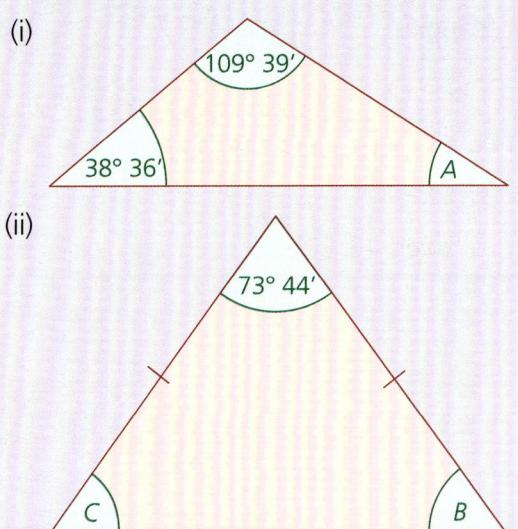

(ii) [Isoceles triangle with apex angle 73° 44', base angles C and B]

(iii) [Parallelogram DEFG with angle 56° 31' at D, angle F marked]

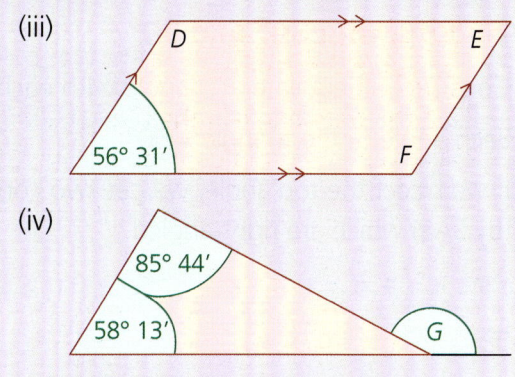

(iv) [Triangle with angles 85° 44', 58° 13', and exterior angle G]

8 Find the following angles in degrees and minutes correct to the nearest minute.

(i) cos A = 0.9123
(ii) tan B = 2.456
(iii) sin D = 0.222
(iv) cos E = 0.444
(v) sin F = 0.888
(vi) tan G = 0.52
(vii) cos H = 0.25

Section 17C Special Angles: 30°, 45° and 60°

Working with an Angle of 45°

If we construct a right-angled triangle with two sides equal to 1 unit, then we can calculate the hypotenuse:

$$x^2 = 1^2 + 1^2$$
$$\Rightarrow x^2 = 2$$
$$\Rightarrow x = \sqrt{2}$$

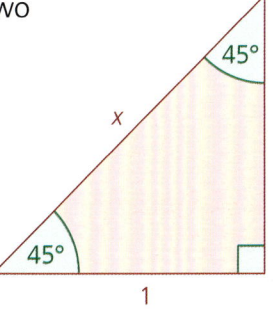

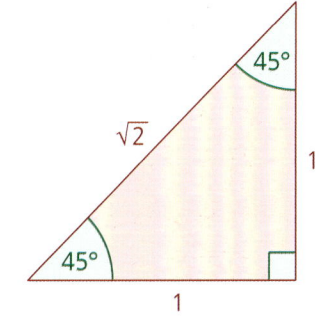

The triangle has two angles = 45°.

Thus, we have the following values:

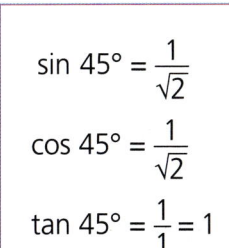

$$\sin 45° = \frac{1}{\sqrt{2}}$$
$$\cos 45° = \frac{1}{\sqrt{2}}$$
$$\tan 45° = \frac{1}{1} = 1$$

17 Working with 30° and 60°

Construct an equilateral triangle with each side equal to 2 units.

Each angle of the triangle = 60°.

If we bisect the top angle, we get two congruent triangles (by SAS) which are right-angled.

$$x^2 + 1^2 = 2^2$$
$$\Rightarrow x^2 = 2^2 - 1^2$$
$$\Rightarrow x^2 = 3$$
$$\Rightarrow x = \sqrt{3}$$

Thus, we get these ratios:

$\sin 30° = \dfrac{1}{2}$	$\sin 60° = \dfrac{\sqrt{3}}{2}$
$\cos 30° = \dfrac{\sqrt{3}}{2}$	$\cos 60° = \dfrac{1}{2}$
$\tan 30° = \dfrac{1}{\sqrt{3}}$	$\tan 60° = \dfrac{\sqrt{3}}{1} = \sqrt{3}$

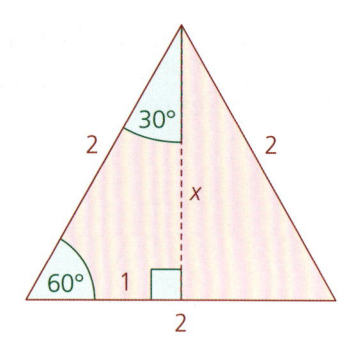

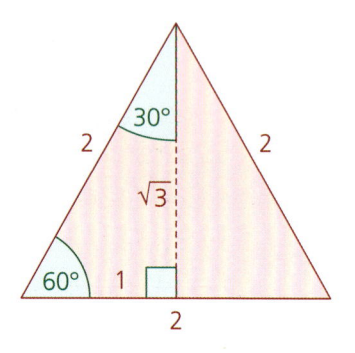

You can see these values in the *Formulae and tables* booklet on page 13.

The ratios for these special angles are given in surd form. As we know, surds are irrational numbers and cannot be written precisely in decimal form. Thus, it is often better to write these ratios in this way.

Example 1

Find the value of x in this diagram. Give your answer in the form $a\sqrt{b}$.

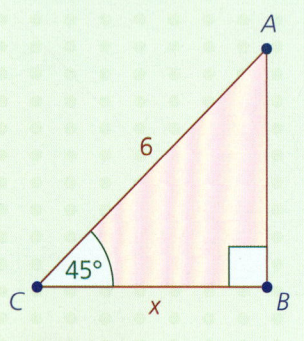

Solution

$$\cos 45° = \frac{\text{adjacent}}{\text{hypotenuse}} = \frac{x}{6}$$
$$\Rightarrow \frac{1}{\sqrt{2}} = \frac{x}{6}$$
$$\Rightarrow \sqrt{2}(x) = 6$$
$$\Rightarrow x = \frac{6}{\sqrt{2}}$$

$$x = \frac{6}{\sqrt{2}} = \frac{6}{\sqrt{2}} \times \frac{\sqrt{2}}{\sqrt{2}} = \frac{6\sqrt{2}}{2} = 3\sqrt{2} \text{ units}$$

Example 2

Find the value of $\cos^2 45° + \sin^2 60° + \tan^2 30°$.

Hint

$\cos^2 45°$ is the same as $(\cos 45°)^2$.

Solution

$$\cos^2 45° + \sin^2 60° + \tan^2 30°$$
$$= \left(\frac{1}{\sqrt{2}}\right)^2 + \left(\frac{\sqrt{3}}{2}\right)^2 + \left(\frac{1}{\sqrt{3}}\right)^2$$
$$= \frac{1}{2} + \frac{3}{4} + \frac{1}{3}$$
$$= \frac{19}{12} \text{ or } 1\frac{7}{12}$$

Activity 17.3

1 (i) Construct the following triangle. You may use any unit of length.

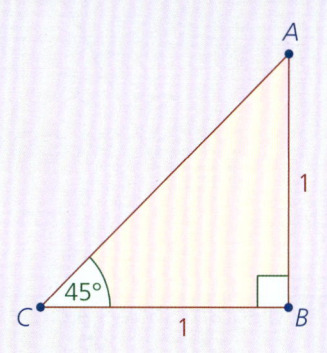

[Triangle ABC with right angle at B, angle 45° at C, sides CB = 1, BA = 1]

(ii) Calculate |AC| and give your answer in surd form.

(iii) Copy this table and use your work in parts (i) and (ii) to complete it. All entries should be integers or in surd form.

A	45°
sin A	
cos A	
tan A	

2 (i) Construct the following triangle and the perpendicular from E onto FG. You may use any unit of length.

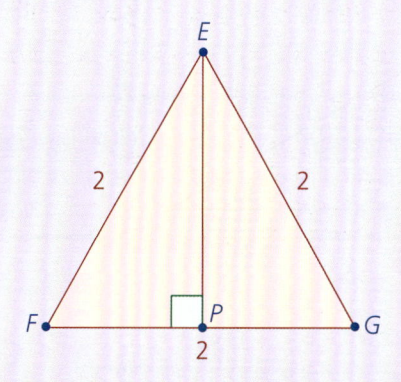

[Triangle EFG with EF = 2, EG = 2, FG = 2, with perpendicular EP from E to FG]

(ii) Prove that the triangles EFP and EPG are congruent.

(iii) Calculate |EP| and fill in the missing angles.

(iv) Copy and complete this table. All entries should be fractions or in surd form.

A	30°	60°
sin A		
cos A		
tan A		

3 Find the value of x in each of the following triangles. Give your answers in the form $a\sqrt{b}$.

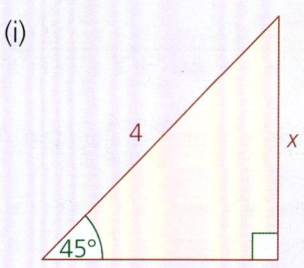

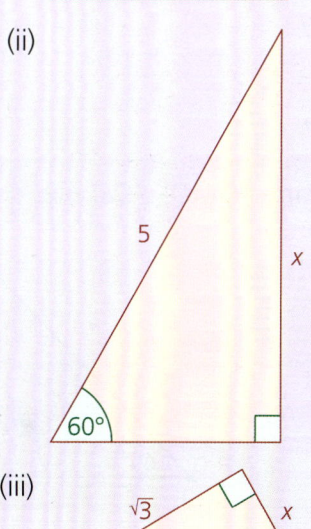

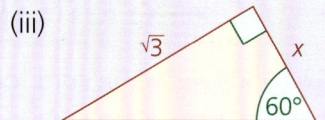

(i) [Right triangle with hypotenuse side 4, angle 45°, side x]

(ii) [Right triangle with side 5, angle 60°, side x]

(iii) [Right triangle with side $\sqrt{3}$, angle 60°, side x]

(iv)

[Triangle with 30° angle at top, hypotenuse 6, side x, right angle at bottom]

4 Find the lengths a and b and the angle θ in the diagram.

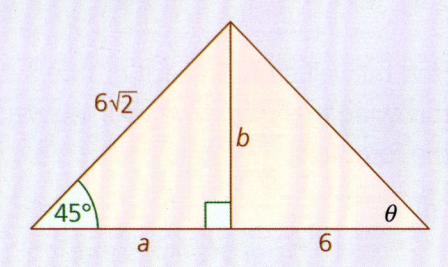

[Triangle with 45° angle at left, hypotenuse $6\sqrt{2}$, altitude b, base split into a and 6, angle θ at right]

5 If $A = 45°$, verify that $\dfrac{\sin A}{\cos A} = \tan A$.

6 Find the value of x in the diagram.

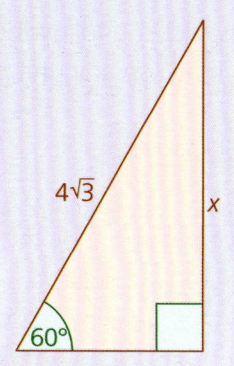

[Right triangle with side $4\sqrt{3}$, hypotenuse x, 60° angle]

7 The diagram shows a circle of centre O. $[DC]$ is a diameter of the circle.

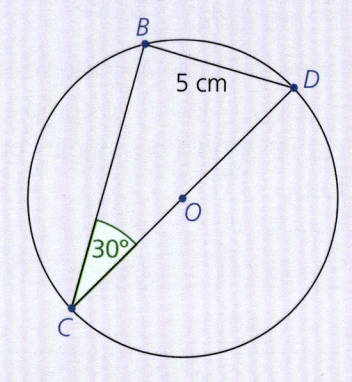

[Circle with points B, D, C on circumference, O centre, BD = 5 cm, angle BCD = 30°]

(i) Name a right angle and give a reason for your answer.

(ii) Find the radius of the circle.

8 In the diagram, $PR \perp QS$. $|QR| = 2$.

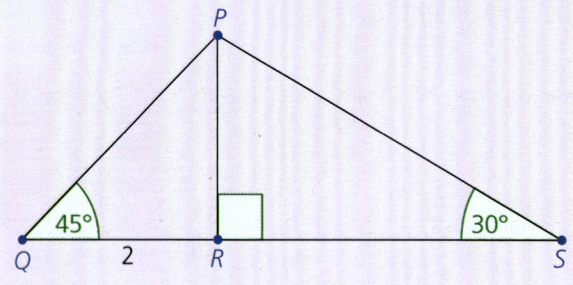

[Triangle PQS with P at top, Q at left with 45° angle, S at right with 30° angle, R on QS with |QR| = 2 and right angle at R]

Find $|RS|$. Give your answer in surd form.

9 If $A = 60°$, verify that $\sin^2 A + \cos^2 A = 1$.

10 (i) If $A = 30°$, find $\sin 2A$ and $2 \sin A$.

(ii) Is $\sin 2A = 2 \sin A$?

11 (i) Find $(\sin 60°)(\cos 30°) + (\cos 60°)(\sin 30°)$.

(ii) Find $\sin (60° + 30°)$.

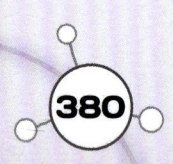

Section 17D Problem Solving

Example 1 below shows how Heron used simple trigonometry and geometry to solve the problem mentioned at the beginning of this chapter.

Example 1

You are an engineer and you want to construct a tunnel under a mountain. You want two teams of workers to start at different ends and to meet somewhere under the mountain.

The teams cannot see each other. How do you ensure that the teams meet?

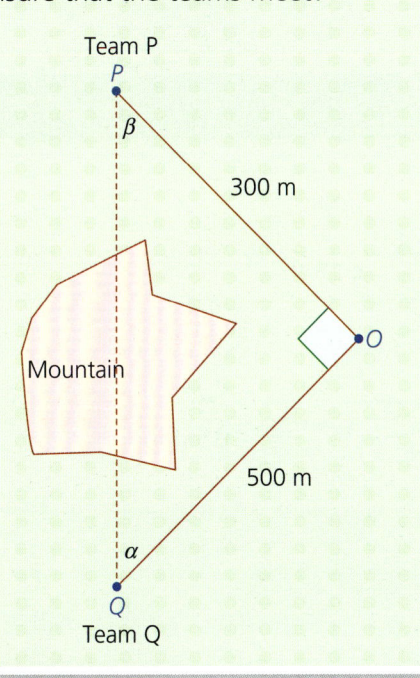

Solution

One team starts from *P* and the other team starts from *Q* so that both teams are visible from a point *O*. *O* is a point such that $|\angle POQ| = 90°$.

Measure the distances |PO| and |OQ|.

Say |PO| = 300 m and |QO| = 500 m.

Find $\angle PQO$:

$$|\angle PQO| = \tan^{-1}\frac{300}{500} = 30°\, 58'$$

Team Q have to dig along a line making this angle with OQ.

The angle for team P is $(90° - 30°\, 58') = 59°\, 2'$. Team P have to dig along a line making this angle with OP.

The two teams then must meet in the middle.

In the 21st century, we would use satellites and GPS systems to sight the teams, but the maths involved is similar.

Example 2

Mary observes the angle of elevation of the top of a cliff 200 m high to be 24°.

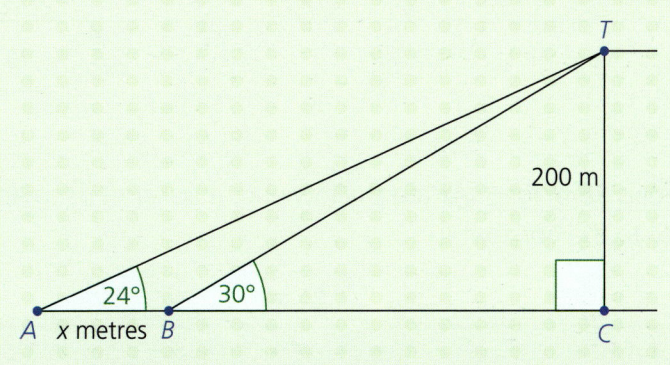

When she moves closer to the cliff by a distance of *x* metres the angle increases to 30°. How far did she travel towards the cliff? Give your answer correct to one decimal place.

Solution

In triangle ATC: $\tan 24° = \dfrac{200}{|AC|}$

$\Rightarrow |AC| \times \tan 24° = 200$

$\Rightarrow |AC| = \dfrac{200}{\tan 24°} = 449.21$ m

In triangle BTC: $\tan 30° = \dfrac{200}{|BC|}$

$\Rightarrow |BC| \times \tan 30° = 200$

$\Rightarrow |BC| = \dfrac{200}{\tan 30°} = 346.41$ m

∴ Mary travelled 449.21 − 346.41 = 102.8 metres.

Activity 17.4

1. The roof of this house has a pitch of 14°. Find the height h of the apex of the roof above the ground. Give your answer to two decimal places.

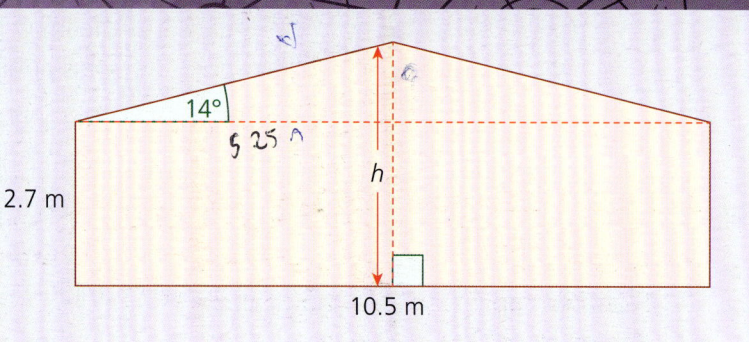

   2.7 m, 14°, 10.5 m

2. Robert used a tree on one bank of a river to mark a point R directly across from it.

   He then walked 70 m along the bank until he reached point S. Using a theodolite, he measured the angle TSR to be 56° 18′.

   Find the width of the river correct to two decimal places.

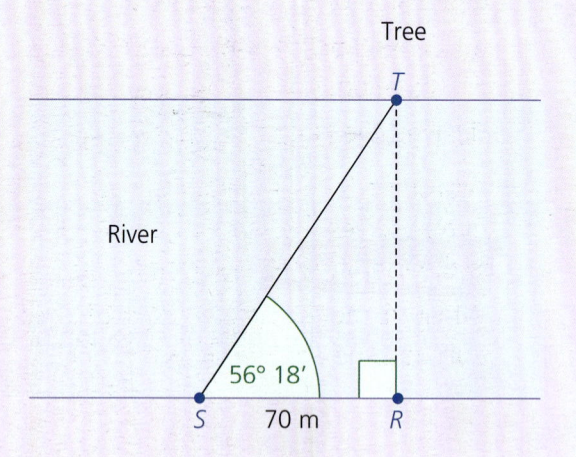

3. A swimming pool is 25 m long. At the shallow end, it is 1.4 m deep and the floor is inclined at 3° 15′ to the horizontal.

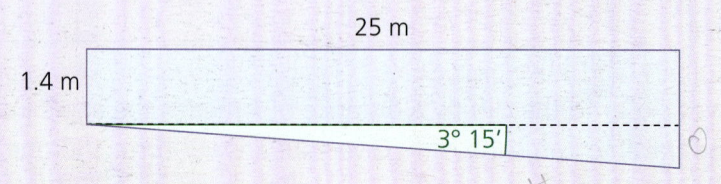

   25 m, 1.4 m, 3° 15′

   Find the depth of water at the deep end.

4 From a rooftop on one side of a street, Charlie observes the angle of elevation of the top of a building to be 21° 48′.

From the same position, the angle of depression of the bottom of the building is 50° 11′.

The building is 25 m distant from Charlie. Find the height of the building correct to two decimal places.

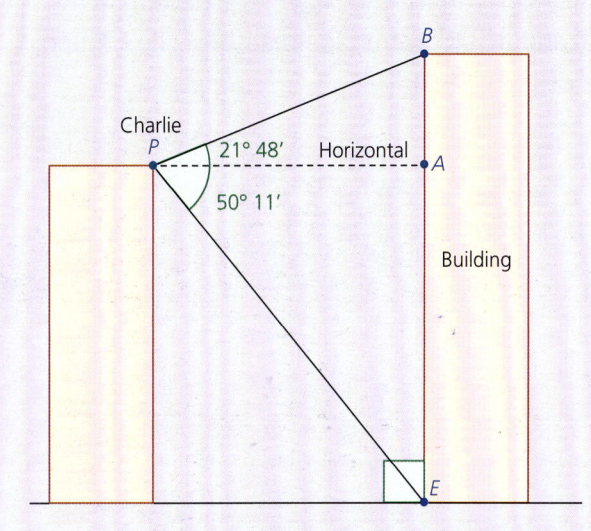

5 A boat is 500 m from the base of a cliff. From the top of the cliff, the angle of depression of the boat is 34°.
  (i) Draw a diagram to represent this situation.
  (ii) Find the height of the cliff.

6 A building is 15 m high. Tom observes the angle of elevation of the top of the building to be 26°. When he moves x metres closer to the building, the angle increases to 44°.

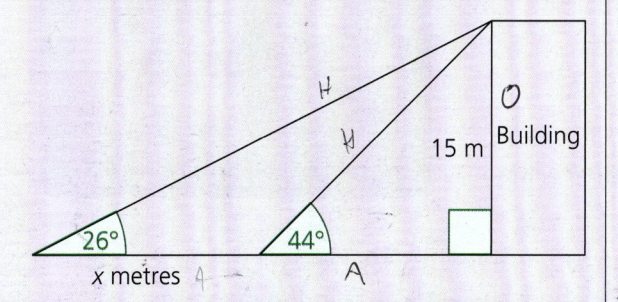

How far did Tom travel, correct to one decimal place?

7 A ladder is 13 m long. It is put against a wall so that it reaches a point on the wall 12.1 metres above the ground.

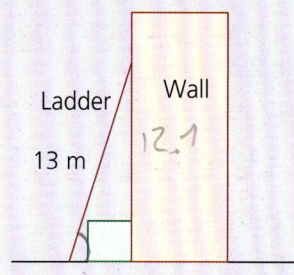

  (i) What angle does the ladder make with the ground?
  (ii) If the ladder were to reach a point 12.6 m high, what angle would the ladder make with the ground?
  (iii) The correct angle for a ladder is 75°. How high will the ladder reach up the wall at this angle?

8 A road sign says that the slope of the road at that point is 10%. What angle does the road make with the horizontal?

9 A vertical pole [AB] is supported by two stay-wires [AC] and [AD]. Points C and D are 20 m apart and in line with the pole. From C, the angle of elevation of the top of the pole is 60°. From D, the angle of elevation of the top of the pole is 30°. Let $x = |CB|$.

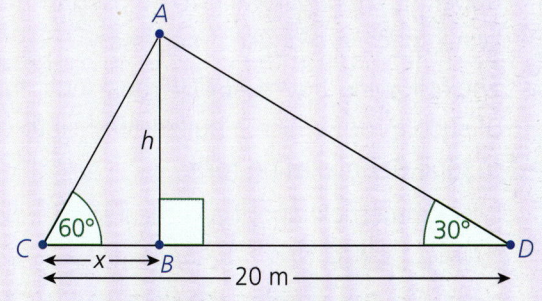

  (i) Use triangle ABC to write h in terms of x.
  (ii) Use triangle ABD to write h in terms of x.
  (iii) Find the value of x.
  (iv) Use your answer to part (iii) to find h, the height of the pole.

10 The diagram shows a circle of centre O with [PQ] as a diameter.
  (i) Name three equal line segments in the diagram.
      Give a reason for your answer.
  (ii) Name a right angle in the diagram.
      Explain your answer.
  (iii) Calculate x and express your answer
      in surd form.

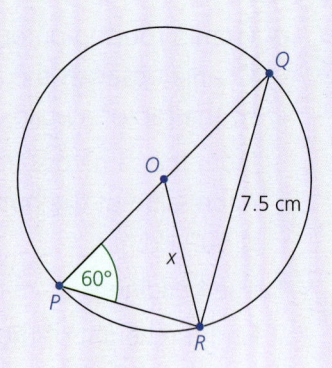

11 Two students want to find the height of a church spire in their locality. They have a clinometer (for measuring angles of elevation) and a 100 metre tape measure. The ground is level and they can get access to the interior of the church.

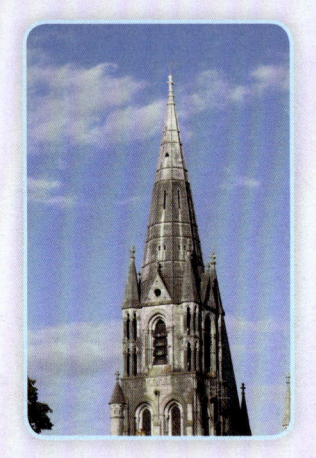

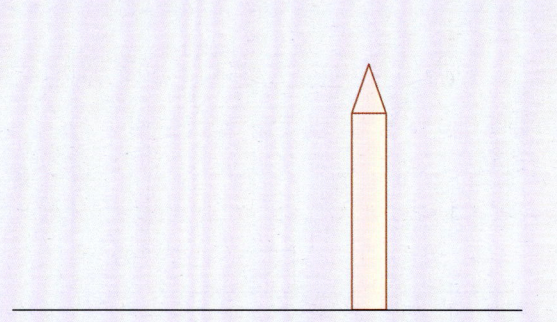

  (i) Explain how they could find the height of the church. Your answer should be illustrated on a diagram like the one shown.
  (ii) Show the point(s) where you think they should take measurements and write down what measurements they should take.
  (iii) Outline briefly how these can be used to find the height of the church.

12 A mansard roof is a four-sided roof having a double slope, with the lower slope much steeper than the upper. Its shape allows it to be used to maximise living space in a house if necessary.

The following figure ABCDE represents the outline of such a roof which a builder wishes to construct to replace an existing roof.

It is symmetrical about a vertical line through C.

A cross-section of a room within the roof is shaded, with [TH] representing the floor and [VW] the ceiling of the room.

The height from the floor to the apex of the roof is 4 metres. |AE| = 6 metres and |AT| = 0.9 metres. The inclination of AB is 22° from the vertical as in the diagram.

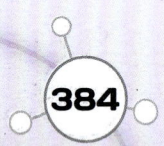

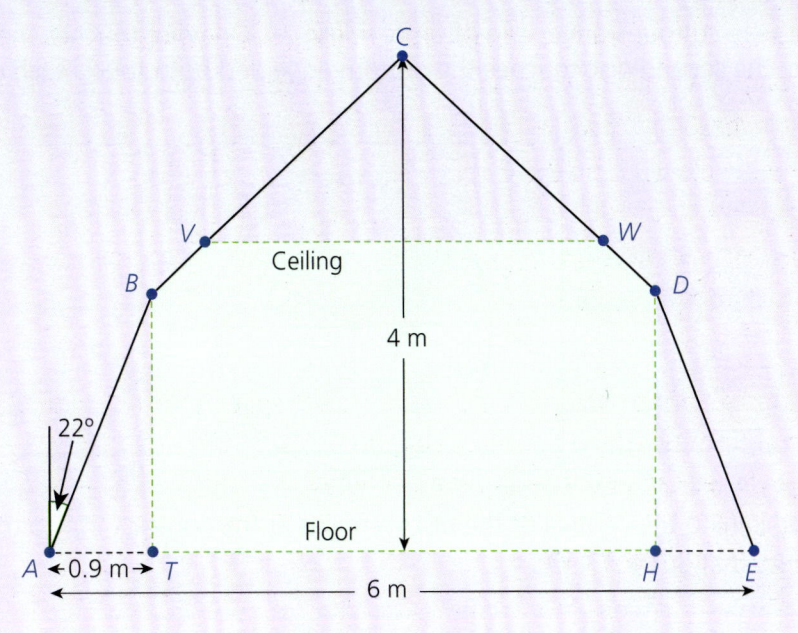

(i) Find |AB|.
(ii) Find the total length of the outline *ABCDE* of the roof correct to two decimal places.
(iii) If the floor to ceiling height is to be at least 2.4 metres, find the maximum length of [*VW*].
(iv) Make an accurate scaled drawing of the outline of the roof, using the scale 1:60. This is, 1 cm on your diagram should represent 60 cm in reality.

13 The diagram below represents a simplified model of a bridge known as a cable-stayed bridge where *PQ* is the supporting tower and *AF* is the carriageway for traffic.

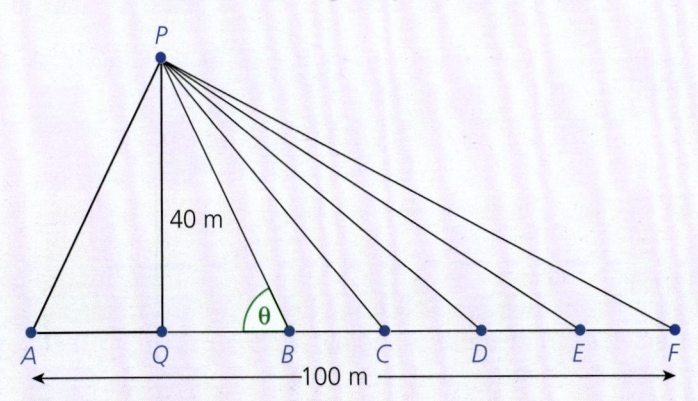

In this particular model, $|\angle APF| = 90°$, $|PQ| = 40$ m and $|AF| = 100$ m.
(i) If *Q* is to be nearer to *A* than *F*, use your knowledge of geometry to explain why there is only one location along *AF* for the tower *PQ* in this model.
(ii) Let $|AQ| = x$. Express $|QF|$ in terms of x.
(iii) Prove that the triangles *APQ* and *PQF* are similar.
(iv) Hence, find x.
(v) The five cables emanating from *P* meet *AF* at equal intervals of y metres at the points *B*, *C*, *D*, *E* and *F*. If $\tan \theta = 2$, where θ is the angle which the shortest cable [*PB*] makes with *AF*, find the value of y.

14 Two discs are cut out from a strip of tin of width 2k. One disc touches the top edge of the strip, the second disc touches the bottom edge and both touch each other, as in the diagram.

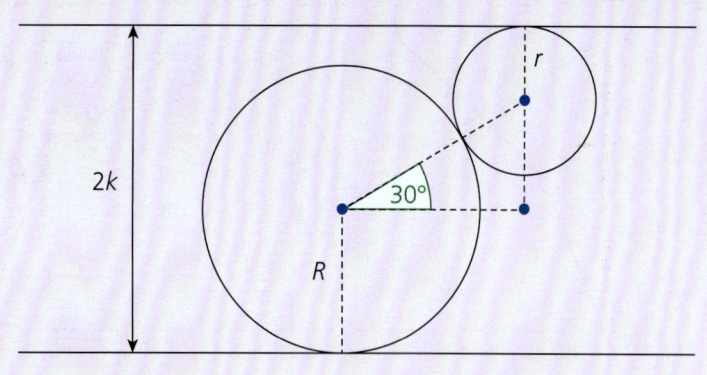

If the line joining the centres of the discs remains at the angle of 30° to the edge of the strip, show that $3(R + r) = 4k$.

Revision Activity 17

1 Find the lengths marked with letters in each of these triangles.

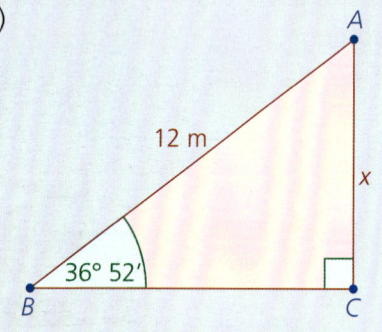

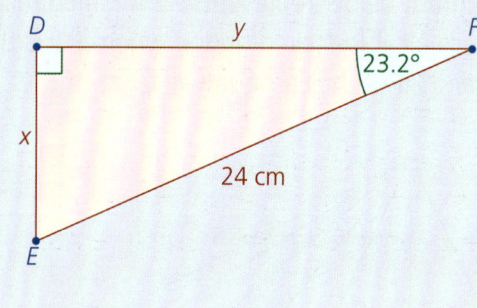

(a) Triangle ABC with angle B = 36° 52', AB = 12 m, BC = x, right angle at C.

(b) Triangle DEF with right angle at D, DE = x, DF = y, EF = 24 cm, angle at F = 23.2°.

2 If $A = 30°$, verify that $\dfrac{\sin A}{\cos A} = \tan A$.

3 Find the angles marked with letters in each of these triangles.

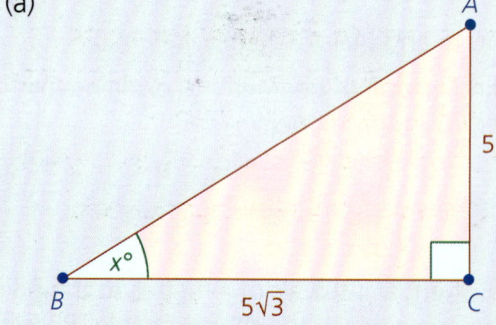

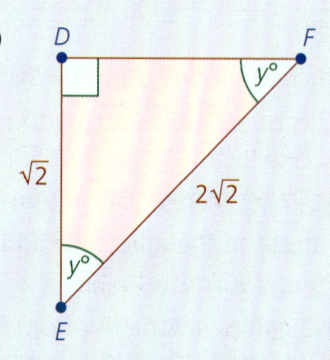

(a) Triangle ABC with angle B = x°, BC = 5√3, AC = 5, right angle at C.

(b) Triangle DEF with right angle at D, DE = √2, EF = 2√2, angles y° at F and at E.

4 If $A = 30°$, verify that $\sin^2 A + \cos^2 A = 1$.

5 Two vertical poles A and B, each of height h, are standing on opposite sides of a level road. They are 24 m apart. The point P, on the road directly between the two poles, is a distance x from pole A. The angle of elevation from P to the top of pole A is 60°.

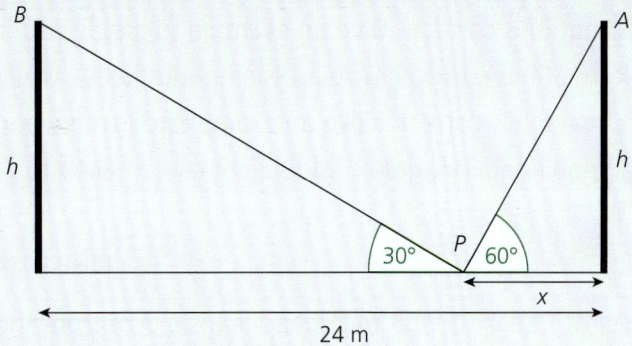

(a) Write h in terms of x.

(b) From P the angle of elevation to the top of pole B is 30°. Find h, the height of the two poles.

6 A group of students wish to calculate the height of the Millennium Spire in Dublin. The spire stands on flat level ground. Maria, who is 1.72 m tall, looks up at the top of the spire using a clinometer and records an angle of elevation of 60°. Her feet are 70 m from the base of spire. Ultan measures the circumference of the base of the spire as 7.07 m.

(a) Explain how Ultan's measurement will be used in the calculation of the height of the spire.

(b) Draw a suitable diagram and calculate the height of the spire, to the nearest metre, using the measurements obtained by the students.

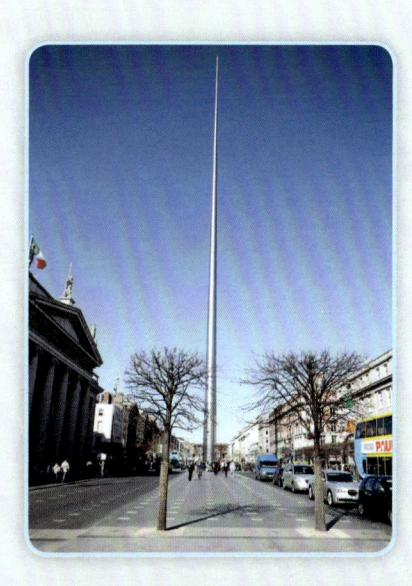

JCHL 2011 Paper 2

Exam-style Questions

1 During a trigonometry lesson, a group of students wrote down some statements about what they expected to happen when they looked at the values of trigonometric functions of some angles. Here are some of the things they wrote down.

(i) The value from any of these trigonometric functions will **always** be less than 1.

(ii) If the size of the angle is doubled, then the value from these trigonometric functions will not double.

(iii) The value from all of the trigonometric functions will increase if the size of the angle is increased.

(iv) I do not need to use a calculator to find sin 60°. I can do it by drawing an equilateral triangle. The answer will be in surd form.

They then found the sin, cos and tan of some angles, correct to three decimal places, to test their ideas.

(a) Do you think that (i) is correct? Give an example to justify your answer.

(b) Do you think that (ii) is correct? Give an example to justify your answer.

(c) Do you think that (iii) is correct? Give an example to justify your answer.

(d) Show how an equilateral triangle of side 2 cm can be used to find sin 60° in surd form.

JCHL 2014 Sample Paper 2

2 The Leaning Tower of Pisa is 55.863 m tall and leans 3.9 m from the perpendicular, as shown below. The tower of the Suurhusen Church in north-western Germany is 27.37 m tall and leans 2.47 m from the perpendicular.

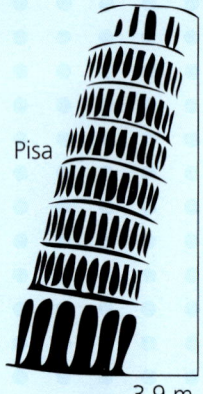

By providing diagrams and suitable calculations and explanations, decide which tower should enter the *Guiness Book of Records* as the **Most Tilted Tower in the World**.

JCHL 2014 Sample Paper 2

KEY WORDS AND PHRASES

- The theorem of Pythagoras
- Right-angled triangle
- Hypotenuse
- Opposite side
- Adjacent side
- Ratio
- Trigonometry ratio
- sin A
- cos A
- tan A
- Angle of elevation
- Angle of depression

Chapter Summary 17

- Three trigonometrical ratios, sine, cosine and tangent:

  $\sin A = \dfrac{\text{Opposite}}{\text{Hypotenuse}}$

  $\cos A = \dfrac{\text{Adjacent}}{\text{Hypotenuse}}$

  $\tan A = \dfrac{\text{Opposite}}{\text{Adjacent}}$

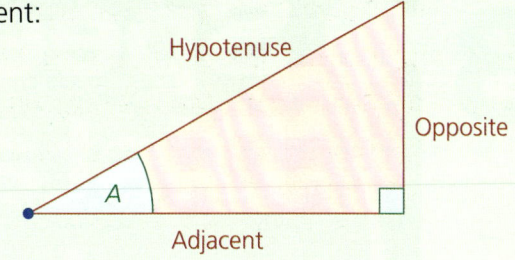

- The angle between the line of sight and the horizontal line is called the **angle of elevation**.

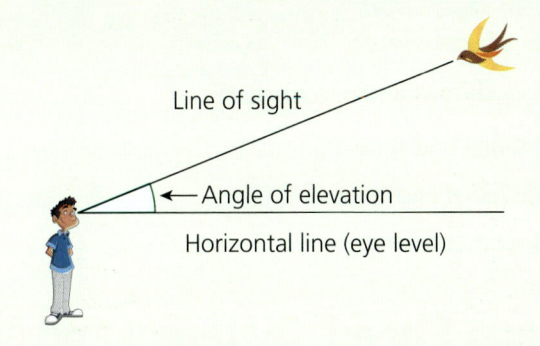

- The angle between the line of sight and the horizontal line is called the **angle of depression**.

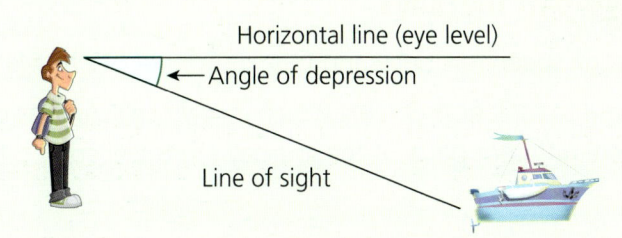

- 34 degrees 42 minutes 14 seconds is written as 34° 42′ 14″.

- Special angles:

  $\sin 45° = \dfrac{1}{\sqrt{2}}$

  $\cos 45° = \dfrac{1}{\sqrt{2}}$

  $\tan 45° = \dfrac{1}{1} = 1$

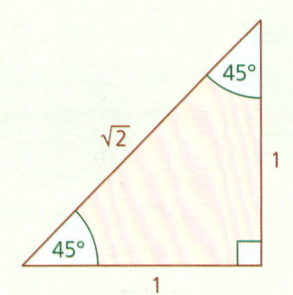

  $\sin 30° = \dfrac{1}{2}$ $\sin 60° = \dfrac{\sqrt{3}}{2}$

  $\cos 30° = \dfrac{\sqrt{3}}{2}$ $\cos 60° = \dfrac{1}{2}$

  $\tan 30° = \dfrac{1}{\sqrt{3}}$ $\tan 60° = \dfrac{\sqrt{3}}{1} = \sqrt{3}$

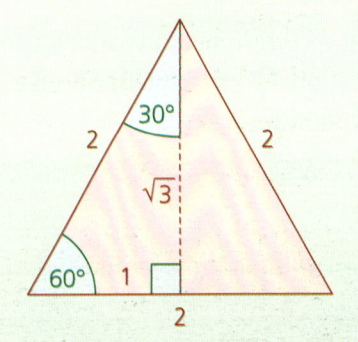

Chapter 18
Speed, Distance, Time and Graphs

Learning Outcomes

In this chapter, you will learn more about:
- Average speed, distance and time
- Graphs involving distance and time
- Graphs involving speed and time

Section 18A Average Speed, Distance and Time

Average Speed for Two-part Journeys

We have already met average speed, distance and time in *Connect With Maths 1*.

In this chapter, we are going to look at problems which involve calculations of speed, distance and time for journeys where different parts of the journey are travelled at different speeds.

> **Key Point**
>
> When a car travels at two different speeds for two different parts of a journey, we can calculate the average speed for the entire journey.
> To do this, we must use the formula:
>
> $$\text{Average speed} = \frac{\text{total distance travelled}}{\text{total time taken}}$$
>
> The average speed **is not** found by finding the average of the two speeds.

Example 1

Jane commutes to work by car and train. It takes 15 minutes to drive to her local train station 10 km from her house. She then takes 30 minutes to travel 30 km to work by commuter train.

(i) What is the average speed in km/h of Jane's car journey?
(ii) What is the average speed in km/h of Jane's train journey?
(iii) What is the average speed in km/h of Jane's total journey to work?

Solution

(i) Average speed of Jane's car journey:

Distance travelled = 10 km

Time taken = 15 minutes = $\frac{15}{60}$ = 0.25 h

Using,

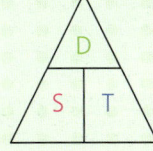

Average speed

= $\frac{\text{distance}}{\text{time}} = \frac{10}{0.25}$ = 40 km/h

(ii) Average speed for the train journey:

Distance travelled = 30 km

Time taken = 30 minutes = 0.5 h

Average speed = $\frac{\text{distance}}{\text{time}}$

= $\frac{30}{0.5}$ = 60 km/h

(iii) Average speed for whole journey

= $\frac{\text{total distance travelled}}{\text{total time taken}}$

= $\frac{10 \text{ km} + 30 \text{ km}}{0.25 \text{ hr} + 0.5 \text{ hr}}$

= $\frac{40}{0.75}$

= $53\frac{1}{3}$ km/h

Connections

We can use our knowledge of algebra to solve problems with speed, distance and time.

Example 2

Mary drove from her home to the shop at a speed of 40 km/h. She drove back from the shop to her home at a speed of 60 km/h. What was her average speed for the whole journey to the shop and back?

Solution

Here we don't know the distance to the shop. Hence, we use a variable.

Let x be the distance from Mary's home to the shop.

- Journey from **home to the shop**:

  Distance travelled = x km

  Speed = 40 km/h

  Time taken = $\frac{x}{40}$ h

- Journey from the **shop back to home**:

  Distance travelled = x km

  Speed = 60 km/h

  Time taken = $\frac{x}{60}$ h

- Total time for **whole journey**

  = $\frac{x}{40} + \frac{x}{60}$

  = $\frac{3x + 2x}{120}$

  = $\frac{5x}{120} = \frac{x}{24}$ h

Average speed for whole journey

= $\frac{\text{total distance}}{\text{total time}} = \frac{2x}{\left(\frac{x}{24}\right)}$

= $\frac{2x(24)}{x}$

= 48 km/h

Units

We have already seen some different units for speed, kilometres per hour (km/h) and metres per second (m/s). Now we will examine problems where we need to convert from one of these units to the other.

Example 3

Convert 108 km/h to m/s.

Solution

Method 1

Unitary method

$$\begin{aligned}
& 108 \text{ km} && \text{in} && 1 \text{ hour} \\
\Rightarrow\ & 108\,000 \text{ m} && \text{in} && (60 \times 60) \text{ seconds} \\
\Rightarrow\ & 108\,000 \text{ m} && \text{in} && 3600 \text{ seconds} \\
\Rightarrow\ & \tfrac{108\,000}{3600} \text{ m} && \text{in} && 1 \text{ second} \\
\Rightarrow\ & 30 \text{ m} && \text{in} && 1 \text{ second}
\end{aligned}$$

i.e. 30 m/s

Method 2

- Convert 108 km to metres.

  1 km = 1000 m

  108 km = 108 × 1000 = 108 000 m

- Convert 1 hour to seconds.

  1 hour = 60 minutes = 60 × 60 seconds
  = 3600 seconds

  $$\text{Speed} = \frac{\text{distance}}{\text{time}}$$
  $$= \frac{108\,000}{3600}$$
  $$= 30 \text{ m/s}$$

Activity 18.1

1. A man travels from Arklow to Blanchardstown, a distance of 90 km. He leaves Arklow at 09:25 and arrives in Blanchardstown at 10:55.

   (i) Calculate his average speed for the journey.

   He continues from Blanchardstown to Cootehill, a distance of 112 km. He increases his average speed by 4 km/h for this section of his journey.

   (ii) At what time does he arrive in Cootehill?

2. Copy and complete the table by filling in the values for x.

Distance	Time	Average speed
100 km	2 hours	x km/h
20 km	20 minutes	x km/h
240 km	x hours	80 km/h
1600 m	x seconds	20 m/s
x km	15 minutes	10 m/s
x m	90 seconds	100 km/h

3. Seán leaves his house at 7.15 am and travels by car to the train station 25 km away arriving at 7.45 am. He then catches the train to Dublin which takes 1 hour and 30 minutes to travel 120 kilometres.

   (i) What is the average speed of Seán's car journey in km/h?

   (ii) What is the average speed of Seán's train journey in km/h?

   (iii) What is the average speed of Seán's complete journey in km/h?

4. A van travels an average speed of 65 km/h for 2 hours and then travels at an average speed of 70 km/h for half an hour. What is the average speed travelled over the $2\frac{1}{2}$ hours?

5. A car travelled a distance of 250 km in 4 hours 24 minutes. The average speed for the first 180 km was 60 km/h. What was the average speed for the remainder of the journey?

6. (i) Convert 54 km/h to m/s.
   (ii) Convert 72 km/h to m/s.
   (iii) Convert 36 km/h to m/s.
   (iv) Convert 126 km/h to m/s.

7. A man walks 2 km to a bus stop at an average speed of 2.5 km/h. He then takes a bus which takes 42 minutes to travel 49 km to his workplace.
   (i) How long in hours did the man take to walk to the bus stop?
   (ii) Find the average speed of the bus journey in km/h.
   (iii) Find the average speed of the complete journey in km/h.

8. To get to a shopping centre, Grace walks 1 km to the bus station and then gets a bus to the shopping centre, which is 7 km from the bus stop. Grace's walking speed is 4 km/h and the average speed of the bus is 35 km/h.
   (i) How long in hours was Grace walking?
   (ii) How long was Grace on the bus?
   (iii) What is the average speed over the full journey? Give your answer correct to two decimal places.

9. Tom cycled from Ballyfore to Newtown against a headwind at a speed of 20 km/h. He cycled back from Newtown to Ballyfore at a speed of 30 km/h. What was his average speed for the complete journey?

10. The distance from Allentown to Balyna is half the distance from Balyna to Courtown. The total distance from Allentown to Courtown, through Balyna, is 60 km.

    A car travels at x km/h from Balyna to Courtown. The total time for the journey is 50 minutes.

    Find the value of x.

Section 18B Distance–Time Graphs with Constant Speed

We can use graphs to tell the story of movement.

> **Key Point**
>
> When looking at any graph, always check what the variables are on both axes.

In distance–time graphs:
- the independent variable (on the *x*-axis) is **time** and
- the dependent variable (on the *y*-axis) is **distance from a point**.

When the rate of change of the distance from some point is constant, the distance–time graph is a straight line.

$$\text{Slope} = \frac{\text{rise}}{\text{run}} = \frac{\text{metres}}{\text{seconds}} = \text{speed in metres per second}$$

Speed, Distance, Time and Graphs

- **Moving away from the point** (distance from the point is increasing and slope is positive):

- **Moving towards the point** (distance from the point is decreasing and slope is negative):

- **Remaining the same distance from the point** (distance from the point is constant and the slope is zero):

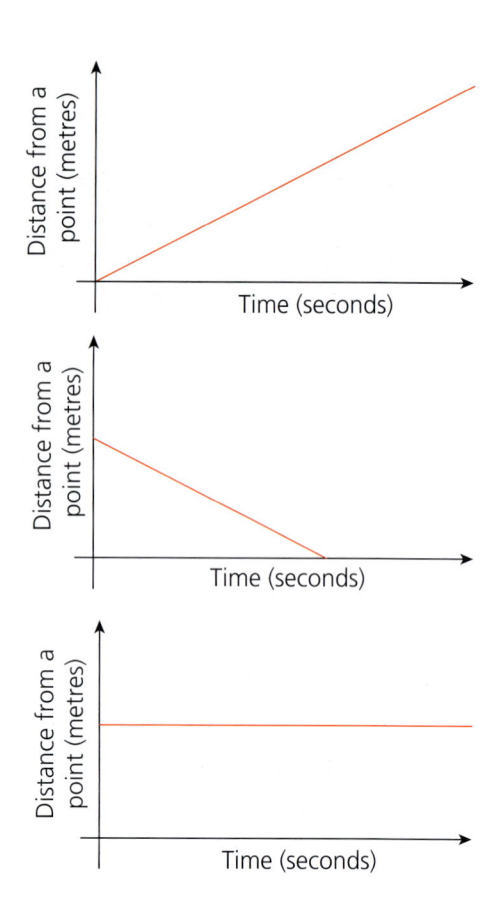

When the rate of change of distance of an object from some point, with respect to time, is zero, the object remains the same distance from the point. Hence, the object is stationary with respect to the point or else is moving in a circle around the point. The option of moving in a circle is possible but unlikely for most contexts.

Combinations of the above graphs can be seen in stories of journeys such as the following example.

Example

The diagram shows the graph of a journey with respect to a point.

(This graph was generated using a motion sensor.)

(i) How can you tell if the person is travelling towards the point or away from the point or staying the same distance from the point at any stage in the journey?

(ii) Tell a possible story for the journey.

(iii) When was the speed greatest?

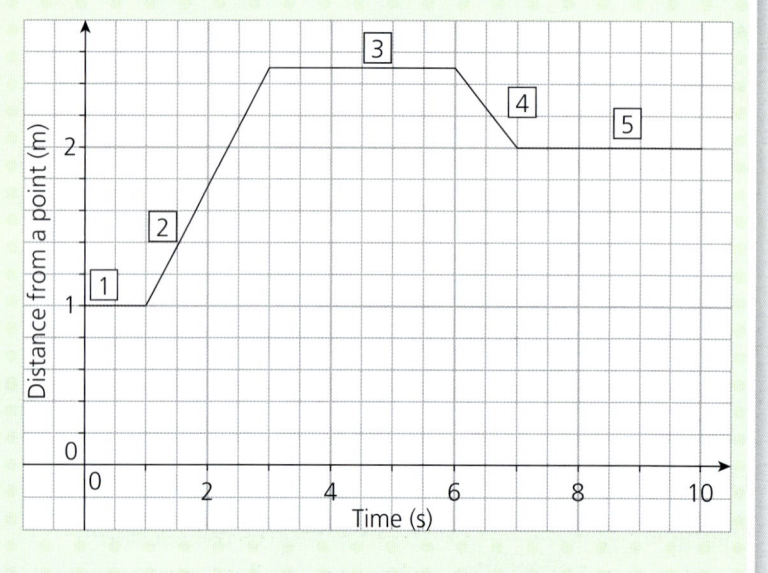

Solution

(i) If the distance from the point is increasing as time increases (i.e. the graph has a positive slope), then the person is travelling **away** from the point.

If the distance from the point is decreasing as time increases (i.e. the graph has a negative slope), then the person is travelling **towards** the point.

If the distance from the point is staying constant as time increases (i.e. the graph has zero slope), then the person is not moving.

(ii) Possible story of the journey:
1. Karl starts at 1 m from some object. He remains stationary for 1 second.
2. He then travels at a constant speed away from the object for two seconds.
3. He remains stationary for 3 seconds at a distance of 2.5 m from the object.
4. He then travels at constant speed towards the object for 1 second.
5. He remains stationary for the next 3 seconds at a distance of 2 metres from the object.

(iii) Speed for part 2 = slope = $\frac{\text{rise}}{\text{run}}$
$= \frac{(2.5 - 1) \text{ m}}{(3 - 1) \text{ s}} = 0.75$ m/s

Speed for part 4 = slope = $\frac{\text{rise}}{\text{run}}$
$= \frac{(2 - 2.5) \text{ m}}{(7 - 6) \text{ s}} = -0.5$ m/s

The speed was greatest for part 2 of the journey at 0.75 m/s.

Constant Flow Rate Graphs

Now we will look at some general graphs that represent the change in height of water for a given container versus the time taken to pour the water into the container.

In these questions, the water is always flowing at a constant rate. However, the graphs will vary due to the different-shaped containers being filled.

For example, let's consider these two cylinders. Which container do you think will fill faster?

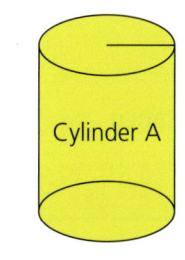

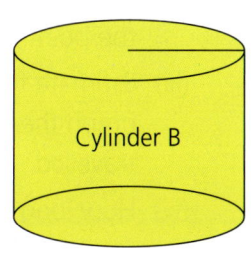

Cylinder A   Cylinder B

Water is poured into both cylinders at the same time and rate.

Let's look at the graphs that represent these cylinders.

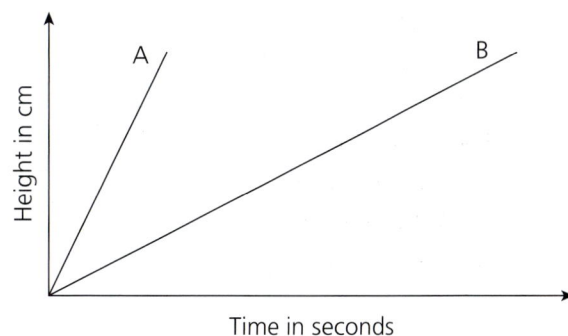

From observation:

- As each cylinder fills up with water, its graph is linear.
- Cylinder A fills faster as it has the smaller base (or radius) of the two cylinders. We can see this on the graph by the fact that the slope of the graph of A is greater than the slope of B.

Activity 18.2

> **Hint**
> › Always note what the variables on each axis are.

1. The graph shows different stages of a journey with respect to a particular point.
   (i) Tell the possible story for the journey.
   (ii) When was the speed greatest? Justify your answer.

2. The graph shows different stages of a journey with respect to a particular point.
   (i) Tell the possible story for the journey.
   (ii) What is the greatest distance travelled from the point A?
   (iii) Estimate from the graph the total distance travelled.
   (iv) How long did the journey take?
   (v) Estimate the average speed for the journey.

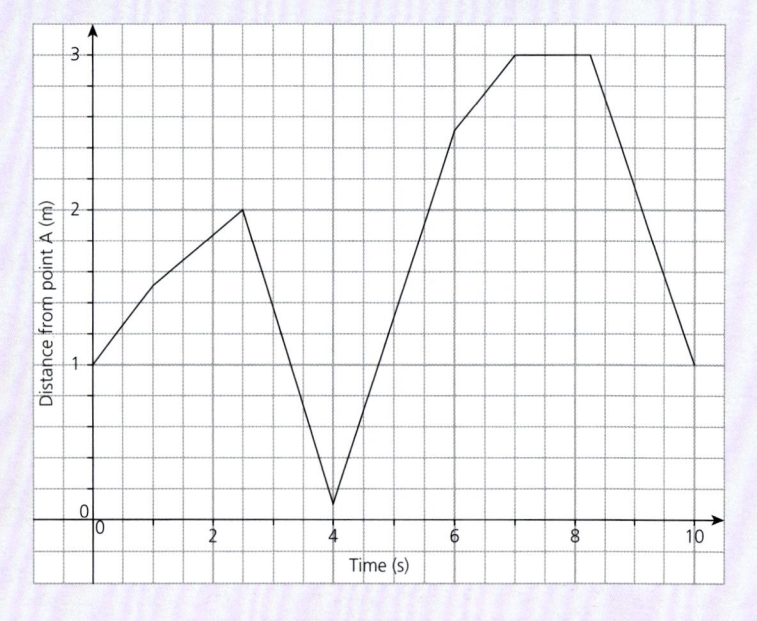

3. If a person walked in a circle of radius r around a flag pole, what would their distance–time graph look like?

4. Amy, Kate, Bernie, Denis, Edwin and Jane all live in the same house and have gone for a cycle ride. Each cycles at constant speed. Draw graphs to represent the journey of each person as described below.
   (i) Amy starts 6 km from home and cycles at 8 km per hour away from home.
   (ii) Kate starts 10 km from home and is 18 km from home after 1.5 hours.
   (iii) Bernie starts 10 km from home, cycles towards home and arrives there in two hours.
   (iv) Denis starts from home and after one hour he is 7 km from home.

(v) Edwin starts 10 km from home and cycles at 12 km per hour away from home.

(vi) Jane starts 3 km from home and cycles towards home. She is home in 10 minutes.

5 Steve left his home and walked at a steady speed to his friend's house, a distance of 500 m. This took 20 minutes.

Steve spent 10 minutes chatting with his friend.

He then walked to the bus stop, a distance of 750 m further away from his home, a journey which took 20 minutes.

Steve waited 10 minutes for the bus.

Steve took the bus and travelled a distance of 2250 m further from home in 4 minutes.

(i) Draw the distance–time graph of Steve's journey.

Answer the following questions, expressing the results in km/h correct to two decimal places.

(ii) What is Steve's average walking speed? Do not include the times he is stopped.

(iii) What is the average speed of the bus?

(iv) What is Steve's average speed for the entire journey?

6 Match the correct story to this graph. Justify your choice.

Story A: John cycled in an easterly direction from his home up a hill. The hill became less steep after a while and when he reached the top he cycled across the top and then cycled quickly down the other side of the hill.

Story B: John went for a walk. He started slowly and then increased his pace. He then walked at a steady pace and at some point he turned around and walked slowly back towards home.

Story C: John set out running from home at a constant speed until he came to rough ground. He immediately reduced his speed and walked at this new constant speed until he came to the end of the track. He stopped for a short while and then he turned back towards home and walked at a constant fast speed towards home.

7 Identify a problem with this distance–time graph. Justify your answer.

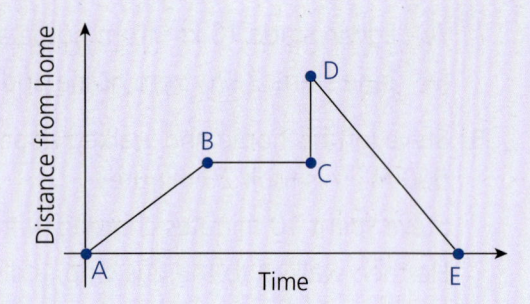

8 The following graphs each represent the distance–time graphs for two runners, Ann and Tom.

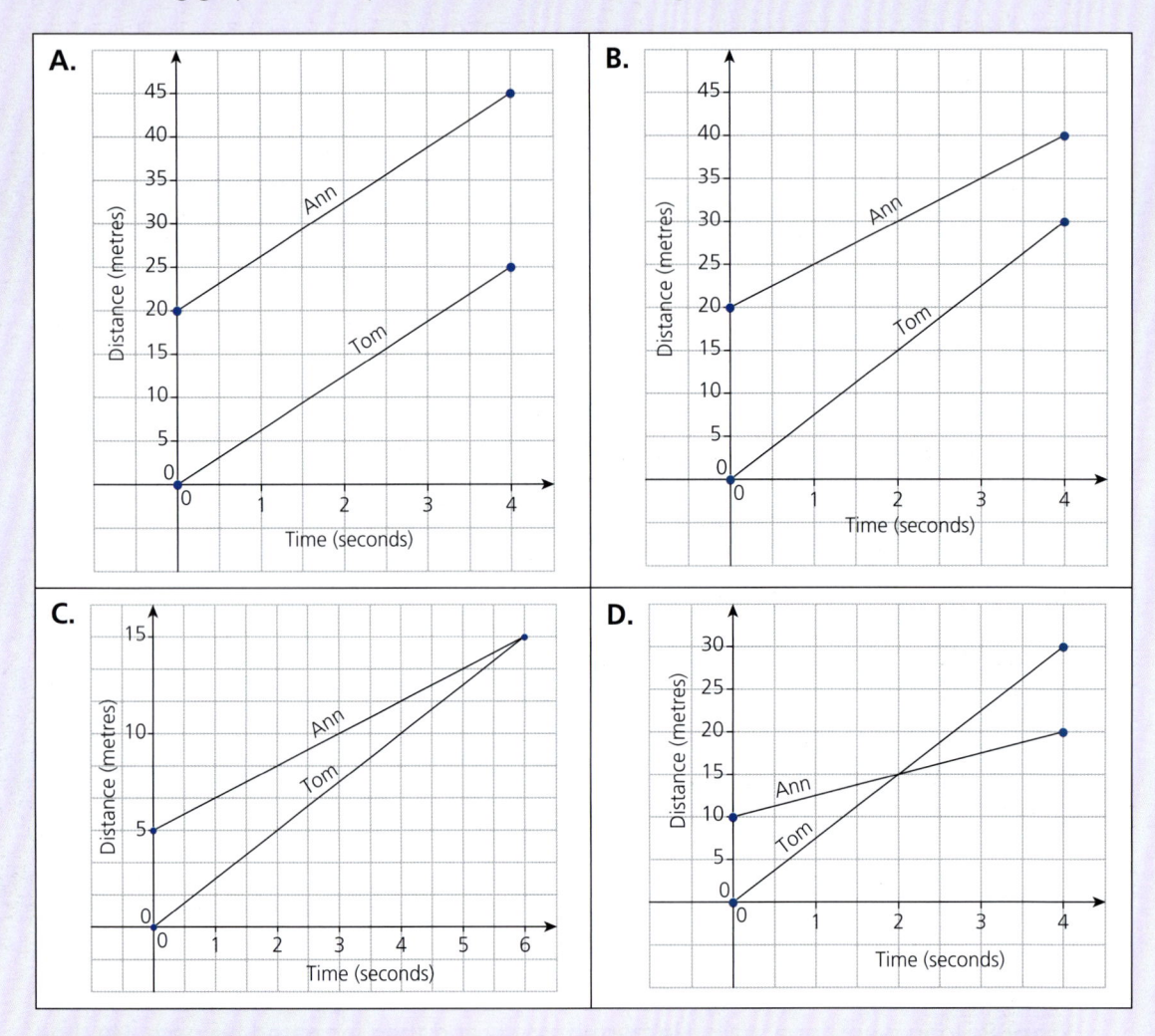

(i) Which of the graphs shows that one runner started 5 metres ahead of the other? Explain.
(ii) In graph C, which runner is moving fastest? Explain your answer.
(iii) In which graph are the runners moving at the same speed? Explain your answer.
(iv) In which graph is one runner going to overtake the other one if they both continue to travel at the same speeds?
(v) In graph D, at what time are the two runners the same distance away from the starting point? Have both runners travelled the same distance at this time? Explain.

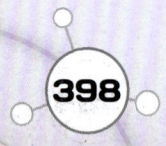

9 Colin and Matthew are two racing drivers in a one-lap motor car race 2.4 km long. Look at the graph of the race and answer the questions which follow.

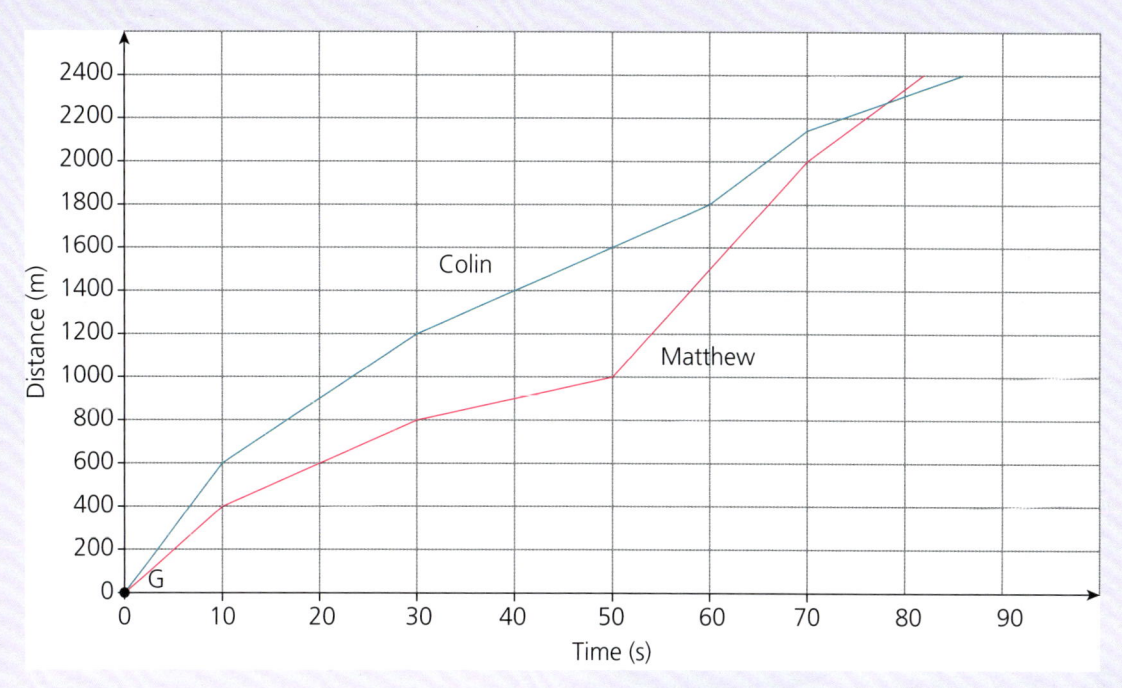

(i) Which driver completed the lap in the fastest time?
(ii) How many different speeds did each driver drive at?
(iii) Estimate the average speed for both drivers.
(iv) Which driver achieved the highest speed in the race? Justify your answer.

10 This distance–time graph shows a comparison between 'walking on the moving walkway' and 'walking on the ground next to the moving walkway' in an airport. Assume that the walking pace is the same for each person.

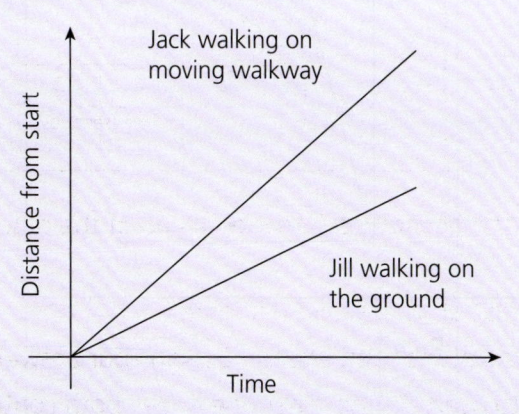

(i) On a copy of the graph, draw a line to represent distance versus time for a person who is standing still on the moving walkway.
(ii) Justify your answer to part (i).

11 The table shows containers of various shapes which are being filled at a constant rate. Match each container with the appropriate graph.

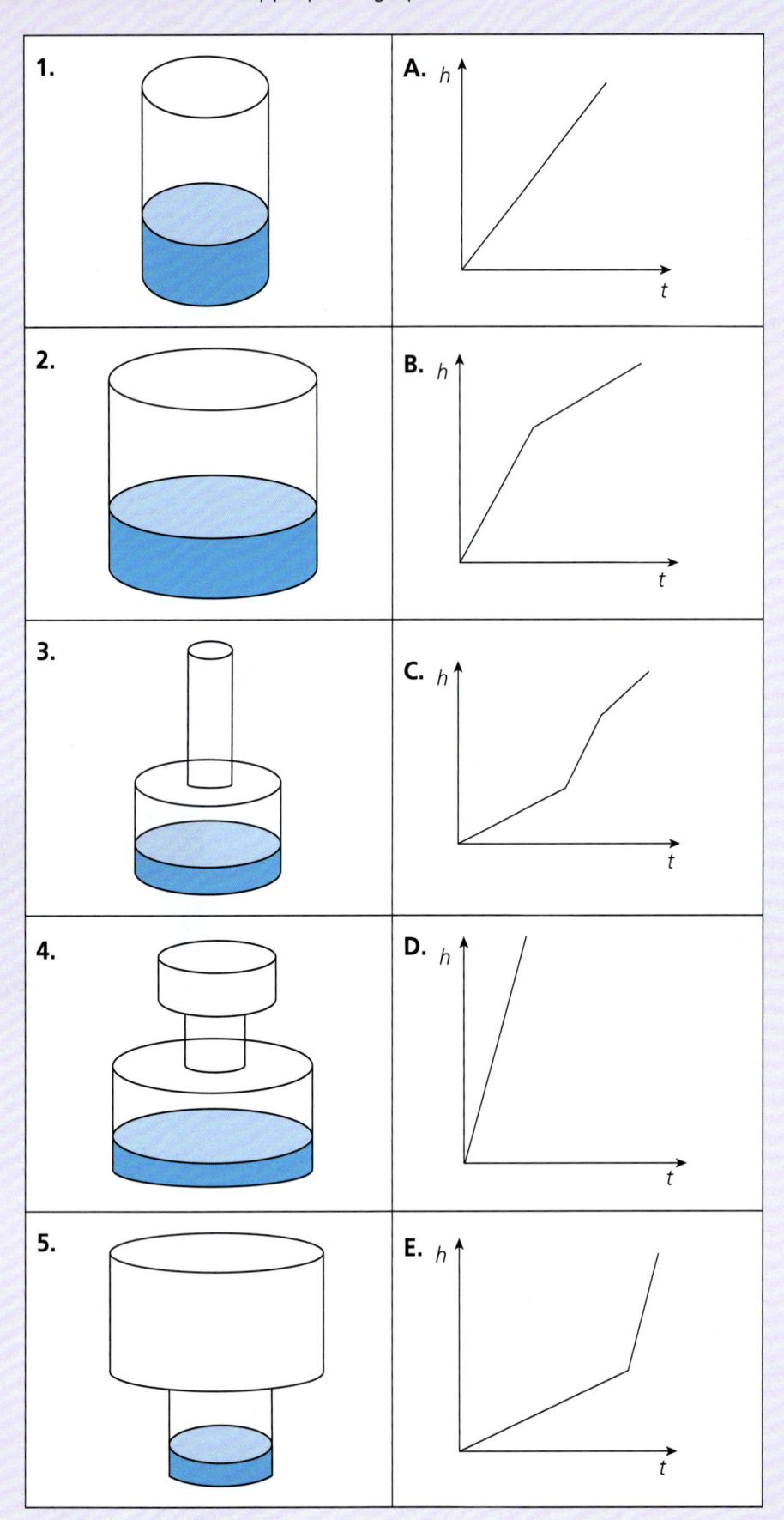

Section 18C Speed–Time Graphs

> **Key Point**
>
> Remember, when looking at any graph, always check what the variables are on both axes.

In speed–time graphs:
- the independent variable (on the *x*-axis) is **time**
- the dependent variable (on the *y*-axis) is **speed**.

Note: Speed in a given direction is referred to as **velocity**.

Example 1

The graph shows the speed changes of a car as it moves from a traffic light at A to a traffic light at D.

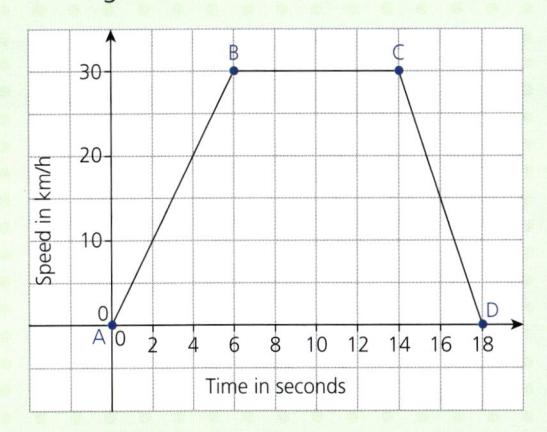

(i) At which part of the journey is the speed of the car increasing?

(ii) At which part of the journey is the speed of the car constant?

(iii) At which part of the journey is the speed of the car decreasing?

(iv) What is the maximum speed of the car?

(v) How long does it take the car to go from A to D?

Solution

(i) The speed of the car is increasing (the car is **accelerating**) between A and B. It goes from 0 km/h to 30 km/h in 6 seconds.

(ii) The speed of the car is constant between B and C.

(iii) The speed of the car is decreasing (the car is **decelerating**) between C and D. It goes from 30 km/h to 0 km/h in 2 seconds.

(iv) The maximum speed of the car is 30 km/h. It stays at this speed for 8 seconds.

(v) It takes 18 seconds to go from A to D.

Example 2

The diagram shows the **distance–time** graph of an object. Sketch the **speed–time** graph of the object. Explain your answer.

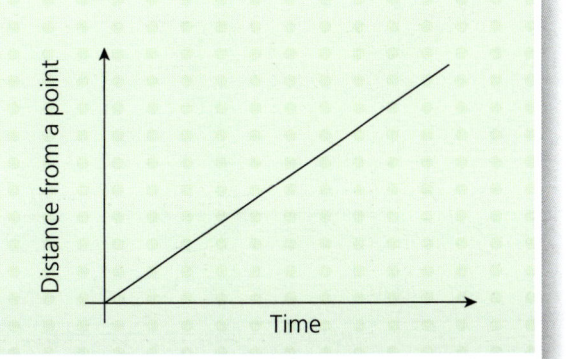

Speed, Distance, Time and Graphs

> **Solution**
>
> The rate of change of distance with time gives the speed. The distance–time graph is a straight line which means that the speed is constant.
>
> Hence, the speed–time graph is a horizontal line.

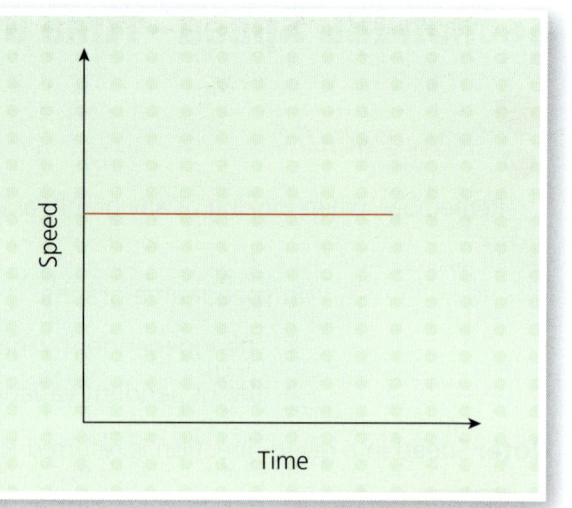

Key Points

- On a linear **distance–time** graph, the constant speed is given by the slope of the graph.
- On a **speed–time** graph, we read the speed directly from the graph.

Activity 18.3

> **Hint**
>
> › Always note what the variables on each axis are.

1 What information is given by the following graphs?

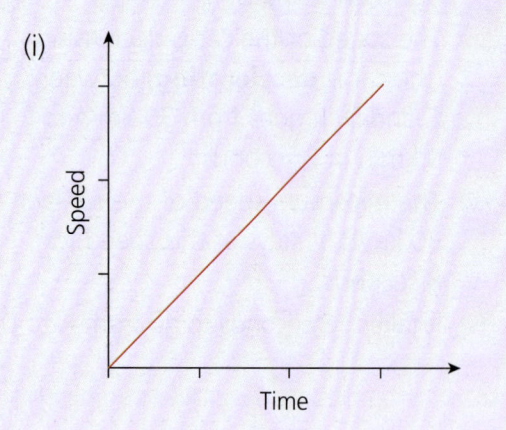

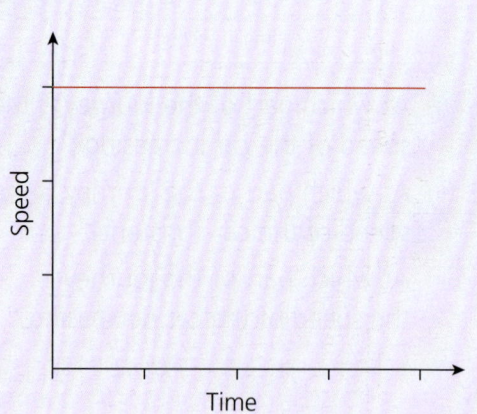

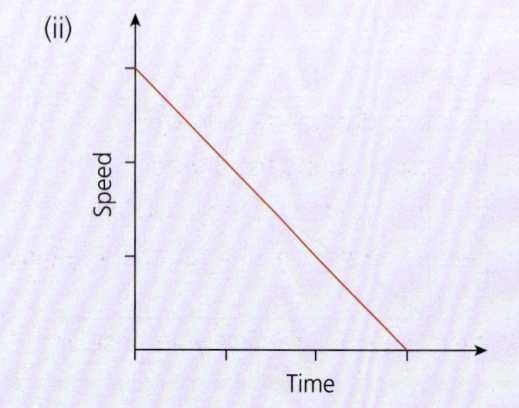

(i) *Speed vs Time — linear increasing line through origin*

(ii) *Speed vs Time — linear decreasing line*

(iii) *Speed vs Time — horizontal line*

2 The graph shows the speed changes of a train as it goes from a station at A to a station at D.

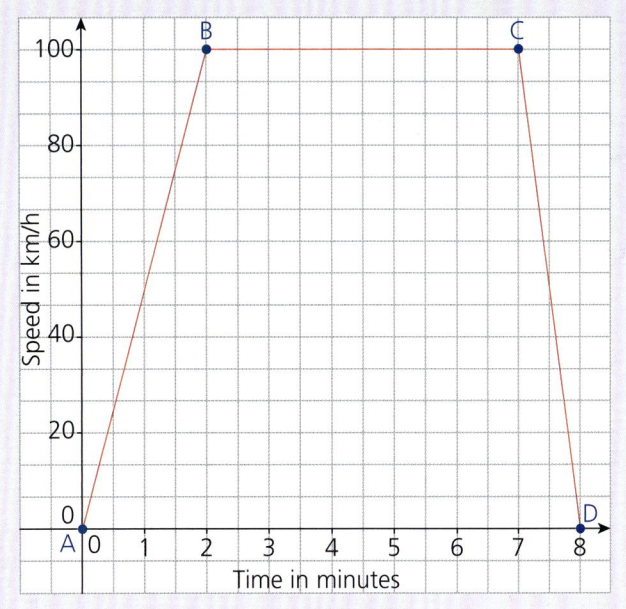

(i) At which part of the journey is the speed of the train increasing?
(ii) At which part of the journey is the speed of the train constant?
(iii) How far did the train travel at a constant speed?
(iv) At which part of the journey is the speed of the train decreasing?
(v) What is the maximum speed of the train?
(vi) How long does it take the train to go from A to D?

3 The graph shows information about a journey taken by Ellen on her bicycle.

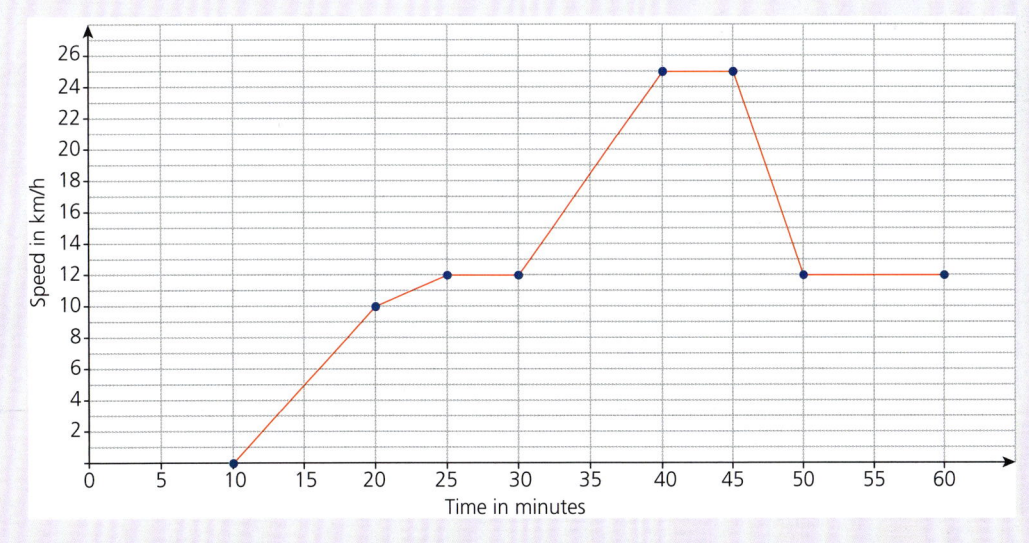

(i) How long did Ellen wait before starting her journey?
(ii) For what intervals of time was Ellen's speed constant during the journey?
(iii) For what intervals of time was Ellen's speed increasing during the journey?
(iv) Did Ellen's speed decrease during any interval of time on the journey? Explain.
(v) For what interval of time was Ellen's speed greatest during the journey and what was that speed?
(vi) How far did Ellen travel when cycling at her maximum speed? Give your answer correct to one decimal place.

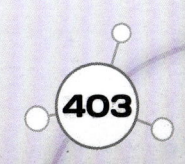

4 The graph shows how the speed of a car varied on a short journey.

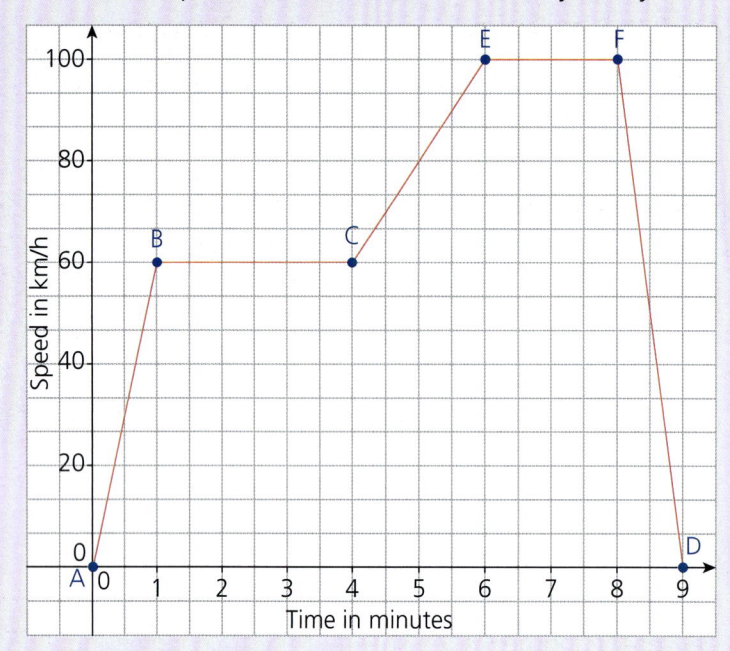

(i) What is the speed of the car after 3 minutes?
(ii) For how long is the speed of the car increasing?
(iii) What is the maximum speed of the car?
(iv) Find the distance travelled by the car at its maximum speed.
(v) What is happening to the speed of the car between 8 and 9 minutes?
(vi) If the total distance travelled is $10\frac{1}{3}$ km, find the average speed of the car over the whole journey.

5 The graph shows the speed of a train during the first minute of its journey as it leaves a station.

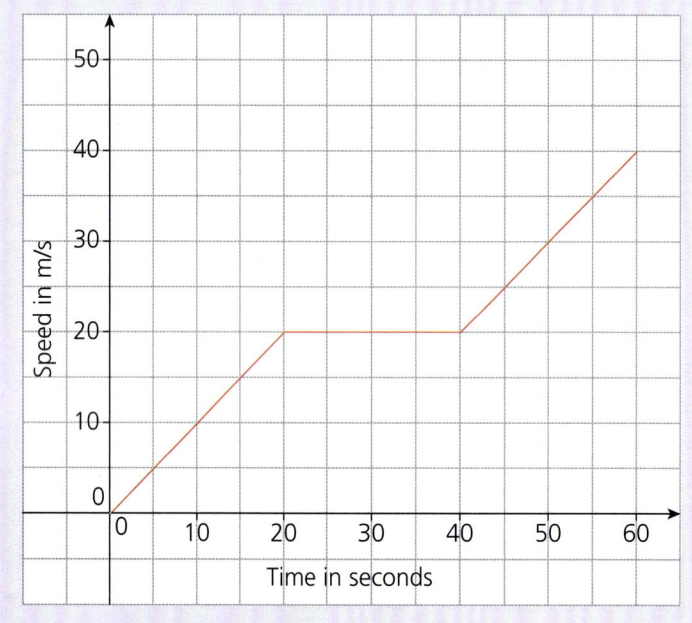

(i) Describe the train's progress during this minute.
(ii) What was the highest speed reached by the train in the first minute? Express this speed in km/h.

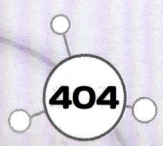

6. An express train's journey from Dublin to Drogheda had the following details.
   - In the first 10 minutes its speed built up uniformly from rest to a speed of 60 km per hour.
   - It maintained this steady speed for 40 minutes.
   - It then reached its destination in the next 10 minutes, reducing its speed uniformly to zero in Drogheda.

   Draw a graph of the train's journey, putting time on the x-axis and speed on the y-axis.

7. A cyclist starts a 100 m race at a speed of 4 m/s and accelerates at a constant rate in 2 seconds to his maximum speed of 16 m/s. He continues at this speed for the rest of the race. The total time for the race is 7 seconds.

   Show the above information on a speed–time graph.

8. A car starts from rest at a traffic light and accelerates (i.e. increases its speed) uniformly at the rate of 3 m/s every second. As it starts it is passed by a cyclist who is moving at a constant speed of 12 m/s.

   Draw a speed–time graph to show the above information and use it to see how long it will take the car to reach the same speed as the cyclist.

9. A tractor and a fast car are stopped at a traffic light. Sketch a speed–time graph to show the speeds of the two vehicles as they move away from the traffic light.

Section 18D Distance–Time Graphs with Varying Speed

When a distance–time graph is linear, it means that the rate of change of the y-variable with respect to the x-variable is constant.

We will now look at distance–time graphs which are not linear.

Example 1

The table gives the approximate distances of a car from a point at different times.

Time (s)	Distance from a point (m)
0	0
1	2
2	8
3	18
4	32
5	50

(i) What does the table tell you about the distance travelled per second by the car for each successive second?

(ii) Draw a distance–time graph for the car's journey in the first 5 seconds.

(iii) What does the graph show about the speed of the car?

Solution

(i) We can see from the table that with each successive second the distance travelled per second by the car is increasing. The car travels 2 m in the first second, 6 m in the 2nd second, 10 m in the 3rd second, 14 m in the 4th second and 18 m in the 5th second. Hence, the speed of the car is constantly increasing.

(ii)

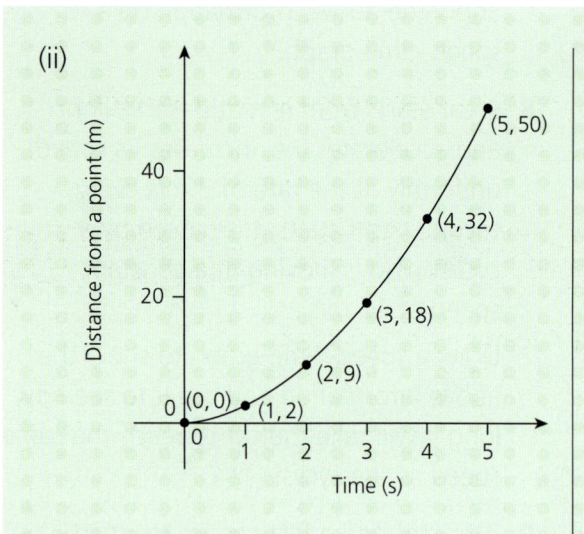

Graph showing distance from a point (m) vs Time (s) with points (0,0), (1,2), (2,9), (3,18), (4,32), (5,50).

(iii) The slope is increasing all the time. Hence, the speed is increasing all the time.

Note: As the distance from the point is increasing, this means that the car is moving away from the point.

Example 2

The table shows the height above the ground for an object which is projected upwards from the ground with an initial speed. It constantly slows down until it reaches its maximum height.

Time (s)	Distance from a point (m)
0	0
1	45
2	80
3	105
4	120
5	125

(i) What does the table tell you about the distance travelled per second by the object for each successive second?

(ii) Draw a distance–time graph for the object's journey in the first 5 seconds.

(iii) What does the graph show about the speed of the object?

Solution

(i) We can see from the table that with each successive second the distance travelled per second by the object is decreasing. The object travels 45 m in the first second, 35 m in the 2nd second, 25 m in the 3rd second, 15 m in the 4th second and 5 m in the 5th second. Hence, the speed of the object is constantly decreasing.

(ii)

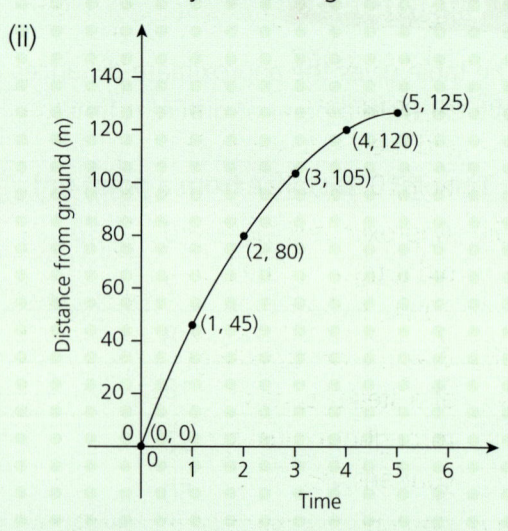

Graph showing distance from ground (m) vs Time with points (0,0), (1,45), (2,80), (3,105), (4,120), (5,125).

(iii) The slope is decreasing all the time. Hence, the speed is decreasing all the time.

> **Key Point**
>
> Distance–time graphs which are curves mean constantly changing slopes and **constantly changing speeds**.

Activity 18.4

1. This is the graph of a horse's run in the first 400 metres of a flat race.
   (i) How long did the horse take to run this distance?
   (ii) Approximately how far did the horse travel in the first 10 seconds?
   (iii) Approximately how far did the horse travel in the last 10 seconds?
   (iv) Was the horse travelling at a steady speed throughout? Justify your answer.
   (v) Describe the speed of the horse during the section of the race shown.

2. The graph shows a short section of a car's journey.
   (i) Approximately how far did the car travel and how long did the car take to do it?
   (ii) Approximately how far did the car travel in the first 10 seconds?
   (iii) Approximately how far did it travel in the last 10 seconds?
   (iv) Was the car travelling at a steady speed throughout? Justify your answer.
   (v) Describe the speed of the car during this part of the journey.

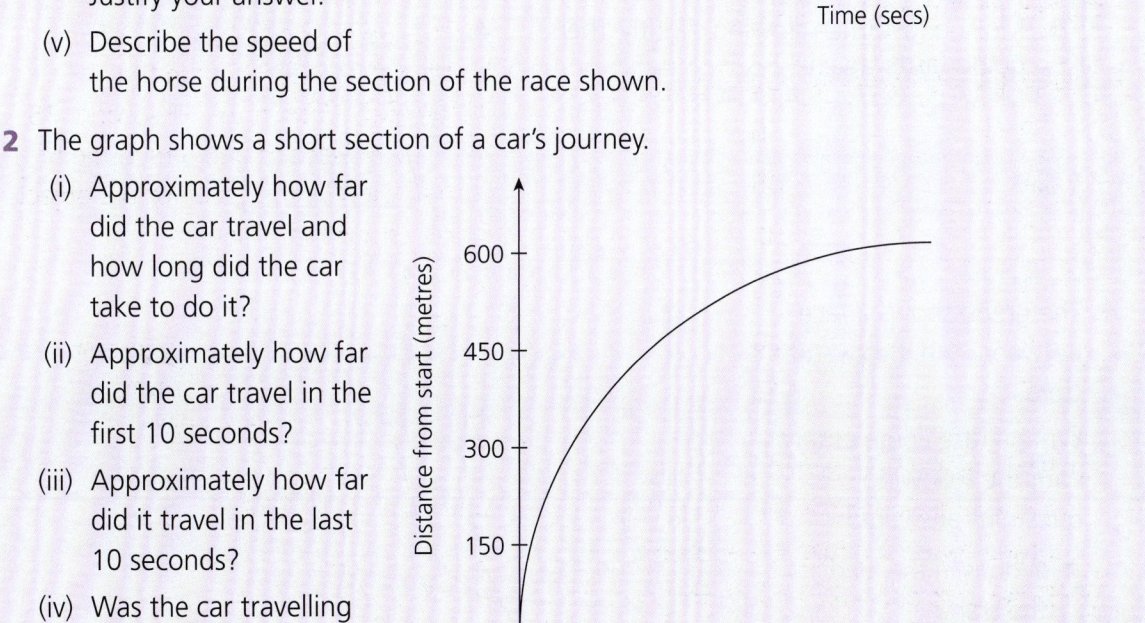

3 Match each of these distance–time graphs with the situation which best fits it.

Situation	Graph
A. Moving at steady moderate pace	**1.** (Distance vs Time: slow-fast-slow S-curve)
B. Moving at a very fast pace then gradually to a slower pace	**2.** (Distance vs Time: straight line)
C. Moving at a fast steady pace	**3.** (Distance vs Time: fast then levelling off)
D. Moving fast, then slowing slightly, then going faster again	**4.** (Distance vs Time: steep increasing curve)

4 The graph shows a race between Ann, Betty and Cora.

Write a race commentary, with the following questions answered:

- Who is in the lead at the start?
- Who overtakes whom and in what order?
- Who won the race?
- Who was second?
- Did they all run at a steady speed or did they all gradually get quicker?

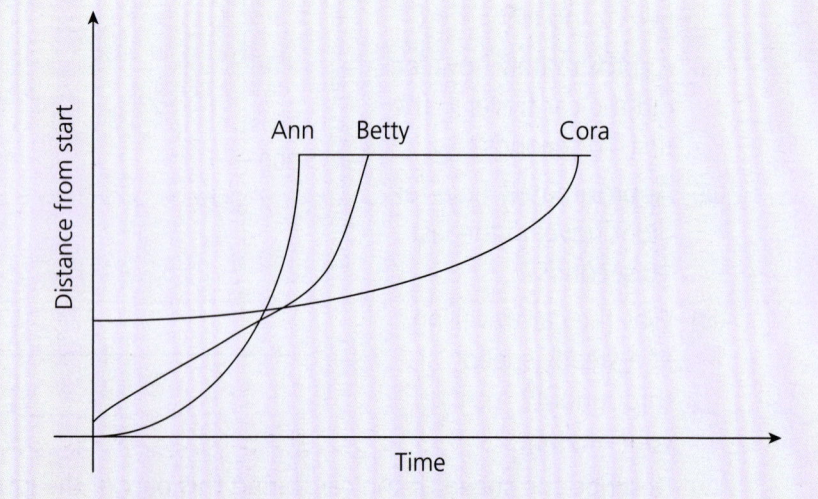

5 The graph shows the journey of three objects A, B and C.

   Write a short paragraph to describe each journey.

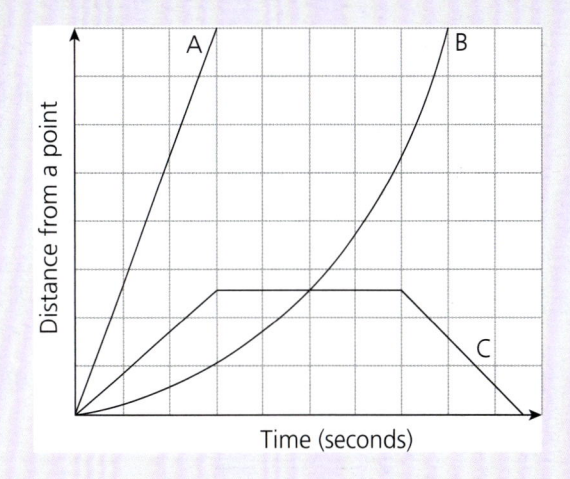

6 The following seven graphs show the change in the height of water in a bathtub with a rectangular cross-section, over time. Match each story with the correct graph.

Graph	Story
1. (Height of water decreasing linearly to zero vs Time)	A. The height of the water is increasing at a constantly increasing rate as the tap is opened more and more.
2. (Height of water decreasing in a concave curve to zero vs Time)	B. The tap is open and the height of the water is increasing at a constant rate.
3. (Height of water increasing in an upward curve vs Time)	C. The bath plug is in, the tap is closed and the height of the water is constant.
4. (Height of water increasing linearly vs Time)	D. The water is draining at a constant rate.
5. (Height of water decreasing rapidly then leveling off vs Time)	E. The height of the water is decreasing, slowly at first but then at a continuously increasing rate.

6. 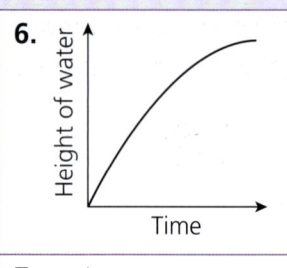 [graph: Height of water increasing, concave down, leveling off vs Time]	F. The height of the water is decreasing, first rapidly and then at a constantly decreasing rate.
7. 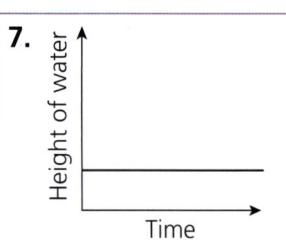 [graph: Height of water constant vs Time]	G. The rate at which the height of the water is increasing reduces as the tap is closed more and more.

7 Match the following graphs with the correct statements.

1. 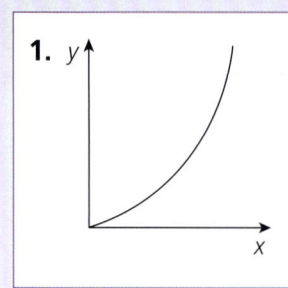 [graph: y vs x, increasing and concave up]	A. The rate of change of y with respect to x is not constant. The rate of change of y with respect to x is slow at first but increases continuously. The graph gets continuously steeper.
2. 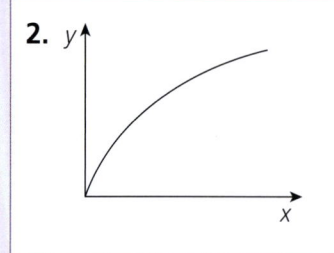 [graph: y vs x, increasing and concave down]	B. The rate of change of y with respect to x is not constant. The rate of change of y with respect to x is slow at first but gradually increases and then it gradually decreases again.
3. 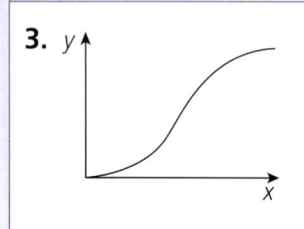 [graph: y vs x, S-shaped curve]	C. The rate of change of y with respect to x is not constant. The rate of change of y with respect to x is fast at first but gradually decreases and then it gradually increases again.
4. 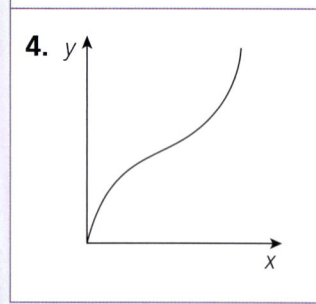 [graph: y vs x, inverse S-shaped curve]	D. The rate of change of y with respect to x is not constant. The rate of change of y with respect to x is fast at first but decreases continuously. The graph continuously becomes less steep.

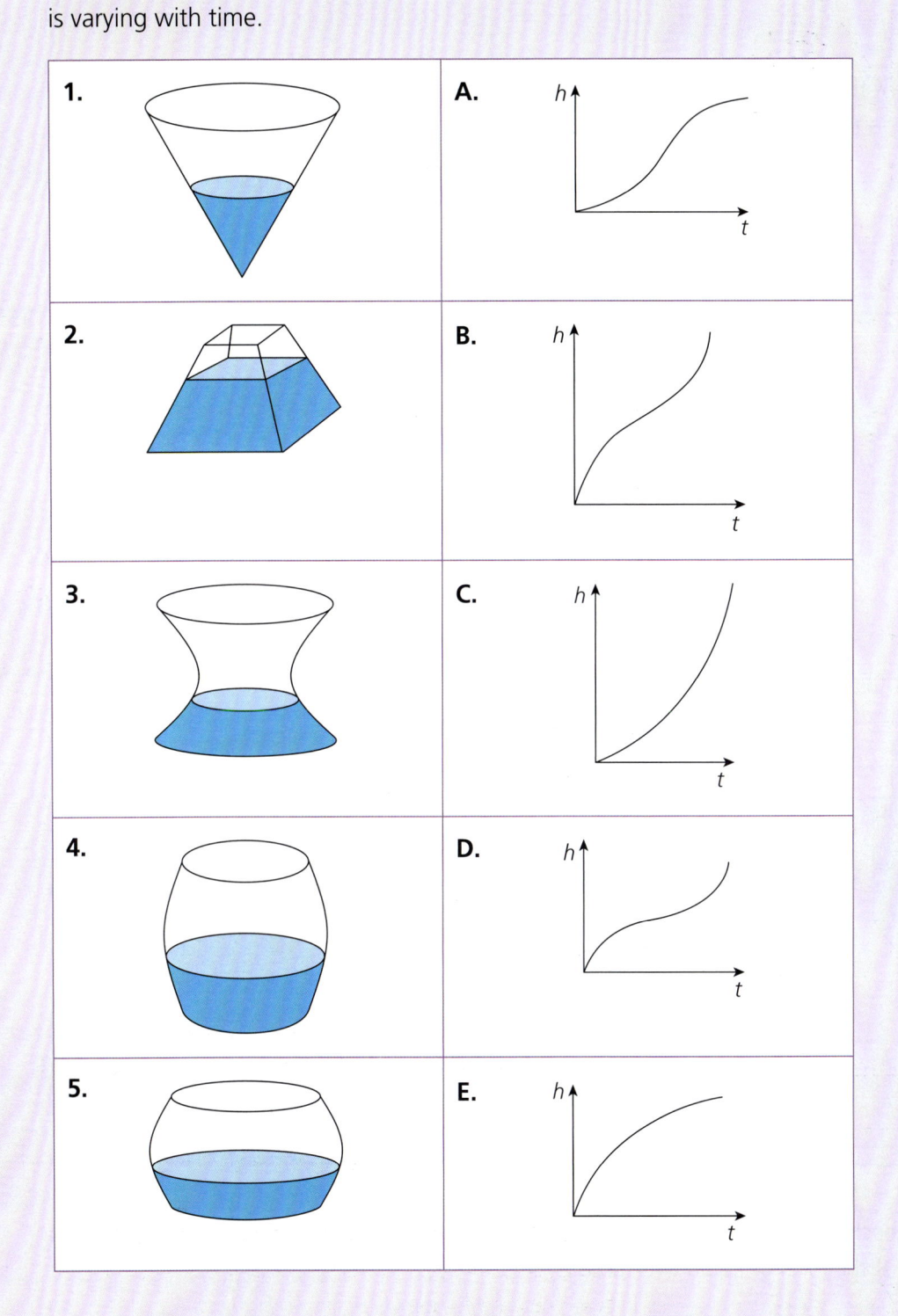

8 The table shows containers of various shapes which are being filled at a constant rate. Match each container to the graph which shows how the height of liquid in the container is varying with time.

1.	(cone, point down)	A.	(h vs t: slow then fast then slow, S-curve leveling)
2.	(truncated pyramid, wider at base)	B.	(h vs t: fast then slow then fast)
3.	(hourglass-like, narrow middle)	C.	(h vs t: increasing, concave up)
4.	(rounded vase)	D.	(h vs t: fast then slow then fast, slight S)
5.	(fishbowl, widest in middle)	E.	(h vs t: increasing, concave down)

Speed, Distance, Time and Graphs

9 A water tank has the shape shown in the diagram. Initially the tank is empty. It is then filled with water at a constant rate.

Which of the following graphs shows how the height of the water surface in the tank changes over time?

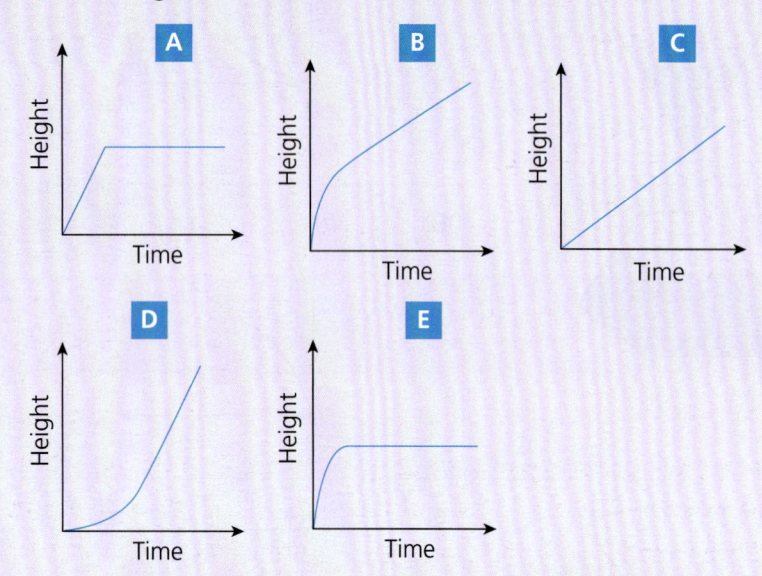

A • B • C • D • E

10 The containers shown are being filled with liquid at a constant rate.

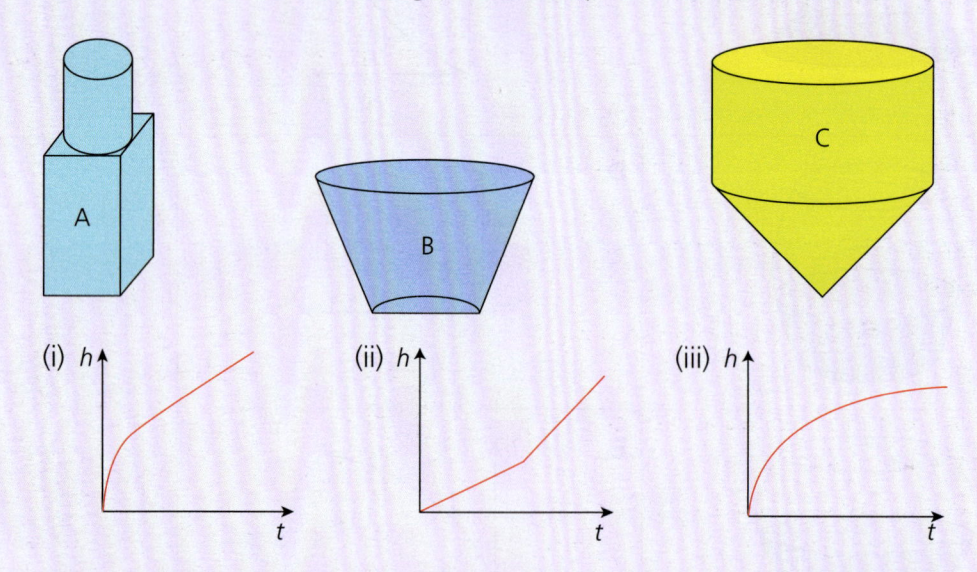

A • B • C

(i) • (ii) • (iii)

Match each of the containers to the correct graphical representation of the change in height of the level of liquid over time.

Revision Activity 18

1 The time taken by Jack to travel from Derry to Waterford, a distance of 378 km, is 6 hours. His return journey from Waterford to Derry, by the same route, takes an extra 45 minutes. By how many km/h is his average speed slower on the return journey?

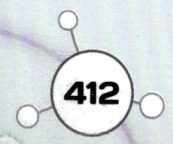

2. The grid shows a distance–time graph representing a practice cycle ride Paul completed one evening.
   (a) What is Paul's average speed between the points C and D?
   (b) Between which points did Paul reach his highest speed and what was the highest speed?
   (c) Between which two points did Paul travel at his lowest speed?
   (d) What is Paul's overall average speed, correct to two decimal places?

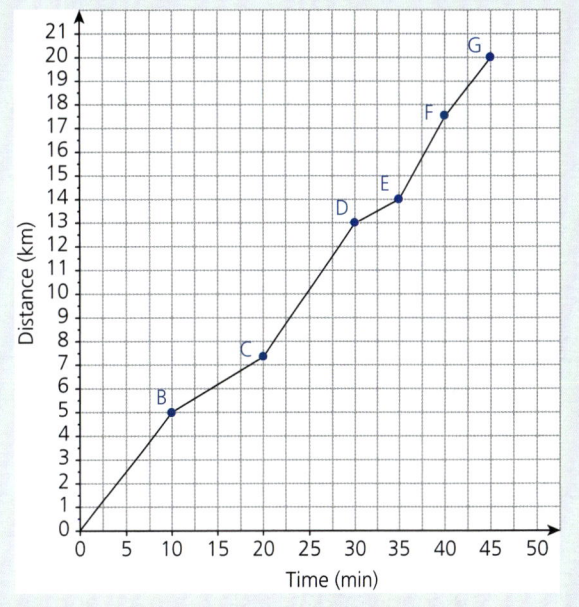

3. Represent the following journey on a distance–time graph and then calculate the overall average speed. Assume that each stage of the journey is travelled at steady speeds.
   Tom travelled from his home to the bus station, a distance of 1 km, in 10 minutes. Tom arrived at the bus station and travelled by bus a distance of 5 km in 25 minutes to reach the city centre. Tom walked the last 500 m in 5 minutes.

4. Given that the speed of sound in air is 330 metres per second, express this speed in km/h.

5. This is the distance–time graph of a cyclist.
   (a) How many stops did the cyclist make throughout the journey?
   (b) How far did the cyclist travel between 12:45 and 1:45?
   (c) How many different speeds did the cyclist go at?
   (d) What is the overall average speed of the cyclist including the stops?
   (e) What is the overall average speed of the cyclist excluding the time spent stopped?

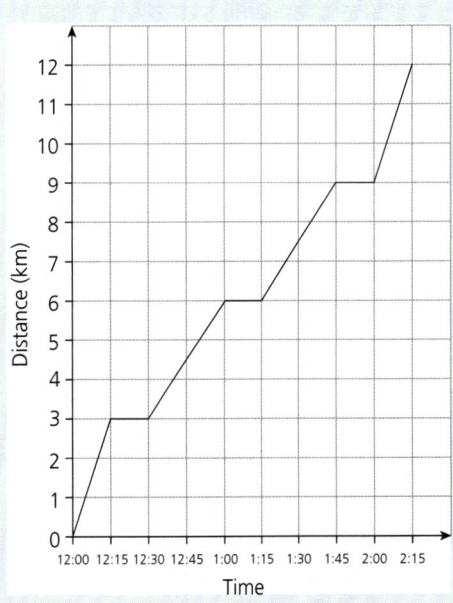

6. Draw the distance–time graph for the following journey.
   Philip left his house to walk to the shop. He travelled 800 m in 10 minutes before stopping for 5 minutes to chat to a friend. Philip then walked 1200 m in 15 minutes to arrive at the shop. Philip spent 10 minutes in the shop. Philip left the shop and walked another 1000 m in 10 minutes to get to another friend's house, where he stayed for 20 minutes.
   Philip was tired at this stage and decided to walk home, it took him 20 minutes to walk the 1000 m to get home.

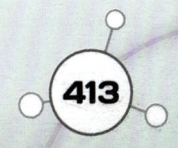

18 Speed, Distance, Time and Graphs

Exam-style Questions

1 Angela leaves home (H) at 5 pm to go to football practice, which is 700 m away. The graph shows her journey, on foot, to football practice.

(a) One of the stories below matches Angela's journey. Place a tick in the box beside the correct matching story. (Note: Only **one** story matches Angela's journey.)

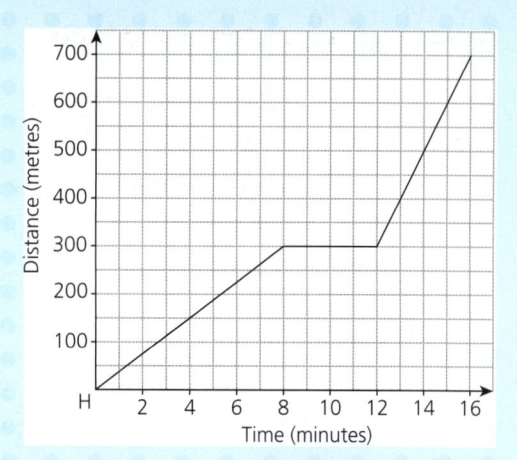

Story	Tick one story (✓)
Angela walks at a constant pace and stops at 5.08 for four minutes. She then walks at a slower pace and arrives at practice at 5.16.	
Angela walks at a constant pace and stops at 5.12 for four minutes. She then walks at a faster pace and arrives at practice at 5.16.	
Angela walks at a constant pace and stops at 5.08 for five minutes. She then walks at a faster pace and arrives at practice at 5.16.	
Angela walks at a constant pace and stops at 5.08 for four minutes. She then walks at a faster pace and arrives at practice at 5.16.	
Angela walks at a constant pace and stops at 5.08 for four minutes. She then walks at the same pace and arrives at practice at 5.16.	

(b) Mary also lives 700 m from football practice, but cycles to practice. She leaves home five minutes after Angela. She cycles at a constant pace and arrives at practice two minutes before Angela.

Represent Mary's journey on the graph above.

JCHL 2013 Paper 1

2 Car A and car B set off from a starting point S at the same time. They travel the same route to destination D, which is 70 km away. Car A travels at an average speed of 50 km/h and car B travels at an average speed of 45 km/h.

How far will car B have travelled by the time car A arrives at destination D?

S————————————————————D

JCHL 2013 Paper

KEY WORDS AND PHRASES

- Average speed
- Distance–time graph
- Speed–time graph

Chapter Summary 18

- **Average speed, distance and time**

    Average speed = $\dfrac{\text{total distance travelled}}{\text{total time taken}}$

    In two-speed problems, the average speed is not found by finding the average of the two speeds.

- When looking at any graph, always check what the variables are on both axes.

- In **distance–time** graphs:
    - the independent variable (on the *x*-axis) is time
    - the dependent variable (on the *y*-axis) is distance from a point.
    - When the rate of change of the distance from some point is constant, the distance–time graph is a straight line.

    Slope = $\dfrac{\text{rise}}{\text{run}}$ = $\dfrac{\text{metres}}{\text{seconds}}$ = speed in metres per second

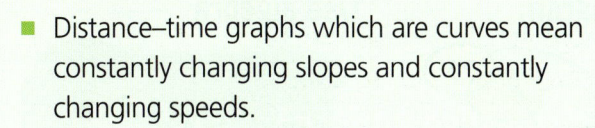

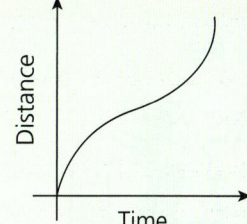

    - Distance–time graphs which are curves mean constantly changing slopes and constantly changing speeds.

- In **speed–time** graphs:
    - the independent variable (on the *x*-axis) is time
    - the dependent variable (on the *y*-axis) is speed.

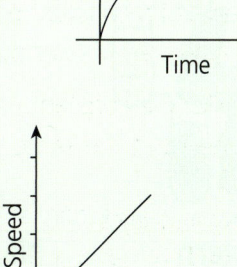

Appendix: Problem Solving

Many mathematicians say that the main purpose of mathematics is to solve problems. All successful engineers, scientists, lawyers, accountants, business managers etc. have to be good problem solvers.

Of course, they meet very different types of problems in their different types of work. But there are common strategies that can help everyone to be better at problem solving. You may be familiar with some of these already. This poster shows some of the strategies we can use to solve problems.

Problem-solving Strategies

- **Guess and test**
- **Draw a diagram**
- **Use algebra** — $5^2 = 3^2 + b^2$
- **Look for a pattern**
- **Make a table or list**
- **Solve a simpler problem** — $30 + 12 = 42$
- **Act it out**
- **Work backwards**
- **Use direct reasoning**

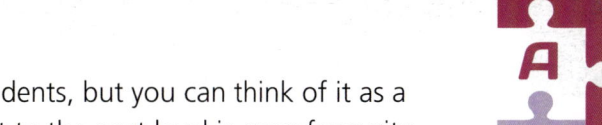

The term 'problem solving' may be off-putting for some students, but you can think of it as a challenge which can be very enjoyable, such as trying to get to the next level in your favourite computer game or solving a crossword puzzle.

Some of the benefits of practising problem solving are:

- It is a way to learn new mathematics
- It is a way to practise your mathematical skills
- It gives you an insight into the work of mathematicians
- It builds confidence
- It encourages you to work with other students
- It is enjoyable!

> The first thing that we should all learn about problem solving is that being 'stuck' is no disgrace and is in fact an honourable state to be in! We all learn by getting stuck, and it is an essential part of learning to improve our thinking.

We learn more by doing harder problems which require a lot of reflection. However, to get the most out of being stuck, you must not just give up after a few minutes. Try every possible way. Discuss the problem with a friend if you need to. Your friend may see things somewhat differently from you.

A famous mathematician, **George Polya**, devoted much of his time to helping students become better problem solvers. He outlined four steps for solving problems:

Step 1: Understand the problem

- Read the question carefully – every word may be important.
- Do you understand all the words?
- Do you know what is given?
- Do you know what the goal is?
- Is there enough information?
- Is there information that is not needed?
- Have I met a similar problem before?

Step 2: Devise a plan

Which of these strategies could you use? See the poster on the previous page.

- Trial and error (guess and test)
- Draw a diagram
- Use an equation
- Look for a pattern
- Make up a table
- Solve a simpler problem
- Act it out
- Work backwards
- Eliminate possible solutions.

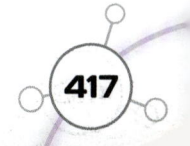

Step 3: Carry out the plan

- Use the strategy you have chosen until the problem is solved or you see that a different course of action is better.
- Give yourself a reasonable amount of time, even days or more. You may get that flash of inspiration just as you are getting on a bus or putting on your jacket. The 'Aha' experience!
  This is how William Rowan Hamilton discovered quaternions.
- Get some hints from friends if you need to – they may know more than you think!
- Don't be afraid to start all over again.

Step 4: Look back

- Have you solved the problem correctly? Does the answer make sense?
- Does your answer satisfy the statement of the problem?
- Have you shown your working?
- Can you see an easier solution?
- Compare your answer to the way other people did it.
- Can you extend your solution to a general case?
- What did you learn from doing the problem?

Learning to use Polya's four steps will be a big help in becoming a good problem solver. In the following sections we will meet methods for tackling problems. We call these 'problem-solving strategies'.

Problem-solving Strategies

Strategy 1: Guess and Test ('Trial and Error')

Example 1

Place the digits 1, 2, 3, 4, 5 and 6 in the circles so that the sum of the three numbers on each side of the triangle is 12.

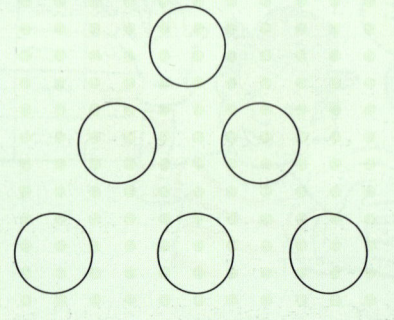

TRY this now before you read on.

Solution

Step 1: Understand the problem

Each number must be used once only; I must get 12 when I add the digits on each side of the triangle.

Step 2: Devise a plan

There are several approaches:

- Try combinations of these six numbers until one works.

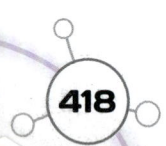

- Keep rearranging the numbers until the solution appears.
- Eliminate some possible answers. I think that the corner circles are important because each of them is on two sides of the triangle. I will try each number in a corner.

Step 3: Carry out the plan

- Try 1 in a corner: then I need two pairs to go with 1 to make 12. 5, 6 is one pair, but I don't have a second pair.
  ∴ 1 cannot go in a corner.
- Try 2 in a corner: then I need two pairs to go with 2 to make 12. 4, 6 is one pair, but I don't have a second pair.
  ∴ 2 cannot go in a corner.
- Try 3 in a corner: then I need two pairs to go with 3 to make 12. 4, 5 is one pair, but I don't have a second pair.
  ∴ 3 cannot go in a corner.
- This means that 4, 5 and 6 are in the corners and I have the solution:

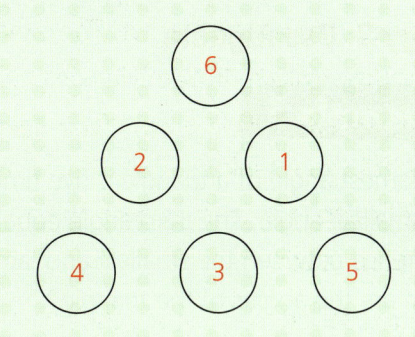

```
        6
      2   1
    4   3   5
```

Step 4: Look back

- We have solved the problem; checking this is easy.
- A general method for doing larger triangles is not apparent.

The 'Trial and Error' strategy may be suitable when:

- There is a reasonably small number of possibilities
- You have a good idea of what the solution is
- You want to understand the problem better
- You can't think of other ways
- Your choice has been narrowed down by using other strategies.

Strategy 2: Draw a Diagram

Example 2

Cut a pizza into 7 pieces with three straight cuts.

TRY this now before you read on.

Solution

Step 1: Understand the problem
Do all the pieces have to be the same size and shape?

Step 2: Devise a plan
I tried to slice it the usual way but only got 6 pieces.

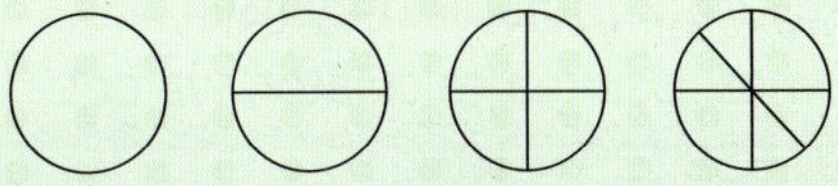

I will try to cut it differently.

Step 3: Carry out the plan

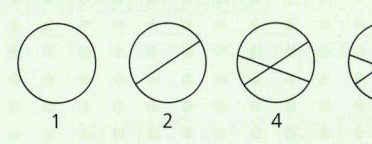

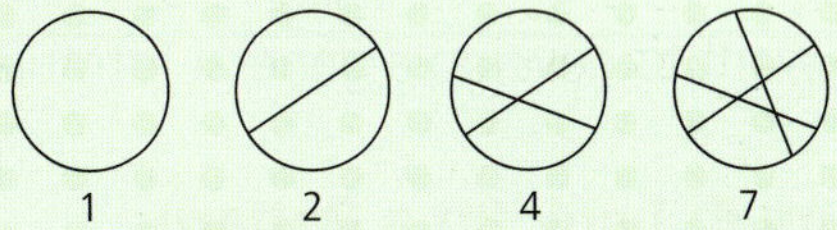

```
  ○    ⊘    ⊕    ✳
  1    2    4    7
```

Step 4: Look back

- We have solved the problem satisfactorily.
- How many pieces can you get with 4 straight cuts?
- How many pieces can you get with 5 straight cuts?

The 'Draw a Diagram' strategy may be suitable when:

- Geometrical shapes or physical situations are involved
- You want to gain a better understanding of the problem
- A diagram is possible.

Strategy 3: Use Algebra

Example 3

The largest angle of a triangle is five times the smallest angle. The third angle equals the difference between the smallest and largest. What are the angles of the triangle?

TRY this now before you read on.

Solution

Step 1: Understand the problem

The three angles add to 180°; I need to use this with the values given.

Step 2: Devise a plan

I could use trial and error, but there seems to be a large number of possibilities.

Let x stand for the smallest angle; that will mean that the largest angle is $5x$ (if I let x be the largest angle, it will involve division of x).

The third angle = $5x - x = 4x$

Step 3: Carry out the plan

Make an equation:

The three angles add to 180° so

$x + 5x + 4x = 180$
$\Rightarrow \quad 10x = 180$
$\Rightarrow \quad x = 18$

Therefore, the angles are 18°, 72° and 90°.

Step 4: Look back

- We have solved the problem satisfactorily.
- I could use this method for any such situation.

The 'Use Algebra' strategy may be suitable when:

- You see a phrase like 'for any number'
- The words 'is equal to' or 'equals' appear in a problem
- A proof or general solution is asked for
- A problem involves consecutive, even or odd whole numbers
- There is a large number of cases involved
- You want to develop a general formula.

Strategy 4: Look for a Pattern

Example 4

Find the units digit in 2^{39}.

TRY this now before you read on.

Solution

Step 1: Understand the problem

2^{39} means 2 multiplied by itself 39 times. Using a calculator, we get $5.497\,558\,139 \times 10^{11}$.

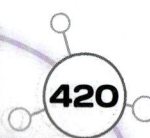

This shows the first digit (5) but not the last (units) digit since there are 11 places to the right of the decimal.

Step 2: Devise a plan

Try powers of 2 to see if there is any pattern forming which might lead to a solution.

i.e. try 2^1, 2^2, 2^3, 2^4, etc.

Step 3: Carry out the plan

$2^1 = 2$ $2^5 = 32$ $2^9 = 512$
$2^2 = 4$ $2^6 = 64$
$2^3 = 8$ $2^7 = 128$
$2^4 = 16$ $2^8 = 256$

In fact, a pattern is emerging in the units digits: 2, 4, 8, 6, 2, 4, 8, 6, 2, …

Whenever the exponent (power) of the 2 is a multiple of 4, the units digit = 6

∴ 2^{40} has a units digit of 6, since 40 is a multiple of 4. The units digit of 2^{39} must be 8, since 8 precedes 6 in the pattern and 2^{39} precedes 2^{40}.

Step 4: Look back

The units digits of other numbers involving powers might be found in the same way.

The 'Look for a Pattern' strategy may be suitable when:
- A list of data is given
- A sequence of numbers is involved
- Listing special cases helps you deal with hard problems
- You can make a table in order to see the information more clearly.

Activity A.1

Use any of the four problem-solving strategies above (or your own) to solve these problems.

1. Read this question **carefully**:
   'As I was going to St. Ives
   I met a man with seven wives.
   Each wife had seven sacks,
   Each sack had seven cats,
   Each cat had seven kittens.
   Kittens, cats, sacks and wives,
   How many were going to St. Ives?'

2. Place the digits 1 to 9 in the circles so that the sum of the numbers on each side of the triangle is 17.

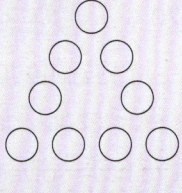

3. Divide a pizza into 11 pieces with just five straight cuts.

4. This puzzle is an example of a cryptarithm, where each letter represents a different digit. The digits in this example are 0, 1, 2, 3, 6, 7 and 9. Work out what digit each letter represents.

   ```
     S U N
   + F U N
   -------
   S W I M
   ```

5. Think of a number. Add 20. Multiply by 3. Add 120. Divide by 3. Subtract your original number. Your result is 60. Why? Explain why this would work for any number.

6. Mary opened her book and said that the product of the page numbers of the two facing pages was 2077. Without doing any calculations, say why Mary was incorrect.

7 Find the units digit in 3^{47}.

8 There are only two rectangles whose sides are whole numbers and whose area and perimeter are the same numbers. What are they?

9 A farmer has a square field of side length 50 m. He has a choice of using one large irrigation system or four smaller ones, as shown.

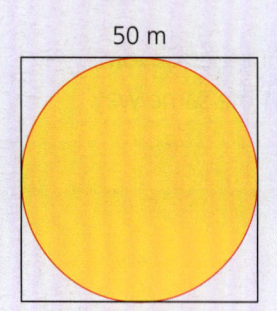

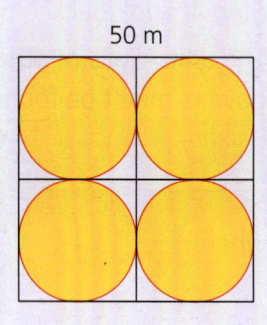

(i) What percentage of the field will the larger system irrigate?
(ii) What percentage of the field will the smaller system irrigate?
(iii) Which system will irrigate more land?
(iv) Can you make a general statement as a result?

10 There are 1000 households in a housing estate. A certain number of the households have one car. Of the other households in the estate, 50% have two cars and the other 50% have no car. How many cars are in the housing estate in total?

More Problem-solving Strategies; Combining Strategies

Strategy 5: Make a Table or List

Example 1

In how many ways can 20 be expressed as the sum of eight odd numbers?

TRY this now before you read on.

Solution

Step 1: Understand the problem

The odd numbers are 1, 3, 5, ... We need to add 8 of these to get 20.

Step 2: Devise a plan

Make a list of all the possible odd numbers. The biggest possible odd number in the list is 13. Start with 13 and work down.

Step 3: Carry out the plan

20 = 13 + 1 + 1 + 1 + 1 + 1 + 1 + 1
20 = 11 + 3 + 1 + 1 + 1 + 1 + 1 + 1
20 = 9 + 5 + 1 + 1 + 1 + 1 + 1 + 1
20 = 9 + 3 + 3 + 1 + 1 + 1 + 1 + 1
20 = 7 + 7 + 1 + 1 + 1 + 1 + 1 + 1
20 = 7 + 5 + 3 + 1 + 1 + 1 + 1 + 1
20 = 7 + 3 + 3 + 3 + 1 + 1 + 1 + 1
20 = 5 + 5 + 5 + 1 + 1 + 1 + 1 + 1
20 = 5 + 5 + 3 + 3 + 1 + 1 + 1 + 1
20 = 5 + 3 + 3 + 3 + 3 + 1 + 1 + 1
20 = 3 + 3 + 3 + 3 + 3 + 3 + 1 + 1

= 11 ways in total

Step 4: Look back

We have solved the problem satisfactorily.

The 'Make a List or Table' strategy may be suitable when:

- You are asked 'in how many ways' something can be done
- Information is easily organised
- You are asked to list the results.

The 'Make a List or Table' strategy is often used with the 'Look for a Pattern' strategy.

Strategy 6: Solve a Simpler Problem

This is a very important strategy for many students.

Example 2

10 people take part in a chess competition. If each person plays each of the other people once, how many games take place?

TRY this now before you read on.

Solution

Step 1: Understand the problem

A plays once against B, C, D, … etc. So each person plays 9 games.

If this is the case, do I simply multiply 10 by 9 to get the number of games? This sounds too easy!

Step 2: Devise a plan

Solve for a smaller number of people and look for a Pattern. See how many games there would be if there were just 2 people, then 3 people, then 4 people, …

Step 3: Carry out the plan

The 'Make a List or Table' and 'Look for a Pattern' strategies will also be useful.

Number of people	Games	Number of games	Pattern
2 (A and B)	A v B	1	The game A v B is the same as the game B v A. The number is half of 2 × 1
3 (A, B, C)	A v B A v C B v C	3	This is half of 3 × 2
4 (A, B, C, D)	A v B A v C A v D B v C B v D C v D	6	This is half of 4 × 3

Now I see that, although all 10 people play 9 games each, I must multiply 10 × 9 and then divide by 2, since the game A v B is the same as the game B v A.

$(10 \times 9) \div 2 = 45$

Thus 45 games are played.

Step 4: Look back

We have solved the problem satisfactorily using a number of strategies together.

The 'Solve a Simpler Problem' strategy may be suitable when:

- The problem has very large or very small numbers
- You want to understand the problem better.

Strategy 7: Act it Out

Example 3

On a long corridor, there is a row of 100 closed lockers numbered 1 to 100.

A student goes down the corridor and opens every locker.

Then a second student goes down the corridor closing every second locker, starting at locker number 2.

A third student goes down the corridor and, starting at locker 3, she opens every third locker that she finds closed and closes every third locker that she finds open.

This continues until a total of 100 students have gone down the corridor opening and closing lockers.

How many lockers are open when the all the students are finished?

TRY this now before you read on.

Solution

Step 1: Understand the problem

Student number 4 will start at locker number 4 and visit every 4th locker. Student number 5 will start at locker number 5 and visit every 5th locker.

Step 2: Devise a plan

We will use the Solve a Simpler Problem strategy first, then Act It Out. Let's imagine that there were just 10 lockers and 10 students. Then act it out to see what happens as each student passes down the corridor.

Step 3: Carry out the plan

Use 10 sheets of paper to represent 10 lockers. Number the 'lockers' from 1 to 10 on both sides. Write 'open' on one side and 'closed' on the other side of each page. Now act out the opening and closing of these 10 lockers as the 10 students pass down the corridor. The Look for a Pattern strategy is of great value here.

(We don't want to spoil this for you, so the final solution is not given here; but you **can** do it!)

Step 4: Look back

- Have you answered the question satisfactorily?
- Can you explain the solution?
- What is special about the numbers on these lockers?
- What is the link to factors and divisors of Natural numbers?

The 'Act It Out' strategy may be suitable when:

- The 'Solve a Simpler Problem' strategy is used
- You want to get a better understanding of the problem.

Strategy 8: Work Backwards

Example 4

Patrick has a box of €1 coins. He has three students. Feeling generous, he gives half of his coins plus one to his eldest student. He then gives half of the remaining coins plus one to his next student and half of the remaining coins plus one to his youngest student. He now has one coin left.

How many coins did he have at the start?

TRY this now before you read on.

Solution

Step 1: Understand the problem

Patrick has one coin at the end. I need to know how many coins he had before giving money to his three students.

Step 2: Devise a plan

The only quantity I have is the €1 coin which Patrick has left at the end, so we could start from there and work backwards.

Step 3: Carry out the plan

Last step	Patrick has 1 coin left
Previous step (youngest student)	Patrick gave away half plus 1, so he must have had $(1 + 1) \times 2 = 4$ coins before this step.
Previous step (middle student)	Patrick gave away half plus 1, so he must have had $(4 + 1) \times 2 = 10$ coins before this step.
Previous step (eldest student)	Patrick gave away half plus 1, so he must have had $(10 + 1) \times 2 = 22$ coins before this step.

Patrick had 22 coins at the start.

Step 4: Look back

We have solved the question satisfactorily.

The 'Work Backwards' strategy may be suitable when:
- The last part of the problem is clear and you need the starting point
- A direct approach involves complicated algebra
- The problem involves a sequence of actions which are reversible.

Strategy 9: Use Direct Reasoning

Example 5

You have a jug of water which contains exactly 8 litres. You also have two empty jugs, one of which can hold 3 litres and the other 5 litres. How can you pour the water so that two of the jugs contain 4 litres?

TRY this now before you read on.

Solution

Step 1: Understand the problem

Only the 8-litre jug contains water at the beginning. I have to pour water into the other empty jugs.

Problem Solving

Step 2: Devise a plan

Think through the problem in a logical way.

- Only the 8-litre and 5-litre jugs are big enough to contain 4 litres.
- This means that, at the end, I need to have 4 litres in each of the bigger jugs and zero litres in the 3-litre jug.
- There will have to be water in the 3-litre jug just before the end to achieve this.
- I can get 4 litres by 3 + 1 or 5 − 1.

Step 3: Carry out the plan

The steps:

Steps	Litres in 8-litre jug	Litres in 5-litre jug	Litres in 3-litre jug
Start	8	0	0
1	5	0	3
2	0	5	3
3	3	5	0
4	3	2	3
5	6	2	0
6	6	0	2
7	1	5	2
8	1	4	3
9	4	4	0

Step 4: Look back

This looks good. Is there a shorter way? Can you do it in fewer steps?

The 'Use Direct Reasoning' strategy may be suitable when:

- A proof is required
- You wish to imply a statement from a collection of given conditions.

Activity A.2

1. See the locker problem in Example 3 above.
   (i) If there are 1000 lockers and 1000 students, which lockers remain open after the 1000th student has passed?
   (ii) Which students touched both lockers 36 and 48?
   (iii) Which lockers were touched by only two students? How do you know?
   (iv) Which lockers were touched by only three students? How do you know?
   (v) Which lockers were switched the most times?

2. There is exactly one three digit positive whole number (so a number between 100 and 999) with the following properties:

   If you subtract 11 from it, the answer is divisible by 11;
   If you subtract 10 from it, the answer is divisible by 10;
   If you subtract 9 from it, the answer is divisible by 9.

   What is the number?

3 Tommy is an elevator operator in the Empire State Building. One morning he went up several floors, then went down 17 floors, then went up 56 floors, went down 85 floors and ended up on the second floor. How many floors did he go up originally?

4 Multiply a number by 4. Then add 12. Divide by 2. Subtract 18. Then divide by 4. If the answer is 6, what was your original number?

5 The last digit of a positive whole number is the digit in the 'ones' position, farthest to the right. For example, the last digit of 156 753 is 3.

What is the last digit of $2004^{1\,000\,000} + 2005^{1\,000\,000}$?

You should not need to work out the actual number!

6 The number 6 has the following property:

If you subtract 2 from it, you get 4 which is a perfect square,

$6 - 2 = 4 = (2 \times 2) = 2^2$

and if you add 2 to it, you get 8 which is a perfect cube,

$6 + 2 = 8 = (2 \times 2 \times 2) = 2^3$.

What is the next whole number, bigger than 6, with this property?
(This means that when you subtract 2 from it, you get a perfect square and when you add 2 to it, you get a perfect cube.)

7 A number like 27 472 or 5665 is called a palindrome because it reads the same backwards as forwards.

How many four-digit palindromes are there?

8 All four-digit palindromes are divisible by some number. Can you find it?

9 There is only one integer such that one less than it is a perfect square and one more than it is a perfect cube. What is the number?

10 Cross out all of the nine dots in the figure using only four straight lines and without lifting your pencil off the paper.

Revision Activity A

Use any problem-solving strategy or a combination of strategies to solve these problems.

1. **Magic Square:** Place the numbers 1 to 9 into the nine cells of the three-by-three square so that: 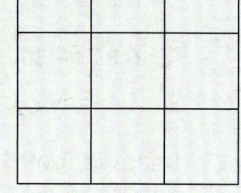
   - The sum of the entries in each row = 15
   - The sum of the entries in each column = 15
   - The sum of the entries in each of the two diagonals = 15.

2. A multiple of 11 I be,
   Not odd, but even, you see.
   My digits, a pair,
   When multiplied there,
   Make a cube and a square
   Out of me. Who am I?

3. When the famous mathematician Gauss was a boy in his first arithmetic class, he was asked by his teacher to do the following problem. He solved it very quickly. Can you work out a quick method to solve it?

   Find the sum of all the Natural numbers from 1 to 100, i.e. find the sum
   $S = 1 + 2 + 3 + 4 + 5 + \ldots + 100$.

4. (a) Express 11 as the sum of two consecutive numbers.
   (b) Express 13 as the sum of two consecutive numbers.
   (c) Can every odd number be expressed as the sum of two consecutive numbers? Explain your answer.

5. If it is possible, find an odd number that can be expressed as the sum of four consecutive Natural numbers. If it is impossible, explain why.

6. Luke and Isla are playing chess. Luke says, 'There are 64 equal squares on the chessboard. But I wonder how many of every size there are.' Isla says that she has read that there are in fact 204 squares on a chessboard. Can you justify Isla's claim?

7. Using the symbols +, −, ×, ÷, fill in the following three spaces to make a true equation (you may use a symbol more than once).

   5___5___5___5 = 11

8. Mary has a square vineyard. She always plants her grape vines in square arrays like those in the diagram. Each year, she plants more vines but always keeps the vineyard square. This year, she planted 41 vines. How many vines does she have in the vineyard now?

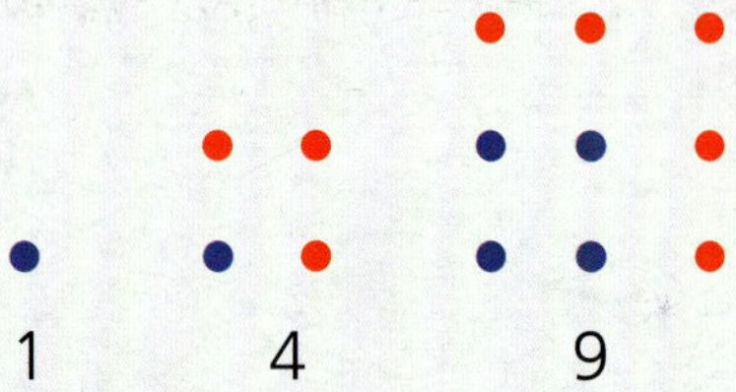

9. If the diagonals of a rectangle are drawn in, how many triangles of all sizes are there in the shape?

10. A, B and C run a 100 m race, each running at a steady speed throughout. A beats B by 10 metres and B beats C by 10 metres. By how much does A beat C?

11. It takes 64 small cubes to completely fill a large cubic container with no top.
    How many cubes are not touching a side or the bottom?

12. Imagine that the Earth is a sphere with a circumference of 40 075 km and that a rope is tied tautly around the Equator. The rope will be 40 075 km long.

    (a) You want to extend the rope so that it will have 1 metre clearance all round the Earth. How much longer will the rope have to be?

    (b) If the Earth were replaced in part (a) by a football with a diameter of 22 cm, how much longer would the rope have to be?

13. In a sale, you get a discount of 30% off a washing machine, but you must pay 23% VAT. Which would you prefer to have applied first, the discount or the tax? Explain your answer.

14. A bag contains 28 red, 31 green, 36 black, 29 orange and 27 yellow wine gums. Michael has been blindfolded so that he cannot see into the bag. What is the smallest number of wine gums that Michael must choose from the bag to guarantee that he has chosen at least two of the same colour?

15. The total cost of a box of chocolates is €11. This includes the cost of the chocolates and the cost of the box.
    If the box costs €7 less than the chocolates, how much do the chocolates cost?

16. There are ten teams in a football league. Each team plays every other team twice, once at home and once away. How many matches are played in total during the season?
    (Be careful that you do not count the same match twice!)

17. Julie and Brendan both have some money and each of them wants to buy a chocolate bar. However, Julie is 2 cent short of the price of the bar while Brendan is 18 cent short (of the price of the same bar). They decide to pool their resources and find that even when they combine their money, they still do not have enough money for the bar.
    How much does the chocolate bar cost?
    (Remember, both of them have **some** money so that each of them has at least one cent.)

18. You have two squares. The lengths of their sides are whole numbers of cm. The total area of the two squares is 34 cm². If you made a rectangle using two sides from one square and two sides from the other, what would its area be?

19. A teacher picks two consecutive whole numbers between 6 and 10. She tells Rashid what one of the numbers is and tells Sheila the other one. Rashid and Sheila then have the following conversation:

Rashid: 'I do not know your number'.

After considering what Rashid said,

Sheila then said, 'I do not know your number'.

What number was given to Sheila?

20. There are 70 students in a year group, 36 girls and 34 boys. At the end of the school year, the students have a choice of two places to go on their school trip: either Galway or Cork. All of the students go on the trip, with 25 students going to Galway and the other 45 going to Cork. How many more girls went to Cork than boys went to Galway?

(You are asked for the difference between the number of girls who went to Cork and the number of boys who went to Galway.)

21. Shuffle a pack of 52 playing cards and then deal out 30 cards to form a pile. Let n be the number of red cards in the pile. Let m be the number of black cards in the reduced deck. What is the value of $n - m$?

Answers

Chapter 1

Activity 1.1
1. C = {the set of months in the year with more than 32 days}. E = {the set of triangles with 5 sides}. 2. Set A (i) {20, 25, 30, 35, 40} Set B (i) {d, i, n, o, v, s} Set C (i) {4, 6, 8, 9, 10} Set D (i) {e, l, o, s, v, w} 3. (i) {1, 2, 3, 6} (ii) { }, {1}, {2}, {3}, {6}, {1, 2}, {1, 3}, {1, 6}, {2, 3}, {2, 6}, {3, 6}, {1, 2, 3}, {1, 2, 6}, {1, 3, 6}, {2, 3, 6}, {1, 2, 3, 6} 4. (i) (a) C = {x, y, z} (b) D = {a, b, c} (c) $C \cup D$ = {a, b, c, x, y, z} (d) $C \cap D$ = { } (ii) (a) 3 (b) 3 (c) 6 5. (i) False (ii) True (iii) True (iv) False (v) True (vi) False (vii) True (viii) True (ix) False 6. (i) $X \cup Y$ Students in the class who are left handed or study Art. (ii) $X \cap Y$ Students in the class who are left handed and study Art. (iii) X' Students in the class who are not left-handed. (iv) $(X \cup Y)'$ Students in the class who are neither left handed nor study Art. (v) $X \backslash Y$ Students in the class who are left handed and do not study Art. 7. (ii) (a) 6 (b) 4 (c) 2 (d) 10 (e) 6 8. (ii) (a) {20, 22, 24, 26, 28, 30, 32, 34} (b) {20, 21, 22, 24, 25, 26, 27, 28, 30, 32, 33, 34, 35} (c) { } (d) {20, 22, 24, 26, 28, 30, 32, 34} (e) {21, 25, 27, 33, 35} (f) {20, 21, 22, 24, 25, 26, 27, 28, 30, 32, 33, 34, 35} 9. (i) 111 (ii) 43 (iii) 21 (iv) 154 10. (ii) 2 11. (ii) 15 12. (i) 23 (ii) 99 13. (i) 27 (ii) 69 14. (i) 8 (ii) 35 15. (ii) (a) 36 (b) 12 (c) 45 16. (ii) (a) 46 (b) 8 (c) 23

Activity 1.2
1. (i) {a, d, e, g, i, m, r} (ii) {a, g, n} (iii) { } (iv) {a, e, g, i, m} (v) {e, i, m} (vi) {a, g} (vii) {e} 2. (i) {2, 3, 4, 10} (ii) {3, 7, 9, 10, 11} (iii) {2, 7, 8, 10, 12} (iv) {2, 3, 4, 7, 8, 10, 12,} (v) {3} (vi) {1, 5, 6, 8, 12} (vii) {4} (viii) { } (ix) {7} 3. (i) {1, 4} (ii) {1, 4, 5, 6} (iii) { } 5. (ii) (a) {h, g, c, i, f, n, l, j, k} (b) {h, g, c, l, j, k} (c) {a, b, m, d} (d) {a, b, d, e, m} (e) {m} (iii) (a) 1 (b) 3 (c) 1 6. (i) 7 (ii) 2 (iii) Prime Numbers 7. (ii) (a) 6 (b) 10 (c) 1 (d) 8 (e) 11 (f) 5 8. (ii) (a) {n, u, m, e, r, i, c, a, l, y} (b) {m, i, r, a, c, l, e} (c) {r, a, l, y} (d) {n, m, e, i, c, u} (e) {m, e, a, r, l} (f) {n, u, m, e, r, i, c, l, y} (g) {n} (h) {n, m, e, r, a, l, y} 9. (i) Students in the class who are afraid of either mice or spiders. (ii) Students in the class who are afraid of mice and wasps. (iii) Students in the class who are afraid of wasps but not spiders. (iv) Students in the class who are afraid of mice and spiders but are not afraid of wasps. (v) Students in the class who are not afraid of mice or spiders or wasps. 10. (i) The people living in Ireland who own a pet or like dogs but don't have pet insurance. (ii) The people living in Ireland who own a pet, like dogs and have pet insurance. (iii) The people living in Ireland who have pet insurance but don't own a pet or like dogs. (iv) The people living in Ireland who don't have a pet or like dogs or have pet insurance. 11. (ii) 9 (iii) (a) 49 (b) 51 (c) 78 (e) 61

Activity 1.3
1. (ii) Yes 4. (i) Distributive Property of **Union over Intersection** (ii) **Commutative property of intersection** (iii) **Associative Property of Intersection** (iv) Distributive Property of **Intersection over Union** (v) **Commutative property of union** (vi) **Associative Property for Union** 5. (i) The people who are married and own a car or own their own home. (ii) The people who own their own home and own a car or who own their own home and are married. (iii) The people who own a car or their own home or are married. 6. (a) (i) {1, 2, 3, 4, 5, 6} (b) {5, 6} (c) {1, 2, 4, 5, 6} (ii) $(P \cup Q) \cap (P \cup R)$

Activity 1.4
1. (ii) 169 (iii) 2 2. (ii) 2 (iii) 12 3. (i) 13 (ii) 13 (iii) 54 (iv) 28 (v) 39 (vi) 20 (vii) 90 (viii) 0 4. (ii) 6 (iii) 12 5. (ii) 3 6. (ii) 15 (iii) 57 7. (i) 6 (ii) 35 8. (i) 15 (ii) 88 9. (ii) $x = 4, y = 3$ 10. (i) $y = 1, x = 3$ (ii) 101

Revision Activity 1
1. (a) (i) {a, b, c, d, e, f} (ii) {e, f, g, h, i} (iii) {a, b, c, d, e, f, g, h, i} (iv) {e, f} (v) {a, b, c, d} (b) (i) 6 (ii) 5 (iii) 9 (iv) 2 (v) 4 2. (b) 370 3. (a) 29 (b) 27 (c) 22 4. (b) $p + q + d - c$ 5. (b) (i) {b, c, e, f} (ii) {b, c, e, f, h, i, k, l} (iii) {a, b, c, d, e, f, g, i, j, k} (iv) {a, d, e, g, i, k} (v) {h, j, l} (vi) {h, j, l} (d) Distributive Property of **Intersection over Union** 6. (a) True (b) False (c) False (d) False (e) True (f) True (g) True (h) False (i) True (j) True (k) False (l) False 7. (a) {1, 2, 3, 4, 5, 6, 8, 9, 10, 11, 12, 13, 14, 16, 17, 18, 19, 20} (b) {5, 7, 9, 14, 15, 17, 19, 20} (c) {2, 4, 8, 12} (d) {3, 13} (e) {1, 10, 16, 18} (f) {2, 3, 12, 13} (g) {3} (h) {2, 12} (i) {5, 6, 9, 11, 13, 14, 17, 19, 20} (j) {1, 2, 4, 5, 6, 7, 8, 9, 10, 11, 12, 13, 14, 15, 16, 17, 18, 19, 20} 9. (b) 7 (c) 36%

Exam-style Questions
1. (b) $P \backslash (E \cup O)$, $P \cap E \cap O$, $E \cap O$, $(E \cap O) \backslash P$ (c) $\frac{1}{5}$
2. (b) Incorrect statements: (iii) or (v) (c) 5

Chapter 2

Activity 2.1
2. (i) $\frac{1}{6}$ (ii) $\frac{1}{18}$ (iii) $\frac{1}{36}$ (iv) $\frac{1}{9}$ 3. (i) €7.80 (ii) €15 (iii) €8 (iv) 3 4. only part (iii) 6. (i) €12.80 (ii) €13.60 (iii) €1.50 7. Answer (iv) 8. (iv) smallest = $\frac{1}{4}$ 9. Tanya is not correct. 10. (i) $\frac{4}{6}$ (ii) $\frac{8}{12}$ 13. (i) 4 (ii) $1\frac{1}{2}$ (iii) $3\frac{2}{3}$ 14. A: 1 square B: 2 squares C: 8 squares D: 4 squares 15. $\frac{7}{10}$ 16. (i) $\frac{5}{8}$ kg (ii) $\frac{5}{24}$ kg 17. (i) $\frac{5}{7}$ (ii) $\frac{7}{5}$

Activity 2.2
1. (i) a^9 (ii) a^4 (iii) a^2 (iv) a^{12} (v) a^9b^6 (vi) a^5b^{20} 2. $\frac{a^7}{a^7} = 1$ 3. $\frac{a^0}{a^5} = \frac{1}{a^5}$ 4. 5 5. $\frac{1}{36}$ 6. 1 7. 4 8. $\frac{1}{5}$ 9. 3 10. $\frac{1}{3}$ 11. 10 12. $\frac{1}{10}$ 13. 10 14. 2 15. $\frac{2}{3}$ 16. 4 17. 3 18. 27 19. 8 20. $\frac{1}{10}$ 21. 1 22. 6 23. 3 24. 3 25. $\frac{1}{3}$ 26. 5 27. 25 28. $\frac{4}{9}$ 29. $\frac{64}{729}$ 30. $\frac{3}{4}$ 31. $\frac{81}{256}$ 32. $\frac{2}{3}$ 33. $\frac{8}{27}$ 34. $\frac{8}{27}$ 35. $\frac{13}{5}$ 36. $\frac{2}{5}$ 37. $\frac{4}{25}$ 38. $\frac{16}{625}$ 39. $\frac{16}{9}$ 40. $\frac{343}{125}$ 41. $\frac{64}{343}$ 42. (i) $x^{\frac{1}{2}}$ (ii) $x^{\frac{3}{2}}$ (iii) $x^{\frac{3}{2}}$ (iv) $x^{\frac{1}{4}}$ (v) $x^{\frac{5}{6}}$ 43. (i) False (ii) True (iii) False (iv) False (v) False (vi) False (vii) False 44. $2^{\frac{5}{2}}$ 45. $3^{\frac{11}{2}}$ 46. $5^{\frac{3}{2}}$

Activity 2.3
1. (i) $x = 3$ (ii) $x = 6$ (iii) $x = 3$ (iv) $x = 3$ (v) $x = 5$ (vi) $x = 1$ (vii) $x = 7$ (viii) $x = 8$ 2. (i) $x = 6$ (ii) $x = 4$ (iii) $x = \frac{3}{2}$ (iv) $x = 2$ (v) $x = 8$ (vi) $x = 1$ (vii) $x = 13$ (viii) $x = 3$ 3. $x = 5$ 4. $x = 3$ 5. $x = 4$ 6. (i) 729 (ii) 3^4 (iii) $x = -10$ 7. (i) 2

(ii) $2^{\frac{1}{2}}$ (iii) $x = 2\frac{1}{2}$ **8.** (i) (a) 2^3 (b) 2^2 (ii) $x = 3$ **9.** (i) (a) 3^5
(b) $3^{\frac{3}{2}}$ (ii) $x = 7$ **10.** (i) 2^5 (ii) $x = 3$ **11.** (i) $5^{\frac{3}{2}}$ (ii) $x = -\frac{3}{2}$
12. $p = -\frac{1}{4}$ **13.** $n = -2$ **14.** $n = -3$

Activity 2.4
1. $x = \frac{2}{9}$ **2.** $x = \frac{2}{3}$ **3.** $x = \frac{45}{99}$ **4.** $x = \frac{23789}{99999}$
5. $x = \frac{5489}{999}$ **6.** $x = \frac{323}{999}$ **7.** $x = \frac{13}{9}$ **8.** No
9. π. Its digits never repeat

Activity 2.5
3. (i) $9\sqrt{5}$ (ii) $8\sqrt{7} + 5\sqrt{3}$ (iii) 30   (iv) −20   (v) $12\sqrt{14}$
(vi) −30   **4.** (i) $13\sqrt{2}$ (ii) $7\sqrt{13} + \sqrt{6}$ (iii) 120   (iv) $-3\sqrt{10}$
(v) $-12\sqrt{34}$ (vi) −105   **5.** (i) $3\sqrt{5}$ (ii) $2\sqrt{6}$ (iii) $3\sqrt{7}$ (iv) $10\sqrt{2}$
(v) $6\sqrt{2}$ (vi) $2\sqrt{2}$ **6.** (i) $\frac{3}{4}$ (ii) $16\sqrt{2}$ (iii) $4\sqrt{5}$ (iv) $5\sqrt{5}$
(v) $3\sqrt{7}$ **7.** (i) $7\sqrt{3}$ (ii) $4\sqrt{5}$ (iii) $7\sqrt{2}$ (iv) $4\sqrt{7}$ **8.** (i) $p = 9$
(ii) $p = 2$ (iii) $p = 16$ (iv) $p = 2$ **9.** (i) 24   (ii) −24   (iii) $18\sqrt{14}$
(iv) −216   (v) $6\sqrt{35}$ **10.** 41   **11.** (i) 7   (ii) 44   (iii) 1
(iv) $27 + 10\sqrt{2}$ **12.** (i) 25   (ii) 5   **14.** $1 + 3\sqrt{10}$ **15.** $3^{\frac{3}{2}}$
17. $8 − 9\sqrt{2}$ **18.** $\frac{1}{2}\sqrt{2}$ **19.** $\frac{2}{3}\sqrt{3}$ **20.** (i) $\sqrt{3} + \frac{1}{3}\sqrt{6}$
(ii) $\frac{1}{2}\sqrt{10} - \frac{1}{2}\sqrt{2}$ (iii) $\sqrt{5} - \frac{1}{5}\sqrt{15}$

Activity 2.6
1. 3.85×10^9 **2.** (i) 7.6×10^2 (ii) 4.62×10^3 (iii) 2.5×10^7
(iv) 3.15×10^5 (v) 1.075×10^9 (vi) 6.3×10^{13} **3.** 8.3812×10^{-26}
4. (i) 8.6×10^{-4} (ii) 4.62×10^{-3} (iii) 2.7×10^7 (iv) 3.26×10^{-7}
(v) 1.077×10^9 (vi) 7.8×10^{-8} **5.** €(5.3×10^9) **7.** 1.2×10^{14} kg
8. 1×10^{-5} **9.** 2.5×10^{-6} **10.** (i) 8.42×10^3 (ii) 1.35×10^4
(iii) 9.7×10^2 (iv) 1.7×10^{-2} (v) 3.9×10^{-3} (vi) 4.9993×10^{-2}
11. (i) 4.16×10^{13} km   (ii) 3.5×10^6 km   **12.** 2×10^{-6}
13. (i) 8.6×10^7 (ii) 2.7×10^{-1} (iii) 2.08×10^2 (iv) 9.9×10^0
14. (i) 2×10^3 (ii) 3.7×10^8 (iii) 8×10^2 (iv) 1.4×10^7
15. (i) 3.1×10^1 (ii) 1.1×10^2 (iii) 1.22×10^{-1} **16.** 5.3×10^6
17. 1.089×10^5 km   **18.** 3.52×10^{-2} **19.** 2.03×10^6 km

Activity 2.7
1. 2, 3, 5, 7, 11, 13, 17, 19, 23, 29, 31, 37, 41, 43, 47   **2.** $2^3 \times 3^2$
3. (i) $6 = 3 + 3$; $8 = 3 + 5$; $10 = 5 + 5$; $12 = 5 + 7$; $14 = 7 + 7$;
$16 = 3 + 13$ (ii) $86 = 43 + 43$ **4.** 3 and 5; 5 and 7; 11 and 13;
17 and 19; 29 and 31; 41 and 43; 59 and 61; 71 and 73;
7. Always even   **9.** Always even   **11.** Always odd
14. Always even   **15.** Always odd   **17.** Always even

Revision Activity 2
1. (a) 1.5×10^8 (b) (i) 3.40; 1.73; 2.97; 1.60; 1.57; 3.50
2. (a) 5.188   (b) 6.56   (c) 10   **3.** (a) $\frac{1}{49}$; 9   (b) 1.68×10^7
4. $3^{\frac{5}{2}}$ **5.** 2^1 **6.** $30\sqrt{2} - 48$ **7.** (a) 512   (b) 16   **8.** $n = 0$
9. (a) 2^{12} (b) 2^5 **10.** $3^{\frac{3}{2}}$

Exam-style Questions
1. (ii) $\sqrt{5}$ is an irrational number; it cannot be written as a fraction.   **2.** (a) −7.3 is negative and is not a whole number.

Chapter 3

Activity 3.1
2. (i) Cost of electricity is 18 cents per unit used plus a fixed charge of €20.   (ii) C and u (iii) 0.18 and 20   (iv) €110
3. (i) Moran $30 + 30x$, Cox $420 + 9x$, Dunne $260 + 10x$, Mulligan $-50 + 25x$ (ii) The Moran family   **4.** (ii) (a) 3
(b) One rule for the number of matchsticks in a pattern is to start with 4 and add 3 matchsticks for every additional pattern   (c) 19   (d) 31   (e) 301   (f) Rule: "the number of matchsticks in any pattern is 4 + 3 times the number of the pattern less one"

(iii) Yes   (iv) 11   **5.** (i) Sunflower A was 12 cm tall at the start and grew by an average of 3 cm per day. Sunflower B was 8 cm tall at the start and grew by an average of 4 cm per day.   (iii) The growth rate is linear because in each case the differences in the heights are constant as the number of days increase one by one.   (iv) Sunflower A is growing at an average rate of 3 cm per day.   (v) Sunflower B is growing at an average rate of 4 cm per day   (viii) The slope of the graph for sunflower A is 3. The slope of the graph for sunflower B is 4.
(ix) 4 days   **6.** (i) 5   (ii) 6   **7.** (i) Coefficient of x^2 is 3; coefficient of x is −4.   (ii) −7   **8.** (i) a, b and c   (ii) Coefficient of ab is 3; coefficient of ac is −5.   (iii) −6   **9.** (i) $(3m^2 - 6m + 2)$ is the most compact.   **10.** $15x + 10y$ **11.** $-6a + 2b$
12. $21 − 14q − 7r$ **13.** $15a^2 − 10ab$ **14.** $-x + 2y$
15. $-10x + 29$ **16.** $-a - 9$ **17.** $5x^2 - 19xy$
18. $15ab - 7ac - 3bc$ **19.** $x^5 - x^4 - x^3 - 2x^2$ **20.** $2p + 11q - 20$
21. $2x^2 + 3x + 5$ **22.** $x^5 - x^4 - 3x^3 + 6x^2 - 3x$ **23.** (i) $8x^2 + 1$
(ii) $4a^3 + 2a^2 - 7a$ (iii) $-6x^2 - 16x + 2$ (iv) $-10x^2 - 11x - 8$
24. (ii) $x^3 + 7x^2 + 14x + 20$ **25.** (i) $2x^2 + x + 4$ (ii) $-5x - 4$
(iii) $3x^2 - 16x - 8$ (iv) $7x^2 - 4x + 8$ **26.** (i) a^4 (ii) $2a$
(iii) $5ab^2$ (iv) $\frac{2x^2}{3y}$ (v) $\frac{4xy^2}{3}$ (vi) a^2 (vii) $\frac{x}{2}$ (viii) $6x^4y^7$
27. $-x + 7$ **28.** $-27a$

Activity 3.2
1. (i) $10x^2 - 11x - 6$ (ii) $-20x^2 - 16x + 4$ (iii) $-9a^2 + 9$
(iv) $-2p^2 + 16p - 30$ **2.** $x^2 + 7x + 10$ **3.** $a^2 + 10a + 24$
4. $y^2 - 6y + 5$ **5.** $3x^2 + 10x - 8$ **6.** $6x^2 - 23x + 20$
7. $10p^2 + 17p + 3$ **8.** $15x^2 + xy - 2y^2$ **9.** $21x^2 + 4xy - y^2$
10. $25x^2 - 4b^2$ **11.** $2x^3 - x^2 - 16x + 15$ **12.** $x^3 - 3xy^2 - 2y^3$
13. $5x^3 - 19x^2 + 12x$ **14.** $x^3 + 3x^2 - 5x - 4$
15. $6x^3 + x^2 - 13x + 4$ **16.** $a = -1$ **17.** $a = -2$ **18.** $a = 4$
19. $6x^2 - 5x - 4$ **20.** (i) $x^2 + 2xy + y^2$ (ii) $x^2 - 2xy + y^2$
21. (i) $x^2 + 4x + 4$ (ii) $x^2 - 6x + 9$ (iii) $a^2 + 8a + 16$
(iv) $a^2 - 10a + 25$ (v) $p^2 - 12p + 36$ (vi) $x^2 + 14x + 49$
22. (i) $a^2x^2 + 2abx + b^2$ (ii) $a^2x^2 - 2abx + b^2$ **23.** (i) $9x^2 + 12x + 4$
(ii) $16x^2 - 8x + 1$ (iii) $4a^2 - 20a + 25$ (iv) $16m^2 + 24m + 9$
(v) $4p^2 - 24p + 36$ (vi) $4x^2 + 4x + 1$

Activity 3.3
1. (i) 27   (ii) 0   (iii) −72   (iv) −66   (v) −18   (vi) 0   (vii) 30
2. (i) −60   (ii) 33   (iii) −4   (iv) −9   **3.** (i) −24   (ii) −4   (iii) 33
(iv) −7   (v) $\frac{1}{2}$ (vi) $\frac{7}{3}$ **4.** (i) 15   (ii) −45   (iii) −223   (iv) −98
(v) 1   (vi) −152   **5.** (i) −11   (ii) −8   (iii) 14   (iv) 4   (v) 108
(vi) 14   **6.** (i) 60   (ii) −94   (iii) −181   (iv) 101   **7.** 3   **8.** 1
9. 3   **10.** $5t$ **11.** $\frac{-1}{12}$ **12.** 4   **13.** $\frac{-6}{5}$

Activity 3.4
1. (i) $5(x + 2y)$ (ii) $3(2x - 3y)$ (iii) $3(p + 5q)$ (iv) $x(x - 5)$
(v) $p(q - m)$ (vi) $3x(y - 4z)$ (vii) $5a(4a - 3b)$ (viii) $5p^2q^2(3q - p)$
(ix) $a(a^2 - a + 1)$ (x) $5xy^2(1 - 3xy + 2y^2)$ **2.** (i) $(x + y)(a + b)$
(ii) $(a + b)(5 + x)$ (iii) $(a + b)(p + q)$ (iv) $(x - 3)(a + b)$
(v) $(a - b)(a + 4)$ (vi) $(y + 1)(x - y)$ (vii) $(a + b)(x - 1)$
(viii) $(a - b)(x^2 - 3y)$ **3.** (i) $(3 - x)(a - b)$ (ii) $(x - 5a)(3 - b)$
(iii) $(2c - d)(2c + 3)$ (iv) $(a + 3)(x - 1)$ (v) $(2 - k)(x - y)$
(vi) $(3a - b)(1 + b)$ (vii) $(3y - 10)(x + b)$ (viii) $(x - 2y)(5x + 1)$
(ix) $(a - 2b)(6p + 2)$ (x) $(x - b)(x + a)$

Activity 3.5
1. $(a + 3)(a + 2)$ **2.** $(x - 3)(x + 2)$ **3.** $(a - 11)(a + 8)$
4. $(m + 14)(m - 3)$ **5.** $(x + 11)(x - 6)$ **6.** $(a - 11)(a + 6)$
7. $(5x - 1)(x - 1)$ **8.** $(3x - 2)(x + 1)$ **9.** $(5x - 2)(2x + 3)$
10. $(4x - 5)(3x - 2)$ **11.** $(3x - 7)(2x + 5)$ **12.** $(11x - 2)(x + 7)$
13. $(6x - 5)(x + 2)$ **14.** $(3m - 4)(3m - 4)$ **15.** $(5x - 3)(5x - 3)$
16. $(a + 1)(a - 1)$ **17.** $(x + 3)(x - 3)$ **18.** $(p + 6)(p - 6)$
19. $(3m + 1)(3m - 1)$ **20.** $(5x + 6y)(5x - 6y)$
21. $(7a + 4b)(7a - 4b)$ **22.** $(12x + 3y)(12x - 3y)$
23. $(13p + 12)(13p - 12)$ **24.** $(m + 100)(m - 100)$
25. $(x + y + z)(x + y - z)$ **26.** $(a + b + 1)(a + b - 1)$
27. $2(x + 3)(x - 3)$ **28.** $(x - 2 + 6y)(x - 2 - 6y)$ **29.** $(5x)(x + 2)$

30. (200)(2) **31.** $6x - 9x^2$ **32.** $12(2x^2 + 1)$ **33.** $\frac{4x}{2x-3}$
34. $(2x - 3)$ **35.** $2[2x + 3y][2x - 3y]$ **36.** (i) $y(17 - 5y)$
(ii) $(3a - 2)(2a - 5)$ **37.** $(3a - 2)(a)$

Activity 3.6
1. $\frac{x}{20}$ **2.** $\frac{8x+18}{15}$ **3.** $\frac{x+11}{3}$ **4.** $\frac{x+10}{5}$ **5.** $\frac{27x-43}{10}$
6. $\frac{34x+3}{12}$ **7.** $\frac{102p-9}{14}$ **8.** $\frac{13k-3}{12}$ **9.** $\frac{5}{2x}$ **10.** $\frac{19}{15k}$
11. $\frac{13x+5}{2x^2+x}$ **12.** $\frac{28x+3}{(3x-2)(2x+3)}$ **13.** $\frac{3x-13}{(3x+1)(2x-4)}$
14. $\frac{-13p+27}{(3p-5)(p+1)}$ **15.** $\frac{3x-18}{(3x+2)(3x-2)}$ **16.** $p = 3$
17. $k = 29$ **18.** (ii) $\frac{1}{x-2}$ **19.** $\frac{2}{x-3}$ **20.** $\frac{-4}{x-4}$
21. $\frac{5x+20}{(2x+5)(x+5)}$ **22.** $k = 17$

Activity 3.7
1. (i) $x + 2$ (ii) $3a + 2$ (iii) $3x + 4$ (iv) $3p + 1$ (v) $3x + 2$
(vi) $x + 8$ (vii) $4x + 5y$ (viii) $3 + 2x$ **2.** $x^2 - 5x - 9$
3. $2x^2 + x - 5$ **4.** $a^2 - 5a - 17$ **5.** $2a^2 - a - 7$ **6.** $2p^2 + 3p + 4$
7. $3k^2 - 4k + 1$ **8.** $x^2 - 2x - 1$ **9.** $x + 4$ **10.** $3k^2 + 6k + 8$
11. $a = 3, b = -4, c = -5$ **12.** (i) $x^2 - 3x$ (ii) $x^2 - 3x$
13. $x^2 + 2x + 4$ **14.** $3 - 5x - 2x^2$

Revision Activity
1. (a) $4x(5y - x)$ (b) $(5x + 1)(x - 2)$ (c) $6(x + 2y)(x - 2y)$
2. $\frac{31}{12}$ **3.** $6x^3 + 7x^2 - 26x + 8$ **4.** (a) $(x - b)(x + a)$
(b) $2(2x + 3y)(2x - 3y)$ **5.** (a) $15x^3 - x^2 - 32x + 12$ (b) 28
6. (a) $3x(3x - 5)$ (b) $(3x - 5)(3x - 3)$ (c) $(y - x)(3 - 4x)$
7. $\frac{2x-1}{(x-3)(x-2)}$ **8.** $2p + 10$ **9.** $\frac{-x+43}{20}$ **10.** (a) $\frac{1}{-20}$
(b) $\frac{5}{8}$ (c) $\frac{-1}{20}$ (d) $\frac{65}{59}$

Exam-style Questions
1. (a) $\frac{x}{20}$ (b) $2x^2 - 5x + 2$ **2.** (a) $5x^2(x - 2)$
(b) $(2x + 9y)(2x - 9y)$ (c) $(a - b)(a + 3)$

Chapter 4

Activity 4.1
1. $x = 3$ **2.** $y = 2$ **3.** $a = -5$ **4.** $x = 6$ **5.** $g = -5$ **6.** $h = 4$
7. $t = -12$ **8.** $z = 10$ **9.** $x = 2$ **10.** $x = 14$ **11.** $w = -29$
12. $y = 25$ **13.** $s = -3$ **14.** $b = 9$ **15.** $l = 1$ **16.** $m = -2$
17. $x = \frac{18}{5}$ **18.** $p = -33$ **19.** $q = 15$ **20.** $n = -2$

Activity 4.2
1. $h = \frac{6}{5}$ **2.** $d = \frac{20}{7}$ **3.** $n = \frac{14}{3}$ **4.** $y = \frac{35}{12}$ **5.** $m = \frac{72}{21} = \frac{24}{7}$
6. $x = \frac{9}{2}$ **7.** $c = -\frac{27}{2}$ **8.** $p = -\frac{25}{3}$ **9.** $v = \frac{28}{3}$ **10.** $z = \frac{108}{7}$
11. $x = \frac{23}{6}$ **12.** $h = \frac{7}{25}$ **13.** $m = \frac{29}{6}$ **14.** $d = \frac{39}{24} = \frac{13}{8}$
15. $k = -\frac{14}{99}$ **16.** $m = \frac{3}{7}$ **17.** $l = \frac{7}{16}$ **18.** $t = \frac{9}{2}$ **19.** $a = \frac{113}{40}$
20. $d = \frac{-6}{53}$ **21.** $b = -\frac{21}{4}$ **22.** $g = -\frac{3}{4}$ **23.** $f = \frac{11}{21}$
24. $c = \frac{101}{51}$ **25.** $k = -\frac{61}{29}$

Activity 4.3
1. (i) 12 (ii) 24 (iii) 27 (iv) 30 (v) 7 (vi) 15
2. The first number = 41, The second number = 42, The third number = 43 **3.** $k = 3$, The lengths of each side are: 3 cm, 4 cm, 5 cm **4.** Josh ran 4 km, Jack ran 8 km **5.** Sean gets €10, Sarah gets €15 **6.** Shoes cost: €55 Trousers cost: €40
7. 96 and 98 **8.** The second side 29 m long, The third side = 58 m long **9.** Harry is 60 years old **10.** 12 and 13

11. (i) $2(5x + 1) = 32$ (ii) $x = 3$ (iii) 11 units (iv) 5 units
(iv) 55 units² **12.** (i) $x + \frac{x}{5} = 48$ (ii) $x = 40$ (iii) 40 years old
(iv) 8 years old **13.** (i) $5x + 2x = 210$ (ii) $x = 30$ (iii) €150
(iv) €60 **14.** (i) $3x(0.69) + x(1.50) = 7.14$ (ii) $x = \frac{7.14}{3.57} = 2$
(iv) 2 (v) 6 **15.** (ii) $A + (2A - 30) = 180$ (iii) $A = 70$ (iv) 70°
(v) 110° **16.** (ii) $0.1 + 0.06(x - 5000) = 1300$
(iii) $0.1x + 0.06(x - 5000) = 1300$; $x = 10\,000$ (iv) Mr Kelly borrowed €10 000 at an interest rate of 10%, Mr Kelly borrowed €10 000 − €5000 = €5000 at an interest of 6%
17. (i) $\frac{2x-5}{2} + 2(w) = \frac{14x-25}{10}$ (ii) (width) = $\frac{x}{5}$ (iii) $\frac{x}{5}$ units
18. (ii) $A + \frac{2A}{3} = 180°$ (iii) $A = 108°$ (iv) 108° (v) 72°
19. (i) $x + \left(\frac{3x}{2}\right) = \frac{25}{2}$ (ii) $x = 5$ (iii) The base length = 5 cm
The length of the 2 equal sides = $\frac{3x}{4} = \frac{3(5)}{4} = \frac{15}{4} = 3.75$ cm
(iv) Add sketch **20.** Time taken for the first part of the journey $\frac{x}{540}$ hr, Time taken for the second part of the journey $\frac{x}{90}$ hr (ii) $\frac{x}{540} + \frac{x}{90} = \frac{7}{10}$ (iii) $x = 54$ (iv) (a) 6 km
(b) 48 km (v) (a) 6 minutes (b) 36 minutes

Revision Activity 4
1. (a) (i) $c = 3$ (ii) $m = 2$ (iii) $y = 8$ (iv) $x = -\frac{37}{9}$ (b) Smaller number = 7, Larger number = 21 **2.** (a) The first number = x, The second number = $x + 1$ (b) $x - \frac{2}{3}(x + 1) = 34$ (c) $x = 104$
(d) The first number = 104, The second number = 105
3. (a) $\frac{3x}{8} + \frac{2x-5}{12}$ + 3rd side = $\frac{17x}{24}$, (b) $\frac{2x+5}{12}$ units
(c) scalene triangle **4.** (a) $5x - 2(20 - x) = 51$ (b) $x = 13$
5. (a) $2 + 1.1x = 20.70$ (b) 17 km (e) €38.30
6. (a) $46x - 18.50 = 234.50$ (b) 5.5 hours (c) €326.50
(d) €1609.50 **7.** (b) $\frac{x}{5}(5) + \frac{3x}{5}(10) + x(20) = 2280$ (c) $x = 80$
(d) Number of €20 notes = 80, Number of €10 notes = 48,
Number of €5 notes = 40 **8.** (a) $\frac{3x}{4}$ (b) $\frac{x}{4}$ (c) $\frac{x}{2} = 432$
(d) $x = 864$ (e) 216 (f) 864 **9.** 9 cars; 28 students

Exam-style Questions
1. (a) $2n = 14$; $2n + 1 = 15$ (c) $x = 42$ **2.** $x = 2$

Chapter 5

Activity 5.2
1. (i) $x > -7$ **2.** (i) $b \geq -12$ **3.** (i) $c < -9$ **4.** (i) $d \leq -7$
5. (i) $f \leq 1$ **6.** (i) $g \leq -1$ **7.** (i) $h > -3$ **8.** (i) $k < \frac{7}{8}$ **9.** (i) $l < -6$
10. (i) $n \geq -3$ **11.** (i) $m \geq 4$ **12.** (i) $p \leq 20$ **13.** (i) $r < -3$
14. (i) $s \geq 2$ **15.** (i) $t < \frac{7}{4}$ **16.** (i) $y < -\frac{4}{3}$

Activity 5.3
1. (i) $2 \leq x \leq 6$ or $1 < x < 7$, $x \in \mathbb{N}$ (ii) $-5 < x < 1$ or $-4 \leq x \leq 0$, $x \in \mathbb{Z}$ (iii) $-5 \leq x < -2$, for $x \in \mathbb{R}$ (iv) $11 \leq x \leq 15$ or $10 < x < 16$, $x \in \mathbb{N}$ (v) $-8 < x < 9$ or $-7 \leq x \leq 8$, $x \in \mathbb{Z}$ (vi) $3 < x \leq 17$, $x \in \mathbb{R}$ **2.** $3 < y < 5$, $y \in \mathbb{N}$ ⎯⎯⎯4⎯⎯⎯

3. $-1 < a < 2$, $a \in \mathbb{Z}$ ⎯⎯0⎯⎯1⎯⎯

4. $-7 \leq c \leq 4$, $c \in \mathbb{R}$
−7 ━━━━━━━━━━ 4

5. $4 \geq d \geq -1$, $d \in \mathbb{R}$
−1 ━━━━━━━━━━ 4

6. $-3 < x < 8$

7. $5 \geq h \geq 1$

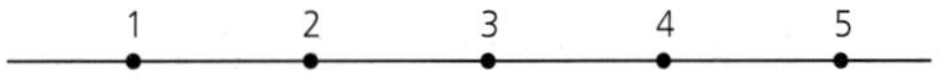

8. $-4 \leq g < 3$

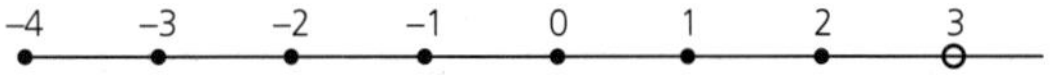

9. $1 > b \geq -\frac{7}{4}$

10. $-\frac{11}{5} \leq c \leq -\frac{1}{5}$

11. $5 \geq f \geq 2$

12. $-\frac{7}{3} \geq h \geq -\frac{16}{3}$

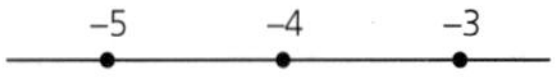

13. $-2 < w < -\frac{8}{7}$

14. $5 \geq b > \frac{17}{8}$

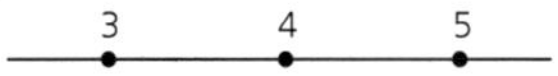

15. $-\frac{3}{2} \leq k < \frac{7}{2}$

Activity 5.4
2. (i) 23°C (ii) 27°C (iii) $23 \leq t \leq 27$ **3.** (i) $1.2 \leq h \leq 5.5$
4. (i) 18.5 (ii) 24.99 (iii) $18.5 \leq b \leq 24.99$
5. (i) 194 beats per minute (ii) Minimum = 164.9 bpm Maximum = 170.7 bpm (iii) $165 \leq x \leq 170$ **6.** (i) 60 bpm (ii) 100 bpm (iii) $60 \leq h \leq 100$ **7.** (i) $50 \leq s \leq 120$
8. (i) 36.5°C (ii) 37.2°C (iii) $36.5 \leq t \leq 37.2$
9. (i) $162 \leq h \leq 193$ (ii) $85 \leq s \leq 100$ **10.** (i) $12.25 \leq l \leq 12.75$ (ii) 12.25 mm (iii) 12.75 mm

Revision Activity 5
1. $q \geq -2, q \in \mathbb{Z}$

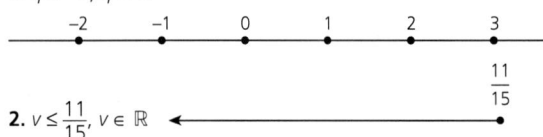

2. $v \leq \frac{11}{15}, v \in \mathbb{R}$

3. $w \geq -1, w \in \mathbb{N}$

4. (a) $x \geq 6$ (b) $x \leq 16$ (c) $\{6,7,8,9,10,11,12,13,14,15,16\}$
5. $x \leq 8.79$ km
6. $-2 \leq x < 6, x \in \mathbb{Z}$

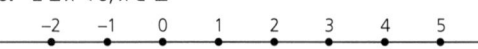

7. (a) $50 \leq 6x + 8 \leq 80$ (b) $7 \leq x \leq 12$
(c) 7 (d) 12 **8.** (a) $600 \leq 15x \leq 1000$ (b) $40 \leq x \leq 66.67$
(c) 40 (d) 66 **9.** (a) $150 \leq 6x^2 \leq 60\,000$ (b) $5 \leq x \leq 100$
(c) 5 cm × 5 cm × 5 cm (d) 1 m × 1 m × 1 m

Exam-style Questions
1. (a) $-1 \leq x \leq 3$ (b) (i) $25 \leq x \leq 50$ (ii) $35 \leq y \leq 60$
2. (a) $2 \leq x < 8$ (b) (i) $3000 - 32x \geq 800$ (ii) 68.75

Chapter 6
Activity 6.1
1. $x = 5; y = 3$ **2.** $a = -2; b = 6$ **3.** $m = 2; n = 6$
4. $s = -1; t = 3$ **5.** $x = -4; y = 7$ **6.** $b = 9; a = 7$
7. $d = 10; c = 1$ **8.** $q = 8; p = 5$ **9.** $v = 11; w = -3$
10. $x = -11; y = -5$ **11.** $b = -\frac{1}{2}; a = 3$ **12.** $f = 7; g = \frac{2}{5}$
13. $n = 4; m = \frac{1}{5}$ **14.** $h = \frac{1}{11}; k = \frac{1}{7}$ **15.** $q = \frac{1}{4}; p = \frac{1}{8}$
16. $x = \frac{1}{2}; y = \frac{2}{3}$ **17.** $x = -1; y = 2$ **18.** $t = -2; s = \frac{2}{3}$
19. $e = \frac{3}{4}; d = -\frac{1}{6}$ **20.** $v = 3; w = -\frac{1}{8}$ **21.** $x = \frac{7}{27}; y = -\frac{1}{54}$
22. $c = -3; h = 8$ **23.** $l = 11; m = \frac{1}{7}$ **24.** $r = \frac{2}{3}; s = -5$
25. $x = -1; y = \frac{3}{-2}$

Activity 6.2
1. (i) $x + y = 40; x - y = 4.6$ (ii) $x = 22.3; y = 17.7$
2. (i) $2x + y = 50; 7x - \frac{y}{2} = 75$ (ii) $x = 12.5; y = 25$
3. (i) $4x - \frac{y}{2} = \frac{13}{2} = 6.5; \frac{x+3}{2} - \frac{y}{3} = \frac{3}{2} = 1.5$ (ii) $x = 2; y = 3$
4. (i) $2x + 3y = 47.50; x + 2y = 27.50$ (ii) Adult ticket costs €12.50; Concession ticket costs €7.50.
5. (i) $0.02x + 0.03y = 650; x + y = 25\,000$ (ii) $y = 15\,000$; $x = 10\,000$ (iv) €10 000; €15 000 (v) €200; €450
6. (i) $x + 4y = 2.00; 2x + 3y = 1.90$ (ii) The cost of a banana is 32 cents; The cost of an apple is 42 cents.
7. (i) $x + y - 10 = y + \frac{x}{3}; y + \frac{x}{3} = 60$ (ii) $y = 55°; x = 15°$
8. (i) $x + 3y = 12.56; x + 2y = 8.87$ (ii) Price of a pack of chicken fillets is €3.69; Price of a bag of stir-fry mix is €1.49.
9. (i) (a) $d - 4s = 20$ (b) $d - 4.2s = 0$ (ii) $s = 100$ km/hr; $d = 420$ km (iv) 100 km/hr (v) 105 km/hr
10. (i) $x + y = 30; x = \frac{y}{4}$ (ii) Width of rectangle = 6 cm; Length of rectangle = 24 cm. (iv) 144 cm² **11.** (i) $x + y = 31\,000$; $0.11x - 0.04y = 560$ (ii) $y = 19\,000; x = 12\,000$
(iv) (a) €12 000 (b) €19 000 (v) €1320 (vi) €760
12. (i) $(x - y) = 110°$, as opposite angles in a parallelogram are equal. (ii) $(x - 3y) = 70°$, as adjacent angles in a parallelogram sum to 180°. (iii) $x - y = 110; x - 3y = 70$ (iv) $x = 130°; y = 20°$
13. (i) (a) $55v - 8d = 0$ (b) $11v - 2d = -330$ (ii) $d = 825$ km; $v = 120$ km/hr (iv) 825 km (v) (a) 120 km/hr (b) 150 km/hr
14. (i) $5 + 22.5d = h; 20 + 20d = h$ (ii) (a) 6 days (b) 140 cm
15. (i) 350 m + 700 = R; 400 m + 400 = R (ii) (a) 7 months (b) €3150

Revision Activity 6
1. (a) 55° (b) $\frac{x}{2} + 2y - 10 = 55; x + y = 55$ (c) $y = 25°; x = 30°$
2. (a) $2x + y = 8.10; 4x + 4y = 18$ (b) $x = 3.60; y = 0.90$
(c) €0.90 (d) €3.60 **3.** (a) $37x + 8y = 423.65$; $37x + 11y = 462.50$ (b) (i) €8.65 (ii) €12.95 **4.** (a) $5x + y = 16$; $x + 2y = 5$ (b) $x = 3; y = 1$ (c) (i) 3 points (ii) 1 point
5. (a) $x + y = 4; 3x - y = 0$ (b) $x = 1; y = 3$ (c) (i) 1 m
(ii) 3 m (e) 3 m² **6.** (a) $x + y = 30; 6x + 8y = 216$
(b) $x = 12; y = 18$ (c) 12 (d) 18 **7.** (c) 4 days (d) Company A
8. (a) (i) $2d - 17s = 0$ (ii) $d - 35s = -2067$ (b) $s = 78; d = 663$
(d) Average speed from Malin head to Mizen head = 78 km/hr; Distance travelled from Malin head to Mizen head = 663 km.
(e) Average speed from Mizen head to Malin head = 16 km/hr; Distance from Mizen head to Malin head = 560 km.

Exam-style Questions
1. A car costs €2.10 to go through the M50 toll; A small van costs €2.90 to go through the M50 toll. **2.** (a) (i) 5 (ii) 1
(b) Teams who win consistently receive more points for a win, which encourages winning. With the new system the ratio of wins to draw is higher which rewards a victory more and might encourage a team to go for a win.

Chapter 7

Activity 7.1
1. Either $a = 0$ or $b = 0$ 2. (i) $x = 4$ or $x = -3$
(ii) $x = -7$ or $x = 3$ (iii) $x = 0$ or $x = 7$ (iv) $x = 5$ or $x = -5$
3. $x = -3$ or $x = 2$ 4. $x = -7$ or $x = -1$
5. $x = -3$ or $x = -1$ 6. $x = 5$ or $x = 1$ 7. $x = 6$ or $x = -3$
8. $x = \frac{3}{2}$ or $x = \frac{-3}{2}$ 9. $x = \frac{13}{15}$ or $x = \frac{-13}{15}$ 10. $x = 0$ or $x = 2$
11. $x = 4$ or $x = -3$ 12. $x = 0$ or $x = \frac{1}{5}$ 13. $x = \frac{5}{2}$ or $x = \frac{-5}{2}$
14. $x = \frac{7}{3}$ or $x = \frac{-7}{3}$ 15. $x = 0$ or $x = 2$ 16. $x = 0$ or $x = \frac{1}{7}$
17. $x = -1$ or $x = \frac{-1}{5}$ 18. $x = \frac{-3}{7}$ or $x = -1$ 19. $x = \frac{-1}{9}$ or $x = -1$
20. $x = \frac{-4}{11}$ or $x = -1$ 21. (i) $x = -7$ or $x = 2$ (ii) $k = -5$ or $k = 4$
22. (i) $x = \frac{1}{3}$ or $x = -2$ (ii) $m = \frac{10}{3}$ or $m = 1$ 23. (i) $p = -5$ or $p = \frac{1}{3}$ (ii) $a = -6$ or $a = \frac{-2}{3}$ 24. $x = -1$ and $x = 3$ 25. $x = -4$ and $x = 3$ 26. $x = \frac{1}{13}$ or $x = 5$ 27. $x = \frac{2}{3}$ or $x = 1$ 28. $x = \frac{3}{4}$ or $x = 1$ 29. $x = \frac{2}{3}$ or $x = \frac{1}{2}$ 30. $x = \frac{2}{5}$ or $x = \frac{-3}{2}$ 31. $x = \frac{-4}{3}$ or $x = \frac{1}{3}$ 32. $x = \frac{5}{8}$ or $x = -1$ 33. $x = \frac{3}{13}$ or $x = -1$
34. $x = \frac{1}{4}$ or $x = -2$ 35. $x = \frac{-1}{2}$ or $x = 4$ 36. $x = 3$ or $x = -1$

Activity 7.2
1. $x^2 - 2x - 3 = 0$ 2. $x^2 + x - 6 = 0$ 3. $x^2 - 7x - 18 = 0$
4. $x^2 + 9x + 20 = 0$ 5. $x^2 - 13x + 42 = 0$ 6. $x^2 + x - 12 = 0$
7. $x^2 - 8x - 33 = 0$ 8. $x^2 - 2x - 80 = 0$ 9. $x^2 + 2x - 8 = 0$
10. $x^2 + 2x - 15 = 0$ 11. $a = 1$, $b = -14$ and $c = 45$
12. $a = 1$, $b = 10$ and $c = -24$ 13. $a = 1$, $b = 8$ and $c = 7$
14. 9 15. $c = 81$

Activity 7.3
1. (i) $x = \frac{-3}{2}$ or $x = \frac{1}{2}$ (ii) $x = \frac{1}{2}, x = \frac{-3}{2}$ 2. (i) $x = \frac{5}{2}, x = -1$
(ii) $x = \frac{5}{2}, x = -1$ 3. $x = 0.851, x = -2.351$ 4. $x = -0.55, x = -5.45$ 5. $x = 4.45, x = -0.45$ 6. $n = 0.36, n = -2.11$
7. $x = 2 \pm \sqrt{7}$ 8. (i) $x = 1 \pm \sqrt{3}$ (ii) $x = 2 \pm \sqrt{3}$ (iii) $x = 2 \pm \sqrt{5}$
9. $t = -1 \pm \sqrt{8}$ 10. $p = \frac{5 + \sqrt{33}}{2}, p = \frac{5 - \sqrt{33}}{2}$ 11. 3.4 or 0.6
12. (i) $x = 3 \pm \sqrt{5}$ (ii) $k = \sqrt{5}, k = -\sqrt{5}$ 13. $x = 2 \pm \sqrt{2}$
(ii) $p = 6 + \sqrt{2}, p = 6 - \sqrt{2}$

Activity 7.4
1. $x = -7$ or $x = 3$ 2. $x = -12$ or $x = 1$ 3. $x = \frac{3}{2}$ or $x = 6$
4. $x = \frac{1}{2}$ or $x = -4$ 5. $x = \frac{3}{2}$ or $x = -2$ 6. $x = \frac{7 \pm \sqrt{273}}{8}$
7. $2 \pm \sqrt{2}$ 8. $x = \frac{5 \pm \sqrt{769}}{12}$ 9. $x = \frac{2}{3}, x = \frac{-7}{2}$
10. $x = \frac{-3 \pm \sqrt{321}}{52}$

Activity 7.5
1. (ii) $x = 15$ (iii) 15 and 17 2. (ii) $x = -26$ or $x = 24$
(iii) -26 and -24, 24 and 26 3. (ii) $L^2 + L - 20 = 0$
(iii) $L = 4$ m (iv) 4 m, 2.5 m 4. (i) $2x^2 - x - 6 = 0$ (ii) $x = 2$
(iii) Base = 2 m Perpendicular Height = 1.5 m (iv) 1.5 m²
5. (i) $2x^2 + 31x - 33 = 0$ (ii) $x = 1$ (iii) 1 m 6. (ii) $4x^2 + 7x - 4 = 0$
(iii) $x = 0.4537$ (iv) Width of border = 0.45 m
7. (ii) $x^2 - 2x - 15 = 0$ (iii) $x = 5$ (iv) 5 cm, 12 cm, 13 cm
8. (ii) 15 cm 9. (ii) 7 m 10. (i) 97.44 m (ii) 24.36 car lengths
(iii) 31.57 km/h

Revision Activity 7
1. (a) $x = 0$ or $x = 16$ (b) $x = 0$ or $x = 9$ (c) $x = 0$ or $x = 32$
(d) $x = 0$ or $x = \frac{1}{2}$ (e) $x = \frac{7}{11}$ or $x = \frac{-7}{11}$ (f) $x = 6$ or $x = -6$
(g) $x = \frac{8}{9}$ or $x = \frac{-8}{9}$ (h) $x = \frac{14}{13}$ or $x = \frac{-14}{13}$ (i) $x = 5$
(j) $x = 9$ or $x = 4$ (k) $x = 7$ or $x = -2$ (l) $x = -8$ or $x = 7$
2. (a) $x = \frac{5}{2}$ or $x = -3$ (b) $x = \frac{2}{3}$ or $x = 3$ (c) $x = \frac{-2}{3}$ or $x = \frac{-1}{3}$
(d) $x = \frac{-7}{4}$ or $x = -1$ (e) $x = \frac{4}{3}$ or $x = \frac{-1}{3}$ (f) $x = \frac{-2}{5}$ or $x = \frac{11}{2}$
(g) $x = \frac{-7}{2}$ or $x = \frac{1}{7}$ (h) $x = \frac{3}{7}$ or $x = \frac{-1}{5}$ 3. $c = 49$
4. $y = 12$ or $y = -2$ 5. (a) $x^2 - 4x - 12 = 0$ (b) $x = 6$ or $x = -2$
(c) -2 or 6 6. (a) $4x^2 + 60x - 99 = 0$ (b) $x = \frac{3}{2}$ (c) 1.5 m

Exam-style Questions
1. $x = \frac{-14}{3}$ or $x = 1$ 2. (a) $2n = 14$, $2n + 1 = 15$
(b) (ii) $x = 42$ 3. $x = 2$ 4. (a) $x = 6$ or $x = -1$ (b) $x = \frac{1}{4}$ or $x = \frac{3}{2}$ (c) $x = \frac{-16}{-8} = 2$ (d) $x = 4.21$ or -0.71

Chapter 8

Activity 8.1
1. (i) $t = 2s - a$ (ii) $t = p - 5q$ (iii) $t = \frac{x}{w}$ (iv) $t = rk$ (v) $t = \frac{f}{gh}$
(vi) $t = \frac{y}{w} + d$ 2. (i) $w = \frac{A}{l}$ (ii) $a = \frac{F}{m}$ (iii) $d = \frac{T}{f}$ (iv) $F = PA$
(v) $m = \frac{W}{g}$ (vi) $t = \frac{W}{P}$ 3. (i) $x = \sqrt{\frac{a}{b}}$ (ii) $x = d - e(s - q)$
(iii) $x = a^2 - g$ (iv) $x = 2p + 2d$ (v) $x = \sqrt{\frac{y - qs^2}{r}}$
(vi) $x = \sqrt{\frac{w}{s - u - t}}$ 4. (i) $h = \frac{E}{mg}$ (ii) $m = \frac{E}{c^2}$ (iii) $a = \frac{v^2 - u^2}{2s}$
(iv) $M = \frac{4\pi^2 R^3}{GT^2}$ (v) $u = \frac{2s - at^2}{2t}$ (vi) $r = \sqrt{\frac{A}{\pi}}$ (vii) $d = \sqrt{\frac{Gm_1 m_2}{F}}$
(viii) $r = \sqrt{\frac{3V}{\pi h}}$ (ix) $g = \frac{4\pi^2 l}{T^2}$ 5. (i) $b = \frac{c}{a - p}$ (ii) $b = \frac{2u}{s + u}$
(iii) $b = \frac{y}{3c - 1}$ (iv) $b = \frac{w}{1 - k}$ (v) $b = \frac{e}{c^4 - 1}$ 6. (i) $l = \frac{qw}{y}$
(ii) $l = \frac{u}{(p - s)}$ 7. (i) $l = \sqrt{A}$ (ii) $R = \sqrt[3]{\frac{GMT^2}{4\pi^2}}$ 8. (i) $w = \frac{p + 4}{3}$
(ii) $w = \frac{p}{(5 - bu)}$

Activity 8.2
1. (i) $K = 310.15$ (ii) $C = K - 273.15$ (iii) $C = 33$
2. (i) $h = \frac{A}{a}$ (ii) $a = \frac{A}{h}$ (iii) 18 cm 3. (i) $a = \frac{2A}{h}$ (ii) 10 m
4. (i) $b = \sqrt{c^2 - a^2}$ (ii) $b = 4$ 5. (i) $u = v - at$ (ii) 10 m/s
6. (i) $m = \frac{F}{a}$ (ii) 700 7. (i) $r = \sqrt[3]{\frac{3V}{4\pi}}$ (ii) 7.6 cm 8. (i) $R = \frac{V}{I}$
(ii) 6 ohms 9. (i) $r = \sqrt{\frac{3V}{\pi h}}$ (ii) 5 10. (i) $F = \frac{9C}{5} + 32$
(ii) 84.2° 11. (i) $m = \rho V$ (ii) 3000 g

Revision Activity 8
1. (a) $A = \frac{F}{P}$ (b) $\frac{W}{m} = g$ (c) $Pt = W$ (d) $\frac{Fd^2}{Gm_1} = m_2$
(e) $h = \frac{E}{mg}$ (f) $c = \sqrt{\frac{E}{m}}$ (g) $u = \sqrt{v^2 - 2as}$ (h) $a = \frac{2s - 2ut}{t^2}$
(i) $R = \sqrt[3]{\frac{T^2 GM}{4\pi^2}}$ (j) $\frac{T^2 g}{4\pi^2} = l$ 2. (a) $\sqrt[3]{\frac{3V}{4\pi}} = r$ (b) 6051.9 km
3. (a) $\sqrt{\frac{2E}{m}} = v$ (b) 2 m/s 4. (a) $h = \frac{A}{2\pi r} - r$ (b) 10.5 cm
5. (a) $\sqrt{\frac{2W}{c}} = v$ (b) 228 v

Exam-style Questions
1. (a) $\frac{10}{3}$ (b) As the denominator increases so the value of the fraction decreases so an increase in P means a decrease in M.
(c) $P = \frac{1}{M} - S$ OR $\frac{1 - MS}{M}$ 2. (a) 1 280 000 Joules (b) $\sqrt{\frac{2W}{C}} = V$

Chapter 9

Activity 9.1
1. (i) 180° (ii) Angles α and β are known as supplementary angles. 2. (i) Angles α and β are known as vertically opposite angles. (ii) 180° (iii) 180° 8. (ii) SSS, SAS and ASA.
(iii) (a) ASA (b) SAS (c) SSS 12. (i) $\angle 3$ and $\angle 6$; $\angle 4$ and $\angle 5$ (ii) These alternate angles are equal. (iii) $\angle 1$ and $\angle 5$; $\angle 7$ and $\angle 3$; $\angle 2$ and $\angle 6$; $\angle 8$ and $\angle 4$ (iv) These corresponding angles are equal. (v) $\angle 3$ and $\angle 5$; $\angle 4$ and $\angle 6$
(vi) 130° = |$\angle 8$| = |$\angle 4$| = |$\angle 1$|; 50° = |$\angle 6$| = |$\angle 2$| = |$\angle 3$|
15. (ii) |$\angle 1$| and |$\angle 3$|; |$\angle 2$| and |$\angle 4$| 18. (iv) A rotation of 180° about the origin. 20. (i) (a) 180° (b) 2 (ii) (a) 360° (b) 4 (iii) (d) N = −4 + 2x where x is the number of sides in the polygon and N is the sum of the angles in terms of right-angles.

Activity 9.2
1. (i) $\alpha = 108°$; $\beta = 45°$; $\gamma = 45°$ (ii) $\beta = 63°$; $\alpha = 63°$; $\gamma = 117°$
(iii) $\beta = 50°$; $\gamma = 50°$ (iv) $\alpha = 108°$; $\gamma = 108°$; $\beta = 108°$
2. $x = 22°$; $y = 10°$ 4. (i) |TU| (ii) |TM| = |MU| = |VU|
(iii) STM and MUV (iv) |$\angle 1$| = |$\angle 4$| (alternate angles); |$\angle 8$| = |$\angle 5$| (alternate angles); |$\angle 2$| = |$\angle 4$| (equal angles of isosceles triangle); |$\angle 7$| = |$\angle 5$| (equal angles of isosceles triangle) 7. (i) |$\angle PQR$| = |$\angle PRQ$| (equal angles of isosceles triangle); |$\angle RNM$| = |$\angle RQP$| (corresponding angles); |$\angle RMN$| = |$\angle RPQ$| (corresponding angles) 9. 145°
10. (iv) |$\angle PSQ$| = |$\angle SQR$|; PS || QR; |$\angle PQS$| = |$\angle QSR$|; PQ || SR; parallelogram.

Activity 9.4
1. (i) $x = 4$ (ii) $x = 5$ 2. 480 m 3. |AG| = |GE| = |ED| |BH| = |HF| = |FC| (iii) |BM| = |ME| (iv) |GN| = |NC| (v) 1.2 m
(vi) 2.33 m (vii) 16.26 m 4. (i) $x = 4.05$ (ii) $x = 4.99$
5. (i) $x = 6$ (ii) $x = \frac{35}{4}$ (iii) $x = \frac{33}{10}$ (iv) $x = \frac{24}{5}$ (v) $x = 5$
(vi) $x = \frac{130}{9}$ 6. (i) 5 : 3 (ii) 8 : 5 (iii) 3 : 8 7. (ii) $x = 7.5$
8. $x = \frac{15}{4}$; $y = \frac{48}{5}$ 9. $w = \frac{35}{9}$ m 10. $x = 7.2$
11. (iii) $h = 13.2$ m 13. (ii) |KR| = |RW| = |TU| = |UV|
14. (iii) 2.3 cm 16. (i) 4.5 17. (ii) $\frac{|AC|}{|AB|} = \frac{|DC|}{|AD|}$ (iii) |DC| = 8

Revision Activity 9
2. $\alpha = 23.5$; $\beta = 83.5$; $\gamma = 23.5$ 3. (b) 120° anti-clockwise or 240° clockwise. (c) 180° rotation about O. Axial symmetry about [FC].

Exam-style Questions
1. (a) [DE] = [EF] because the compass arcs used to find E were drawn with the same radius (b) Triangles Δ DFB and Δ BFE are congruent (SSS) 2. (b) No, because if [AB] is ≠ [AC], |$\angle B$| ≠ |$\angle C$|

Chapter 10

Activity 10.1
1. (i) $c^2 = a^2 + b^2$ (ii) $e^2 = c^2 + d^2$ (iii) $k^2 = g^2 + h^2$ 2. (i) 8 (ii) 10 cm
(iii) 37 mm 3. (i) 75 cm (ii) $\frac{7}{24}$ 4. $d = 169.2$ m 6. (i) 27.2 m
(iii) 42.1 m 8. (i) $4\sqrt{2}$ m (ii) $4\sqrt{3}$ m 9. (i) $a^2 = 2$
(ii) $b^2 = 3$; $c^2 = 4$ (iii) 3

Activity 10.2
1. (i) 60° (ii) 55° (iii) 34° (iv) 100° (v) 90° (vi) 70°
(vii) 51° (viii) 120° 2. (i) 50° (ii) 50° 3. (ii) 75° (iii) 210°
(iv) 105° (v) 180° 4. (i) $\theta = 75°$ (ii) $\theta = 50°$ (iii) $\theta = 130°$
(iv) $\theta = 90°$ (v) $\theta = 61°$ (vi) $\theta = 60°$ (vii) $\theta = 45°$ (viii) $\theta = 50°$
5. (i) 140° (ii) 30° 6. (i) 100° (ii) 40° 8. (i) 20° (ii) 55°
12. 119.5°

Revision Activity 10
1. 17 m 4. (a) 4 (c) $\frac{24}{5}$

Exam-style Questions
1. (a) a = 16; b = 30; c = 34

Chapter 11

Activity 11.1
1. (i) 48 cm² (ii) 60 cm² (iii) 120 cm² 2. (i) $9\sqrt{3}$ units²
(ii) $25\sqrt{3}$ units² (iii) $36\sqrt{3}$ units² 3. (i) 6 units² (ii) 60 units²
(iii) 630 units² 4. (a) (i) 60 cm² (ii) 40 cm (b) (i) 420 cm²
(ii) 100 cm (c) (i) $\frac{49\sqrt{3}}{4}$ cm² (ii) 21 cm (d) (i) 24 cm²
(ii) $21 + 3\sqrt{17}$ cm 5. (i) 9 units² (iv) 18 units² 6. (i) 36 units²
(iv) 72 units² (v) |Base| × |Perpendicular height|

Activity 11.2
1. (i) 286 units² (ii) 780 units² 2. (i) $b = 32$ units
(ii) $h = 17.33$ units (iii) $b = 13.6$ units 3. (i) 104 cm²
(ii) 52.5 cm² (iii) 63.59 cm² (iv) 144 cm² (v) 37.68 cm²
4. (i) (a) 43.98 cm (b) 153.94 cm² (ii) (a) 62.83 cm
(b) 314.16 cm² (iii) (a) 34.56 cm (b) 95.03 cm² (iv) (a) 31.54 cm
(b) 45.24 cm² (v) (a) 33.57 cm (b) 69.40 cm² (vi) (a) 9.28 m
(b) 4.71 m² 5. (i) (a) 44 cm (b) 101 cm² (ii) (a) 72.8 cm
(b) 201 cm² (iii) (a) 58.3 cm (b) 235.2 cm² (iv) (a) 172.5 cm
(b) 1300.9 cm² (v) (a) 82.3 cm (b) 54.9 cm² 6. (i) 8 cm
(ii) 12 cm (iii) 3 m (iv) 135.65° 7. (i) 177 cm² (ii) 314 cm²
(iii) 97 cm² 8. 145 cm² 9. (i) 85.84 cm² (ii) 78.54%
10. (i) 28 cm (ii) 176 cm (iii) 440 m 11. (i) 360 m²
(ii) 36 m² (iii) 102 m² (iv) 197 m² (v) 45% 12. (i) 45.3 cm
(ii) 1951.45 cm² (iii) 33%

Activity 11.3
1. (i) 900 cm² (ii) 1800 cm³ (iii) 1.8 litres 2. B, D
3. (i) Volume = 231; Total surface area = 227
(ii) Volume = 1012.5; Total surface area = 612
(iii) Volume = 336 000; Total surface area = 29 200
(iv) Volume = 3.456; Total surface area = 13.92
(v) Volume = 0.25; Total surface area = 2.417 (vi) Width = 16; Total surface area = 1534 (vii) Length = 4.6; Total surface area = 124.08 (viii) Height = 8; Total surface area = 544
(ix) Width = 28.5; Volume = 14820; (x) Length = 33.5; Volume = 8858.07 4. (i) 58.34 litres (ii) 14.73 litres
(iii) 4032 litres (iv) 174.72 litres 5. (i) (b) 3.54 m² (c) 5.31 m³
(d) 22.98 m² (ii) (b) 204 cm² (c) 8160 cm³ (d) 3768 cm²
(iii) (b) 1.38 m² (c) 3.45 m³ (d) 16.01 m² 7. (i) (a) 83.14 cm³
(b) 157.86 cm² (ii) (a) 25200 cm³ (b) 12060 cm²
(iii) (a) 1092 cm³ (b) 896 cm² 8. (i) (a) 5040 cm³ (b) 2436 cm²
(ii) (a) 420.66 m³ (b) 394.12 m² (iii) (a) 436800 cm³
(b) 37960 cm² 9. (i) 3.5 m (ii) 26 cm (iii) 17.5 cm
11. E is opposite A, C is opposite H, B is opposite G, D is opposite F 13. D 14. A, B, D 15. (ii) 1980 cm³
(iii) 396 cm³ (iv) 11 cm 16. (i) 1136 m³ (ii) 76 trips

Activity 11.4
1. (i) Volume = 75.36 cm²; Total surface area = 100.48 cm²
(ii) Volume = 125π m³; Total surface area = 100π m²
(iii) Volume = 38808 cm³; Total surface area = 6468 cm²
(iv) Radius = 9.5 cm; Total surface area = 985.29 cm²
(v) Height = 13.5 m; Volume = 952.56 π m³ (vi) Radius = 4.5 m; Total surface area = 166.73 m² (vii) Height = 5.42 cm; Volume = 4878π cm³ (viii) Height = 24 mm;
Total surface area = 11880π mm² (ix) Height = 10 cm;
Volume = 1540 cm³ (x) Height = 55 cm; Total surface area = 17483.52 cm² (xi) Height = 9 cm; Volume = 854.87 cm³
(xii) Height = 0.29 cm; Total surface area = 7756.74 cm²
2. 54 glasses 4. (i) 125.7 cm² (ii) 157.08 cm³
(iii) Length = 15 cm, Width = 5 cm Height = 8 cm
5. (i) D (ii) 117.1 cm² 6. (i) 14 : 75 (ii) 21 : 64 (iii) 1 : 4
(iv) 2057 : 2925 7. (i) 3322.23 litres (ii) He can wrap the new tank with 2 layers of insulation. 8. $r = 2$

Activity 11.5
1. (i) Volume = 1436.027 m³; Curved surface area = 615.44 m²
(ii) Radius = 1.435 cm; Volume = 12.383 cm³
(iii) Radius = 5.524 m; Volume = 705.715 m³
(iv) Volume = 179.594 cm³; Curved surface area = 153.938 cm²
(v) Volume = 14137.167 cm³; Curved surface area = 2827.433 cm²
(vi) Radius = 17.171 cm; Curved surface area = 3706.601 cm²
2. (i) 56.55 cm³   (ii) $h = 8$ cm to the nearest cm   (iii) 11 cm
3. (i) 25000 cm²   (ii) 0.30 m³   4. (i) 110592 cm³   (ii) 24 cm
(iii) The sculptor will not meet the requirement.
(iv) 71623.34 cm³   5. (i) 280π cm²   (ii) 427π cm²
6. (i) 121.5π cm³   (ii) 182.25π cm³   7. (i) 6 cm   (ii) 658.19 cm³
(iii) 23.82%

Activity 11.6
1. (i) Volume = 201.06 units³; Total Surface Area = 209.22 units²
(ii) Volume = 75.40 units³; Total Surface Area = 232.31 units²
(iii) Volume = 65.97 units³; Total Surface Area = 100.05 units²
(iv) Radius = 9 units; Total Surface Area = 614.34 units²
(v) Height = 10 units; Total Surface Area = 1556.40 units²
(vi) Height = 8.47 units; Volume = 79.83 units³
(vii) Radius = 5 units; Total Surface Area = 201.22 units²
(viii) Radius = 12 units; Total Surface Area = 1092.16 units²
(ix) Height = 124.63 units; Volume = 42285.96 units³
2. (i) (a) 301.59 cm³   (b) 301.59 cm²   (ii) (a) 314.16 cm³
(b) 282.74 cm²   3. (i) 2.7 m   (ii) 98.84 m³   (iii) 8%   4. (i) $8\pi R^3$
(ii) $4R, 4R, 6R$ (iii) $96R^3$ 5. 318.25 cm³   6. (i) 1385.18 cm³
(ii) 706.86 cm²   7. 30π cm³, 75π cm³, 45π cm³   8. (i) 8 : 27
(ii) 4 : 27   (iii) 3 : 2   (iv) 2873 : 245   9. 12801.99 cm³
10. (i) 1152π cm³   (ii) 64π cm³   (iii) 17

Activity 11.7
1. 24   2. 81 cm   3. 2144.661 cm³   4. 20.25 cm
5. 0.72 cm   6. 2.2 cm   7. 74.667 cm   8. 1 cm   9. 66.67%
10. (i) 0.2 m³   (ii) 1.8 m³   (iii) 392.7 cm³   (iv) 76 minutes
11. (i) 98.96 cm³   (ii) 48.762 seconds

Revision Activity 11
1. (a) 126 m²   (b) €106   2. (a) 54643.73 cm³
(b) 10661.25 cm²   3. D is opposite F, C is opposite H, B is opposite G, A is opposite E   4. 8.45 cm   5. 1.22 cm
6. (a) 904.78 cm³   (b) 11.389 cm   7. (a) 24 cm   (b) 3888 cm²
(c) 216 boxes   (d) 72 balls   8. 160 litres

Exam-style Questions
1. (a) 13 m   (b) 30 m²   (c) 169 m²   (d) 508 flagstones
2. (a) 1 : 4   (b) 1 : 8   3. 2 cm

Chapter 12

Activity 12.1
1. (ii) $|AC| = 6$, $|BC| = 3$ (iii) $\sqrt{45}$ units   (iv) $\sqrt{45}$ units
2. (v) The mid-point between two points = (average of the x coordinates, average of the y coordinates)   3. (ii) $\sqrt{58}$ units
(iii) $\left(1\frac{1}{2}, 4\frac{1}{2}\right)$ (iv) $\sqrt{14.5}$ units   7. (iii) $|AB| = |A'B'| = \sqrt{13}$ units
9. (ii) 10.2 km   (iii) 8.6 km   (iv) (6.5, 4.5)   10. (i) 72.11 m
(ii) (−30, −20)   (iv) 28.28 m   (v) 20 m

Activity 12.2
2. (ii) −1   6. $\sqrt{3}$ 7. (i) 2   (ii) 63°   8. (i) $\frac{1}{10}$
9. (i) $|\angle CEF| = 22.5°$ and $|\angle ECF| = 67.5°$ (ii) 0.414

Activity 12.3
1. Line B   3. (i) Line 3   (ii) Line 1 and Line 4
(iii) Line 2 and Line 5   (iv) Line 5   10. (ii) −3   11. (ii) 3

Activity 12.4
1. (i) $y = -\frac{2}{3}x - 2$ (ii) $-\frac{2}{3}$ 2. (I) Slope = 3   (ii) Slope = $\frac{1}{2}$
(iii) Slope = −2   (iv) Slope = $\frac{3}{2}$ (v) Slope = $\frac{1}{4}$ (vi) Slope = 0

(vii) Slope = $\frac{2}{7}$ (viii) Slope is undefined   (ix) Slope = $\frac{1}{2}$
(x) Slope = −3   6. (i) (c)   (ii) (a)   (iii) (b)   (iv) (a)   (v) (a)   (vi) (b)
(vii) (c)   7. (i) The equation of line p is $y = 4$, The equation of line q is $y = 3$, The equation of line r is $y = 2$, The equation of line n is $x = 3$ (ii) A(3, 4), B(3, 3), C(3, 2)   9. (i) $\frac{5}{2}$ 10. (i) $\frac{3}{2}$
(ii) $3x - 2y - 17 = 0$ 11. (i) −4   (ii) $x - 4y + 9 = 0$
12. (i) $\frac{1}{3}$ (ii) $x - 3y - 1 = 0$ 13. (i) $\frac{3}{2}$ (ii) $2x + 3y - 10 = 0$

Activity 12.5
1. (ii) (4, −5)   (iii) (4, −5)   2. (ii) (2, 0)   (iii) (2, 0)
(iv) These are perpendicular lines   3. (4, 2)   4. (3, 2)
5. $\left(4\frac{1}{2}, 4\frac{1}{2}\right)$ 6. (−4, 4)   7. (3, −1)

Revision Activity 12
1. (b) B(3, 0)   (c) −1   (d) $y = -x + 3$ (e) −1   (f) $x + y + 2 = 0$
(g) ABCD is a parallelogram   2. (a) $\sqrt{98}$ units   (b) $\left(-\frac{1}{2}, \frac{3}{2}\right)$
(c) −1   (d) $x + y - 1 = 0$ 3. (a) $2x - 3y = 9$ 4. $y = \sqrt{3}x - 2\sqrt{3}$
5. (a) $\frac{3}{2}$ (b) $2x + 3y + 7 = 0$ 6. (b) $3x - y - 12 = 0$ (c) $\left(\frac{7}{2}, -\frac{3}{2}\right)$
7. (a) $\frac{2}{3}$ (b) $2x - 3y = 14$ (c) (−2, −6)   8. (a) The equation of first street is $y = 1$, The equation of second street is $y = 2$.
(b) The equation of fifth avenue is $x = 5$ (c) $3x + 2y = 12$
9. (c) 15.81 km   (d) $3y = x$ (g) 9.487 km   (h) The ship is travelling in a direction East 18.43° North

Exam-style Questions
(a) 7.07 km   (b) 3 km   (c) $3x - 4y + 31 = 0$
(d) $4x + 3y - 92 = 0$ (e) (11, 16)   (f) 22 km

Chapter 13

Activity 13.1
1. (i) A: Very unlikely; B: Very likely; C: Very likely; D: Evens chance; E: Impossible   2. (i) 500   (ii) 500   (iii) 0   3. (i) $\frac{1}{2}$
(ii) $\frac{1}{4}$ (iii) 0.3   (iv) 80%   4. (i) 0.4   (ii) 0.6   5. (ii) 80   (iii) $\frac{1}{4}$
(iv) $\frac{1}{80}$ 6. (i) (a) 0   (b) 1   (c) $\frac{1}{2}$ (ii) (c) A number from 1 to 6 inclusive turns up.   7. (ii) (a) Group Y   (b) 78 times   (c) $\frac{128}{175}$
8. (i) $\frac{15}{32}$ (ii) $\frac{17}{32}$ 9. (i) $\frac{4}{11}$ (ii) $\frac{7}{11}$ 10. (i) 6   (ii) (W, W), (W, B), (B, W), (B, B), (C, W), (C, B)   11. (i) $\frac{3}{7}$ (ii) $\frac{2}{3}$ (iii) $\frac{5}{18}$ (iv) $\frac{5}{8}$
12. (i) $\frac{1}{8}$ (ii) $\frac{1}{8}$ 13. $\frac{16}{25} = 0.64$ 14. (i) 2, 3, 4; 2, 4, 3; 3, 2, 4; 3, 4, 2; 4, 2, 3; 4, 3, 2   (ii) $\frac{1}{6}$ (iii) $\frac{1}{3}$ 15. (i) 16   (ii) $\frac{1}{16}$
(iii) $\frac{1}{4}$ (iv) $\frac{3}{4}$ 16. (i) $\frac{17}{96}$ (ii) $\frac{47}{96}$ (iii) $\frac{1}{8}$ (iv) $\frac{59}{96}$ 17. (ii) $\frac{35}{76}$
(iii) $\frac{83}{152}$ (iv) $\frac{31}{69}$ (v) $\frac{19}{41}$ 18. (i) $\frac{1}{6}$ (ii) + (iii) The number 4 appeared 179 times.   19. (i) 0.25   20. 0.375

Activity 13.2
1. (i) (a) (H, H); (H, T); (T, H); (T, T)   (c) (ii) $\frac{1}{4}$ (iii) 200 times
(iv) This is not likely   (v) 50–50 chance   2. (i) $\frac{1}{2}$ (iv) Incorrect
3. (ii) $\frac{1}{12}$ (iii) $\frac{1}{6}$ (iv) Not very likely   4. (iii) $\frac{1}{8}$ (iv) $\frac{7}{8}$ (v) $\frac{1}{2}$
5. (i) $\frac{3}{5}$ 6. (ii) $\frac{1}{8}$ (iii) $\frac{1}{2}$ (iv) $\frac{1}{2}$ 7. (i) $\frac{1}{16}$ 8. (i) $\frac{1}{8}$ (ii) $\frac{1}{4}$
9. (iii) $\frac{1}{6}$ 10. (ii) $\frac{1}{12}$ (iii) $\frac{1}{6}$ (iv) $\frac{1}{3}$ 11. (i) Ben is incorrect
(ii) Chloe is also incorrect   12. (i) 0.94   (ii) 0.06   13. (ii) $\frac{1}{4}$
(iii) $\frac{1}{4}$ (iv) $\frac{1}{2}$

Activity 13.3

1. (i) 12   (ii) $\frac{3}{7}$ (iii) $\frac{1}{4}$ 2. (ii) (a) $\frac{5}{26}$ (b) $\frac{11}{26}$ (c) $\frac{145}{442}$ 3. (ii) $\frac{1}{7}$
(iii) $\frac{9}{35}$ (iv) $\frac{5}{7}$ 4. (ii) $\frac{5}{12}$ (iii) $\frac{49}{180}$ 5. (ii) $x = 16$ (iii) $\frac{1}{20}$ (iv) $\frac{1}{40}$
6. (ii) 0.8   7. (ii) $\frac{13}{24}$ (iii) $\frac{5}{13}$ (iv) $\frac{5}{9}$ 8. (ii) $\frac{2}{27}$ (iii) $\frac{19}{54}$ (iv) $\frac{31}{54}$

Revision Activity 13

2. (b) 23   (c) $\frac{1}{36}$ (d) 0   3. (a) (i) 55%   (ii) 16%   (c) (i) 240
(ii) 6720   (iii) 1280   4. (a) $\frac{3}{7}$ (b) $\frac{1}{4}$ (c) $\frac{3}{28}$ (d) $\frac{1}{4}$ 5. (a) $\frac{1}{7}$
(b) $\frac{1}{49}$ (c) $\frac{1}{49}$ 6. (a) $\frac{2}{5}$ (b) $\frac{3}{20}$ (c) $\frac{1}{4}$ 7. (a) 89   (b) Yes
(c) 150 times   8. (a) $\frac{2}{3}$ (b) $\frac{1}{6}$ (c) $\frac{1}{3}$

Exam-style Questions

1. (b) (i) 3   (ii) $\frac{5}{12}$ 2. (a) $\frac{1}{100}$ (b) 10%   (c) 84%

Chapter 14

Activity 14.1

4. (i) Numerical continuous   (ii) Categorical nominal
(iii) Numerical discrete   (iv) Numerical continuous
(v) Categorical nominal   (vi) Numerical discrete   (vii) Numerical discrete   (viii) Categorical nominal   (ix) Categorical ordered

Activity 14.2

4. AB, AC, AD, BC, BD, CD   5. (ii) No   6. (iv)   8. (ii) Answer 2

Activity 14.3

1. No   2. (iv)

Activity 14.4

1. (i) 49 years   (ii) 67%   (iii) 26   (iv) 0   2. (ii) 165 to 170 cm
(iii) 165 to 170 cm   (iv) 166 cm   3. (iii) 1.4 days   4. (iii) 100 kg
(iv) 96 kg   (v) (100 − y) kg   5. (i) 13   (ii) 87.5%   (iii) €45.2
6. (i) 250 cm   (ii) 240 cm   (iii) 100 cm; 250 cm   7. (i) 60%
(ii) 55–70 marks   (iii) 59 marks   8. (ii) 20–25 years   (iii) 7%
(iv) 34.09 years; 34.32 years

Activity 14.5

1. (i) Group 1: There are two modes: €22 and €34, median = €23, mean = €30; Group 2: There is no mode. Median = €16, mean = €16   (iii) Group 1: range = €90; Group 2: range = €19   (iv) Group 1: Q_1 = €21, Q_3 = €34, IQR = €13; Group 2: Q_1 = €11, Q_3 = €21, IQR = €10
2. (ii) Median age: 82 years; Mean age = 79   (iv) 45 years
(v) Q_1 = 73, Q_3 = 85.5 years, IQR = 12.5 years
3. (ii) Mean = 16 minutes, median = 15 minutes   (iv) 36 minutes
(v) Lower quartile = 10 minutes, upper quartile = 20 minutes, IQR = 10 minutes   (vi) 50%   4. (i) Group 1: Mean = 7; median = 7; Group 2: Mean = 7; median = 7   (ii) Group 1: Range = 4; Q_1 = 6; Q_3 = 8; IQR = 2; Group 2: Range = 6; Q_1 = 5; Q_3 = 9; IQR = 4   6. (i) Numerical discrete data   (iv) 74%
(vi) 11 and 19   (ix) 4

Activity 14.6

1. (ii) No outliers (iii) Mean = 169.2 cm, median = 169 cm
2. (i) Skewed right   (ii) Cluster: 60 kg–75 kg; Gap: 85 kg–110 kg
(iii) 110–115 kg is an outlier   3. (i) 30 drivers   (iii) Skewed left
(iv) The mean will be less than the median.   (v) The mean = 108.7 km/h; The median = 110 km/h   4. (iii) 46, 47, 48 years
(iv) Mean = 42 years: Median = 45 years   5. (iii) 65
(iv) Mean = 63.6 marks; Median = 65

Activity 14.7

2. (ii) 12 people at John's party 39 people at Sorcha's party.
(iii) The ages of people at John's party are from 28 to 40 which is a range of 12 years. The ages of people at Sorcha's party are from 0 to 92 years which is a range of 92 years.   3. (ii) Yes. One student was absent.   4. (i) 21 students on the first day and 22 students on the second day.   (vii) 57.6 m
(viii) Error = 4.5 m   (ix) 7.3%

Revision Activity 14

1. (a) 50   (b) The minimum time interval was 90–100 minutes and the maximum time interval was 190–200 minutes.
(e) 120 to 130 minutes   3. (a) 824 schools   (b) No
5. (b) Range = £72 million   (c) 515%   (d) Mean = £40.0 million
7. (a) 14 competitors in 2011 and 12 competitors in 2012
(b) 50 pucs in 2011 and 39 pucs in 2012   (d) 2011: Median = 58 pucs 2012: Median = 48 pucs   (e) 2011: Mean = 58 pucs 2012: Mean = 48 pucs   8. (a) Q1 with histogram B, Q2 with histogram C and Q3 with histogram A   9. (a) (i) 34 (ii) 28.5
(iii) 26.4   (c) Mode = 31, Median = 25.5, Mean = 23.4
11. (d) Median = 47 years; IQR = 23 years   (e) Median 39 years; IQR = 15.5 years   13. (b) 38%   14. (a) 5 students
15. (b) 2–4 hours

Exam-style Questions

1. (b) 38 people; 30 people   (c) Mean or mode
2. (a) 1460   (b) 30%   (c) 108°

Chapter 15

Activity 15.1

1. (i) % Profit on a single bed = 20%   (ii) % Profit on a double bed = 15%   (iii) % Profit on a king-size bed = 25%
2. (i) Selling Price of frying pan = €51.75   (ii) Selling Price of food mixer = €113.28   (iii) Selling Price of vegetable strainer = €7.20   3. (i) Laptop Cost Price = €472.73   (ii) External Hard Drive Cost Price = €103.45   (iii) Cost Price of Computer Mouse = €9.17   4. (i) (a) Profit = €2.50   (b) Mark-up = 25%
(c) Margin = 20%   (ii) (a) Profit = €1.20   (b) Mark-up = 20%
(c) Margin = 16.67%   (iii) (a) Profit = €18.00
(b) Mark-up = 40%   (c) Margin = 28.57%   5. (i) Cost Price = €13.99   (ii) Cost Price = €32.49   (iii) Cost Price of Headphones = €60   6. (i) Selling Price of Shirt = €13.80
(ii) Selling Price of Jumper = €18   (iii) Selling Price of Jeans = €63.70   7. (i) Selling Price = €522.06   (ii) Margin = 15%
8. (i) Cost Price of the television = €521.99   (ii) The Mark-up for the television is 72.42%   9. (i) Cost Price of the tablet = €249.91   (ii) Mark-up on the tablet = 144%   10. (i) Profit = €0.86   (ii) Mark-up = 253%   (iii) Margin = 72%
11. (i) Cost Price of Car = €17 757   (ii) Cost Price of Car = €16 522   12. (i) €11 per kilogram   (ii) Mark-up = 275%
(iii) Margin = 73%   13. (i) Selling Price = €281.40
(ii) Selling Price = €318.18   14. (i) Selling Price of Bike = €97.28
(ii) Selling Price of the Bike = €105.56

Activity 15.2

1. (ii) €13 403.30   2. (a) (i) €67.49   (ii) €208.96   (iii) €3517.75
(iv) €22 676.77   (v) €218 661.76   (vi) €1 367 128.13
(b) (i) €7.49   (ii) €33.96   (iii) €1017.75   (iv) €5376.77
(v) €79 761.76   (vi) €286 928.13   3. (i) F = €669.11
(ii) F = €1 937.20   (iii) F = €15 529.24   4. (i) F = €23 850
(ii) F = €21 942   (iii) F = €20 406.06   5. (i) F = €8164.80
(ii) F = €7838.21   (iii) F = €7681.45   6. €3389.88
7. €2410.89   8. €203 544   9. (i) €26 896   (ii) 14%
10. (i) €220 800   (ii) 12.6%   11. (i) i = 6%   (ii) i = 8%
(iii) i = 6%   12. (i) P = €1000   (ii) P = €2650   (iii) P = €5000
(iv) P = €40 000   13. P = €1557.41   14. P = €6550
15. (i) 4.2%   (ii) €4273.94

Activity 15.3

1. (i) Amount Charged 252.40; Tax 252.40 Amount Charged 77.08; Tax 77.08; Gross Tax Due 329.48   (ii) €266.02
(iii) €1183.98   (iv) €61 566.96   2. Scenario A: (i) €29 352
(ii) €26 052   (iii) €66 948; Scenario B: (i) €10 492   (ii) €7192
(iii) €39 808; Scenario C: (i) €15 744   (ii) €12 444   (iii) €59 556

3. Scenario A: (i) €114 (ii) €82.27 (iii) €487.73; Scenario B: (i) €826.50 (ii) €551.50 (iii) €3248.50; Scenario C: (i) €1307.90 (ii) €1032.90 (iii) €4957.10 **4.** (i) Income charged at 41% is €5097.56 (ii) Gross Income = €37 897.56
5. (i) Income charged at 41% is €14 487.80 (ii) Gross Income = €56 287.80 **6.** (i) Net Income = €28 981.50 (ii) Gross Income = €35 323.73 **7.** (i) Tax Credits = €1650
(ii) Gross Income = €42 300 (iii) Net Income = €33 495
8. (i) Net Tax = €21 372 (ii) Net Income = €53 628
(iii) Kathy's new gross income = €81 400 **9.** (i) (a) €0
(b) €578.80 (ii) (a) €307.84 (b) €1138.60 (iii) (a) €1627.84
(b) €3448.80 (iv) (a) €2747.84 (b) €5408.80 **10.** (i) Gross Tax = €16 625.50 (ii) Tax Payable = €14 975.50
(iii) PRSI due = €1561.84 (iv) €3333.30 (v) Total deductions = €21 220.64 (vi) Net Income = €36 129.36 **11.** (i) Gross Tax = €24 354 (ii) Tax Payable = €21 054 (iii) PRSI Due = €2987.84 (iv) €5828.80 (v) Total deductions = €30 630.64
(vi) Net Income = €62 369.36 **12.** (i) Gross Tax = €371.83
(ii) Tax Payable = €340.10 (iii) PRSI = €35.12 (iv) €73.00
(v) €476.22 (vi) €753.78 (vii) €39 196.56 **13.** (i) €1810.50
(ii) €1535.50 (vi) €186.99 (iv) €377.23 (v) €2479.72
(vi) €3720.28 **14.** (i) €53 160.98 (ii) €12 418 (iii) €1394.28
(iv) €3040.07 (v) €36 308.63 **15.** (i) €68 600 (ii) €42 029.46

Revision Activity 15

1. (a) Selling Price – Cost Price (b) Cost Price – Selling Price
(c) $\frac{\text{Profit Amount}}{\text{Cost Price}} \times 100$ (d) $\frac{\text{Loss Amount}}{\text{Cost Price}} \times 100$
2. (a) 50% (b) 33.33% (c) 50% **3.** (a) €9.74 (b) 100%
4. (a) He must repay €6014.44 at the end of year 3 to repay his loan. (b) He would need to repay €3280.50 at the end of year 4 and 5 in order to clear his loan. (c) Total interest paid = €1961 **5.** (a) €12 480 (b) 6% **6.** (a) €5100.50
(b) Interest Rate = 4.9% **7.** (a) €8200 (b) €49 300
8. (a) Amount of income charged at the higher rate is €14 487.80
(b) €56 287.80 **9.** (a) €6837 (b) €52 000 (c) €42 758

Exam-style Questions

1. (b) €8.13 (c) No **2.** (a) €2468.80 (b) €3300
(c) €8262 (d) €34 269.20

Chapter 16

Activity 16.1

1. (i) 35 (ii) 8 (iii) $t^2 + 4t + 3$ (iv) $t = -\frac{3}{2}$ **2.** (i) $k = -2$
(ii) $x = 0$ or $x = -\frac{3}{4}$ **3.** (ii) (0.5, 10.5) (iii) $x < 0.5$ (iv) $x > 0.5$
(v) $x = 0.5$ **4.** (ii) 4 (iii) $x = 0.6, x = 2.9$ (iv) $x = 0.15, x = 3.35$
(v) $0.15 < x < 3.35, x \in \mathbb{R}$ **5.** (i) $3b - c = 18$ Equation 1;
$2b + c = -8$ Equation 2 (ii) $b = 2; c = -12$ (iii) $(0, -12)$
(iv) (2.6, 0) and (−4.6, 0) **6.** (i) 5 = c (ii) $3a - b = 3$ Equation 1;
$5a + b = 5$ Equation 2 (iii) $a = 1; b = 0$ **7.** (ii) $c = -12$
8. (i) (a) $x = \frac{1}{2}$ or $x = -3$ (b) $x = 2$ (c) $x = 0$ or $x = 3$
(ii) Graph 1 corresponds to $h(x)$; Graph 3 corresponds to $g(x)$;
Graph 5 corresponds to $f(x)$ **9.** (iii) $x = -5.3$ and $x = 2.3$
10. (ii) (a) 6.1 (b) $x = -2$ and $x = 1.5$ (c) $\{-2 \le x \le 1.5\}$

Activity 16.2

1. (i) $l = 140 - 2x$ (iii) (a) 2450 m² (b) 1650 m²
2. (ii) (a) 61 metres (b) 41 metres (c) $t_1 \approx 0.6s, t_2 \approx 6.4s$
3. (i) $x = 2$ (ii) Find where the graph of $f(x) = 2x^2 + 25x - 58$ cuts the positive x-axis. (iii) $x = 2$ **4.** (i) Approximately 3.2 seconds
(v) 3.16 sec (vi) $h = 45$ m (vii) 7.75 sec **5.** (i) 0 m above ground (iii) 18 seconds (v) 9 seconds (vi) 405 metres
6. (i) $w = 18 - x$ (ii) Length of the inner section = $(x - 3)$ m; Width of the inner section = $(15 - x)$ m **7.** (i) €420
(ii) €$(520 - 20n)$ (iii) $520n - 20n^2$ (v) The company makes a loss of €2400 if they take 30 people for the tour.
(vii) $n = 0$ or $n = 26$ (viii) $n = 13$ (ix) €3380 **8.** (ii) The relationship between height and time is linear.

(iii) Tank A: 2 cm/s; Tank B: −2 cm/s (v) (50, 0) means that after 50 seconds the volume of Tank B is zero. (vi) Tank A: $h = 15 + 2t$, h = height of water in cm, t = time in seconds; Tank B: $h = 100 - 2t$, h = height of water in cm, t = time in seconds (viii) 57.75 cm
9. (ii) $21000x - 500x^2$ (iii) $x = 0$ or $x = 42$ (v) $x = €21$; €220 500
(vi) €16 (vii) €12 500 (viii) No

Activity 16.3

1. (iv) (0, 1) (v) y is increasing (vi) $3^{10} = 59 049$;
$3^{20} = 3 486 784 401$; $3^{30} = 2.058911321 \times 10^{14}$ **2.** (i) 3 (ii) x
(iii) The exponent (iv) The base 3 (v) Real numbers $\mathbb{R}$
(vi) There are no values (vii) All the positive real numbers
(viii) As x decreases the output gets closer and closer to 0 but never equals 0. (ix) No **3.** (iii) (0, 2) (iv) $2(3^{10}) = 118 098$;
$2(3^{20}) = 6 975 568 802$ **4.** (ii) $x = 2$ **5.** (ii) 262 144
6. (i) 50 (ii) 136 221 **7.** (i) $k = 2; a = 3$ (ii) 4374
8. Graph C: $f(x)$; Graph B: $g(x)$; Graph A: $h(x)$; Graph D: $j(x)$
9. (i) $a = 4; b = 3$ (ii) $1.129718146 \times 10^{12}$ (iii) 1.1×10^{12}
(iv) 1.1 billion bacteria (taking 1 billion to be 1 million million)
(v) $t = 10.052$ hours **10.** (ii) $x = -0.2$ and 3.1 (iii) $k \approx 1.89$
(iv) $g(k) \approx 29$

Activity 16.4

2. (iii) y-intercepts are at 0, −2, −4, and −5 respectively.
8. $f(x) = (x + 1)^2 - 3$; $g(x) = (x - 2)^2 - 3$ **9.** (i) $k = +3$
(ii) (a) (3, −4) (b) $x = 3$ **10.** (i) $h = 2$ (ii) (a) (−2, 3) (b) $x = -2$

Revision Activity 16

1. (a) $b = 1, c = -6$ (b) $x = -1.5$ **3.** (b) $x = 0.5$ and $x = 2.4$
(c) $k \approx 1.3$. Using the calculator $k \approx 1.26$ (d) $g(1.3) \approx 13.5$
4. (b) (i) 160 (ii) 320 (c) No **5.** (a) €5000
(c) $-x^2 + 60x - 500$ (d) A loss of €500 (e) $x = 10$ and $x = 50$
(g) 30 items (h) €400 **6.** (b) Between 4 and 5 seconds
(c) 4.45 seconds (e) 2 sec (f) About 4 seconds
(g) $0 \le t \le 4.45, t \in \mathbb{R}$ (h) $0 \le h \le 30, h \in \mathbb{R}$

Exam-style Questions

1. (a) $5a - b = 29$ Equation 1; $2a + b = -1$ Equation 2
(b) $a = 4; b = -9$ (c) (0, −9) (d) (1.6, 0) and (−5.6, 0)
3. (b) Roots of (x): $x = -4; x = 0$; Roots of $g(x)$: $x = 1; x = 5$
(d) $h = +5$ (e) $x = 5$ **5.** (b) $f(x)$: Diagram 3; $g(x)$: Diagram 5; $h(x)$: Diagram 2

Chapter 17

Activity 17.1

1. (i) 13 (ii) (a) $\frac{5}{13}$ (b) $\frac{12}{13}$ (c) $\frac{5}{12}$ (d) $\frac{12}{13}$ (e) $\frac{5}{13}$ (f) $\frac{12}{5}$
2. (i) (a) $\frac{y}{x}$ (b) $\frac{y}{x}$ (c) $\frac{z}{x}$ (d) $\frac{z}{x}$ (ii) $\tan A = \frac{y}{z}$; $\tan B = \frac{z}{y}$;
$\tan A$ is the reciprocal of $\tan B$ **3.** $|AC| = 6 \tan 30°$
4. (ii) $\cos A = \frac{\sqrt{51}}{10}$ **6.** $h = 7.3144$ m **7.** Statement (ii) is correct; Statement (iv) is correct **8.** (i) 7 cm (ii) $|CR| = 2.4$ cm; $|BQ| = 5.1$ cm; $|AP| = 6.5$ cm (v) The value of the sine of an angle can never exceed 1 **9.** (i) $|OR| = 6.5$ cm; $|OQ| = 4.6$ cm; $|OP| = 2.3$ cm (iv) The value of the cosine of an angle can never exceed 1

Activity 17.2

1. (i) 15° 45′ (ii) 35° 30′ (iii) 86° 15′ (iv) 45° 24′ (v) 33° 20′
(vi) 41° 13′ **2.** (i) 17.7° (ii) 49.9° (iii) 22.4° (iv) 82.3°
(v) 3.6° (vi) 85.4° **3.** (i) 64° 38′ (ii) 32° 18′ (iii) 54° 52′
(iv) 31° 50′ (v) 78° 13′ (vi) 69° 50′ (vii) 7° 43′ (viii) 85° 30′
4. (i) 0.5334 (ii) 1.0446 (iii) 0.0616 (iv) 0.2918 (v) 0.8921
(vi) 0.5719 (vii) 0.9861 (viii) 0.7455 **5.** 97° 25′ **6.** 86° 56′
7. (i) 31° 45′ (ii) 53° 8′ (iii) 123° 29′ (iv) 143° 57′
8. (i) 24° 10′ (ii) 67° 51′ (iii) 12° 50′ (iv) 63° 38′ (v) 62° 37′
(vi) 27° 28′ (vii) 75° 31′

Activity 17.3

1. (ii) |AC| = $\sqrt{2}$ units **2.** (iii) $\sqrt{3}$ units **3.** (i) $x = 2\sqrt{2}$
(ii) $x = \dfrac{5\sqrt{3}}{2}$ (iii) $x = 1$ (iv) $x = 3\sqrt{3}$ **4.** $b = 6$; $a = 6$; $\theta = 45°$
6. $x = 6$ **7.** (i) |CBD| = 90° (ii) Radius = 5 **10.** (i) $\sin 2A = \dfrac{\sqrt{3}}{2}$;
$2\sin A = 1$ (ii) $\sin 2A \neq 2\sin A$ **11.** (i) 1 (ii) 1

Activity 17.4

1. $h = 4.01$ m **2.** 104.96 m **3.** 2.82 m **4.** 39.99 m
5. (ii) 337.25 m **6.** 15.2 m **7.** (i) $\theta = 68.56°$ (ii) 75° 45'
(iii) 12.56 m **8.** 5° 43' **9.** (i) $h = x\sqrt{3}$ (ii) $h = (20 - x)\dfrac{1}{\sqrt{3}}$
(iii) $x = 5$ (iv) $h = 8.66$ m **10.** (i) |OQ| = |OR| = |OP|
(ii) |∠PRQ| = 90° (iii) $x = \dfrac{15}{2\sqrt{3}}$ m **11.** (iii) 107.72
12. (i) |AB| = 2.402 m (ii) 10.3 m (iii) 3.79 m **13.** (iv) 20 m
(v) 15 m

Revision Activity 17

1. (a) $x = 7.2$ m (b) $x = 9.45$ cm; $y = 22.06$ cm **3.** (a) 30°
(b) 45° **5.** (a) $h = x\sqrt{3}$ (b) 8.66 m **6.** (b) 125 m

Exam-style Questions

1. (a) Not correct (b) Correct (c) Not correct
2. Suurhusen is the most tilted

Chapter 18

Activity 18.1

1. (i) 60 km/h (ii) 12:40 **3.** (i) 50 km/h (ii) 80 km/h
(iii) 72.5 km/h **4.** 66 km/h **5.** 50 km/h **6.** (i) 15 m/s
(ii) 20 m/s (iii) 10 m/s (iv) 35 m/s **7.** (i) 48 mins (ii) 70 km/h
(iii) 34 km/h **8.** (i) 15 min (ii) 12 min (iii) 17.78 km/h
9. 24 km/h **10.** 48 km/h

Activity 18.2

1. (i) Part (4) **2.** (ii) 3 metres (iii) 7.8 m (iv) 10 seconds
(v) 0.78 m/s **5.** (ii) 1.88 km/h (iii) 33.75 km/h (iv) 4.77 km/h
8. (i) Graph C (ii) Tom is fastest (iii) Graph A (iv) Graph B
(v) After 2 seconds **9.** (i) Matthew (ii) Matthew: 5 different
speeds; Colin: 5 different speeds (iii) Matthew's average
speed: 29.27 m/s; Colin's average speed: 28.24 m/s
(iv) Matthew in Part (4) **11.** 1 → D, 2 → A, 3 → E, 4 → C, 5 → B

Activity 18.3

2. (i) A to B (ii) B to C (iii) 8.33 km (iv) C to D (v) 100 km/h
(vi) 8 minutes **3.** (i) 10 minutes (ii) 25 to 30 minutes, 40 to
45 minutes and 50 to 60 minutes (iii) 10 to 20 minutes,
20 to 25 minutes and 30 to 40 minutes (iv) Yes (v) 40 to
45 minutes; Speed = 25 km/h (vi) 2.1 km **4.** (i) 60 km/h
(ii) 3 minutes (iii) 100 km/h (iv) 3.3 km (vi) 68.9 km/h
5. (ii) 144 km/h **8.** 4 seconds

Activity 18.4

1. (i) 30 seconds (ii) 20 m approximately (iii) 300 m
approximately (iv) No **2.** (i) 620 m approximately in
30 seconds approximately (ii) 450 m approximately
(iii) 40 m approximately **3.** A → 2, B → 3, C → 4, D → 1
6. 1D, 2E, 3A, 4B, 5F, 6G, 7C **7.** 1A, 2D, 3B, 4C **8.** 1E, 2C,
3A, 4B, 5D **9.** B **10.** A(ii), B(iii), C(i)

Revision Activity 18

1. 63 km/h; 56 km/h; 7 km/h **2.** (a) 0.55 km/min (b) E to F:
speed = 0.7 km/min (c) D to E: speed = 0.2 km/min
(d) 0.44 km/min **3.** 9.75 km/h **4.** 1188 km/h **5.** (a) 3 stops
(b) 4.5 km (c) Two (d) $5\dfrac{1}{3}$ km/h (e) 8 km/h

Exam-style Question

2. 1.4 h; 63 km